W9-DII-450

040 DISCARDED

Queensbury, N.Y.

CRITICAL SURVEY
OF
SHORT FICTION

CRITICAL SURVEY

OF

SHORT FICTION

Second Revised Edition

Volume 2

Italo Calvino - Louise Erdrich

Editor, Second Revised Edition

Charles E. May

California State University, Long Beach

Editor, First Edition

Frank N. Magill

SALEM PRESS, INC.

Pasadena, California   Hackensack, New Jersey

Managing Editor: Christina J. Moose
Research Supervisor: Jeffry Jensen
Acquisitions Editor: Mark Rehn
Photograph Editor: Philip Bader
Manuscript Editors: Lauren M. Mitchell
Melanie Watkins
Research Assistant: Jeff Stephens
Production Editor: Cynthia Beres
Layout: Ross Castellano

Copyright © 2001, by Salem Press, Inc.

All rights in this book are reserved. No part of this work may be used or reproduced in any manner whatsoever or transmitted in any form or by any means, electronic or mechanical, including photocopy, recording, or any information storage and retrieval system, without written permission from the copyright owners except in the case of brief quotations embodied in critical articles and reviews. For information, address the publisher, Salem Press, Inc., P.O. Box 50062, Pasadena, California 91115.

∞ The paper used in these volumes conforms to the American National Standard for Permanence of Paper for Printed Library Materials, Z39.48-1992(R1997).

Library of Congress Cataloging-in-Publication Data

Critical survey of short fiction / editor, Charles E. May.—2nd rev. ed.
7 v. ; cm.
First edition edited by Frank Northen Magill.
Includes bibliographical references and index.
ISBN 0-89356-006-5 (set : alk. paper) — ISBN 0-89356-007-3 (v. 1 : alk. paper) —
ISBN 0-89356-008-1 (v. 2 : alk. paper) — ISBN 0-89356-009-X (v. 3 : alk. paper) —
ISBN 0-89356-010-3 (v. 4 : alk. paper) — ISBN 0-89356-011-1 (v. 5 : alk. paper) —
ISBN 0-89356-012-X (v. 6 : alk. paper) — ISBN 0-89356-013-8 (v. 7 : alk. paper)
1. Short story. 2. Short story—History and criticism. 3. Short story—Bio-bibliography.
I. May, Charles E. (Charles Edward) 1941 -   . II. Magill, Frank Northen, 1907-1997.

PN3321 .C7 2001
809.3′1—dc21

00-046384

Fourth Printing

PRINTED IN THE UNITED STATES OF AMERICA

CONTENTS

COMPLETE LIST OF AUTHORS

Volume I

Volume II

Volume III

Volume IV

Volume V

Volume VI

CRITICAL SURVEY
OF
SHORT FICTION

ITALO CALVINO

Born: Santiago de las Vegas, Cuba; October 15, 1923

Died: Siena, Italy; September 19, 1985

PRINCIPAL SHORT FICTION

Ultimo viene il corvo, 1949 (partial trans., *Adam, One Afternoon, and Other Stories*, 1957)

La formica Argentina, 1952 (*The Argentine Ant*, 1957)

L'entrata in guerra, 1954

La nuvola di smog, 1958 (*Smog*, 1971)

I racconti, 1958

La giornata d'uno scrutatore, 1963 (*The Watcher and Other Stories*, 1971)

Marcovaldo: Ovvero, Le Stagioni in città, 1963 (*Marcovaldo: Or, The Seasons in the City*, 1983)

Le cosmicomiche, 1965 (*Cosmicomics*, 1968)

Ti con zero, 1967 (*T Zero*, 1969)

Gli amore difficili, 1970 (*Difficult Loves*, 1984)

Sotto il sole giaguaro, 1986 (*Under the Jaguar Sun*, 1988)

OTHER LITERARY FORMS

Spanning some forty years, Italo Calvino's literary production includes highly diverse novels, adaptations, translations, edited texts, critical essays, newspaper articles, and lectures. Calvino selected some of these latter essays for inclusion in *Una pietra sopra: Discorsi di letteratura e societa* (1980; *The Uses of Literature*, 1986). After his death, his wife collected essays that he had been preparing for the 1985-1986 Charles Eliot Norton Lectures at Harvard University. The five lectures in *Sulla fiaba* (1988; *Six Memos for the Next Millennium*, 1988, the sixth apparently never written) explore the distinctive values that Calvino believed literature alone imparts to humanity as it faces a dubious future. (The sixth lecture, on consistency, was apparently never written.)

ACHIEVEMENTS

An innovative traditionalist, Calvino imaginatively fuses the two major modes of fiction—realism and fantasy—by using both poetic association and scientific reasoning. As he observed in 1970:

> What is at the heart of narration for me is not the explanation of a strange fact, but the *order of things* this extraordinary fact or event develops in and around itself . . . , the network of images deposited around it, as in the formation of a crystal.

While best known for this crystalline blend of mundane and magical, of logical and impossible, Calvino is also a critically acclaimed realist and master fabulist. His first novel, *Il sentiero dei nidi di ragno* (1947, 1957, 1965; *The Path to the Nest of Spiders*, 1956), a boy's wartime experiences narrated in neorealistic manner, won the Premio Riccione, while in 1972, he received the Premio Feltrinelli per la Narrativa—Italy's equivalent of the Pulitzer Prize—for the historical fantasy, *Le città invisibili* (1972; *Invisible Cities*, 1974). *I racconti* (short stories) won the prestigious Bagutta Prize in 1958.

BIOGRAPHY

Born outside Havana, Cuba, Italo Calvino was two years old when his Italian parents, an agronomist and a botanist, returned to the ancestral farm in San Remo, on the Italian Riviera. The influence of their mature, enlightened skepticism is discernible both in Calvino's art and in his life. Unconvinced by fascism, for example, Calvino deserted the army to join the Resistance when drafted in 1943, two years after enrolling in the University of Turin. His wartime experiences later provided much material for his pen.

The war over, he returned in 1945 to Turin to complete his degree. Altered by recent events and stimulated by his new environment, he made several far-reaching decisions: He changed his major from agronomy to English literature (his thesis was on Joseph Conrad), he began writing fiction, and he joined the staff at the Einaudi publishing house. There, encouraged by coworkers Elio Vittorini, Cesare Pavese, and Natalia Ginzburg, he became a member of the

Italo Calvino (©Jerry Bauer)

neorealist movement and also became increasingly active in the Communist Party.

Calvino's earliest works focus on the war, and, although "slice of life" realism predominates in both his first novel and the short stories of *Ultimo viene il corvo*, his own proclivities directed his fiction into increasingly fantastic territory. The 1950's saw some of his most original and popular prose, with the historical fantasy novellas—*Il visconte dimezzato* (1952; *The Cloven Viscount*, 1962), *Il barone rampante* (1957; *The Baron in the Trees*, 1959), and *Il cavaliere inesistente* (1959; *The Nonexistent Knight*, 1962), released in 1960 as the trilogy *I nostri antenati* (our forefathers)—among his most famous and typical works. These novels are in many ways highly imaginative, idiosyncratic mirrorings of the forms and themes of the storytelling tradition, which Calvino was also pursuing in a more scholarly manner. *Fiabe italiane: Raccolte della traizione popolare durante gli ultima cento anni e transcritte in lingua dai vari dialetti* (1956; *Italian Fables*, 1959), which consists of two volumes, collects and retells hundreds of tales from all over Italy. Immersion in this tradition led to the creation of ominously modern counterparts, such

as *The Argentine Ant* and *Smog*, two novellas appearing in *The Watcher and Other Stories*.

Disenchanted with communism, Calvino quit the party around 1958; his interpretation of the complexities of political action informs the novella *The Watcher*. The note that prefaces it, "The substance of this book is based on fact, but the characters are all entirely imaginary," could be applied equally well to the realistic but poignantly comic vignettes in *Marcovaldo: Or, The Seasons in the City.*

Calvino moved to Paris in 1964, the same year that he married a translator for UNESCO from Argentina; in 1965, they had a daughter. Although Calvino stayed in Paris for the next sixteen years, he retained his Italian contacts, including his position with the publishing house Einaudi. The loosely joined short-story collections and wildly experimental novels from this period—*Cosmicomics, T zero, Il castello dei destini incrociati* (1973; *The Castle of Crossed Destinies*, 1976), *Invisible Cities*, and *Se una notte d'inverno un viaggiatore* (1979; *If on a Winter's Night a Traveler*, 1981)—all demonstrate the influence of acquaintances such as Claude Lévi-Strauss and Roland Barthes and of literary experiments such as the New Novel. His teasing parody of this latter, *If on a Winter's Night a Traveler*, became an international success.

Calvino and his family relocated to Rome in 1980. His final novel, *Palomar* (1983; *Mr. Palomar*, 1985), appearing in English around the time of his death from cerebral hemorrhage, bears the possibly prescient dedication: "For Gore [Vidal], these last meditations about Nature. Italo." Significantly, the novel's protagonist, Mr. Palomar—like the telescope for which he is named and like the man who created him—is an observer, a being dedicated to scrupulously recording the complexity of existence. The posthumously published *Under the Jaguar Sun* shares *Mr. Palomar*'s emphasis on the sensory, with each story dominated by taste, hearing, or smell. The wide-ranging, often metaphysical perspectives opened by sensory perception in his fiction are evident in *Six Memos for the Next Millennium* as well. In concentrating upon literature's unique contribution to humanity through the millennia in these essays, Calvino also divulges the essential characteristics of his own considerable intellectual and creative legacy.

ANALYSIS

Although he maintained close attention to concrete, realistic detail—both physical and psychological—throughout his career, Italo Calvino, like his fellow neorealists, was quick to point out that his realism was actually quite different from naturalism. Not content simply to describe the visible and tangible, Calvino always sought to arrive at the intangible reality—symbolic, psychological, historical, social, mythic—that concrete phenomena both reveal and conceal.

"ADAM, ONE AFTERNOON"

"Un pomeriggio, Adamo" ("Adam, One Afternoon"), one of his most discussed early stories, admirably demonstrates his understated skill in this complex endeavor. Maria-nunziata, a young kitchen maid, spies the exotic new gardener's boy from her window. Her jovial, childlike curiosity is aroused by the odd young man, who wears the short pants of a little boy and the long, tied-back hair of a girl. Liberoso ("Liberty" in Esperanto) beckons and asks if she wants to see—and receive—something nice. Unsure but intrigued, she cautiously follows Liberoso into the garden, even though he refuses to answer her insistent questions. Leading her deeper into shadows, he finds the spot that he had already carefully chosen. Pushing aside some foliage, the half-naked youth reveals to Maria—a toad. Revolted and superstitiously afraid, Maria refuses his unusual gift. However, remaining enticed by Liberoso (who is as desirable and incomprehensible as he finds her), she continues to accompany him through the Edenic garden. Their curious quest is apparently never fulfilled, though, for the discoveries that they make provoke wonder and delight in Liberoso but disgust or dread in Maria. Through the process, however, Maria—increasingly trusting yet continually mystified—experiences some of the heady, perilous freedom that Liberoso embodies.

With little in the way of plot, action, or character development—a common characteristic in Calvino— "Adam, One Afternoon" is memorable for its magical atmosphere. Full of tension and ambiguity, innocence and sensuality, the story organically portrays both the light sweetness of the idyll and the weighty symbolism of myth. The abrupt, cryptic ending, with its riotous invasion of Maria's world by Liberoso, encourages a variety of interpretations.

"THE CROW COMES LAST"

"Ultimo viene il corvo" ("The Crow Comes Last") is perhaps Calvino's most famous early story. Containing the same curious mixture of innocence, magic, and danger as "Adam, One Afternoon," it is set in wartime. It begins with a nameless, "apple-faced" boy fearlessly appropriating a partisan's gun to shoot at targets—trout, birds, rabbits—in an expert display of marksmanship. Perceiving the usefulness of the boy's gift, the commander entices him to join up with them. This the boy does without hesitation, for he is eager to see new things, "all at those false distances, the distances that could be filled by a shot swallowing the air in between."

Because he is ignorant of the natural laws of cause and effect, uncaring if his target is inanimate or animate, the boy's ritualized play, without thought or effort, soon progresses to firing at increasingly significant targets. Like an amoral god or natural force, the boy is oblivious to the consequences of his actions; he does not understand that death follows his magical filling of space between gun barrel and living being. Thus, when he spies a new challenge on the road below—the indistinct insignia on the uniforms of German soldiers—he fires. His shots rouse the sleeping partisans, who ironically interpret his attack on the enemy as heroic; interpretation, the gap between being and seeming, is a favorite device (and theme) of Calvino.

By recording meticulously a final, fatal game of cat and mouse, the concluding pages intensify the detached dreaminess and moral ambiguity of the story. Jumping abruptly into the mind of the German soldier about to die, the narrative exposes the psychological toll of fear and hope: Lucid reason imperceptibly becomes hallucination—or revelation. It is for the reader to decide.

"THE ADVENTURE OF A BATHER"

Calvino's narratives—whether humorous, like *Marcovaldo: Or, The Seasons in the City*, or gently melancholic, like "Sleeping Like Dogs," or profoundly disturbing, like "The House of the Beehives"—all have as their focus the complex relationship between the inner and outer realms of human experience. A painfully poignant group, "Stories of Love and Loneliness," uses the anguished context not of war but of daily life to probe delicately connections between the real and the imagined, the actual and the potential.

"L'avventura di una bagnante" ("The Adventure of a Bather") is a typical example of this kind of story. In it, a middle-class matron loses the bottom half of her suit while swimming alone on vacation. At first calm, she grows increasingly desperate; her distressing nakedness produces not only physical contortions but also intellectual and emotional gyrations. Magnifying and symbolically interpreting even the smallest incident (like his preoccupation with "signs," this is a favorite thematic strategy of Calvino's), the signora's agony translates not into logical action but rather into the logic of association: Instead of calling for help, she muses about the complexities of body image, the threatening sexual undercurrent of interpersonal relations, and the internalization of religious dogma such as original sin. These are clearly not mere flights of fancy, for all significantly illuminate her experience of her situation. Feeling "cast out by the whole world," with she alone "chosen to pay for all," the bather, now a sacrificial lamb, prepares to meet death in the chill, darkening waters. A young fisherman, who has discovered her plight with his underwater mask, however, suddenly deflects both tragedy and comedy by becoming the agent of her salvation—and of her unexpected encounter with grace. Provided with clothes and a ride back to shore, the lady suddenly, perhaps miraculously, no longer feels ill at ease with the physical reality of her own being.

The provocative multiplicity of the physical phenomena that she observes on the return to shore is explored—this time on a truly cosmic scale—by Calvino in the quirky tales gathered in *Cosmicomics*. Through the narrative of Qfwfq, who is an ageless, protean being, a breathtaking cosmos of matter, experience, thought, and feeling is spread before the reader. Hard science, fantasy, myth, human psychol-ogy, and virtuous literary exercises mutually illuminate one another, blending and leading the reader through possible and impossible realms.

"GAMES WITHOUT END"

Like all these narratives, "Giochi senza fine" ("Games Without End") begins with a dry, scientific headnote: "When the galaxies become more remote, the rarefaction of the universe is compensated for by the formation of further galaxies composed of newly created matter." This note provides the basis of the story, for this freshly created matter is imaginatively interpreted as shiny, new, atom-marbles, with which youthful Qfwfq and Pfwfp play and over which they fight. The mighty laws of physics introducing the story soon affect both game and players as well, for the curves of space offer Qfwfq unfair advantage. Fleeing a Pfwfp "green with rage," Qfwfq declares ruefully: "So there I was, with nothingness in front of me, and that nasty-faced Pfwfp after me: an unpleasant sight either way." Caught in an endless hall of mirrors—"after every Qfwfq there was a Pfwfp, and after every Pfwfp a Qfwfq, and every Pfwfp was chasing a Qfwfq, who was pursuing him and vice versa"—Qfwfq ends his narrative with the cynical yet wistful observation: "We had lost all pleasure in this game of chase, and we weren't children any more for that matter, but now there was nothing else we could do."

Impossibly, wonderfully alive, Qfwfq synthesizes the rational and irrational, the human and nonhuman; his is perhaps Calvino's most masterful creation. The scientific apparatus through which he and his worlds are presented neither diminishes nor contains his quintessentially humanistic perspective; rather, the collision of ancient and modern, alien and familiar, intimate and distant, provides the framework for sensitive and provocative exploration of human realities. In fact, Qfwfq's last lines in "Lo zio acquatico" ("The Aquatic Uncle"), a merry tale of devolution, are unexpectedly imbued with the same grave beauty informing Italian Renaissance humanism: "They all had something, I know, that made them somehow superior to me, sublime, something that made me, compared to them, mediocre. And yet I wouldn't have traded places with any of them."

"UNDER THE JAGUAR SUN"

While certain stories, such as "Ti con zero" ("t zero") and "Il guidatore notturno" ("The Night Driver"), both from *T Zero, Cosmicomics'* companion collection, are abstract intellectual conundrums similar to those wrought by Jorge Luis Borges, Calvino's unflagging interest in "the multiplicity of possible things" most typically arises out of their human significance and value. One of his last stories, "Under the Jaguar Sun," exemplifies many of the literary values—"Lightness," "Quickness," "Exactitude," "Visibility," and "Multiplicity"—that Calvino had singled out for his 1985 Harvard lectures. With admirable economy and his trademark curious perspective, Calvino uses the most universal of experiences—eating—as entry into a multifaceted world, simultaneously idiosyncratic and personal, archetypal and universal.

While vacationing in Mexico, the unidentified narrator and his wife divide their time between visiting historical sites and eating. The complexities of native cuisine provoke impassioned discussion along the way, its diverse ingredients, modes of preparation, and flavors becoming interwoven—in ways romantic, ineffable, and grotesque—with the dramas of history, religion, and private life. Besides providing the story with its subject, plot, and dialogue, food performs other vital functions: It defines personality (the narrator describes his "insipidness" as a "flavor more discreet and restrained than that of red peppers"), it promotes intimate communication ("the pleasures of existence could be appreciated only if we shared them"), it excites or displaces sexual desire, and, most important, it vivifies and makes love concrete, both sacred and profane.

Calvino uses transcendent love—tinged with "horror, sacredness, and mystery"—as the frame (a favorite narrative and structural device) of the story. He also employs associated motifs—self-renunciation, convoluted logic, voluptuousness, the "flavor" and meaning of the sacred—to integrate masterfully his multiple tangible and intangible realities. The ultimate result of his orchestrations is unveiled with a fascinated revulsion at the story's close: "Our eyes stared into each other's with the intensity of serpents'—serpents concentrated in the ecstasy of swallowing each other in turn . . . in the universal cannibalism that leaves its imprint on every amorous relationship and erases the lines between our bodies." This erasing of boundaries, of paradoxically dissolving yet finding the self in the other, is clearly related to the goal that most of Calvino's fictions share: to transform the mundane into the magical, the familiar into the alien, and so to open the reader to the infinite potential and multiformity of being.

OTHER MAJOR WORKS

LONG FICTION: *Il sentiero dei nidi di ragno*, 1947, 1957, 1965 (*The Path to the Nest of Spiders*, 1956); *Il visconte dimezzato*, 1952 (novella; *The Cloven Viscount*, 1962); *Il barone rampante*, 1957 (novella; *The Baron in the Trees*, 1959); *Il cavaliere inesistente*, 1959 (novella; *The Non-Existent Knight*, 1962); *I nostri atenati*, 1960 (*Our Ancestors*, 1980; includes *The Cloven Viscount, The Non-Existent Knight*, and *The Baron in the Trees*); *Il castello dei destini incrociati*, 1969, 1973 (*The Castle of Crossed Destinies*, 1976); *La città invisibili*, 1972 (*Invisible Cities*, 1974); *Se una notte d'inverno un viaggiatore*, 1979 (*If on a Winter's Night a Traveler*, 1981); *Palomar*, 1983 (*Mr. Palomar*, 1985).

NONFICTION: *Una pietra sopra: Discorsi di letteratura e societa*, 1980 (*The Uses of Literature*, 1986); *Collezione di sabbia*, 1984; *The Literature Machine: Essays*, 1986; *Sulla fiaba*, 1988 (*Six Memos for the Next Millennium*, 1988); *Perché leggere i classici*, 1991 (*Why Read the Classics?*, 1999).

EDITED TEXTS: *La letteratura americana e altri saggi*, 1951; *Fiabe italiane: Raccolte della traizione popolare durante gli ultimi cento anni e transcritte in lingua dai vari dialetti*, 1956 (*Italian Fables*, 1959); *Cesare Pavese: Lettere, 1926-1950*, 1966; *L'Uccel Belverde e altre fiabe italiane*, 1972 (*Italian Folk Tales*, 1975).

BIBLIOGRAPHY

Adler, Sara. *Calvino: The Writer as Fablemaker.* Potomac, Md.: Ediciones Turanzas, 1979. A valuable introduction to the themes, techniques, images in—and critical perspectives on—Calvino's works. Presents the author as an explorer on fabulous, sometimes horrifying journeys, who provides rich, mythical perspectives on the world. Secondary bibliography, index.

Carter, Albert. *Italo Calvino: Metamorphoses of Fantasy.* Ann Arbor: UMI Research Press, 1987. This masterful analysis of Calvino the fantasist explores his contribution to what is possible in literature by analyzing his use of the contrafactual realms of imagination, speculation, and hypothesis. Excellent bibliography.

Fenwick, Julie. "Sex, Language, and Narrative Continuity and Discontinuity in Italo Calvino's 'Meiosis.'" *Studies in Short Fiction* 27 (Spring, 1990): 203-209. Shows how Calvino's story is poststructuralist in that the essential self disappears before the narrator's speculations, just as the essential text disappears under poststructuralist criticism. Asserts Calvino's characters are caught in a paradox of discontinuity because they are incapable of real contact, and continuity, in that they are chained to the past.

Gabriele, Tommasina. *Italo Calvino: Eros and Language.* Madison, N.J.: Fairleigh Dickinson University Press, 1994. Explores Calvino's language of love and his treatment of sex, language, and laughter. Includes notes and bibliography.

Hume, Kathryn. *Calvino's Fictions: Cogito and Cosmos.* Oxford, England: Clarendon Press, 1992. Explores Calvino's treatment of the cosmos and of cosmogony. Includes notes and bibliography.

_____. "Sensuality and the Senses in Calvino's Fiction." *Modern Language Notes* 107 (January, 1992): 160-177. Argues that sensual material is largely lacking in Calvino's work because of his lack of interest in constructing simulations of everyday reality. Discusses Calvino's treatment of the senses and his unusual handling of sensuous experiences; categorizes treatment of senses in Calvino's fiction.

McLaughlin, Martin. *Italo Calvino.* Edinburgh, Scotland: Edinburgh University Press, 1998. A very detailed study of Calvino's fiction, beginning with his early stories and his development of a neorealistic style. Includes a chronology of Calvino's fictions and a bibliography.

Olken, I. T. *With Pleated Eye and Garnet Wing: Symmetries of Italo Calvino.* Ann Arbor: University of Michigan Press, 1984. A perceptive analysis of the various "symmetries" (structural, thematic, natural, configural) in Calvino's work, as well as his balancing of diverse elements: traditional and innovative, rational and absurd, roguish and grotesque. Notes, index.

Re, Lucia. "Calvino and the Value of Literature." *MLN* 113 (January, 1998): 121-137. Claims that the issues of readership and high and low culture have always been important to Calvino; discusses the relevance of Calvino's thought to the current crisis of literary studies and literature's devaluation. Discusses Calvino's belief that literature is educational, but only if indirect and difficult.

Review of Contemporary Fiction 6 (Summer, 1986). Special issue on Calvino, with essays on his framed narratives, his minimalist narratives, his aesthetics, and both his long and short fictions.

Wood, Michael. "Hidden in the Distance: Reading Calvino Reading." *The Kenyon Review,* n.s. 20, no. 2 (Spring, 1998): 155-170. Discusses Calvino's belief that language is more often failure than success. Argues that Calvino's fiction is an example of one of literature's most significant half-truths: When you write, you always write the wrong book.

Terri Frongia

ALBERT CAMUS

Born: Mondovi, Algeria; November 7, 1913
Died: Near Villeblevin, France; January 4, 1960

PRINCIPAL SHORT FICTION

L'Exil et le royaume, 1957 (*Exile and the Kingdom*, 1958)

OTHER LITERARY FORMS

Albert Camus was an important novelist and playwright as well as a philosophical essayist and journalist. He translated and adapted the works of Spanish, Russian, and American writers such as Pedro Calderón de la Barca, Lope de Vega, Fyodor Dostoevski, William Faulkner, and James Thurber. During World War II, he was the anonymous editor of *Combat*, and he often practiced the trade of journalism during his brief life.

ACHIEVEMENTS

At the early age of forty-four, Albert Camus accepted the Nobel Prize in Literature. He had already been feted by the literary elite of Paris and had himself become the center of a *cause célèbre* due to his criticism of Soviet Marxism and its concomitant lack of a humanistic face. More than thirty years after Camus's death, the philosophic and aesthetic values found in his writings continue to attract a wide audience, from American high school students to deconstructionists. Few contemporary writers have provoked more thoughtful discussion concerning the human condition and the themes of absurdity, revolt, and fraternity found in the human struggle. Perhaps Camus's principal achievement centers on his refusal to make a distinction between his writings and his own actions. In his works, these actions take "form" in his protests against racism, intolerance, and human indignity, wherever they may be found. Camus's durability may, in the final analysis, rest as much on the character of the writer as on his art.

BIOGRAPHY

Albert Camus was born of a peasant mother of Spanish descent and an Alsatian father who was killed in World War I. He received a degree in philosophy from the University of Algiers in 1936. He had a brief membership in the Communist Party at that time. He pursued a varied career as actor, producer, journalist, and schoolteacher. An active participant in the French underground during World War II, he first came into national prominence after the war, when it was revealed that he had been the editor of the famed clandestine newspaper *Combat*. He made many political and literary enemies after the war by chastising the Communists and his erstwhile friend and fellow writer Jean-Paul Sartre. A position as editor in a publishing house, lecture tours in the United States and South America, and government posts followed until his untimely death in an automobile accident in 1960.

ANALYSIS

Albert Camus published a single collection of short stories entitled *Exile and the Kingdom* near the end of his life. Its six stories are an important encapsulation of Camus's humanistic philosophy enveloped in his quasirealistic style and dramatized by exotic backgrounds. According to Camus's recondite views, the universe is meaningless; however, the human beings in it may become significant (even happy) if they can acquire and maintain a clear awareness of its ultimate absurdity. Each story in *Exile and the Kingdom* unfolds a situation which brings the protagonist to an intimation of the lack of lawfulness and coherence in his or her life and depicts the protagonist's response to this traumatic realization. Some of the stories go no further than this; others move away from understatement and describe wrongheaded or perverse reactions; and the last story offers a solution which seems to step beyond mere awareness of absurdity.

Readers of Camus's novels and plays will recognize the cavalcade of alienated heroes, the metaphysical paradoxes, and Camus's own preoccupation with criminals and their police counterparts—all tendered

Albert Camus, Nobel Laureate for Literature in 1957 (©The Nobel Foundation)

in lucid, tight prose which differentiates him from the strained cerebralisms of more philosophically rigorous existentialists such as Sartre. This collection of short stories also avoids the imperious eloquence and plain sententiousness which often mar Camus's longer works.

"THE ADULTEROUS WOMAN"

"The Adulterous Woman," first published in English in *Redbook* magazine, portrays the mounting depression of a housewife (Janine) traveling with a husband (Marcel) who is almost wholly absorbed in selling wools and silks to disdainful, according to Marcel, Arabs who are reluctantly emerging from the wintry Algerian landscape.

Janine is pictured as tall and "thick," yet possessing a languid sensuality which attracts the desultory

glances of bus passengers, pedestrians, and hotel guests. She often returns a look, and in spite of the characteristic prejudices of her class against Arabs she can spontaneously admire one of that race who is striking in his slender virility. She frequently counters the ennui of the endless bus rides by basking in the adoration of her husband. He can speak of little else but the volume of dry goods he can move, how much profit he will reckon by dispensing with the middleman, and how much he loathes his customers. He has made Janine his refuge from the sordidness and triviality of his life, however, and becomes instantly solicitous when prodded.

Thus, after another day of selling in yet another ordinary town, Janine rebels at the thought of retiring to their icy room for the customary nap before supper. She proposes to follow the hotel manager's suggestion to "climb up to the terrace around the fort to see the desert," and Marcel automatically assents. A marvelous description of the twilight desertscape is counterposed against Marcel's impatient complaint that he is cold and there is nothing to see anyway.

That night, however, Janine slips out of bed to return to the fort. There, alone under the chilly and vast firmament, she suffers a moment of awareness—an epiphany. She feels the sensual presence of her body, and she encompasses the sky full of stars stretched out over her as she lies against the cold parapet. This encounter with the night sky is her act of "adultery," which she does not share with Marcel, who is oblivious of her absence and only awakes to reach for a bottle of mineral water.

In all this, however, there is a note of disconcerting ambivalence. The distant tone of the narration raises the possibility that the reader has been "taken": Is this story actually only revelatory of Janine's disconsolate banality? More important, has Camus played a joke on readers by forcing them to choose between two diversely wretched characters?

"THE GUEST"

These questions also arise in "The Guest," the best story in *Exile and the Kingdom*, also set in North Africa—specifically in the snows of the Atlas Mountains in Algeria. Daru, an Algerian schoolteacher of French extraction, has fully provisioned himself to weather an expected blizzard which has emptied his one-room schoolhouse of its Arab pupils. He is comfortably awaiting its onset when he observes two figures, one on horseback, toiling up the steep slope leading toward the school building. The man on horseback is Balducci, a gendarme dragging behind him a trussed and cowering shepherd who killed his cousin with a billhook during a squabble over a share of grain.

Balducci asks the astonished Daru to safeguard the prisoner for the night and deliver him the next morning to police headquarters at Tinguit, twenty kilometers away. He explains that the Algerian revolt is on and police manpower is stretched thinly over the plateau. When Daru protests that delivering criminals is not his job, Balducci counters by insisting bitterly that "In wartime people do all kinds of jobs." Then he leaves Daru a revolver and departs.

Daru has little physical fear of the obviously spent murderer but knows full well that he is caught in an impossible situation: Delivering his charge will assure the probably lethal (in view of his isolated circumstances) enmity of the local Arab population; releasing him will make him a rebel and a traitor to his European countrymen. In the first case, his life would be in jeopardy, in the second his career and perhaps his freedom. Daru also feels morally affronted by the repugnant nature of his imposed task. The next day Daru escorts the felon to a trail juncture where he hands him a food package and a thousand francs. He gives him the choice of walking east for two hours to Tinguit and the police, or walking south across the plateau where nomads will shelter him according to their laws of hospitality.

On the way back to his schoolhouse Daru looks behind him and discerns the black dot of the Arab moving toward the police station. Arriving at the schoolhouse he reads a message chalked over his drawing of the four main rivers of France: "You handed over our brother, you will pay for this."

Thus the paradoxical title of this collection is explained. Daru, like his "guest," was born and has lived his life in this inhospitable plateau—this is his kingdom. Yet an accidental turn of events has transformed his kingdom into a place of exile. His strategy for eluding this onrushing absurdity has been unavailing; worse, Daru will become a casualty with little time left to savor his newly acquired awareness of the meaninglessness of the universe.

"The Guest," because of its artistic virtuosity, is a landmark which forces comparisons for English-speaking readers with such pinnacles of the adventure story with moral and epistemological overtones as Jack London's "To Build a Fire" and Stephen Crane's "The Blue Hotel." Apropos of this analysis, however, "The Guest" is an excellent and mercifully succinct distillation of Camus's outlook and provides a take-off point for an important criticism of it in line with the previous discussion of "The Adulterous Woman."

At least one critic, John K. Simon, writing in *Studies in Short Fiction*, shifts the focus of attention from the unsolvable quandary facing Daru to an assertion that Daru himself is morally flawed for abandoning the Arab under the pretense of giving him a choice when it is patent that this outcast is neither morally, psychologically, nor physically (a walk to the police station is shorter than one across the plateau) able to decide on a proper course of action. Daru's obsession with solitude—as exemplified by the fact that at one point Balducci calls him "cracked," and also by the puzzling observation that Daru's hostility toward the Arab and toward his new role as policeman cannot be fully accounted for within the text—explains his abandonment of the prisoner and reinforces the suspicion that Daru does not understand social process. If all this is true, then Camus's philosophic message becomes irrelevant and Daru is not a victim of an indifferently cruel universe, but rather he is a man who has been consistently guilty of social omissions and blunders.

"THE GROWING STONE"

The last story in the collection, "The Growing Stone," has an overtly neopagan motif, a recurring interest of Camus which critics have attributed to his North African upbringing. D'Arrast, a French engineer descended from an aristocratic family, is chauffeured by a Brazilian named Socrates across the jungle to a seaside town where he will build much-needed jetties and roads. During the all-night drive they pass through the town of Registro, which is populated by Japanese immigrants who still dress in their kimonos. Arriving at Iguape, D'Arrast is effusively received by the town officials, who are grateful for his services. The welcome is spoiled, however, by the inexplicable belligerence of the drunken police chief, who loutishly proclaims that D'Arrast's passport is not in order. D'Arrast insists on touring the quarters where his future laborers reside, and while there, he encounters a ship's cook who tells him that he survived a shipwreck after making a promise to St. George to carry a one-hundred-pound stone at the forthcoming procession.

D'Arrast also meets a "black Diana" who lures him to a ceremonial dance held the night before the procession. The poor of the town crowd into a large hut and engage in a frenetic, obscene, grotesque, and at times sinister ritual which at first nauseates D'Arrast but then bewitches him. At a certain point, D'Arrast is asked to leave. The ship's cook, contrary to his resolve to get a good night's sleep, stays on. The next day the weary cook falters while carrying the rock to the church. In an inspired moment D'Arrast wrests a cork mat from the encouraging crowd and shoulders the stone. Being young, strong, and well rested, he bears it easily; but nearing the portals of the church he veers away from them dramatically and, ignoring the enraged and mystified commands of the mob which dins "to the church," he heads for the cook's hovel and hurls the rectangular block onto the glowing fire in the center of the room, where it immediately becomes another idol.

This then is Camus's tentative answer to the problem of absurdity: In the face of the prevailing incongruity, arbitrariness, and disorganization, human beings can strive for an emotional coherence which sidesteps the question of absurdity, which Camus now views as merely an intellectual problem.

"THE RENEGADE" AND "THE SILENT MEN"

"The Renegade" depicts in the first person the psychotic state of mind of a missionary who, after mental and physical torture, surrenders morally to the Saharan heathens he has come to civilize. His tongue cut out, the renegade conducts a frenzied interior monologue as he waits to ambush the priest sent to replace him. Is this tour de force Camus's revenge upon Christianity? Can it also be construed as an attack upon the paganism which is more favorably presented in "The Growing Stone"? "The Silent Men" is more mundane. Set in a French city, it narrates how a crew of coopers returning to work after a failed strike decide not to communicate with their boss in an attempt to salve their humiliation. In spite of Camus's socialist sympathies, this story remains one of his few treatments of skilled craftsmen who, in this case, practice an obsolete craft.

"THE ARTIST AT WORK"

Finally, "The Artist at Work" is notable only because it contains the only humor in the collection. It is an overlong cataloging of the distractions of wife, children, and zealous friends, all of whom drive a moderately talented painter to isolation and artistic impotence. "The Artist at Work," like the other stories in *Exile and the Kingdom*, presents themes that are central to Camus's philosophy. They demonstrate the world of human suffering, solitude, humiliation, and isolation in an absurd world.

OTHER MAJOR WORKS

LONG FICTION: *L'Étranger*, 1942 (*The Stranger*, 1946); *La Peste*, 1947 (*The Plague*, 1948); *La Chute*, 1956 (*The Fall*, 1957); *La Mort heureuse*, 1971 (written 1936-1938; *A Happy Death*, 1972); *Le Premier homme*, 1994 (*The First Man*, 1995).

PLAYS: *Caligula*, wr. 1938-1939, pb. 1944 (English translation, 1948); *Le Malentendu*, pr., pb. 1944 (*The Misunderstanding*, 1948); *L'État de siège*, pr., pb. 1948 (*State of Siege*, 1958); *Les Justes*, pr. 1949 (*The Just Assassins*, 1958); *Caligula and Three Other Plays*, pb. 1958.

NONFICTION: *L'Envers et l'endroit*, 1937 ("The Wrong Side and the Right Side"); *Noces*, 1938 ("Nuptials"); *Le Mythe de Sisyphe*, 1942 (*The Myth of Sisyphus*, 1955); *L'Homme révolté*, 1951 (*The Rebel*, 1953); *L'Été*, 1954 ("Summer"); *Carnets: Mai 1935-février 1942*, 1962 (*Notebooks*, 1963); *Carnets: Janvier 1942-mars 1951*, 1964 (*Notebooks*,

1963); *Lyrical and Critical Essays*, 1968 (includes "The Wrong Side and the Right Side," "Nuptials," and "Summer").

BIBLIOGRAPHY

Bloom, Harold, ed. *Albert Camus*. New York: Chelsea House, 1989. A collection of essays written by some of the principal scholars of Camus's oeuvre. Among the contributors are Victor Brombert, Roger Shattuck, Paul de Man, Patrick McCarthy, and David R. Ellison. Harold Bloom's introduction, though brilliant in its own virtuosity, may lack a certain humanistic understanding.

Brée, Germaine. *Camus*. New York: Harcourt, Brace & World, 1964. A comprehensive study of the inner life and fictional universe of Camus. While drawing a sympathetic portrait of the writer, Brée gives particular importance to the aesthetic values in Camus's works. Also includes a chapter on the short story "The Renegade" from *Exile and the Kingdom*.

Cruickshank, John. *Albert Camus and the Literature of Revolt*. London: Oxford University Press, 1959. An important early book on Camus as writer and philosopher. Includes a general discussion of his principal ideas as they relate to the literature and historical events of the period. Offers some interesting comments concerning American literary influences on Camus.

Dunwoodie, Peter. *Camus: "L'Envers et L'endroit" and "L'Exil et le royaume."* London: Grant and Cutler, 1985. Presents an introductory discussion of the short story as genre and then looks for—in the best treatment in a single volume—the central themes and metaphors of the short stories contained in *Exile and the Kingdom*.

Hurley, D. F. "Looking for the Arab: Reading the Readings of Camus's 'The Guest.'" *Studies in Short Fiction* 30 (Winter, 1993): 79-93. A detailed, close reading that argues against the prevailing critical notion that the Arab prisoner in Camus's story is an idiot or a beast.

Jackson, Tommie Lee. *The Existential Fiction of Ayi Kwei Armah, Albert Camus, and Jean-Paul Sartre*. Lanham, Md.: University Press of America, 1997. Examines the existential writings of the three authors. Includes bibliographical references and an index.

Lazere, Donald. *The Unique Creation of Albert Camus*. New Haven, Conn.: Yale University Press, 1973. In his chapter on short fiction, Lazere finds the style of the interior monologue in "The Renegade" the most impressive technical feat in the collection and "The Growing Stone" the weakest piece of writing because of its mixing of a realistic and a symbolic style. Lazere contends that the collection shows that Camus did not master the short-story form.

Lottman, R. Herbert. *Albert Camus*. Garden City, N.Y.: Doubleday, 1979. The most comprehensive biography of Camus, especially important for its recounting of Camus's formative years in Algeria. Remains very useful for understanding the influence that the author's private life may have had on his fiction.

Suther, Judith D., ed. *Essays on Camus's "Exile and the Kingdom."* University, Miss.: Romance Monographs, 1981. An important collection of translated critical pieces written by international scholars using different literary approaches to the short stories of Camus. Interesting introductions by Germaine Brée and the editor.

Tarrow, Susan. *Exile from the Kingdom: A Political Rereading of Albert Camus*. University: University of Alabama Press, 1985. Combines a study of Camus's journalism with his fiction. As the title indicates, particular emphasis is placed on Camus's short stories.

Todd, Olivier. *Albert Camus: A Life*. Translated by Benjamin Ivry. New York: Alfred A. Knopf, 1994. Making use of material such as unpublished letters made available after the death of Camus's widow, this detailed biography reveals much about Camus's love affairs and his many important friendships.

Julian Grajewski, updated by James Gaash

ETHAN CANIN

Born: Ann Arbor, Michigan; July 19, 1960

PRINCIPAL SHORT FICTION

Emperor of the Air, 1988
The Palace Thief, 1994

OTHER LITERARY FORMS

Although Ethan Canin is the author of the novels *Blue River* (1991) and *For Kings and Planets* (1998), he is most acclaimed for his short fiction.

ACHIEVEMENTS

Ethan Canin received the Henfield/*Transatlantic Review* Award in 1989, the Houghton Mifflin Literary Fellowship in 1988, and a National Endowment for the Arts grant in 1989.

BIOGRAPHY

Ethan Canin's talents as a writer were first recognized by popular romance author Danielle Steel, who taught at Canin's private high school before her own novels became successful. After high school, Canin attended Stanford University, where he studied physics and then switched to English. After graduating from Stanford in 1982, he went on to get an M.F.A. from the prestigious writing program at the University of Iowa. Discouraged by his experience at the Iowa workshop, where he learned about many of the negative aspects of a writer's life, and feeling a need to be useful, Canin elected to attend Harvard's medical school. He was in the midst of his exams at medical school when the publishing company Houghton Mifflin proposed that he prepare a collection of short stories. This volume, titled *Emperor of the Air*, became a best-seller, rare among short-story collections. Canin's success has been such that he has published every story he wrote from his first acceptance in 1987. Although he received his M.D. from Harvard in 1992 and was a resident at a San Francisco hospital for a time, Canin left medicine to devote himself exclusively to writing.

ANALYSIS

Ethan Canin's short stories are characterized by a humorous and empathic approach to his characters and their situations and by a polished literary style. Family life is a favorite subject, although the members of Canin's families are almost always at odds with one another. Often Canin's stories turn on the exploration of two characters who, even if friends or members of the same family, approach life with differing values and modes of perception. As the paths of these characters diverge, Canin introduces a larger, more reflective aspect to his stories that allows the reader to consider such issues as sanity and normality, delinquency and conventionality, science and art.

The construction of a viable male identity is a strong concern in Canin's work. Whether they are concerned with fathers and sons, students and teachers, peers or brothers, Canin's stories often portray men whose characters or values clash. Of special concern is the contrast between the man who conforms to a fairly traditional role and the man who has chosen a more offbeat and unconventional way of life. Canin's mavericks can be frightening or they can be inspiring, but they always exist as a possibility in the psyche of his male characters.

The contrast between a scientific, secular America, whose primary value is material well-being, and a more imaginative, rebellious, or spiritual vision of life is also an important theme in Canin's work. In this theme readers can see the exquisite contrast between the medical and literary sides of Canin himself. In exploring the tensions in contemporary American life, however, Canin avoids an easy, journalistic topicality, so that his stories engage larger moral and philosophical issues and begin to function as timeless parables.

EMPEROR OF THE AIR

Although the stories in *Emperor of the Air* feature characters suffering from heart disease, epilepsy, and birth defects, these illnesses serve larger themes involving the tensions between father and son and between the practical mind and the poetic imagination.

In "Star Food," a young boy must resolve his father's wish that he help in his grocery store and learn to work for a living with the encouragement to dream coming from his mother, who feels that the time the boy spends on the roof looking at the stars will one day make him a great man. Competing perspectives are also the subject of "American Beauty." In this story, which features characters that return in Canin's novel *Blue River*, tensions between the creative Darienne and her two brothers, who are more interested in motorcycle mechanics, also contrast romantic and practical views of the world. Whereas the young boy in "Star Food" is able to balance these two perspectives, the divisions in this family end with revelations of psychopathology on the part of the older, dominant brother, who claims his brutal behavior as one of the prerogatives of masculinity.

Male role models are also the topic of "The Year of Getting to Know Us." The father's philandering and preoccupation with work and golf have made him an inaccessible parent, and his son reacts with acts of vandalism. Nevertheless, the remote father suggests that his emotional distance is actually, sadly, teaching his son how to be a man. The title story, "Emperor of the Air," gives readers a brighter look at the father-son relationship but once again explores the tensions between realistic and romantic perspectives. In this story, an old man suffering from heart disease fights to rescue an unhealthy old elm tree from his neighbor, a young man who wants to sacrifice it in the interests of three saplings growing in his yard. This contest between the old generation and the new is complicated by the fact that the old man is a former high school science teacher who has had no children, whereas the young father, who knows nothing about science, has a son. The young father invents for his son a magical story about one of the constellations in the sky, which he identifies as a sword that belongs to "the emperor of the air"; the future, in this story, seems to belong to the imaginative storyteller and not to the realistic man of science. A similar tribute to the poetic imagination, "We Are Nighttime Travelers," features a retired couple who have grown apart but who rediscover the love that brought them together when the husband takes up writing poetry.

Ethan Canin (©Miriam Berkley)

THE PALACE THIEF

Canin's next collection consists of four long stories, each featuring two men who are linked in one way or another but who represent contrasting perspectives and whose lives have widely diverged. "Accountant" is told from the perspective of Abba Roth, whose careful, even voice reveals a deeply conventional man with a steady, if dull, life as an accountant and family man. His opposite is Eugene Peters, a boyhood friend whose free spirit and enthusiasm for auto mechanics have provided him with a lucrative business. In middle age, Roth and Peters both attend a fantasy baseball camp overseen by the great former baseball player Willie Mays. Although Roth is an excellent ballplayer, his inability to get into the spirit of the game ends in Mays's awarding a pair of prized baseball socks not to the tiresome Roth but to the lively Peters. A resentful Roth steals one of the socks, but this one act of uncharacteristic daring cannot change the fact that he knows he has traded a life with a potential for passion, spontaneity, and adventure for a life of material security and comfort.

"Batorsag and Szerelem" returns to one of Canin's favorite themes, namely, the tensions between a brilliant and eccentric young man and his admiring kid brother. The title refers to words invented by the older brother, Clive, a math prodigy who has developed a secret language he shares only with his best friend Eddie. The words in the title are eventually associated with sexual secrets in Clive's life that so shock and upset his previously indulgent parents that their discovery begins what Clive's brother describes as "the great unturning," in which he becomes the favored son and the free-spirited Clive the outcast whose great promise is never fulfilled.

Like "Accountant," the third story, "City of Broken Hearts," features both baseball and a defeated, middle-aged businessman. Wilson Kohler, who has lost his wife to someone higher up in the company, is a lonely man who seeks consolation in devoting himself to the fortunes of the Boston Red Sox baseball team. Wilson is baffled by the life of his son Brent, an idealistic college student who wears an earring and whose sensitivity to the feminine side has led him to work during his summer vacation at a shelter for battered women. Representative of a new and different generation of men, Brent also has an almost magical role in the life of his father, gently bringing his father out of the past and into a love affair that will give him a new lease on life,

The title story, "The Palace Thief," is narrated by Hundert, a retired history teacher at a fashionable West Virginia preparatory school. Although he prides himself on his integrity and his role as the molder of the young, Hundert was once manipulated by a powerful senator into making allowances for his ne'er-do well son, whom Hundert knows to have cheated and whose dishonesty he has never exposed. The unscrupulous son in turn becomes a powerful political and economic force in the state, and also manipulates the now-retired professor into helping him become elected senator. Hundert constantly draws on analogies between his situation and the Augustan age of the Roman Empire, but he does not realize that, far from being a principal player, he is merely a slave, serving the interests of the wealthy and the powerful.

OTHER MAJOR WORKS

LONG FICTION: *Blue River*, 1991; *For Kings and Planets*, 1998.

EDITED TEXT: *Writers Harvest 2*, 1996.

BIBLIOGRAPHY

Frucht, Abby. "Grand Delusions." *The New York Times* (February 20, 1994). Review of *The Palace Thief* discusses each of the four stories in detail. Although she terms the stories highly intellectual, she does not feel that this distracts from their effectiveness in depicting lives that are disintegrating. She characterizes all four protagonists as "antiheroes" who seem either foolish or delusional about their lives and find that, instead of an expected safety and security, they have found themselves in a vast psychological minefield.

Gurewich, David. "Breaking Away from the Brat Pack." *The New Leader* (March 21, 1988): 21-22. This review of *Emperor of the Air* examines several stories in detail, pointing out their depiction of the American family as troubled and unsettled. Gurewich does not feel Canin is a trailblazer, noting the similarity to the stories of John Cheever, but also describes Canin as a "postminimalist" who moves the short story into the future.

Leavitt, David. "As Children and Others See It." *The New York Times Book Review* (February 14, 1988): 7. In this mixed review of *Emperor of the Air*, Leavitt, a well-known novelist and short-story writer, discusses a number of the stories in this collection. While suggesting the stories are overly artful and sentimental, Leavitt also praises Canin s talent as prodigious and admits that he admires his skill and imagination.

Lehmann-Haupt, Christopher. *Emperor of the Air*. *The New York Times* (January 23, 1988): C34. Important review by the noted critic discusses a number of the stories from *Emperor of the Air* in detail, praising the stories as remarkable and as preoccupied with matters of ultimate concern— life and death, youth and age, wealth and poverty.

_____. "Errors in Judgment and Ripples Thereof." *The New York Times*, February 3, 1994. Review of *The Palace Thief* singles out the first story, "The

Accountant," as the best of the four and provides a lengthy analysis of it. Notes that although the subject matter is contemporary, characters and plots are traditional. Applauds the collection as a commanding performance that surpasses Canin's two previous books and calls him one of the most satisfying writers on the contemporary scene.

Michener, Charles. "The Palace Thief." *The New York Times* (March 21, 1994): 76. Describes the stories as old-fashioned tales that echo past masters Henry James and John O'Hara but praises Canin's natural assurance of voice, his acuity, the steadiness of his moral compass, and his often humorous detail.

Yardley, Jonathan. "Canin's Mature Miracles." *Washington Post*, January 20, 1988, p. C2. An important review of *Emperor of the Air* by one of the United States' most influential literary critics, this essay praises Canin's maturity. Pointing out especially his insights into the relationship between father and son and also into the mysteries of the solitary, individual psyche, Yardley sums up his achievement by saying that in studying the health of the body, Canin has also discovered much about the human heart.

Margaret Boe Birns

KAREL ČAPEK

Born: Malé Svatoňovice, Bohemia, Austro-Hungarian Empire (now Czech Republic); January 9, 1890

Died: Prague, Czechoslovakia (now Czech Republic); December 25, 1938

PRINCIPAL SHORT FICTION

Zářivé hlubiny, 1916 (with Josef Čapek; *The Luminous Depths*, 1916)

Bozímuka, 1917

Krakonošova zahrada, 1918 (with Josef Čapek)

Trapné povídky, 1921 (*Money and Other Stories*, 1929)

Povídky z jedné kapsy and *Povídky z druhé kapsy*, 1929 (*Tales from Two Pockets*, 1932)

Devatero pohádek, 1931 (*Fairy Tales*, 1933)

Kniha apokryfů, 1946 (*Apocryphal Stories*, 1949)

OTHER LITERARY FORMS

Karel Čapek, who earned his living as a journalist, is best known for his futuristic drama, *R.U.R.: Rossum's Universal Robots* (with Josef Čapek, 1921; English translation, 1923), which brought into the language the word "robot," coined by his brother Josef. Besides his collections of short stories, Čapek published seven novels and a book of travel sketches. Six of his plays were produced.

ACHIEVEMENTS

Karel Čapek, recognized as one of Czechoslovakia's leading literary figures, is remembered for works of science fiction in which he expresses concern for the human race in a rapidly changing, increasingly technological society. Elected president of the PEN Club of Prague in 1925, Čapek chose not to serve, although a decade later he was persuaded to succeed H. G. Wells as president of the International PEN Club. Unable to attend his inauguration in Latin America, Čapek failed to assume office. Čapek was a serious contender for the Nobel Prize in Literature in 1937 and 1938. The Nobel Committee, however, fearful of offending German Chancellor Adolf Hitler, passed him over.

BIOGRAPHY

The son of Antonin Čapek, a physician, and Božena Čapková, a woman much interested in folklore, Karel Čapek was the youngest of their three children. Born in Malé Svatoňovice, a rural community in the Krakonose Mountains not far from Czecho-

Karel Čapek (Archive Photos)

slovakia's border with Austria and Germany, Karel was a sickly child. Božena entertained her children with folktales, many of which eventually made their way into the writing of her sons, Karel and Josef.

Karel and Josef were seldom apart during their lifetimes, although in 1910 Karel went to Berlin to study and Josef went to Paris. Karel had already studied philosophy at Prague's Charles University under Thomas G. Masaryk, who became president of Czechoslovakia in 1918, holding that position until 1935. He and the Čapek brothers were close friends, who met every Friday night at the double house that Karel and Josef built in 1925 and in which they lived side by side for the rest of their lives.

The rise of Hitler in Germany troubled the Čapeks greatly. Karel, severely depressed by the oppressive political climate, failed physically and, on Christmas Day, 1938, less than a year before World War II began, succumbed to pneumonia. His widow, Olga, burned his papers, fearing that in the political climate that then existed they might incriminate his friends.

Shortly after Karel died, Nazi officials arrived at his house with a warrant for his arrest.

ANALYSIS

Karel and Josef Čapek frequently collaborated in their writing. Their early collection *The Luminous Depths* is a collaboration, although some of the stories in it were the sole work of Karel. The stories in this collection are charged with a forceful vitality. They affirm that life is worthwhile but then question whether humans are capable of appreciating the value of life. The collection begins with a cynical and ironic tone but soon moves toward optimism. Before the end, however, the tone is clearly pessimistic as the Čapeks consider the status of humans in society and their ability to adapt naturally to their lots.

The metaphysical tales in Čapek's collection *Bozímuka* reflect the author's delving into aesthetics, particularly the aesthetics of French philosopher Henri Bergson. They are also much influenced by the pragmatism of American educator and philosopher William James. Karel published *Pragmatismus* (1918) shortly after this collection and published his doctoral dissertation *Musaion* (1920-1921), which focused on aesthetics.

The tales in *Bozímuka*, among his deepest and most serious work philosophically, are precursors of some of Čapek's later science-fiction writing. They raise doubts about Bergson's optimism and James's pragmatism. Čapek was searching for absolutes that neither Bergson nor James could provide. This collection, reflecting Čapek's pessimism resulting largely from his concerns about World War I, reveal his sadness, indeed his personal agony, at failing in his search for God.

The collaborative *Krakonošova zahrada* is less reflective than *Bozímuka*. It is a collection of the brothers' earlier writing to which they added an autobiographical preface. Much of the folklore they learned at their mother's knee is found in the tales included in this collection. The preface reveals two gifted young men who contemplate devoting their lives to literature.

Čapek's next collection, *Money and Other Stories*, is often regarded as his most pessimistic work, although it moves beyond *Bozímuka*, suggesting that if the search for God is futile, then a renewed sympathy for humankind is a logical alternative. The establishment of a new humanitarianism is clearly the thrust of this volume. Its tales reflect a relative rather than an absolute judgment of human actions.

Čapek's later collections, often focusing on crime and detective work, are less philosophical than these seminal early works. The former grew largely out of his work as a journalist, yet nevertheless go beyond being mere detective fiction. Allegorically they deal with humankind's search for truth.

"A Scandal and the Press"

Among the stories in *The Luminous Depths* is "Skandál a žurnalistika" ("A Scandal and the Press"), presumably written in 1911 when Karel spent the summer in Paris with Josef, who was studying there. This story is important because it represents a new genre of narrative fiction suggestive of Truman Capote's *In Cold Blood* (1965), which is often referred to as a nonfiction novel.

Essentially, this story is the report of how a French aristocrat orchestrated the false report of his own suicide so that he could run away with his children's governess. The story, in all its sensationalism, was reported in the Paris press when Karel was visiting his brother in the French capital. Appropriating the news story to his own purposes, Čapek retells it, using the actual names in the news reports but adding to the story an ironic twist that is actually a commentary on reporting techniques. In this story, besides moving toward the development of a new genre, Čapek shows early signs of his fascination with crime reporting, which enters into his writing quite fully several years later in *Povídky z jedné kapsy* and *Povídky z druhé kapsy* (1929; *Tales from Two Pockets*, 1932).

Money and Other Stories

This collection is composed largely of a number of short stories Čapek published between 1918 and 1920. These stories are reminiscent of some of Anton Chekhov's stories, although they possess an irony not found in Chekhov. In this respect, they are more similar in tone to some of the stories of Guy de Maupassant or O. Henry.

All of these stories place their protagonists in impossible predicaments to which there is no reasonable solution. The protagonists are forced to choose between good and evil, imposing upon them a moral decision that is both painful and unsatisfying. Having failed in his search for the absolute good he sought in *Bozímuka*, Čapek now realizes that human beings are victims of a world in which all values are relative. This situation forces people to choose between one good and another.

Čapek had reached the point of believing that all people have their own truths. He sought in these tales to depict human beings in states of humiliation and weakness but to do so without debasing their value as humans. He acknowledges human frailties such as cowardice, cruelty, and disloyalty, but he makes no judgments about the people who reflect such frailties.

"Tribunal"

One of the stories in *Money and Other Stories*, "Tribunal," deviating from the realism of the collection's other stories, is worth noting. This tale recounts how a military judge quite justifiably has condemned a soldier for murdering and robbing a comrade who has fallen in battle. Despite the justness of his sentence, the judge suddenly grows aware of an inner voice that questions whether law and justice, conscience and God, exist.

This revelation makes him consider his condemnation of the soldier arbitrary and tyrannical. Stripped by this revelation of his moral authority, the judge turns into a weak, pitiful person. This story makes an extreme statement reflecting the personal philosophical skepticism that led Čapek from his quest for absolutes to his acknowledgment that morality is relative, a conclusion at which he arrived with no small degree of personal anguish.

Fairy Tales

In the final volume of his fiction, *Fairy Tales*, the reader finds a smattering of short pieces that Čapek wrote for newspapers. Although most of these tales are somewhat shallow and suffer from lack of revision, a few of them rise above the others in their content.

Probably the best of the pieces in this collection is "Hamlet, Prince of Denmark," written in 1931. This tale is a stinging satire on unilateral newspaper reporting. The journalist in the story reports on the tragedy at Elsinor, casting Polonius as the hero. This tale reflects clearly Čapek's continuing struggle that grew out of his lost faith in absolutes and his grudging acceptance of moral relativism. He is forced to admit that Truth with a capital "T" does not exist and that point of view determines moral values.

OTHER MAJOR WORKS

LONG FICTION: *Továrna na absolutno*, 1922 (*The Absolute at Large*, 1927); *Krakatit*, 1924 (English translation, 1925); *Hordubal*, 1933 (English translation, 1934); *Provětroó*, 1934 (*Meteor*, 1935); *Obyčejný život*, 1934 (*An Ordinary Life*, 1936); *Válka a mloky*, 1936 (*The War with the Newts*, 1937); *Privni parta*, 1937 (*The First Rescue Party*, 1939); *Život a dílo skladatele Foltýna*, 1939 (*The Cheat*, 1941).

PLAYS: *Lásky hra osudná*, wr. 1910, pr. 1930 (with Josef Čapek); *Loupezník*, pr. 1920 (*The Robber*, 1931); *Ze života hmyzu*, pb. 1920 (with Josef Čapek; *The Insect Play*, 1923; also known as *And So Infinitum: The Life of the Insects*); *Věc Makropulos*, pb. 1920 (*The Macropulos Secret*, 1925); *R.U.R.: Rossum's Universal Robots*, pr. 1921 (with Josef Čapek, 1921; English translation, 1923); *Adam Stvořitel*, pb. 1927 (with Josef Čapek; *Adam the Creator*, 1929); *Bílá nemoc*, pr. 1937 (*Power and Glory*, 1938; also known as *The White Plague*, 1988); *Matka*, pr. 1938 (*The Mother*, 1939); *Bilá nemoc*, pr. 1937 (*Power and Glory*, 1938).

NONFICTION: *Pragmatismus*, 1918; *Kritika slov*, 1920; *O nejbližších vecech*, 1920 (*Intimate Things*, 1935); *Muscaion*, 1920-1921; *Italské listy*, 1923 (*Letters from Italy*, 1929); *Anglické listy*, 1924 (*Letters from England*, 1925); *Hovory s T. G. Masarykem*, 1928-1935 (3 volumes; *President Masaryk Tells His Story*, 1934; also as *Masaryk on Thought and Life*, 1938); *Zahradníkův rok*, 1929 (*The Gardener's Year*, 1931); *Výlet do Španěl*, 1930 (*Letters from Spain*, 1931); *Marsyas*, 1931 (*In Praise of Newspapers*, 1951); *O věcech obecných: Čili, Zóon politikon*, 1932; *Obrázky z Holandska*, 1932 (*Letters from Holland*, 1933); *Dášeóka*, 1933 (*Dashenka*, 1940); *Cesta na sever*, 1936 (*Travels in the North*, 1939); *Měl jsem psa a kočku*, 1939 (*I Had a Dog and a Cat*, 1940);

Obrázky z domova, 1953; *Veci kolemnás*, 1954; *Poznámky o tvorbě*, 1959; *Viktor Dyk-S. K. Neumannbratří Č.: Korespondence z let 1905-1918*, 1962.

TRANSLATION: *Francouzská poesie nové doby*, 1920 (of French poetry).

BIBLIOGRAPHY

Bradbrook, Bohuslava R. *Karel Čapek: In Pursuit of Truth, Tolerance, and Trust*. Portland, Oreg.: Sussex Academic Press, 1998. A critical study of the works of Čapek. Includes a bibliography and an index.

_____. "Karel Čapek's Contribution to Czech National Literature." In *Czechoslovakia Past and Present*, edited by Miloslav Rechcigl. The Hague: Mouton, 1968. Clearly places Čapek high on the list of notable Czech authors, demonstrating how much his writing affected other literary production in the country as well as making a political impact. Remarks perceptively on Čapek's inventiveness and on his ability to work in several genres.

Harkins, William E. *Karel Čapek*. New York: Columbia University Press, 1962. Despite its age, this carefully researched and well-written critical biography of Karel Čapek remains the best available full-length source on the author. Harkins depicts with considerable accuracy the social tensions that arose in Czechoslovakia and much affected Čapek during Hitler's rise to power.

Heé, Veronika. "The Pocket-Stories of Karel Čapek." *Studia Slavica* 22, nos. 3/4 (1976): 401-411. Focuses on the means Čapek uses to convey his philosophical ideas through the detective stories included in *Tales from Two Pockets*. A good critical analysis of how these pieces succeed as detective stories while simultaneously reaching beyond that genre to shed light on more serious matters.

Mann, Erika. "A Last Conversation with Karel Čapek." *The Nation* 149 (January 14, 1939): 68-69. Although brief, this account by Thomas Mann's daughter of her last meeting with Čapek at about the time of the Munich Pact comments on the pressures Čapek found building up all around him, causing him to undergo a physical decline that eventually led to his death. She senses and comments on Čapek's sickness of the spirit that left him unwilling to continue living in the face of Hitler's growing fanaticism and power.

Matuska, Alexander. *Karel Čapek: An Essay.* Translated by Cathryn Alan. London: Allen & Unwin, 1964. The best account in print of Čapek's artistry. It discusses how he develops his themes, shapes his characterization, fashions his plots, and handles the details that underlie the structure of his work. Despite its age, this book is a valuable resource for those interested in this author.

Wellek, Rene. *Essays on Czech Literature.* The Hague: Mouton, 1963. Wellek's essay on Karel Čapek that appears in this book was originally published in 1936. It is among the most searching and insightful assessments of the author written during his lifetime. Wellek considered Čapek at the height of his powers in 1936.

R. Baird Shuman

TRUMAN CAPOTE
Truman Streckfus Persons

Born: New Orleans, Louisiana; September 30, 1924
Died: Bel-Air, California; August 25, 1984

PRINCIPAL SHORT FICTION
A Tree of Night and Other Stories, 1949
Breakfast at Tiffany's: A Short Novel and Three Stories, 1958
One Christmas, 1983
I Remember Grandpa: A Story, 1986

OTHER LITERARY FORMS
In addition to stories and short novels, Truman Capote wrote travel sketches and various kinds of nonfiction, much of which has been collected, along with some of Capote's short stories and novellas, in *A Capote Reader* (1987). The volume *Local Color* (1950), on the other hand, is a collection solely of travel essays. Capote also did some screenwriting, including critically well-received scripts for *Beat the Devil* (1954) and *The Innocents* (1961), an adaptation of the Henry James story *The Turn of the Screw* (1898), and an adaptation of *Breakfast at Tiffany's*, which became a well-known film in 1961.

In Cold Blood (1966), probably his most famous work, is a "nonfiction novel," a documented re-creation of the murder of a family in Kansas. The novel was both a critical and a popular success, and the television film version won an Emmy Award in 1967. Capote's last work, another nonfiction novel, *Answered Prayers: The Unfinished Novel* (1986), set off a social scandal with its gossipy revelations. Capote finished his writing career in ignominy.

ACHIEVEMENTS
The best of Truman Capote's writing is regarded as elegant prose, noted for its lucidity, although at its worst it became an example of vain excess and gossip. Yet Capote was one of the United States' leading post-World War II writers. He pioneered the genre of the "nonfiction novel" with *In Cold Blood* and gained renown for his short stories and novellas. His story "Miriam" won the O. Henry Memorial Award in 1943, and "Shut a Final Door" won the same prize in 1946. Although much of his work has been both critically and popularly praised, Capote was rarely formally recognized during his writing career.

BIOGRAPHY
Because his parents were divorced when he was four years old, Truman Capote was reared by aunts and cousins in a small town in Alabama. At seventeen, he moved to New York City and worked his way up from mailroom clerk to feature writer for *The New Yorker*. Capote's early promise seemed fulfilled with

Truman Capote (Library of Congress)

the success of *In Cold Blood*, and he spent many years traveling around the world as a celebrated author. He became the pet celebrity for a number of high-society women, most notably Barbara "Babe" Paley and Lee Bouvier Radziwill, sister of Jacqueline Kennedy Onassis. His charmed life seemed to fade, however, under the pressure of trying to produce another successful novel. During the 1970's and early 1980's, Capote's health was ruined by alcoholism and drug dependency.

The downslide began in 1975, however, when *Esquire* magazine published Capote's story "La Côte Basque: 1965." The story was a thinly veiled exposé of the scandals of the rich and famous, and its targets did not appreciate the publicity. Capote's friends immediately ostracized him, and he became *persona non grata* in many of the places he had previously frequented. Depressed by the reaction that his story generated, Capote became reclusive. His work deteriorated even more, and he did not produce anything to rival his earlier writing before he died at the home of his longtime friend Joanne Carson in 1984.

ANALYSIS

Truman Capote's stories are best known for their mysterious, dreamlike occurrences. As his protagonists try to go about their ordinary business, they meet with unexpected obstacles—usually in the form of haunting, enigmatic strangers. Corresponding to some childhood memory or to someone the protagonist once knew, these people take on huge proportions and cause major changes in the character's life. The central figures of these stories are usually people who have left their hometowns, who travel, or who live alone, for they seem most vulnerable to chance encounters. Their isolation gives them the time, and their loneliness gives them the motivation to see these experiences through to their conclusions—and often with great risk.

Capote was a careful craftsman. His words are meticulously chosen for their evocative power, and, at their best, they create highly charged images and symbols. His descriptions of the seasons or weather further heighten the effects he wants to create. Snow, rain, dusk, and sunlight serve to separate the particular setting from a larger landscape, thus reinforcing the self-reflexive nature of his stories. Attics, kitchens, one-room walk-ups, and isolated apartments are typical settings that also provide sequestered settings. The atmosphere, location, characters, and events present a touching but often chilling and ominous beauty. The combination of reality and dream also produces an eerie beauty.

"A TREE OF NIGHT"

In "A Tree of Night," one of his finest stories, Kay is a young, attractive student returning to college after the funeral of an uncle. It is late on a winter night, bare and icy, when she boards the train from the deserted platform. Taking the only available seat, she sits opposite an odd-looking couple. The woman is in her fifties, with a huge head and a dwarfish body, while the man is mute, with marblelike eyes and an expressionless face. Although Kay is initially polite, she hopes to be left alone, but the woman wants company and conversation. Kay tries to remain distant, but the woman and man are persistent and aggressive. Without any warning, the man reaches toward Kay and strokes her cheek. Her reaction is immediate but confused: She is repelled by the boldness of the gesture while, at the same time, she is touched by the delicacy.

From this point on, Kay seems to view the man and woman as harbingers of danger. Capote's style remains realistic and his tone objective, but the couple behave as though they are part of Kay's nightmare. The woman talks endlessly, always wanting a response from her listener. She forces Kay to drink liquor with her and even grabs her wrist. As in a nightmare, Kay wants to scream and awaken the other passengers, but no sounds come out. Trying to escape from the woman's irritating voice, Kay has a reverie as she stares into the void face of the man, and suddenly his face and her uncle's dead face blend. She sees, or imagines that she sees, a shared secret and a stillness. This association of the stranger with someone from her past is deadly, preparing the reader for the end of the story.

By degrees, the man assumes control over Kay. He takes from his pocket a peach seed and fondles it gently. The woman insists that he only wants Kay to purchase it as a good-luck charm, but Kay is frightened, interpreting his action as some kind of warning. Trying to avoid the man, she leaves her seat for the observation platform and fresh air, but soon she senses someone beside her and knows that it must be the man. Now, without the distracting annoyance of the woman, Kay understands why she finds him so threatening. Unable to speak or to hear, he is like her uncle, dead, and the dead can haunt. She further recognizes him as a figure from her childhood dreams, the boogeyman, the "wizard-man," the mysterious personage that could bring alive "terrors that once, long ago, had hovered above her like haunted limbs on a tree of night." Kay's submission is unquestionable, but precisely what she submits to is left ambiguous. Together, she and the man return to their seats, and she gives him money for the peach seed. Then the woman takes possession of Kay's whole purse and, although Kay wants to shout, she does not. Finally the woman takes Kay's raincoat and pulls it "like a shroud" over her head. No longer struggling, Kay sinks into a strange passivity.

"A Tree of Night" raises many questions but provides few answers. The characters are realistically presented, but eccentric, to say the least. Kay is not wholly convincing, yet is still three-dimensional. It is rather the events themselves that appear unlikely and nightmarish, but since Capote delights in paradox, his story cannot be classified as either pure dream or simple reality. Why does Kay not protest? To what extent do she and the mute actually communicate? Is the submission of the young girl carefully planned by the couple? Are the two travelers real passengers who want to do her harm, or can they be projections from Kay's psyche? Or are they merely two unique strangers to whom Kay attributes much more power than they really have? These ambiguities are the source of both the story's weaknesses and its strengths; they enrich the encounter and abstract it, but they also leave the reader feeling baffled. Nevertheless, Capote seems to imply that human beings are extremely vulnerable to destructive instincts. Perhaps beginning with a memory or fear from deep within the psyche, one projects it and expands it until it acquires a frightening degree of reality. In fact, it may become a deadly kind of reality. Kay essentially wills herself first into isolation from other passengers and finally into submission. She returns from the observation platform accompanied by the stranger. She chooses neither to change her seat nor to scream. Eventually, she chooses not to struggle. Human beings are delicate creatures, and the power of the "wizard-man" is enough to cause Kay to sink into nightmarish and unnecessary helplessness.

"MASTER MISERY"

The mysterious realm of dream can invade the workaday world and then consume it. This is precisely what happens in "Master Misery" when Sylvia leaves her hometown of Easton to stay with married friends who live in New York City. Soon she becomes frustrated with her daily routine and her "namby-pamby, bootsytotsy" friends. Hoping to earn money to find her own apartment, Sylvia overhears a conversation in the Automat. As unlikely as it sounds, a certain Mr. Revercomb purchases dreams. Intrigued, Sylvia visits his Fifth Avenue brownstone and discovers that Mr. Revercomb does indeed purchase dreams for cash. As she continues to visit his office, events take an unfortunate turn. The more Sylvia sees him, the more he seems eccentric, even unnatural. One time as she whispers her dream, Mr. Revercomb bends forward to brush her ear with his lips, apparently in a sexual approach.

Sylvia becomes so obsessed with selling her dreams that everything else in her life loses significance. She cuts off communication with her married friends, quits her office job, and rents a dingy studio apartment. Her only friend is Oreilly, a former clown whom she meets in Mr. Revercomb's waiting room. They have much in common, for Oreilly used to sell his dreams also, but now Mr. Revercomb has no use for them. Although he spends most of his time drunk, Oreilly has the foresight to warn his new companion against the man he calls the Master of Misery, who is so adept at convincing people that parting with a dream is worth five dollars. He explains to Sylvia that she must not lose her independence or her private world of memory and dream, and he compares Mr. Revercomb with the demon of childhood nightmare, the ominous figure who haunted the trees, chimneys, attics, and graveyards of make-believe. Like the mute in "A Tree of Night," Revercomb is "a thief and a threat," for after he appropriates one's dreams, it is a short passage to one's subconscious and one's soul.

Sylvia's life contracts to unhappy proportions. She moves from Revercomb's waiting room back to Oreilly, her waiting companion, who commiserates with her shrinking self before consuming the liquor she buys with her dream-money. He does, however, advise her to ask Revercomb for her dreams back, provided that she gradually returns the money over a period of time. Sylvia agrees, for her life has become miserable and isolated, but this is a Faustian story, and what was spent cannot be retrieved. Revercomb informs Sylvia that under no circumstances would he return what she has sold and, besides, he has already used them up. Walking home in the falling snow, Sylvia acknowledges that she is no longer her own master and has no individuality; soon she will not have even Oreilly, who will go his own way. Thinking she used Revercomb, it turns out that he has used her, and now they are inseparable—until he discards her as he did Oreilly. The story concludes as Sylvia overhears

footsteps following behind. There are two boys, who have followed her from the park and continue to do so. Sylvia is frightened, but like Kay in "A Tree of Night," she becomes passive and submissive, for there is "nothing left to steal."

As in much of Capote's short fiction, the individual tacitly gives a stranger enormous power. Once Sylvia abdicates full responsibility for herself and enters Revercomb's world, she becomes vulnerable and he becomes omniscient. Gradually she is emptied of friends, an orderly routine, ambition, desire, and, finally, of self-possession. The reader can never be sure who Revercomb is or what he does with dreams, but Sylvia, not the Master of Misery, is the focus of interest. She allows him to create her misery, leaving her with no one, not even her former self.

Capote's early work especially makes use of the gothic tradition, but because the details remain realistic and controlled, the mysterious elements are subtle and therefore even more insidious. The "wizardman" is Capote's archetype—the mute in "A Tree of Night," Mr. Revercomb in "Master Misery," the young girl in "Miriam," Mr. Destronelli in "The Headless Hawk." This figure transforms the actual world of the protagonist, usually in undesirable and irreversible ways. Whether the encounter with this stranger is a final retreat into narcissism or a submission to a purely external presence may not be clarified, but the fragility of the human psyche is all too clear.

OTHER MAJOR WORKS

LONG FICTION: *Other Voices, Other Rooms*, 1948; *The Grass Harp*, 1951; *A Christmas Memory*, 1956 (serial); *In Cold Blood*, 1966; *The Thanksgiving Visitor*, 1967 (serial); *Answered Prayers: The Unfinished Novel*, 1986.

PLAYS: *The Grass Harp: A Play*, pr., pb. 1952; *House of Flowers*, pr. 1954 (with Harold Arlen).

SCREENPLAYS: *Beat the Devil*, 1954 (with John Huston); *The Innocents*, 1961.

NONFICTION: *Local Color*, 1950; *The Muses Are Heard*, 1956; *Observations*, 1959 (with Richard Avedon); *The Dogs Bark: Public People and Private Places*, 1973.

MISCELLANEOUS: *Selected Writings*, 1963; *Trilogy: An Experiment in Multimedia*, 1969 (with Eleanor Perry and Frank Perry); *Music for Chameleons*, 1980; *Three by Truman Capote*, 1985; *A Capote Reader*, 1987.

BIBLIOGRAPHY

Brinnin, John Malcolm. *Truman Capote: Dear Heart, Old Buddy*. Rev. ed. New York: Delacorte Press, 1986. This expansion on an earlier memoir of Capote (which can be found in Brinnin's *Sextet*, 1981) chronicles Capote's life from before the success of *In Cold Blood* to his ruin from alcoholism and drugs. Most useful is the insight into the literary circles in which Capote moved. Includes an index.

Clarke, Gerald. *Capote: A Biography*. New York: Simon & Schuster, 1988. Probably the definitive biographical work on Capote, this lengthy text covers all the ups and downs of his career. In particular, Clarke recounts the effect that the short story "La Côte Basque: 1965" (later published as part of *Answered Prayers: The Unfinished Novel*) had on his life. Contains copious references and an index.

Dunphy, Jack. *"Dear Genius": A Memoir of My Life with Truman Capote*. New York: McGraw-Hill, 1987. In this biography, Dunphy reminisces about Capote and discusses the self-destructive streak that perhaps led the writer to alienate almost everyone who loved him. Supplemented by an index.

Garson, Helen S. *Truman Capote: A Study of the Short Fiction*. New York: Twayne, 1992. An introduction to Capote's short fiction, arranged chronologically. Provides brief analyses of his major stories and includes critical essays by a number of other critics.

Grobel, Lawrence. *Conversations with Capote*. New York: New American Library, 1985. This biography uses interview material to flesh out its information. Grobel covers Capote's life from childhood to his fall from society's grace and his subsequent death. In chapter 4, entitled "Writing," Capote discusses his writing career and the authors who he believed had the greatest influence on him. Includes a brief primary bibliography that lists films that Capote scripted and an index.

Hardwick, Elizabeth. "Tru Confessions." *The New York Review of Books* 45 (January 15, 1998): 4-5. Discusses George Plimpton's recording the remarks of those who came into contact with Capote's journey to literary fame; notes that Plimpton arranges these voices to produce the effect of the unrehearsed, companionable exchange at a cocktail party; argues that the method and result suit their subject, given that Capote, when not writing, was partying, forever receiving and producing banter.

Inge, M. Thomas, ed. *Truman Capote: Conversations*. Jackson: University Press of Mississippi, 1987. This book is a collection of interviews with Capote done by interviewers who range from Gloria Steinem to George Plimpton to Capote himself, in a section called "Self-Portrait." The index allows the reader to find specific references to individual short stories.

Plimpton, George. *Truman Capote: In Which Various Friends, Enemies, Acquaintances, and Detractors Recall His Turbulent Career*. New York: Doubleday, 1997. As the subtitle warns, this work is about a controversial author. As an oral biography based on interviews, it provides dramatic, primary information, but it also must be checked against the more reliable biography by Gerald Clarke. Includes biographies of contributors and a chronology.

Windham, Donald. *Lost Friendships: A Memoir of Truman Capote, Tennessee Williams, and Others*. New York: William Morrow, 1987. A friend of the major literary lights of the 1950's and 1960's, as well as a novelist himself, Windham dedicates the first half of *Lost Friendships* to his relationship with Capote and its subsequent decline. No reference material is included.

Miriam Fuchs, updated by Jo-Ellen Lipman Boon

ORSON SCOTT CARD

Born: Richland, Washington; August 24, 1951

Capitol: The Worthing Chronicle, 1979
Unaccompanied Sonata and Other Stories, 1981
Cardography, 1987
The Folk of the Fringe, 1989
The Worthing Saga, 1990
Maps in a Mirror: The Short Fiction of Orson Scott Card, 1990
Magic Mirror, 1999 (illustrated by Nathan Pinnock)

OTHER LITERARY FORMS

A prolific author in many forms, Orson Scott Card has written, in addition to his many short stories, more than a dozen novels, as well as plays, poetry, video and audiotape productions, nonfiction books, and essays on biography, history, Mormonism, the craft of writing, computing, science fiction and fantasy, and other topics. His most honored works are series of novels, especially a science-fiction series that consists of *Ender's Game* (1985), *Speaker for the Dead* (1986), *Xenocide* (1991), *Children of the Mind* (1996), and *Ender's Shadow* (1999), and a fantasy series, *Tales of Alvin Maker*, the first volumes of which are *Seventh Son* (1987), *Red Prophet* (1988), *Prentice Alvin* (1989), *Alvin Journeyman* (1995), and *Heartfire* (1998).

ACHIEVEMENTS

Within the genres of fantasy and science fiction, Orson Scott Card achieved eminence early in his career. Before his fortieth birthday, he not only had joined the small group of science-fiction writers to receive both the Nebula and Hugo Awards—the most prestigious in the field—for the same work, *Ender's Game*, but also had become one of only two writers to capture both awards two years in a row, when *Speaker for the Dead* won them in 1986. Card won the Hugo Award again in 1991 for his nonfiction work *How to Write Science Fiction and Fantasy* (1990).

Science fiction and fantasy tend to gain relatively little attention from the reviewers whose reviews appear in general-circulation media. Card, like Ursula K. Le Guin, is one of the few authors to attract a wider readership and receive the notice of critics outside the science-fiction and fantasy magazines and journals.

BIOGRAPHY

Orson Scott Card was born on August 24, 1951, in Richland, Washington, the son of Willard Richards, a teacher, and Peggy Jane Park Card, an administrator. He earned his B.A. at Brigham Young University in 1975, interrupting his studies to spend two years as a volunteer Mormon missionary in Brazil, from 1971 to 1973. His experience in Brazil is reflected in several of his stories and novels, perhaps most vividly in *Speaker for the Dead*, though more literally in the short story "America." He married Kristine Allen on May 17, 1977.

Card began his artistic career at Brigham Young University, writing and producing a number of plays on Mormon themes during his college years. After college, he began publishing short stories in science-fiction and fantasy magazines. Completing his M.A. in 1981, he began a doctoral program in literature at the University of Notre Dame with the idea of becoming a teacher and writer, but he abandoned this program to devote himself to writing fiction. When Card won the Hugo and Nebula best novel awards two years in a row, 1985 and 1986, he was firmly established as one of the best young writers in science fiction. The appearance of the first volume of *Tales of Alvin Maker* in 1987 won for him a wider audience, especially among younger readers and their teachers. In 1990, Card published a collection of short fiction entitled *Maps in a Mirror*, bringing together stories that had appeared in ephemeral sources or that had been absorbed into his novels, as well as his best stories that were no longer in print. During the 1990's Card continued to add to both the Ender saga and the Alvin Maker series. He also completed the five-volume Homecoming series and branched out into historical fiction: *Stone Tables* (1997), the supernatural thriller *Homebody* (1998), the modern fantasy *Enchantment* (1999), and the illustrated fairy tale *Magic Mirror*. Card and his wife settled in Greensboro, North Carolina, with their five children: Geoffrey, Emily, Charles, Zina Margaret, and Erin Louisa.

ANALYSIS

Orson Scott Card is most often praised as an absorbing storyteller. He creates characters of great depth and places them in morally complex situations. The result is fiction that grips and entertains the reader in the ways expected in popular fiction, while provoking thought about his major themes: a religious view of humanity and the cosmos, the exploration of ideal conceptions of human community and the struggles of individuals to realize such communities, examination of the forms of spiritual poverty that repeatedly threaten individual fulfillment, and the realization of living communities. In interviews, Card made clear his commitment to Mormonism, and his reviewers noted how Card's religious beliefs permeate his work. Michael R. Collings compares Card's work to that of an important influence on Card, C. S. Lewis in his seven-volume Chronicles of Narnia series, showing that both writers produce stories that are enriched by their religious beliefs without being explicitly didactic.

Card's short fiction includes a variety of kinds, though most stories fall within popular genres. He divides *Maps in a Mirror* into groups of horror stories, speculative fiction, fables and fantasies, religious tales, and a miscellaneous group that includes stories and a poem that have grown into novels as well as several exemplary stories for religious, family readers. The stories in *The Worthing Saga* are closer to traditional science fiction, while those in *The Folk of the Fringe* speculate about a postnuclear holocaust world in the Mormon West. While nearly all these stories have been well received, the most interesting and moving of them tend to be the fantasies and speculative fiction that explore themes of human spirituality.

"KINGSMEAT"

"Kingsmeat" was first published in 1978 and later collected in *Maps in a Mirror*. Though it is a story of the liberation of a conquered human colony on another planet, these events are not the central interest of the story. The story of the conquest and release is revealed at the human shepherd's trial for collaboration with the alien king and queen. The king and queen are multilimbed alien life-forms with an advanced technology that allows them to dominate human colonists. Their usual procedure is to conquer a colony and then feed off it, eating the humans until they are gone, then moving to another colony. At some point, they reproduce a large number of new pairs to spread the species. The shepherd discovers a way to save the human colony from this fate. He succeeds in communicating with the king and queen and then persuades them to accept a procedure by which he will provide them an endless supply of human flesh. He thereby preserves the colony until its rescue by cutting off body parts of the colonists, using tools provided by the king and queen that allow painless surgery, and saving the colonists' lives at the cost of their physical wholeness.

On the day the king and queen are defeated, the shepherd supplies their order of breast-in-butter by cutting off the breasts of a fifteen-year-old mother of a newborn, then overseeing the cooking and serving of this delicacy. After a rescue party destroys the king and queen, there is a trial of the collaborators, mainly the shepherd, whom the colonists have hated and feared for years. The trial supplies the reader with the background of the conquest and with a detailed account of how the shepherd came to occupy his position. The trial is conducted by telepathic means, there being a machine for this purpose. As a result, the entire colony as well as the accused participate, and every participant feels what the witnesses and the accused feel as they remember these events. The court is moved to compassion by the shepherd's story. While it is true he has committed atrocities, his doing so has saved all the lives that could be saved, for the shepherd never took a life. The court decides that for his sacrifice, the shepherd is to be preserved, cared for, and honored annually by the colonists.

The story ends, however, with what proves to be its most horrific image. The colonists cannot forgive the shepherd for having remained whole while he dismembered them. Therefore, they remove all of his limbs and his genitals. They carry out the court's order to the letter, caring for him, preserving his life as long as possible, and honoring him annually with visits and gifts. They leave him his tongue because he never speaks and his eyes because they want him to see them smile as he once smiled when he was their shepherd.

"Kingsmeat" is a powerful tale that suggests meanings on several levels. The testimony in the trial can hardly fail to evoke images of the Jewish Holocaust of World War II, specifically the problem of collaborating with evil to mitigate it. The narrative voice of the story is always sympathetic to the shepherd, emphasizing how much he tries to be kind to his flock even as he makes them into food, how he endures their hatred and fear in order to save them. His final fate suggests a living crucifixion, the figure of a savior who cannot be forgiven for his necessary actions. Card says that as he developed this story, he found himself focusing on "an area of unbearable ambiguity. . . . [T]he one who suffered and died to save others is depicted as one who also inflicts suffering; it is a way to explicitly make the Christ figure take upon himself, in all innocence, the darkest sins of the world."

The final image is so horrifying because those he saved prove unable to show him the same mercy he won for them. In the end, they prove more vicious than the king and the queen, whose morality did not require that they value humans any more than humans value the animals they use and eat. By obeying the letter rather than the spirit of the law, his tormentors fail to understand their human condition, revealing that they need but do not deserve the mercy they deny the shepherd.

Card said in the extensive commentary included in *Maps in a Mirror* that he considered science fiction the ideal genre for dealing with the basic religious questions. While he was not always aware that this was happening in his fiction, the more experience and success he gained, the clearer it became to him that he preferred science fiction as a genre, in part because it allowed him to explore metaphysical issues without having to choose or favor the point of view of a particular religion. In "Kingsmeat," Card is able to explore aspects of the problem of the affirmation of community values—life, wholeness, suffering, and sacrifice—in an ultimate, yet fictional, situation. The reader is given a means of thinking about these issues concretely but without having to connect them to actual historical events or institutions that often demand loyalties that would fix one's perspective.

"THE PORCELAIN SALAMANDER"

Card saw science fiction as an ideal genre for the exploration of religious issues because the genre as a whole is committed to a scientific worldview at the same time that it is open to the representation of alien cultures. Fantasy, because it usually occurs in a world where supernatural powers operate, is less well suited to the exploration of religious questions, but Card saw it as ideal for the creation of myths about the values by which communities are defined. One of Card's best stories of this kind is "The Porcelain Salamander," first published in 1981 and collected in *Maps in a Mirror*.

"The Porcelain Salamander" tells how a curse is spoken and then lifted. It takes place in a beautiful land, where all are said to be as happy as humans can be. Princess Kiren is singled out for special unhappiness. Because her father's much-beloved wife died in giving birth to Kiren, he cursed the child: "May you never move a muscle in your life, until you lose someone you love as much as I loved her!" In Kiren's world, magic and curses work, but partially and unpredictably. Kiren is not really paralyzed, but she is so weak that she can move only with great difficulty and is soon exhausted by any activity. Though he almost immediately regrets his curse, her father is unable to take it back, so Kiren lives for eleven years in enforced passivity.

Her father travels to foreign lands for relief from his guilt, and on one of his trips meets a magician, Irvass, who sells him a cure for the curse, a porcelain salamander magically endowed with motion and, as Kiren learns later, the power of speaking to her alone. Should the salamander ever stop moving, her father tells her, it will be frozen forever, an ordinary piece of porcelain. The salamander changes her life, helping her to become more lively herself by the cheerfulness of its constant motion and by talking to her. Eventually, she comes to love it more, she says, than her father or even the dream of her mother. This declaration brings Irvass to her door to reclaim the salamander. Irvass does not simply take it away but creates a magical situation: A wall encloses Kiren and her pet while they are playing in the forest and gradually squeezes in upon them, until the salamander tells her that she can escape only by standing on him, and she can stand on him only if he holds still. Instantly, he becomes a porcelain statue. When she climbs over the wall, it and the salamander disappear, and she becomes physically whole.

The story does not end, however, with her cure, for to achieve it, she has had to suffer exactly what her father suffered upon losing his wife. This, it turns out, was the real curse, and how she deals with her grief becomes a central theme of this fable, opening it out to all readers who will suffer bereavement as an inheritance of mortality. When Irvass comforts Kiren for her loss, he offers the usual platitudes that, at first glance, are not particularly consoling to the bereaved: The salamander, always in motion, needed and welcomed rest; the salamander's life ended with the motives of a generous action frozen in its memory; it will live more vibrantly in her memory now than had it continued longer. As Kiren grows older, she comes to understand this more deeply, and she learns in this way what her father forgot when he cursed her: "The moment when he [the salamander] decided, without love, that it would be better for his life, such as it was, to end than to have to watch Kiren's life end. It is such a moment that can be lived with for eternity." She has her father's grief but not his guilt, and he would have been happier had he known or remembered this. Grief cannot be avoided, but it is better to believe that one suffers alone than to cause another to suffer.

"The Porcelain Salamander" is a charming fable, told in an intimate and humorous voice. Its moral content is complex, even though the tale seems simple, and it is subtly conveyed, allowing the reader the pleasure of discovery. Furthermore, it is so structured as to allow for repeated discoveries of meaning on several levels. For example, charming and humorous as it is, the story is absolutely uncompromising in its presentation of the inevitability and pain of the loss of loved ones. Not a living being, not capable of love, the salamander will give up its claim to life rather than suffer bereavement, yet the human characters cannot choose death over grief, because to do so bereaves the others who love them. Card considered this to be one of his three best stories: "If my career had to be encapsulated in only three stories, I believe I would choose 'The Porcelain Salamander,' 'Unaccompanied Sonata,' and 'Salvage' as the three that did the best job, together, of saying all I had to say."

MAGIC MIRROR

Magic Mirror is a contemporary adult fable disguised as an illustrated children's fairy tale. It epitomizes one of Card's primary themes, the family in crisis. His stories often demonstrate how family members influence each other and should be the primary source for solving life's problems. On the surface, *Magic Mirror* is the tale of Heather, who, as a young princess, dreamed of contributing to the success of her dashing prince, Richard. Now that the children have grown, she laments her lonely existence as a stay-at-home queen. In order to placate her, Richard has given her a magic mirror that allows her to communicate with their son, Jason, who is away at school. Lonely and despondent, Heather turns to the mirror to fill the hours of her life, first for news and information, finally for companionship. Stephen, a compassionate wizard, becomes her truest friend and confidant. Then her life is upended when Stephen reveals that Richard has taken a mistress.

What seems like an ordinary, even mundane fantasy is given a contemporary interpretation by means of Nathan Pinnock's illustrations. Working from detailed descriptions provided by Card, Pinnock provided illustrations that interpret the story by ingeniously combining medieval and modern settings. Heather's home is a cross between a castle and a suburban house, but anachronisms are used for both time periods. In an illustration depicting a mostly modern setting, some conveniences are replaced by medieval devices (a gnome washing dishes instead of a dish-washer), while a mostly medieval setting contains modern devices (a luxury sedan instead of a gallant steed). King Richard fights corporate battles but slays real dragons. The magic mirror is a computer wired to the Internet. Card's fairy tale is thereby a metaphor for the destructive forces facing the contemporary family. For example, the so-called evidence of Richard's affair is actually a series of digital images manipulated by a vengeful enemy pretending to be a wise confidant.

Nowhere, however, does Card decry the obvious. He does not lament the modern family. Contemporary challenges are presented as simple facts of life. Instead, Card's tale is redemptive. It is never too late for family members to recognize the forces that have separated them and to make decisions that enable them to heal.

Card pointedly writes for a popular audience, yet he is uncompromising in his moral seriousness. Like "Kingsmeat," "The Porcelain Salamander," and *Magic Mirror*, most of his fiction is accessible to younger and adult readers alike. There is often humor and epic adventure, and there is often the grimness of the human suffering no person evades, sometimes in its darkest hues, as when the shepherd removes the young mother's breasts or when those he saved through atrocity come to mock him in his age. Card's striving to tell an interesting story that speaks profound truth helped to make him one of the best writers to work in the genres of fantasy and science fiction.

OTHER MAJOR WORKS

LONG FICTION: *A Planet Called Treason*, 1979 (revised as *Treason*, 1988); *Songmaster*, 1980; *The Worthing Chronicle*, 1983; *Hart's Hope*, 1983; *A Woman of Destiny*, 1984 (also published as *Saints*, 1988); *Ender's Game*, 1985; *Speaker for the Dead*, 1986; *Seventh Son*, 1987; *Wyrms*, 1987; *Red Prophet*, 1988; *Prentice Alvin*, 1989; *The Abyss*, 1989; *Xenocide*, 1991; *Lost Boys*, 1992; *The Memory of Earth*, 1992; *The Call of Earth*, 1993; *Lovelock*, 1994; *The Ships of Earth*, 1994; *Alvin Journeyman*, 1995; *Earthfall*, 1995; *Earthborn*, 1995; *Children of the Mind*, 1996; *Pastwatch: The Redemption of Christopher Columbus*, 1996; *Treasure Box*, 1996; *Stone Tables*, 1997; *Heartfire*, 1998; *Homebody*, 1998; *Enchantment*, 1999.

NONFICTION: *"Listen, Mom and Dad . . .": Young Adults Look Back on Their Upbringing*, 1977; *Saintspeak: The Mormon Dictionary*, 1981; *Ainge*, 1982; *Characters and Viewpoint*, 1988; *How to Write Science Fiction and Fantasy*, 1990; *A Storyteller in Zion: Essays and Speeches*, 1993.

BIBLIOGRAPHY

Collings, Michael R. *In the Image of God: Theme, Characterization, and Landscape in the Fiction of Orson Scott Card*. New York: Greenwood Press, 1990. Dealing mainly with Card's major novels, Collings's book is a good introduction to Card's themes, interests, aims, and influences. There is considerable attention to ways in which Mormonism influences his work. Collings quotes and summarizes generously from Card's interviews and essays. Includes bibliographies of Card's works and of secondary writing about Card.

DeCandido, Grace Anne Andreassi, and Keith Decandido. *Publishers Weekly* 237 (November, 1990): 54-55. Discusses *Maps in a Mirror: The Short Fiction of Orson Scott Card*, noting that he writes stories that turn on issues of moral choice. Card discusses the importance of challenging readers in science fiction and contends that, at its best, the genre changes the world's moral imperatives.

Hantke, Steffen. "Surgical Strikes and Prosthetic Warriors: The Soldier's Body in Contemporary Science Fiction." *Science-Fiction Studies* 25 (November, 1998): 495-509. Discusses how the technologically augmented body in the science fiction of Card and others raises issues about what it means to be male or female, or even human, since the use of prosthetics to heal or strengthen the body is accompanied by the dissolution of the body.

Heidkemp, Bernie. "Responses to the Alien Mother in Post-Maternal Cultures: C. J. Cherryl and Orson Scott Card." *Science-Fiction Studies* 23

(November, 1996): 339-354. Discusses Card's use of the Queen Mother archetype as a literary manifestation of the pre-Oedipal mother figure. Argues that in his work protagonists react as infants to this archetypal mother image in gendered ways.

Van Name, Mark L. "Writer of the Year: Orson Scott Card." *Science Fiction and Fantasy Book Review Annual*, edited by Robert A. Collins and Robert Latham. Westport, Conn.: Meckler, 1988. This combination interview and review essay provides an introduction to Card's career as well as helpful insights into his ideas about life and writing. The richest source of such information, however, remains *Maps in a Mirror*, which includes long and interesting introductions and afterwords for each group of stories.

Terry Heller, updated by Gerald S. Argetsinger

PETER CAREY

Born: Bacchus Marsh, Victoria, Australia; May 7, 1943

PRINCIPAL SHORT FICTION
The Fat Man in History, 1974
War Crimes, 1979
The Fat Man in History and Other Stories, 1981
Collected Stories, 1995

OTHER LITERARY FORMS

Peter Carey is best known for his novels; he has also published children's literature and autobiographical essays.

ACHIEVEMENTS

Peter Carey is one of the most famous Australian authors worldwide. His collection *War Crimes* won a New South Wales Premier's Literary Award, and his novel *Bliss* (1981) garnered that award and a National Book Council Award. *Bliss* also won an AWGIE Award and awards for best film and best screenplay from the Australian Film Institute. His novel *Illywhacker* (1985) received *The Age* Book of the Year Award, the Victorian Premier's Literary Award, and a National Book Council Award, as well as a nomination for the Booker McConnell Prize. Carey received the Booker McConnell Prize for *Oscar and Lucinda* (1988) and the Commonwealth Writers Prize as well as the Australian Miles Franklin Award for *Jack Maggs* (1997). He has also published a children's book and a short, autobiographical memoir.

BIOGRAPHY

Peter Carey was born in suburban Melbourne, where he grew up the son of a prominent local car dealer. He graduated from Geelong Grammar School, one of the most prestigious high schools in Australia, which later was attended by Prince Charles, the heir to the British throne. In 1961, Carey matriculated at the University of Sydney, where at first he studied biology. Though his original ambition was to be a scientist, he soon realized his ambitions were in the literary sphere. He spent about a decade working in advertising, for two years in London and for the rest of the time in Australia. He also spent some years living in an alternative commune in southern Queensland. In 1985, he married theater director Alison Summers, with whom he had two children. In 1999, they settled in New York City, making frequent visits back to Australia.

ANALYSIS

Peter Carey's short stories are closer to fantasy and science fiction than his novels, which are more aptly categorized as historical or Magical Realist. The only novel by Carey that is close to the vision of the short stories is *The Unusual Life of Tristan Smith* (1994). In the stories, plot and psychologically well-rounded characterization are given less priority than atmosphere and audacity of conception. They are set in surreal, strange environments. Many of the stories take place in alternate histories where people are ruled by nondemocratic governments. These settings assist Carey in establishing an atmosphere of distortion and exaggeration where everything is at risk and no horror is inconceivable. The reader is put into a suspenseful mood, kept on edge. "Room No. 5 (Escribo)" is typical in this regard. This story was inspired by Carey's visit to Spain in the early 1970's, during the last years of the authoritarian government there. The story hauntingly imagines the conditions of life in a society filled with fear, degradation, and uncertainty. Everyone is waiting for the aged dictator Timoshenko to die. The narrator and his girlfriend, whom he has met on his travels, tentatively explore their relationship in the grimy atmospheric squalor of a country in which they are strangers. This sense of alienation and dislocation, often laced with humor, is characteristic of Carey's early stories. Though nothing dramatic happens in "Room No. 5 (Escribo)," the reader is left with the record of a journey not only to a different land but also to an often unexplored area of experience. This is true of many of Carey's short stories, which read like postcards from the untraveled realm, full of foreboding and apprehension but also pulsing with imaginative vigor. Carey has suggested that this vision may owe something to the history of his native Australia. Its European settlement pioneered by convicts, criminals whom Britain had rejected and exiled, Australia had its origins in the degradation suffered by outcasts. Carey's short stories, though, show some un-Australian influences, particularly those of the Latin American writers Gabriel García Márquez and Carlos Fuentes, whose depictions of nightmarish dictatorships surely influenced Carey's.

"DO YOU LOVE ME?"

"Do You Love Me" is set in an imaginary world governed by the Cartographers, whose mapmaking can control activity in the real world. They travel all around, keeping track of what is going on, and thus have a tremendous amount of power and social privilege. The narrator's father, with whom he has always

had a distant and difficult relationship, is a Cartographer. When society is faced with a crisis, the sudden vanishing of several major buildings and eventually the dematerialization of individual people, the father is unperturbed. As a Cartographer, he is accustomed to being able to control events. When people begin disappearing en masse, the narrator grows concerned and asks his girlfriend, Karen, if she loves him. The father realizes intellectually that only the portions of the world that are not needed or loved are disappearing, but he cannot translate that realization to an emotional level. The son also resents his father for having affairs with other women and for flirting with his own girlfriend. When his father starts disappearing, the son declares his love for his father, but as he does not really mean it, the father disappears nonetheless. The idea of "disappearance" is in some ways a metaphor for death.

"KRISTU-DU"

"Kristu-Du" concerns an architect, Gerrard Haflinger, hired to construct a huge edifice in the capital of a backward country ruled by a fierce dictator. The architect is intent on finishing this building, called "Kristu-Du," the purpose of which is not only

Peter Carey (©Miriam Berkley)

to house individuals or offices but also to serve as an emblem of the dictator's power, inspire awe and fear in the people, and unify the country's disparate tribes. This will be the capstone of his career; it will be not just a building but also a vision of how public life can be brought together and made meaningful. Yet Haflinger, as his name may connote, is only "half" a person. His wife, repulsed by his working for a dictator, has left him, and he has a very detached relationship with his son, to whom he writes a letter that he never finishes. Haflinger is increasingly isolated, alienated from the other Europeans in the country, who are mainly skilled workers underpaid by the government, and who see Haflinger as a symbol of their exploitation. There is also a man named Wallis, nicknamed "Mr. Meat," who, like Haflinger, is employed by the government (in Wallis's case making propaganda films) but who is even more cynical about his role. In an unexpected development, Mr. Meat warns Haflinger that there is an incipient rebellion against the dictator and that rebellious tribes are gathering for his overthrow. Not heeding this advice Haflinger remains, thinking that the tribes will converge on Kristu-Du and, in this building, come together to create a new, free society. Just as the dictator seems about to be overthrown, however, the building closes in on the frenzied population. Kristu-Du is in fact a prison that the dictator had envisioned for the precise purpose of containing this sort of dissent. Haflinger has a short while to realize this before he goes mad, betrayed by the folly of his pride.

"THE FAT MAN IN HISTORY"

Like so many of Carey's stories, "The Fat Man in History" takes place after a revolution. Alexander Finch is a fat man and a cartoonist by trade who had been fiercely opposed to the now-overthrown Danko dictatorship. The new postrevolutionary government, though, has singled out fat people for persecution. Fat people, in its view, are symbols of indolence and wealth and should be held up as negative examples in an age of social equality and leveling. Finch is one of six fat men living in a run-down boardinghouse. They are led by a fat man named Fantoni, who is more charismatic than any of them except for a possibly suspicious, unnamed man who is one of their com-

pany. They are without female companionship (some of their wives have left them) except for the woman they call Florence Nightingale, who collects their rent and serves as their intermediary to the hostile world outside. The fat men decide to blow up a public statue as an act of counterrevolutionary defiance. Later, they amend this goal and decide to eat Florence Nightingale, eating being a symbol of the pleasure-seeking and indulgence forbidden by the revolution. Florence Nightingale is in fact Nancy Bowlby, a government researcher who is studying the group of fat men in an effort to control dissent. She strikes up a sexual relationship with the unnamed man which is hidden from the other five until the couple are found out as the woman is about to be eaten. With her sociological acumen and government-instilled propaganda techniques, Nancy Bowlby convinces the men to eat Fantoni instead. The unnamed man becomes the new leader (and assumes the name Fantoni, which evidently goes with this role). The resistance will be contained, and the revolution is securely in power.

"WITHDRAWAL"

"Withdrawal" is a story set on the fringes of the Australian drug scene of the 1970's, but the withdrawal spoken of in the title is not one from drug addiction but from an obsession with death. Eddie Rayner is a shop proprietor who traffics in the minutiae of death, selling photographs of dead people and objects associated with the dead to powerful people who have a morbid fascination with them. Eddie not only makes money doing this but also seduces the mistress of a cabinet minister, who is one of his customers; the mistress subsequently becomes his girlfriend. Yet through all this Eddie has never himself seen a dead body. He thus is psychologically cordoned off from the reality of death even though he exploits it. Two heroin addicts move in with Eddie, bringing with them a pig that eats human excrement. This symbolizes the ultimate degradation of Eddie, which is heightened when he decides to reconstruct an entire tableau of the life of a dead old woman, exhibiting her body and her entire life (including private letters, records of past love affairs) to the public. Finally repulsed, Eddie's girlfriend runs off with the heroin addicts, finding their grisly existence superior to Eddie's, and Eddie is left to confront his own utter loss of humanity.

"AMERICAN DREAMS"

"American Dreams" concerns a small Australian town that sees itself as a remote backwater far away from anything interesting. The only inspiration comes from watching American movies and dreaming of the glamorous life. The town is intrigued when the pharmacist, Mr. Gleason, suddenly hires a group of laborers, begins building a huge wall on top of a hill, and isolates himself behind it. When Mr. Gleason dies, Mrs. Gleason has the wall torn down. When the townspeople come to see what is behind the wall, they find Mr. Gleason has built a small-scale model of the town and all its inhabitants. Moreover, he has penetrated into the deepest secrets of the townspeople. When one model house's roof is lifted off, the figures unearthed are of a woman having an extramarital affair. The townspeople realize that their lives will never be the same because their inner identities have been "caught" by Mr. Gleason. Moreover, the town has now become a tourist attraction, and the very Americans about whom the townspeople had once fantasized now come to see it, making it into a theme-park-like locale with little regard for the real lives of the inhabitants. Carey discloses that the privilege of imagination can also be a peril, that dreams can become life-altering nightmares.

OTHER MAJOR WORKS

LONG FICTION: *Bliss*, 1981; *Illywhacker*, 1985; *Oscar and Lucinda*, 1988; *The Tax Inspector*, 1991; *The Unusual Life of Tristan Smith*, 1994; *The Big*

Bazoohley, 1995; *Jack Maggs*, 1997.

SCREENPLAY: *Bliss*, 1986.

NONFICTION: *A Letter to Our Son*, 1994.

BIBLIOGRAPHY

Callahan, David. "Whose History Is the Fat Man's? Peter Carey's *The Fat Man in History*." *SPAN* 40 (1995): 34-53. The best single article on the mood and technique of Carey's short stories. Occasionally difficult but still worth exploring.

Hassall, Anthony. *Dancing on Hot Macadam: Peter Carey's Fiction*. St. Lucia: University of Queensland Press, 1998. Clearly written introductory work. Gives a capsule discussion of every published short story by Carey; analysis is more in-depth on some stories than on others. Particularly good on "Kristu-Du."

Huggan, Graham. *Peter Carey*. New York: Oxford University Press, 1996. A student-level introduction to Carey; gives considerable emphasis to the short stories, although Huggan is not totally sympathetic to Carey's stance as a writer.

Kane, Paul. "Postcolonial/Postmodern: Australian Literature and Peter Carey." *World Literature Today* 67, no. 3 (1993): 519-522. An accessible introduction to Carey's significance within contemporary theoretical debates.

Woodcock, Bruce. *Peter Carey*. New York: Manchester University Press, 1996. Another introductory work; gives thorough coverage of Carey's career, although it stresses the novels.

Nicholas Birns

WILLIAM CARLETON

Born: Prillisk, Ireland; March 4, 1794
Died: Dublin, Ireland; January 30, 1869

PRINCIPAL SHORT FICTION

Father Butler, The Lough Dearg Pilgrim: Being Sketches of Irish Manners, 1829
Traits and Stories of the Irish Peasantry, 1830-1833 (5 volumes)
Tales of Ireland, 1834
The Fawn of Spring-Valve, The Clarionet, and Other Tales, 1841 (3 volumes)
The Battle of the Factions and Other Tales of Ireland, 1845
Characters and Sketches of Ireland and the Irish, 1945
Denis O'Shaughnessy Going to Maynooth, 1845
Parra Sastha: Or, The History of Paddy Go-Easy and His Wife Nancy, 1845
Roddy the Rover: Or, The Ribbon Man, 1845
Art Maguire: Or, The Broken Pledge, 1847
The Irishman at Home, 1849
The Clarionet, The Dead Boxer, and Barney Branagan, 1850
Alley Sheridan and Other Stories, 1858
The Double Prophecy: Or, Trials of the Heart, 1862 (2 volumes)
The Silver Acre and Other Tales, 1862
The Fair of Emyvale and The Master and Scholar, 1870
The Red Haired Man's Wife, 1889

OTHER LITERARY FORMS

William Carleton's reputation largely rests on the short-fiction collection in the two series of his *Traits and Stories of the Irish Peasantry*. He was also, however, a prolific novelist. Works such as his *Fardorougha the Miser: Or, The Convicts of Lisnamona* (1839), *Valentine McClutchy, the Irish Agent: Or, Chronicles of the Castle Cumber Property* (1845), and *The Black Prophet: A Tale of Irish Famine* (1847) are extensions of the themes and venues of his short stories. Carleton is also the author of an incomplete autobiography, published posthumously as *The Life of William Carleton* (1896). It is one of the more significant cultural documents to emerge from early nineteenth century Ireland.

ACHIEVEMENTS

William Carleton was the first Irish writer to depict from the inside the lives of the Irish peasantry, an achievement for which he was well qualified by birth and background. As a son of the soil, almost totally lacking in formal education, Carleton gave a voice to a people whose existence was previously unknown to fiction in English. The story of how he did so, and its literary and cultural repercussions, makes Carleton's career at once exemplary and cautionary.

In view of its unlikely origins and undoubted originality, Carleton's work has often been valued more for its historical significance than for its literary interest. This verdict has also been reinforced by the excessive exuberance of Carleton's style and the supercharged melodrama of his plots. Such superficial blemishes, while obviously detracting from the artistic refinement of Carleton's fiction, also express very graphically the difficulties he was obliged to negotiate in order to establish the perspective and sense of form adequate to convey the social plight and moral vigor of his subjects.

BIOGRAPHY

Born to a poor, Catholic, rural family skilled in oral traditional literature and music, William Carleton was never formally educated; instead, he attended haphazard hedge schools along the roadside or in small buildings, operated by itinerant schoolmasters. Abandoning his peasant environment for Dublin, Carleton was eventually given the opportunity to write anti-Catholic stories and sketches. These became the basis for his *Traits and Stories of the Irish Peasantry*. He converted to Protestantism, married, and begot a large family, the support of which by his pen alone occasioned much hackwork. In time, Carleton's work appeared in support of the whole spectrum of nineteenth century Irish cultural and ideological life, from the Tory *Dublin University Magazine* to the republican *The Nation*. Not even the granting, partly on political grounds, of a civil list pension alleviated his financial distress, and by the time of his death Carleton was a broken and embittered man.

ANALYSIS

The most popular of William Carleton's short stories are contained in *Traits and Stories of the Irish Peasantry*, read and appreciated by diverse artists such as Alfred, Lord Tennyson and Edgar Allan Poe. Fairy tales, local legends, and episodes from his life and the lives of his neighbors constitute the subject matter of Carleton's short fiction. Years after he left his native province, Carleton still wrote about it; in one story, "Ned M'Keown," the characters' names are the real names of his neighbors.

Of the nineteen tales edited for the five volumes of *Traits and Stories of the Irish Peasantry*, most record an event in the community, including "Shane Fadh's Wedding," "Larry M'Farland's Wake," "The Battle of the Factions," "The Party Fight and Funeral," "Tubber Derg," "The Hedge School," "The Station," "The Midnight Mass," "The Horse Stealers," "An Essay on Irish Swearing," "Wildgoose Lodge," "Denis O'Shaughnessy Going to Maynooth," and "Phelim O'Toole's Courtship." Carleton also describes people in stories such as "Mickey M'Rory, the Country Fiddler," "Neal Malone," "Rose Moan," "Mary Murray, the Irish Match-Maker," "Buckram-Back, the Country Dancing Master," and "Bob Pentland, the Irish Smuggler." Carleton's fairy tales, a mixture of the real and the unreal, are generally not of a fantastic nature; "The Three Tasks: Or, The Little House Under the Hill," "Frank Martin and the Fairies," and "The Pudding Bewitched," for example, dramatize the relationship between the country people and characters from the spirit world. Carleton presents a panoramic view of his culture, colored by his own perception of people and events. "The Three Tasks: Or, The Little House Under the Hill," "The Lough Derg Pilgrim," "Phelim O'Toole's Courtship," and "Tubber Derg" represent the range of his fiction.

"THE THREE TASKS"

In the first series of *Traits and Stories of the Irish Peasantry*, the lead story, Ned M'Keown, introduces characters who, like Geoffrey Chaucer's pilgrims, tell stories to one another as they sit around Ned's fireplace. The characters are not fictitious but are actual people who lived in the region described, and who are recollected from the author's youth. "The Three Tasks: Or, The Little House Under the Hill" is the tale Ned M'Keown tells to entertain his visitors on a stormy night at Kilrudden. In the story, Jack Magennis meets a dark man and a pipe-smoking talking dog who offer Jack riches if he wins a card game but servitude if he loses. Since Jack "heard of men being made up entirely by the fairies, till there was no end to their wealth," he agrees to play. When he loses, Jack asks for a year's grace so he can provide for his widowed mother. At the appointed hour, the dog appears with a green ribbon and a spyglass about his neck and Wellington boots upon his hind legs to take Jack to the dark man's castle.

At the castle, Jack is shown a long room with 365 hooks, all but one holding a man's head. By nightfall, if he is to avoid decapitation, Jack must clean a stable that has not been cleaned in seven years. Unable to clean the stable, in his frustration Jack sings an Irish song and dances the hornpipe at triple time, attracting the attention of a beautiful young lady. Magically, she gets the task done, and Jack's life is spared. He must accomplish two other tasks, however: to catch a wild filly and to rob a crane's nest high in a tree on an island. The beautiful lady helps Jack to bridle the filly and get the crane's eggs. In his haste, Jack leaves one of the lady's toes, used to climb the tree, on the island. The master will know who has helped Jack, so the lady informs him that she must flee from the castle or be killed. Now in love with each other, the couple escapes on the filly's back.

Following the traditional folk motifs of the chase, the pair eludes the pursuing villain and his party. On three occasions, Jack delays their progress. From the filly's right ear, a dry stick, a pebble, and a drop of green water produce a forest, rocky roads, and finally a lake to drown the dark man. Arriving safely in Ireland, the beauty tells Jack that a cache of gold lies buried near his mother's cottage. He finds it but forgets about the lady. Rich and famous, Jack is to marry the daughter of a nobleman. At the wedding feast, the talking dog appears followed by a man on horseback who claims the bride-to-be was pledged to him. Then Jack, his lips touched by the dog's paw, suddenly remembers his adventures and finds his beautiful benefactor. A double wedding takes place. As Jack is to join his bride in the nuptial chamber, he is awakened by his mother from a long dream. He loses his bride but finds the gold, accounting for the Magennis wealth.

"The Three Tasks: Or, The Little House Under the Hill" illustrates the dual nature of the fairies; some will help people and others will harm them, a characteristic of the Irish oral literary tradition. Unlike the Scots, whose fairies are usually demonic, and the English, whose fairies were banished during the Age of Enlightenment, the Irish treasure them and invent a variety of adventures between humans and the good and bad inhabitants of the woods, water, and the air. Folk beliefs, because of the cultural acceptance of a preternatural world, are naturally a part of Irish realistic tales. Such stories often have three dominant themes: the relationship of the people to their church, land, and family, as demonstrated in "The Lough Derg Pilgrim," "Phelim O'Toole's Courtship," and "Tubber Derg."

"THE LOUGH DERG PILGRIM"

"The Lough Derg Pilgrim," first published in 1828 as "A Pilgrimage to Patrick's Purgatory" in *The Christian Examiner*, an anti-Catholic journal of the Church of Ireland, appeared under Carleton's pseudonym, Wilton. It was actually coauthored by Caesar Otway, the journal's editor and an ardent foe of Catholic Emancipation. When the tale was later published as "The Lough Derg Pilgrim," the objectionable inflammatory passages of Otway were deleted. This story, however, and the others that appeared in *The Christian Examiner*—"The Broken Oath," "Father Butler," "The Station," "The Death of a Devotee," "The Priest's Funeral," "The Brothers," "Lachlin Murray and the Blessed Candle," "The Lianhan Shee," "The Illicit Distiller: Or, The Force of Conscience," "History of a Chimney Sweep," "The Mate-

rialist," and "Denis O'Shaughnessy Going to Maynooth"—branded Carleton as an anti-Catholic writer who ridiculed his people. These stories were categorized as "Sketches of the Irish Peasantry," "Popular Romish Legends," and Irish superstitions, a serious break in the Irish literary tradition which never considered its people to be peasants or its legends to be Romish and superstitious.

Eventually, Carleton outgrew the condemnation, but he has yet to assume the role that Charles Dickens enjoys in England. The abridged edition of "The Lough Derg Pilgrim" begins with the narrator, a thinly disguised version of Carleton in his nineteenth year, describing his religious practices prior to his pilgrimage to Lough Derg (Irish for Red Lake). To prepare himself for a walk across water, the young man fasts and prays for three days. Then in a "pitch of superstitious absurdity," he places his foot on a water lily in his father's pond and sinks up to his neck. Crestfallen but undaunted, he sets out for Lough Derg within a month, dressed in a black suit and mistaken for a priest by the Catholics, who bow to him. On the road, he overtakes two women wearing gray cloaks with striped red-and-blue petticoats.

Because of the detailed description of the travelers, the inns, food served, and natural scenery, the reader becomes a listener and an onlooker to the pilgrimage. The two women talk to the "priest" in reverential tones and treat him differently, but not because of their piety. As the pilgrims converge on Lough Derg, they represent a wide variety of people, young and old, male and female, holy and unholy. Crowds of folks reach the island in Lough Derg where the chapel, or "Prison," is located. There they undergo physical pain which includes walking on sharp rocks, praying throughout an entire night and being kept awake by blows to the head by other pilgrims, and fasting. On his way home, the young pilgrim is robbed of his clothing and money by the two women, who were seasoned pilgrims there for the plunder.

"PHELIM O'TOOLE'S COURTSHIP"

Not all Irishmen had the religious fervor satirized in "The Lough Derg Pilgrim," but most of them loved Ireland. That love permeates Carleton's fiction. Poor or rich, the Irish, attached to their land, were concerned about passing on their holdings to posterity. "Phelim O'Toole's Courtship," a comic tale, demonstrates this concern. Phelim, an only child, is heir to "a snug estate of half an acre." His parents, loving and spoiling him, deny him nothing that their poverty can afford. By the age of ten, Phelim has become the village thief, liar, and troublemaker—a source of anxiety to his honest parents. At twenty, he is uneducated, unemployed, fond of women and whiskey, and a fugitive from the law. His parents think it is time for Phelim to marry and beget an heir for the half acre, which has been in the O'Toole family for three generations.

In a series of comic episodes, Phelim proposes to Bridget Doran, the priest's housekeeper. She is older than Phelim's mother but the source of money for his future adventures. Next, Phelim proposes to Sally Flattery, a thief and the daughter of a thief with whom Phelim operates. She tricks Phelim into believing that her father has been jailed and will not implicate Phelim in the crime if he takes care of her. Meanwhile, his father is preparing for a match with Peggy Donovan. After much wrangling with her father about the dowry to match the half acre, it is agreed that a marriage is to take place. On the following Sunday, the banns of marriage are announced between Phelim and Bridget, Sally, and Peggy. The congregation is amused, expecting this sort of behavior from Phelim, but the women are furious. They, along with relatives, rush over to the half acre, fighting it out with one another and the O'Tooles. Tricked by the village fool, Phelim is jailed while his matrimonial fate is being decided. Unable to lie his way out of jail, he is convicted and transported for life. His aged parents eventually lose the land and join the army of beggars, recollecting that they should have been more careful about Phelim's moral education.

"TUBBER DERG"

In a much more somber tone, Carleton in "Tubber Derg" discusses the land and a family's connection with it, placing more emphasis on the family and the father's responsibilities for his children. This story tells of the poverty and sufferings of Owen M'Carthy and his family, a reality all too common in nineteenth century Ireland. Once a prosperous farmer and the descendant of an ancient and honest family, Owen, his wife, and their young children face eviction because they are unable to pay the inflated rent on their farm. By walking to Dublin to see the absentee landlord, Owen believes he can postpone the eviction. With much tenderness, Owen bids his family farewell, speaking in Irish and holding back tears. His trip to Dublin does not stay the eviction; Owen, derided by the servants, does speak to the landlord, who refers him to the agent. The fact that the M'Carthys had farmed the estate for more than two hundred years does not impress the landlord or the agent.

Returning to Tubber Derg (meaning Red Well), Owen discovers that his young daughter has died and that his family is living in a neighbor's barn. Within a year they all leave home to beg in a strange part of the country where the proud M'Carthys are unknown. They are turned away from the homes of the rich and fed by poor families fortunate enough to have a roof and some food. Despite great odds, the family survives until the three eldest boys are hired out to herd cows, and the daughter works as a maid in a farm house. The two youngest children remain with their parents. From the children's earnings and the alms, within a few years, Owen can rent a small cottage, and the homeless begging days are over. Owen goes back to Tubber Derg to find a productive, small farm for rent. Both he and his wife want to lie beside their dead daughter in the ancient burial grounds of the M'Carthys.

At Tubber Derg, he visits the home of the family that befriended him after the eviction and goes on to his daughter's grave site. His sorrow turns to indignation when he sees a tombstone in the graveyard, wondering who would dare to bury upon the M'Carthy Mores of Tubber Derg. Shocked, Owen sees that it is his daughter's headstone, erected by a widow and her son out of respect for the M'Carthys who helped her in her distress. Then in a fresh burst of sorrow, Owen, speaking in Irish with the feeling and figurative language of the old Irish families, delivers his own greeting and that of his wife to their child, wishing she were part of the family again. That not being possible, Owen asks his child for her prayers before God to look with favor and compassion upon her family.

Sixteen years after leaving Tubber Derg, Owen and his family return with cattle and furnishings to begin anew their lives among old friends at the site of their ancestral home. Like so many other stories, "Tubber Derg" contains frequent authorial passages criticizing the avaricious landlords and agents who rack-rent the tenants, producing starvation and misery among the independent farmers. Carleton also points out that this type of land management leads to violence, for not all tenants are as meek as Owen M'Carthy. The violent reaction to eviction is best illustrated in "Wildgoose Lodge," in which murder and executions follow the evictions.

Carleton, categorized a decade ago as a minor Victorian writer, is a major Irish writer whose best work was written by 1850. In all his work he sings the praises of his people, damns their indolence, and mourns their sorrows. The simplistic solution to the woes of rural Ireland, according to Carleton, was a return of the landed gentry to harmonize the relationship of the working population between their church and family. Carleton's tales illustrate his belief that a good life is possible following great tragedies.

OTHER MAJOR WORKS

LONG FICTION: *Fardorougha the Miser: Or, The Convicts of Lisnamona*, 1839; *Valentine McClutchy, the Irish Agent: Or, Chronicles of the Castle Cumber Property*, 1845; *The Black Prophet: A Tale of Irish Famine*, 1847; *The Emigrants of Ahadarra: A Tale of Irish Life*, 1848; *The Tithe-Proctor*, 1849; *The Squanders of Castle Squander*, 1852 (2 volumes); *Red Hall: Or, The Baronet's Daughter*, 1852 (3 volumes); *Willy Reilly and His Dear Cooleen Bawn: A Tale Founded upon Fact*, 1855 (3 volumes); *The Evil Eye: Or, The Black Spectre*, 1860; *Redmont, Count O'Hanlon: The Irish Rapparee*, 1862.

NONFICTION: *The Life of William Carleton*, 1896 (2 volumes).

BIBLIOGRAPHY

Chesnutt, Margaret. *Studies in the Short Stories of William Carleton*. Göteburg, Sweden: Acta Universitatis Gothoburgensis, 1976. Discussion of Carleton's combination of folk sources and nine-teenth century narrative techniques. Argues that "Confessions of a Reformed Ribbonman" is mere literary sensationalism, and as much an example of propaganda as many of Carleton's weaker stories.

Flanagan, Thomas. *The Irish Novelists, 1800-1850*. New York: Columbia University Press, 1959. A pioneering work that still has much to offer to those unfamiliar with the literary history of Carleton's period. The study concludes with a section on Carleton. Kiely's biographical approach is adapted to provide a broader perspective. The resulting sense of historical context is critical to an appraisal of Carleton's significance.

Hayley, Barbara. *Carleton's "Traits and Stories" and the Nineteenth Century Anglo-Irish Tradition*. Totowa, N.J.: Barnes & Noble Books, 1983. A detailed discussion of the revisions that Carleton made to the stories from their original periodical publication to their publication in the *Traits and Stories of the Irish Peasantry*.

Kiely, Benedict. *Poor Scholar*. Dublin: Talbot Press, 1947. Remains the best study of Carleton. The approach is uniquely informative and sympathetic for being written by a short-story writer and novelist from the same part of Ireland as Carleton. Kiely's approach is largely biographical. The degree to which Carleton's fiction dovetails with his life is explored in the light of Carleton's autobiography. The author's acutely sensitive ear is helpfully attuned to Carleton's language.

O'Donoghue, D. J. *The Life of William Carleton*. 2 vols. London: Downey, 1986. The one essential work for Carleton scholars, largely because volume 1 consists of Carleton's autobiography. The second volume is a pallid, informative account of Carleton's Dublin years. While uncritical, volume 2 contains important information about Carleton's struggle for survival. The second volume also contains some essays by Carleton, which have not otherwise been reprinted.

Orel, Harold. *The Victorian Short Story*. Cambridge, England: Cambridge University Press, 1986. In the chapter on Carleton, Orel discusses Carleton's use of the folk tradition, his belief in the inextricable mixture of fact and fiction, his use of historical and eye-witness materials, and his experimentation with narrative techniques.

Sullivan, Eileen A. *William Carleton*. Boston: Twayne, 1983. A general introduction to Carleton's life and art. Summarizes and critiques critical reception of *Traits and Stories of the Irish Peasantry*; discusses the best-known stories in the collection such as "The Linahan Shee" and "The Three Tasks." Dis-

cusses Carleton's mingling of oral folktale and modern short-story techniques.

Wolff, Robert Lee. *William Carleton, Irish Peasant Novelist: A Preface to His Fiction*. New York: Garland, 1980. A brief, incisive overview of Carleton's stories and novels. The approach is chronological and biographical.

Eileen A. Sullivan, updated by George O'Brien

ALEJO CARPENTIER

Born: Havana, Cuba; December 26, 1904
Died: Paris, France; April 24, 1980

PRINCIPAL SHORT FICTION
Guerra del tiempo, 1958 (*War of Time*, 1970)

OTHER LITERARY FORMS

In contact with avant-garde groups in Havana and Paris, Alejo Carpentier wrote poetry as well as opera libretti and texts for other theatrical enterprises in his early years. Involved in publishing, broadcasting, and cinema for virtually all his life, he has contributed hundreds of articles of criticism on literature and the fine arts, especially music, some of which have been republished in book form. He is best known for his novels, which have been widely translated and studied.

ACHIEVEMENTS

Considered a pioneer and a continuing advocate of the New Novel in Latin America, Alejo Carpentier contributed a steady stream of fiction from the early 1930's until his death in 1980. His wide scope of interests, which range from politics and botany to the mythology and music of primitive Native American civilizations, is evident in his highly complex novels.

In his famous and influential essay, "De lo real maravilloso americano" (1962; "On the Marvelous Reality of America"), which grew out of the prologue to *El reino de este mundo* (1949; *The Kingdom of*

This World, 1957), Carpentier provides an alternative to the realistic "nativismo" style then popular in Latin American fiction and describes his theory of the quality of Latin American literature, which depicts a reality infused with magic and myth. In 1977, he was awarded the Cervantes Prize for literature by the Royal Academy of Spain.

BIOGRAPHY

Alejo Carpentier, the son of French and Russian parents, was educated in France as well as Cuba, studying architecture and music. A journalist during the 1920's, he became fascinated with Afro-Cuban culture, publishing his first novel, which dealt with this theme, shortly after being exiled for political activities. During the 1930's he moved among avant-garde coteries in Paris, including the surrealists, although he later rejected doctrinaire surrealism. His reencounter in 1939 with the Caribbean—Venezuela, Mexico, Haiti—initiated his finest years of literary production. In 1959, he began serving the Castro government in a wide assortment of cultural offices, and he was without question the most prestigious Cuban to lend it such support. Carpentier died in Paris, France, on April 24, 1980.

ANALYSIS

Alejo Carpentier's "Semejante a la noche" ("Like the Night") is indicative of one of the prominent al-

Alejo Carpentier (Archive Photos)

ternatives for sociological literature in the mid-twentieth century, an alternative that has had an enormous impact on the so-called new Latin American narrative. This is a mode of writing that is depersonalized, structurally geometric, and virtually allegorical in its thematic otherness. Unlike the social realism of the 1930's and 1940's in Latin America that shared with American and European counterparts a sentimentality and idealization that often bordered on kitsch and the trite, the committed literature represented by Carpentier's stories aspires, by eschewing all rhetoric of empathy, to a Brechtian intellectual and analytical contemplation. The goal may be to prevent contaminating the object—the verbal message and its sociopolitically definable meaning—with trivial emotional responses, but the artistic effect is equally to render ostensible "propositional" meaning less transparent and to increase the density of the symbolic texture. In short, fiction like Carpentier's, as properly ideological as it may be, is more complex and, therefore, less

assimilable to reductionary meanings than are its ancestors in a literature of sociopolitical commitment.

"LIKE THE NIGHT"

"Like the Night" deals with the oppressively ideological myths of war. Three separate time frames and three separate nuclei of incident and event are seamlessly worked together to project a holistic image of war as an enterprise that engulfs a certain class of young men in convenient commonplaces concerning adventure, ennobling sacrifice, and righteous strife. Men subscribe to these ideological myths in a gesture of unconscious self-betrayal to the interests of power structures that use war not only as a means of conquest and subjugation but also as an instrument for self-serving lies that provide the masses with a unifying and "noble" cause.

The three time frames are the Trojan War, the Spanish Conquest, and the French Conquest of the New World. In each case, an innocent youth prepares to embark by ship on an adventure that has been justified for him by his superiors. In each case, the explanation of the just cause is an ideological cliché that the reader associates with the particular culture at issue. "I breathe in deeply the breeze that came down from the olive tree groves, thinking how beautiful it would be to die in such a just cause, in the very cause of reason." These are the words of the young Trojan warrior. The Spanish sailor thinks:

> They were millions of souls that we would win for our holy religion, thereby fulfilling Christ's mandate to his Apostles. We were soldiers of God at the same time we were soldiers of the king, and through those Indians baptized and claimed, freed of their barbarous superstitions by our work, our nation would know the prize of an unbreakable greatness that would give us happiness, riches and power over all of the kingdoms of Europe.

Finally, the French legionnaire claims:

> We were going to carry out a great civilizing task in those immense wooded territories that extended from the burning Gulf of Mexico to the regions of Chicagúa, teaching new skills to the nations that lived there.

In each case the youth utters these self-serving commonplaces of an imperialistic ideology as he takes leave of a familiar and comforting personal reality: the familiar sounds and smells of his hometown, his betrothed.

Thus, from a semiological point of view, the four segments of the story (one for each of the three settings; the last returns to close the cyclical pattern) arrange an opposition for the reader, in the persons of a series of innocent and uncritical youths, between familiar and comforting knowns and the threatening unknowns of exploration, war, and conquest explained and given importance by patriotic slogans. To be sure, the story depends on the reader's accepting for himself a greater perceptivity than that of the three overlapping narrators. That is, it is the reader who must realize that the thoughts of the youths which so stir their minds and hearts are so many political bromides by which governments seek to ennoble the ignoble slaughter and subjugation of their military campaigns.

The cyclical nature of the narrative is an important ingredient in the rhetorical demand for such a perception on the part of the reader. In the first place, the contemporary reader—aware (thanks to historical interpretations and popular legends) that the three campaigns described by Carpentier's story were not the heroic gests that the protagonists believed them to be—is asked to perceive the thoughts of the youths as ideological clichés. In the second place, the repetition of a nucleus of narration—the preparations for a heroic adventure, the excitement of the hustle and bustle, the heightened emotions, and the patriotic claims for the adventure—in a variety of times and places serves to suggest, rather than its unique transcendence, its quality as commonplace.

This dual semiological strategy—the appeal to the reader's cultural knowledge and the repetition of a commonplace—is enhanced by what in the original Spanish is a subtle linguistic parody. If readers recognize the key thoughts of the one-in-three narrators as political commonplaces, they also recognize the texture of the three first-person narrations as kitschy recreations of the expressive style of the different periods and cultures. Thus, the text of the Trojan has a neutral "Attic" quality that stresses, in a way reminiscent of passages of Homer, the cumulative details of

epic campaigns. The text of the Spanish youth abounds in the archaisms of fifteenth century Spanish, in the pithy and earthy proverbs of the peasant, and in reference to the clamorous sounds and pungent smells of late-medieval Mediterranean locales. By contrast the text of the French warrior is characterized by the *sermo gravis*, the measured periods, and the self-sufficient cultural superiority characteristic of French classicism; it is also the longest of the three narrations.

In order to confirm the demythificational, anti-ideological reading suggested to the reader by the three strategies mentioned, the conclusion is "revisionist" in that the Trojan narrator, to whom Carpentier returns in the fourth and final segment, suffers a moment of sudden critical reflection:

> Now it would be the bugles, the mud, the wet bread, the arrogance of the chiefs, the blood spilled in error, the gangrene smelling of infected syrups. I was no longer so sure that my courage would increase the greatness and fortunes of the long-haired Achaeans. An older soldier going off to war as a job, with no more enthusiasm than the shearer of sheep heading for the stables, was telling anyone who cared to listen how Helen of Sparta was very happy in Troy and how when she lay with Paris her groans of pleasure reddened the cheeks of the virgins who dwell in Priamos's palace. It was said that the whole story of the sad captivity of Leda's daughter, offended and humiliated by the Trojans, was merely the propaganda of war, spread by Agamemnon with Menelaus' consent.

Thus Carpentier ensures his reader's "proper reading" of the separate but overlapping narrations. Carpentier's rhetoric strategies are not simply a clever artistic device for structural originality, although whatever aesthetic reaction that may derive from contemplating the neatness of the meshing narrations is certainly a legitimate response to the story. Rather, these strategies are elements in an overall narrative configuration in which Carpentier's story is in semiologically productive clash with the stories of the narrator participants. This irony vanishes suddenly in the closure of the text when the naïveté of the young warrior, challenged by the hardened soldier's cynicism, yields suddenly to a shock of recognition that confirms in a demythifying "reading" of the events and slogans surrounding the military preparations the demythifying reading of the individual narrations that the structure of Carpentier's text sets out to encourage in the reader. It is in this subtle and complex narrative texture that "Like the Night" is eminently paradigmatic of alternatives for Marxist and committed fiction in the new Latin American narrative that eschews the broadside approach of classical social realism.

OTHER MAJOR WORKS

LONG FICTION: *¡Ecué-Yamba-O! Historia Afro-Cubana*, 1933; *El reino de este mundo*, 1949 (*The Kingdom of This World*, 1957); *Los pasos perdidos*, 1953 (*The Lost Steps*, 1956); *El acoso*, 1956 (*Manhunt*, 1959); *El siglo de las luces*, 1962 (*Explosion in a Cathedral*, 1963); *El derecho de asilo*, 1972; *El recurso del método*, 1974 (*Reasons of State*, 1976); *Concierto barroco*, 1974 (*Concert Baroque*, 1976); *La consagración de la primavera*, 1978; *El arpa y la sombra*, 1979 (*The Harp and the Shadow*, 1990).

POETRY: *Dos poemas afro-cubanos*, 1930; *Poèmes des Antilles*, 1931.

NONFICTION: *La música en Cuba*, 1946; *Tientos y diferencias*, 1964; *Afirmación literaria latinoamericana*, 1978; *La novela latinoamericana en vísperas del nuevo siglo*, 1981.

MISCELLANEOUS: *El milagro de Anaquillé*, 1928 (ballet scenario); *Obras completas de Alejo Carpentier*, 1983-1990 (14 volumes).

BIBLIOGRAPHY

Adams, M. Ian. *Three Authors of Alienation: Bombal, Onetti, Carpentier.* Austin: University of Texas Press, 1975. The intent of this work is to study alienation as a literary theme in the works of these three authors. Each of them modifies traditional literary forms in order to present different aspects of the theme. The history of the concept is followed by a short description of modern alienation. Section devoted to Carpentier is subtitled "Alienation, Culture, Myth, and 'Marvelous Reality.'" Select bibliography.

Brotherston, Gordon. *The Emergence of the Latin American Novel.* Cambridge, England: Cambridge University Press, 1977. Intended as an introduction to the Latin American novel, particularly from the 1950's to the 1970's, this is a scholarly work that is also accessible to the general reader. The chapter on Carpentier discusses the historical, cultural, and mythic dimensions of the author's work. Contains a general bibliography of secondary works on Latin American literature as well as a list of works by and on the major authors mentioned in the text.

Figueredo, Danilo H. "Beyond the Boom: García Márquez and the Other Latin American Novelists." *Wilson Library Bulletin* 69 (February, 1995): 36-40. Notes that although Gabriel García Márquez is the most famous Latin American novelist, many of his predecessors and contemporaries, such as Jorge Luis Borges, Juan Rulfo, and Carpentier, refined *belles lettres* and invented a literature that did not wish to duplicate reality; notes that Borges, Rulfo, and Carpentier sought universality and employed experimental literary techniques.

González Echevarría, Roberto. *Alejo Carpentier: The Pilgrim at Home.* Austin: University Press of Texas, 1990. A sustained consideration of Carpentier's works and their overall significance, both within the field of Latin American literature and in the broader context of contemporary literature. Comes to terms with the basic question posed by his fiction as well as with the larger theoretical questions about literary modernity and history. A good introduction to Carpentier's work. Contains a bibliography of primary works and a select bibliography of secondary works.

Harvey, Sally. *Carpentier's Proustian Fiction: The Influence of Marcel Proust on Alejo Carpentier.* London: Tamesis, 1994. Examines the themes and style in Carpentier that are derived from Proust. Includes bibliographical references and an index.

Peden, Margaret Sayers, ed. *The Latin American Short Story.* Boston: Twayne, 1983. The essays in this insightful collection chart the main currents and principal figures of the historical mainstream of the Latin American short story, suggesting the outlines of the great depth and breadth of the genre in these lands. The section devoted to Carpentier focuses on the story "Semejante a la noche." Includes a select list of authors, and collections and critical studies in English.

Shaw, Donald L. *Alejo Carpentier.* Boston: Twayne, 1985. The first adequate critical work in English dealing with the entire body of Carpentier's writing. The work's primary aim is to present an overview of Carpentier's entire fictional production. Offers a balanced appraisal of Carpentier's development from his earliest work, through his discovery of "marvelous realism," to his last, apparently

Marxist, stance. Supplemented by an annotated bibliography and a chronology.

Unruh, Vicky. "The Performing Spectator in Alejo Carpentier's Fictional World." *Hispanic Review* 66 (Winter, 1998): 57-77. Argues that Carpentier uses the concept of performance to explore subjectivity and identity; asserts he was interested in performance because of his interest in switching identities; claims his theater activity is a key to understanding his fictional world, in which spectatorship is an important way of experiencing the world.

David W. Foster, updated by Genevieve Slomski

JOHN DICKSON CARR

Born: Uniontown, Pennsylvania; November 30, 1906
Died: Greenville, South Carolina; February 27, 1977

PRINCIPAL SHORT FICTION

The Department of Queer Complaints, 1940 (as Carter Dickson)
Dr. Fell, Detective, and Other Stories, 1947
The Exploits of Sherlock Holmes, 1954 (with Adrian Conan Doyle)
The Third Bullet and Other Stories, 1954
The Men Who Explained Miracles, 1963
The Door to Doom and Other Detections, 1980

OTHER LITERARY FORMS

John Dickson Carr's prolific and lengthy career produced seventy-one novels, four novelettes, several radio plays, two nonfiction works, and numerous articles in addition to six short-story collections (one of which was compiled posthumously by Douglas G. Greene). His work has been translated into at least a dozen languages—everything from the standard French, German, Italian, and Spanish to the more exotic Greek, Hungarian, Serbo-Croatian, and Turkish.

ACHIEVEMENTS

John Dickson Carr is best known for his contribution to the genre of detective fiction, specifically, to the tiny subgenre known as that of the "impossible crime." Under his pseudonym Roger Fairbairn, Carr also is credited with having been among the first to write a historical detective novel, *Devil Kinsmere* (1934). One of his early radio plays, *Cabin B-13* (1943), for the Columbia Broadcasting System series *Suspense*, later became the basis of a film called *Dangerous Crossing* (1953), which starred Michael Rennie and Jeanne Crain.

Carr was the recipient of many honors for his work, including an award from *Ellery Queen's Mystery Magazine* for "The Gentleman from Paris," a 1949 Edgar Allan Poe Award for *The Life of Sir Arthur Conan Doyle*, and a 1962 Grandmaster Award from the Mystery Writers of America.

BIOGRAPHY

Born in Uniontown, Pennsylvania, John Dickson Carr came from a respectable, well-to-do family. His father, Wood Nicholas Carr, was a lawyer and, later, a postmaster who also enjoyed a career in politics: He was elected to the House of Representatives, as a

Democrat, in 1912. The family spent four years in Washington, D.C., from 1913 to 1916. Perhaps inspired by his grandfather, who was a partial owner of a newspaper in Uniontown, Carr began writing articles on court proceedings and murder cases at the age of eleven. By age fifteen, he had his own column—about boxing.

From 1921 to 1925, Carr attended a preparatory school called the Hill School, where he wrote for the literary magazine. In 1925, he started at Haverford College, in Haverford, Pennsylvania. There, he became associate editor (in April, 1926) and then editor (in June of the same year) of *The Haverfordian*, although most of his literary contributions have been described as "tales of historical adventure." English and European history remained among Carr's principal interests, although he also commanded detailed knowledge about true crime, fencing, and other, as one critic called them, "curious bits of learning."

In 1928, Carr went to Paris, ostensibly to attend the Sorbonne, but it was during this time that Carr wrote *Grand Guignol* (1929), a short novel that served as the basis for his later *It Walks by Night* (1930). After the success of the latter novel, Carr married an Englishwoman named Clarice Cleaves, and the couple moved to England, where Carr instituted his now-legendary regimen of producing three to five novels a year. He and Clarice had three daughters, Julia (named for his mother), Bonita, and Mary.

ANALYSIS

John Dickson Carr's abundant output throughout his writing career is best characterized by his reply to a friend who asked if he had much trouble with inventing plots: "I've had exactly a hundred and twenty complete plots outlined, for emergencies, since I was eleven years old." This natural propensity for puzzles perhaps explains why Carr always restricted his writing to the locked-room murder in particular or the "impossible crime" in general, rather than branching out into other categories of mystery writing.

Carr was influenced at an early age by the Father Brown stories of G. K. Chesterton. In fact, Carr himself said that one of his most popular detectives, Dr. Gideon Fell, was based on Chesterton, as that author

John Dickson Carr (Library of Congress)

and his Father Brown series were the idols of Carr's boyhood.

For Carr, detective fiction was a "hoodwinking contest, a duel between author and reader" as he wrote in his essay "The Grandest Game in the World." Yet Carr despaired at the turn writers in the genre had taken by the 1960's. He believed that the authors were not taking enough care to craft a fair and reasonable story that would not purposely mislead the reader. Carr believed that all the writer had to do was to state his or her evidence, "and the reader [would] mislead himself."

Carr's oeuvre is most easily divided by detective. His three most famous creations were Henri Bencolin, prefect of police and later *juge d'instruction* in Paris; Dr. Gideon Fell, whose career as an amateur detective spanned twenty-three novels and five short stories as well as a number of radio plays; and Sir Henry Merrivale, a genteel chief of the Military Intelligence Department in the War Office. There were various other detectives whom Carr tried over the years but usually discarded after one or two outings.

Henri Bencolin is unique as a Carr creation in that he is the only detective whom Carr uses who is officially connected with the police department. He appeared in only a few stories and novels before being retired by Carr. Yet, according to critic Douglas G. Greene, in 1937 Carr revived Bencolin in *The Four False Weapons* to demonstrate that "the original Bencolin of the short stories was the genuine version of the detective."

"THE SHADOW OF THE GOAT"

In "The Shadow of the Goat," Bencolin, while vacationing in England, becomes involved in a case unofficially when a Frenchman is murdered. Carr sets the scene for the story complete with thick London fog and swirls of tobacco smoke. Bencolin calls on his English friend Sir John Landervorne, a man with unofficial connections to both Whitehall and Scotland Yard, to see if he can glean more details about the murder of Monsieur Jules Fragneau.

The supernatural aspects to this story are emphasized by Carr's own clues to the reader. Sir John states that the probable murderer was locked in a room while he himself (as well as some others) watched the door and that "nobody had either entered or left that door." Carr finishes that section of the story with the italicized line, *"And, as later events proved, Sir John spoke the absolute truth."* The conclusion is that the explanation to this story's puzzle is most likely one beyond the ken of rationality. Yet very few of Carr's stories ever bear out that conclusion. Most of the time, as in "The Shadow of the Goat," the murderer proves to be all too human.

"THE DOOR TO DOOM"

In "The Door to Doom," Carr does incorporate the supernatural as at least partial explanation for foul play. Instead of using one of his more famous detectives, Carr introduces the character of Peter Maynard, a hapless American tourist lost on the road to Chartres. Advised by two local peasants to take a shortcut through the woods, Maynard finds himself staying at a most peculiar inn called the Inn of the Beautiful Prospect, although its original name seems to have been something much less enticing.

Despite its name, this inn turns out to be less than salubrious for Maynard's future: He ends up in a struggle against the innkeeper and his friends, who lure unsuspecting American and English guests to a "crushing" end. They then take the tourists' money, making it look as if they have been crushed by falling into the local ravine and thus lulling any police suspicions. Fortunately for Maynard, help arrives in a form that proves to be Carr's trump card in this story, for it appears that vengeance on the perpetrators is taken from beyond the grave, and Carr's ending does not dispute this supernatural interpretation.

Not all Carr's stories are so overtly violent. In his Department of Queer Complaints stories, for example, Carr's detective Colonel March takes pride in handling situations that hint at foul play, although in "William Wilson's Racket," there is not even a murder to solve. In "The Empty Flat," the Department of Queer Complaints' Colonel March handles a bona fide death, but the question arises as to whether it was murder.

"ALL IN A MAZE"

"All in a Maze" (originally entitled "Ministry of Miracles" when first published in *Housewife*, in 1955) is a long short story that showcases the talents of Sir Henry Merrivale, generally known by his admirers as "the old man" or "H. M." Merrivale holds an ambiguous government position in a somewhat mysterious department that technically is called Central Office Eight but that goes by the nom de guerre of the Ministry of Miracles.

Yet Merrivale is not ostensibly the main protagonist of the story. Carr has his detective take a backseat to two characters, Tom Lockwood and Jennifer Holden, one of whom is the actual and one of whom is the seemingly intended victim of a ventriloquist-murdering Frenchman. Merrivale does manage to get at least a mention, however, even in the scenes in which he does not actually appear. For example, upon first hearing the suggestion that she should seek help from Merrivale, Jenny cries, "But he is awful! He is fat and bald, and he swear [sic] and carry on and throw people out of windows."

Ultimately, however, Merrivale is asked to handle the case and proceeds to dispatch the mysteries that keep developing. He does so with such prosaic solutions that he himself admits to the disappointment that people feel upon discovering that the miracle is merely a tawdry work of human design—which only adds to the humor of his character.

"THE INCAUTIOUS BURGLAR"

It is Carr's detective Dr. Fell who features in "The Incautious Burglar" (originally entitled "A Guest in the House" when it was first published in *The Strand Magazine*, in 1940). Fell is an idiosyncratic detective, as different from Henri Bencolin as possible. Physically, Fell is similar to Rex Stout's Nero Wolfe—that is, he is impressively large. In "The Incautious Burglar," he "settled back massively in the wicker settee, so that its frame creaked and cracked like a ship's bulkhead in a heavy sea." Carr himself, however, has said that the inspiration for Fell came from G. K. Chesterton, creator of the Father Brown mysteries. In "Invisible Hands" (originally entitled "King Arthur's Chair" when it was first published in *Lilliput*, in 1957), Carr writes about Dr. Fell: "Into the room, wheezing and leaning on a stick, lumbered a man so enormous that he had to maneuver himself sideways through the door. . . . His big face would ordinarily have been red and beaming, with chuckles animating several chins."

"The Incautious Burglar" is noteworthy not only for Fell's appearance but also for Carr's careful setup of the murder victim as a criminal. The description of the murdered man implies that art collector Marcus Hunt set out to steal his own collection but was murdered in the process. Both his attire and his fatal wound are carefully described, and with these clues, Carr gives the reader—and Dr. Fell—enough to solve the mystery. The brilliance of Carr's stories lies in their simplicity; Carr always lays out his hand for the careful reader to study.

OTHER MAJOR WORKS

LONG FICTION: *Grand Guignol*, 1929; *It Walks by Night*, 1930; *The Lost Gallows*, 1931; *Castle Skull*, 1931; *The Corpse in the Waxworks*, 1932 (also known as *The Waxworks Murder*); *Poison in Jest*, 1932; *Hag's Nook*, 1933; *The Mad Hatter Mystery*, 1933; *The Bowstring Murders*, 1933 (first edition as Carr Dickson and subsequent editions as Carter Dickson); *The Eight of Swords*, 1934; *The Plague Court Murders*, 1934 (as Carter Dickson); *The Blind Barber*, 1934; *The White Priory Murders*, 1934 (as Carter Dickson); *Devil Kinsmere*, 1934 (as Roger Fairbairn); *Death-Watch*, 1935; *The Red Widow Murders*, 1935 (as Carter Dickson); *The Three Coffins*, 1935 (also known as *The Hollow Man*); *The Unicorn Murders*, 1935 (as Carter Dickson); *The Arabian Nights Murder*, 1936; *The Punch and Judy Murders*, 1936 (as Carter Dickson; also known as *The Magic-Lantern Murders*); *The Burning Court*, 1937; *The Peacock Feather Murders*, 1937 (as Carter Dickson; also known as *The Ten Teacups*); *The Four False Weapons*, 1937; *To Wake the Dead*, 1937; *The Judas Window*, 1938 (as Carter Dickson; also as *The Crossbow Murder*); *Death in Five Boxes*, 1938 (as Carter Dickson); *The Crooked Hinge*, 1938; *Fatal Descent*, 1939 (with John Rhode, pseudonym of Cecil John Charles Street, and as Carter Dickson; also as *Drop to His Death*); *The Problem of the Green Capsule*, 1939 (also as *The Black Spectacles*); *The Reader Is Warned*, 1939 (as Carter Dickson); *The Problem of the Wire Cage*, 1939; *The Man Who Could Not Shudder*, 1940; *Nine—And Death Makes Ten*, 1940 (as Carter Dickson; also as *Murder in the Submarine Zone* and *Murder in the Atlantic*); *And So to Murder*, 1941 (as Carter Dickson); *The Case of the Constant Suicide*, 1941; *Seeing Is Believing*, 1941 (as Carter Dickson; also as *Cross of Murder*); *Death Turns the Tables*, 1941 (also known as *The Seat of the Scornful*); *The Gilded Man*, 1942 (as Carter Dickson; also as *Death and the Gilded Man*); *The Emperor's Snuff-Box*, 1942; *She Died a Lady*, 1943 (as Carter Dickson); *He Wouldn't Kill Patience*, 1944 (as Carter Dickson); *Till Death Do Us Part*, 1944; *The Curse of the Bronze Lamp*, 1945 (as Carter Dickson); *He Who Whispers*, 1946; *My Late Wives*, 1946 (as Carter Dickson); *The Sleeping Sphinx*, 1947; *The Skeleton in the Clock*, 1948 (as Carter Dickson); *Below Suspicion*, 1949; *A Graveyard to Let*, 1949 (as Carter Dickson); *The Bride of Newgate*, 1950; *Night at the Mocking Widow*, 1950 (as Carter Dickson); *The Devil in Velvet*, 1951; *Behind the Crimson Blind*, 1952 (as Carter Dickson); *The Nine Wrong Answers*, 1952; *Captain Cut-Throat*, 1955; *Fear Is the Same*, 1956 (as Carter Dickson); *Patrick Butler for the Defence*,

1956; *Fire, Burn!*, 1957; *The Dead Man's Knock*, 1958; *Scandal at High Chimneys*, 1959; *In Spite of Thunder*, 1960; *The Witch of the Low-Tide*, 1961; *The Demoniacs*, 1962; *Most Secret*, 1964; *The House at Stan's Elbow*, 1965; *Panic in Box C*, 1966; *Dark of the Moon*, 1967; *Papa Là-bas*, 1968; *The Ghosts' High Noon*, 1969; *Deadly Hall*, 1971; *The Hungry Goblin*, 1972.

RADIO PLAYS: *The Bride Vanishes*, 1942; *The Devil in the Summerhouse*, 1942; *Will You Make a Bet with Death?*, 1942; *Cabin B-13*, 1943; *The Hangman Won't Wait*, 1943; *The Phantom Archer*, 1943; *The Dead Sleep Lightly*, 1983.

NONFICTION: *The Murder of Sir Edmund Godfrey*, 1936; *The Life of Sir Arthur Conan Doyle*, 1949.

EDITED TEXT: *Great Stories*, 1959 (by Sir Arthur Conan Doyle).

BIBLIOGRAPHY

Greene, Douglas G. *John Dickson Carr: The Man Who Explained Miracles*. New York: Otto Penzler, 1995. A brief biographical sketch, followed by a survey of Carr's works, commenting on the high consistency of his fiction, his focus on the locked-room mystery convention, and the romantic and fantastic atmosphere that distinguishes his books from those of other detective writers.

_____. "A Mastery of Miracles: G. K. Chesterton and John Dickson Carr." *Chesterton Review* 10 (August, 1984): 307-315. This article pays homage to Carr's work particularly as it relates to that of G. K. Chesterton. Greene concentrates on Carr's short fiction but includes some biographical information too. Notes on sources are given at the end of the article.

Joshi, S. T. *John Dickson Carr: A Critical Study*. Bowling Green, Ohio: Bowling Green State University Popular Press, 1990. Joshi's text is the main full-length critical study available. He discusses in detail Carr's short fiction while also including some biographical information. Joshi gives publishing information for Carr's individual stories as well as for the collections. His detailed notes, bibliographies (both primary, including translations, and secondary), and index make this text an excellent starting place for research.

Panek, LeRoy. *An Introduction to the Detective Story*. Bowling Green, Ohio: Bowling Green State University Popular Press, 1987. References to Carr's work—in particular, his short fiction—are scattered throughout this text. Good for setting Carr in the context of his time. An index and a list of reference works are given at the end, and a separate list of history and criticism texts is also included.

_____. "John Dickson Carr." In *Watteau's Shepherds: The Detective Novel in Britain, 1914-1940*. Bowling Green, Ohio: Bowling Green University Popular Press, 1979. Despite Carr's nationality, he is considered one of the finest British mystery writers. In his text, Panek devotes a detailed chapter to Carr, covering Carr's most famous detectives and works, including both long and short fiction. An appendix outlines the structure of the detective story. Supplemented by a chronology of Carr's works, notes on the Carr chapter, and an index.

Taylor, Robert Lewis. "Two Authors in an Attic, Part I." *The New Yorker* 27 (September 8, 1951): 39-44, 46, 48.

_____. "Two Authors in an Attic, Part II." *The New Yorker* 27 (September 15, 1951): 36-40, 42, 46, 48, 51. This pair of articles is extremely useful for detailed biographical information as well as for Carr's own thoughts on his writing. Carr discusses with Taylor which writers influenced him most and goes into detail about his political and philosophical views. Invaluable for getting a personal look at Carr, despite its lack of references.

Jo-Ellen Lipman Boon

ANGELA CARTER
Angela Olive Stalker

Born: Eastbourne, Sussex, England; May 7, 1940
Died: London, England; February 16, 1992

PRINCIPAL SHORT FICTION

Fireworks: Nine Profane Pieces, 1974
The Bloody Chamber and Other Stories, 1979
Black Venus, 1985 (pb. in U.S. as *Saints and Strangers*, 1986)
American Ghosts and Old World Wonders, 1993
Burning Your Boats, 1995

OTHER LITERARY FORMS

Angela Carter is best known as a novelist, having won several awards for her long fiction. Her earliest novels were surreal without being overtly supernatural, but after *Heroes and Villains* (1969) she made increasing use of fantastic devices, developing phantasmagorical symbolic landscapes of an extraordinary complexity in *The Infernal Desire Machines of Doctor Hoffman* (1972) and *The Passion of New Eve* (1977). She also wrote a great deal of journalistic criticism, collected in *Shaking a Leg* (1997).

ACHIEVEMENTS

Angela Carter won the John Llewelyn Rhys Memorial Prize for *Several Perceptions* in 1968, the Somerset Maugham Award for *The Magic Toyshop* in 1969, the Kurt Maschler Award (for children's fiction) in 1982, and the James Tait Black Memorial Prize for *Nights at the Circus* in 1985. Following her untimely death in 1992—which allowed her work to be included in the syllabi of those British universities reluctant to venerate living writers—Carter was immediately hailed as the most important English fantasist of her generation.

BIOGRAPHY

Angela Olive Carter was born Angela Olive Stalker in Eastbourne, soon after the outbreak of World War II. She was evacuated to Yorkshire to live with her grandmother, returning south after the war's end to attend school in Balham in south London. After leaving school she worked as a junior reporter on the *Croydon Advertiser*. She married Paul Carter in 1960. She read English at the University of Bristol from 1962 to 1965 and published her first novel, *Shadow Dance*, a year after graduating.

Carter lived in Japan for more than two years before her divorce in 1972, and there was a distinct hiatus in her work thereafter, although her productivity increased again after she became the Arts Council Fellow in creative writing at the University of Sheffield in 1976—an appointment she held for two years. She returned to London thereafter, eventually settling with Mark Pearce, the father of her son Alexander, who was born in 1983. During the 1980's she taught creative writing for brief periods at a number of universities, including Brown University in Providence, Rhode Island, the University of Adelaide in Australia, and the University of East Anglia in England. She died of lung cancer in 1992.

ANALYSIS

Angela Carter's interest in the usefulness of fantastic devices increased markedly while she was writing the shorter pieces making up her first collection, *Fireworks*, between 1970 and 1973. She described these items as "tales" rather than "stories," explaining in her introduction that

> Formally the tale differs from the short story in that it makes few pretenses at the imitation of life. The tale does not log everyday experience, as the short story does; it interprets everyday experience through a system of imagery derived from subterranean areas behind everyday experience, and therefore . . . cannot betray its readers into a false knowledge of everyday experience.

Carter's introduction goes on to locate her short work within the gothic tradition, readily admitting that tradition's links with "subliterary forms," such as pornography, ballads, and dreams.

All of Carter's subsequent collections consist of

tales rather than stories, according to this characterization, and all of them are firmly set in the gothic tradition. They are surreal even when they are not frankly supernatural or outrightly phantasmagorical, and they offer commentaries on quotidian existence rather than depictions of it. They make little use of dialogue, sometimes tending toward essaylike discourses imaginatively reconstructing the states of mind and existential plights of their central characters. These include several real individuals: Charles Baudelaire's mistress Jeanne Duval in "Black Venus" (1980); America's most famous murderess, Lizzie Borden, in "The Fall River Axe Murders" (1981) and "Lizzie's Tiger" (1981); and the greatest master of the gothic tale in "The Cabinet of Edgar Allan Poe" (1982). All the tales in *The Bloody Chamber and Other Stories*—described by Salman Rushdie as her "masterwork"—and some of those in her subsequent collections apply the same method to various imaginary figures, including all the classic female stereotypes to be found in popular fairy tales.

"REFLECTIONS"

"Reflections" is the longest of the items in *Fireworks*. Unlike the mildly phantasmagorical "The Loves of Lady Purple" and "Flesh and the Mirror," it does not draw directly upon Carter's experiences in Japan, but it has motifs in common with both of those stories. It is an account of a dream whose protagonist, while walking in a wood, is led by a siren song to discover a mysterious seashell. The shell turns out to have strayed from the Sea of Fertility: a "reversed system," accessible through a mirror in a house where a lone androgyne plays the reality-weaving role delegated in Greek myth to the three Fates.

The dreamer passes through the mirror to the world beyond, where she is raped by the siren. Her retaliation and subsequent shattering return through the mirror break the thread which connects the two worlds and puts an abrupt end to the patient weaving of fate. There is no awakening, as such, at the end of the tale, but the implication is that the protagonist has finally broken free of the oppressive pattern that has hitherto confined and restricted her life. That kind of breakthrough recurs throughout Carter's work, usually represented in more explicit but equally fantastic

terms as the triumphant empowerment of a female character, who has belatedly seized control of her own sexuality.

"THE COMPANY OF WOLVES"

Most of the stories in *The Bloody Chamber* rework the imagery of classic fairy tales in such a way as to reverse the traditional message that female fulfilment can only be found in submission to the authority of males. The title story offers a new account of the defeat of Bluebeard, while "The Courtship of Mr. Lyon" and "The Tiger's Bride" rework "Beauty and the Beast." "The Lady of the House of Love" is a version of "Sleeping Beauty," which subjects tales of vampiric femmes fatales to a similarly ironic but less straightforward revision. The most famous tales in the collection, however, are the two accounts of female lycanthropy that were adapted into the script of the 1984 film, directed by Neil Jordan, which took its title from "The Company of Wolves."

"The Company of Wolves" is a version of "Little Red Riding Hood," a traditional tale, whose easily decoded erotic imagery has always seemed to some readers to be peculiar if not perverse. The heroine of Carter's story easily recognizes that the wolf is "car-

Angela Carter (©Miriam Berkley)

nivore incarnate," whose hunger can be appeased only by "immaculate flesh," but she refuses to be intimidated by the prospect of lying down with him in her grandmother's bed. She joins him there, not merely willingly but avid, gladly becoming a feral child like the ones in "Wolf-Alice"—the wolf-girl story from *The Bloody Chamber* that was left out of the film—and "Peter and the Wolf," a later variant on the theme from *Black Venus*.

BLACK VENUS

All of the tales in *Black Venus* are biographies of a sort, ranging in complexity from "The Kiss," a brief account of Tamburlaine's wife, to "Overture and Incidental Music for 'A Midsummer Night's Dream,'" an account of the mythic characters of William Shakespeare's play as seen from the viewpoint of the mercurial Golden Herm. "Our Lady of the Massacre" (originally published as "Captured by the Red Man"), though entirely fictitious, is one of the more naturalistic items in the book. It borrows some inspiration for its account of the early phases of an English whore's career from Daniel Defoe's *Moll Flanders* (1722) but is primarily concerned with the narrator's adventures among the Native Americans, who give her the dignity and social position denied her by the Puritan colonists to whom she is indentured after transportation.

The narrator attempts to warn her adopted tribe that their new neighbors are more dangerous than they imagine—or can imagine—but to no avail. In the end, the Puritans reclaim her and restore her to what they consider to be her due status. The nature of the collection ensures that several of the items therein are tragedies of some sort, thus contrasting its overall tone with the celebratory ambience of the tales of exotic liberation assembled in *The Bloody Chamber*, but "Our Lady of the Massacre" is the angriest and most harrowing in its condemnations of patriarchy.

AMERICAN GHOSTS AND OLD WORLD WONDERS

It is hardly surprising that *American Ghosts and Old World Wonders*, a posthumous assembly of remnants, is the least unified of Carter's four collections. The inclusion of "Lizzie's Tiger" suggests that Carter might have toyed with the idea of building a novel on the foundation of "The Fall River Axe Murders,"

while "Gun for the Devil" is a reworking of a screenplay that would have reformulated Johann Apel's tale "Der Freischutz" as a Western. "Ashputtle: Or, The Mother's Ghost" recalls the method of the tales in *The Bloody Chamber* in offering three new versions of the often reworked tale of Cinderella, but all three are more downbeat in tone than their predecessors and their arrangement—longest first, shortest last—is such that their impetus seems to be dwindling away by degrees.

The first of the three tales is a cynical account of the way in which the replacement mother mutilates her own children in the hope of making their feet fit the crucial slipper, and how their bloodstains still pollute the slipper as the rightful owner steps into her heritage. The second tale focuses on the dead mother of the heroine and the manner in which she obtains a problematic "revenge" against the one who took her place. The third tale does likewise but offers an even more graphic account of the way in which luckless daughters are forced to follow in their mothers' footsteps. The tale is too early to have been affected by the author's knowledge of her own impending death, but it is undoubtedly colored by her own experiences as a mother. Although the tone of the story is far darker than its analogues in *The Bloody Chamber*, it retains the same blithely dark humor, and it is written with exactly the same poetic elegance. It confirms, as do all of Carter's short fictions, that she was a brilliant wordsmith, one who loved to stretch the resources of the English language in the construction of fabulous imagery and fervent morality plays.

OTHER MAJOR WORKS

LONG FICTION: *Shadow Dance*, 1966 (pb. in U.S. as *Honeybuzzard*, 1967); *The Magic Toyshop*, 1967; *Several Perceptions*, 1968; *Heroes and Villains*, 1969; *Love*, 1971, revised 1987; *The Infernal Desire Machines of Doctor Hoffman*, 1972 (pb. in U.S. as *War of Dreams*, 1972); *The Passion of New Eve*, 1977; *Nights at the Circus*, 1984; *Wise Children*, 1991.

SCREENPLAYS: *The Company of Wolves*, 1984 (with Neil Jordan); *The Magic Toyshop*, 1987.

RADIO PLAYS: *Vampirella*, 1976; *Come unto These Yellow Sands*, 1979; *The Company of Wolves*, 1980;

Puss in Boots, 1982; *Come Unto These Yellow Sands: Four Radio Plays*, pb. 1985 (includes previous four plays).

NONFICTION: *The Sadeian Woman: And the Ideology of Pornography*, 1978; *Nothing Sacred: Selected Writings*, 1982; *Expletives Deleted*, 1992; *Shaking a Leg: Collected Writings*, 1997.

CHILDREN'S LITERATURE: *Miss Z, the Dark Young Lady*, 1970; *Moonshadow*, 1982.

TRANSLATION: *The Fairy Tales of Charles Perrault*, 1977.

EDITED TEXTS: *Wayward Girls and Wicked Women*, 1986; *The Virago Book of Fairy Tales*, 1990 (pb. in U.S. as *The Old Wives' Fairy Tale Book*).

BIBLIOGRAPHY

Day, Aidan. *Angela Carter: The Rational Glass*. Manchester, England: Manchester University Press, 1998. A good overview of Carter's work, although more attention is paid to the novels than to short fiction. Chapter 5 is an extended study of the tales in *The Bloody Chamber and Other Stories*.

Gamble, Sarah. *Angela Carter: Writing from the Front Line*. Edinburgh: Edinburgh University Press, 1997. A comprehensive account of Carter's life and works, which includes discussions of all four short-story collections as well as detailed individual analyses of a handful of quasi-autobiographical tales.

Jordan, Elaine. "Enthralment: Angela Carter's Speculative Fictions." In *Plotting Change: Contemporary Women's Fiction*, edited by Linda Anderson. London: Edward Arnold, 1990. An analysis of Carter's use of mythological and fairy-tale motifs in parables of sexual liberation.

Sage, Lorna. *Angela Carter*. Plymouth, England: Northcote House, 1994. An essay in the British Council-sponsored Writers and Their Work series, less detailed than the full-length studies by Day or Gamble but at least their equal in the sensitivity of its analysis.

Sage, Lorna, ed. *Flesh and the Mirror: Essays on the Art of Angela Carter*. London: Chatto & Windus, 1994. A collection of thirteen essays on various aspects of Carter's work, including several devoted wholly or partly to the short fiction.

Brian Stableford

RAYMOND CARVER

Born: Clatskanie, Oregon; May 25, 1938
Died: Port Angeles, Washington; August 2, 1988

PRINCIPAL SHORT FICTION

Put Yourself in My Shoes, 1974
Will You Please Be Quiet, Please?, 1976
Furious Seasons and Other Stories, 1977
What We Talk About When We Talk About Love, 1981
Cathedral, 1983
Where I'm Calling From, 1988

OTHER LITERARY FORMS

Raymond Carver distinguished himself as a short-story writer and poet, and he wrote in both forms until his death. His poetry has been published in the following collections: *Near Klamath* (1968), *Winter Insomnia* (1970), *At Night the Salmon Move* (1976), *Two Poems* (1982), *Fires: Essays, Poems, Stories* (1983), *If It Please You* (1984), *This Water* (1985), *Where Water Comes Together with Other Water* (1985), *Ultramarine* (1986), and *A New Path to the Waterfall* (1989).

ACHIEVEMENTS

Raymond Carver's greatest achievement was overcoming his economically and culturally disadvantaged background to become an author of world renown. He made the short story a viable literary form; since Carver, short-story collections have again become a marketable commodity in the book trade. Both as a model and as a teacher, he had such an influence on younger fiction writers that author Jay McInerney could truthfully say (alluding to a famous statement that Fyodor Dostoevski made about Nikolai Gogol) that there is hardly a single American short-story writer younger than Carver who did not "come out of Carver's overcoat."

With only a bachelor's degree and mediocre grades, Carver was invited to teach at distinguished universities and became a professor of English at Syracuse University in 1980. He received many honors during his lifetime, including a Strauss Living Award, which guaranteed him an annual stipend of thirty-five thousand dollars and enabled him to devote all his time to writing during the last years of his life. Just before his death, he received a doctorate of letters from the University of Hartford.

Raymond Carver (Marion Ettlinger)

BIOGRAPHY

Raymond Carver grew up in a sparsely populated corner of the Pacific Northwest. This rustic environment had an indelible effect upon his character and writing. Like Ernest Hemingway, one of the writers who influenced him, he loved the purity and freedom of the American wilderness, and he also respected the simplicity, honesty, and directness of the men and women who earned meager and precarious livelihoods in that primitive setting. He married young and had two children to support by the time he was twenty. He had wanted to be a writer from the time he was in the third grade, but the responsibilities of parenthood made it extremely difficult for him to find time to write. His limited education forced him to take menial jobs for which he was temperamentally unsuited. He was unable to consider tackling anything as ambitious as a full-length novel, so he spent his odd free hours writing short stories and poetry. He managed to get some of his work published in little magazines, but these publications paid little or nothing for his work, so he was haunted by financial problems for much of his life.

One of the most important influences in Carver's life was John Gardner, who taught creative writing at California State University at Chico and said, "You cannot be a great writer unless you feel greatly." The idealistic Gardner introduced his students to the literary magazines that represented the cutting edge in contemporary American fiction and poetry, and he urged them to write honestly about what they knew, as opposed to turning out formula fiction in an attempt to make money. This is exactly what Carver did, and, ironically, he found that the hardships and distractions that were preventing him from writing were the very things that provided him with material to write about. This may account for the characteristic stoical humor to be found in many of his stories.

Another profound influence in his life was alcohol. One of Carver's distinguishing traits as a writer is his astonishing candor, and anyone who reads a dozen of his short stories will get a good idea of what his life was like for nearly two decades. His drinking caused serious domestic and financial problems, which led to feelings of guilt and more drinking.

Amazingly, his strong constitution and unwavering motivation enabled him to continue producing stories and poems.

With the publication of *What We Talk About When We Talk About Love* in 1981, Carver achieved critical and popular fame. His financial problems were ameliorated because he was receiving valuable grants and teaching assignments and was also selling his work to high-paying slick magazines such as *Esquire, Harper's Bazaar, Playgirl*, and *The New Yorker*. Collections of his short stories sold well. He was earning money teaching creative writing courses and appearing as a featured attraction at many workshops and seminars.

By the late 1970's, Carver had separated from his first wife and was living with the poet and teacher Tess Gallagher. She helped him cope with his drinking problem and provided a much-needed stabilizing influence. Carver, always a heavy cigarette smoker, died of lung cancer in 1988. By that time, his works had been published all over the world in more than twenty languages.

ANALYSIS

Nearly everything written about Raymond Carver begins with two observations: He is a minimalist, and he writes about working-class people. Even when the critic is sympathetic, this dual categorization tends to stigmatize Carver as a minor artist writing little stories about little people. Although it is true that most of Carver's characters belong to the working class, their problems are universal. Carver writes about divorce, infidelity, spiritual alienation, alcoholism, bankruptcy, rootlessness, and existential dread; none of these afflictions is peculiar to the working class, and in fact, all were once more common to members of the higher social classes.

Carver was a minimalist by preference and by necessity. His lifelong experience had been with working-class people. It would have been inappropriate to write about simple people in an ornate style, and, furthermore, his limited education would have made it impossible for him to do so effectively. The spare, objective style that he admired in some of Hemingway's short stories, such as "The Killers" and "Hills Like White Elephants," was perfectly suited to Carver's needs.

The advantage and appeal of minimalism in literature is that it draws readers into the story by forcing them to conceptualize missing details. One drawback is that it allows insecure writers to imply that they know more than they know and mean more than they are actually saying. This was true of the early stories that Carver collected in *Will You Please Be Quiet, Please?* A good example of Carver's strengths and weaknesses is a short story in that volume titled "Fat."

"FAT"

As the title suggests, "Fat" is about a fat man. It is little more than a character sketch; nothing happens in the story. Throughout his career, Carver based stories and poems on people or incidents that he observed or scraps of conversation that he overheard; these things seemed to serve as living metaphors or symbols with broader implications. Carver frames his story by setting it in a restaurant and by describing the fat man from the point of view of a waitress. She says that she has never seen such a fat person in her life and is somewhat awestruck by his appearance, by his gracious manners, and by the amount of food that he can consume at one sitting. After she goes home at night, she is still thinking about him. She says that she herself feels "terrifically fat"; she feels depressed, and finally ends by saying, "My life is going to change. I feel it."

The reader can feel it too but might be hard pressed to say what "it" is. The story leaves a strong impression but an ambiguous one. No two readers would agree on what the story means, if anything. It demonstrates Carver's talent for characterization through dialogue and action, which was his greatest asset. Both the waitress and her fat customer come alive as people, partially through the deliberate contrast between them. His treatment of the humble, kindly waitress demonstrates his sensitivity to the feelings of women. His former wife, Maryann Carver, said of him, "Ray loved and understood women, and women loved him."

"Fat" also shows Carver's unique sense of humor, which was another trait that set him apart from other writers. Carver was so constituted that he could not help seeing the humorous side of the tragic or the grotesque. His early, experimental short stories most closely resemble the early short stories of William Saroyan reprinted in *The Daring Young Man on the Flying Trapeze and Other Stories* (1934) and subsequent collections of his stories that appeared in the 1930's. Saroyan is perhaps best remembered for his novel *The Human Comedy* (1943), and it might be said that the human comedy was Carver's theme and thesis throughout his career. Like the early stories of Saroyan, Carver's stories are the tentative vignettes of a novice who knows very well that he wants to be a writer but still does not know exactly what he wants to say.

"NEIGHBORS"

Will You Please Be Quiet, Please? includes the tragicomic "Neighbors," the first of Carver's stories to appear in a slick magazine with a large circulation. Gordon Lish, editor of the men's magazine *Esquire*, recognized Carver's talent early but did not immediately accept any of his submissions. Lish's welcome encouragement, painful rejections, and eventual acceptance represented major influences in Carver's career. "Neighbors" deals with ordinary people but has a surrealistic humor, which was to become a Carver trademark.

Bill and Arlene Miller, a couple in their thirties, have agreed to feed their neighbors' cat and water the plants while they are away. The Stones' apartment holds a mysterious fascination, and they both find excuses to enter it more often than necessary. Bill helps himself to the Chivas Regal, eats food out of their refrigerator, and goes through their closets and dresser drawers. He tries on some of Jim Stone's clothes and lies on their bed masturbating. Then he goes so far as to try on Harriet Stone's brassiere and panties and then a skirt and blouse. Bill's wife also disappears into the neighbors' apartment on her own mysterious errands. They fantasize that they have assumed the identities of their neighbors, whom they regard as happier people leading fuller lives. The shared guilty adventure arouses both Bill and Arlene sexually, and they have better lovemaking than they have experienced in a long while. Then disaster strikes: Arlene discovers that she has inadvertently locked the

Stones' key inside the apartment. The cat may starve; the plants may wither; the Stones may find evidence that they have been rummaging through their possessions. The story ends with the frightened Millers clinging to each other outside their lost garden of Eden.

This early story displays some of Carver's strengths: his sense of humor, his powers of description, and his ability to characterize people through what they do and say. It also has the two main qualities that editors look for: timeliness and universality. It is therefore easy to understand why Lish bought this piece after rejecting so many others. "Neighbors" portrays the alienated condition of many contemporary Americans of all social classes.

"Neighbors," however, has certain characteristics that have allowed hostile critics to damn Carver's stories as "vignettes," "anecdotes," "sketches," and "slices-of-life." For one thing, readers realize that the terror they briefly share with the Millers is unnecessary: They can go to the building manager for a passkey or call a locksmith. It is hard to understand how two people who are so bold about violating their neighbors' apartment should suddenly feel so helpless in the face of an everyday mishap. The point of the story is blunted by the unsatisfactory ending.

WHAT WE TALK ABOUT WHEN WE TALK ABOUT LOVE

The publication of the collection titled *What We Talk About When We Talk About Love* made Carver famous. These short, rather ambiguous stories also got him permanently saddled with the term "minimalist." Carver never accepted that label and claimed that he did not even understand what it meant. He had a healthy mistrust of critics who attempted to categorize writers with such epithets: It was as if he sensed their antagonism and felt that they themselves were trying to "minimize" him as an author. A friend of Carver said that he thought a minimalist was a "taker-out" rather than a "putter-in." In that sense, Carver was a minimalist. It was his practice to go over and over his stories trying to delete all superfluous words and even superfluous punctuation marks. He said that he knew he was finished with a story when he found himself putting back punctuation marks that he had previously deleted. It would be more accurate to call Carver a perfectionist rather than a minimalist.

"WHY DON'T YOU DANCE?"

One of the best short stories reprinted in *What We Talk About When We Talk About Love* is "Why Don't You Dance?" It is one of the most representative, the most "Carveresque" of all Carver's short stories. A man who is never given a name has placed all of his furniture and personal possessions outside on the front lawn and has whimsically arranged them as if they were still indoors. He has run an extension cord from the house and hooked up lamps, a television, and a record player. He is sitting outside drinking whiskey, totally indifferent to the amazement and curiosity of his neighbors. One feels as if the worst is over for him: He is the survivor of some great catastrophe, like a marooned sailor who has managed to salvage some flotsam and jetsam.

A young couple, referred to throughout the story as "the boy" and "the girl," drive by and assume that the man is holding a yard sale. They stop and inquire about prices. The man offers them drinks. The boy and girl get into a party spirit. They put old records on the turntable and start dancing in the driveway. The man is anxious to get rid of his possessions and accepts whatever they are willing to offer. He even makes them presents of things that they do not really want. Weeks later, the girl is still talking about the man, but she cannot find the words to express what she really feels about the incident. Perhaps she and her young friends will understand the incident much better after they have worked and worried and bickered and moved from one place to another for ten or twenty years.

"Why Don't You Dance?" is a humorous treatment of a serious subject, in characteristic Carver fashion. The man's tragedy is never spelled out, but the reader can piece the story together quite easily from the clues. Evidently there has been a divorce or separation. Evidently there were financial problems, which are so often associated with divorce, and the man has been evicted. Judging from the fact that he is doing so much drinking, alcoholism is either the cause or the effect of his other problems. The man has given up all hope and now sees hope only in other

people, represented by this young couple just starting out in life and trying to collect a few pieces of furniture for their rented apartment.

Divorce, infidelity, domestic strife, financial worry, bankruptcy, alcoholism, rootlessness, consumerism as a substitute for intimacy, and disillusionment with the American Dream are common themes throughout Carver's stories. The symbol of a man sitting outside on his front lawn drinking whiskey, with all of his worldly possessions placed around him but soon to be scattered to the four winds, is a striking symbol of modern human beings. It is easy to acquire possessions but nearly impossible to keep a real home.

Carver did not actually witness such an event but had a similar episode described to him by a friend and eventually used it in this story. A glance at the titles of some of Carver's stories shows his penchant for finding in his mundane environment external symbols of subjective states: "Fat," "Gazebo," "Vitamins," "Feathers," "Cathedral," "Boxes," "Menudo." The same tendency is even more striking in the titles of his poems, for example, "The Car," "Jean's TV," "NyQuil," "My Dad's Wallet," "The Phone Booth," "Heels."

In his famous essay "The Philosophy of Composition," Edgar Allan Poe wrote that he wanted an image that would be "emblematical of Mournful and Never-ending Remembrance," so he created his famous raven perched on the bust of Pallas Athena and croaking the refrain "nevermore." To highlight the difference in Carver's method, Carver might have seen a real raven perched on a real statue, and it would have suggested mournful and never-ending remembrance. This kind of "reverse symbolism" seems characteristic of modern American minimalists in general, and Carver's influence on their movement is paramount.

Poe states that he originally thought of using a parrot in his famous poem but rejected that notion because it did not seem sufficiently poetic and might have produced a comical effect; if Carver had been faced with such a choice, he probably would have chosen the parrot. What distinguishes Carver from most minimalists is a sense of humor that is impervious to catastrophe: Like the man on the front lawn, Carver had been so far down that everyplace else looked better. He would have concurred heartily with William Shakespeare's often-quoted lines in *As You Like It* (1599-1600):

> Sweet are the uses of adversity,
> Which, like a toad, ugly and venomous,
> Wears yet a precious jewel in his head

On a different level, "Why Don't You Dance?" reflects Carver's maturation as a person and an author. The responsibilities of parenthood as well as the experience of teaching young students were bringing home to him the fact that his personal problems could hold instructional utility for others. As a teacher of creative writing, placed more and more in the limelight, interacting with writers, editors, professors, and interviewers, he was being forced to formulate his own artistic credo. The older man in the story sees himself in his young yard-sale customers and wants to help them along in life; this is evidently a reflection of the author's own attitude. Consequently, the story itself is not merely an autobiographical protest or lament like some of Carver's earlier works but is designed to deliver a message—perhaps a warning—for the profit of others. The melancholy wisdom of Carver's protagonist reflects Carver's own mellowing as he began to appreciate the universally tragic nature of human existence.

"WHERE I'M CALLING FROM"

"Where I'm Calling From" is a great American short story. It originally appeared in the prestigious *The New Yorker*, was reprinted in the collection titled *Cathedral*, and appears once again as the title story in the best and most comprehensive collection of Carver's stories, *Where I'm Calling From*. The story is narrated by an alcoholic staying at a "drying-out facility," an unpretentious boardinghouse where plain meals are served family style and there is nothing to do but read, watch television, or talk. The bucolic atmosphere is strongly reminiscent of the training-camp scenes in one of Hemingway's most brilliant short stories, "Fifty Grand."

The narrator in Carver's story tells about his drinking problems and interweaves his own biography with that of a friend he has made at the drying-out facility, a man he refers to as J. P. The only thing unusual about their stories is that J. P. is a chimney sweep and is married to a chimney sweep. Both J. P. and the narrator ruined their marriages through their compulsive drinking and are now terrified that they will be unable to control their craving once they get out of the facility. They have made vows of abstinence often enough before and have not kept them. They have dried out before and gone right back to the bottle.

Carver manages to convey all the feelings of guilt, remorse, terror, and helplessness experienced by people who are in the ultimate stages of alcoholism. It is noteworthy that, whereas his alcoholic protagonists of earlier stories were often isolated individuals, the protagonist-narrator of "Where I'm Calling From" not only is actively seeking help but also is surrounded by others with the same problem. This feature indicates that Carver had come to realize that the way to give his stories the point or meaning that they had previously often lacked was to suggest the existence of large-scale social problems of which his characters are victims. He had made what author Joan Didion called "the quantum leap" of realizing that his personal problems were actually social problems. The curse of alcoholism affects all social classes; even people who never touch a drop can have their lives ruined by it.

"THE BRIDLE"

"The Bridle" first appeared in *The New Yorker* and was reprinted in *Cathedral*. It is an example of Carver's mature period, a highly artistic story fraught with social significance. The story is told from the point of view of one of Carver's *faux-naïf* narrators. Readers immediately feel that they know this good-natured soul, a woman named Marge who manages an apartment building in Arizona and "does hair" as a sideline. She tells about one of the many families who stayed a short while and then moved on as tumbleweeds being blown across the desert. Although Carver typically writes about Northern California and the Pacific Northwest, this part of Arizona is also "Carver Country," a world of freeways, fast-food restaurants, Laundromats, mindless television entertainment, and transient living accommodations, a homogenized world of strangers with minimum-wage jobs and tabloid mentalities.

Mr. Holits pays the rent in cash every month, suggesting that he recently went bankrupt and has neither a bank account nor credit cards. Carver, like minimalists in general, loves such subtle clues. Mrs. Holits confides to Marge that they had owned a farm in Minnesota. Her husband, who "knows everything there is about horses," still keeps one of his bridles, evidently symbolizing his hope that he may escape from "Carver Country." Mrs. Holits proves more adaptable: She gets a job as a waitress, a favorite occupation among Carver characters. Her husband, however, cannot adjust to the service industry jobs, which are all that are available to a man his age with his limited experience. He handles the money, the two boys are his sons by a former marriage, and he has been accustomed to making the decisions, yet he finds that his wife is taking over the family leadership in this brave new postindustrial world.

Like many other Carver males, Holits becomes a heavy drinker. He eventually injures himself while trying to show off his strength at the swimming pool. One day the Holitses with their young sons, pack and drive off down the long, straight highway without a word of explanation. When Marge trudges upstairs to clean the empty apartment, she finds that Holits has left his bridle behind.

The naïve narrator does not understand the significance of the bridle, but the reader feels its poignancy as a symbol. The bridle is one of those useless objects that everyone carts around and is reluctant to part with because it represents a memory, a hope, or a dream. It is an especially appropriate symbol because it is so utterly out of place in one of those two-story, frame-stucco, look-alike apartment buildings that disfigure the landscape and are the dominant features of "Carver Country." Gigantic economic forces beyond the comprehension of the narrator have driven this farm family from their home and turned them into the modern equivalent of the Joad family in John Steinbeck's classic novel *The Grapes of Wrath* (1939).

There is, however, a big difference between Carver and Steinbeck. Steinbeck believed in and prescribed the panacea of socialism; Carver has no prescriptions to offer. He seems to have no faith either in politicians or in preachers. His characters are more likely to go to church to play bingo than to say prayers or sing hymns. Like many of the contemporary minimalists, he seems to have gone beyond alienation, beyond existentialism, beyond despair. God is dead; so what else is new?

Carver's working-class characters are far more complicated than Steinbeck's Joad family. Americans have become more sophisticated in the past fifty years as a result of the influence of radio, motion pictures, television, the Internet, more abundant educational opportunities, improved automobiles and highways, cheap air transportation, alcohol and drugs, more leisure time, and the fact that their work is less enervating because of the proliferation of labor-saving machinery. Many Americans have also lost their religious faith, their work ethic, their class consciousness, their family loyalty, their integrity, and their dreams. Steinbeck saw it happening and showed how the Joad family was splitting apart after being uprooted from the soil; Carver's people are the Joad family a half-century down the road. Oddly enough, Carver's mature stories do not seem nihilistic or despairing because they contain the redeeming qualities of humor, compassion, and honesty.

"BOXES"

Where I'm Calling From is the most useful volume of Carver's short stories because it contains some of the best stories that had been printed in earlier books plus a generous selection of his later and best efforts. One of the new stories reprinted in *Where I'm Calling From* is "Boxes," which first appeared in *The New Yorker*. When Carver's stories began to be regularly accepted by *The New Yorker*, it was an indication that he had found the style of self-expression that he had been searching for since the beginning of his career. It was also a sign that his themes were evoking sympathetic chords in the hearts and minds of *The New Yorker*'s middle and upper-class readership, the people at whom that magazine's sophisticated advertisements for diamonds, furs, highrise condominiums, and luxury vacation cruises are aimed.

"Boxes" is written in Carver's characteristic tragicomic tone. It is a story in which the *faux-naïf* narrator, a favorite with Carver, complains about the eccentric behavior of his widowed mother who, for one specious reason or another, is always changing her place of residence. She moves so frequently that she usually seems to have the bulk of her worldly possessions packed in boxes scattered about on the floor. One of her complaints is the attitude of her landlord, whom she calls "King Larry." Larry Hadlock is a widower and a relatively affluent property owner. It is evident through Carver's unerring dialogue that what she is really bitter about is Larry's indifference to her own fading charms. In the end, she returns to California but telephones to complain about the traffic, the faulty air-conditioning unit in her apartment, and the indifference of management. Her son vaguely understands that what his mother really wants, though she may not realize it herself, is love and a real home and that she can never have these things again in her lifetime no matter where she moves.

What makes the story significant is its universality: It reflects the macrocosm in a microcosm. In "Boxes," the problem touched on is not only the rootlessness and anonymity of modern life but also the plight of millions of aging people, who are considered by some to be useless in their old age and a burden to their children. It was typical of Raymond Carver to find a metaphor for this important social phenomenon in a bunch of cardboard boxes.

Carver uses working-class people as his models, but he is not writing solely about the working class. It is simply the fact that all Americans can see themselves in his little, inarticulate, bewildered characters that makes Carver an important writer in the dominant tradition of American realism, a worthy successor to Mark Twain, Stephen Crane, Sherwood Anderson, Theodore Dreiser, Willa Cather, John Steinbeck, and William Faulkner, all of whom wrote about humble people. Someday it may be generally appreciated that, despite the odds against him and despite the antipathy of certain mandarins, Raymond Carver managed to become the most important American fiction writer in the second half of the twentieth century.

OTHER MAJOR WORKS

SCREENPLAY: *Dostoevsky*, 1985.

POETRY: *Near Klamath*, 1968; *Winter Insomnia*, 1970; *At Night the Salmon Move*, 1976; *Two Poems*, 1982; *Fires: Essays, Poems, Stories*, 1983; *If It Please You*, 1984; *This Water*, 1985; *Where Water Comes Together with Other Water*, 1985; *Ultramarine*, 1986; *A New Path to the Waterfall*, 1989.

ANTHOLOGY: *American Short Story Pieces*, 1987 (with Tom Jenks).

BIBLIOGRAPHY

Adelman, Bob, and Tess Gallagher. *Carver Country: The World of Raymond Carver*. Introduction by Tess Gallagher. New York: Charles Scribner's Sons, 1990. Produced in the spirit of a photographic essay, this book contains excellent photographs of Carver, his relatives, people who served as inspirations for characters in his stories, and places that were important in his life and work. The photographs are accompanied by excerpts from Carver's stories and poems.

Barth, John. "A Few Words About Minimalism." *The New York Times Book Review*, December 28, 1986, 2. A prominent American writer who is considered a leading exponent of the maximalist style of fiction writing defines minimalism in art and concludes that there is a place for both maximalism and minimalism in literature. He regards Carver as the prime shaper of "the new American Short Story."

Bugeja, Michael. "Tarnish and Silver: An Analysis of Carver's Cathedral." *South Dakota Review* 24, no. 3 (1986): 73-87. Discusses the revision of an early Carver story, "The Bath," which was reprinted in *Cathedral* as "A Small Good Thing." The changes made throughout the story, and especially the somewhat more positive resolution, reflect Carver's evolution as a writer.

Campbell, Ewing. *Raymond Carver: A Study of the Short Fiction*. New York: Twayne, 1992. An introduction to Carver's stories that focuses on such issues as myth and archetype, otherness, and the grotesque. Discusses the difference between "early" and "late" versions of the same story, such as "So Much Water Close to Home" and "The Bath" and "A Small Good Thing." Includes Carver's own comments on his writing as well as articles by other critics who challenge the label of minimalist for Carver.

Carver, Raymond. "A Storyteller's Shoptalk." *The New York Times Book Review*, February 15, 1981, 9. In this interesting article, Carver describes his artistic credo, evaluates the work of some of his contemporaries, and offers excellent advice to aspiring young writers. The article reveals his perfectionism and dedication to his craft.

Gentry, Marshall Bruce, and William L. Stull, eds. *Conversations with Raymond Carver.* Jackson: University Press of Mississippi, 1990. A wide-ranging collection of interviews covering Carver's career from the early 1980's until just before his death.

Halpert, Sam, ed. *When We Talk About Raymond Carver.* Layton, Utah: Gibbs Smith, 1991. A collection of transcripts of interviews with ten writers who knew Carver on a personal basis, including a fascinating interview with Carver's first wife, Maryann, who provides a fresh perspective on the incidents on which many of Carver's stories were based.

Kesset, Kirk. *The Stories of Raymond Carver.* Athens: Ohio University Press, 1995. An intelligent discussion of Carver's stories, focusing on Carver's development of his own moral center.

Mullen, Bill. "A Subtle Spectacle: Televisual Culture in the Short Stories of Raymond Carver." *Critique* 39 (Winter, 1998): 99-114. Discusses the relationship between television—both as an influence on and a subject of—Carver's fiction. Argues that in both structure and tone, Carver's stories constitute a critique of television culture based on the medium's ability to eliminate class consciousness; discusses "Will You Please Be Quiet, Please?"

Powell, Jon. "The Stories of Raymond Carver: The Menace of Perpetual Uncertainty." *Studies in Short Fiction* 31 (Fall, 1994): 647-656. Discusses the sense of menace Carver creates by leaving out or only providing clues to central aspects of his stories. Argues that this technique forces both the characters and the readers to try to understand the clues.

Runyon, Randolph Paul. *Reading Raymond Carver.* Syracuse, N.Y.: Syracuse University Press, 1992. Analyzes Carver's stories as "intratextual" and argues that they should be read in relationship to each other. Claims that in *Will You Please Be Quiet, Please?* and *Cathedral* each story is linked to the immediately preceding story and the one after it.

Saltzman, Arthur M. *Understanding Raymond Carver.* Columbia: University of South Carolina Press, 1988. A short overview of Carver's life and work with the emphasis on Carver's short stories and one chapter devoted to his poetry. Contains a valuable bibliography of works by and about Carver.

Scofield, Martin. "Story and History in Raymond Carver." *Critique* 40 (Spring, 1999): 266-280. Shows how three late Carver stories—"Intimacy," "Blackbird Pie," and "Elephant"—embody a new experimental technique for integrating fiction and autobiographical or historical events.

Stull, William L. "Raymond Carver." In *Dictionary of Literary Biography*, edited by Jean W. Ross. Detroit: Gale Research, 1985. This article covers Carver's life and work up until shortly before his death and attempts to analyze his poetry and fiction techniques. It contains a fairly comprehensive list of Carver's books and miscellaneous publications as well as a list of articles about Carver.

Wolff, Tobias. "Raymond Carver Had His Cake and Ate It Too." *Esquire* 112 (September, 1989): 240-248. A friend and fellow author and teacher relates a series of anecdotes about Carver in his wild drinking days. The essay highlights Carver's zest for life, his kindly interest in people, and his unconcealed delight with the recognition that he received toward the end of his life.

Bill Delaney

R. V. CASSILL

Born: Cedar Falls, Iowa; May, 17, 1919

PRINCIPAL SHORT FICTION

15 × 3, 1957 (with Herbert Gold and James B. Hall)
The Father and Other Stories, 1965
The Happy Marriage and Other Stories, 1966
Collected Stories, 1989
The Unknown Soldier, 1991
Late Stories, 1995

OTHER LITERARY FORMS

Although R. V. Cassill has won high praise for his short stories, he has also written more than twenty novels, the first of which, *The Eagle on the Coin*, was published in 1950. He has also written nonfiction, including *Writing Fiction* (1962) and *In an Iron Time: Statements and Reiterations, Essays* (1969), many articles, and more than one hundred book reviews for periodicals. As editor, he has worked on *The Norton Anthology of Short Fiction* (1977) and *The Norton Anthology of Contemporary Fiction* (1988). His most critically recognized novel is *Clem Anderson* (1961).

ACHIEVEMENTS

R. V. Cassill has been noted mainly for his short stories, the first of which, "The Conditions of Justice," won second place in the *Atlantic Monthly* "Firsts" contest for the short story in 1947. Despite the fact that he has written more than twenty novels, the only one that has received wide critical attention has been *Clem Anderson* (1961). It could perhaps be argued that the attention his short stories have been given has overshadowed such a collection of novels, but both genres demonstrate Cassill's diversity, range, and depth. His literary subjects explore the tensions between the individual and society, between the forces of moral conviction and practical expression, between power and sex. Cassill's own convictions have been expressed in not only his stories but also his career. The protagonist of Cassill's novel *Clem Anderson*, which portrays the struggles of an American poet (Clem), in some ways represents Cassill's own struggle to fit a literary voice of integrity and moral conviction into a world becoming increasingly institutionalized and anonymous. The novel, like the writer, gives the literary world much to savor, much to consider, though critics may disagree on the true value of what Cassill has to offer.

BIOGRAPHY

Before World War II, Ronald Verlin Cassill studied art, planning to become a professional painter, and won some regional art contests in Iowa in 1939 and 1940. He began to write fiction after serving as an army officer in the South Pacific during the war. The beginning of his professional writing career was marked by his winning second place in the *Atlantic Monthly* "Firsts" contest of 1947. Several of his stories have been included in *The Best American Short Stories* and in *Prize Stories: The O. Henry Awards*. He earned B.A. and M.A. degrees from the University of Iowa, studied at the Sorbonne, and received a Fulbright fellowship, Rockefeller grant, and John Simon Guggenheim Memorial Foundation grant. He has taught at Iowa, the New School for Social Research, Purdue, Columbia, Harvard, and Brown.

Although he wrote less in his later years, his long career as writer, editor, and professor of literature and fiction writing has assured his voice an echoing resonance across the landscape of twentieth century literature since World War II. He settled in Providence, Rhode Island, where he remained professor emeritus at Brown University.

ANALYSIS

Writers whom R. V. Cassill especially admires are Gustave Flaubert, Henry James, D. H. Lawrence, and James Joyce. Their influence is not verifiable from the features of a given story so much as it is a cumulative force in Cassill's writing. His work often manifests the rich hues and texture of Flaubert's visual imagery, the complex internal conflicts of characters presented by Flaubert and James, the agonies of initiation from Joyce, and the energy and obsession of the characters of Lawrence. Considering his background in art, it is natural for Cassill to share the painterly qualities which all of these men, except the nearly blind Joyce, exhibited throughout their works. Cassill does not neglect color, shape, composition, and fine detail.

His stories, usually set in the Midwest, present rather common situations of youthful initiation, frustrated dreams, family conflict, and harbored delusion. The stories might be considered in terms of two broad types: those that examine the effects of youthful passions and those that reveal the destructiveness of self-delusion in adults. The most lyrical language and imagery in Cassill's short fiction appears in the stories of youthful initiation. Good examples of this type are "The Biggest Band" and "In the Central Blue," both of which present boyhood passions which are so strong that achieving them becomes the focal point of a boy's life. Given such a frame of mind, whatever happens to the boys in these stories is bound to be disappointing; either they fail to get what they want, or they succeed and find that the thing desired is not so valuable after all. Perhaps Cassill's most complex dramatic problems appear in the stories about adults such as "The Crime of Mary Lynn Yager" and "The Sunday Painter." In both of these pieces the protagonists are unable to face inadequacies within themselves.

"THE BIGGEST BAND"

In most of the stories of the first type, locale is crucial, as is the case with "The Biggest Band." This story, Cassill's own favorite, grows out of the small-town environment and financial straits of Davisburg, Iowa, during the Depression. The reflective first-person narrator (called Buddy in childhood) speaks as an adult about his experiences with the Corn State Southern Band, and what he knows now strikes a telling contrast to what he felt as a boy.

The plan to assemble a state-wide band to travel to Chicago and play at the 1933 World's Fair is promoted by Lothar Smith, whose nominal resemblance to Lothario (deceiver and seducer) carries over into his character. He resembles Meredith Wilson's "Music Man"; however, his ambition and musical ability far exceed those of "Professor" Harold Hill. A more important difference is that, despite all the appearances of a massive confidence game, the trip does take place, the band does play at the world's fair, and Smith goes broke realizing his dream. Finally, he appears to have been more a grand dreamer than a self-server. In this regard he and Buddy are alike.

The vital factor in the success of Smith's plan is the imagination of the people, and it is a historical commonplace that hard times produce ardent dreamers. Part of the plan is to sell instruments to people who want to make the trip but do not have an instrument and, therefore, usually cannot play one. Buddy's parents buy him a trombone that he must learn to play; he is later required to sell two "excursion tickets" in order to make the trip, and every appearance of a swindle is present. Buddy becomes so obsessed that he even suggests that his father should borrow money to buy the tickets. Buddy fails to sell the tickets, and his mother, who has known Smith since childhood, forces him to honor his initial promise. Buddy goes, the band plays at odd times and poorly, and the whole affair is a predictable failure. He does not discover what he expected, just as he fails to see the evasively nude Sally Rand; nevertheless, he learns more than he will admit, even in retrospect.

Buddy's selfish obsession with going to Chicago, like Smith's big plans, is presented negatively at first because both of them expect others to sacrifice for their personal fulfillment. In the end, however, Smith has given far more than he has taken, and Buddy feels "oddly free to do [his] best now that it didn't seem to count for anything." He narrates the story from adulthood and speaks laughingly of the band as "an altogether preposterous blunder committed against nature and a fine art," but he also admits the clean beauty of a performance given at dawn before a stadium which contained only a few janitors. He describes how he would have told the story to Mrs. Packer, who shared his dream, if she had been alive when he returned, and the story ends with a burst of images embodying youthful zeal and true art:

> From their staffs over the national pavilions the ultramarine and lemon and scarlet pennants streamed out like dyes leaking out into an oceanic current. It was

only the empty sky that watched us—but my God, my God, how the drums thundered, how we blew.

"In the Central Blue" also deals with youthful obsession, this time the more common one of sex. The location is changed to Chesterfield, Nebraska, but the place is essentially similar. Also, as in "The Biggest Band," the proportions of the boy's desire exceed any gratification he might achieve. The first-person narrator says of the girl desired, "I loved her ignorantly, impurely and intermittently." Yet his desire is far more than a physical one:

> But it was not a physical assault on her that I planned or needed. I was going to ravish her mind. With the aid of this powerful movie plus a few tickles and kisses and afterward, I was going to wheedle her mind right away into the realm of wish and nonsense, where I was so lonely all by myself.

What he really wants is escape from the fearful self-doubt and loneliness of adolescence, but, like the World War I aviator-heroes of the movies and like all mortals, he finds himself condemned to "soaring in the central blue."

In the process of the story he discovers his identity as an uneasy inhabitant of the middle space between heaven and hell. More important than dealing with his frustrated desire to take "Hudson's blonde and titless cousin Betty" home and share kisses, tickles, and isolation is the discovery he makes about himself. Through the whim of his older brother, he is not allowed to go along in the car to take Betty home and fulfill his hopes. When he realizes what is being done to him, he puts up a fight to stay in the car and his father comes outside. His father, walking into the house with him, tells him he is too old to cry. In his frustration and his desire to be punished for his stupidity, he shouts back, "Well, I'm crying, you bastard." With obvious effort his father controls the urge to strike him, causing a discovery: "Maybe for the first time, I saw him in his human dimension, bewildered and tugged in contrary directions like me." Even his father lives in the central blue of divided feelings. As in "The Biggest Band," the boy has not achieved what he was looking for, but he has found something more important in its place.

"THE SUNDAY PAINTER"

Representative of the other broad type of Cassill's stories is "The Sunday Painter," in which detail and delusion are interwoven to create a vivid, amusing, and ironic story. In this third-person narrative limited to the viewpoint of Joe Becker, businessman and unfulfilled amateur artist, there is a theme that works on at least two levels. First, Becker is self-deluded regarding his skill as a painter, thinking that "What had been so painful twenty years ago had mellowed and changed without being totally lost." Second, after months of painting works which are rendered with fine visual detail, Becker convinces himself that he has "explored art clean down to its sterile origin." Implicitly Cassill states that the sterility is not in art but in Becker himself. Quite like some artists in many forms of expression, Becker has transferred his own failing to art in general. In a comic and powerful final scene, he goes berserk and starts painting all over objects in his house and ends up painting the babysitter from next door. She, who mocked his serious earlier efforts for lacking the bizarre, quickly comes to his defense as the neighbors pull him off her: "I don't think you should persecute him. . . . Artists have enough troubles as it is." Her misunderstanding of art mirrors his. The story can also be viewed as a satire of those writers and artists who complain that traditional approaches to art have become "sterile" and meaningless. Interpreted along these lines, the story argues that the fault lies not with art but with the complaining artists themselves. In the reference work *Contemporary Novelists of the English Language* (1972), Cassill comments, "As I grow older I love the commonplace of traditional thought and expression with growing fervor."

"THE CRIME OF MARY LYNN YAGER"

"The Crime of Mary Lynn Yager" presents the problem of self-deception in more serious terms. Clarissa Carlson, who plans to marry Joe Meadow and leave Iowa with him once he finishes his degree and begins his promising business career, has the course of her life altered when one of her second-grade children drowns. Mary Lynn Yager, the girl Clarissa always disliked, drowns on a school outing at the lake. When Clarissa finds that the drowned child is Mary Lynn and not one of her "good ones," she feels a relief that leads to guilt later. The guilt which engulfs Clarissa in the story emanates from her refusal to face the unfairness of her attitude toward Mary Lynn. The third-person point of view is slanted through Clarissa's perception in order to heighten the effect of her turmoil. Even though Clarissa has convinced herself that the child was a "wrong little girl," it becomes clear that there was very little basis for this attitude. The teacher blames Mary Lynn's contrary nature for causing the accident because she cannot admit her own prejudice and thereby remove her submerged guilt. She is doomed to struggle subconsciously with both her guilt over the child's drowning and her guilt over having misjudged her. An underlying question is implanted in the story as to whether people's lives can be fated by the attitudes of others.

The unconfronted guilt makes Clarissa quarrelsome, driving off Joe, and one problem leads to another. She marries LeRoy Peterson, who blames her for his business troubles just as she had unjustly blamed Mary Lynn. With her confidence destroyed by LeRoy's accusations, she wonders "what was to blame for the decay of her life" and begins to agree with him "that it was she who had brought it on them." Their marriage degenerates to "protracted hostility" and ends when LeRoy deserts her.

After years of absence she returns to Iowa where she discovers that one of her "good children," Bobbie Tenman, is in trouble with the law. In fact, it becomes clear that he was better than Mary Lynn only in Clarissa's mind. She is relieved that he receives a suspended sentence for vandalism, feeling, "In the maimed frustration of her loneliness any evasion of just punishment [is] a sign of hope." As Mary Lynn was misunderstood, so is Clarissa when she kisses Bobbie in an attempt to keep him innocent and unblemished in her mind. Bobbie's wife, who also happens to be one of Mary Lynn's sisters, discovers Clarissa and shoves her to the ground. The girl has no idea who Clarissa is but assumes the worst of her. In Clarissa's eyes, "Mary Lynn's play with her teacher's life had been foul play," when the foul play actually has been in Clarissa's self-deception. At the end of the story she is still haunted by a picture of Mary Lynn which she has long since destroyed, and she envies the child her peace in death.

In his conscientious presentation of characters caught up in their passions and delusions, Cassill has given much to the short story. He develops irony by setting his characters in a common milieu, then twisting them slightly on their axis to reveal their agony and their worth.

OTHER MAJOR WORKS

LONG FICTION: *The Eagle on the Coin*, 1950; *Clem Anderson*, 1961; *Pretty Leslie*, 1963; *The President*, 1964; *La Vie Passionnée of Rodney Buckthorne*, 1968; *Dr. Cobb's Game*, 1970; *The Goss Women*, 1974; *Hoyt's Child*, 1976; *Flame*, 1980; *Labors of Love*, 1980; *Patrimonies*, 1988.

NONFICTION: *Writing Fiction*, 1962; *In an Iron Time: Statements and Reiterations, Essays*, 1967.

EDITED TEXTS: *The Norton Anthology of Short Fiction*, 1977; *The Anthology of Contemporary Fiction*, 1988.

BIBLIOGRAPHY

The Antioch Review 30, nos. 3-4 (1970). "Second thoughts" persuaded the editors to mention Cassill's novel *Dr. Cobb's Game*, which they admit they find "outrageous but nonetheless unforgettable." They conclude: "A repugnant reading experience—so be it. Evil is evil and must be nothing less than frightening."

Cassill, Kay, Orin E. Cassill, and Kurt Johnson, eds. *R. V. Cassill*. Chicago, 1981. A collection of articles, reminiscences, commentaries, and analyses of Cassill's work by friends, admirers, and members of his family.

Grumbach, Doris. "Fine Print: *The Goss Women*." *The New Republic* 170 (June 29, 1974): 33. Grumbach looks at this Cassill novel in the light of feminine sexuality, claiming that Cassill's female characters are "extrasexual perceptive." Although she finds the author's technical skills quite developed, she says the novel ultimately results in "ennui."

Roberts, David. "The Short Fiction of R. V. Cassill." *Critique: Studies in Modern Fiction*, no. 1 (1966):

56-70. Roberts searches out "a continuous vision" in Cassill's short fiction. He studies Cassill's short stories, analyzing some of them individually, finds "excellence" in the body of short fiction as a whole, and concludes Cassill is "eminently deserving of further critical attention."

Yates, Richard. "R. V. Cassill's *Clem Anderson.*" *Ploughshares* 14, nos. 2-3 (1988): 189-196. A

critical study of Cassill's most widely acclaimed novel. Analyzes the main character, Clem, as representative of Cassill's own struggle as writer and poet to find meaning in the academic world, and links that struggle to the author/narrator's search for new forms of expression.

James Curry Robison,
updated by David J. Thieneman

WILLA CATHER

Born: Back Creek Valley, near Gore, Virginia; December 7, 1873
Died: New York, New York; April 24, 1947

PRINCIPAL SHORT FICTION
The Troll Garden, 1905
Youth and the Bright Medusa, 1920
Obscure Destinies, 1932
The Old Beauty and Others, 1948
Willa Cather's Collected Short Fiction: 1892-1912, 1965
Uncle Valentine and Other Stories: Willa Cather's Collected Short Fiction, 1915-1929, 1973

OTHER LITERARY FORMS

Willa Cather is best known as a novelist, but she wrote prolifically in other forms, especially as a young woman; she had been publishing short stories for more than twenty years before she published her first novel. Although her fame rests largely on her twelve novels and a few short stories, she has a collection of poetry, several collections of essays, and hundreds of newspaper columns and magazine pieces to her credit. Only one of her books, *A Lost Lady* (1923), was filmed in Hollywood; after that one experience, Cather would not allow any of her work to be filmed again.

ACHIEVEMENTS

Willa Cather was one of America's first modern writers to make the prairie immigrant experience an

important and continuing subject for high-quality fiction. Although her setting is often the American western frontier, she masterfully locates the universal through the specific, and her literary reputation transcends the limitations of regional or gender affiliation. In her exploration of the human spirit, Cather characteristically defends artistic values in an increasingly materialistic world, and she is known for her graceful rendering of place and character.

Praised in the 1920's as one of the most successful novelists of her time, Cather was sometimes criticized in the next decade for neglecting contemporary social issues. Later, however, and especially since her death, she was recognized as a great artist and one of the most important American writers of the twentieth century. In 1923, she was awarded the Pulitzer Prize for the novel *One of Ours* (1922). She also received the Howells Medal for fiction from the Academy of the National Institute of Arts and Letters in 1930, the Prix Fémina Américain for *Shadows on the Rock* (1931) in 1933, and the gold medal from the National Institute of Arts and Letters in 1944. With time, interest in Cather's fiction continued to increase, rather than diminish, and she enjoys appreciative audiences abroad as well as in her own country.

BIOGRAPHY

Willa Sibert Cather moved with her family from Virginia to Nebraska when she was only nine years old, a move that was to influence her mind and art throughout her life. As a student at the University of

Willa Cather (Library of Congress)

Nebraska, she wrote for various college magazines; she also became a regular contributor to the *Nebraska State Journal*, publishing book, theater, and concert reviews, as well as commentary on the passing scene. Even after she moved to Pittsburgh to take an editorial job, she continued to send columns home to the *Nebraska State Journal*. Later she also began contributing to the Lincoln *Courier*. She taught English in Pittsburgh (an experience that became the source for one of her most famous short stories, "Paul's Case") and then moved to New York to take a position with *McClure's Magazine*. After the publication of her first novel, *Alexander's Bridge*, in 1912, she left *McClure's Magazine* to devote full time to her creative work.

ANALYSIS

Willa Cather was always conscious of a double urge in herself, toward art and toward the land. As long as her parents were living, she found herself torn between the Western prairie and the cultural centers of the East and Europe. That basic polarity appears again and again in her stories, some of which deal with the artist's struggle against debilitating influences, and some with both the pleasant and the difficult aspects of the prairie experience. Perhaps only in her work did Cather achieve a comfortable reconciliation of these polarities, by making the prairie experience the subject of her art.

All of Cather's work is consistently value-centered. She believed in characters who are good, artists who are true to their callings, people who can appreciate and use what is valuable from the past, and individuals who have a special relationship with the land. Her chief agony lay in what she saw as a general sell-out to materialism—in the realm of art, in the prairie and desert, in the small town, in the city.

The struggle of the artist to maintain integrity against an unsympathetic environment and the forces of an exploitative materialism is explored in three stories that are particularly important in the Cather canon. Two of them, "The Sculptor's Funeral" and "Paul's Case," have been widely anthologized and are well known. The third, "Uncle Valentine," is an important later story.

"THE SCULPTOR'S FUNERAL"

"The Sculptor's Funeral" is about the return in death of a world-renowned sculptor to the pinched little prairie town from which he somehow miraculously sprang. Harvey Merrick's body arrives by train in the dead of winter, accompanied by one of his former students. There to meet the coffin are several prominent townsmen, among them a brusque, red-bearded lawyer named Jim Laird. Only he can appreciate the magnitude of Harvey Merrick's achievement. The watchers around the body chuckle and snort over poor Harvey's uselessness as a farm hand, over his inability to "make it" in the only things that count for them—money-making ventures in Sand City. Jim Laird, in a storm of self-hatred for having become the scheming lawyer these harpies wanted him to be, enters the room and blasts them mercilessly. He reminds the town elders of the young men they have ruined by drumming "nothing but money and knavery into their ears from the time they wore knickerbockers." They hated Harvey, Laird says, because he left them and rose above them, achieving in a world they were not fit to enter. He reminds them that Harvey "wouldn't have given one sunset over your marshes" for all of their material properties and possessions. Laird is too drunk the next day to attend the funeral, and it is learned that he dies some years later from a cold he caught while "driving across the Colorado mountains to defend one of Phelps's sons who had got into trouble there by cutting government timber."

Harvey Merrick is not the tragic figure of the story, for he, thanks to a timid father who sensed something special about this one son, managed to escape destruction. He became the artist he was destined to be, in spite of his unlikely beginnings. The money-grubbing first citizens of Sand City can wag their tongues feebly over his corpse, but they cannot touch him or detract from his accomplishment. If there is a tragic element in the story, it is the life of Jim Laird. Like Harvey, he went away to school full of idealistic fire; like Harvey, he wanted to be a great man and make the hometown people proud of him. Instead, he says, "I came back here to practice, and I found you didn't in the least want me to be a great man. You wanted me to be a shrewd lawyer." He became that shrewd lawyer and lost his soul in the process. The dead artist, imposing and serene in his coffin, serves as a perfect foil for Jim Laird, and the story stands as one of Cather's most powerful treatments of the conflict between artistic ideals and materialistic value systems.

"PAUL'S CASE"

"Paul's Case" presents a somewhat different view of that conflict. Paul, a high school youngster, is not a practicing artist, but he has an artistic temperament. He loves to hang around art galleries and concert halls and theaters, talking with the performers and basking in their reflected glory. It is glitter, excitement, and escape from the dripping taps in his home on Pittsburgh's Cordelia Street that Paul craves. A hopeless "case," Paul is finally taken out of high school by his widowed father because his mind is never on his studies. Forced from his usher's job at the concert hall and forbidden to associate with the actors at the theater, he loses the only things he had lived for and cared about. When he is denied those vital outlets for his aesthetic needs and sent to do dull work for a dull company, he carries out a desperate plan. One evening, instead of depositing his firm's receipts in the bank, he catches a train for New York. With swift determination, he buys elegant clothes and installs himself in a luxurious hotel suite, there to live for a few brief days the life he had always felt himself suited for. Those days are lovely and perfect, but the inevitable reckoning draws near: He learns from a newspaper that his father is en route to New York to retrieve him. Very deliberately Paul plots his course, even buying carnations for his buttonhole. Traveling to the outskirts of town, he walks to an embankment above the Pennsylvania tracks. There he carefully buries the carnations in the snow, and when the appropriate moment comes, he leaps into the path of an oncoming train.

A sensitive youngster with limited opportunity, Paul is not an artist in the usual sense. His distinction is that he responds to art, almost any art, with an unusual fervor. To him, anything associated with the world of art is beautiful and inspiring, while anything associated with lower-middle-class America is ugly and common. He is wrong about both worlds. With eyes only for the artificial surface glitter that spangles the world of art, he never sees the realities of hard work and struggle that define the life of every artist. Clearly, Cordelia Street is not as bad as Paul imagines it to be; it is, in fact, a moderately nice neighborhood where working people live and rear their families. Cordelia Street, however, has inadvertently taught him that money is the answer to all desires, that it can buy all the trappings that grace the world of art. Cordelia Street's legendary heroes are the Kings of Wall Street.

In spite of his blindness, Paul captures the reader's sympathies because he feels trapped in an aesthetic wasteland to which he cannot and will not return; the reader realizes at the end that perhaps Paul's only escape lies in his final choice. The Waldorf, after all, provided temporary breathing space at best. His only real home is, as Cather tells us, in the "immense design of things."

"UNCLE VALENTINE"

Valentine Ramsay, the title character in "Uncle Valentine," is like Paul in many ways: He is sensitive, charming, flighty, unpredictable, temperamental, and intolerant of commonness. Unlike Paul, however, Valentine is a true artist, a gifted composer; it is not the artificial shell of art that he values, but the very heart of it. After several years abroad, he decides to return to Greenacre, his family home in the lush Pennsylvania countryside. He feels that perhaps at Greenacre he can shut out the world and find the peace he needs to write music.

He and the neighbors next door, with whom he shares a special affection, both artistic and social, have a magnificent year together, a "golden year." They roam the fields and woods, they share music, and they increase in aesthetic understanding. Casting a tragic shadow over this happy group, however, is the figure of Valentine's uncle, who haunts the premises like a grieving ghost. A child prodigy, he had left home to pursue his art, but for reasons never disclosed, he gave up his music and returned, burying himself in the ashes of his ruined life.

As a young man, Valentine had made a bad marriage to a rich woman whose materialistic coarseness became a constant affront to him; her very presence beside him in a concert hall was enough to shatter his nerves and obliterate the music he came to hear. Valentine has escaped from her, but she is destined to destroy his peace once again. He and his neighbors discover that she has purchased the large piece of property next to theirs, the property they had loved and tramped through for endless days. She intends to move in soon, bringing her fortune, her brash assertiveness, and Valentine's only son. She, along with the encroaching factory smoke down-river, spells the end of the blessed life the little group of art fanciers has known at Greenacre. Valentine is forced to flee again, and we learn that he is killed while crossing a street in France.

Cather's message is clear. The important things in life—art and the sharing of its pleasures, friendships, a feeling for land and place, a reverence for the past—are too often destroyed in the name of progress. When economic concerns are given top priority,

whether on the prairie or in Pennsylvania, the human spirit suffers. Happily, in a much-loved story called "Neighbor Rosicky," Cather affirms that material temptations can be successfully resisted. Valentine is defeated, but Rosicky and his values prevail.

"NEIGHBOR ROSICKY"

Anton Rosicky, recognizable as another rendering of Ántonia's husband in Cather's best-known novel *My Ántonia* (1918), has instinctively established a value system that puts life and the land above every narrow-minded material concern. For example, when his entire corn crop is destroyed in the searing heat one July day, he organizes a little picnic so that the family can enjoy the few things they have left. Instead of despairing with his neighbors, Rosicky plays with his children. It is no surprise that he and his wife Mary agree without discussion as to what things they can let go. They refuse to skim the cream off their milk and sell it for butter because Mary would "rather put some colour into my children's faces than put money into the bank." Doctor Ed, who detects serious heart trouble in Rosicky, observes that "people as generous and warm-hearted and affectionate as the Rosickys never got ahead much; maybe you couldn't enjoy your life and put it into the bank, too."

"Neighbor Rosicky" is one of Cather's finest tributes to life on the Nebraska prairie, to a value system that grows out of human caring and love for the land. Rosicky had lived in cities for many years, had known hard times and good times there, but it occurred to him one lonely day in the city that he had to get to the land. He realized that "the trouble with big cities" was that "they built you in from the earth itself, cemented you away from any contact with the ground," so he made his decision and went West.

The only thing that disturbs his sleep now is the discontentment of his oldest son. Rudolph is married to a town girl, Polly, and he wants to leave the farm and seek work in the city. Rosicky understands Rudolph's restlessness and Polly's lonesomeness and looks for every opportunity to help the young couple find some recreation time in town. In spite of his efforts, however, Polly continues to dislike farm life and to find the Rosickys strange and "foreign." Then one day Rosicky suffers a heart attack near Rudolph's place. No one is there to care for him but Polly, and that day something lovely happens between the two of them: She has a revelation of his goodness that is "like an awakening to her." His warm brown hand somehow brings "her to herself," teaches her more about life than she has ever known before, offers her "some direct and untranslatable message." With this revelation comes the assurance that at last all will be well with Rudolph and Polly. They will remain on the land and Rosicky's spirit will abide with them, for Polly has caught the old man's vision. It is fitting that Rosicky's death a few months later is calmly accepted as a natural thing, and that he is buried in the earth he loved. That way there will be no strangeness, no jarring separation.

Rosicky is Cather's embodiment of all that is finest in the human character. He had been a city man, a lover of opera and the other cultural advantages of city life, but he found his peace in the simple life of a Nebraska farm. By contrast, Harvey Merrick, the sculptor, had been a country boy, a lover of the prairie landscape, but he found his peace in the art capitals of the world. Nevertheless, Merrick and Rosicky would have understood each other perfectly. One's talent lay in molding clay, the other's in molding lives.

Cather is sometimes accused of nostalgia, of denying the present and yearning for the past. What seems clear in her work, however, is not that she wants to live in the past, but that she deplores a total rejection of the values of the past. She fears a materialistic takeover of the human heart, or a shriveled view of human life. She is convinced that the desire for money and the things money can buy corrupts character, cheapens life, destroys the landscape, and enervates art. In her exploration of the conflicts engendered by a destructive materialism, in her celebration of art and the land, Willa Cather's devotion to an enduring system that spans time and space to embrace the good, the beautiful, and the true is made evident.

OTHER MAJOR WORKS

LONG FICTION: *Alexander's Bridge*, 1912; *O Pioneers!*, 1913; *The Song of the Lark*, 1915; *My Ántonia*, 1918; *One of Ours*, 1922; *A Lost Lady*,

1923; *The Professor's House*, 1925; *My Mortal Enemy*, 1926; *Death Comes for the Archbishop*, 1927; *Shadows on the Rock*, 1931; *Lucy Gayheart*, 1935; *Sapphira and the Slave Girl*, 1940.

POETRY: *April Twilights*, 1903.

NONFICTION: *Not Under Forty*, 1936; *Willa Cather on Writing*, 1949; *Willa Cather in Europe*, 1956; *The Kingdom of Art: Willa Cather's First Principles and Critical Statements, 1893-1896*, 1966; *The World and the Parish: Willa Cather's Articles and Reviews, 1893-1902*, 1970 (2 volumes).

MISCELLANEOUS: *Writings from Willa Cather's Campus Years*, 1950.

BIBLIOGRAPHY

Arnold, Marilyn. *Willa Cather's Short Fiction*. Athens: Ohio University Press, 1984. In this indexed volume, Arnold discusses all Cather's known short fiction chronologically. The detailed investigations will be helpful both for readers new to Cather's stories and those who are more familiar with them. Discussions of stories which have received little critical attention are especially useful. Includes a selected bibliography.

Gerber, Philip L. *Willa Cather*. Rev. ed. New York: Twayne, 1995. In this revised edition, Gerber focuses more on Cather's short fiction than in the first edition, as well as on the resurgence of criticism of her work. Discusses the major themes of the experience of the artist and life in rural Nebraska in major Cather short stories.

Harris, Jeane. "Aspects of Athene in Willa Cather's Short Fiction." *Studies in Short Fiction* 28 (Spring, 1991): 177-182. Discusses Cather's conflict between her gender and her inherited male aesthetic principles and how this is reflected in some of her early short stories by "manly" female characters modeled after the Greek goddess Athene. Maintains that Cather's androgynous females represent her dissatisfaction with traditional notions of femininity and masculinity.

Meyering, Sheryl L. *A Reader's Guide to the Short Stories of Willa Cather*. New York: G. K. Hall, 1994. Discusses individual Cather stories, focusing on publishing history, circumstances of composition, sources, influence, relationship to other Cather works, and interpretations and criticism. Deals with her debt to Henry James, the influence of her sexual orientation on her fiction, and the influence of Sarah Orne Jewett.

Murphy, John J., ed. *Critical Essays on Willa Cather*. Boston: G. K. Hall, 1984. Among the thirty-five essays in this substantial collection are reprinted reviews and articles by Eudora Welty, Katherine Anne Porter, Leon Edel, Blanche H. Gelfant, and Bernice Slote. It also includes original essays by David Stouck, James Leslie Woodress, Paul Cameau, and John J. Murphy. The introduction offers a history of Cather scholarship.

Rosowski, Susan J. *The Voyage Perilous: Willa Cather's Romanticism*. Lincoln: University of Nebraska Press, 1986. This thematic study interprets Cather's writing within the literary tradition of Romanticism. Although the main focus is on her novels (with a chapter devoted to each), the volume also investigates the stories in *The Troll Garden* and includes a chapter on *Obscure Destinies*. See also *Cather Studies*, a forum for scholarship and criticism, which is edited by Rosowski and published biennially by the University of Nebraska Press.

Seaton, James. "The Prosaic Willa Cather." *The American Scholar* 67 (Winter, 1998): 146-150. Argues that Gary Saul Morson's concept of prosaics, which implies the most important events may be the most banal and common ones, should be used to understand Cather's view of romantic love and normal family life.

Shanley, J. Lyndon. "Willa Cather's Fierce Necessity." *The Sewanee Review* 102 (Fall, 1994): 620-630. Notes that Cather's stories are about ordinary people and that one of her most important themes is youthful dreams; discusses Cather's clear prose and the apparent simplicity of her stories.

Thomas, Susie. *Willa Cather*. Savage, Md.: Barnes & Noble Books, 1990. This feminist study, which draws extensively on Cather's unpublished letters, focuses on the particular contributions Cather made as a woman writing about America and analyzes how her cultural awareness influenced the development of her style. The volume includes a short biography and chapters on Cather's major novels and works of short fiction.

Wasserman, Loretta. *Willa Cather: A Study of the Short Fiction*. Boston: Twayne, 1991. Part of Twayne's Studies in Short Fiction series, this volume focuses on selected short stories that the author feels are the most challenging and lend themselves to different critical approaches. Includes interviews with Cather, one of Cather's essays on the craft of writing, samples of current criticism, a chronology, and a select bibliography.

Woodress, James. *Willa Cather: A Literary Life*. Lincoln: University of Nebraska Press, 1990. This definitive biography extends previous studies of Cather, including Woodress's own earlier work (*Willa Cather: Her Life and Art*, 1970), with fuller accounts of Cather's life and includes new and expanded critical responses to her work, taking feminist criticism into account. In preparing the volume, Woodress was able to use the papers of Cather scholar Bernice Slote. Scholars and students will appreciate the extensively documented sources. Includes photographs of Cather, as well as of people and places important to her.

Marilyn Arnold, updated by Jean C. Fulton

MIGUEL DE CERVANTES

Born: Alcalá de Henares, Spain; September 29, 1547
Died: Madrid, Spain; April 23, 1616

PRINCIPAL SHORT FICTION

Novelas ejemplares, 1613 (*Exemplary Novels*,
   1640)

OTHER LITERARY FORMS

Miguel de Cervantes is best known to readers in all languages as the author of *El ingenioso hidalgo don Quixote de la Mancha* (1605, 1615; *The History of the Valorous and Wittie Knight-Errant, Don Quixote of the Mancha*, 1612-1620; better known as *Don Quixote de la Mancha*). That work was not only one of the first novels, but also the first truly modern novel (and one of the many wonders attendant upon its publication is the fact that such a book came so early in the life of the form); its influence appears in such disparate works as *Madame Bovary* (1857) and *Gravity's Rainbow* (1973). Cervantes's achievement is even more remarkable in view of the idiosyncratic nature of the book, its many and complex allusions to the history of Spain and the Jews in Spain, and the fact that most scholars believe that it did, indeed, start out as satire and only later, in part 2, complete the move from art through parody of art to art through imitation of nature.

Cervantes's first novel, written when he was a young man, was *La Galatea* (1585; *Galatea: A Pastoral Romance*, 1833). One eminent Cervantes scholar advises readers to forget the story, characters, and structure and imagine listening to it being read by skillful actors in a pleasant garden well furnished with wine and music. Cervantes's last novel, *Los trabajos de Persiles y Sigismunda* (1617; *The Travels of Persiles and Sigismunda: A Northern History*, 1619), finished only days before his death, is a strange, wintry book composed in the kind of balanced, poetic, but tough Castilian that reminds one forcefully of William Shakespeare's diction in *King Lear* (1605); in fact, until the nineteenth century, its reputation was almost as great as that of *Don Quixote de la Mancha*.

In the Spain of his day, however, Cervantes was better known as a dramatist. After being freed from slavery in North Africa, he returned to Spain and wrote twenty to thirty plays for the theaters in Madrid. From 1580 to about 1587, all were produced and, as Cervantes said later, "were received without cucumbers or other things suitable for throwing." We have the titles of only nine of the plays, and Cervantes preserved only two in the collection of plays he published in 1615, which includes six *comedias* and eight *entremeses*, all written more than twenty years later. Cervantes's dramatic reputation rests on the *entremeses* (interludes between acts), which are spiritually very close to the short stories of *Exemplary Novels*. In one, "Elrufian viudo," a pimp named Trampagos is mourning the death of his best girl until those in the crowd suggest he pick another from the whores gathered at the wake, which he does amidst scenes of low humor and drunken high spirits.

Cervantes had turned to drama to make money quickly, but he was unlucky enough to be competing against Lope de Vega, whose rambunctious, verbally dazzling, thoroughly anticlassical plays soon swept the stage; in fact, Lope de Vega wrote four hundred plays that have been preserved. Cervantes then turned to fiction. His later plays were less ambitious, more finely crafted, and were probably written more for art's sake. The *entremeses* are still performed today. Besides his short stories, Cervantes's other works include two volumes of poetry; the only one still read, *El Viaje del Parnaso* (1614; *The Voyage to Parnassus*, 1870), is about meeting his fellow poets on Mt. Parnassus.

ACHIEVEMENTS

Miguel de Cervantes was the first modern novelist. His influence on the novel has been recognized for centuries, not only by scholars but also by novelists themselves. His masterpiece, *Don Quixote de la Mancha*, achieved immediate and lasting success, making Cervantes one of the unquestioned great figures of world literature. Cervantes also launched the modern short story. Just as in his masterpiece *Don Quixote de la Mancha*, Cervantes transformed prose fiction through his short stories, collected in *Novelas ejemplares*. His characters are personalities who are independent of their author. He was the first fiction writer to utilize dialogue to allow his characters to portray themselves. According to E. C. Riley, he was the first writer to theorize extensively on the novel. His most memorable prose presents reality as complex and ambiguous. This style has had a pervasive and ongoing influence on literature in the West.

BIOGRAPHY

Scholars have begun to realize that the three greatest premodern Spanish writers were all of Jewish origin: They were *conversos*, in the ethnic jargon of the day—Jews converted to Christianity—and Miguel de Cervantes Saavedra was one of them. Many Jews had come to Spain with the Muslim conquerors of the Peninsula. In Spain, at first, they were well treated and often rose to positions of importance. From the Great Pogrom of 1391 in Spain onward, however, many had converted, nominally or in fact, to Christianity, realizing that once Spain was

reconquered, they would be needed by neither the government nor the populace. All Jews still living in Spain and following Judaism were expelled in 1492 and dispersed to all parts of the Mediterranean, becoming the Sephardim. Only the *conversos* remained. The main problem for *conversos* in Cervantes's lifetime was that their status as *hidalgos* might be questioned by the courts and the community. A *hidalgo* was not subject to arrest for ordinary (non-Royal) debt; Cervantes's claims must have been deficient, for he and his father and his grandfather were arrested for debt many times. It was the attitude that *conversos* were somehow second-class citizens which probably accounts for all the illegitimacies among the Cervantes girls: They were considered fair game for sexual adventurers.

Miguel was one of seven Cervantes children of Rodrigo and Leonor de Cortinas, five of them born, as he was, in the pleasant university town of Alcalá de Henares. What Cervantes studied as a youth has never been settled by Spanish scholars, and it is not believed he attended any university, but his description of student life as "amicable, fantastic, intrepid, free and easy, amorous, spendthrift, diabolical and amusing" surely owes something to his observations of Alcalá, or those made by his family. When Miguel was still rather young, the family moved to Valladolid, where after a few months Rodrigo was thrown into the same prison where his father had been incarcerated—the son for debt, however, rather than over a matter of honor. The list of goods seized by Rodrigo's creditors is rather pitiful: a table, three benches, three chairs (two broken), eight sheets, six blankets, and two of his three books. The next move was to Córdoba, at the time one of the most impressive cities in Europe, where Juan de Cervantes, Miguel's grandfather, lived; he was prosperous and could be counted on to help Rodrigo and his family. Miguel's education began there, at the Jesuit College of Santa Clara. There were more moves, but by 1564, the family was in Seville, where Cervantes studied at another Jesuit school. Including his final year of schooling at the City School of Madrid, Cervantes had only six years of schooling between the ages of six and twenty.

Miguel de Cervantes (Library of Congress)

Cervantes was forced into exile in 1568, when he wounded a construction foreman while apparently defending his sister Andrea's nonexistent honor; unfortunately the incident occurred on the grounds of the royal palace in Madrid and thus involved unsheathing a blade in the presence of the King, a crime harshly punished all over Europe. A warrant for his arrest was issued on September 15, 1569, which specified that his right hand was to be cut off and that he was to be exiled for ten years. His pursuers had to give up their search for him when a rebellion broke out in Spain, and Cervantes escaped to Rome. His exact movements in Italy are a mystery, but he was there in 1570, serving Bishop Giulio Acquaviva, a friend of a cousin. Then he joined a Spanish regiment stationed in Naples, which belonged then to Spain, and went off to fight the Turks; he served aboard the galley *Marguesa* in the Battle of Lepanto. Two days away from his twenty-fourth birthday, Cervantes lost his left hand in the battle and took two bullets in the chest. When he had recuperated, he and his brother Rodrigo boarded the galley *Sol* returning to Spain, only to be captured on September 26, 1574, by Moorish pirates and taken to Algiers as slaves. This episode, which lasted six years, was the watershed in Cervantes's life. He tried to escape his horrible conditions three times; amazingly, his only punishment was the severe beatings his captors administered. Finally, in October of 1580, he was ransomed by Trinitarian monks. Cervantes was thirty-three; he had been absent from Spain for twelve years.

During the next few years, Cervantes wrote *La Galatea* and twenty to thirty other plays. Finally, he landed a job as commissary for the navy. This job was not without its perils: He was temporarily excommunicated when he seized some corn the Church had claimed, and he was thrown into prison when his banker went bankrupt and fled, leaving his depositors owing their creditors. It was while he was in jail in Seville in 1595, being punished for his banker's malfeasance, that he began *Don Quixote de la Mancha*; it was printed in January, 1605, by the bookman Robles. The fame of the book was immediate; only a month after its publication in Spain, Don Quixote and Sancho Panza were figures on a float in the Peruvian

Mardi Gras parade. When the Madrid theaters were reopened in 1607, Cervantes wrote *Los Baños de Argel, El Gallardo Español, La Gran Sultana*, and *Pedro de Urdemalas*, which are all included in *Ocho comedias y ocho entremeses* (1615). He wrote two more *comedias* and then discovered his form: the *entremes*. Two of his earlier plays, the six *comedias*, and his eight *entremeses* were now gathered into a book. *Exemplary Novels* was published in 1613 and the collection of plays in 1615. Whether in the *entremeses* he adapted himself to the traditions of the farce or tapped a fertile imagination fettered by the conventions of the longer plays is still an open question, but the one-act plays belong to what one scholar has called the period of his "supreme creativity."

Cervantes, while suffering from some undiagnosed malady thought by some modern scholars to be diabetes, finished *The Travels of Persiles and Sigismunda* just before his death on April 23, 1616, in Madrid. He was buried by his confreres in the Tertiary Order of St. Francis, and his body was taken to a nearby convent. No marker was put on his grave and its location has been lost.

ANALYSIS

Miguel de Cervantes's models for *Exemplary Novels* were Giovanni Boccaccio and Matteo Bandello. There had been short fictions before in Cervantes's work. "Meddlesome Curiosity" had been embodied in *Don Quixote de la Mancha*, as had "The Captive's Tale," and there had been short stories in *La Galatea*. The stories in *Exemplary Novels* were written to stand alone, neither to interrupt, however fruitfully, a longer narrative, nor to form part of a cycle. *Novela* in the Spanish of the time meant "deceit" or "happening" and only secondarily, and as a neologism, "short story"; thus the oxymoronic nature to Cervantes and his contemporaries of the title *Exemplary Deceits*, a *concetto* that opens up his purpose and themes to the reader who has this understanding of Golden Age Spanish. The pieces were not written as tales (*contes*) or as anecdotes or as tall tales, but as something akin to the modern novella. Concerning them, Cervantes wrote: "My intention has been to place in the marketplace of our commonwealth a billiard table [*mesa de trucos*], at which everyone can entertain himself without threat to body or soul, for innocent recreation does good rather than harm." Since moralists in Spain did not like novels, which were characterized as trash fit only for the lower orders, Cervantes called his tales "exemplary." *Exemplary Novels* was an instant commercial success, going through four editions in two months, one a pirated edition from Barcelona and the other a Portuguese forgery.

"COLLOQUY OF THE DOGS"

Amezúa, the modern editor of "Colloquy of the Dogs," places the composition of the story in 1603 or 1604 and "before the spring of 1605." The story opens as Berganza and Cipión, two big watchdogs, find themselves suddenly gifted with the power of speech in the hospital where they serve as the watchdogs of Mahudes, a collector of alms at the Hospital of the Resurrection in Valladolid. The story is written as if it were a play; there are no stage directions, however, and we are given no exposition by the author. The speakers must set the mood, provide the tone, and move the action linguistically rather than structurally. Berganza, who has something in him of the village philosopher, begins speaking and never relinquishes the floor. His earliest memories are of a Seville slaughterhouse from which his first experience of crime and corruption, malfeasance and defalcation, comes: The butchers and their wives and girlfriends always take choice cuts of meats for themselves and smuggle them out of the slaughterhouse. One of the butchers trains him to take things to one of his girls, but the other intercepts the dog, takes what he was entrusted with, and beats him, so Berganza runs away and goes to the shepherds outside the city.

Thus one of the themes of the story is set, and it becomes a kind of allegory of the condition of those on the bottom of society in Spain—the *conversos, moriscos*, gypsies, thieves, soldiers, whores, and foreigners. Berganza never gets into a scrape that could not be explained if he could speak. It has been suggested that the great works of literature tap into the feelings of the child, especially his feelings of helplessness and his anxieties about the future, and, by resolving the problem set forth in the story, prepare the child to take his place in the world. "Colloquy of the Dogs" certainly captures vividly the feelings of powerlessness and anxiety that those who are weak and ignorant feel.

The dog's second sojourn is with a group of shepherds, who, Berganza soon discovers, have a nice racket worked out: In the middle of the night they cry, "Wolf! Wolf!" and the dogs dash up to see a mauled sheep; then they are sent out by their masters to chase the wolf. One night, suspicious, Berganza remains behind and sees the shepherds maul a sheep exactly as a wolf would. When the master of the shepherds comes up later and demands to know what happened, the shepherds blame the lazy dogs for not protecting the flock. The temptation here to see the shepherds as the Inquisitors, the mauled sheep as the *conversos*, and the nonexistent wolves as nonexistent Judaizing is irresistible. In fact, when the Inquisition was beginning, Isabella found it politic to write the Pope that she was not beginning the Inquisition to seize the wealth of the *conversos* (which was probably less than the truth). Cervantes had already taken a shot at the Inquisition in one of his *entremeses*.

Berganza finds a much happier home; in fact the description of it is one of the warmest parts of the tale. He makes himself indispensable to a merchant by becoming his watchdog—his analysis of human psychology is quite amusing—and eventually so ingratiates himself with the family that he accompanies the family's little boy to the Jesuit school. There Berganza does tricks and is fed from the boys' lunches and in general becomes such a clown that the Jesuits send him home; once home, he is chained between the inner and outer doors. He soon finds that his sleep is disturbed and his job compromised by the black maid who must pass by him on her way to see her lover. Usually she scrimps on his food but on the nights she has a rendezvous, she feeds him. He takes the first few bribes, but he is not happy with himself, and one night, without barking, he mauls her severely. After that she offers him a sponge fried in lard, which will kill him, then tries to starve him. He sees how things are going to fall out, so, reluctantly, he escapes through a hole in the wall around the family's compound.

The wall may as well be the limits of society, for now Berganza will live among the marginal people, the outcasts and criminals and atheists and witches of Spain. He has eleven masters, counting Mahudes. Seven of the eleven (seven itself being a cabalistic number) will be the forces spurned or outlawed by society. Berganza meets a constable named Nicolás the Snubnose and is given a brass collar. The metal collar in classical times, certainly in North Africa during Cervantes's captivity, and later in the New World, was the emblem of the slave. After his first trinity of owners, the producers, middlemen, and consumers of meat, Berganza slips into the company of marginal men and wears the emblem of the slave.

The constable and the scrivener make their living walking the constable's rounds and playing the badger game, in cooperation with the whores who are their girls. One night, as they are rousting a Breton caught with the constable's whore, Berganza smells some food in the victim's pants and drags them outside; but this also removes the money the constable had hoped to extort from the victim, and in the ensuing fracas, the Chief of Police has to be called in. The constable's next adventure is defeating six thieves in a swordfight. Then Berganza accompanies the constable to the lair of Monipodio, the *éminence grise* of the thieves of Seville, and discovers that Monipodio had arranged the whole thing. Berganza is now disgusted, and when given a chance later to fall upon his master, he does so, then disappears.

He next falls in with a drummer serving in a company of soldiers marching to take ship. Berganza is taught to perform some tricks, which he finds humiliating, and in consequence of his new talents, he is dubbed the Wise Dog. One night in Montilla, an old witch named Cañizares comes to him and calls him Montiel and takes him to her room, where she tells him the story of his birth as she disrobes and rubs on a magic salve that will enable her spirit to fly away to a witches' coven. The famous witch of the age had indeed been from Montilla and was called La Camacha and was burned at the stake by the Inquisition. This woman and Berganza's mother, according to his new patroness, had been La Camacha's disciples.

This is the part of the story that Berganza had

wanted to tell first, but he had relented at the insistence of Cipión, something of a traditionalist. Now we learn that the dog's mother, according to the witch, was Montiela, one of the witch's cohorts and fellow disciples. La Camacha made her twin sons be born as puppies and took them off with her, but now Montiel has been "recognized." Cervantes leaves the door open, with his careful ambiguity, to the possibility that she is telling the truth; from this we can make the further inference that the other dog is Cipión, another human in dog's skin and thus equally able to assume that human characteristic, speech.

Berganza reacts adversely to the witch's revelations and tries to kill her. The townspeople believe he is the devil in human form and chase him. Once again, he is on the run, but our feeling that his rendezvous with Cañizares was the purpose of his life is heightened by the fact that the woman is the middle of his eleven masters, that the episode happens almost in the middle of the book, and that we have been warned by the narrator himself that this is the most important part of his story.

The obvious allegory of "The Colloquy of the Dogs" is to Cervantes's life; he would have been called *perro* (dog) himself, as Christian slaves of the Arabs and Turks were. This allegory holds up when the reader considers that the main nexus between writer and reader is the scene with the witch, for art itself is a kind of sorcery. Another allegory comes to mind when we recall that Protestantism traveled from belief in salvation through faith in the Trinity (the "good" masters are a trinity) to salvation through works—and that in the process it caused wars and an upsurge of witchcraft because people still hungered for the rituals and images of liturgical worship and for the intercession of the myriad saints and the buying of masses and favors from the priests and the orders. The story is also a fable for the critics and an exemplar of how to explore the lower depths without the juridical deadness of the picaroon novel. For whatever reason, this story, with its lively action and constant invention, still stands out as one of the best, most moving, wittiest, and most absorbing short stories ever written; it is a marvel of diction, compression, and depth.

"The Glass Scholar"

To some, "The Glass Scholar" is a dull story, useful only as a medium for some of Cervantes's apothegms. Others see it as truly outstanding, and still others hail it as the first surrealist short story. All three judgments are correct to a degree.

The plot is simple: Two students at an unspecified university find an eleven-year-old boy sleeping under a tree, and they ask him his name. He replies, with the evasiveness we have come to expect of Cervantes's characters, that he will not give his real name until he can bring glory to it. Meanwhile, he calls himself Tomás Rodaja (which means *little wheel*). From this and other things, the students assume he is the son of a poor peasant. In those days the servants of students, and this was especially true at Salamanca, could also be enrolled as undergraduates, and soon Rodaja is thus enrolled.

One day, riding back to the university, he is joined on the road by an officer of infantry who extols the delights of army life to him, although Cervantes wryly notes that he leaves out the fleas, hunger, and danger which to the majority are all that constitute military life. The student decides to accompany the army, but not join it, and there follows a travelogue which covers most of the Italian cities and ends in Flanders. Then Rodaja goes back to Salamanca.

At the university, a woman falls in love with him, but he rejects her, and she feeds him a poisoned quince. He sickens immediately and lies in his bed for six months. When he is coherent again, he believes that he is made of glass and that he will shatter if handled too roughly. It terrifies him when his friends embrace him. He says the soul is more efficient in a body of glass than of heavy earth. There is no doubt religious symbolism in his statement, but it is indecipherable. In the winter, Rodaja, ever consistent, sleeps as bottles are packed: *in straw up to the neck*.

He is finally taken to court for all to gawk at and ask questions of, for he is very good at epigrams ("good painters imitate nature but bad ones vomit it forth"). Finally, he is cured by an Hieronymite friar, possibly because his creator had run out of apothegms. He renames himself Rueda (*wheel; vidriera* means

glass) and attempts to follow his profession, the law, but ironically, no one wants him now that he is sane and serious; so he enlists in the army and is killed in Flanders. This is a delightful tale, especially if one likes epigrams and apothegms, and almost all of them are good. Moreover, it was and is an audacious story which unites realistic writing with a surrealist premise.

Whether Cervantes used an anecdote from the *Miscelánea* (c. 1590) of Luís de Zapata de Chaves as the basis for his story "Rinconete and Cortadillo" or whether he met the originals in prison on one of his frequent trips there, is difficult to say. The most important thing about the story is that here, as a scholar says, we can find the germ of *Don Quixote de la Mancha*, the "contrast, the humorous incongruity, between the world as it is and the world as it ought to be, which constitutes Cervantes's major theme and forms the basis of his finest art . . . close-to-life realism, which in itself will doubtless suffice for many but which holds a deeper meaning for those who seek it."

Rincón and Cortado are between fourteen and sixteen years old when they meet at the inn of Molinillo on the border of the plains of Alcudia on the road from Castile to Andalusia (there was an inn there and the topography of the countryside around Seville and the city itself is exact). They have no capes or stockings, and their shoes are almost falling off; they are obviously runaways. Each perceives that the other is a criminal.

The younger and smaller one says at first, when the older and larger one questions him, "I do not know the name of my country" and "my land is not my land." (Again, this is the kind of ambiguity Cervantes cherished.) He eventually admits he is Diego Cortado. *Cortado* is the past participle of *cortar* (*to cut*, either a piece of cloth or a deck of cards; it also means to dilute, as in *to cut wine with water*); so even this information is less than revealing. He was born between Salamanca and Medina del Campo, and has been, as it turns out, a cutter for his tailor father as well as a cutpurse (thief). The older boy, Pedro de Rincón (which means *nook* or *corner* in Spanish), is a native of Fuenfrida, today's Fuenfría, and his father sold papal indulgences. One day Rincón stole his father's bag of money and went to Madrid and spent it all. There, after various misadventures, he was caught and flogged and denied entrance to the city for four years. He has occupied himself since then by dealing blackjack. The deck he carries is crooked and will produce an ace whenever he wants it to.

The two boys skin a muleteer with Rincón's crooked deck; when the man tries to take his money back from them, thinking this will be easy because they are only boys, one pulls a shortsword and the other a yellow-handled cattle knife. They go next to Seville with a caravan, and as thanks to their fellow-travelers, steal two shirts from one of them and sell them in the flea market for spending money. It is summer, the season for provisioning the outgoing fleet. Porters are needed, and the two boys see that this trade will gain them admittance to big houses; they need not pass an examination, and they only need two bags for bread and three palm-fiber baskets.

The first day on the job, Cortado steals a student's purse. Another young man, also a thief, notices the two and their real (as opposed to nominal) trade, and tells them they will have to "register" with Monipodio, the prince—or perhaps the prior—of thieves. Their "Vergil" tells them that Monipodio insists that part of the swag be used to light candles in front of a local icon the thieves hold sacred, to pay officials and to hold masses for the dead parents of the members of the gang. Furthermore, many of them do not steal on Friday or speak to a woman named Mary on Saturday. It is heavy irony, but Cervantes also uses this speech to capture the peculiarly Andalusian mixture of brigandage and piety that is one of the presiding ironies of the tale. They go to a house where they meet the "coarsest and most hideous barbarian in the world." He christens them Rinconete and Cortadillo, much in the manner of an abbot giving vocational names to new novices in a religious order. We see the house and its furnishings, the courtyard, the dress of the thieves, whores, and cutthroats who frequent the place; there is even an old moll praying to a cheap print of Our Lady.

This story has no real plot. Sluts beaten by their pimps seek justice from Monipodio, lists of beatings

and acid-throwings and cuttings bought from Monipodio are subcontracted, and a young man who wanted a fourteen-stitch cut put in the face of a merchant demands his money back because the thug in charge of the job decided the merchant's face was too small for fourteen, so gave the fourteen to his lackey instead. Monipodio negotiates the case with a gangster's jurisprudential principles, but the legal reasoning employed is as fine as any employed in chancery courts. The atmosphere is part of the very real charm of the piece, but to Cervantes's contemporaries most of this story would have been a shocking, journalistic exposé of the Sevillean underworld. Cervantes may have been interested in showing that this criminal welfare state was far better regulated and more humane than the straight world. Some notice of this could hardly have escaped the contemporary audience.

The day ends and all retire, Cervantes closing his story with the promise that the boys' further adventures in Seville will furnish "edifying" anecdotes—thus making this tale one of postponed exemplariness. It has a far wider importance to us: These boys are the dim creatures of Maxim Gorky's *The Lower Depths* (1902), the fathers of Fyodor Dostoevski's heroes, and the ancestors of the human wrecks scattered along Raymond Chandler's mean streets.

OTHER MAJOR WORKS

LONG FICTION: *La Galatea*, 1585 (*Galatea: A Pastoral Romance*, 1833); *El ingenioso hidalgo don Quixote de la Mancha*, 1605, 1615 (*The History of the Valorous and Wittie Knight-Errant, Don Quixote of the Mancha*, 1612-1620; better known as *Don Quixote de la Mancha*); *Los trabajos de Persiles y Sigismunda*, 1617 (*The Travels of Persiles and Sigismunda: A Northern History*, 1619).

PLAYS: *El trato de Argel*, pr. 1585 (*The Commerce of Algiers: A Comedy*, 1870); *Ocho comedias y ocho entremeses nuevos*, pb. 1615 (includes *Pedro de Urdemalas*, 1615, *Pedro the Artful Dodger*, 1807; *El juez de los divorcios*, *The Divorce Court Judge*, 1919; *Los habladores*, *Two Chatterboxes*, 1930; *La cueva de Salamanca*, *The Cave of Salamanca*, 1933; *La elección de los alcaldes de Daganzo*, *Choosing a*

Councilman in Daganzo, 1948; *La guarda cuidadosa, The Hawk-eyed Sentinel*, 1948; *El retablo de las maravillas, The Wonder Show*, 1948; *El rufián viudo llamada Trampagos, Trampagos the Pimp Who Lost His Moll*, 1948; *El viejo celoso, The Jealous Old Husband*, 1948; and *El vizcaíno fingido, The Basque Imposter*, 1948); *El cerco de Numancia*, pb. 1784 (written 1585; *Numantia: A Tragedy*, 1870); *The Interludes of Cervantes*, pb. 1948.

POETRY: *El Viaje del Parnaso*, 1614 (*The Voyage to Parnassus*, 1870).

BIBLIOGRAPHY

Clamurro, William H. *Beneath the Fiction: The Contrary Worlds of Cervantes's "Novelas ejemplares."* New York: Peter Lang, 1997. Examines the settings of the stories. Includes bibliographical references and an index.

Dunn, Peter N. "Framing the Story, Framing the Reader: Two Spanish Masters." *The Modern Language Review* 91 (January, 1996): 94-106. Shows how Cervantes fragments and internalizes narrative frames and thus poses basic questions about the way that narrative establishes boundaries. Cervantes defeats our expectation about order and culture by disturbing our sense of what is stable in his narrative frames.

Duran, Manuel. *Cervantes*. New York: Twayne, 1974. This excellent general study provides a background on the Spain of Cervantes's time and discusses his influence on world literature. It dedicates a chapter to his short fiction and includes a select bibliography.

El Saffar, Ruth S. *Novel to Romance: A Study of Cervantes' "Novelas ejemplares."* Baltimore: The Johns Hopkins University Press, 1974. El Saffar analyzes the exemplary tales in terms of Cervantes's development as man and artist to demonstrate how his fiction evolves from novel to romance—that is, from tales of individual alienation to idealistic tales in which the characters overcome adversity and achieve their goals. Supplemented by a bibliography and an index.

Hart, Thomas R. *Cervantes' Exemplary Fictions: A Study of the Novelas Ejemplares*. Lexington: The University Press of Kentucky, 1994. A reading of Cervantes's stories in the context of the knowledge of everyday life and literary conventions shared by Cervantes's contemporaries. Concludes that speculations of how old books were read when they were new cannot tell us how they should be read today.

Nelson, Lowry, Jr., ed. *Cervantes: A Collection of Critical Essays*. Englewood Cliffs, N.J.: Prentice-Hall, 1969. A collection of ten essays featuring contributions by the novelist Thomas Mann, the poet W. H. Auden, and venerable figures of Cervantes studies such as Leo Spitzer and Edwin Honig. The essays discuss *Don Quixote de la Mancha*, the picaresque in Cervantes's fiction, the one-act plays, and *Los trabajos de Persiles y Sigismunda*. Supplemented by a short select bibliography.

Predmore, Richard L. *Cervantes*. London: Thames and Hudson, 1973. This biography of Cervantes contains frequent references to the history of the period. Makes liberal use of quotes from Cervantes's writings to depict the events of his life. Includes illustrations of personalities, places, documents, and historical events of the period. Complemented by notes, a bibliography, and an index.

Riley, E. C. *Cervantes's Theory of the Novel*. Oxford, England: Clarendon Press, 1962. A detailed examination of Cervantes's views on questions of literary practice in terms of traditional issues in poetics, such as art and nature, unity, and purpose and function of literature. Includes a bibliography and indexes of names and topics.

Stierle, Karlheinz. "Three Moments in the Crisis of Exemplarity: Boccaccio, Petrarch, Montaigne, and Cervantes." *Journal of the History of Ideas* 59 (October, 1998): 581-595. Discusses Boccaccio's response to the exemplum as a form of narration that presumes more similarity in human behavior than diversity. Discusses Cervantes's *Exemplary Novels* as attempts to combine exemplary figures with the unique and the morally ambiguous.

Weber, Alison. "Pentimento: The Parodic Text of *La Gitanilla*." *Hispanic Review* 62 (Winter, 1994):

59-75. Argues that Cervantes imagines Preciosa free from class and family, but that when she is returned to her patriarchal family, she is once again bound to the values of her class.

Weiger, John G. "Cervantine Kinesics: Gestures as an Element of Cervantes's Narrative Technique." *Journal of Medieval and Renaissance Studies* 25 (Spring, 1995): 271-304. Argues that gesture to communicate states of mind is a basic aspect of Cervantes's narrative technique. Asserts the gradual transition from oral to print culture removed the human body from the act of reading, forcing the writer to convey the kinesics of the plot through language.

_____. *The Substance of Cervantes*. London: Cambridge University Press, 1985. Provides valuable insights into Cervantes's craft as a writer by exploring questions such as the relationship of art and reality, the functions of authors and readers, the elusive nature of truth, the dynamics of society, and the significance of the individual and of communication between individuals. Augmented by a bibliography and an index.

Williamson, Edwin, ed. *Cervantes and the Modernists: The Question of Influence*. London: Tamesis, 1994. Explores the novelist's impact on such twentieth century writers as Marcel Proust, Thomas Mann, Primo Levi, Carlos Fuentes, and Gabriel García Márquez. No index or bibliography.

John Carr, updated by Evelyn Toft

MICHAEL CHABON

Born: Washington, D.C.; May 24, 1963

PRINCIPAL SHORT FICTION

A Model World and Other Stories, 1991
Werewolves in Their Youth: Stories, 1999

OTHER LITERARY FORMS

Michael Chabon's literary career began in 1988 with the publication of his first novel, *The Mysteries of Pittsburgh*. He also published travel sketches in magazines such as *Vogue*, as well as essays in *The New Yorker* and *Civilization*. In 1995, his first novel, *Wonder Boys*, was published, followed by another in 2000, *The Amazing Adventures of Kavalier and Clay*.

ACHIEVEMENTS

When Michael Chabon's adviser in the master's of fine arts program at the University of California at Irvine submitted *The Mysteries of Pittsburgh* to an agency in 1987, the novel created such a sensation that the right to publish was sold at auction. The publisher William Morrow paid a record $155,000 for publication rights. Foreign publishers were eager to obtain rights, and by the time the novel appeared, Chabon was already at work under contract on a film adaptation. He wrote other screenplays, which were sold but not produced, and the film rights to *Wonder Boys* (1995) were purchased after that novel's release. In 1987, his short stories began to appear in *Mademoiselle* and *The New Yorker*, which subsequently bought most of the stories that appear in *A Model World and Other Stories*.

BIOGRAPHY

Michael Chabon (pronounced "shaybin") was born in Washington, D.C. He graduated with a B.A. from the University of Pittsburgh and went on to study creative writing as a Regents Fellow at the University of California at Irvine. He submitted his first novel, *The Mysteries of Pittsburgh*, to his graduate adviser, novelist MacDonald Harris, who then recommended it to his literary agent. The book was accepted for publication when Chabon was twenty-three years old. Chabon subsequently completed his master's of fine arts degree. The success of his first novel plunged Chabon into a glamorous world of endorsement offers (deals from the Gap and *People* magazine)—all of which he rejected. He settled with his first wife, Lolly Groth, in Seattle, Washington. After their divorce he married Ayelet Waldman and settled first in San Francisco, then in Los Angeles.

Michael Chabon (©Miriam Berkley)

ANALYSIS

Michael Chabon's distinctive strength in storytelling is a command of style that reminds his reviewers of F. Scott Fitzgerald. Chabon creates an engaging surface of epigrams, wit, and telling comparisons. His subjects are also similar to Fitzgerald's, dealing mainly with young people trying to find their way through morally ambiguous and confusing situations. Though his style calls attention to the surface of his stories, they are, nevertheless, moving, mainly because his characters are realized fully enough and their problems and dilemmas are serious enough to involve the reader. *A Model World* is divided into two parts. "Part 1: A Model World" contains six stories

on varied subjects. "Part 2: The Lost World" is a group of five stories about Nathan Shapiro, a boy who grows up while dealing with his parents' divorce. Looking closely at three stories, "S ANGEL," "A Model World," and "The Little Knife," will illustrate Chabon's characteristics.

"S ANGEL"

In "S ANGEL," Ira Wiseman, a twenty-one-year-old senior drama student at the University of California, Los Angeles, goes to the wedding of his cousin, Sheila, in Los Angeles. A young romantic, Ira is waiting for fate to bring him together with the right woman: "Ira never went anywhere without expecting that when he arrived there he would meet the woman with whom he had been destined to fall in love." His ideas of falling in love are confused, a mixture of unsatisfied sexual desire and idealism, but the world that he finds at the wedding seems dominated by sexual exploitation and economics.

At the reception, following the wedding, Ira feels uncomfortable and lonely. A woman attracts his notice: "Her body had aged better than her fading face, which nonetheless he found beautiful, and in which, in the skin at her throat and around her eyes, he thought he read strife and sad experience and a willingness to try her luck." Is she attractive because suffering has deepened her character or her romantic appeal, or because she might prove willing to engage in sex? The narrative voice makes fairly clear that the advice that he gets from his lesbian cousin, Donna, is right; Carmen, a neurotic, abused divorcée, is not a good prospect for Ira's first love affair.

As Ira approaches, meets, and attempts to begin a friendship with Carmen, he witnesses events that sketch out his activities and attitudes. He sees, and others confirm, that after two hours of wedded bliss, Sheila remains uncertain that marrying is what she wants. He overhears a conversation in which a non-Jew, Jeff Freebone, who affects Jewish speech and mannerisms, and who has rapidly become wealthy in the real-estate business, talks about firing an employee: "I should have done it the day it happened. Ha ha. Pow, fired in her own bed." Later, this same man commands the "carnal" affections of the group of Jewish women at Ira's table, including Carmen, his wealth overcoming even the unabashed lesbianism of Donna and her girlfriend and Carmen's history of abuse by a husband not unlike Freebone. He takes them away from the reception to view Carmen's house, which she would like to sell. These and other incidents underline Ira's naïve attitudes toward sex and love. Left alone again, Ira receives the assignment of locating the bride, who is supposed to cut the cake but has disappeared. Ira finds her alone, and they sympathize with each other, seemingly renewing an old sexual attraction between them. The story ends with their kiss.

As the story of a young idealist looking for romantic love in what turns out ironically to be an inappropriate place, at a wedding, "S ANGEL" is light in tone. There are no great defeats or losses in the story, and Ira does not lose his sweet, idealistic side. Nevertheless, the threats to people such as Ira and Sheila are serious. They believe that they are looking for authentic relationships, untainted by sexual exploitation and the struggle for wealth and status, but virtually everyone around them seems to be the way Sheila feels at her wedding, like "a big stupid puppet or something, getting pulled around." They may both be victims of rather silly romantic illusions about love. Chabon achieves this lightness of tone in part through his style, especially in sentences that carry readers over long thoughts containing interesting turns and amusing surprises. When Ira pretends to go to the bar in order to walk by Carmen's table for a closer look at her, he is described: "Ira swung like a comet past the table, trailing, as he supposed, a sparkling wake of lustfulness and Eau Sauvage, but she seemed not to notice him, and when he reached the bar he found, to his surprise, that he genuinely wanted a drink." Here, Chabon captures the contrast between Ira's dream of his attractiveness and Carmen's jaded response, which converts his pretense of going for a drink into a reality.

The story's title refers to a misfolded map of Los Angeles in Carmen's purse. Ira is following a metaphorical map of romantic love, believing that he knows the signposts: "He had yet to fall in love to the degree that he felt he was capable of falling, had never written villanelles or declarations veiled in careful metaphor, nor sold his blood plasma to buy champagne or jonquils. . . ." This only begins his list of the signs of love. Carmen has the map in a disorganized purse that reflects her lost life, and she apparently used it to find the location of the wedding, whereas Ira got lost and was late in arriving. This metaphor implies that Carmen, abused, divorced, depressed, and still looking for another rich husband, knows the road much better than Ira.

"A MODEL WORLD"

"A Model World" shows Chabon setting up a complex social situation that might remind one of the parties that Fitzgerald created in *The Great Gatsby* (1925). Smith, the narrator, and his friend, Levine, are physics students at a Southern California university. Smith is working on subatomic particles with brief lives: "Evanescence itself was the object of my studies." Levine is working on cloud dynamics, research that should lead toward the ability to control internal cloud movements. Both areas of study involve modeling, attempting to describe phenomena that are virtually impossible to measure and manipulate. This motif of modeling parts of the world turns up in a variety of ways, from the central image of a model of the greenhouse effect on Baldwin's computer through the modeling of social life in drama and on television to the telling of stories, fictional models of human life. The story culminates in a dinner party at the home of Baldwin, Levine's thesis adviser. There, social tensions mount as in a storm cloud until Smith manages to give them the spin that eases tension and contributes to changing the course of several people's lives.

The tensions arise from the secrets shared between various pairs at the dinner party, secrets that amount to attempts to give shapes to different aspects of the relationships among these people. Having lost the excitement of science while working on his dissertation, Levine discovers in a used bookstore an obscure study of Antarctic clouds that completely and persuasively demonstrates the thesis toward which he has been working. This book arouses his passion, for it seems to have suffered the fate that he fears: "It was the horror of death, of the doom that waited all his efforts, and it was this horror, more than anything else . . . that determined him to commit the mortal sin of Academe." The sin is to plagiarize the book. By doing so, he will escape the prison of his fruitless studies so that he can go to New Mexico to make ceramic wind chimes and forget about measuring and controlling wind in clouds. In the process of plagiarizing, however, "his faith in the stoic nobility of scientific endeavor" is restored, and he once again dreams of a scientific career. This leads him to want to confer with Baldwin, to learn whether he has any real chance of getting away with plagiarizing. At this point, an academic reader might wonder why Levine does not simply use the book in the usual way, giving the author credit for his or her work instead of stealing it.

Smith's dissertation is going well enough, but he has become interested in an attractive drama student, Jewel, who turns out to be Julia, Baldwin's wife. She is currently enthralled by a French Egyptian theater guru, Mehmet Monsour. When Levine is invited to the dinner party, Mrs. Baldwin asks that he bring his friend, Smith. The dinner party then consists of Monsour, Levine, Smith, Baldwin, and Julia. Monsour seems mainly interested in absorbing a variety of American experiences and transforming them into drama. Levine wants to find out whether his plagiarism will work without revealing that he has plagiarized. Smith wants a sexual encounter with Julia. Julia, it turns out, wants mainly to plague her husband. Baldwin wants to triumph over Julia in some way and, perhaps, to humiliate himself in the process, since he wants to confront and expose the affair that he has detected but that he mistakenly believes is between Julia and Monsour. During a private talk with Baldwin, Levine again despairs that he can get away with plagiarism, as he realizes that the book he is copying, though published by a vanity press and probably very rare, still exists for someone to find sometime. Out of this despair, he betrays Smith, revealing what he discovers in the course of his conversation with Baldwin, that Smith, not Monsour, is Julia's lover.

The dinner proceeds with all of these tensions in operation. Monsour observes and talks volubly; Smith is unaware of his danger but observes that Julia

sees him as an instrument to use against her husband rather than as a lover; Levine is aware that he can probably succeed in his plagiarism but that he has, perhaps, bought this security by betraying his friend; Baldwin thinks he has gained power over Julia with his knowledge that Smith is her lover. These tensions come to a crisis when, at Baldwin's instigation, Monsour begins a game that is one of his theater exercises, in which each person must tell, truthfully, the worst thing that he or she 'has ever done. Smith is chosen to go first. He says that he had good sense enough to tell the truth. From among the most obvious choices—acquiescing in plagiarism, adultery, being an instrument in a marital battle—he chooses none but instead remembers a childhood action that he has most regretted—the wanton, unmotivated destruction of a neighbor child's toy—depending on his undeserved reputation for goodness as a shield from discovery and punishment. He tells the story so well that no one believes him, perhaps in part because it concerns none of them and is not what they expected to hear. The immediate effect of the story, nevertheless, is to bring an end to the game, to the tensions, and to the evening. The longer-term effects are also interesting: an end to Smith's affair with Julia and the beginning of his own very successful theater career, the end of Levine's vacillation about plagiarism and the beginning of his rapid ascent in the academic study of meteorology.

Like "S ANGEL," this story is light in tone, though in the crisis the stakes for the main characters are fairly high. The tone is maintained in part by Chabon's witty style and in part by the distance that he maintains from the characters. In this story, the moral ambiguities of the social world that he presents seem foregrounded while the characters remain relatively flat, which is another similarity with some of the best-known fiction of Fitzgerald, such as *The Great Gatsby*. The central effect of the story seems to be the irony of a world in which truth seems like fiction, where plagiarism and social lies may lead just as surely to success as telling the truth. The complexity of this irony becomes clear when one considers that while Levine steals his dissertation, he also rescues from loss the valuable work of another scientist, and when one considers that although Smith may tell a true story from his childhood, it is a difficult matter to judge whether breaking a child's toy was worse than committing adultery or failing to report plagiarism.

"THE LITTLE KNIFE"

Chabon maintains his light surface tone even in the sad and moving story that begins his series of Nathan Shapiro as he lives through and adjusts to his parents' divorce. The contrast between subject and tone is exemplified in the opening sentence of "The Little Knife": "One Saturday in that last, interminable summer before his parents separated and the Washington Senators baseball team was expunged forever from the face of the earth, the Shapiros went to Nag's Head, North Carolina, where Nathan, without planning to, perpetrated a great hoax." This contrast parallels the ironic distance between ten-year-old Nathan's perceptions about that vacation and the reader's more adult view.

This vacation brings the elder Shapiros to the realization that their marriage has come to an end. Mrs. Shapiro, though she says that her husband is a liberal and generous man, is looking for means of fulfillment in addition to marriage, and Dr. Shapiro has come to see these explorations into yoga, bonsai, and real estate as affronts to himself. They have fights, overheard by Nathan and his little brother, Ricky, in which Dr. Shapiro buries his wife "under a heap of scorn and ridicule." The fight that cuts their vacation short at midweek leads her to assert herself and implies that the marriage is over as far as she is concerned. By the middle of the day, Dr. Shapiro seems to have realized and accepted this, too.

Nathan, however, as the point-of-view character, has a child's mixed and somewhat vague understanding of what is happening, his vision typified by the equation of separating parents and the demise of the Washington Senators. His first reaction to his parents' fighting is a wish to return home, a step in the development of the nostalgia that becomes one of his leading characteristics throughout the stories in this series. He feels his parents are coming apart and wants to return to, or somehow preserve, a past that he remembers as more comfortable, when he was not in danger of being abandoned.

He actually perpetrates two hoaxes on their last day at Nag's Head. In the first, he walks alone along the beach on his heels, leaving impossible tracks, then returns to the spot later with his parents. To divert them from the realization that they must separate, he points to these tracks, and they go along with his game, pretending not to know what monster made them, though Ricky realizes immediately and Nathan must stifle him. When they announce that they are "unwell" and must cut the vacation short, Nathan thinks—or perhaps pretends to believe—that the strange tracks are the cause of this decision. When he asks them not to leave and claims responsibility, they react to quite another message, for they believe that he understands they are going to separate and believes himself to blame. This hoax creates a complexly moving moment of family unity and probably leads him to commit the second hoax.

At breakfast, his mother admired an especially handy little knife that is part of the furnishing of their beach cottage. His father suggests that she just take it, and this sets off the latest explosion in this last phase of their disintegration. She says that she will not let Dr. Shapiro make her dishonest. Nathan does not know what this means, but he arranges to be alone to pack his things while the rest of the family takes a last walk on the beach. While they are gone, he gathers up the seashells that they have found in a shoe box, and finally, he puts in the little knife, "where it swam, frozen, like a model shark in a museum diorama." As he looks at it, he looks forward to his parents fighting over it: "He foresaw, recalled, and fondly began to preserve all the discord for which, in his wildly preserving imagination, he was and would always be responsible." At least in discord, they are all together, and his "wildly preserving imagination" wishes to hold that togetherness, even at the price of discord.

Chabon's control of imagery in this story is especially notable. For example, as the family walks on the beach, they give seashells to Dr. Shapiro to hold, so that they come to jingle in his hands like money. When Mrs. Shapiro repeats "never again," her husband lets the shells fall: "He rubbed his hands together and then stared at them as though waking from a dream in which he had been holding a fortune in gold." The depth of this image is enhanced when Nathan reads it in the same way the reader is told to read it and responds quickly with his first hoax.

"WEREWOLVES IN THEIR YOUTH"

The title story of *Werewolves in Their Youth* opens with: "I had known him as a bulldozer, as a samurai . . . as a Peterbilt truck . . . but it was as a werewolf that Timothy Stokes finally went too far." Timothy clings to the imaginative world of most boys with a greater tenacity, ultimately at greater risk to himself. The narrator, Paul Kovel, is Timothy's reluctant neighbor, a boy who tries to avoid him at any cost. Paul struggles with obesity and, most profoundly, a violent father whose wife has tossed him out of their home. Both the school administrators and Timothy's mother, Mrs. Stokes, rely on Paul to wrest the boy from his conviction that he is a werewolf.

Paul's mother, who used to take the time to make him healthy meals, is now out selling real estate. When Paul finds her in the basement ready to throw away the last of his father's belongings—his Panama hat, his experiments as a research chemist for the Food and Drug Administration—it is all too much for the boy. He calls his father at work and lies about getting expelled from school to trick him into coming to the house. Then Paul steals a box of his father's possessions, including the notebook containing the formulas for his experiments, and hides it outside Timothy's house.

When Paul goes to retrieve the box later, he runs into Timothy, who carries Paul's father's notebook and wears a "rifle strapped across his back and a plastic commando knife in his boot." Timothy, having decided that Paul's father has been poisoning his son slowly, offers him an antidote, Coca-Cola and something else that burns his throat going down. Returning to the Kovel house, the boys are shocked to see Paul's parents locked in an amorous embrace. They throw up the antidote, and Paul tells Mrs. Stokes that Timothy has a real gun; he then helps his father load the rest of his things in the car. The following morning, Paul watches Timothy board a bus bound for the "special school" for boys who do not fit in elsewhere.

"Werewolves in Their Youth" is redolent of those boyhoods in which parents are too busy with their own dilemmas to be of any significant use to their children. Chabon reveals a masterful eye for detail, such as the pancakes that Mrs. Stokes makes for her disturbed son which "sounded okay until you found out that she put things in them like carrots and leftover pieces of corn." In less skillful hands, "Werewolves in Their Youth" could fall prey to vilifying the parents while painting the boys as hapless victims. It is not that simplistic, however. Chabon portrays Mrs. Kovel as a woman trying to do her best in an untenable situation. By the same token, Paul's father, although a drinker and wife beater, is limited by his own inability to confront his addiction and mercurial temper. The boys are both inventive and complex, funny and maddening. Such tales of domestic discord are Chabon's trademark.

OTHER MAJOR WORKS

LONG FICTION: *The Mysteries of Pittsburgh*, 1988; *Wonder Boys*, 1995; *The Amazing Adventures of Kavalier and Clay*, 2000.

BIBLIOGRAPHY

Benedict, Elizabeth. "Sorrow at the Mall." Review of *A Model World and Other Stories*, by Michael Chabon. *The New York Times Book Review*, May 26, 1991, 7. In this review of Chabon's first short-story collection, Benedict praises the author's narrative skills and descriptive powers. For Benedict, Chabon in the second half of the collection seems to be "delving below the surface of his fluent, astonishingly vivid prose and reaching deeper into his characters."

Chabon, Michael. "Smashing the Dishes." Interview by Laurel Graeber. *The New York Times Book Review*, May 26, 1991, 7. This brief interview focuses on Chabon's art of storytelling. Basing his stories on "real episodes," Chabon explains that "you have these gives. But to write an interesting story you have to depart from them." Includes a photograph of Chabon.

Fowler, Douglas. "The Short Fiction of Michael Chabon: Nostalgia in the Very Young." *Studies in Short Fiction* 32 (Winter, 1995): 75-82. Suggests that Chabon's stories are best when he deals with memory and when he makes use of light comic irony and sophisticated prose. Argues that the tales in "The Lost World" sequence of *A Model World* are the best place to examine Chabon's exploration of the child within us all.

Giles, Jeff. "He's a Real Boy Wonder." *Newsweek* 125 (April 10, 1995): 76-77. Discusses Chabon's literary celebrity status in 1988 at the age of twenty-four after the publication of *The Mysteries of Pittsburgh*, which he wrote as a master's thesis. Discusses a number of Chabon projects, including screenplays.

See, Lisa. "Michael Chabon: Wonder Boy in Transition." *Publishers Weekly* 242 (April 10, 1995): 44-45. Discusses Chabon's rise to late 1980's "brat packer"; in this informal interview, Chabon discusses his struggles with his second novel and the pressures of being a successful young writer.

Terry Heller, updated by Nika Hoffman

RAYMOND CHANDLER

Born: Chicago, Illinois; July 23, 1888
Died: La Jolla, California; March 26, 1959

PRINCIPAL SHORT FICTION

Five Murderers, 1944
Five Sinister Characters, 1945
Finger Man and Other Stories, 1946
Red Wind, 1946
Spanish Blood, 1946
Trouble Is My Business, 1950
The Simple Art of Murder, 1950
Pick-up on Noon Street, 1952
Smart-Aleck Kill, 1953
Pearls Are a Nuisance, 1958
Killer in the Rain, 1964 (Philip Durham, editor)
The Smell of Fear, 1965
The Midnight Raymond Chandler, 1971

OTHER LITERARY FORMS

Raymond Chandler is best known for his hard-boiled detective novels featuring Philip Marlowe. Chandler often used material from his short stories to create the novels, and Philip Marlowe's character grew out of the various detectives in the short tales. This archetypal hero has been further popularized through many major motion pictures. Chandler wrote screenplays for six works by others. His works have been selected for Book-of-the-Month Club members, and his stories and novels have been collected in a number of editions. He also wrote criticism on the art of detective fiction and in his early years conventional poems and essays.

ACHIEVEMENTS

Raymond Chandler may undoubtedly be considered second only to Dashiell Hammett as the writer who raised the reputation of the hard-boiled detective novel from its humble origins in popular culture to the level of serious literature. The seven novels he wrote are classics of the genre; the ten films made from his novels are equally well known. Together, the novels and films have made Chandler's major literary creation, Philip Marlowe, one of America's most popular icons. Cynical, tough, yet curiously sentimental and moral, this detective figure seems particularly appealing as a lone fighter against heavy odds in a violent world.

Chandler's screenplay *The Blue Dahlia* (1946) won the Edgar Allan Poe Award from Mystery Writers of America and an Academy Award nomination in 1946. One of his seven novels, *The Long Goodbye* (1953), won another Edgar Allan Poe Award in 1954.

BIOGRAPHY

Raymond Thornton Chandler, although he was

born in Chicago and spent his first seven years in the Middle West, received an English Public School education (Dulwich College) when his mother took him to England after her divorce. He traveled in Europe, spent an unsatisfying few months in the British civil service, and set out to become a writer. After publishing a number of poems and essays, he returned to America in 1912. He worked at various jobs and in 1917 joined the Canadian Army and served in France. After the war, he became a successful oil executive in California and married Cissy Pascal, who was eighteen years his senior. Chandler's dissatisfaction and drinking left him jobless in 1932. He turned to writing again and became the best of the *Black Mask* pulp writers before turning to novels with *The Big Sleep* in 1939. He was a successful and highly paid Hollywood screenwriter throughout the 1940's. Following Cissy's death in 1954, Chandler resumed his rootless life and heavy drinking. He visited England several times. When he died he was president of the Mystery Writers of America and was at work on another Philip Marlowe novel.

Raymond Chandler (Library of Congress)

ANALYSIS

Joseph T. Shaw, editor of *Black Mask*, the leading pulp detective magazine of the 1930's, remarked upon receiving Raymond Chandler's first story that the author was either a genius or crazy. He must have decided in favor of genius, for he accepted "Blackmailers Don't Shoot" in 1933 and paid Chandler the standard rate of a penny a word, or $180.00.

Chandler reveals in his letters that he taught himself to write for the pulps by reading back issues. He gives full credit to Dashiell Hammett, who wrote stories that commented on contemporary life using the detective story or puzzle framework. Chandler, however, surpasses his mentor in his use of the language. His ability to hear the American vernacular and to transfer it onto the printed page may be his strongest point as a writer. This trait helps to explain Chandler's often aimless sentences and strange word order. His classical education in England made him aware of the finer points of language and of the uses of slang. His characters reveal themselves through their language. Since his fiction describes the interplay between levels or classes in society, the speech of his characters as identifying labels is paramount.

Chandler's major themes also deserve consideration. His close examination, in both short stories and novels, of society at large reveals a concern for humanity equal to that of Mark Twain. He wrote in almost every work of fiction about human behavior. True, his characters often came from the criminal element, but his works show that the criminal element (or at least the vices of that element) extends into all levels of society, that greed, pride, and violence have no basis in economic or social status. His revelation of Southern California of the 1930's to 1950's offers a view not found in other media of that era.

Chandler's ability to set a scene or mood is also remarkable. "Red Wind" takes its title from the prevailing weather phenomenon present at the time of the story.

There was a desert wind blowing that night. It was one of those hot dry Santa Anas that come down through the mountain passes and curl your hair and make your nerves jump and your skin itch. On nights like that every booze party ends in a fight. Meek little wives feel the edge of the carving knife and study their husbands' necks. Anything can happen.

Although the wind does not figure in the events of the story, it sets a mood in which the story seems plausible, in spite of several coincidences that the reader may wonder over. As if Chandler realizes this, he seems to joke with the reader:

> "There's a hell of a lot of coincidences in all this business," the big man said.
> "It's the hot wind," I grinned. "Everybody's screwy tonight."

Chandler never lets the reader wonder about a room or a house. The unusual Southern California locations for his scenes seem to be designed as if for a Hollywood set.

> We sat down and looked at each other across a dark floor, on which a few Navajo rugs and a few dark Turkish rugs made a decorating combination with some well-used overstuffed furniture. There was a fireplace, a small baby grand, a Chinese screen, a tall Chinese lantern on a teakwood pedestal, and gold net curtains against lattice windows. The windows to the south were open. A fruit tree with a white-washed trunk whipped about outside the screen, adding its bit to the noise from across the street.

Chandler felt that such detail helped to build character as well as set the scene. He considered that many readers wanted more than the barest plot filled with action, and his success bears him out.

Chandler's humor is an important element of his work. Perhaps realizing that stories filled with violence and murder need some relief, he frequently allows his narration to entertain the reader. When a man is shot in a bar in "Red Wind," Dalmas relates that "the guy took a week to fall down." In describing the beautiful girl in the story, he tells readers: "She had brown wavy hair under a wide-brimmed straw hat with a velvet band and loose bow. She had wide blue eyes and eyelashes that didn't quite reach her chin." As a car leaves the scene of a murder, Dalmas "got its license number the way I got my first million." He doesn't "like being a witness" because "the

pay's too low." The humor presented through the first-person narrator makes him human; he remains a believable, if somewhat exaggerated, character; and he remains a stabilizing force in an otherwise inhuman world. Chandler was aware of the extent of the exaggeration called for by the formula. He wrote "Pearls Are a Nuisance" as a deliberate parody of the type.

Chandler's private eyes invariably find much more action and a more involved plot than the reader suspects, a fact which makes his stories difficult to synopsize. The detective follows one lead to another and ends up walking a narrow path between the mob and the police as new characters appear on the scene. Although the citizen being protected is usually female, Chandler was not afraid to include a woman as the villain. Carol Donovan in "Goldfish" is meaner and tougher than her male rivals, but Carmady (another Marlowe prototype) is equal to the task. Someone else shoots Carol, but only after Carmady has slugged her in the jaw to provide the opportunity.

Chandler is best known as a writer of detective fiction, and he deserves much credit for the phenomenal growth of the genre in popular literature, but his contributions to serious literature and film continue to be recognized by readers and scholars. His revelation of Southern California to the world is unique among his writing peers; his view of human behavior moves his stories into a context encompassing all of the corrupt world of his vision; and his influence will continue to be felt as long as detective stories and crime tales are written.

"BLACKMAILERS DON'T SHOOT"

In his early stories, Chandler attempted to master the hard-boiled style of writing while still saying something of value about society and human behavior. "Blackmailers Don't Shoot" is a story about an actress, Rhonda Farr, who is being blackmailed because of a bundle of reckless letters she wrote. The detective character in the story, Mallory, is hired by the actor-turned-gangster recipient of the letters to get them back and to identify the blackmailer. The chase leads Mallory, who is imported to Los Angeles from Chicago for the case, to crooked cops, Rhonda Farr's crooked lawyer, and assorted gangsters. Four men are killed in a short space of time; Rhonda Farr is kidnapped (by the blackmailers) and recovered (by Mallory). The actress turns out to want as much publicity as possible, and she seems only slightly penitent in her reaction to the beatings, killings, and trouble created by her letters. Landry, the actor-gangster, seems to have created the whole caper in an attempt to recapture the affections of Rhonda Farr. In the aftermath of this plot, two more hoods are killed and one wounded, and Mallory is wounded. He gets a clean slate from the local police, who manage to tie up all the loose ends with ease, including a complete cover-up of the illegal activities of their own men. Mallory decides that he might stay in Los Angeles instead of returning to Chicago.

The action of this story is fast, furious, and somewhat confusing. Mallory uses some deductive reasoning to figure out the details of the case, but he is much more involved in threatening, hitting, and shooting than in deducing. The story exposes the unreasonable desire for publicity in Hollywood, even bad publicity. "You don't know much about this Hollywood racket, do you, darling?" Rhonda Farr chides Mallory. "Publicity has to hurt a bit out here. Otherwise nobody believes it."

The corrupt elements of society are well represented here as well. Practically every character who enters the story has a gun and is willing to use force to have his way over someone else. Chandler wrote that it is the "smell of fear" in the detective tale that ties it to real life. His chief target for criticism seems to be those who, by whatever means, try to rule others unjustly. Since the world of the criminal is built around injustice—toward individuals, society, or its institutions—Chandler found a remarkable wealth of material about which to write.

In the midst of the chaotic world of Los Angeles crime and violence, there is always the good man, the man who tries to bring order. As Chandler wrote later: "Down these mean streets a man must go who is not himself mean, who is neither tarnished nor afraid." Mallory considers himself "the nearest thing to an honest stranger," and he is basically upright. The Chicago police verify that he has "a clean sheet—damn' clean."

Mallory is the direct predecessor of Philip Marlowe, Chandler's famous private eye. Marlowe did not appear as the central detective character until Chandler began writing novels in 1939. His detective in the earlier short stories—whatever his name—is, however, usually the same man. Chandler probably found it a minor task to change most of the names to Philip Marlowe in later stories and collected printings of the early stories.

"RED WIND"

Thus John Dalmas in "Red Wind" becomes Marlowe in later printings—the only change, incidentally, in the story. It is not true, as some have reported, that all book versions of the stories use the revised Marlowe name. The collection *Red Wind* (World Publishing Company, 1946) keeps the original names used in magazine texts.

Chandler is a moral writer. His detective, even before Marlowe, is a man who sees the truth and works to set things right, often without pay and always alone. He is disappointed in himself and in the world when he is unable to succeed. John Dalmas in "Red Wind" suffers dejection at the breakup of a marriage, even though he knows the husband and wife have been equally unfaithful. As a final act of decency, he protects the wife from the knowledge that her dead lover had been "just another four-flusher." Dalmas substitutes a set of obviously fake pearls for the seemingly real pearls given her. Dalmas/Marlowe protects her memory of her lover at considerable expense and trouble to himself. In so doing, he assumes the grief, which we see as he throws the pearls into the Pacific one by one.

"GUNS AT CYRANO'S"

An unusual character for Chandler is Ted Malvern in "Guns at Cyrano's." Unlike the typical hard-boiled detective, Malvern is wealthy and essentially idle. He is generous with his wealth, because, as we learn at the story's conclusion, he considers it "dirty money." The money is inherited from his father, who made it

out of crooked sewerage and paving contracts, out of gambling concessions, appointment payoffs, even vice, I daresay. And when it was made and there was nothing to do but sit and look at it, he died and left it to me. It hasn't brought me any fun either. I always hope it's going to, but it never does.

Malvern compensates, in his own hard-boiled fashion, for living on his father's "crooked dough" by consorting with the rougher elements in society and helping to rid the world of at least one crooked politician.

THE CHANDLER DETECTIVE

Chandler's detective (even when he is not a licensed private investigator) works against tremendous odds to clean up a small corner of the world. He seldom gets paid, he almost never gets the girl, and he knows that the next case will produce just as many seedy and malevolent characters to be dealt with. He does not contemplate his old age or retirement. His violent world is not provided with such sureties. He knows he is alone and that he will probably remain so.

The hard-boiled formula as created by Dashiell Hammett and Raymond Chandler includes an almost automatic confrontation with the police. Thus the detective is the true guardian of morality, between abusive police and equally abusive criminals. He risks arrest and beatings from the former for not revealing his clients' interests, and he risks physical violence and death from the latter for daring to enter the nether world of mobsters and crooks—which he inevitably must do in the course of his work.

His home is not his castle. He lives alone, usually in a spare, if not spartan, apartment. He is likely to find either a pair of unfriendly and incompetent police detectives or a mob of violent gangsters in his living room when he arrives home intent only on a slug of whiskey and much-needed sleep. His office is equally spartan, with no secretary and no fellow workers. He has a waiting room, a desk—with an "office bottle" in one drawer—and a telephone.

Many writers of mystery and detective fiction have been influenced by Raymond Chandler. The violence visited upon Chandler's detective hero may be the source of the almost constant threats, beatings, and incarcerations used by Dick Francis. The security—or lack of it—of the home may help to explain the elaborate system of checks that Travis McGee has

installed on his houseboat to see if anyone is or has been aboard. Robert B. Parker has said that he learned to write detective novels by reading Hammett and Chandler.

Chandler has placed the hard-boiled detective firmly in American literature as a remarkable and enduring character type. The many imitations, exaggerations, and developments upon Philip Marlowe speak well of his profound influence on fiction and the popular arts. Chandler's importance and his craft do not stop there, however; Chandler wanted to be considered a serious writer. He was pleased that the British critics considered him a major writer, and he would no doubt be pleased now to know that he is ever being "discovered" by new generations of American readers and critics.

OTHER MAJOR WORKS

LONG FICTION: *The Big Sleep*, 1939; *Farewell, My Lovely*, 1940; *The High Window*, 1942; *The Lady in the Lake*, 1943; *The Little Sister*, 1949; *The Long Goodbye*, 1953; *Playback*, 1958.

NONFICTION: *The Blue Dahlia*, 1946 (Matthew J. Bruccoli, editor); *Raymond Chandler Speaking*, 1962 (Dorothy Gardiner and Katherine Sorely Walker, editors); *Chandler Before Marlowe: Raymond Chandler's Early Prose and Poetry*, 1973 (Matthew J. Bruccoli, editor); *The Notebooks of Raymond Chandler and English Summer*, 1976 (Frank MacShane, editor); *Selected Letters of Raymond Chandler*, 1981 (Frank MacShane, editor).

BIBLIOGRAPHY

Hamilton, Cynthia S. "Raymond Chandler." In *Western and Hard-Boiled Detective Fiction: From High Noon to Midnight*. Iowa City: University of Iowa Press, 1987. This study provides an unusual insight into Chandler's detective fiction from the historical and generic perspective of the American Western novel. It includes three chapters on the study of formula literature. Complemented by a bibliography and an index.

Hiney, Tom. *Raymond Chandler: A Biography*. New York: Atlantic Monthly Press, 1997. A brief biography of Chandler that discusses his education in

England, his relationship to Los Angeles, and the plots and characters of his most important detective novels and stories.

Jameson, F. R. "On Raymond Chandler." In *The Poetics of Murder: Detective Fiction and Literary Theory*, edited by Glenn W. Most and William W. Stowe. San Diego: Harcourt Brace Jovanovich, 1983. This critic starts with the observation that Chandler's English upbringing in essence gave him an outsider's view of American life and language. A useful discussion of the portrait of American society that emerges from Chandler's works.

Knight, Stephen. "'A Hard Cheerfulness': An Introduction to Raymond Chandler." In *American Crime Fiction: Studies in the Genre*, edited by Brian Docherty. New York: St. Martin's Press, 1988. This is a discussion of the values and attitudes that define Philip Marlowe and that make him unusual in the genre of hard-boiled American crime fiction.

Lehman, David. "Hammett and Chandler." In *The Perfect Murder: A Study in Detection*. New York: Free Press, 1989. Chandler is represented in this comprehensive study of detective fiction as one of the authors who brought out the parable at the heart of mystery fiction. A useful volume in its breadth and its unusual appendices, one a list of further reading, the other, an annotated list of the critic's favorite mysteries. Includes two indexes, one of concepts, and one of names and titles.

Simpson, Hassell A. "'So Long, Beautiful Hunk': Ambiguous Gender and Songs of Parting in Raymond Chandler's Fictions." *Journal of Popular Culture* 28 (Fall, 1994): 37-48. Discusses the sexual ambiguity of Chandler's Philip Marlowe.

Skinner, Robert E. *The Hard-Boiled Explicator: A Guide to the Study of Dashiell Hammett, Raymond Chandler, and Ross Macdonald*. Metuchen, N.J.: Scarecrow Press, 1985. This volume is indispensable for the scholar interested in tracking down unpublished dissertations as well as mainstream criticism. Brief introductions of each author are followed by annotated bibliographies of books, articles, and reviews.

Steiner, T. R. "The Origin of Raymond Chandler's 'Mean Streets.'" *ANQ*, n.s. 7 (October, 1994): 225-227. Suggests that the origin of the expression "mean streets" is Arthur Morrison's *Tales of Mean Streets*, a classic of late Victorian slum literature. The phrase referred to the lack of purpose and joy in the East End of London.

Van Dover, J. K., ed. *The Critical Response to Raymond Chandler*. Westport, Conn.: Greenwood Press, 1995. A collection of essays examining Chandler's literary output. Includes bibliographical references and an index.

Thomas D. Lane, updated by Shakuntala Jayaswal

LAN SAMANTHA CHANG

Born: Appleton, Wisconsin; 1965

PRINCIPAL SHORT FICTION

Hunger: A Novella and Stories, 1998

OTHER LITERARY FORMS

Hunger: A Novella and Stories is Lan Samantha Chang's first book.

ACHIEVEMENTS

Lan Samantha Chang was awarded a Wallace Stegner Fellowship at Stanford University in 1993. "Pippa's Story" was selected for the annual publication *The Best American Short Stories* in 1994; "The Eve of the Spirit Festival" appeared in *The Best American Short Stories* in 1996. She won a Truman Capote Fellowship, a National Endowment for the Arts grant, and first place for fiction in The Bay Area Book Reviewers Association Awards.

BIOGRAPHY

Lan Samantha Chang's parents both lived in China during the Japanese occupation of that country in World War II; they came to the United States separately, met in New York, and settled in Appleton, Wisconsin, where Chang was born in 1965. Following her parents' wishes, Chang attended Yale University as a premedical student but changed her mind and earned a degree in East Asian studies. She then attended Harvard University's Kennedy School of Government; however, after taking a number of classes in economics, she decided she wanted to be a writer and began taking creative writing classes in Boston and later earned an M.F.A. at the University of Iowa. She attended Stanford University for two years as a Wallace Stegner Fellow and stayed on there as a teacher.

ANALYSIS

Among the almost universally positive reviews that Lan Samantha Chang's first book received, there were some that inevitably compared her to other Asian women writers, such as Amy Tan and Maxine Hong Kingston. It is true that Chang charts some of the same thematic territory as did those established novelists, especially the familiar Asian American conflict between parents and children, the Old World and the New. However, those reviewers who liken Chang to Bernard Malamud or James Joyce are perhaps more accurate. Like those masters of the modern short story, Chang is a consummate stylist, more concerned with tightly structured aesthetic form than with abstract social issues, such as marginality, cultural diversity, and the status of the immigrant.

Also like past masters of the short story, Chang is often oblique in her narrative presentation, frequently situating the heart of the story in places other than where the reader first assumes it to be. Thus, while the title novella *Hunger* seems to be about the ambitious hunger of the husband, it is really about the lyrically implied hunger of the wife; and while the prize-winning "Pippa's Story" seems to be about the escape of the daughter into the future, it is really about the hold the mother has on her through the past.

The fact that Chang's stories have been received with wide praise for their universality, lyricism, and formal control rather than for their cultural particularity and postcolonial political stance perhaps signals that, in the late 1990's, the multicultural and the marginal are not praised for exoticism alone; if Chang's reception is indicative, the focus in contemporary fiction seems to be on what unites us as human beings rather than what separates us as multicultural individuals.

HUNGER

More than half of Chang's first collection of stories is taken up by this novella of a Chinese immigrant violinist, his wife, and their two daughters. Although the plot focuses on Tian's "hunger" to be a professional musician in America, the psychological interest of the novella centers on the narrator, his wife Min, on whom Tian's passionate desire has the greatest impact. Tian's account of swimming half a mile across the Taiwan Strait from mainland China to a refugee ship, holding his precious violin out of the water, is a central image of the hunger at the core of the story, but Min's hunger, revealed indirectly by her simple, lyrical voice, resonates throughout the story and colors everything. Although Tian is obsessively passionate, first about playing the violin himself and then about compelling his daughters to learn to play, it is Min, hungry for the love denied to her by her self-obsessed family, who lives her life destined to receive very little of what her mother calls *yuanfen*— "the apportionment of love" destined for one in the world.

What also makes the story more than a domestic tragedy of one man's unfulfilled immigrant ambitions is Min's sense of the magic and mystery of human passion and transcendent reality; she is like a finely tuned violin, quiescent until her own passion is evoked. When Tian gives up on becoming a professional musician and loses his job at the school where he has been teaching, he turns his attentions to Anna, the oldest daughter, only to discover that she has a poor ear for music. By next directing his teaching attentions to Ruth, the younger daughter, he puts Anna in the same situation Min has endured, yearning for his love. Min identifies both with Anna, who feels shut out, and with Ruth, who hates the violin and wants to leave their closed-in world for someplace else.

The story works itself out in classically tragic fashion: Ruth runs away; Tian dies unfulfilled; Anna seems destined to be alone; Min, ill with cancer, has only the past from which to gain sustenance. However, in spite of this darkness at the end of *Hunger*, what remains is Min's endurance. Although she fears that there may come a time when no one will remember their lives, the story she has just told is a guarantee that this is not true.

"THE UNFORGETTING"

This is Chang's most explicit, almost parabolic, treatment of the familiar Asian immigrant story—the tension between hanging on to the traditions of the Old World and wholeheartedly embracing those of the New. The Hwangs are the prototypical Asian family, who move to the heartland of the Midwest to forget what they no longer need to know and learn what they do need to know. When their son Charles is born, they forget even more, replacing all useless memories with thoughts of him. Still, their memories persist, the world of their past growing larger and larger. When Charles decides to go away to school, the mother blames the father for making him like other Americans who leave their parents and create their own homes. In a bitter scene in which they blame each other for the loss of Charles, the couple break every plate in the kitchen. At the end of the story they both realize that the world they once knew now lives only inside them and that they are the end of that world. "They had no solace, and no burden, but each other."

"THE EVE OF THE SPIRIT FESTIVAL"

Chang again presents the conflict between generations in this story, although not in such stark terms as in "The Unforgetting." The Chinese father has aspirations for academic promotion and invites his colleagues over for drinks, "watching the Americans and studying to become one." As in *Hunger*, two daughters are involved: Claudia, who narrates the story, and Emily, who berates her father for mimicking the Americans. Although Claudia tries to be a good daughter, Emily puts on makeup, dresses in pants, and goes out with boys against her father's wishes. After Emily has gone away to college and the father has died, the focus of the story shifts to the two sisters—the good daughter, who has stayed home, and the prodigal one, who has returned. In the climactic scene, Emily asks Claudia to cut off her long, black hair, and Claudia, who has scraggly, brownish hair, enjoys it. When she is awakened that night by Emily's screams, Claudia understands that her father's ghost will never visit her, but she lies awake waiting anyway.

"PIPPA'S STORY"

"Pippa's Story" is the only story in *Hunger* that is not based on immigrants in America. Although the plot centers on a young woman who leaves her Chinese village to work for a wealthy family in Shanghai, the thematic heart of the story is the relationship between the girl and her mother, who stays home. The mother works in charms and is a powerful figure in her village; the girl thinks she will disappear if she cannot escape her mother's shadow. When she leaves, the mother gives her a small stone and makes her promise to find the heart of the house where Wen, the man for whom she is going to work, lives and to hide the stone there. Although the girl does not know the story behind the promise, it is clear that even though she is leaving, the shadow of her mother accompanies her.

The daughter gets rid of the stone when she arrives, but later she hears the story behind it—how Wen desired her mother when they were young and murdered her father just before she was born. Although she insists that she will not keep her promise to her mother, that none of the story has anything to do with her, she begins to think that even her flight from her mother fits into some incomprehensible design. She finds the stone and, when Wen sexually assaults a friend, hides it in his bed.

The story mixes history and folklore; when the Communists enter the city, they execute Wen, as a result of either the mother's curse or Wen's political leanings. The narrator says her story is a small one compared with the larger events of the Communist occupation of China. However, in its delicate treatment of the past's impingement on the present and in its complex combination of the political, the personal, and the supernatural, the story reflects, the narrator says, how our buried pasts are like ginseng roots, all with different shapes.

BIBLIOGRAPHY

Carter, Emily. "Chang Debuts with Uneven Stories." *Minneapolis Star Tribune*, November 22, 1998, p. 18F. In practically the only negative review of *Hunger*, Carter says that Chang's writing is basic, writing-school fare and that her psychological insights are simple; argues that Chang stays close to the themes of assimilation and forgetfulness with which immigrant parents want to escape the past while the children want to understand it.

Chang, Lan Samantha. "Out of Parents' Silence Comes a Daughter's Tales." Interview by Scott Martelle. *Los Angeles Times*, December 21, 1998, p. E3. In this interview/feature story, Chang talks about her parents' reticence about the past and her

creation of stories that allowed her to work through questions about them. Martelle discusses the universality of the stories, which Chang says are about things that happen over and over again. Chang discusses the conflict in her stories between children who wish to know their parents and parents who want to make new lives in America for their children.

Messud, Claire. "A Hole in Our House." *The New York Times*, October 25, 1998, pp. 7, 24. In this review, Messud says that Chang offers no easy resolution for the immigrant experience; says her stories express internal struggles in a complex way; discusses several stories, praising Chang's ability to create concrete descriptions of the abstract.

Rubin, Sylvia. "A Hunger for Heritage." *The San Francisco Chronicle*, December 2, 1998, p. E1. In this biographical sketch/review/interview, Chang says she writes from a position of deep incomprehension; Chang discusses how her parents' secrets about their past have allowed her to use her imagination to re-create that past for herself. Also describes how her parents disapproved of her decision to be a writer rather than a doctor or a lawyer.

Ryan, Suzanne C. "Immigrants in *Hunger* Starved of Their Past." *The Boston Globe*, October 9, 1998, p. D10. Notes that while the stories focus on the Chinese immigrant experience, they could really be about any race or nationality; Ryan says the desire for love, prosperity, parental approval, and strong family ties in Chang's stories is universal. Notes the common theme in the stories of well-meaning parents who, despite sacrifices, cannot give their children what they need most—a firm foundation of cultural and family history.

Salm, Arthur. "Author Taps into Immigrant Experiences." *The San Diego Union-Tribune*, November 15, 1998, p. E4. An interview/biographical sketch in which Chang talks about what she thinks is central to the immigrant experience—the artifacts of personal history—and laments that she has nothing to represent her grandparents' lives in China. Chang discusses the way she writes, the relationship between the short story and the novel, and her work on her first novel.

Wan, Helen C. "Children of Broken Dreams." *The Washington Post*, October 18, 1998, p. X11. Wan argues that Chang's stories go beyond the current appeal of ethnicity and are truly universal in their significance; discusses how the stories focus on fragility and family relationships rather than merely the immigrant experience; argues that they emphasize universal themes of loneliness, longing, unfulfilled ambition, love and loss, and memory and forgetting.

Charles E. May

FRED CHAPPELL

Born: Canton, North Carolina; May 28, 1936

PRINCIPAL SHORT FICTION

Moments of Light, 1980
More Shapes than One, 1991
The Lodger, 1993

OTHER LITERARY FORMS

Fred Chappell is an award-winning poet whose works include the four-volume *Midquest* cycle and two collections of critical essays on poetry. He has written eight novels, including a quartet featuring the multigenerational Kirkman family: *I Am One of You Forever* (1985), *Brighten the Corner Where You Are* (1989), *Farewell, I'm Bound to Leave You* (1996), and *Look Back All the Green Valley* (1999).

ACHIEVEMENTS

Fred Chappell has been honored with grants from both the Rockefeller Foundation and the National Institute of Arts and Letters. He was awarded the Prix de Meilleur des Lettres Étranger by the French Academy in 1971 for his novel *Dagon* (1968), the Sir Walter Raleigh Award in 1973 for his novel *The Gaudy Place* (1972), and the Bollingen Prize in poetry from the Yale University Library in 1985. He received the Ragan-Rubin Award from the North Carolina English Teachers Association and the Thomas H. Carter award. He is also a recipient of the Ingersoll Foundation's T. S. Eliot Prize for Creative Writing and a two-time recipient of the World Fantasy Award for short fiction (1992, 1994). His poetry is the subject of a tribute anthology of essays, *Dream Garden: The Poetic Vision of Fred Chappell* (1997).

BIOGRAPHY

Fred Davis Chappell was born in Canton, North Carolina, on May 28, 1936, and was raised on his grandparents' farm in the mountains outside Asheville. He attended Canton High School and enrolled at Duke University but was expelled at the beginning of his junior year for misconduct. In 1959, he married his high school sweetheart, Susan Nicholls, and the following year their son Heath was born. He returned to Duke to finish his studies and graduated with a B.A. in English in 1961.

Chappell enrolled in the graduate English program at Duke on a three-year National Defense Education Act fellowship and was completing his master's thesis when he was approached by a New York publisher to write a novel. *It Is Time, Lord*, which he wrote in six weeks, was published in 1963. The following year he published his first short story in *The Saturday Evening Post* and received his M.A. Chappell began teaching English at the University of North Carolina in Greensboro, a position he was offered while still a graduate student at Duke. The World Between the Eyes, the first of more than a dozen volumes of his poetry, was published in 1971.

ANALYSIS

Like his contemporaries Reynolds Price and Peter Taylor, Fred Chappell draws on his rural southern background for much of his fiction. However, Chappell is not easily pigeonholed as a "southern writer." His short fiction includes, in addition to tales in the southern folk tradition, period stories with European settings, and tales of the supernatural. The forms Chappell's stories take also vary widely, from realistic drama to biblical allegory, gothic fantasy, and whimsical humor.

Most of Chappell's stories are character-driven and concerned with personal ideals challenged by private experience. John Lang, in his essay "Illuminating the Stricken World: Fred Chappell's *Moments of Light*," locates the dramatic core of Chappell's stories in the "conflict between transcendent and temporal values" that ensues when characters cling to noble beliefs that are either naïve or outmoded in the world at large. This conflict manifests as a tension between opposites incarnated in the story's different characters: the traditional and the modern, the sacred and the profane, the civilized and the primitive, the artistic and the scientific, the rational and the irrational. Chappell's stories often focus on family relationships, notably fathers and sons embarked on rites of passage from childhood innocence to adult experience. Notwithstanding the "fallen world" that Lang feels this clash of values presupposes, Chappell's outlook is essentially optimistic. His innocent characters are rarely crushed by their experiences. They emerge edified, rather than disillusioned, and with a broadened base of experience.

"THE MAKER OF ONE COFFIN"

"The Maker of One Coffin" is typical of Chappell's tales in the southern folk tradition, presenting a slice of rural life with gentle humor that softens its account of young Jess's passage from childhood innocence to adult experience through an early encounter with death. Uncle Runkin, a visiting relative from Jess's mother's side of the family, is a death-obsessed man who sleeps in a coffin and reads tombstone epitaphs for amusement. Joe Robert, Jess's practical-minded father, teases Uncle Runkin relentlessly for his morbidness. Uncle Runkin and Joe Robert represent the opposite extremes of attitudes toward death between which Jess must choose or find a middle ground. As a joke, Jess and his father

Fred Chappell (©Miriam Berkley)

put a skeleton borrowed from the local school in the coffin, hoping to scare Uncle Runkin.

The next day, Runkin gives no clue that the prank has worked, but the skeleton is missing. Jess sneaks into Runkin's room to look for the skeleton and, attracted to Runkin's coffin, climbs into it and has a comforting vision of death, which is interrupted when the startled Runkin walks in on him. Uncle Runkin leaves the next day, to his and the family's relief, and the mystery of the skeleton is solved when it is discovered that he has disarticulated it and secreted all of the bones in 3,034 hiding places around the house. An older Jess muses how, for the next twenty years, "When you went looking for a Mason jar rubber or a length of string you would turn up a toebone or a metacarpal"—a lesson, perhaps, that even when we choose to ignore it, death *is* an inescapable part of life.

"BLUE DIVE"

The themes of Chappell's stories often resonate with myth and legend, giving them a timelessness. "Blue Dive," set in a southern roadhouse in the 1970's, is a variation on the folktale of John Henry in which Chappell explores the clash of traditional and modern values. Elderly African American blues guitarist Stovebolt Johnson arrives in a small southern town to take a job offer made three years earlier to perform regularly at the Blue Dive roadhouse. The roadhouse has since been sold to Locklear Hawkins, a progressive, young, African American man, who prefers a jukebox for music. Stovebolt offers to provide an evening of free entertainment to prove that he can outplay the jukebox. He gives an inspired performance that pleases the Blue Dive patrons, but Locklear is implacable: He wants nothing to do with Stovebolt and the old ways of southern blacks that Stovebolt and his blues music represent. Stovebolt leaves dejected but dignified, knowing that, like John Henry, he has outperformed the machine. The story ends with him composing a blues song about his trial at the Blue Dive, adding a new chapter of his own to the legacy of misery and suffering memorialized in the blues.

"MOMENTS OF LIGHT"

"Moments of Light" is one of several period stories in which Chappell uses compassionate and sympathetic portraits of historical personalities to explore universal human concerns and ideals. Events center on a meeting between the composer Franz Joseph Haydn and his contemporary, astronomer William Herschel, both expatriate Germans living in England in the latter half of the eighteenth century. Both men are geniuses in their fields and share similar tastes and interests, but Haydn postpones the much anticipated meeting with the astronomer out of his unspoken fear that Herschel's perspective-shifting discoveries are inimical to the principles of harmony on which Haydn's music is based. At the meeting, Haydn finds Herschel a gracious host with a genuine respect for what he calls "the Harmony of the Universe." When Herschel treats Haydn to a demonstration of his telescope, Haydn feels his spirit drawn from his body to the remote celestial body he is view-

ing. There he discovers a world of indescribable beauty that supports a harmonious music equivalent to his own. Back in his own body, Haydn realizes that Herschel's discoveries describe a vast and orderly cosmic score in which Haydn's art and Herschel's science contribute équally to the harmonic music of the spheres. Coincidentally or not, Haydn composes some of his most inspired music in the years that follow.

"THE LODGER"

Winner of the World Fantasy Award, "The Lodger" is a humorous fantasy that allegorically addresses one of Chappell's favorite themes, the challenges that the mundane world poses to the creative spirit. Librarian Robert Ackley is an average man with ordinary tastes and a boring job transferring card catalog entries to a computer system. A book lover with wide-ranging interests, he chances upon a volume of verse by the obscure early twentieth century poet Lyman Scoresby and accidentally resurrects his spirit. Scoresby, an arrogant man with an exaggerated sense of his own importance, lodges in Ackley's subconscious and tries to turn Ackley into an appropriate vessel for his soul by subliminally cultivating decadent passions, such as a taste for absinthe and a desire for unconventional sex. Ackley attempts to exorcise Scoresby by indulging in behavior that he hopes will disgust the poet: eating junk food, watching bad television programs, and reading poetry worse than Scoresby's. Ackley succeeds only when he begins reading postmodern literary criticism that is more impenetrable and self-important than Scoresby's verse. Surprisingly, he discovers a latent talent for such writing and becomes a critic himself. Having exorcised the poet from his soul, he becomes a crippled version of the poet he might have been.

MORE SHAPES THAN ONE

The title of *More Shapes than One* derives from John Milton's essay *Areopagitica* (1644) and refers to the variety of forms Truth takes in the world. The majority of the stories in the book are fantasies, yet as the title suggests, fantasy is but one of a variety of possible approaches Chappell uses to explore the ideas that inform his fiction.

A theme that predominates in the thirteen stories

is the fallen world in which ideals of beauty and order have been subverted. Characters who seek to transcend the corrupted forms of these ideals find themselves thwarted and often forced to make compromises. The first story, "Linnaeus Forgets," sets the tone for the tales that follow. It tells of eighteenth century botanist Carl Linnaeus, who is ridiculed by his colleagues as prurient for his sexual classifications of plants. Linnaeus is vindicated during an experience he later dismisses as a dream in which he studies an exotic plant and discovers an entire world in its leaves that transcends human notions of morality. This theme finds its most exquisite expression in the World Fantasy Award-winning story "The Somewhere Doors," about an underappreciated writer of fantasy and science-fiction stories who is told by a mysterious visitor that sometime in the future he will be given a choice of two doors, each of which leads to a different reality. The writer spends much of his life waiting expectantly to see the doors, only to realize years later that he has already explored the possibilities each offers but at the expense of "the entrance to the world in which he already lived." Although much has passed him by, he remains hopeful that "much awaited him still."

The book's more sober efforts are counterbalanced by an equal number of comical treatments of the same ideas. In "The Adder," a book of occult knowledge manifests its corrupting power by poisoning the text of any book shelved next to it, turning Milton's beautifully measured verse into drunken doggerel that gets laughably worse each time the narrator inspects it. "Mankind Journeys Through Forests of Symbols" grapples with the idealized in a banal setting, imagining some of the problems a rural police force might encounter trying to get rid of a symbolist who materializes in the middle of the main highway leading into town.

OTHER MAJOR WORKS

LONG FICTION: *It Is Time, Lord*, 1963; *The Inkling*, 1965; *Dagon*, 1968; *The Gaudy Place*, 1972; *I Am One of You Forever*, 1985; *Brighten the Corner Where You Are*, 1989; *Farewell, I'm Bound to Leave You*, 1996; *Look Back All the Green Valley*, 1999.

POETRY: *The World Between the Eyes*, 1971; *River*, 1975; *The Man Twice Married to Fire*, 1977; *Bloodfire*, 1978; *Awakening to Music*, 1979; *Wind Mountain*, 1979; *Earthsleep*, 1980; *Driftlake: A Lieder Cycle*, 1981; *Midquest*, 1981 (includes *River*, 1975; *Bloodfire*, 1978; *Wind Mountain*, 1979; *Earthsleep*, 1980); *Castle Tzingal*, 1984; *Source*, 1986; *First and Last Words*, 1989; *C: Poems*, 1993; *Spring Garden: New and Selected Poems*, 1995; *Family Gathering*, 2000.

NONFICTION: *Plow Naked: Selected Writings on Poetry*, 1993; *A Way of Happening: Observations of Contemporary Poetry*, 1998.

MISCELLANEOUS: *The Fred Chappell Reader*, 1987.

BIBLIOGRAPHY

Broughton, Irv. "Fred Chappell." In *The Writer's Mind: Interviews with American Authors*. Vol. 3. Fayetteville: University of Arkansas Press, 1990. Far-ranging interview in which Chappell discusses influences on his writing and the differences between writing fiction and poetry. Discussion of his short fiction touches upon his historical short stories as attempts to liberate historical personalities from the history books and make them seem living human beings.

Chappell, Fred. "First Attempts." *Turnstile* (1992): 71-84. Discusses the changes that being objective about subjective feelings makes in a writer and how a young writer comes to appreciate this. As a young man, Chappell wrote science-fiction stories because "plotting real experiences proved impossible; plotting what I made up proved to be fairly easy." Once he learned how to combine analysis with vision, his interest shifted from stories of the fantastic to stories based on his personal life.

Chappell, Fred. "Fred Chappell." Interview by Tersh Palmer. *Appalachian Journal* (Summer, 1992): 402-410. Interview that touches on all aspects of Chappell's creative efforts, including his poetry and novels. Of his short fiction, Chappell observes that critics tend to divide his work into realistic stories and fantasies, but he sees "no need to distinguish between what is imaginary and what is objective . . . both ways of writing are ways to try to deal with reality on the plane of literature."

Dillard, Annie. Foreword to *Moments of Light*. Raleigh, N.C.: New South Company, 1980. Critical exegesis of the stories in Chappell's first collection, which Dillard interprets as a history of human experience. In Dillard's view, the parable-like stories in the first half of the book establish a theoretical and historical framework for the morally complex stories with contemporary settings that make up the second half. Recurring themes in the stories include one's search for a just moral order in a fallen world, one's longing for transcendence of the temporal world, and one's use of art to reconcile the "hope of harmony with his experience of chaos."

Dziemianowicz, Stefan. "Fred Chappell." In *The St. James Guide to Horror, Ghost and Gothic Writers*, edited by David A. Pringle. Detroit, Mich.: St. James, 1998. Brief exploration of Chappell's weird fiction and his debt to H. P. Lovecraft in his novel *Dagon* and his short stories "Weird Tales" and "The Adder." Discusses Chappell's work as an extension of the southern gothic tradition.

Lang, John. "Illuminating the Stricken World: Fred Chappell's *Moments of Light*." *South Central Review* (Winter, 1986): 95-103. Close reading of Chappell's first short-fiction collection, *Moments of Light*, the eleven stories of which the author views as interrelated by the themes of lost innocence and the quest for justice. Follows the arc the stories describe as they move from biblical allegory to historical parable and finally to contemporary realism. Concludes that Chappell's stories all elaborate the concept of a fallen world in which humanity is forever seeking transcendence.

Stefan Dziemianowicz

GEOFFREY CHAUCER

Born: London(?), England; c. 1343
Died: London, England; October 25(?), 1400

PRINCIPAL SHORT FICTION

Book of the Duchess, c. 1370
Romaunt of the Rose, c. 1370 (translation, possibly not by Chaucer)
Hous of Fame, 1372-1380
The Legends of St. Cecilia, 1372-1380 (later used as "The Second Nun's Tale")
Tragedies of Fortune, 1372-1380 (later used as "The Monk's Tale")
Anelida and Arcite, c. 1380
Parlement of Foules, 1380
Palamon and Ersyte, 1380-1386 (later used as "The Knight's Tale")
Legend of Good Women, 1380-1386
Troilus and Criseyde, 1382
The Canterbury Tales, 1387-1400

OTHER LITERARY FORMS

In addition to the works listed above, Geoffrey Chaucer composed *Boece* (c. 1380), a translation of Boethius's *The Consolation of Philosophy* (523), which Boethius wrote while in prison. Chaucer also wrote an astrological study, *A Treatise on the Astrolabe* (1387-1392), and a miscellaneous volume entitled *Works* (1957).

ACHIEVEMENTS

Geoffrey Chaucer is generally agreed to be the most important writer in English literature before William Shakespeare. Recognized internationally in his own time as the greatest of English poets and dubbed "the father of English poetry" by John Dryden as early as 1700, his central position in the development of English literature and even of the English language is perhaps more secure today than it has ever been. One of the keys to Chaucer's contin-

Geoffrey Chaucer (Library of Congress)

ued critical success is the scope and diversity of his work, which extends from romance to tragedy, from sermon to dream vision, from pious saints' lives to bawdy *fabliaux*. Readers from every century have found something new in Chaucer and learned something about themselves.

BIOGRAPHY

Household records seem to indicate that as a boy, Geoffrey Chaucer served as a page for the Countess of Ulster, wife of Edward III's son Lionel, Duke of Clarence. Chaucer undoubtedly learned French and Latin as a youth, to which languages he later added Italian. Well versed in both science and pseudo-science, Chaucer was familiar with physics, medicine, astronomy, and alchemy. Spending most of his life in government service, he made many trips abroad on diplomatic missions and served at home in such important capacities as Comptroller of Customs for the Port of London, Justice of the Peace for the County of Kent, and Clerk of the King's Works, a position that made him responsible for the maintenance of certain public structures. He married Philippa de Roet, probably in 1367, and he may have had two

daughters and two sons, although there is speculation concerning the paternity of some of those children believed to have been Chaucer's. Since Chaucer's career was his service to the monarchy, his poetry was evidently an avocation which did not afford him a living.

ANALYSIS

Geoffrey Chaucer's best-known works are *Troilus and Criseyde* and the unfinished *The Canterbury Tales*, with the *Book of the Duchess*, the *Hous of Fame*, the *Parlement of Foules*, and the *Legend of Good Women* positioned in the second rank. In addition to these works and to *Boece* (c. 1380; translation of Boethius's *The Consolation of Philosophy*, c. 523-524) and the *Romaunt of the Rose*, there exist a number of shorter and lesser-known poems, some of which merit brief attention.

These lesser-known poems demonstrate Chaucer's abilities in diverse but typically medieval forms. Perhaps the earliest extant example of Chaucer's work is "An ABC to the Virgin"; this poem, primarily a translation from a thirteenth century French source, is a traditional series of prayers in praise of Mary, the stanzas of which are arranged in alphabetical order according to the first letter of each stanza. Another traditional form Chaucer used is the "complaint," or formal lament. "A Complaint to His Lady" is significant in literary history as the first appearance in English of Dante's terza rima, and "The Complaint unto Pity" is one of the earliest examples of rime royal; this latter poem contains an unusual analogy which represents the personified Pity as being buried in a heart. "The Complaint of Mars" illustrates Chaucer's individuality in treating traditional themes and conventions; although the poem purports to be a Valentine poem, and akin to an aubade, its ironic examination of love's intrinsic variability seems to make it an anti-Valentine poem. Chaucer similarly plays with theme and form in *To Rosemounde*, a ballade in which the conventions of courtly love are exaggerated to the point of grotesquerie; the narrator says, for example, that he is as immersed in love as a fish smothered in pickle sauce. Finally, Chaucer's poem "Gentilesse" is worthy of note for its presentation of a theme, developed in "The Wife of Bath's Tale" and in "The Clerk's Tale," which posits that "gentilesse" depends not on inheritance or social position but on character. In sum, these poems, for most of which dates of composition cannot be assigned, represent a variety of themes and forms with which Chaucer may have been experimenting; they indicate not only his solid grounding in poetic conventions but also his innovative spirit in using new forms and ideas and in treating old forms and ideas in new ways.

BOOK OF THE DUCHESS

Of those poems in the second rank, the *Book of the Duchess* was probably the earliest written and is believed to have been composed as a *consolation* or commemoration of the death of Blanche, Duchess of Lancaster and wife of John of Gaunt, with whom Chaucer was associated. The poem uses the technique of the dream vision and the device of the fictional narrator as two means of objectifying the subject matter, of presenting the consolation at a remove from the narrator and in the person of the bereaved knight himself. The poem thus seems to imply that true consolation can come only from within; the narrator's human sympathy and nature's reassurance can assist in the necessary process of acceptance of and recovery from the loss of a loved one, but that movement from the stasis of deprivation to the action of catharsis and healing can occur only within the mourner's own breast.

The poem is told by a lovesick narrator who battles his insomnia by reading the story of Ceyx and Alcyone. Finally falling asleep, he dreams that he awakens in the morning to the sounds of the hunt and, following a dog, comes upon a distinguished young knight dressed in black who laments his lost love. In response to the dreamer's naïve and persistent questions, the knight is eventually prodded into telling of his loss; he describes his lady in love-filled superlatives, reveals that her outer beauty was symbolic of her inner nobility, and acknowledges the great happiness they enjoyed in their mutual love. At the end of this lengthy discourse, when the narrator inquires as to the lady's whereabouts, the knight states simply that she is dead, to which the narrator replies, "Be God, hyt ys routhe!"

The poem thus blends the mythological world, the natural world, and the realm of human sympathy to create a context within which the mourner can come to accept his loss. The dreamer's lovesickness causes him to have a natural affinity with the knight, and, by posing as stupid, naïve, and slow-witted, the dreamer obliges the knight to speak and to admit his loss, a reality he must acknowledge if he is to move beyond the paralysis caused by his grief to a position where he is accessible to the consolation that can restore him. This restoration is in part accomplished by the dreamer's "naïve" questions, which encourage the knight to remember the joys he experienced with his lady and the love which they shared. The knight is then able to be consoled and comforted by the corrective and curative powers of his own memories.

The poem thus offers a psychologically realistic and sophisticated presentation of the grief process, a process in which the dreamer-narrator plays a crucial role, since it is the dreamer who, through his seemingly obtuse questioning, propels the knight out of the stasis to which his grief has made him succumb; the cathartic act of speaking to the dreamer about his lost love renders the knight open to the healing powers available in human sympathy and the natural world. The poem, even as it is elegiac in its tribute to the lost lover, is in the genre of the *consolatio* as it records the knight's conversion from unconsolable grief to quiet acceptance and assuagement. In establishing the persona of the apparently naïve and bumbling narrator, Chaucer initiates a tradition which not only has come to be recognized as typical of his works but also has been used repeatedly throughout literature. Probably the earliest English writer to use such a narrative device, Chaucer thereby discovered the rich possibilities for structural irony implicit in the distance between the author and his naïve narrator.

HOUS OF FAME

In contrast to the well-executed whole that is the *Book of the Duchess*, the *Hous of Fame*, believed to have been composed between 1372 and 1380, is an unfinished work; its true nature and Chaucer's intent in the poem continue to elude critics. Beyond the problems posed by any unfinished work is the question of this particular poem's unity, since the connections between the three parts of the poem which Chaucer actually finished are tenuous. In the first book of the poem, the narrator dreams of the Temple of Venus, where he learns of Dido and Aeneas. The second book, detailing the narrator's journey, in the talons of a golden eagle, to the House of Fame, and the contrast between the eagle's chatty friendliness and volubility and the obviously terrified narrator's monosyllabic responses as they swoop through the air, provides much amusement. The third book, describing the House of Fame and its presiding goddess, demonstrates the total irrationality of fame, which the goddess awards according to caprice rather than merit. After visiting the House of Rumor, the narrator notices everyone running to see a man of great authority, at which point the poem breaks off.

Critical opinion differs considerably as to the poem's meaning. Some believe it attempts to assess the worth of fame or perhaps even the life of the poet, in view of the mutability of human existence; others believe the poem intends to consider the validity of recorded history as opposed to true experience; yet other critics believe the poem attempts to ascertain the nature of poetry and its relationship to love. Although scholars have certainly not as yet settled on the poem's meaning, there is agreement that the flight of the eagle and the narrator in book 2 is one of literature's most finely comic passages. Beyond this, it is perhaps wisest to view the poem as an experiment with various themes which even Chaucer himself was apparently disinterested in unifying.

PARLEMENT OF FOULES

In contrast to the *Hous of Fame*, the *Parlement of Foules*, composed around 1380, is a finely crafted and complete work in which Chaucer combines several popular conventions, such as the dream vision, the parliament of beasts, and the *demande d'amour* to demonstrate three particular manifestations of love: divine love, erotic love, and procreative love, or natural love. The fictional narrator is here a person who lacks love, who knows of it only through books, and whose very dreams even prove emotionally unsatisfying. The narrator recounts his reading of Scipio Africanus the Younger, who dreamed that his ancestor came to him, told him of divine justice and the life

hereafter, and urged him to work to the common profit. Having learned of the nature of divine love, the narrator dreams that Scipio comes to him as he sleeps to take him to a park where there are two gardens, one the garden of Venus and the other the garden of Nature. The garden of Venus is clearly the place of erotic or carnal love; it is located away from the sun and consequently is dark, and it has an illicit and corrupt atmosphere. In addition to such figures as Cupid, Lust, Courtesy, and Jealousy, the narrator sees Venus herself, reclining half-naked in an atmosphere that is close and oppressive.

In contrast, the garden of Nature is in sunlight; it is Valentine's Day, and the birds have congregated to choose their mates. In addition to the natural surroundings, the presence of Nature herself, presiding over the debate, helps to create an atmosphere of fertility and creativity. The choice of mates is, however, impeded by a quarrel among three male eagles who love a formel. Each eagle has a different claim to press: The first asserts that he has loved her long in silence, the second stresses the length of his devotion, and the third emphasizes his devotion's intensity, pointing out that it is the quality rather than the length of love that matters. Since the lower orders of birds cannot choose mates until the eagles have settled their quarrel, the lesser birds enter the debate, aligning themselves variously either for or against the issues of courtly love which are involved. When the various birds' contributions deteriorate into invective without any positive result, Nature intervenes to settle the matter, but the formel insists upon making her own choice in her own time, that is, at the end of a year. The other birds, their mates chosen, sing a joyful song which ends the dream vision. When the narrator awakes he continues to read, hoping to dream better.

The poem, then, presents love in its divine, erotic, and procreative forms. Although the narrator sees these various manifestations of love, he is unable to experience them since all are unavailable to him. He is, in some ways, thus akin to the eagles and in contrast to the lower orders of birds who obviously fare well, since at the end of the parliament they are paired with their mates and blissfully depart. The eagles and the formel, however, because of the formel's need to deliberate upon and choose among her courtly lovers, are in a kind of emotional limbo for a year; in effect, they are all denied for a relatively long period love's natural expression. Thus, even as the system of courtliness raises and ennobles love, the system also provides an impediment to the ultimate realization of love in mating. Although there seems to be a movement in the debate from the artificiality of courtly love to the naturalness of pairing off, this movement does not affect the eagles, who remain constrained, in large part because of their commitment to the courtly code. The poem examines, then, not merely the various faces of love but the nature of courtly love in particular and its seemingly undesirable effects upon its adherents.

LEGEND OF GOOD WOMEN

Like the *Hous of Fame*, the *Legend of Good Women* is unfinished; although the poem was intended to contain a prologue and a series of nineteen or twenty stories telling of true women and false men, the extant material consists of two versions of the prologue and only nine legends. The poem purports to be a penance for the poet's offenses against the God of Love in writing of the false Criseyde and in translating the antifeminine *Romaunt of the Rose*.

In the prologues, Chaucer uses the techniques of the dream vision and the court of love to establish a context for his series of tales, which are much akin to saints' lives. In fact, the poem seems to parody the idea of a religion of love; the poet, although he worships the daisy as the God of Love's symbol, commits by his work heresy against the deity and must therefore repent and do penance by writing of women who were saints and martyrs in love's service. The two prologues differ in the degree to which they use Christian conventions to describe the conduct of love; the "G" prologue, believed to be later than the "F" prologue, has lessened the strength of the analogy to Christian worship. The legends, however, are very much in the hagiographic tradition, even to the extent of canonizing women not customarily regarded as "good," such as Cleopatra and Medea. Evidently wearying of his task, however, Chaucer did not complete the poem, perhaps because of the boredom inherent in the limited perspective.

TROILUS AND CRISEYDE

Of Chaucer's completed work, *Troilus and Criseyde* is without question his supreme accomplishment. Justly considered by many to be the first psychological novel, the poem places against the epic background of the Trojan War the tragedy and the romance of Troilus, son of Priam, and Criseyde, daughter of Calchas the soothsayer. Entwined with their lives is that of Pandarus, friend of Troilus and uncle of Criseyde, who brings the lovers together and who, in consequence, earns lasting disapprobation as the first panderer. In analyzing the conjunction of these three characters' lives, the poem considers the relationship of the individual to the society in which he or she lives and examines the extent to which events in one's life are influenced by external circumstances and by internal character. At a deeper level, the poem assesses the ultimate worth of human life, human love, and human values. Yet the poem does not permit reductive or simplistic interpretation; its many thematic strands and its ambiguities of characterization and narrative voice combine to present a multidimensional poem which defies definitive analysis.

The poem's thematic complexity depends upon a relatively simple plot. When callow Troilus is stricken with love for Criseyde, he follows all the courtly rules: He suffers physically, loves her from a distance, and rises to great heights of heroism on the battlefield so as to be worthy of her. When Troilus admits to Pandarus that his misery can only be cured by Criseyde's love, Pandarus is only too happy to exercise his influence over his niece. By means of a subtle mix of avuncular affection, psychological manipulation, and veiled threats, Pandarus leads Criseyde to fall in love with Troilus. The climax of Pandarus's machinations occurs when he arranges for Troilus and Criseyde to consummate their love affair, ostensibly against the stated will of Criseyde and in spite of Troilus's extremely enfeebled condition. Until this point the poem, reflecting largely the conventions of *fabliau*, has been in the control of Pandarus; he generates the action and manipulates the characters much as a rather bawdy and perhaps slightly prurient stage manager. With the love scene, however, the poem's form shifts from that of *fabliau* to that of romance;

Pandarus becomes a minor figure and the love between Troilus and Criseyde achieves much greater spiritual significance than either had anticipated.

Although the tenets of courtly love demand that the lovers keep their affair secret, they enjoy for three years a satisfying and enriching relationship which serves greatly to ennoble Troilus; the poem's shape then shifts again, this time from romance to tragedy. Calchas, having foreseen the Trojan defeat and having therefore defected to the Greeks, requests that a captured Trojan be exchanged for his daughter. The distraught lovers discover that the constraints placed upon them by their commitments to various standards and codes of behavior combine with the constraints imposed upon them by society to preclude their preventing the exchange, but Criseyde promises within ten days to steal away from the Greek camp and return to Troilus. Once in the Greek camp, however, Criseyde finds it difficult to escape; moreover, believing that the Greek Diomede has fallen in love with her, she decides to remain in the Greek encampment until the grief-stricken Troilus eventually has to admit that she has, indeed, betrayed him.

At the end of the poem, having been killed by Achilles, Troilus gazes from the eighth sphere upon the fullness of the universe and laughs at those mortals who indulge in earthly endeavor. In his bitter wisdom he condemns all things of the earth, particularly earthly love, which is so inadequate in comparison with heavenly love. This section of the poem, erroneously called by some "the epilogue," has been viewed as Chaucer's retraction of his poem and a nullification of what has gone before. Chaucer's poetic vision, however, is much more complex than this interpretation supposes; throughout the poem he has been preparing the reader to accept several paradoxes. One is that even as human beings must celebrate and strive for secular love, which is the nearest thing they have to divine love, they must nevertheless and simultaneously concentrate on the hereafter, since secular love and human connections are, indeed, vastly inferior to divine love. A second paradox is that humans should affirm the worth of human life and human values while at the same time recognizing their mutability and their inferiority to Christian values. The poem

also presents courtly love as a paradox since, on the one hand, it is the system which inspires Troilus to strive for and achieve a vastly ennobled character even though, on the other, the system is proven unworthy of his devotion. Criseyde is similarly paradoxical in that the narrator portrays her as deserving of Troilus's love, even though she proves faithless to him.

These paradoxes are presented against a classical background which contributes to the poet's juxtaposition of several oppositions. The world of the classical epic provides the setting for a medieval courtly romance so that, although the characters exist in a pagan environment, they are viewed from the Christian medieval perspective which informs the poem. The poem's epic setting and its romance form, then, like its pagan plot and its Christian point of view, seem thus to be temporally misaligned; this misalignment does not, however, lead to dissonance but instead contributes to the poem's thematic ambiguity.

The characters also contribute significantly to the poem's ambiguity. Criseyde, particularly, resists classification and categorization. The ambivalent narrator encourages the reader to see Criseyde in a variety of contradictory postures: as a victim, but also as a survivor, one who takes the main chance; as a weak and socially vulnerable person, but also as a woman who is self-confident and strong; as an idealistic and romantic lover, but also as a careful pragmatist; as a greatly self-deceived character, but also as a self-aware character who at times admits painful truths about herself.

Also ambiguous, but to a lesser degree, is Pandarus, whose characterization vacillates between that of the icily unsentimental cynic and that of the sensitive human being who bemoans his failures to achieve happiness in love and who worries about what history will do to his reputation. He seems to see courtly love as a game and to disbelieve in the total melding of two lives, but he betrays his own sentimentality when he indicates that he longs to find such love for himself.

Although his mentor seems not to take courtly love seriously, to Troilus it is the center of his life, his very reality. His virtue lies in large part in his absolute commitment to courtly ideals and to Criseyde.

The solidity of that commitment, however, prevents Troilus from taking any active steps to stop the exchange, since such action would reveal their love affair, soil Criseyde's reputation, and violate the courtly love code. In this sense, Troilus is trapped by his own nobility and by his idealism, so that his course of action is restrained not only by external forces but also by his own character.

In fact, the poem seems to show that both Troilus and Criseyde are ultimately responsible for what happens to them; the role of fate in their lives is relatively insignificant because their very characters are their fate. As Troilus is governed by his dedication to heroic and courtly ideals, Criseyde is governed by the fact that she is "slydynge of corage." It is her nature to take the easiest way, and because of her nature she is untrue to Troilus.

From the poet's point of view, however, Criseyde's faithlessness does not invalidate for Troilus the experience of her love. Because of his own limited perspective, Troilus is himself unable to assess the worth of his life, his love affair, and the values to which he subscribed; the parameters of his vision permit him to see only the inadequacy and imperfection of earthly experience in comparison with the experience of the divine. The poet's perspective, however, is the one which informs the poem, and that perspective is broader, clearer, and more complex, capable of encompassing the poem's various paradoxes and oppositions. In consequence, even though Troilus at the end discounts his earthly experience, the poem has proven its worth to an incontrovertible degree; human life, even though inferior to the afterlife, nevertheless affords the opportunity for experiences which, paradoxically, can transcend their earthly limitations. Ultimately, then, the poem affirms the worth of human life, human love, and human idealism.

THE CANTERBURY TALES

Although Chaucer never completed *The Canterbury Tales*, it is his most important work and the one for which he is best known. In its conceptual richness, in its grace and precision of execution, and in its broad presentation of humanity, *The Canterbury Tales* is unequaled. The poem occupied Chaucer for the last one and a half decades of his life, although several of the stories date from an earlier period; it was not until sometime in the middle 1380's, when he conceived the idea of using a framing device within which his stories could be placed, that the work began to assume shape. That shape is the form of a springtime pilgrimage to Canterbury to see the shrine of Thomas à Becket. The fictional party consists of some thirty pilgrims, along with the narrator and the host from the Tabard Inn; each pilgrim was to tell two stories en route to Canterbury and two on the return trip, making an approximate total of 120 tales. There are extant, however, only the prologue and twenty-four tales, not all of which are completed; moreover, the sources of these extant tales (more than eighty manuscript fragments) contain considerable textual variations and arrange the tales in many differing orders. Thus, it is impossible for critics to determine the order which Chaucer envisioned for the tales.

The notion of using the pilgrimage as a frame device was a stroke of narrative brilliance, since the device provides infinite possibilities for dramatic action while it simultaneously unifies a collection of widely disparate stories. In response to the host's request for stories of "mirth" or "doctryne," the pilgrims present an eclectic collection of tales, including romances, fabliaux, beast-fables, saints' lives, tragedies, sermons, and exempla. The frame of the pilgrimage also permits the poet to represent a cross section of society, since the members of the party range across the social spectrum from the aristocratic knight to the bourgeois guild members to the honest plowman. Moreover, since the tales are connected by passages of dialogue among the pilgrims as they ride along on their journey, the pilgrimage frame also permits the characters of the storytellers to be developed and additional dramatic action to occur from the pilgrims' interaction. These "links" between the tales thus serve to define a constant fictional world, the pilgrimage, which is in juxtaposition to and seemingly in control of the multiple fictional worlds created in the tales themselves; the fictional world of the pilgrims on their pilgrimage thereby acquires a heightened degree of verisimilitude, especially because the pilgrims' interchanges with one another often help to place them at various recognizable points on the road to Canterbury.

The pilgrimage frame also permits the creation of an exquisitely ironic tension between the fictional narrator and the poet himself. The narrator is Chaucer's usual persona, naïve, rather thick-witted, and easily and wrongly impressed by outward show. This narrator's gullible responses to the various pilgrims are contrasted to the attitude of the poet himself; such use of the fictional narrator permits the poet not only to present two points of view on any and all action but also to play upon the tension deriving from the collision of those two perspectives. The device of the pilgrimage frame, in sum, allows the poet virtually unlimited freedom in regard to form, content, and tone.

The context of the pilgrimage is established in the poem's prologue, which begins by indicating that concerns both sacred and secular prompt people to go on pilgrimage. Those people are described in a formal series of portraits which reveals that the group is truly composed of "sondry folk" and is a veritable cross section of medieval society. Yet the skill of the poet is evident in the fact that even as the pilgrims are "types"—that is, they are representative of a body of others like themselves—they are also individuals who are distinguished not simply by the realistic details describing their external appearances but more crucially by the sharply searching analysis which penetrates their external façades to expose the actualities of character that lie beneath.

"THE KNIGHT'S TALE"

The tales begin with a group which has come to be seen as Chaucer's variations on the theme of the love-triangle and which consists of "The Knight's Tale," "The Miller's Tale," and "The Reeve's Tale." Like *Troilus and Criseyde*, "The Knight's Tale" superimposes a romance against the background of the classical world as it tells of Palamon and Arcite, knights of Thebes who are captured by Theseus during his battle with Creon and sentenced to life imprisonment in Athens. While imprisoned they fall in love with Emily, over whom they quarrel; since Palamon, who saw and loved her first, thought she was a goddess, Arcite, who saw her second but who loved her as a woman, insists that his is the better claim. Several years later, Arcite having been freed and Palamon

having escaped from prison, the knights meet and again quarrel, agreeing to settle the matter with a duel. When Theseus comes upon them he stops the duel and decrees that they must instead meet a year later with their troops to decide the matter in a tournament.

For this tournament Theseus erects a magnificent stadium with temples to Venus, Mars, and Diana. When the stadium is completed and the time for the tournament has arrived, the three members of the love-triangle pray for the assistance of their particular gods: Palamon asks Venus for Emily or for death; Arcite asks Mars for victory; and Emily asks Diana to permit her to remain a virgin or, failing that, to be wedded to the one who most loves her. These various petitions cause a quarrel between Venus and Mars which Saturn resolves by announcing that Palamon shall have his lady even though Mars assists Arcite to victory. Arcite, in consequence, wins the tournament, but in the midst of his victory parade, his horse rears, and he is mortally injured. From his deathbed Arcite summons both Palamon and Emily and commends them to each other, but they continue to grieve during the next several years. Finally, Theseus summons Palamon and Emily to him and tells them that since grief should end and life go on, they are to marry and thus make joy from sorrows.

The poem's plot, then, concerns the resolution of the love-triangle typical of romance. This plot, however, is in the service of a more serious conflict, that between order and chaos. Theseus serves as the civilizing instrument, the means by which order is imposed on the anarchy of human passion. In actuality, by assuming control over the hostility between Palamon and Arcite, Theseus reshapes their primitive emotional conflict into a clearly defined ritual; by distancing it as well in time and space, Theseus forces that conflict into a shape and an expression which is socially acceptable and which poses no threat to the culture's peaceful continuance. Theseus thus makes order and art out of raw emotion and violent instincts.

"THE MILLER'S TALE"

The love conflict which in "The Knight's Tale" serves to develop this cosmic theme is in "The

Miller's Tale" acted out on the smaller scale and in the more limited space of the sheerly natural world and thus serves no such serious or noble end. Again there is a triangle, but the romantic discord among the aristocratic Palamon, Arcite, and Emily becomes in "The Miller's Tale" the bawdy comedy of the *fabliau* as it arises from the interaction of the young clerk Nicholas and the effeminate dandy Absolon, both of whom desire Alison, the young wife of John, an old and jealous carpenter. At the same time that the amorous Absolon serenades her nightly and sends her gifts in an effort to win her, Alison agrees to give her love to Nicholas as soon as he can create the opportunity. In fact, however, no elaborate stratagem is needed to make possible the encounter Alison and Nicholas both desire. Since Alison's husband is away all day working, and since Nicholas as a student who boards with the couple is at home with Alison all day, there really are no obstacles preventing the lovers from acting on their passions immediately. Alison's insistence, then, that Nicholas devise a plan whereby they can give rein to their passions, reflects an important stylistic and thematic connection between the tale and "The Knight's Tale." In the latter tale, Theseus controls the passions of Palamon and Arcite by postponing their encounter and dictating its arena; the distancing in time and space results in a civilized, restrained expression of their passions. In "The Miller's Tale," by contrast, the distancing Alison demands parodies the conventions of romance and courtly love. This distance in actuality simply ennobles base instincts, for Alison and Nicholas inhabit not a courtly world but a natural one, and their intellectual, spiritual, and romantic pretensions constitute only a thin veneer covering their healthy animalism. By using distance as a means of ennobling base instincts, "The Miller's Tale" parodies not only the world and the theme of "The Knight's Tale" but also its poetic treatment.

Nicholas's seduction plan plays upon both the strengths and the weaknesses of the carpenter's character. Telling John that another flood is coming, Nicholas convinces the carpenter that he must hang three barrels from the rafters in which Nicholas, John, and Alison can remain until the waters rise,

then they will cut themselves free to float away. The carpenter's pretensions to spiritual and theological superiority cause him to accept this prophecy unquestioningly, but at the same time his genuine love for his wife causes his first reaction to be fear for her life. When all three on the appointed night have ostensibly entered their barrels, Nicholas and Alison sneak down to spend a night in amorous play.

At this point the plot is entered by Absolon, who comes to Alison's window to serenade her; pleading for a kiss, he finds himself presented with Alison's backside. Bent then on avenging his misdirected kiss, he brings a hot colter and asks for another kiss; presented this time with the backside of Nicholas, Absolon smacks it smartly with the red-hot colter, causing Nicholas to cry out "Water!" which in turn causes the carpenter to cut the rope on his barrel and crash to the ground, injuring both his person and his dignity. Whereas in "The Knight's Tale" the three major characters ultimately obtain what they desire most—Arcite, victory; Palamon, Emily; and Emily, the man who loves her most—"The Miller's Tale" reverses this idea; John, the jealous carpenter, is cuckolded and humiliated in front of the entire town, the fastidious Absolon has kissed Alison's "nether ye," and Nicholas has lost a hand's-breadth of skin from his backside. Only Alison remains unscathed, but then, she must spend her life being married to John.

The poem thus parodies the romance tradition, the idealistic notion that civilized or courtly processes can elevate and ennoble fundamental human passions. Even as it transfers various themes, mechanisms, and perspectives from "The Knight's Tale," "The Miller's Tale" transforms these and reflects them negatively. The generic differences between the two poems, however, demand that content and tone differ. "The Knight's Tale," combining epic and romance, deals seriously with serious considerations, whereas "The Miller's Tale," by virtue of its being a fabliau, has as one of its purposes the humorous depiction of human shortcomings.

"THE REEVE'S TALE"

"The Knight's Tale" and "The Miller's Tale" are different tales which have structural similarities;

"The Reeve's Tale," which completes the poem's first thematic grouping, shares with "The Miller's Tale" the fabliau form but the two differ considerably in tone. The Reeve's story results from his outrage at the Miller's story, which has belittled carpenters; in angry retaliation the Reeve relates the popular fabliau concerning the two students who, cheated by a dishonest miller, exact revenge by sleeping with both his wife and his daughter. The plot, which hangs in part upon the device of the misplaced cradle, has as its end the unsophisticated students' triumph over the social-climbing miller. The tone of "The Reeve's Tale," therefore, is bitter and vindictive, told, the Reeve acknowledges, solely to repay the Miller.

Chaucer uses the romance and the fabliau, the two forms with which he begins his series of tales, again and again in the course of the poem. Other romances are the unfinished "The Squire's Tale," which has an Asian setting; "The Man of Law's Tale," which blends romance and a saint's life in the story of the unfortunate Constance; and "The Wife of Bath's Tale," "The Clerk's Tale," and "The Franklin's Tale," which will be discussed together as "the marriage group." The genre of the fabliau is also further represented in "The Shipman's Tale" of the debt repaid by the adulterous monk to his lender's wife, and in "The Friar's Tale" and "The Summoner's Tale," stories which are attacks on each other's professions and which are told to be mutually insulting.

USE OF SAINT'S LIVES

Another popular genre Chaucer employs in his collection is that of the saints' lives, a type used in "The Second Nun's Tale" of St. Cecilia and in "The Prioress's Tale" of the martyred Christian boy slain by Jews. While both tales conventionally concern "miracles of the virgin," the tale of the Prioress is of particular interest because of the nature of the storyteller. Although she is supposed to be a spiritual being, a guardian of other spiritual beings, she is described in the same manner as the heroine of a courtly romance; moreover, although her description points to sensitivity and charity, her moral sensibility is clearly faulty. She worries over a little mouse but tells a violent tale of religious intolerance. Moreover, the ironies implicit in the engraving on her brooch—

"Amor vincit omnia"—are extensive, as are the ironies deriving from the conflicting perspectives of the narrator, who naïvely admires her for all the wrong reasons, and the poet, who clearly sees her as possessed of many shortcomings.

"THE NUN'S PRIEST'S TALE"

Another popular genre in the Middle Ages was the beast-fable, a form which Chaucer uses brilliantly in "The Nun's Priest's Tale." The story concerns Chauntecleer and Pertelote, a cock and hen owned by a poor widow. When Chauntecleer one night dreams of a fox, he and Pertelote have an extended discussion on the validity of dreams. Believing that dreams are caused by bile or overeating, Pertelote advises the use of a laxative; Chauntecleer, however, holding a different opinion, tells a story wherein a dream is proven prophetic. At this point the fox appears, whom the Nun's Priest likens to such other traitors as Simon and Judas Iscariot. Even as he insists that his antifeminine statements are not his own but the cock's, the Nun's Priest clearly believes that woman's counsel often brings misfortune and points with relish to the fox's sudden appearance as proof of this belief.

The encounter between the fox and the cock reveals the weaknesses of both. Relying hugely on flattery, the fox persuades Chauntecleer to relax his guard, close his eyes, and stretch his neck, providing the perfect opportunity to seize Chauntecleer and race off. As the widow and her household set chase, Chauntecleer advises the fox to tell the pursuers to turn back because he will soon be eating Chauntecleer in spite of them; when the fox opens his mouth to do this, Chauntecleer escapes. Although the fox tries to persuade Chauntecleer to come down out of the tree, Chauntecleer wisely declares that he will not again be fooled by flattery and that no one should prosper who closes his eyes when he should watch. The fox, as one might expect, disagrees, declaring that no one should prosper who talks when he should hold his peace.

The poem thus uses the beast-fable's technique of personifying animals to the end of revealing human truths; it also uses the conventions and the rhetoric of epic and courtly romance to talk about the lives of chickens, thus creating a parody of the epic form and a burlesque of the courtly attitude. The poem is also, to a degree, homiletic in treating the dangers inherent in succumbing to flattery; each character suffers as a result of this weakness, the cock by having foolishly permitted himself to be captured, and the fox by having gullibly permitted himself to be hoodwinked by one pretending affinity.

"THE WIFE OF BATH'S TALE"

Having begun the discussion of *The Canterbury Tales* with an analysis of the group of tales concerned with the love-triangle, it seems fitting to end the discussion with an analysis of those tales referred to as "the marriage group." "The Wife of Bath's Tale," "The Clerk's Tale," "The Merchant's Tale," and "The Franklin's Tale" bring to that group several perspectives on women and the relation between the sexes. The Wife of Bath, in complete opposition to the traditional view of women, presents one extreme point of view which advocates sensuality and female authority. An excellent example of what she advocates, the wife is strong and lusty and insists on dominance in her marriages. In her lengthy prologue to her story she takes issue with patristic doctrine concerning chastity and female inferiority and uses scriptural allusions to buttress her opinions. Her prologue thus provides a defense of women and of sensuality.

Her tale, an exemplum illustrating the argument contained in her prologue, concerns a knight who must, in order to save his life, find out what women desire most. Despairing over his inability to get a consensus of opinion, he one day comes upon a "loathly lady" who offers to give him the answer if he in turn will do what she requests. Gratefully agreeing, he learns that women most want "sovereynetee" and "maistrie" over their husbands; he is less pleased, however, to learn that her request is that he marry her. Having kept his promise, the knight on their wedding night is understandably distant from his new wife; when pressed for an explanation, he notes that she is ugly, old, and lowly born. She in turn explains that nobility comes not from wealth or birth, that poverty is virtuous, and that her age and ugliness ensure her chastity. She gives the knight a choice: He can have her ugly and old but faithful, or young and pretty but untrue. The knight chooses, however, to transfer this

decision and consequently the control of the marriage to her, whereupon she announces that she will be not only young and pretty but also faithful, thus illustrating the good that comes when women are in control.

"THE CLERK'S TALE"

The Wife's tale, and the wife herself, with her heretical opinions concerning marriage and sexual relations, outrage the Clerk, who tells a tale to counter the Wife's; his tale reinforces the doctrine that male dominance on earth conforms to the order of the divine hierarchy. His story treats the patient Griselda, who promises her husband, Walter, to do everything he wishes and never to complain or in any way indicate disagreement. When a daughter is born to them, Walter, who is an Italian marquis, tells Griselda that since the people are complaining about her low birth, he must have the child killed, to which Griselda meekly agrees; Walter, however, sends the child secretly to a relative to be reared. When a son is born, Walter again does the same thing, again to test her obedience, and again Griselda is perfectly submissive. Twelve years later Walter secretly sends for the two children and tells Griselda that since he is divorcing her in order to marry someone else, she must return to her father. Moreover, he insists that she return to her father just as she had left him, that is, naked, since Walter had provided her with clothes. Griselda, with great dignity, requests at least a shift as recompense for the virginity which she had brought to him but which she cannot take away with her. When asked later to come and make arrangements for Walter's new bride, Griselda cheerfully complies, although she does, at this point, give some indication of the great price she has paid for her obedience and her faithfulness to her vow; she asks Walter not to torment his new wife as he tormented her, the bride-to-be having been tenderly reared and therefore not so well able to withstand such adversity. Walter, finally satisfied as to Griselda's steadfastness, restores her as his wife and reunites her with her children. The Clerk concludes by noting that it is hard to find women like Griselda nowadays.

The tale is one with which critics have long grappled, since it presents seemingly insurmountable interpretive problems. The story can hardly be taken as realistic, even though the Clerk, through his efforts to give Walter psychological motivation, attempts to provide verisimilitude. Although the poem may be intended as allegory, to illustrate that one must be content in adversity, it seems also to have a tropological level of meaning, to illustrate the proper attitude for wives. The narrator's own uncertainty as to whether he tells a tale of real people, a saint's life, or an allegory, contributes to the difficulty one has in assessing the poem's nature and purpose. It is obvious, though, that the Clerk's intended corrective to "The Wife of Bath's Tale" is perfectly accomplished through his tale of the impossibly patient Griselda.

"THE MERCHANT'S TALE"

At the end of his tale the Clerk appears to switch directions; he advises that no husband should try what Walter did, and that furthermore wives should be fierce to their husbands, should provoke their jealousy, and should make them weep and wail. The Merchant picks up this notion and echoes the line in the first sentence of his own remarks, which are intended to counter the Clerk's presentation of the saintly wife. The Merchant's own unhappy marriage experience adds a painfully personal coloration to his tale of the old husband and the young wife.

His story of May, Januarie, and the pear tree is well known in the history of the fabliau. Immediately after wedding the sixty-year-old Januarie, whose lovemaking she considers not "worth a bene," May meets and falls in love with Damian, who loves her in return. When Januarie becomes temporarily blind, the lovers plot to consummate their love in the pear tree above Januarie's head. Pluto and Proserpina, debating how men and women betray each other, decide to restore Januarie's sight but to give May a facile tongue. Consequently, when Januarie's sight returns and he sees May and Damian making love in the pear tree, May explains that her struggling in a tree with a man was an effort to restore his sight, which is obviously as yet imperfect. Placated, Januarie accepts her explanation, and they are reconciled.

The three tales thus present varying views of woman as lascivious termagant, as obedient saint, and as clever deceiver; marriage, accordingly, is seen as a struggle for power and freedom between combat- ants who are natural adversaries. It remains for Chaucer in "The Franklin's Tale" to attempt a more balanced view, to try to achieve a reconciliation of the oppositions posed in the tales of the Wife of Bath, the Clerk, and the Merchant.

"THE FRANKLIN'S TALE"

"The Franklin's Tale" is a particular kind of romance called a Breton lai, which conventionally is concentrated, imaginative, and exaggeratedly romantic. While the tale is interesting in its depiction of an integrity which rests upon absolute commitment to the pledged word, the intricacies of the poem's moral issues are ultimately resolved, in a rather disappointing fashion, by something akin to a *deus ex machina*. The tale, nevertheless, has been seen traditionally to function as the reconciliation of the marriage group because of the more balanced relationship portrayed between Arveragus, a knight, and Dorigen, his wife. The couple agree that he will show no sovereignty except for that semblance of it which may be necessary for his dignity, and that their effort will be for freedom, harmony, and mutual respect in marriage, rather than for mastery. In this regard, they represent an ideal example of marriage which is totally antithetical to those of the preceding marriage tales; in Dorigen and Arveragus, Chaucer seems to be exploring the possibility that chivalric ideals and middle-class virtues can be compatible in marriage. Whether the poet really believes this is possible, however, is placed in question by the tale's romance form and by its contrived ending.

While Arveragus is away on knightly endeavors, Dorigen mourns and grieves, worrying particularly about the black rocks which make the coastline hazardous. When Aurelius, who has loved her long, pleads for her attentions, she explains that she will never be unfaithful to her husband but adds, in jest, that if he will remove the rocks she will love him. Two years after Arveragus has come home, Aurelius, made ill by his long-frustrated passion, finds a magician who, for a large fee, creates the illusion that the rocks have vanished. Asked then to fulfill her end of the bargain, the horrified Dorigen contemplates suicide to avoid this dishonor, but her miserably unhappy husband, declaring that "Trouthe is the hyeste thyng that man may kepe," sends Dorigen to fulfill her promise. Pitying them, Aurelius releases her from her promise and is in turn released from his debt by the magician; the tale ends by asking who was the most generous.

Although Dorigen and Arveragus have a marriage based on respect, honesty, and love, and although they share a moral sensibility and agree on the importance of honor to them individually and to their marriage, the artificial resolution of the plot by totally unexpected elements—the decisions of both Aurelius and the magician not to press their just claims—would seem to suggest that the poet himself dared not treat in a realistic fashion the unpleasant and probably disastrous results of the plot which he had created. In effect, he established an ideal marriage situation, set up a test of that marriage's strength, but then decided not to go through with the test. In placing his attempted solution of the marriage problem in the form of a Breton lai, in failing to pursue to the end the very questions he himself raises, and in providing a typical romance ending, the poet seems to indicate that any real solution to the problems pertaining to women and to marriage are not going to be so easily attained.

The Canterbury Tales, then, represents one of the earliest collections of short stories of almost every conceivable type. In addition to being a generic compendium, the poem is also a compendium of characters, since the pilgrims who tell the stories and the people who inhabit the stories together constitute the widest possible representation of character types. In framing his collection of tales with the pilgrimage, Chaucer permitted himself an eclecticism in form, content, and treatment which was unprecedented in English literature. There are those who would eagerly affirm that the grace of vision which permeates *The Canterbury Tales* makes the work not only one which was unprecedented but also one which has not since been equaled.

OTHER MAJOR WORKS

NONFICTION: *Boece*, c. 1380 (translation of Boethius's *The Consolation of Philosophy*); *A Treatise on the Astrolabe*, 1387-1392.

MISCELLANEOUS: *Works*, 1957 (second edition, F. N. Robinson, editor).

BIBLIOGRAPHY

Bowden, Muriel. *A Commentary on the General Prologue to "The Canterbury Tales."* 2d ed. New York: Macmillan, 1967. Restricted in scope to the general prologue, the most widely read (and taught) of Chaucer's writings. Provides a detailed explication that explores the prologue virtually line by line, collecting and arranging all significant discussions of the text. A valuable reference for the specialist, while remaining clear enough to be accessible to the general reader.

Condren, Edward I. *Chaucer and the Energy of Creation: The Design and the Organization of "The Canterbury Tales."* Gainesville: University Press of Florida, 1999. Examines the motives behind Chaucer's layout of the stories.

Gittes, Katherine S. *Framing the Canterbury Tales: Chaucer and the Medieval Frame Narrative Tradition.* Westport, Conn.: Greenwood Press, 1991. Analyzes the influence of the Asian frame narrative tradition on *The Canterbury Tales*; argues that what was once taken for incompleteness is the result of the influence of Eastern modes of narrative structure.

Harding, Wendy. "The Function of Pity in Three Canterbury Tales." *The Chaucer Review* 32 (1997): 162-174. Discusses the variability of pity in "The Knight's Tale," "The Clerk's Tale," and "The Parson's Tale." Argues that in different ways, all three deal with the role of pity in hierarchical relations.

Howard, Donald R. *Chaucer.* New York: E. P. Dutton, 1987. The most comprehensive and authoritative biography, by a renowned critic, valuable for both the novice and the advanced student. Combines biographical and historical material with insightful commentary on the poetry. A thorough yet readable introduction to Chaucer, his work, and his world.

Narkiss, Doron. "The Fox, the Cock, and the Priest: Chaucer's Escape from Fable." *The Chaucer Review* 32 (1997): 46-63. Examines Chaucer's reworking of Aesop's fable in "The Nun's Priest's

Tale." Argues that Chaucer moves the fable away from the realm of learning and wisdom to mockery and a way of reading that in "The Nun's Priest's Tale" fable is extended by characterization and action. Claims that Chaucer's use of the fable suggests doubling, repetition, and substitutions.

Payne, Robert O. *Geoffrey Chaucer*. 2d ed. Boston: Twayne, 1986. A concise introduction to Chaucer and his period for the beginning student by one of the leading scholars in the field. Addressed to readers who have no previous background in medieval literature or cultural studies.

Rossignol, Rosalyn. *Chaucer A to Z: The Essential Reference to His Life and Works*. New York: Facts on File, 1999. An indispensable guide for the student of Chaucer.

Rowland, Beryl, ed. *Companion to Chaucer Studies*. Rev. ed. New York: Oxford University Press, 1979. Especially valuable for the student or teacher with little ready access to a research library. Contains twenty-two essays, each followed by an extensive bibliography, by major authorities in the field. Surveys the history of Chaucer criticism in a wide range of topics, beginning with Chaucer's biography and influences, to his style. Contains six chapters on *The Canterbury Tales* and individual chapters on the more important minor poems.

Schoeck, Richard, and Jerome Taylor, eds. *Chaucer Criticism*. 2 vols. Notre Dame, Ind.: University of Notre Dame Press, 1960-1961. Volume 1, *The Canterbury Tales*, assembles some of the most important early studies of Chaucer's masterpiece, including John Matthews Manly's "Chaucer and the Rhetoricians" and George Lyman Kittredge's seminal "Chaucer's Discussion of Marriage." A valuable introduction to major critics and approaches. Volume 2, *"Troilus and Criseyde" and the Minor Poems*, contains an introduction to "The System of Courtly Love" by William George Dodd, followed by twelve essays on *Troilus and Criseyde*. Also includes essays on individual shorter poems.

Storm, Mel. "Speech, Circumspection, and Orthodontics in the Manciple's Prologue and Tale and the Wife of Bath's Portrait." *Studies in Philology* 96 (Spring, 1999): 109-126. Asserts that Chaucer's "The Manciple's Tale" is his apologia for his life as a poet. Suggests that "The Wife of Bath's Tale" is balanced both thematically and dramatically in "The Manciple's Tale."

Taavitsainen, Irma. "Narrative Patterns of Affect in Four Genres of the Canterbury Tales." *The Chaucer Review* 30 (1995): 191-210. Discusses four genres: sermons, saints' lives, courtly romances, and fabliaux. Argues that an assessment of inherent linguistic patterns of genres reveals new ways of seeing how the audience is manipulated, how their emotions are provoked, and how narrative suspense is sustained.

Evelyn Newlyn, updated by William Nelles

JOHN CHEEVER

Born: Quincy, Massachusetts; May 27, 1912
Died: Ossining, New York; June 18, 1982

PRINCIPAL SHORT FICTION

The Way Some People Live, 1943
The Enormous Radio and Other Stories, 1953
The Housebreaker of Shady Hill and Other Stories, 1958
Some People, Places, and Things That Will Not Appear in My Next Novel, 1961
The Brigadier and the Golf Widow, 1964
The World of Apples, 1973
The Stories of John Cheever, 1978

OTHER LITERARY FORMS

Believing that "fiction is our most intimate and acute means of communication, at a profound level, about our deepest apprehensions and intuitions on the meaning of life and death," John Cheever devoted himself to the writing of stories and novels. Although he kept voluminous journals, he wrote only a handful of essays and even fewer reviews, and only one television screenplay, *The Shady Hill Kidnapping*, which aired January 12, 1982, on the Public Broadcasting Service. A number of Cheever's works have also been adapted by other writers, including several early short stories such as "The Town House" (play, 1948), "The Swimmer" (film, 1968), "Goodbye, My Brother" as *Children* (play, 1976), and "O Youth and Beauty," "The Five-Forty-Eight," and "The Sorrows of Gin" (teleplays, 1979). Benjamin Cheever has edited selections of his father's correspondence, *The Letters of John Cheever* (1988), and journals, *The Journals of John Cheever* (1991).

ACHIEVEMENTS

A major twentieth century novelist, John Cheever has achieved even greater fame as a short-story writer. He published his first story, "Expelled," in *The New Republic* when he was only eighteen. Reviewers of his first collection, *The Way Some People Live*, judged Cheever to be a promising young writer. Nu-

merous awards and honors followed: two John Simon Guggenheim Memorial Foundation grants (1951, 1961), a Benjamin Franklin award for "The Five-Forty-Eight" (1955), an O. Henry Award for "The Country Husband" (1956), election to the National Institute of Arts and Letters in 1957, elevation to the American Academy in 1973, a National Book Award in 1958 for *The Wapshot Chronicle* (1957), the Howells Medal in 1965 for *The Wapshot Scandal* (1964), cover stories in *Time* (1964) and *Newsweek* (1977), the Edward MacDowell Medal in 1979, a Pulitzer Prize and a National Book Critics Circle award (both in 1978), an American Book Award (1979) for *The Stories of John Cheever*, and the National Medal for Literature (1982). Cheever's achievements, however, cannot be measured only in terms of the awards and honors that he has received (including the honorary doctorate bestowed on this high school dropout), for his most significant accomplishment was to create, with the publication of *The Stories of John Cheever*, a resurgence of interest in, and a new respect for, the short story on the part of public and publishers alike.

BIOGRAPHY

The loss of his father's job in 1930, followed by the loss of the family home and the strained marital situation caused, John Cheever believed, by his mother's growing financial and emotional dependence, all had a lifelong effect on Cheever. When he was expelled from Thayer Academy at the age of seventeen, Cheever was already committed to a writing career. His career, however, would do little to assuage his sense of emotional and economic insecurity. Although he liked to claim that "fiction is not crypto-autobiography," from the beginning, his stories were drawn from his personal experiences. They have even followed him geographically: from New England, to New York City, through his military service, to the suburbs (first Scarborough, then Ossining), with side trips to Italy (1956-1957), the Soviet Union (on three government-sponsored trips), and Sing Sing prison, where he taught writing (1971-1972). The stories have, more importantly, followed Cheever over hazardous emotional terrain, transforming personal obsessions into published fictions: alcoholism, bisexuality, self-doubts, strained marital relations, and the sense of "otherness." The stories also evidence the longing for stability and home that manifested itself in three of the most enduring relationships of his fifty-year career: with the Yaddo writers' colony in Saratoga Springs, New York (beginning in 1934); with *The New Yorker* (which began publishing his work in 1935); and with his wife Mary Winternitz Cheever (whom he met in 1939 and married two years later, and with whom he bickered over the next forty years).

Cheever did not become free of his various fears and dependencies—including his nearly suicidal addiction to alcohol—until the mid-1970's. After undergoing treatment for alcoholism at Smithers Rehabilitation Center, he transformed what might well have become his darkest novel into his most affirmative. *Falconer* (1977) was both a critical and a commercial success. Like its main character, Cheever seemed for the first time in his life free, willing at least to begin talking about the private life that he had so successfully guarded, even mythified before, when he had played the part of country squire. The triumph was, however, short-lived: two neurological seizures in 1980, a kidney operation and the discovery of cancer in 1981, and, shortly after the publication of his fifth novel, the aptly and perhaps whimsically titled *Oh What a Paradise It Seems* (1982), his death on June 18, 1982.

ANALYSIS

John Cheever has been called both "the Chekhov of the exurbs" and "Ovid in Ossining"—which suggests both the variety and the complexity of the man and his fiction. Accused by some of being a literary lightweight—a writer merely of short stories and an apologist for middle-class life—he has been more often, and more justly, praised as a master chronicler of a way of life that he both celebrates and satirizes in stories that seem at once conventional and innovative, realistic and fantastic. His stories read effortlessly,

John Cheever in 1981 (©Nancy Crampton)

yet their seeming simplicity masks a complexity that deserves and repays close attention. The line "The light from the cottage, shining into the fog, gave the illusion of substance, and it seems as if I might stumble on a beam of light," for example, only appears simple and straightforward. It begins with a conventional image, light penetrating darkness, thus illuminating the way to truth, but the next five words undermine the "illusion" first by calling attention to it, then by paradoxically literalizing the metaphor, making this substantive light a stumbling block rather than a source of spiritual and/or philosophical truth.

"A MISCELLANY OF CHARACTERS THAT WILL NOT APPEAR IN MY NEXT NOVEL"

Nothing in Cheever's fiction of stark contrasts— light and dark, male and female, city and country— ever exists independent of its opposite. His stories proceed incrementally and contrapuntally, at times in curiously indirect ways. In "A Miscellany of Characters That Will Not Appear in My Next Novel," for example, Cheever's narrator banishes seven kinds of characters and situations from his fiction, including alcoholics, homosexuals, and "scornful descriptions of American landscapes." However, not only did his next novel, as well as much of the rest of his fiction, include all three, but also the very act of listing them in this "miscellany" confirms their power, giving them a prominence that far outweighs their hypothetical banishment from any later work. This play of voices and positions within individual works also exists between stories.

The same narrative situations will appear in various Cheever stories, handled comically in some, tragically in others. In effect, the stories offer a series of brilliant variations on a number of basic, almost obsessive themes, of which the most general and the most recurrent as well as the most important is the essential conflict between his characters' spiritual longings and social and psychological (especially sexual) nature. "What I wanted to do," one of his narrator-protagonists says, is "to grant my dreams, in so incoherent a world, their legitimacy," "to celebrate," as another claims, "a world that lies spread out around us like a bewildering and stupendous dream." Their longings are tempered not only by the incoherence of their world but also by a doubt concerning whether what they long for actually exists or is rather only an illusion conjured out of nothing more substantial than their own ardent hopes for something or some place or someone other than who, what, and where they presently are. Even when expressed in the most ludicrous terms possible, the characters' longings seem just as profound as they are ridiculous, as in the case of "Artemis the Honest Well Digger" searching "for a girl as pure and fresh as the girl on the oleomargarine package." The line seems both to affirm and to qualify the yearning of a character who may confuse kitsch with Kant, advertising copy with lyrical longings, but who nevertheless seems as much a holy fool as a deluded consumer.

Whether treated comically or tragically, Cheever's characters share a number of traits. Most are male, married, and white-collar workers. All—despite their Sutton Place apartments or, more often, comfortable homes in affluent Westchester communities—feel confused, dispossessed, lost; they all seem to be what the characters in Cheever's Italian stories actually are: expatriates and exiles. Physical ailments are rare, emotional ones epidemic. Instead of disease, there is the "dis-ease" of "spiritual nomadism." They are as restless as any of Cheever's most wayward plots and in need of "building a bridge" between the events of their lives as well as between those lives and their longings. Trapped in routines as restricting as any prison cell and often in marriages that seem little more than sexual battlefields, where even the hair curlers appear "bellicose," his characters appear poised between escaping into the past in a futile effort to repeat what they believe they have lost and aspiring to a lyrical future that can be affirmed, even "sung," though never quite attained. Even the latter can be dangerous. "Dominated by anticipation" (a number of Cheever's characters hope excessively), they are locked in a state of perpetual adolescence, unwilling to grow up, take responsibility, and face death in any form. Although their world may lie spread out like a bewildering and stupendous dream, they find it nevertheless confining, inhospitable, even haunted by fears of emotional and economic insecurity and a sense of personal inadequacy and inconsequentiality, their sole inheritance, it seems, from the many fathers who figure so prominently in the stories, often by virtue of their absence from the lives of their now middle-aged sons. Adrift in an incoherent world and alone in the midst of suburbs zoned for felicity, they suffer frequent blows to their already fragile sense of self-esteem, seeing through yet wanting the protection of the veneer of social decorum and ceremoniousness that is the outward and visible sign of American middle-class aspiration and which Cheever's characters do not so much court as covet.

"THE ENORMOUS RADIO"

The thinness of that veneer is especially apparent in "The Enormous Radio," a work that shows little trace of the Hemingway style that marks many of Cheever's earlier stories. The story begins realistically enough. Jim and Irene Westcott, in their mid-thirties, are an average couple in all respects but one: their above-average interest in classical music (and, one assumes, in the harmony and decorum that such music represents). When their old radio breaks down, Jim generously buys an expensive new one to which Irene takes an instant dislike. Like their interest in music, which they indulge as if a secret but harmless vice, this small disruption in their harmonious married life seems a minor affair, at least at first. The radio, however, appearing "like an aggressive intruder," shedding a "malevolent green light," and possessing a "mistaken sensitivity to discord," soon becomes a divisive, even diabolical presence, but the evil in this story, as in Nathaniel Hawthorne's "Young Goodman Brown," to which it has often been compared, comes from *within* the characters, not from without (the radio). When the radio begins to broadcast the Westcotts' neighbors' quarrels, lusts, fears, and crimes, Irene becomes dismayed, perversely entertained, and finally apprehensive; if she can eavesdrop on her neighbors' most intimate conversations, she thinks that perhaps they can listen in on hers. Hearing their tales of woe, she demands that her husband affirm their happiness. Far from easing her apprehensiveness, his words only exacerbate it as he first voices his own previously well-guarded frustrations over money, job prospects, and growing old, and as he eventually exposes his wife's own evil nature. As frustration explodes into accusation, the illusion of marital happiness that the Westcotts had so carefully cultivated shatters. As with so many Cheever stories, "The Enormous Radio" has its origin in biographical fact: While writing in the basement of a Sutton Place apartment house, Cheever would hear the elevator going up and down and would imagine that the wires could carry his neighbors' conversations down to him.

"GOODBYE, MY BROTHER"

"Goodbye, My Brother" derives from another and far more pervasive biographical fact, Cheever's relationship with his elder brother, Fred, the father figure to whom he developed too close an attachment. Fred turned to business and for a time supported Cheever's writing but, like Cheever, eventually became an alcoholic. Beginning with "The Brothers" and culminating in the fratricide in *Falconer*, relations between brothers figure nearly as prominently in Cheever's fiction as those between spouses. Just as stories such as "The Enormous Radio" are not simply about marital spats, "Goodbye, My Brother" is not just about sibling rivalry. Just as the relationship between Irene and the malevolent radio is actually about a condition within the marriage and more especially within Irene herself, the external relationship between the story's narrator and his brother Lawrence is actually about the narrator's own Dr. Jekyll and Mr. Hyde personality—in psychological terms, a matter of split personality and projection. The narrator objectifies in Lawrence his own fears, frustrations, and self-loathing. Lawrence and the narrator are two of the Pommeroys who have gathered on Laud's Head in August for their annual family vacation. Like his sister, just back after her divorce, and their widowed mother, who drinks too much while trying to keep up the family's upper-crust pretensions, the narrator needs these few weeks of respite from the grind of his dead-end teaching job. Together they swim, play cards and tennis, drink, and go to costume dances, where in an almost Jungian freak of chance, all the men come dressed as football players and all the women as brides, as eloquent a statement of the sadness of their blighted but still aspiring lives as one can imagine. Lawrence partakes in none of it. A lawyer moving from one city and job to another, he is the only family member with prospects and the only one unable to enjoy or even tolerate the illusion of happiness that the family seeks to maintain. He is also the only one willing, indeed eager, to detect the flaws and fakery in the Pommeroys' summer home, its protective sea wall, and its equally protective forms of play. Gloomy and morose as well as critical, Lawrence is, to borrow the title of another Cheever story, the worm in the Pommeroy apple. He is the messenger bearing the bad news, whom the narrator nearly kills with a blow to the head as the two walk along the beach. He strikes not only to free himself from his brother's morbid presence but also to extirpate the Lawrence side of his own divided self: Cain and Abel, murderer and good Samaritan. Once Lawrence and his sickly looking wife and daughter leave, the narrator turns to the purifying water and the triumphant vision of his mythically named wife and sister, Helen and Diana, rising naked from the sea. The story closes on a lyrically charged note that seems both to affirm all that the Pommeroys have sought and, by virtue of the degree of lyrical intensity, to accentuate the gap between that vision and Lawrence's more factual and pessimistic point of view.

"O YOUTH AND BEAUTY"

"O Youth and Beauty" makes explicit what virtually all Cheever's stories imply, the end of youth's promise, of that hopeful vision that the ending of "Goodbye, My Brother" sought to affirm. Thus it seems ironically apt that "O Youth and Beauty" should begin with a long (two-hundred-word) Whitmanesque sentence, which, in addition to setting the scene and establishing the narrative situation, subtly evokes that Transcendental vision that Walt Whitman both espoused and, in his distinctive poetic style, sought to embody. Beginning "At the tag end of nearly every long, large Saturday night party in the suburb of Shady Hill," it proceeds through a series of long anaphoric subordinate clauses beginning with the word "when" and ending with "then Trace Bearden would begin to chide Cash Bentley about his age and thinning hair." The reader is thus introduced to what, for the partygoers, has already become something of a suburban ritual: the perfectly named Cash Bentley's hurdling of the furniture as a way of warding off death and reliving the athletic triumphs of the youth that he refuses to relinquish. When Cash, now forty, breaks his leg, the intimations of mortality begin to multiply in his morbid mind. Although he may run his race alone, and although the Lawrentian gloominess that comes in the wake of the accident may make him increasingly isolated from his neighbors and friends, Cash is not at all unique, and his fears are extreme but nevertheless representative of a fear that pervades the entire community and that evidences itself in his wife's trying to appear younger and slimmer than she is and her "cutting out of the current copy of *Life* those scenes of mayhem, disaster, and violent death that she felt might corrupt her children." It is rather ironic that a moment later she should accidentally kill her husband in their own living room with the starter's pistol, as he attempts to recapture the past glories of all those other late Saturday night races against time and self in an attempt

always, already doomed, to recapture the past glories of his days as a young track star. The track is in fact an apt symbol for Cash's circular life, in which, instead of progress, one finds only the horror of Nietzschean eternal recurrence.

"THE FIVE-FORTY-EIGHT"

Upon first reading, "The Five-Forty-Eight" seems to have little in common with the blackly humorous "O Youth and Beauty." A disturbed woman, Miss Dent, follows Blake, whose secretary she had been for three weeks and whose lover she was for one night, some six months earlier. She trails him from his office building to his commuter train. Threatening to shoot him, she gets off at his stop and forces him to kneel and rub his face in the dirt for having seduced and abandoned her six months earlier. One of Cheever's least likable characters, Blake gets what he deserves. Having chosen Miss Dent as he has chosen his other women (including, it seems, his wife) "for their lack of self-esteem," he not only had her fired the day after they made love but also took the afternoon off. Miss Dent fares considerably better, for in choosing not to kill Blake she discovers "some kindness, some saneness" in herself that she believes she can put to use. Blake too undergoes a change insofar as he experiences regret for the first time and comes to understand his own vulnerability, which he has heretofore managed to safeguard by means of his "protective" routines and scrupulous observance of Shady Hill's sumptuary laws. Whether these changes will be lasting remains unclear; he is last seen picking himself up, cleaning himself off, and walking home, alone.

"The Five-Forty-Eight" is quite literally one of Cheever's darkest stories; only the dimmest of lights and the faintest of hopes shine at its end. Although it too ends at night, "The Housebreaker of Shady Hill" is one of Cheever's brightest and most cheerful works, full of the spiritual phototropism so important in *Falconer*, the novel that *Newsweek* hailed as "Cheever's Triumph." The housebreaker is thirty-six-year-old Johnny Hake, kindly and comical, who suddenly finds himself out of work, at risk of losing his house, his circle of friends, and the last shreds of his self-esteem. Desperate for cash, he steals nine hundred dollars from a neighbor, a theft that transforms his vision of the world. Suddenly, he begins to see evil everywhere and evidence that everyone can see him for what he now is. The "moral bottom" drops out of his world but in decidedly comic fashion: Even a birthday gift from his children—an extension ladder—becomes an acknowledgment of his wrong-doing (and nearly cause for divorce). Chance, however, saves Johnny. Walking to his next victim's house, he feels a few drops of rain fall on his head and awakens from his ludicrous nightmare, his vision of the world restored. Opting for life's simple pleasures (he is after all still unemployed), he returns home and has a pleasant dream in which he is seventeen years old. Johnny cannot get his youth back, but he does get his job (and he does return the money he has stolen). The happy endings proliferate as the story slips the yoke of realism and romps in the magical realm of pure fairy tale, where, as Cheever puts it far more sardonically in his third novel, *Bullet Park* (1969), everything is "wonderful wonderful wonderful wonderful."

"THE COUNTRY HUSBAND"

Comic exaggeration and hyperbolically happy endings characterize many of the stories of the late 1950's and early 1960's. In "The Hosebreaker of Shady Hill," it is losing his job that starts Johnny Hake on his comical crime spree; in "The Country Husband," it is nearly losing his life that sends Francis Weed on an ever more absurdly comical quest for love and understanding. Weed has his brush with death when his plane is forced to make an emergency landing in a field outside Philadelphia. The danger over, his vulnerability (like Blake's) and mortality (like Cash Bentley's) established, the real damage begins when Weed can find no one to lend a sympathetic ear—not his friend, Trace Bearden, on the commuter train, not even his wife, Julia (too busy putting dinner on the table), or his children (the youngest are fighting and the oldest is reading *True Romance*). With his very own True Adventure still untold, Weed goes outside, where he hears a neighbor playing "Moonlight Sonata," *rubato*, "like an outpouring of tearful petulance, lonesomeness, and self-pity—of everything it was Beethoven's greatness not to know," and everything it will now be Weed's comic

misfortune to experience as he embarks upon his own True Romance with the rather unromantically named Anne Murchison, his children's new teenage babysitter.

Playing the part of a lovesick adolescent, the middle-aged Weed acts out his midlife crisis and in doing so jeopardizes his family's social standing and his marriage. The consequences are potentially serious, as are the various characters' fears and troubles (Anne's alcoholic father, Julia's "natural fear of chaos and loneliness," which leads to her obsessive partygoing). What is humorous is Cheever's handling of these fears in a story in which solecisms are slapstick, downfalls are pratfalls, and pariahs turn out to be weeds in Cheever's suburban Garden of Eden. When Francis finally decides to overcome his Emersonian self-reliance, to confide in and seek the help of a psychiatrist (who will do what neither friends nor family have thus far been willing to do—that is, listen), the first words Weed tearfully blurts out are, "I'm in love, Dr. Harzog." Since "The Country Husband" is a comedy, Weed is cured of his "disease" and able to channel his desires into more socially acceptable ways (conjugal love and, humorously enough, woodworking). The story ends with a typically Cheeveresque affirmation of Fitzgerald-like romantic possibilities, no less apparent in Shady Hill than in the *Great Gatsby*'s (1925) West Egg. It is an affirmation, however, tempered once again by the tenuousness of the characters' situation in a "village that hangs, morally and economically, from a thread."

"THE DEATH OF JUSTINA"

The thread will break—although still comically—in "The Death of Justina." Here, the focus is double, on the parallel plights of the authorial narrator, a fiction writer, and the protagonist-narrator of the story that he writes (like "The Housebreaker of Shady Hill," in oral style), also a writer (of advertising copy). Briefly stated, their shared predicament is this: how (for the one) to write about and (for the other) to live in a world that seems to grow increasingly chaotic and preposterous. As the authorial narrator explains, "Fiction is art and art is the triumph over chaos (no less) and we can accomplish this only by the most vigilant exercise of choice, but in a world that changes more swiftly than we can perceive there is always the danger that our powers of selection will be mistaken and that the vision we serve will come to nothing." The authorial narrator then offers Moses' account of the death of his wife's cousin Justina as "one example of chaos." Ordered by his doctor to stop smoking and drinking and by his boss to write copy for a product called Elixircol (something of a cross between Geritol and the Fountain of Youth), Moses suddenly finds himself at a complete loss when he tries to arrange for Justina's funeral, for Justina has died in his house and his house is an area of Proxmire Manor not zoned for death. No doctor will issue a death certificate, and the mayor refuses to sign an exemption until a quorum of the village council is available, but when Moses threatens to bury Justina in his yard, the mayor relents. Victorious but still shaken, Moses that night has a strange dream set in a vast supermarket where the shoppers stock their carts with unlabeled, shapeless packages, which are then, much to their shame, torn open at the checkout counters by brutish men who first ridicule the selections and then push the shoppers out the doors into what sounds much like Dante's inferno. The scene is amusing but, like the ludicrously comical scenes in Franz Kafka's works, also unsettling. The story does not affirm the shoppers any more than it does the village council that drew up the zoning laws, but it does understand what compels them even as it sympathetically satirizes the inadequacy of their means. As Moses points out, "How can a people who do not mean to understand death hope to understand love, and who will sound the alarm?"

"THE BRIGADIER AND THE GOLF WIDOW"

"The Brigadier and the Golf Widow" makes a similar point in a similar way. Here too, the authorial narrator is perplexed, wondering what the nineteenth century writers Charles Dickens, Anton Chekhov, Nikolai Gogol, and William Makepeace Thackeray would have made of a fallout shelter (bizarrely decorated and disguised with gnomes, plaster ducks, and a birdbath). He also understands, however, that fallout shelters are as much a part of his mid-twentieth century landscape as are trees and shrubbery. The shelter in question belongs to Charlie Pastern, the country

club general who spends his time calling loudly for nuclear attacks on any and all of his nation's enemies. His world begins to unravel when, by chance, he begins an affair with a neighbor whose own fears and insecurity lead her first to promiscuity and then to demanding the key to the Pasterns' shelter (a key that the local bishop also covets). Apparently the last words of "The Death of Justina," taken verbatim from the Twenty-third Psalm, about walking through the shadow of the valley of death and fearing no evil, no longer apply.

For all the good cheer, hearty advice, biblical quotations, comical predicaments, and lyrical affirmations, there lies at the center of Cheever's fiction the fear of insufficiency and inadequacy—of shelters that will not protect, marriages that will not endure, jobs that will be lost, threads that will not hold.

"THE SWIMMER"

That the thread does not hold in "The Swimmer," Cheever's most painstakingly crafted and horrific work, is especially odd, for the story begins as comedy, a lighthearted satire, involving a group of suburban couples sitting around the Westerhazys' pool on a beautiful midsummer Sunday afternoon talking about what and how much they drank the night before. Suddenly Neddy Merrill, yet another of Cheever's middle-aged but youthfully named protagonists, decides to swim home pool to pool. More than a prank, it is for him a celebration of the fineness of the day, a voyage of discovery, a testament to life's romantic possibilities. Neddy's swim will cover eight miles, sixteen pools, in only ten pages (as printed in *The Stories of John Cheever*). Although he encounters some delays and obstacles—drinks graciously offered and politely, even ceremoniously, drunk, a thorny hedge to be gotten over, gravel underfoot—Neddy completes nearly half the journey in only two pages (pages 3-4; pages 1-2 are purely preparatory). The story and its reader move as confidently and rapidly as Neddy, but then there are a few interruptions: a brief rain shower that forces Neddy to seek shelter, a dry pool at one house, and a for-sale sign inexplicably posted at another. Midway through both journey and story, the point of view suddenly and briefly veers away from Neddy, who now looks pitifully exposed and foolishly stranded as he attempts to cross a divided highway. His strength and confidence ebbing, he seems unprepared for whatever lies ahead yet unable to turn back. Like the reader, he is unsure when his little joke turned so deadly serious. At the one public pool on his itinerary, he is assaulted by crowds, shrill sounds, and harsh odors. After being very nearly stalled for two pages, the pace quickens ever so slightly but only to leave Neddy still weaker and more disoriented. Each "breach in the succession" exposes Neddy's inability to bridge the widening gap between his vision of the world and his actual place in it. He is painfully rebuffed by those he had previously been powerful enough to mistreat—a former mistress, a socially inferior couple whose invitations he and his wife routinely discarded. The apparent cause of Neddy's downfall begins to become clear to the reader only as it begins to become clear to Neddy—a sudden and major financial reversal—but Neddy's situation cannot be attributed to merely economic factors, nor is it susceptible to purely rational analysis. Somewhere along Neddy's and the reader's way, everything has changed: The passing of hours becomes the passage of whole seasons, perhaps even years, as realism gives way to fantasy, humor to horror as the swimmer sees his whole life pass before him in a sea of repressed memories. Somehow Neddy has woken into his own worst dream. Looking into his empty house, he comes face to face with the insecurity that nearly all Cheever's characters fear and the inadequacy that they all feel.

The stories (and novels) that Cheever wrote during the last two decades of his life grew increasingly and innovatively disparate in structure. "The Jewels of the Cabots," for example, or "The President of the Argentine" matches the intensifying disunity of the author's personal life. Against this narrative waywardness, however, Cheever continued to offer and even to extend an affirmation of the world and his protagonists' place in it in a lyrically charged prose at once serene and expansive ("The World of Apples," *Falconer*). In other words, he continued to do during these last two decades what he had been doing so well for the previous three: writing a fiction of celebration and incoherence.

OTHER MAJOR WORKS

LONG FICTION: *The Wapshot Chronicle*, 1957; *The Wapshot Scandal*, 1964; *Bullet Park*, 1969; *Falconer*, 1977; *Oh What a Paradise It Seems*, 1982.

SCREENPLAY: *The Shady Hill Kidnapping*, 1982.

NONFICTION: *The Letters of John Cheever*, 1988 (Benjamin Cheever, editor); *The Journals of John Cheever*, 1991.

BIBLIOGRAPHY

Bosha, Francis J. *John Cheever: A Reference Guide.* Boston: G. K. Hall, 1981. Especially useful for its annotated listing of works about Cheever and for its brief overview of the critical response to Cheever's fiction. For a more complete listing of primary works, see Dennis Coale's checklist in *Bulletin of Bibliography* (volume 36, 1979) and the supplement in Robert G. Collins's book (below). Robert A. Morace's exhaustive assessment of all available biographical, bibliographical, and critical materials appears in *Contemporary Authors: Bibliographical Series: American Authors* (1986) and can be updated by reference to *American Literary Annual* (1985-   ).

_____, ed. *The Critical Response to John Cheever.* Westport, Conn.: Greenwood Press, 1994. A collection of reviews and critical essays on Cheever's novels and short-story collections by various commentators and critics.

Collins, Robert G., ed. *Critical Essays on John Cheever.* Boston: G. K. Hall, 1982. Reprints an excellent sampling of reviews, interviews, and early criticism (including many dubbed "new" that are in fact only slightly reworked older pieces). Of the truly new items, three deserve special mention: Collins's biocritical introduction, Dennis Coale's bibliographical supplement, and particularly Samuel Coale's "Cheever and Hawthorne: The American Romancer's Art," arguably one of the most important critical essays on Cheever.

Dessner, Lawrence Jay. "Gender and Structure in John Cheever's 'The Country Husband.'" *Studies in Short Fiction* 31 (Winter, 1994): 57-68. Argues that the story is structured as a comedy with a farcical narrow escape and a tension between the domestic and the wild; contends the plot pattern dissolves pain into laughter.

Donaldson, Scott. *John Cheever: A Biography.* New York: Random House, 1988. Scrupulously researched, interestingly written, and judiciously argued, Donaldson's biography presents Cheever as both author and private man. Donaldson fleshes out most of the previously unknown areas in Cheever's biography and dispels many of the biographical myths that Cheever himself encouraged. The account is sympathetic yet objective.

Donaldson, Scott, ed. *Conversations with John Cheever.* Jackson: University Press of Mississippi, 1987. Until his final years a rather reticent man, Cheever granted relatively few interviews. The most important ones are reprinted here, along with the editor's thorough chronology and brief but useful introduction.

Hipkiss, Robert. "'The Country Husband': A Model Cheever Achievement." *Studies in Short Fiction* 27 (Fall, 1990): 577-585. Analyzes the story as a prose poem filled with imagery of war, myth, music, and nature. Argues that the elaborate image pattern makes us realize how rooted in our American value system the protagonist's final fate really is.

Meanor, Patrick. *John Cheever Revisited.* New York: Twayne, 1995. The first book-length study of Cheever to make use of his journals and letters published in the late 1980's and early 1990's. Focuses on how Cheever created a mythopoeic world in his novels and stories. Includes two chapters on his short stories, with detailed analyses of stories in *The Enormous Radio* and *The Brigadier and the Golf Widow.*

O'Hara, James E. *John Cheever: A Study of the Short Fiction.* Boston: Twayne, 1989. In addition to reprinting five important reviews and critical essays and providing a detailed chronology and annotated selected bibliography, this volume offers a 120-page analysis of Cheever as a writer of short stories that goes well beyond the introductory level. O'Hara's discussion of the early unanthologized stories is especially noteworthy.

Salwak, Dale, and Paul David Seldis, eds. *Dragons and Martinis: The Skewed Realism of John Cheever,* by Michael D. Byrne. San Bernardino, Calif.: Borgo Press, 1993. Focuses on Cheever's style in his fiction. Includes bibliographical references and an index.

Robert A. Morace

ANTON CHEKHOV

Born: Taganrog, Russia; January 29, 1860
Died: Badenweiler, Germany; July 15, 1904

PRINCIPAL SHORT FICTION
Skazki Melpomeny, 1884
Pystrye rasskazy, 1886
Nevinnye rechi, 1887
V sumerkakh, 1887
Rasskazy, 1888
The Tales of Tchehov, 1916-1922

OTHER LITERARY FORMS

Anton Chekhov's literary reputation rests as much on his drama as on his stories and sketches, despite the fact that he was a far more prolific writer of fiction, having written only seventeen plays but almost six hundred stories. *Chayka* (1896, rev. 1898; *The Seagull,* 1909), *Dyadya Vanya* (1897; *Uncle Vanya,* 1914), *Tri sestry* (1901; *Three Sisters,* 1920), and *Vishnyovy sad* (1904; *The Cherry Orchard,* 1908), Chekhov's chief dramatic works, are universally considered classics of modern theater. Chekhov was also an indefatigable correspondent, and his letters, along with his diaries and notebooks, form an important segment of his writing. He also wrote numerous journal articles and one long work, *Ostrov Sakhalin* (serialized in 1893 and 1894), a scholarly exposé of an island penal colony that Chekhov visited in 1890.

ACHIEVEMENTS

In his lifetime, Anton Chekhov gained considerable critical acclaim. In 1888, he won the Pushkin Prize for his fiction, and in 1900, he was selected to honorary membership in the Russian Academy of Sciences for both his fiction and his drama.

Chekhov's fiction departs from the formulaic, heavily plotted story to mirror Russian life authentically, concentrating on characters in very ordinary circumstances that often seem devoid of conflict. A realist, Chekhov treads a fine line between detachment and a whimsical but sympathetic concern for his subjects. In his mature work, he is perhaps the most genial of Russian masters, compassionate and forgiving, seldom strident or doctrinaire. Equally important, that mature work reflects very careful artistry, worthy of study for its technique alone.

BIOGRAPHY

Anton Pavlovich Chekhov, the third of six Chekhov children, was born on January 29, 1860, in Taganrog, a provincial city in southern Russia. His father, Pavel Egorovich Chekhov, son of a serf, ran a meager grocery store, which young Anton often tended in his neglectful father's absence. A religious fanatic and stern disciplinarian, Pavel gave his children frequent beatings and forced them to spend long hours in various devotional activities. For Anton, who did not share his father's zeal, it was a depressing, gloomy childhood.

Although the family was poor and Pavel's marginal business was slowly failing, Anton was able to get some schooling, first at a Greek parochial school, then at the boys' gymnasium, or high school. In 1875, after a bout with acute peritonitis, young Chekhov decided to become a physician. His future brightened when, in 1876, his father, trying to evade his credi-

tors, secretly moved the family to Moscow, leaving Anton to finish school.

In 1879, Anton moved to Moscow, entered the medical school of the University of Moscow, and almost immediately began publishing stories in various magazines and newspapers. A very prolific apprentice, by 1884, when he was graduated from medical school, he had published his first collection of short fiction. By 1886, Chekhov had begun his long association and friendship with A. S. Suvorin, the owner of an influential conservative newspaper to which Chekhov contributed dozens of pieces. Recognized as a significant new author, Chekhov devoted more time to writing and less and less to his medical practice, which, in time, he would abandon altogether.

His greatly improved finances allowed Chekhov to buy a better Moscow house and gave him time to travel, which he frequently did, despite ill health. In 1887, he journeyed to the Don Steppe, and two years later crossed Asia to visit the Russian penal colony on Sakhalin Island. The next year he traveled to Europe with Suvorin. In 1892, Chekhov purchased Melikhovo, an estate outside Moscow. It became a

Anton Chekhov (Library of Congress)

gathering place for family, relatives, and associates. There, too, Chekhov practiced medicine, more as a human service to poor villagers than as a necessary source of income.

In 1896, Chekhov had his first theatrical success with *The Seagull*, although the reaction of the opening-night audience greatly distressed the author. Suffering from tuberculosis, by the mid-1890's he began coughing up blood, and in 1897 he had to be hospitalized. In 1898, Chekhov began his propitious association with the newly formed Moscow Art Theater and its great director, Konstantin Stanislavski. He also met Olga Leonardovna Knipper, a young actress. Despite his ill health and his frequent sojourns to Yalta, they carried on a love affair and were married in 1901.

The last six years of Chekhov's life, from 1898 to 1904, brought him as much recognition as a dramatist as his earlier career had brought him as a writer of fiction. *Uncle Vanya, Three Sisters*, and *The Cherry Orchard*, his last significant work, were all major successes. In 1904, in one last attempt to stay the course of his disease, Chekhov and his wife went to Germany, where, at Badenweiler, he died on July 15.

ANALYSIS

Anton Chekhov published his earliest stories and sketches in various popular magazines under pseudonyms, the most often used being "Antosha Chekhonte." As that pen name hints, he was at first an unassuming and relatively compliant "hack," willing to dash off careless pieces fashioned for the popular reader. Most are light, topical studies of social types, often running less than a thousand words. Many are mere sketches or extended jokes, often banal or cynical. Some are farces, built on caricatures. Others are brief parodies of popular genres, including the romantic novel. Few display much originality in subject. Still, in their technique, economy of expression, and themes, the early pieces prefigure some of Chekhov's most mature work. In them, Chekhov experimented with point of view and most particularly the use of irony as a fictional device. He also established his preference for an almost scientific objectivity in his depiction of character and events, an insistence

that, in the course of his career, he would have to defend against his detractors.

Chekhov's penchant for irony is exemplified in his very first published story, "Pis'mo k uchenomu sosedu" ("A Letter to a Learned Neighbor"), which appeared in 1880. The letter writer, Vladimirovich, is a pompous, officious oaf who makes pretentious statements about science and knowledge with inane blunders in syntax, spelling, and diction, inadvertently revealing his boorish stupidity while trying to ingratiate himself with his erudite neighbor.

As does this sketch, many of Chekhov's first pieces lampoon types found in Russian society, favorite satirical targets being functionaries in the czarist bureaucracy and their obsequious regard for their superiors. One sketch, "Smert' chinovnika" ("The Death of a Government Clerk"), deals with a civil servant named Chervyakov who accidentally sneezes on a general and is mortified because he is unable to obtain the man's pardon. After repeated rebukes, he resigns himself to defeat, lies down, and dies. His sense of self-worth is so intricately bound up in his subservient role that, unpardoned, he has no reason to continue living.

In another story, "Khameleon" ("The Chameleon"), Ochumelov, a police officer, vacillates between placing blame on a dog or the man whom the dog has bitten until it can be confirmed that the dog does or does not belong to a certain General Zhigalov. When it turns out that the dog belongs to the general's brother, the officer swears that he will get even with the dog's victim. Like so many other characters in Chekhov's fiction, Ochumelov is a bully to his subordinates but an officious toady to his betters.

Other stories, not built on irony or a momentous event in the central character's life, are virtually plotless fragments. Some chronicle the numbing effects of living by social codes and mores rather than from authentic inner convictions, while others record human expectations frustrated by a sobering and often grim reality. In several stories, Chekhov deals with childhood innocence encountering or narrowly evading an adult world that is sordid, deceitful, or perverse. For example, in "V more" ("At Sea"), a man decides to provide a sex education for his son by having him observe a newly married couple and a third man through a bulkhead peep hole. Presumably to satisfy his own puerile interest, the father peeps first and is so mortified by what he sees that he does not allow his son to look at all.

Sometimes severely restricted by magazine requirements, Chekhov learned to be direct and sparse in statement. Many of his early stories have little or no exposition at all. The main character's lineage, elaborate details of setting, authorial incursions—all disappear for economy's sake. In his precipitous openings, Chekhov often identifies a character by name, identifies his class or profession, and states his emotional condition, all in a single sentence. Others open with a snippet of conversation that has presumably been in progress for some time. When he does set a scene with description, Chekhov does so with quick, deft, impressionistic strokes, with only the barest of details.

Chekhov also learned the value of symbols as guides to inner character. In "Melyuzga," a pathetic clerk named Nevyrazimov is trying to write a flattering Easter letter to his superior, whom, in reality, he despises. Hoping for a raise, this miserable underling must grovel, which contributes to his self-loathing and self-pity. As he tries to form the ingratiating words, he spies a cockroach and takes pity on the insect because he deems its miserable existence worse than his own. After considering his own options, however, and growing more despondent, when he again spies the roach he squashes it with his palm, then burns it, an act which, as the last line divulges, makes him feel better. The destruction of the roach is a symbolic act. It seems gratuitous and pointless, but it reveals the dehumanizing effect that *chinopochitanie*, or "rank reverence," has on the clerk. In destroying the roach, Nevyrazimov is able to displace some of the self-loathing that accompanies his self-pity. His misery abates because he is able, for a moment, to play the bully.

Despite the limitations that popular writing imposed, between 1880 and 1885 there is an advance in Chekhov's work, born, perhaps, from a growing tolerance and sympathy for his fellow human beings. He gradually turned away from short, acrid farces toward more relaxed, psychologically probing studies of his characters and their ubiquitous misery and infrequent joy. In "Unter Prishibeev" ("Sergeant Prishibeev"), Chekhov again develops a character who is unable to adjust to change because his role in life has been too rigid and narrow. A subservient army bully, he is unable to mend his ways when returned to civilian life and torments his fellow townspeople through spying, intimidation, and physical abuse. His harsh discipline, sanctioned in the military, only lands him in jail, to his total astonishment.

By 1886, Chekhov had begun to receive encouragement from the Russian literati, notably Dmitrí Grigorovich, who, in an important unsolicited letter, warned Chekhov not to waste his talents on potboilers. The impact on Chekhov was momentous, for he had received the recognition that he desired. Thereafter, he worked to perfect his craft, to master the *literature nastroenija*, or "literature of mood," works in which a single, dominant mood is evoked and action is relatively insignificant.

This does not mean that all Chekhov's stories are plotless or lack conflict. "Khoristka" ("The Chorus Girl"), for example, is a dramatic piece in method akin to the author's curtain-raising farces based on confrontation and ironic turns. The singer, confronted by the wife of one of her admirers, an embezzler, gives the wife all of her valuables to redeem the philanderer's reputation. His wife's willingness to humble herself before a chorus girl regenerates the man's love and admiration for his spouse. He cruelly snubs the chorus girl and, in rank ingratitude, leaves her alone in abject misery.

Other stories using an ironic twist leave the principal character's fate to the reader's imagination. "Noch' pered sudom" ("The Night Before the Trial") is an example. The protagonist, who narrates the story, makes a ludicrous blunder. On the eve of his trial for bigamy, he poses as a doctor and writes a bogus prescription for a woman. He also accepts payment from her husband, only to discover at the start of his trial that the husband is his prosecutor. The story goes no further than the man's brief speculation on his approaching fate.

In yet another, more involved story, "Nishchii" ("The Beggar"), a lawyer, Skvortsov, is approached by a drunken and deceitful but resourceful beggar, Lushkov, whom he unmercifully scolds as a liar and a wastrel. He then sets Lushkov to work chopping wood, challenging him to earn his way through honest, hard work. Before long, Skvortsov persuades himself that he has the role of Lushkov's redeemer and manages to find him enough work doing odd jobs to earn a meager livelihood. Eventually, growing respectable and independent, Lushkov obtains decent work in a notary's office. Two years later, encountering Skvortsov outside a theater, Lushkov confides that it was indeed at Skvortsov's house that he was saved—not, however, by Skvortsov's scolding but by Skvortsov's cook, Olga, who took pity on Lushkov and always chopped the wood for him. It was Olga's nobility that prompted the beggar's reformation, not the pompous moral rectitude of the lawyer.

In 1887, when Chekhov took the time to visit the Don Steppe, he was established as one of Russia's premier writers of fiction. With the accolades, there inevitably came some negative criticism. A few of his contemporaries argued that Chekhov seemed to lack a social conscience, that he remained too detached and indifferent to humanity in a time of great unrest and need for reform. Chekhov never believed that his art should serve a bald polemical purpose, but he was sensitive to the unjust critical opinion that he lacked strong personal convictions. In much of his mature writing, Chekhov worked to dispel that misguided accusation.

For a time Chekhov came under the spell of Leo Tolstoy, his great contemporary, not so much for that moralist's religious fervor but for his doctrine of nonresistance to evil. That idea is fundamental to "The Meeting." In this tale, which in tone is similar to the didactic Russian folktales, a thief steals money from a peasant, who had collected it for refurbishing a church. The thief, baffled by the peasant's failure to resist, gradually repents and returns the money.

"THE STEPPE"

In 1888, Chekhov wrote and published "Step'" ("The Steppe"), inspired by his journey across the Don Steppe. The story, consisting of eight chapters,

approaches the novella in scope and reflects the author's interest in trying a longer work, which Grigorovich had advised him to do. In method, the piece is similar to picaresque tales, in which episodes are like beads, linked only by a common string—the voyage or quest.

The main characters are a merchant, Kuznichov, his nine-year-old nephew, Egorushka, and a priest, Father Christopher, who set out to cross the steppe in a cart. The adults travel on business, to market wool, while Egorushka is off to school. The monotony of their journey is relieved by tidbits of conversation and brief encounters with secondary characters in unrelated episodes. Diversion for young Egorushka is provided by various denizens of the steppe. These minor characters, though delineated but briefly, are both picturesque and lifelike.

Some of the characters spin a particular tale of woe. For example, there is Solomon, brother to Moses, the Jewish owner of a posting house. Solomon, disgusted with human greed, has burned his patrimony and now wallows in self-destructive misery. Another miserable figure is Pantelei, an old peasant whose life has offered nothing but arduous work. He has nearly frozen to death several times on the beautiful but desolate steppe. Dymov, the cunning, mean-spirited peasant, is another wretch devoid of either grace or hope.

The story involves a realistic counterpart to the romantic quest, for the merchant and the priest, joined by the charming Countess Dranitskaya, seek the almost legendary figure, Varlamov. Thus, in a quiet, subdued way, the work has an epic cast to it. Its unity depends on imagery and thematic centrality of the impressions of Egorushka, whose youthful illusions play off against the sordid reality of the adult world. The journey to the school becomes for Egorushka a rite of passage, a familiar Chekhovian motif. At the end of the story, about to enter a strange house, the boy finally breaks into tears, feeling cut off from his past and apprehensive about his future.

"The Steppe" marks a tremendous advance over Chekhov's earliest works. Its impressionistic description of the landscape is often poetic, and though, like most of Chekhov's fiction, the work is open plotted, it is structurally tight and very compelling. The work's hypnotic attraction comes from its sparse, lyrical simplicity and timeless theme. It is the first of the author's flawless pieces.

"A BORING STORY"

Another long work, "Skuchnaia istoriia" ("A Boring Story"), shifts Chekhov's character focus away from a youth first encountering misery in the world to an old man, Nikolai Stepanovich, who, near the end of life, finally begins to realize its stupefying emptiness. The professor is the narrator, although, when the story starts, it is presented in the third rather than the first person. It soon becomes apparent, however, that the voice is the professor's own. The story is actually a diary, unfolding in the present tense.

The reader learns that although Stepanovich enjoys an illustrious reputation in public, of which he is extremely proud, in private he is dull and emotionally handicapped. Having devoted his life to teaching medicine, the value of which he never questions, the professor has sacrificed love, compassion, and friendship. He has gradually alienated himself from family, colleagues, and students, as is shown by his repeated failures to relate to them in other than superficial, mechanical ways. He admits his inability to communicate to his wife or daughter, and although he claims to love his ward, Katya, whom his wife and daughter hate, even she finally realizes that he is an emotional cripple and deserts him to run off with another professor who has aroused some jealousy in Nikolai.

The professor, his life dedicated to academe, has become insensitive to such things as his daughter Liza's chagrin over her shabby coat or her feelings for Gnekker, her suitor, who, the professor suspects, is a fraud. Unable to understand his family's blindness to Gnekker, whom he perceives as a scavenging crab, Nikolai sets out to prove his assumption. He goes to Kharkov to investigate Gnekker's background and confirms his suspicions, only to discover that he is too late. In his absence, Liza and Gnekker have married.

Bordering on the tragic, "A Boring Story" presents a character who is unable to express what he feels. He confesses his dull nature, but, though honest with himself, he can confide in no one. Detached, he

is able to penetrate the illusions of others, but his approach to life is so abstract and general as to hinder meaningful interpersonal relationships. Near the end of life, he is wiser but spiritually paralyzed by his conviction that he knows very little of human worth. One notes in "A Boring Story" Chekhov's fascination with the fact that conversation may not ensure communication, and his treatment of that reality becomes a signatory motif in Chekhov's later works, including his plays. Characters talk but do not listen, remaining in their own illusory worlds, which mere words will not let them share with others.

"THE DUEL"

"Duel" ("The Duel"), a long story, is representative of Chekhov's most mature work. Its focal concern is with self-deception and rationalization for one's failures. It pits two men against each other. The one, Laevsky, is a spineless, listless, and disillusioned intellectual who has miserably failed in life. The other, Von Koren, is an active, self-righteous zoologist who comes to despise the other man as a parasite.

In his early conversations with his friend Dr. Samoilenko, Laevsky reveals his tendency to place blame on civilization for human failings, a notion espoused by Jean-Jacques Rousseau and a host of other romantic thinkers. The doctor, whose mundane, pragmatic values simply deflect Laevsky's lament, cannot understand his friend's ennui and disenchantment with his mistress, Nadezhda Feydorovna. Laevsky perceives himself as a Hamlet figure, one who has been betrayed by Nadezhda, for whom he feels an increasing revulsion, which he masks with hypocritical sweetness. He envisions himself as being caught without purpose, vaguely believing that an escape to St. Petersburg without Nadezhda would provide a panacea for all of his ills.

Laevsky's antagonist, Von Koren, is next introduced. Von Koren is a brash, outspoken, vain man who believes that Laevsky is worthy only of drowning. He finds Laevsky depraved and genetically dangerous because he has remarkable success with women and might father more of his parasitical type. During their encounters, Von Koren is aggressive and takes every chance to bait Laevsky, who is afraid of him.

Laevsky's situation deteriorates when Nadezhda's husband dies, and she, guilt ridden, looks to him to save her. Laevsky wants only to escape, however, and he runs off to Samoilenko, begging the doctor for a loan so he might flee to St. Petersburg. After confessing his depravity, he swears that he will send for Nadezhda after he arrives in St. Petersburg, but in reality he has no intention of doing so.

Caught up in his own web of lies and half truths, Laevsky must deal with those of Nadezhda, who is carrying on affairs with two other men and who has her own deceitful plans of escape. Convinced that Samoilenko has betrayed him through gossiping about him, Laevsky starts an argument with him in the presence of Von Koren, who supports the doctor. The heated exchange ends with a challenge to a duel, gleefully accepted by Von Koren. The night before the duel, Laevsky is extremely frightened. He is petrified by the prospect of imminent death, and his lies and deceit weigh upon him heavily. He passes through a spiritual crisis paralleled by a storm that finally subsides at dawn, just as Laevsky sets out for the dueling grounds.

The duel turns into a comic incident. The duelists are not sure of protocol, and before they even start they seem inept. As it turns out, Laevsky nobly discharges his pistol into the air, and Von Koren, intent on killing his opponent, only manages to graze his neck. The duel has a propitious effect on both men. Laevsky and Nadezhda are reconciled, and he gives up his foolish romantic illusions and begins to live a responsible life. He is also reconciled to Von Koren, who, in a departing confession, admits that a scientific view of things cannot account for all life's uncertainties. There is, at the end, a momentary meeting of the two men's minds.

"The Duel" is representative of a group of quasi-polemical pieces that Chekhov wrote between 1889 and 1896, including "Gusev" ("Gusev"), "Palata No. 6" ("Ward Number Six"), and "Moia zhizn" ("My Life"). All have parallel conflicts in which antagonists are spokespersons for opposing ideologies, neither of which is capable of providing humankind with a definitive epistemology or sufficient guide to living.

"ROTHSCHILD'S FIDDLE"

Other mature stories from the same period deal with the eroding effect of materialism on the human spirit. "Skripka Rotshil'da" ("Rothschild's Fiddle") is a prime example. In this work, Yakov Ivanov, nicknamed Bronze, a poor undertaker, is the protagonist. Yakov, who takes pride in his work, also plays the fiddle and thereby supplements his income from coffin-making.

For a time, Yakov plays at weddings with a Jewish orchestra, whose members, inexplicably, he comes to hate, especially Rothschild, a flutist who seems determined to play even the lightest of pieces plaintively. Because of his belligerent behavior, after a time the Jews hire Yakov only in emergencies. Never in a good temper, Yakov is obsessed with his financial losses and his bad luck. Tormented by these matters at night, he can find some respite only by striking a solitary string on his fiddle.

When his wife, Marfa, becomes ill, Yakov's main concern is what her death will cost him. She, in contrast, dies untroubled, finding in death a welcome release from the wretchedness that has been her lot married to Yakov. In her delirium, she does recall their child, who had died fifty years earlier, and a brief period of joy under a willow tree by the river, but Yakov can remember none of these things. Only when she is buried does Yakov experience depression, realizing that their marriage had been loveless.

Sometime later Yakov accidentally comes upon and recognizes the willow tree of which Marfa had spoken. He rests there, beset by visions and a sense of a wasted past, regretting his indifference to his wife and his cruelty to the Jew, Rothschild. Shortly after this epiphany, he grows sick and prepares to die. Waiting, he plays his fiddle mournfully, growing troubled by not being able to take his fiddle with him to the grave. At his final confession, he tells the priest to give the fiddle to Rothschild, in his first and only generous act. Ironically, the fiddle for Rothschild becomes a means of improving his material well-being.

As "Rothschild's Fiddle" illustrates, Chekhov continued his efforts to fathom the impoverished spirit of his fellow man, often with a sympathetic, kindly regard. Most of his last stories are written in that vein. Near the end of the 1890's, Chekhov gave increasing attention to his plays, which, combined with his ill health, reduced his fictional output. Still, between 1895 and his last fictional piece, "Nevesta" ("The Bride"), published in 1902, he wrote some pieces that rank among his masterpieces.

As in "Rothschild's Fiddle," Chekhov's concern with conflicting ideologies gives way to more fundamental questions about human beings' ability to transcend their own nature. He examines characters who suffer desperate unhappiness, anxiety, isolation, and despair, experienced mainly through the characters' inability either to give or to accept love. He also, however, concerns himself with its antithesis, the suffocating potential of too much love, which is the thematic focus of "Dushechka" ("The Darling").

"THE DARLING"

In this story, Olenka, the protagonist, is a woman who seems to have no character apart from her marital and maternal roles. She is otherwise a cipher who, between husbands, can only mourn, expressing her grief in folk laments. She has no important opinions of her own, only banal concerns with petty annoyances such as insects and hot weather. She comes to life only when she fulfills her role as wife and companion to her husband, whose opinions and business jargon she adopts as her own, which, to her third husband, is a source of great annoyance.

Ironically, alive and radiant in love, Olenka seems to suck the life out of those whom she adores. For example, her love seems to cause the demise of her first husband, Kukin, a wretched, self-pitying theater manager. Only in the case of her last love, that for her foster son, Sasha, in her maternal role, does Olenka develop opinions of her own. Her love, however, ever suffocating, instills rebellion in the boy and will clearly lead to Olenka's downfall.

"THE BRIDE"

By implication, the comic, almost sardonic depiction of Olenka argues a case for the emancipation of women, a concern to which Chekhov returns in "Nevesta" ("The Bride"). This story deals with a young woman, Nadya, who attempts to find an identity independent of roles prescribed by traditional mores and the oppressive influence of her mother, Nina, and her grandmother.

Nadya, at twenty-three, is something of a dreamer. As the story begins, she is vaguely discontent with her impending marriage to Andrew, son to a local canon of the same name. Her rebellion against her growing unhappiness is encouraged by Sasha, a distant relative who becomes her sympathetic confidant. He constantly advises Nadya to flee, to get an education and free herself from the dull, idle, and stultifying existence that the provincial town promises.

When Andrew takes Nadya on a tour of their future house, she is repulsed by his vision of their life together, finding him stupid and unimaginative. She confides in her mother, who offers no help at all, claiming that it is ordinary for young ladies to get cold feet as weddings draw near. Nadya then asks Sasha for help, which, with a ruse, he provides. He takes Nadya with him to Moscow and sends her on to St. Petersburg, where she begins her studies.

After some months, Nadya, very homesick, visits Sasha in Moscow. It is clear to her that Sasha, ill with tuberculosis, is now dying. She returns to her home to deal with her past but finds the atmosphere no less oppressive than before, except that her mother and grandmother now seem more pathetic than domineering. After a telegram comes announcing Sasha's death, she leaves again for St. Petersburg, resolved to find a new life severed completely from her old.

As well as any story, "The Bride" illustrates why Chekhov is seen as the chronicler of twilight Russia, a period of stagnation when the intelligentsia seemed powerless to effect reform and the leviathan bureaucracy and outmoded traditions benumbed the people and robbed the more sensitive of spirit and hope. While the contemporary reader of Chekhov's fiction might find that pervasive, heavy atmosphere difficult to fathom, particularly in a comic perspective, no one can doubt Chekhov's mastery of mood.

With Guy de Maupassant in France, Chekhov is rightly credited with mastering the form, mood, and style of the type of short fiction that would be favored by serious English language writers from Virginia Woolf and James Joyce onward. His impact on modern fiction is pervasive.

OTHER MAJOR WORKS

PLAYS: *Ivanov*, pr., pb. 1887 (English translation, 1912); *Medved*, pr., pb. 1888 (*A Bear*, 1909); *Predlozhiniye*, pr. 1889 (*A Marriage Proposal*, 1914); *Leshy*, pr. 1889 (*The Wood Demon*, 1925); *Svadba*, pb. 1889 (*The Wedding*, 1916); *Yubiley*, pb. 1892 (*The Jubilee*, 1916); *Chayka*, pr. 1896, rev. pr. 1898 (*The Seagull*, 1909); *Dyadya Vanya*, 1897 (based on his play *The Wood Demon; Uncle Vanya*, 1914); *Tri sestry*, pr., pb. 1901 (*Three Sisters*, 1920); *Vishnyovy sad*, pr., pb. 1904 (*The Cherry Orchard*, 1908); *Platonov*, pb. 1923 (English translation, 1930); *The Plays of Chekhov*, pb. 1923-1924 (two volumes); *Nine Plays*, pb. 1959.

NONFICTION: *Ostrov Sakhalin*, 1893-1894; *Letters on the Short Story, the Drama, and Other Literary Topics*, 1924; *The Selected Letters of Anton Chekhov*, 1955.

MISCELLANEOUS: *The Works of Anton Chekhov*, 1929; *Polnoye sobraniye sochineniy i pisem A. P. Chekhova*, 1944-1951 (twenty volumes); *The Portable Chekhov*, 1947; *The Oxford Chekhov*, 1964-1980 (nine volumes).

BIBLIOGRAPHY

Flath, Carol A. "The Limits to the Flesh: Searching for the Soul in Chekhov's 'A Boring Story.'" *Slavic and East European Journal* 41 (Summer, 1997): 271-286. Argues that "A Boring Story" affirms the value of art and offers comfort against the harshness of the truth about ordinary life and death.

Johnson, Ronald J. *Anton Chekhov: A Study of the Short Fiction*. New York: Twayne, 1993. An introduction to Chekhov's short stories, from his earliest journalistic sketches and ephemera to his influential stories "Gooseberries" and "Lady with a Dog." Discusses Chekhov's objective narrative stance, his social conscience, and his belief in the freedom of the individual. Includes excerpts from Chekhov's letters in which he talks about his fiction, as well as comments by other critics who discuss Chekhov's attitude toward religion and sexuality.

Kirk, Irina. *Anton Chekhov*. Boston: Twayne, 1981. This solid study in the Twayne series offers a good departure point for serious further inquiry. In addition to provocative interpretations of selected fictional and dramatic works, it includes a useful chronology and select bibliography. The study is most helpful in delineating the guiding principles of Chekhov's art.

Lantz, K. A. *Anton Chekhov: A Reference Guide to Literature*. Boston: G. K. Hall, 1985. Lantz offers an indispensable tool for the researcher. The work provides a brief biography, a checklist of Chekhov's published works with both English and Russian titles, chronologically arranged, and a very useful annotated bibliography of criticism through 1983.

McMillin, Arnold. "Chekhov and the Soviet Village Prose Writers: Affinities of Fact and Fiction." *The Modern Language Review* 93 (July, 1998): 754-761. Discusses Chekhov's influence on Soviet village prose writers.

Martin, David W. "Chekhov and the Modern Short Story in English." *Neophilologus* 71 (1987): 129-143. Martin surveys Chekhov's influence on various English-language writers, including Katherine Mansfield, Virginia Woolf, James Joyce, Sherwood Anderson, and Frank O'Connor. He compares selected works by Chekhov with pieces by those he has influenced and discusses those Chekhovian traits and practices revealed therein. He credits Chekhov with showing how effete or banal characters or circumstances can be enlivened with the dynamics of style. The article is a good departure point for further comparative study.

Pritchett, V. S. *Chekhov: A Spirit Set Free*. New York: Random House, 1988. Pritchett's study is a critical biography and a good general introduction to Chekhov. Himself a writer of fiction, Pritchett has a very readable, engaging style. His discussions of selected works, though helpful, are prone to summary rather than extensive analysis. The work is not recommended as a guide for further study. It has no bibliography or other aids.

Prose, Francine. "Learning from Chekhov." *Western Humanities Review* 41 (1987): 1-14. Prose's article is an appreciative eulogy on the staying power of Chekhov's stories as models for writers. She notes that while Chekhov broke many established rules, his stress on objectivity and writing without judgment is of fundamental importance. The piece would be of most help to creative writers.

Rayfield, Donald. *Anton Chekhov: A Life*. New York: Henry Holt, 1998. A detailed and highly documented biography by a noted Chekhov scholar. Comments on his relationship with his family; discusses the sources of his work; describes his literary friendships; provides a context for his work in prerevolutionary Russia.

Troyat, Henri. *Chekhov*. Translated by Michael H. Heim. New York: E. P. Dutton, 1986. Troyat's biography, drawing heavily on Chekhov's letters, is a much more detailed and comprehensive study of Chekhov's life than is V. S. Pritchett's (above). It is less a critical biography, however, and is mainly valuable for its intimate portrayal of Chekhov the man. It is well indexed and documented by Chekhov's correspondence. Illustrated with photographs.

John W. Fiero

CHARLES WADDELL CHESNUTT

Born: Cleveland, Ohio; June 20, 1858
Died: Cleveland, Ohio; November 15, 1932

PRINCIPAL SHORT FICTION

The Conjure Woman, 1899
The Wife of His Youth and Other Stories of the Color Line, 1899

OTHER LITERARY FORMS

Charles Waddell Chesnutt achieved his literary reputation and stature as a short-story writer. His scholarly bent and indelible concern for human conditions in American society, however, occasionally moved him to experiment in other literary forms. Based on his study of race relations in the American South, he wrote the novel *The Marrow of Tradition* (1901). As a result of the critical acclaim for this novel and for his first, *The House Behind the Cedars* (1900), Chesnutt became known not only as a short-story writer but also as a first-rate novelist. He wrote two other novels, *The Colonel's Dream* (1905) and "The Quarry," which remains unpublished.

In 1885, Chesnutt published several poems in *The Cleveland Voice*. The acceptance of his essay "What Is a White Man?" by the *Independent* in May of 1889

began his career as an essayist. Illustrating his diverse talent still further and becoming an impassioned voice for human justice, he wrote essays for a major portion of his life. Chesnutt demonstrated his skill as a biographer when he prepared *The Life of Frederick Douglass* (1899) for the Beacon biography series.

ACHIEVEMENTS

One of Chesnutt's most significant achievements was his own education. Self-taught in the higher principles of algebra, the intricate details of history, the linguistic dicta of Latin, and the tenets of natural philosophy, he crowned this series of intellectual achievements by passing the Ohio bar examination after teaching himself law for two years.

A man of outstanding social reputation, Chesnutt received an invitation to Mark Twain's seventieth birthday party, an invitation "extended to about one hundred and fifty of America's most distinguished writers of imaginative literature." The party was held on December 5, 1905, at Delmonico's, in New York City. Chesnutt's greatest public honor was being chosen as the recipient of the Joel E. Springarn Medal, an award annually bestowed on an American citizen of African descent for distinguished service.

Charles Waddell Chesnutt (Cleveland Public Library)

December of 1885 with the printing of the story "Uncle Peter's House" in the *Cleveland News and Herald*. Several years passed and "The Goophered Grapevine" was accepted by *The Atlantic Monthly* and published in 1888. Continuing his dual career as a man of letters and a businessman/attorney for more than a decade after his reception as a literary artist, Chesnutt decided, on September 30, 1899, to devote himself full-time to his literary career. From that moment on he enjoyed a full and productive career as a man of letters.

At the beginning of the twentieth century, Chesnutt became more politically active as a spokesman for racial justice. He toured the South and its educational institutions such as Tuskegee Institute and Atlanta University. He joined forces with black leaders such as Booker T. Washington and W. E. B. Du Bois. In May of 1909, he became a member of the National Negro Committee, which later became the National Association for the Advancement of Colored People (NAACP). The last two decades of Chesnutt's life were less active because his health began to fail him in 1919. He was, however, elected to the Cleveland Chamber of Commerce in 1912. Chesnutt continued to write until his death on November 15, 1932.

BIOGRAPHY

Charles Waddell Chesnutt was born in Cleveland, Ohio, on June 20, 1858. He attended Cleveland public schools and the Howard School in Fayetteville, North Carolina. Having distinguished himself academically early in his schooling, Chesnutt was taken into the tutelage of two established educators, Robert Harris of the Howard School and his brother, Cicero Harris, of Charlotte, North Carolina. He later succeeded Cicero Harris as principal of the school in Charlotte in 1877 and followed this venture with an appointment to the Normal School in Fayetteville to train teachers for colored schools.

On June 6, 1878, Chesnutt was married to Susan Perry. Shortly after his marriage, he began his training as a stenographer. Even at this time, however, his interest in writing competed for his energies. He spent his spare time writing essays, poems, short stories, and sketches. His public writing career began in

ANALYSIS

The short fiction of Charles Waddell Chesnutt embraces traditions characteristic of both formal and folk art. Indeed, the elements of Chesnutt's narrative technique evolved in a fashion that conspicuously parallels the historical shaping of the formal short story itself. The typical Chesnutt narrative, like the classic short story, assumes its heritage from a rich oral tradition immersed in folkways, mannerisms, and beliefs. Holding true to the historical development of the short story as an artistic form, his early imaginative narratives were episodic in nature. The next stage of development in Chesnutt's short fiction was a parody of the fable form with a folkloric variation. Having become proficient at telling a story with a unified effect, Chesnutt achieved the symbolic resonance characteristic of the Romantic tale, yet his awareness of the plight of his people urged him toward an increasingly realistic depiction of social conditions. As a mature writer, Chesnutt achieved depth of characterization, distinguishable thematic features, and a rare skillfulness in creation of mood, while a shrewdly moralizing tone allowed him to achieve his dual goal as artist and social activist.

"THE GOOPHERED GRAPEVINE"

Chesnutt's journal stories constituted the first phase of his writing career, but when *The Atlantic Monthly* published "The Goophered Grapevine" in 1888, the serious aspects of his artistic skill became apparent. "The Goophered Grapevine" belongs to a tradition in Chesnutt's writings which captures the fable form with a folkloric variation. These stories also unfold with a didactic strain which matures significantly in Chesnutt's later writings. To understand clearly the series of stories in *The Conjure Woman*, of which "The Goophered Grapevine" is one, the reader must comprehend the allegorical features in the principal narrative situation and the thematic intent of the mythic incidents from African American lore.

The Conjure Woman contains narratives revealed through the accounts of a Northern white person's rendition of the tales of Uncle Julius, a former slave. This storytelling device lays the foundation for Chesnutt's sociological commentary. The real and perceived voices represent the perspectives he wishes to expose, those of the white capitalist and the impoverished, disadvantaged African American. The primary persona is that of the capitalist, while the perceived voice is that of the struggling poor. Chesnutt skillfully melds the two perspectives.

Chesnutt's two volumes of short stories contain pieces which are unified in theme, tone, and mood. Each volume also contains a piece which might be considered the lead story. In *The Conjure Woman*, the preeminent story is "The Goophered Grapevine." This story embodies the overriding thematic intent of the narratives in this collection. Chesnutt points out the foibles of the capitalistic quest in the post-Civil War South, a venture pursued at the expense of the newly freed African American slave. He illustrates this point in "The Goophered Grapevine" by skillfully intertwining Aunt Peggy's gains as a result of her conjurations and Henry's destruction as a result of man's inhumanity to man. Chesnutt discloses his

ultimate point when the plantation owner, McAdoo, is deceived by a Yankee horticulturist and his grape vineyard becomes totally unproductive.

Running episodes, such as Aunt Peggy's conjurations to keep the field hands from consuming the grape crop and the seasonal benefit McAdoo gains from selling Henry, serve to illustrate the interplay between a monied white capitalist and his less privileged black human resources. McAdoo used Aunt Peggy to deny his field laborers any benefit from the land they worked, and he sold Henry every spring to increase his cash flow and prepare for the next gardening season.

The central metaphor in "The Goophered Grapevine" is the bewitched vineyard. To illustrate and condemn man's inhumanity to man, Chesnutt contrasts the black conjure woman's protection of the grape vineyard with the white Yankee's destruction of it. McAdoo's exploitation of Henry serves to justify McAdoo's ultimate ruin. Through allegory, Chesnutt is able to draw attention to the immorality of capitalistic gain through a sacrifice of basic humanity to other people.

"PO' SANDY"

Following the theme of inhumanity established in "The Goophered Grapevine," "Po' Sandy" highlights the abuse of a former slave laborer. Accordingly, a situation with a folkloric variation is used to convey this message. Sandy, Master Marabo's field hand, is shifted from relative to relative at various points during the year to perform various duties. During the course of these transactions, he is separated from his second common-law wife, Tenie. (His first wife has been sent to work at a distant plantation.) Tenie is a conjurer. She transforms Sandy into a tree, and she changes him back to his original state periodically so that they can be together. With Sandy's apparent disappearance, Master Marabo decides to send Tenie away to nurse his ailing daughter-in-law. There is therefore no one left to watch Sandy, the tree. The dehumanizing effects of industrialization creep into the story line at this point. The "tree" is to be used as lumber for a kitchen at the Marabo home. Tenie returns just in time to try to stop this transformation at the lumber mill, but she is deemed "mad."

Sandy's spirit thereafter haunts the Marabo kitchen, and no one wants to work there. The complaints are so extensive that the kitchen is dismantled and the lumber donated toward the building of a school. This structure is then haunted, too. The point is that industrialization and economic gain diminish essential human concerns and can lead to destruction. The destruction of Sandy's marital relationships in order to increase his usefulness as a field worker justifies this defiant spirit. In his depiction of Sandy as a tree, Chesnutt illustrates an enslaved spirit desperately seeking freedom.

"THE CONJURER'S REVENGE"

"The Conjurer's Revenge," also contained in *The Conjure Woman*, illustrates Chesnutt's mastery of the exemplum. The allegory in this work conveys a strong message, and Chesnutt's evolving skill in characterization becomes apparent. The characters' actions, rather than the situation, contain the didactic message of the story. Some qualities of the fable unfold as the various dimensions of characters are portrayed. Consequently, "The Conjurer's Revenge" is a good example of Chesnutt's short imaginative sketch. These qualities are also most characteristic of Chesnutt's early short fiction.

"The Conjurer's Revenge" begins when Primus, a field hand, discovers the conjure man's hog alone in a bush one evening. Concerned for the hog and not knowing to whom the animal belongs, Primus carries it to the plantation where he works. Unfortunately, the conjurer identifies Primus as a thief and transforms Primus into a mule. Chesnutt uses this transformation to reveal Primus's personality. As a mule, Primus displays jealousy when other men show an attraction to his woman, Sally. The mule's reaction is one of shocking violence in instances when Sally is approached by other men. The mule has a tremendous appetite for food and drink, an apparent compensation for his unhappiness. Laying the foundation for his exemplum, Chesnutt brings these human foibles to the forefront and illustrates the consequences of even the mildest appearance of dishonesty.

The conjurer's character is also developed more fully as the story progresses. After attending a religious revival, he becomes ill, confesses his act of vengeance, and repents. During the conjurer's metamorphosis, Chesnutt captures the remorse, grief, and forgiveness in this character. He also reveals the benefits of human compassion and concern for other human beings. A hardened heart undergoes reform and develops an ability to demonstrate sensitivity. Nevertheless, the conjurer suffers the consequences of his evil deed: He is mistakenly given poison by a companion and he dies before he completely restores Primus's human features, a deed he undertakes after repenting. The conjurer dies prematurely, and Primus lives with a club-foot for the rest of his life.

Features of Chesnutt's more mature writing emerge in the series of narratives which make up *The Wife of His Youth and Other Stories of the Color Line*. The stories in this collection center on the identity crisis experienced by African Americans, portraying their true human qualities in the face of the grotesque distortions wrought by racism. In order to achieve his goal, Chesnutt abandons his earlier imaginative posture and embraces realism as a means to unfold his message. The dimensions of his characters are therefore appropriately self-revealing. The characters respond to the stresses and pressures in their external environment with genuine emotion; Mr. Ryder in "The Wife of His Youth" is no exception.

"THE WIFE OF HIS YOUTH"

"The Wife of His Youth" follows the structural pattern which appears to typify the narratives in the collection. This pattern evolves in three phases: crisis, character response, and resolution. The crisis in "The Wife of His Youth" is Mr. Ryder's attempt to reconcile his new and old ways of life. He has moved North from a southern plantation and entered black middle-class society. Adapting to the customs, traditions, and mores of this stratum of society is a stressful challenge for Mr. Ryder. Tensions exist between his old life and his new life. He fears being unable to appear as if he belongs to this "blue vein" society and exposing his lowly background. This probable eventuality is his constant preoccupation.

The "blue veins" were primarily lighter-skinned blacks who were better educated and more advantaged than their darker counterparts. Relishing their perceived superiority, they segregated themselves from their brothers and sisters. It is within this web of social clamoring and essential self-denial that Mr. Ryder finds himself. The inherent contradictions of this lifestyle present a crisis for him, although a resolution is attained during the course of the narrative.

Mr. Ryder's efforts to fit into this society are thwarted when his slave wife appears at his doorstep on the day before a major social event that he has planned. He is about to introduce the Blue Vein Society to a widow, Mrs. Dixon, upon whom he has set his affections. The appearance of Liza Jane, his slave wife, forces Mr. Ryder to confront his new life. This situation also allows Chesnutt to assume his typically moralizing tone. Mr. Ryder moves from self-denial to self-pride as he decides to present Liza Jane to his society friends instead of Mrs. Dixon. The narrative ends on a note of personal triumph for Mr. Ryder as he proudly introduces the wife of his youth to society.

"THE PASSING OF GRANDISON"

Chesnutt does not totally relinquish his allegiance to the use of myth in *The Wife of His Youth and Other Stories of the Color Line*. The myth of the ascent journey, or the quest for freedom, is evident in several stories in the collection, among them "The Passing of Grandison" and "Wellington's Wives." Following the structured pattern of crisis, character response, and resolution, "The Passing of Grandison" is a commentary on the newly emerging moral values of the postbellum South. Colonel Owens, a plantation owner, has a son, Dick, who is in love with a belle named Charity Lomax. Charity's human values reflect the principles of human equality and freedom, and the challenge that she presents to Dick Owens becomes the crisis of the narrative.

Dick is scheduled to take a trip North, and his father insists on his being escorted by one of the servants. Grandison is selected to accompany his young master. Charity Lomax challenges Dick to find a way to entice Grandison to remain in the North and receive his well-deserved liberation. Charity's request conflicts with the values held by Dick and Grandison. Dick believes that slave/master relationships are essential to the survival of the South. Grandison holds that servants should be unequivocally loyal to their masters.

In spite of Dick's attempts to connect Grandison unobtrusively with the abolitionist movement in the North, the former slave remains loyal to Dick. Grandison's steadfastness perplexes Dick because his proposed marriage to Charity is at risk if he does not succeed in freeing Grandison. After a series of faulty attempts, Dick succeeds in losing Grandison. Dick then returns home alone and triumphant. Grandison ultimately returns to the plantation. He had previously proven himself so trustworthy that goodwill toward him is restored. To make the characterization of Grandison realistic, however, Chesnutt must have him pursue his freedom.

In a surprise ending typical of Chesnutt, Grandison plans the escape of all of his relatives who remain on the plantation. They succeed, and in the last scene of the narrative, Colonel Owens spots them from a distance on a boat journeying to a new destination. "The Passing of Grandison" successfully achieves the social and artistic goals of *The Wife of His Youth and Other Stories of the Color Line*. Chesnutt creates characters with convincing human qualities and captures their responses to the stresses and pressures of their environment. While so doing, he advocates the quest for human freedom.

"UNCLE WELLINGTON'S WIVES"

"Uncle Wellington's Wives" contains several of the thematic dimensions mentioned above. The story concerns the self-identity of the African American and the freedom quest. Wellington Braboy, a lightskinned mulatto, is determined to move North and seek his freedom. His crisis is the result of a lack of resources, primarily financial, to achieve his goal.

Braboy is portrayed as having a distorted view of loyalty and commitment. He justifies stealing money from his slave wife's life savings by saying that, as her husband, he is entitled to the money. On the other hand, he denies his responsibility to his slave wife once he reaches the North. In order to marry a white woman he denies the legality of a slave marriage.

Chesnutt takes Braboy on a journey of purgation and catharsis as he moves toward resolution. After being subjected to much ridicule and humiliation as a result of his mixed marriage, Braboy must honestly confront himself and come to terms with his true identity. Abandoned by his wife for her former white husband, Braboy returns to the South. This journey is also a symbolic return to himself; his temporary escape from himself has failed.

Milly, Braboy's first wife, does not deny her love for him, in spite of his previous actions. Milly receives and accepts him with a forgiving spirit. Chesnutt capitalizes on the contrast between Braboy's African and Anglo wives. The African wife loves him unconditionally because she has the capacity to know and understand him, regardless of his foibles. Braboy's Anglo wife was frustrated by what she considered to be irreparable inadequacies in his character and abandoned him.

"CICELY'S DREAM"

In his character development, Chesnutt repeatedly sought to dispel some of the stereotypical thinking about African Americans. An example of his success in this effort is found in "Cicely's Dream," set in the period of Reconstruction. Cicely Green is depicted as a young woman of considerable ambition. Like most African Americans, she has had very little education and is apparently limited in her capacity to achieve. She does have, however, many dreams.

Cicely's crisis begins when she discovers a wounded man on her way home one day. The man is delirious and has no recollection of who he is. Cicely and her grandmother care for the man until his physical health is restored, but he is still mentally distraught. The tenderness and sensitivity displayed by Cicely keep the stranger reasonably content. Over a period of time, they become close and eventually pledge their love to each other. Chesnutt portrays a caring, giving relationship between the two lovers, one which is not complicated by any caste system which would destroy love through separation of the lovers. This relationship, therefore, provides a poignant contrast to the relationships among blacks during the days of slavery, and Chesnutt thereby exposes an unexplored dimension of the African American.

Typically, however, there is a surprise ending: Martha Chandler, an African American teacher, enters the picture. She teaches Cicely and other black youths for one school term. During the final program of the term, the teacher reveals her story of lost love.

Her lover had been killed in the Civil War. Cicely's lover's memory is jolted by the teacher's story, and he proves to be the teacher's long-lost love. The happy reunion is a celebration of purely committed love. Again, Chesnutt examines qualities in African Americans which had largely been ignored. He emphasizes the innate humanity of the African American in a natural and realistic way, combining great artistic skill with a forceful moral vision.

OTHER MAJOR WORKS

LONG FICTION: *The House Behind the Cedars*, 1900; *The Marrow of Tradition*, 1901; *The Colonel's Dream*, 1905.

NONFICTION: *The Life of Frederick Douglass*, 1899.

BIBLIOGRAPHY

Chesnutt, Charles Waddell. *"To Be an Author": Letters of Charles W. Chesnutt, 1889-1905*. Edited by Joseph R. McElrath, Jr., and Robert C. Leitz III. Princeton, N.J.: Princeton University Press, 1997. The six-part organization is particularly useful to a student of Chesnutt's fiction and of his career development: "Cable's Protégé in 1889-1891," "A Dream Deferred, 1891-1896," "Page's Protégé in 1897-1899," "The Professional Novelist," "Discontent in 1903-1904," "The Quest Renewed, 1904-1905." Includes a comprehensive introduction and detailed index.

Delma, P. Jay. "The Mask as Theme and Structure: Charles W. Chesnutt's 'The Sheriff's Children' and 'The Passing of Grandison.'" *American Literature* 51 (1979): 364-375. Argues that the story exploits the theme of the mask: the need to hide one's true personality and racial identity from self and others. Delma argues that because Chesnutt uses the mask theme, the story is not a run-of-the-mill treatment of the long-lost-son plot.

Filetti, Jean. "The Goophered Grapevine." *Explicator* 48 (Spring, 1990): 201-203. Discusses the use of master-slave relationships within the context of storytelling and explains how Chesnutt's "The Goophered Grapevine" relates to this tradition. Indicates that one of Chesnutt's concerns was inhumanity among people, but the story is told from a humorous perspective with the newly freed slave outwitting the white capitalist.

Gleason, William. "Chesnutt's Piazza Tales: Architecture, Race, and Memory in the Conjure Stories." *American Quarterly* 51 (March, 1999): 33-77. Argues that in the second phase of the Conjure Tales, Chesnutt uses piazzas as a central imaginative space for African American memory. Argues that Chesnutt counters historical amnesia with concrete memories from the piazza that represents a simpler past.

Heermance, Noel. *Charles Chesnutt: America's First Great Black Novelist*. Hamden, Conn.: Archon Books, 1974. This book is a good introduction to the overall life and themes of Chesnutt. It discusses Chesnutt's short fiction, his novels, and his other writings, and it asserts that Chesnutt was the first great African American novelist.

Kulii, Elon A. "Poetic License and Chesnutt's Use of Folklore." *CLA Journal* 38 (December, 1994): 247-253. Discusses Chesnutt's use of the hoodoo tradition in "Goophered Grapevine." Claims that Chesnutt communicates the inner tale as a story from the hoodoo tradition, but that the episodic core of the tale is not of the oral tradition.

McFatter, Susan. "From Revenge to Resolution: The (R)evolution of Female Characters in Chesnutt's Fiction." *CLA Journal* 42 (December, 1998): 194-211. Discusses the theme of female revenge in Chesnutt's fiction, showing how female characters respond to racism and patriarchal paradigms in various ways. Argues that Chesnutt's women use intelligence and instinct for survival to manipulate their repressive environments.

Render, Sylvia. *Charles W. Chesnutt*. Boston: Twayne, 1980. A good general introduction to the life and writing of Charles Chesnutt. Render discusses Chesnutt's major concerns with narrative technique, social justice, and the place of the African American in American society.

_____. *The Short Fiction of Charles Chesnutt*. Washington, D.C.: Howard University Press, 1974. Discusses the collected short fiction of Chesnutt and indicates that it came out of the storytelling tradition of African Americans and was written within the conventions of local humor that were popular at the time.

Sollers, Werner. "Thematics Today." In *Thematics Reconsidered: Essays in Honor of Horst S. Daemmrich*, edited by Frank Trommler. Amsterdam: Rodopi, 1995. A detailed discussion of the themes in "The Wife of His Youth." Argues that contemporary thematic readings that stress race and gender are less likely to identify other themes such as marriage, fidelity, and age difference. Suggests that Chesnutt's special way of treating the race and age themes needs more attention.

Wonham, Henry B. "Plenty of Room for Us All? Participation and Prejudice in Charles Chesnutt's Dialect Tales." *Studies in American Fiction* 26 (Autumn, 1998): 131-146. Argues that the dialect tales deal in a subtle way with the restriction of African American rights in post-Reconstruction South; asserts Chesnutt focuses on a historical moment between Reconstruction and the return of white racism.

Patricia A. R. Williams,
updated by Earl Paulus Murphy

G. K. CHESTERTON

Born: London, England; May 29, 1874
Died: Beaconsfield, England; June 14, 1936

PRINCIPAL SHORT FICTION

The Tremendous Adventures of Major Brown, 1903
The Club of Queer Trades, 1905
The Man Who Was Thursday, 1908
The Perishing of the Pendragons, 1914
The Man Who Knew Too Much and Other Stories, 1922
Tales of the Long Bow, 1925
Stories, 1928
The Sword of Wood, 1928
The Moderate Murder and the Honest Quack, 1929
The Poet and the Lunatics: Episodes in the Life of Gabriel Gale, 1929
Four Faultless Felons, 1930
The Ecstatic Thief, 1930
The Paradoxes of Mr. Pond, 1936

OTHER LITERARY FORMS

From 1901 until his death in 1936, G. K. Chesterton worked as a journalist in London. He was a prolific essayist and literary critic, and his 1909 book on his close friend George Bernard Shaw is still held in the highest esteem. He wrote several volumes of poetry, foremost of which was his 1911 *The Ballad of the White Horse*. After his conversion to Catholicism in 1922, he became a fervent but tactful apologist for his new faith. His 1925 book *The Everlasting Man* and his 1933 study on Thomas Aquinas reveal the depth of his insights into the essential beliefs of Catholicism. His *Autobiography* was published posthumously in late 1936.

ACHIEVEMENTS

Chesterton was a man of letters in the finest sense of the term. He expressed effectively and eloquently his ideas on a wide variety of literary, social, and religious topics. He was a master of paradox and always encouraged his readers to reflect on the subtle differences between appearance and reality. Reading his

well-crafted short stories is a stimulating aesthetic experience because he makes readers think about the moral implications of what they are reading.

Although his critical writings on literature and religion reveal the depth of his intellect, Chesterton's major achievement was in the field of detective fiction. Between 1911 and 1935, he published five volumes of short stories in which his amateur sleuth is a Catholic priest named Father Brown. Unlike such famous fictional detectives as Arthur Conan Doyle's Sherlock Holmes and Edgar Allan Poe's Auguste Dupin, Father Brown relied not on deductive reasoning but rather on intuition in order to solve perplexing crimes. Father Brown made judicious use of his theological training in order to recognize the specious reasoning of criminals and to lead them to confess their guilt. His Father Brown stories explored moral and theological topics not previously treated in detective fiction.

BIOGRAPHY

Gilbert Keith Chesterton was born on May 29, 1874, in London. He was the second of three children born to Edward and Marie Louise Chesterton. Edward Chesterton was a realtor. Gilbert's older sister, Beatrice, died at the age of eight, in 1877, and two years later his brother, Cecil, was born. Everything seems to indicate that Edward and Marie Louise were loving parents.

In 1982, Gilbert was graduated from St. Paul's School in London. For the next three years, he studied at London's Slade Art School, but he finally realized that he would never develop into a truly creative artist. From 1895 until 1900, he worked for a publishing firm. From 1901 until his death, in 1936, he served as a journalist and editor for various London newspapers and magazines.

In 1901, he married Frances Blogg. Gilbert and Frances had no children. Theirs was a good marriage, each helping the other. Frances survived her husband by two years. During the first decade of the twentieth century, Chesterton met the writers Hilaire Belloc and Shaw, who became his lifelong friends. Although Belloc and Shaw seemed to have little in common because Belloc was an apologist for Catholicism and Shaw was an agnostic, Chesterton liked them both very much. Several times, Belloc organized lively but good-natured debates in which Shaw and Chesterton discussed religion and politics. Throughout his adult life, Chesterton supported the Liberal Party in Great Britain, but gradually he became disillusioned with the leadership of the Liberal prime minister David Lloyd George. After the coalition government run by Lloyd George fell apart in 1922, Chesterton lost much interest in politics. During the last fourteen years of his life, his major interests were literature and religion.

Before World War I began, Chesterton was already a well-known English writer, but he had not yet explored profound philosophical and religious themes. Two unexpected events forced Chesterton to think about his mortality and the reasons for his existence. In late 1914, he fell into a coma, which lasted four months. The cause of this coma was never fully explained to the public. After his recovery, he was a changed man. His view of the world became very serious. Then, less than one month after the end of World War I, Chesterton suffered a terrible personal loss when his only brother, Cecil, died from nephritis in a military hospital in France.

After's Cecil's death, Chesterton felt a void in his life. His friend Father John O'Connor, who was the apparent inspiration for Father Brown, spoke to him at length about Catholicism, and Chesterton became a Catholic on July 30, 1922. Four years later, his wife Frances joined him in the Catholic church. The last decade of his life was a very productive period. He continued to write his Father Brown stories, but he also found much pleasure in writing and giving speeches on religious topics. Although firmly convinced that Catholicism was essential for his own spiritual growth and salvation, he was always tolerant and respectful of friends such as H. G. Wells and Shaw, who did not share his religious beliefs. Soon after he had completed his *Autobiography* in early 1936, he developed serious heart problems. He died at his home in Beaconsfield, England, on June 14, 1936, at the age of sixty-two.

G. K. Chesterton (Library of Congress)

ANALYSIS

Before he began writing his Father Brown stories, G. K. Chesterton had already published one book of detective fiction. In *The Man Who Was Thursday*, Chesterton created a detective named Gabriel Syme, who infiltrates an anarchist group in which each of the seven members is named for a different day of the week. Syme replaces the man who had been Thursday. At first, this group seems strange to Syme because he does not understand what the anarchists wish to accomplish. This paradox is resolved when Chesterton explains that all seven "anarchists" were, in fact, detectives assigned separately to investigate this nonexistent threat to society. Although *The Man Who Was Thursday* does demonstrate Chesterton's ability to think clearly in order to resolve a problem, the solution to this paradox is so preposterous that many readers have wondered why Chesterton wrote this book, whose ending is so odd. It is hardly credible that all seven members of a secret organization could be police officers. Critics have not been sure how they should interpret this work. Chesterton's own brother, Cecil, thought that it expressed an excessively optimistic view of the world, but other reviewers criticized *The Man Who Was Thursday* for its pessimism. This book lacked a central focus.

In his Father Brown stories, this problem of perspective does not exist because it is the levelheaded Father Brown who always explains the true significance of scenes and events that had mystified readers and other characters as well. The other characters, be they detectives, criminals, suspects, or acquaintances of the victim, always come to the conclusion that Father Brown has correctly solved the case.

"THE SECRET OF FATHER BROWN"

In his 1927 short story "The Secret of Father Brown," Chesterton describes the two basic premises of his detective. First, Father Brown is very suspicious of any suspect who utilizes specious reasoning or expresses insincere religious beliefs. Father Brown senses intuitively that a character who reasons incorrectly might well be a criminal. Second, Father Brown strives to "get inside" the mind of "the murderer" so completely that he is "thinking his thoughts, wrestling with his passions." Father Brown needs to understand what drives the guilty party to commit a specific crime before he can determine who the criminal is and how the crime was committed.

Most critics believe that the best Father Brown stories are those that were published in Chesterton's 1911 volume *The Innocence of Father Brown*. Although his later Father Brown stories should not be neglected, his very early stories are ingenious and have remained popular with generations of readers. Several stories in *The Innocence of Father Brown* illustrate nicely how Father Brown intuitively and correctly solves crimes.

"THE BLUE CROSS"

In "The Blue Cross," Aristide Valentin (the head of the Paris police) is sent to London to arrest a notorious thief named Flambeau, who is a master of disguises. Valentin knows that Flambeau is well over six feet tall, but he does not know how Flambeau is dressed. As Valentin is walking through London, his attraction is suddenly drawn to two Catholic priests. One is short and the other is tall. The short priest acts strangely so that he would attract attention. He deliberately throws soup on a wall in a restaurant, upsets

the apples outside of a grocery store, and breaks a window in another restaurant. This odd behavior disturbs the merchants, who consequently, ask police officers to follow the priests, who are walking toward the Hampstead Heath. Readers soon learn that the short priest wants to be followed for his own protection. Just as the tall priest, who is, in fact, Flambeau, orders Father Brown, the short priest, to turn over a sapphire cross that he was carrying to a church in Hampstead, Father Brown tells him that "two strong policemen" and Valentin are waiting behind a tree in order to arrest Flambeau. The astonished Flambeau asks Father Brown how he knew that he was not a real priest. Readers learn that Father Brown's suspicion began when, earlier in the story, the tall priest affirmed that only "modern infidels appeal to reason," whereas true Catholics have no use for it. Father Brown tells Flambeau: "You attacked reason. It's bad theology." His intuition told him that his tall companion could not have been a priest, and he was right.

Father Brown is not merely an amateur detective. He is above all a priest whose primary responsibility is to serve as a spiritual guide to upright people and sinners alike. Although he brought about Flambeau's arrest, Flambeau soon turned away from a life of crime. After his release from prison, he became a private detective, and his closest friend became Father Brown. This transformation can be attributed only to the religious teaching that Flambeau received from his spiritual mentor, Father Brown.

"THE EYE OF APOLLO"

The tenth story in *The Innocence of Father Brown* is entitled "The Eye of Apollo." At the beginning of this short story, Flambeau has just opened his detective agency in a new building located near Westminster Abbey. The other tenants in the building are a religious charlatan named Kalon, who claims to be "the New Priest of Apollo," and two sisters, who are typists. Flambeau and Father Brown instinctively distrust Kalon, who has installed a huge eye of Apollo outside his office. Pauline Stacey, the elder of the two sisters, is attracted to Kalon, whom Joan Stacey dislikes intensely. One afternoon, Pauline falls down an elevator shaft and dies. Flambeau concludes hastily that this was an accident, but Father Brown wants to examine her death more thoroughly. He and Flambeau decide to talk with Kalon before the police officers arrive. Kalon presents the preposterous argument that his "religion" favors life, whereas Christianity is concerned only with death. Father Brown becomes more and more convinced that Kalon is a murderer. To the astonishment of Flambeau, Father Brown proves that Pauline "was murdered while she was alone." Pauline was blind, and Kalon knew it. As Kalon was waiting in the elevator, he called Pauline, but suddenly he moved the elevator, and the blind Pauline fell into the open shaft. Flambeau wonders, however, why Kalon killed her. Readers learn that Pauline had told Kalon that she was going to change her will and leave her fortune of five hundred thousand pounds to him. Kalon did not realize, however, that her pen had run out of ink before she could finish writing her will. When he first hears Kalon speak, Father Brown knows instantly that this hypocrite is a criminal. At the end of the story, he tells Flambeau: "I tell you I knew he [Kalon] had done it even before I knew what he had done." Once again Father Brown's intuition is perfectly correct.

"THE SECRET GARDEN"

Father Brown has the special ability to recognize the true meaning of seemingly insignificant clues, which other characters see but overlook. In *The Innocence of Father Brown*, there are two other stories, "The Secret Garden" and "The Hammer of God," that illustrate the effectiveness of Father Brown's powers of intuition and that also contain rather unexpected endings. Just as they are in "The Blue Cross," Valentin and Father Brown are major characters in "The Secret Garden." As the head of the Paris police, Valentin has been so successful in arresting criminals that many men whom he sent to prison have threatened to kill him as soon as they regain their freedom. For his own protection, Valentin has very high walls built around his garden, with the only access to it being through his house. His servants guard the entrance to his house at all times. One evening, Valentin holds a reception, which is attended by Father Brown, a medical doctor, an American philanthropist named Julius Brayne, Commandant O'Brien from the French Foreign Legion, Lord and Lady Galloway,

and their adult daughter Lady Margaret. Father Brown learns that Valentin is especially suspicious of all organized religions, especially Catholicism, and Julius Brayne likes to contribute huge sums of money to various religions. During the party, a body with a severed head is found in the garden. All the guests are mystified because the head found next to the body does not belong to any of Valentin's servants or to any of the guests.

After much reflection on this apparent paradox, Father Brown proves that the head and the body belong to different men. The body was that of Julius Brayne, and the head belonged to a murderer named Louis Becker, whom the French police had guillotined earlier that day in the presence of Valentin, who had obtained permission to bring Becker's head back to his house. Valentin killed Brayne because of a rumor that Brayne was about to become a Catholic and donate millions to his new church. His hatred for Christianity drove Valentin mad. Father Brown explains calmly that Valentin "would do anything, *anything*, to break what he calls the superstition of the Cross. He has fought for it and starved for it, and now he has murdered for it." Valentin's butler Ivan could not accept this explanation, but as they all went to question Valentin in his study, they found him "dead in his chair." He had committed suicide by taking an overdose of pills. The ending of this short story is surprising because readers of detective fiction do not suspect that a police commissioner can also be a murderer.

"THE HAMMER OF GOD"

In "The Hammer of God," readers are surprised to learn from Father Brown that the murderer is not a violent madman but rather a very respected member of the community. The Reverend Wilfred Bohun could no longer stand the scandalous behavior of his alcoholic brother Norman, who blasphemed God and humiliated Reverend Bohun in the eyes of his parishioners. Chesterton states that Wilfred and Norman Bohun belong to an old noble family whose descendants are now mostly "drunkards and dandy degenerates." Rumor has it that there has been "a whisper of insanity" in the Bohun family. Although Father Brown empathizes with Reverend Bohun, he nevertheless believes that he should express Christian charity toward his brother. When the body of Norman Bohun is found outside his brother's church, Father Brown begins to examine the case. Father Brown finally comes to the conclusion that Reverend Bohun killed his brother by dropping a hammer on him from the church tower. The murderer tried to frame the village idiot because he knew that the courts would never hold an idiot responsible for murder. At the end of this story, Reverend Bohun and Father Brown have a long conversation, and Father Brown dissuades Reverend Bohun from committing suicide because "that door leads to hell." He persuades him instead to confess his sin to God and admit his guilt to the police. In prison, Reverend Bohun, like Flambeau, may find salvation. In both "The Blue Cross" and "The Hammer of God," Father Brown hates the crime but loves the sinner. Readers are left with the definite impression that Father Brown is absolutely essential for the spiritual growth and eventual salvation of Flambeau and Reverend Bohun.

Several critics have remarked that the character of Father Brown did not change much in the four volumes of detective fiction that Chesterton wrote after *The Innocence of Father Brown*. This stability represents, however, strength and not weakness. It would have been inappropriate for a member of the clergy to have stopped caring about the spiritual life of others. Father Brown knows that evil exists in the world, but he also believes that even sinners and murderers can be reformed in this life and saved in the next. Father Brown is a fascinating fictional detective who uses his own religious beliefs in order to solve crimes and express profound insights into the dignity of every person.

OTHER MAJOR WORKS

LONG FICTION: *The Napoleon of Notting Hill*, 1904; *The Man Who Was Thursday: A Nightmare*, 1908; *The Ball and the Cross*, 1909; *The Innocence of Father Brown*, 1911; *Manalive*, 1912; *The Flying Inn*, 1914; *The Wisdom of Father Brown*, 1914; *The Incredulity of Father Brown*, 1926; *The Secret of Father Brown*, 1927; *The Return of Don Quixote*, 1927; *The Floating Admiral*, 1931 (with others); *The Scan-*

dal of Father Brown, 1935; *The Vampire of the Village*, 1947.

PLAYS: *Magic: A Fantastic Comedy*, pr., pb. 1913; *The Judgment of Dr. Johnson*, pb. 1927; *The Surprise*, pr., pb. 1953.

POETRY: *Greybeards at Play: Literature and Art for Old Gentlemen—Rhymes and Sketches*, 1900; *The Wild Knight and Other Poems*, 1900, revised 1914; *The Ballad of the White Horse*, 1911; *A Poem*, 1915; *Poems*, 1915; *Wine, Water, and Song*, 1915; *Old King Cole*, 1920; *The Ballad of St. Barbara and Other Verses*, 1922; (*Poems*), 1925; *The Queen of Seven Swords*, 1926; *Gloria in Profundis*, 1927; *Ubi Ecclesia*, 1929; *The Grave of Arthur*, 1930.

NONFICTION: *The Defendant*, 1901; *Twelve Types*, 1902 (revised as *Varied Types*, 1903; also as *Simplicity and Tolstoy*); *Thomas Carlyle*, 1902; *Robert Louis Stevenson*, 1902 (with W. Robertson Nicoll); *Leo Tolstoy*, 1903 (with G. H. Perris and Edward Garnett); *Charles Dickens*, 1903 (with F. G. Kitton); *Robert Browning*, 1903; *Tennyson*, 1903 (with Richard Garnett); *Thackeray*, 1903 (with Lewis Melville); *G. F. Watts*, 1904; *Heretics*, 1905; *Charles Dickens: A Critical Study*, 1906; *All Things Considered*, 1908; *Orthodoxy*, 1908; *George Bernard Shaw*, 1909, revised 1935; *Tremendous Trifles*, 1909; *What's Wrong with the World*, 1910; *Alarms and Discursions*, 1910; *William Blake*, 1910; *The Ultimate Lie*, 1910; *Appreciations and Criticisms of the Works of Charles Dickens*, 1911; *A Defence of Nonsense and Other Essays*, 1911; *The Future of Religion: Mr. G. K. Chesterton's Reply to Mr. Bernard Shaw*, 1911; *The Conversion of an Anarchist*, 1912; *A Miscellany of Men*, 1912; *The Victorian Age in Literature*, 1913; *Thoughts from Chesterton*, 1913; *The Barbarism of Berlin*, 1914; *London*, 1914 (with Alvin Langdon Coburn); *Prussian Versus Belgian Culture*, 1914; *Letters to an Old Garibaldian*, 1915; *The So-Called Belgian Bargain*, 1915; *The Crimes of England*, 1915; *Divorce Versus Democracy*, 1916; *Temperance and the Great Alliance*, 1916; *A Shilling for My Thoughts*, 1916; *Lord Kitchener*, 1917; *A Short History of England*, 1917; *Utopia of Usurers and Other Essays*, 1917; *How to Help Annexation*, 1918; *Irish Impressions*, 1920; *The Superstition of Divorce*, 1920; *Charles Dickens Fifty Years After,*

1920; *The Uses of Diversity*, 1920; *The New Jerusalem*, 1920; *Eugenics and Other Evils*, 1922; *What I Saw in America*, 1922; *Fancies Versus Fads*, 1923; *St. Francis of Assisi*, 1923; *The End of the Roman Road: A Pageant of Wayfarers*, 1924; *The Superstitions of the Sceptic*, 1925; *The Everlasting Man*, 1925; *William Cobbett*, 1925; *The Outline of Sanity*, 1926; *The Catholic Church and Conversion*, 1926; *A Gleaming Cohort, Being from the Words of G. K. Chesterton*, 1926; *Social Reform Versus Birth Control*, 1927; *Culture and the Coming Peril*, 1927; *Robert Louis Stevenson*, 1927; *Generally Speaking*, 1928; *(Essays)*, 1928; *Do We Agree? A Debate*, 1928 (with George Bernard Shaw); *The Thing*, 1929; *G. K. C. as M. C., Being a Collection of Thirty-seven Introductions*, 1929; *The Resurrection of Rome*, 1930; *Come to Think of It*, 1930; *The Turkey and the Turk*, 1930; *At the Sign of the World's End*, 1930; *Is There a Return to Religion?*, 1931 (with E. Haldeman-Julius); *All Is Grist*, 1931; *Chaucer*, 1932; *Sidelights on New London and Newer York and Other Essays*, 1932; *Christendom in Dublin*, 1932; *All I Survey*, 1933; *St. Thomas Aquinas*, 1933; *G. K. Chesterton*, 1933 (also as *Running After One's Hat and Other Whimsies*); *Avowals and Denials*, 1934; *The Well and the Shallows*, 1935; *Explaining the English*, 1935; *As I Was Saying*, 1936; *Autobiography*, 1936; *The Man Who Was Chesterton*, 1937; *The End of the Armistice*, 1940; *The Common Man*, 1950; *The Glass Walking-Stick and Other Essays from the "Illustrated London News," 1905-1936*, 1955; *Lunacy and Letters*, 1958; *Where All Roads Lead*, 1961; *The Man Who Was Orthodox: A Selection from the Uncollected Writings of G. K. Chesterton*, 1963; *The Spice of Life and Other Essays*, 1964; *Chesterton on Shakespeare*, 1971.

EDITED TEXTS: *Thackeray*, 1909; *Samuel Johnson*, 1911 (with Alice Meynell); *Essays by Divers Hands*, 1926; *G. K.'s*, 1934.

MISCELLANEOUS: *Stories, Essays, and Poems*, 1935; *The Coloured Lands*, 1938.

BIBLIOGRAPHY

Clipper, Lawrence J. *G. K. Chesterton*. New York: Twayne, 1974. In this useful introduction to the works of Chesterton, Clipper does a fine job of describing the recurring themes in Chesterton's fictional and nonfictional writings. He analyzes very well Chesterton's poetry and literary criticism. Contains an excellent annotated bibliography.

Conlon, D. J., ed. *Chesterton: A Half Century of Views*. New York: Oxford University Press, 1987. Contains numerous short essays on Chesterton published during the first fifty years after his death. The wide diversity of positive critical reactions shows that not only his popular fiction but also his writings on literature and religion continue to fascinate readers.

Crowe, Marian E. "G. K. Chesterton and the Orthodox Romance of Pride and Prejudice." *Renascence* 49 (Spring, 1997): 209-221. Argues that Chesterton used the word "romance" to refer to three different concepts: erotic love, adventure stories, and orthodox faith.

Hollis, Christopher. *The Mind of Chesterton*. Coral Gables, Fla.: University of Miami Press, 1970. This especially thoughtful study explores above all Chesterton's evolution as a writer before his conversion to Catholicism in 1922. In his final chapter, entitled "Chesterton and His Survival," Hollis explains why Chesterton's work continues to fascinate readers who do not share his religious beliefs.

Horst, Mark. "Sin, Psychopathology and Father Brown." *The Christian Century* 104 (January 21, 1987): 46-47. Compares Chesterton's detective Father Brown to Will Graham, a character in Michael Mann's film *Manhunt*. Argues that although both sleuths use introspection to pursue criminals, when Father Brown looks within himself, he sees sin, a universal reality, whereas when Will Graham looks within, he sees psychopathology, an aberration.

Lauer, Quentin. *G. K. Chesterton: Philosopher Without Portfolio*. New York: Fordham University Press, 1988. This volume is a thought-provoking study of Chesterton's philosophical reflections on the uses and limitations of reason, Christian humanism, religious tolerance, and moral values.

Pearce, Joseph. *Wisdom and Innocence: A Life of*

G. K. Chesterton. San Francisco: Ignatius Press, 1996. A scholarly and well-written biography of Chesterton. Contains many quotes from his works and good analysis of them, as well as useful data on his family and friends.

Royal, Robert. "Our Curious Contemporary, G. K. Chesterton." *The Wilson Quarterly* 16 (Autumn, 1992): 92-102. Notes that although his works were once highly popular, Chesterton's reputation has fallen since his death; argues that postmodern consciousness could give today's readers a new and better appreciation of Chesterton, for his work anticipates such postmodern obsessions as the fragmentation of meaning and language, the dissolution of identity, and the attempt to construct a humane society.

Schwartz, Adam. "G. K. C.'s Methodical Madness: Sanity and Social Control in Chesterton." *Renascence* 49 (Fall, 1996): 23-40. Part of a special issue on G. K. Chesterton. Argues that his view shifts from focus on mental condition of an individual to the way societies define sanity and make "insanity" a means of bourgeois class control.

Tadie, Andrew A., and Michael H. Macdonald, eds. *Permanent Things: Toward the Recovery of a More Human Scale at the End of the Twentieth Century*. Grand Rapids, Mich.: William B. Eerdmans, 1995. This volume includes a fairly thorough discussion of Chesterton's writing, along with works of T. S. Eliot and C. S. Lewis, looking primarily at its ethical and religious components.

Ward, Maisie. *Gilbert Keith Chesterton*. New York: Sheed & Ward, 1943. This well-researched book remains the essential biography of Chesterton. Ward had full access to Chesterton's manuscripts and spoke with many people who had known him personally. Reveals much about his evolution as a writer and the importance of friendship in his life.

Edmund J. Campion

KATE CHOPIN

Born: St. Louis, Missouri, February 8, 1851
Died: St. Louis, Missouri, August 22, 1904

PRINCIPAL SHORT FICTION
Bayou Folk, 1894
A Night in Acadie, 1897

OTHER LITERARY FORMS

In addition to the short stories which brought her some fame as a writer during her own lifetime, Kate Chopin published two novels, *At Fault* (1890) and *The Awakening* (1899), the latter of which was either ignored or condemned because of its theme of adultery and frank depiction of a woman's sexual urges. Chopin also wrote a few reviews and casual essays and a number of undistinguished poems.

ACHIEVEMENTS

Kate Chopin's short stories, published in contemporary popular magazines, won her fame as a local colorist with a good ear for dialect and as a writer concerned with women's issues (sexuality, equality, independence). After the publication of *The Awakening* in 1899, however, her popularity waned, in part because of the furor over the open treatment of adultery and sex in the novel. She wrote few stories after 1900, and her work was largely neglected until the rediscovery of *The Awakening* by feminist critics. Criticism of that novel and new biographies have spurred a new interest in her Creole short stories, which have been analyzed in detail in terms of their regionalism and their treatment of gender. Influenced by Guy de Maupassant, she did not exert any literary influence on later short-story writers, at least until the rediscovery of *The Awakening*.

BIOGRAPHY

Kate Chopin was born Katherine O'Flaherty in St. Louis, Missouri, in 1851. Her mother's family was Creole, descended from French settlers, and her father, a successful merchant, was an Irish immigrant. She was educated at the Academy of the Sacred Heart in St. Louis beginning in 1860, five years after her father's accidental death, and was graduated in 1868. In 1870, she married Oscar Chopin, who took her to live in Louisiana, first in New Orleans and later in Natchitoches Parish, the setting for many of her stories. In 1882, Oscar died of swamp fever; Kate Chopin managed her husband's properties for a year and in 1884 returned to St. Louis. The next year her mother died, and in 1888 Chopin began writing out of a need for personal expression and to help support her family financially. Her stories appeared regularly in popular periodicals, and she published a novel, *At Fault*, in 1890. *Bayou Folk*, a collection of stories and sketches, appeared in 1894, the year her widely anthologized "The Story of an Hour" was written. *A Night in Acadie* followed, and she was identified as one of four outstanding literary figures in St. Louis by the *Star-Times*. Her celebrated novel, *The Awakening*, received hostile reviews that upset her, though reports about the book being banned were greatly exaggerated. She did, however, write relatively little after this controversy and died five years later in St. Louis, where she was attending the world's fair.

ANALYSIS

Until the 1970's, Kate Chopin was known best literarily, if at all, as a "local colorist," primarily for her tales of life in New Orleans and rural Louisiana. Chopin manages in these stories (about two-thirds of her total output) to bring to life subtly the settings and personalities of her characters, usually Creoles (descendants of the original French settlers of Louisiana) or Cajuns (or Acadians, the French colonists who were exiled to Louisiana following the British conquest of Nova Scotia). What makes Chopin especially important for modern readers, however, is her insight

Kate Chopin (Missouri Historical Society)

into human characters and relationships in the context of their societies whether Creole, Cajun, or Anglo-Saxon—and into the social, emotional, and sexual roles of women within those societies.

Chopin's desire and hope for female independence can be seen in two of her earliest stories, "Wiser Than a God" and "A Point at Issue!" (both 1889). In the first story, the heroine Paula Von Stoltz rejects an offer of marriage in order to begin a successful career as a concert pianist because music is the true sole passion of her life; it is an act which anticipates the actions of Edna Pontellier in *The Awakening*. In the second story, Eleanor Gail and Charles Faraday enter into a marriage based on reason and equality and pursue their individual careers in separate places. This arrangement works very well for some time, but finally each of the two succumbs to jealousy; in spite of this blemish in their relationship, Chopin's humorous tone manages to poke fun at traditional attitudes toward marriage as well.

"THE STORY OF AN HOUR"

This questioning though humorous attitude is strongly evident in one of Chopin's most anthologized and best-known tales, "The Story of an Hour" (1894). Mrs. Mallard, a woman suffering from a heart condition, is told that her husband has been killed in a train accident. She is at first deeply sorrowful, but soon realizes that even though she had loved and will mourn her husband, his death has set her free: "There would be no powerful will bending hers in that blind persistence with which men and women believe they have a right to impose a private will upon a fellow-creature." As Mrs. Mallard descends the stairs, however, the front door is opened by her husband, who had never been on the train. This time her heart gives out and the cause ironically is given by the doctors as "the joy that kills."

"LA BELLE ZORAÏDE"

It is in her Louisiana stories, however, that Chopin's sympathy for female and indeed human longings emerges most fully, subtly blended with a distinct and evocative sense of locale and folkways. "La Belle Zoraïde" (1893) is presented in the form of a folktale being told by a black servant, Manna-Loulou, to her mistress, Madame Delisle (these two characters also are central to the story "A Lady of Bayou St. John," 1893). The tale itself is the story of a black slave, Zoraïde, who is forbidden by her mistress to marry another slave with whom she has fallen in love because his skin is too black and her mistress intends her for another, more "gentlemanly" servant. In spite of this, and although the slave she loves is sold away, she bears his child and refuses marriage to the other slave. Her mistress falsely tells Zoraïde that her child has been born dead, and the slave descends into madness. Even when her real daughter is finally brought back to her, Zoraïde rejects her, preferring to cling to the bundle of rags which she has fashioned as a surrogate baby. From then on,

> She was never known again as la belle Zoraïde, but ever after as Zoraïde la folle, whom no one ever wanted to marry. . . . She lived to be an old woman, whom some people pitied and others laughed at—always clasping her bundle of rags—her 'piti.'

The indirect narration of this story prevents it from slipping into the melodramatic or the maudlin. Chopin's ending, presenting the conversation of Manna-Loulou and Madame Delisle in the Creole dialect, pointedly avoids a concluding moral judgment, an avoidance typical of Chopin's stories. Instead, the reader is brought back to the frame for the tale and concentrated upon the charm of the Creole dialect even while he or she retains pity and sympathy for Zoraïde.

"DÉSIRÉE'S BABY"

In spite of their southern locale, Chopin's stories rarely deal with racial relations between whites and blacks. One important exception is "Désirée's Baby" (1892). Désirée Valmondé, who was originally a foundling, marries Armand Aubigny, a plantation owner who is proud of his aristocratic heritage but very much in love with Désirée. He is at first delighted when she bears him a son, but soon begins to grow cold and distant. Désirée, puzzled at first, soon realizes with horror that her child has Negro blood. Armand, whose love for Désirée has been killed by "the unconscious injury she had brought upon his home and his name," turns her out of the house, and she disappears with her child into the bayou, never to be seen again. Later, in a surprise ending reminiscent of Maupassant, Armand is having all reminders of Désirée burned when he discovers a letter from his mother to his father which reveals that his mother had had Negro blood. In this story we see the continuation of Chopin's most central theme, the evil that follows when one human being gains power over another and attempts to make that person conform to preset standards or expectations.

As suggested earlier, Chopin finds that power of one person over another is often manifested in the institution of marriage. Yet, as even her earliest stories suggest, she does not always find that marriage necessarily requires that a wife be dominated by her husband, and she demonstrates that both men and women are capable of emotional and spiritual growth.

"ATHÉNAÏSE"

That possibility for growth is perhaps best seen in the story "Athénaïse" (1895). Athénaïse, an emotionally immature young woman, has married the planter Cazeau, but has found that she is not ready for marriage. She runs back to her family, explaining that she does not hate Cazeau himself:

> It's jus' being married that I detes' an' despise. . . . I can't stan' to live with a man; to have him always

there; his coats and pantaloons hanging in my room; his ugly bare feet—washing them in my tub, befo' my very eyes, ugh!

When Cazeau arrives to bring her back, however, she finds that she has to go with him. As the couple rides home, they pass an oak tree which Cazeau recalls was where his father had once apprehended a runaway slave: "The whole impression was for some reason hideous, and to dispel it Cazeau spurred his horse to a swift gallop."

Despite Cazeau's attempt to make up and live with Athénaïse at least as friends, she remains bitter and unhappy and finally runs away again, aided by her romantic and rather foolish brother Montéclin. Cazeau, a sensitive and proud man, refuses to go after her again as though she too were a runaway slave: "For the companionship of no woman on earth would he again undergo the humiliating sensation of baseness that had overtaken him in passing the old oak-tree in the fallow meadow."

Athénaïse takes refuge in a boarding house in New Orleans where she becomes friendly with Mr. Gouvernail, a newspaper editor. Gouvernail hopes to make Athénaïse his lover, but he refrains from forcing himself on her: "When the time came that she wanted him . . . he felt he would have a right to her. So long as she did not want him, he had no right to her,—no more than her husband had." Gouvernail, though, never gets his chance; Athénaïse has previously been described to us as someone who does not yet know her own mind, and that such knowledge will not come through rational analysis but "as the song to the bird, the perfume and color to the flower." This knowledge does come to her when she discovers that she is pregnant. As she thinks of Cazeau, "the first purely sensuous tremor of her life swept over her. . . . Her whole passionate nature was aroused as if by a miracle." Thus, Athénaïse returns to reconciliation and happiness with her husband.

Chopin's story illustrates that happiness in a relationship can come only with maturity and with mutual respect. Cazeau realizes that he cannot force his wife to love him, and Athénaïse finally knows what she wants when she awakens to an awareness of her own sexuality. If Cazeau has to learn to restrain himself, though, Mr. Gouvernail learns the need to take more initiative as well; not having declared his love for Athénaïse he suffers when she goes back home. The tone of the entire story is subtly balanced between poignancy and humor, allowing us to see the characters' flaws while remaining sympathetic with each of them.

The importance of physical passion and of sexual self-awareness which can be found in "Athénaïse" can also be found in many of Chopin's stories and is one of the characteristics which make her writing so far ahead of its time. It is this theme which, as the title suggests, is central to her novel *The Awakening* and which was partly responsible for the scandal which that novel provoked. Chopin's insistence not merely on the fact of women's sexual desires but also on the propriety and healthiness of those desires in some ways anticipates the writings of D. H. Lawrence, but without Lawrence's insistence on the importance of male dominance.

"THE STORM"

Sexual fulfillment outside of marriage without moral judgments can be found in "The Storm," written in 1898, just before *The Awakening*, but not published until 1969. The story concerns four characters from an earlier tale, "At the 'Cadian Ball" (1892). In that earlier story, a young woman, Clarisse, rides out in the night to the 'Cadian Ball to declare her love for the planter Alcée Laballière. Alcée is at the ball with an old girlfriend of his, Calixta, a woman of Spanish descent. Clarisse claims Alcée, and Calixta agrees to marry Bobinôt, a man who has been in love with her for some time.

"The Storm" is set several years later. Calixta and Bobinôt have had a child, and Alcée and Clarisse have been happily married. One day, while Bobinôt and his son are out on an errand, a huge storm breaks out. Alcée takes refuge at Calixta's house, and the old passion between the two is rekindled; as the storm breaks about them in mounting intensity, the two make love, Calixta's body "knowing for the first time its birthright." While the storm mirrors the physical passion of the couple, neither it nor the passion itself is destructive. Where one would expect some retribution for this infidelity in a story, the results are only beneficial: Calixta, physically fulfilled, happily welcomes back her returning husband and son; Alcée writes to Clarisse, off visiting relatives, that he does not need her back right away; and Clarisse, enjoying "the first free breath since her marriage," is content to stay where she is for the time. Chopin's ending seems audacious: "So the storm passed and every one was happy."

Although written about a century ago, Chopin's stories seem very modern in many ways. Her concern with women's place in society and in marriage, her refusal to mix guilt with sexuality, and her narrative stance of sympathetic detachment make her as relevant to modern readers as her marked ability to convey character and setting simply yet completely. In the little more than a decade in which she produced most of her work, her command of her art grew ever stronger as did her willingness to deal with controversial subjects. It is unfortunate that this career was cut so short by the reaction to *The Awakening* and her early death; but it is fortunate that Chopin left us the writing that she did, and that it has been preserved.

OTHER MAJOR WORKS

LONG FICTION: *At Fault*, 1890; *The Awakening*, 1899.

MISCELLANEOUS: *The Complete Works of Kate Chopin*, 1969 (Per Seyersted, editor, 2 volumes).

BIBLIOGRAPHY

Beer, Janet. *Kate Chopin, Edith Wharton and Charlotte Perkins Gilman: Studies in Short Fiction.* London: Macmillan, 1997. This book includes three chapters on Chopin's short fiction. In one, Beer argues that Chopin's Louisiana is post-colonial rather than post-bellum; in another, she discusses how erotic desire expresses the lives of women; and in the third, she examines the authorial voice in Chopin's short-shory fables.

Boren, Lynda S., and Sara de Saussure Davis, eds. *Kate Chopin Reconsidered: Beyond the Bayou.* Baton Rouge: Louisiana State University Press, 1992. Although most of these essays focus on *The Awakening*, several discuss such stories as "Charlie," "After the Winter," and "At Cheniere Caminada." Other essays compare Chopin with playwright Henrik Ibsen in terms of domestic confinement and discuss her work from a Marxist point of view.

Brown, Pearl L. "Awakened Men in Kate Chopin's Creole Stories." *ATQ*, n.s. 13, no. 1 (March, 1999). Argues that in Chopin's Creole stories, in intimate moments women discover inner selves buried beneath socially imposed ones and men discover subjective selves buried beneath public personas.

Erickson, Jon. "Fairytale Features in Kate Chopin's 'Désirée's Baby': A Case Study in Genre Cross-Reference." In *Modes of Narrative*, edited by Reingard M. Nischik and Barbara Korte. Würzburg: Königshausen and Neumann, 1990. Shows how Chopin's story conflicts with the expectations set up by the fairy-tale genre on which it is based; for example, the prince turns out to be the villain. Argues that the ending of the story is justified, for in the fairy tale the mystery of origin must be solved and the villain must be punished.

Koloski, Bernard. *Kate Chopin: A Study of the Short Fiction.* New York: Twayne, 1996. Discusses Chopin's short stories in the context of her bilingual and bicultural imagination; provides readings of her most important stories, examines her three volumes of stories, and comments on her children's stories. Also includes excerpts from Chopin's literary criticism and brief discussions by other critics of her most familiar stories.

Seyersted, Per. *Kate Chopin: A Critical Biography.* Baton Rouge: Louisiana State University Press, 1980. Seyersted's biography, besides providing invaluable information about the New Orleans of the 1870's, examines Chopin's life, views, and work. Provides lengthy discussions not only of *The Awakening* but also of her many short stories. Seyersted sees her as a transitional literary figure, a link between George Sand and Simone de Beauvoir.

Seyersted, Per, and Emily Toth, eds. *A Kate Chopin Miscellany.* Natchitoches, La.: Northwestern State University Press, 1979. This volume contains some previously unpublished stories, some poems, two of Chopin's diaries, Chopin's letters and those written to her, and a translation of Cyrille Arnavon's introduction to a 1953 edition of *The Awakening*. Contains also an excellent annotated bibliography, arranged chronologically, of Chopin scholarship from 1890 to 1979, and several photographs of Chopin's family.

Skaggs, Peggy. *Kate Chopin*. Boston: Twayne, 1985. Skaggs reads Chopin's work in terms of the theme of the search for identity, which pervades the two chapters devoted to Chopin's short fiction. Also included in this helpful overview of Chopin's life and work are a biographical chapter, a chronology, and a select bibliography. The book is indispensable for readers of Chopin's short fiction.

Taylor, Helen. *Gender, Race, and Religion in the Writings of Grace King, Ruth McEnery Stuart, and Kate Chopin*. Baton Rouge: Louisiana State University Press, 1989. Taylor divides her chapter on Chopin between the novels and the short stories, some of which are given extensive feminist readings. Taylor focuses on Chopin as a local

colorist who uses regional and historical themes to explore gender issues. The book is invaluable in its material on literary influences, particularly Guy de Maupassant, and the intellectual climate of the time.

Toth, Emily. *Kate Chopin*. New York: William Morrow, 1990. Toth's thoroughly documented, exhaustive work is the definitive Chopin biography. She covers not only Chopin's life but also her literary works and discusses many of the short stories in considerable detail. Toth updates Per Seyersted's bibliography of Chopin's work, supplies a helpful chronology of her life, and discusses the alleged banning of *The Awakening*. The starting point for Chopin research.

_____. *Unveiling Kate Chopin*. Jackson: University Press of Mississippi, 1999. Using newly discovered manuscripts, letters, and diaries of Chopin, Toth examines the source of Chopin's ambition and passion for her art, arguing that she worked much harder at her craft than previously thought.

Donald F. Larsson, updated by Thomas L. Erskine

CHRÉTIEN DE TROYES

Born: France; c. 1150
Died: France(?); c. 1190

PRINCIPAL SHORT FICTION

Erec et Enide, c. 1164 (English translation, 1913)
Cligés: Ou, La Fausse Morte, c. 1164 (*Cligés: A Romance*, 1912)
Lancelot: Ou, Le Chevalier à la charrette, c. 1168 (*Lancelot: Or, The Knight of the Cart*, 1913)
Yvain: Ou, Le Chevalier au lion, c. 1170 (*Yvain: Or, The Knight with the Lion*, c. 1300)
Perceval: Ou, Le Conte du Graal, c. 1180 (*Perceval: Or, The Story of the Grail*, 1844)

OTHER LITERARY FORMS

Chrétien de Troyes, whose complete works are listed above, is acknowledged as the first writer of Arthurian romance in the vernacular. He is also the originator of the Arthurian version of the Grail legend, although his is not a fully Christianized version.

ACHIEVEMENTS

One of the first poets to treat the legend of King Arthur, Chrétien is widely regarded as the founder of the medieval romantic tradition. More than anyone else, Chrétien defined the characteristics of romance for later generations. For example, his use of humor, irony, and symbolism influenced romantic authors such as Marie de France, Gottfried von Strassburg, and Wolfram von Eschenbach. His *Perceval*, which contains the earliest known use of the Grail legend in the Arthurian tradition, continued to be a model for romantic works as late as Richard Wagner's *Parsifal* (1986). Moreover, Chrétien's use of the supernatural inspired those who revived the Romantic and gothic traditions at the beginning of the nineteenth century.

The code of courtly love seen in Chrétien's works is similar to that described in Andreas Capellanus's *The Art of Courtly Love* (1969). Chrétien's knights embody Christian virtues and combine physical strength with romantic devotion. Other values represented by the heroes of Chrétien's poems are similar to the aristocratic code embraced by the author's wealthy and well-educated audience.

BIOGRAPHY

Although details of Chrétien de Troyes's life are unknown, he names himself in his romances and gives a list of his writings to date in the *Cligés*. His dialect is that of Champagne. There have been many hypotheses concerning his identity, but no significant evidence in support of any of them has been brought forward. That he was attached to the courts of Marie de Champagne and possibly of Phillipe of Flanders may be detected from the texts of *Lancelot* and *Perceval*, respectively. Stylistic traits such as the use of formal rhetorical techniques indicate clerical training, and he may have been in holy orders, although not necessarily higher than the diaconate. If, indeed, he was an inhabitant of Troyes, the site of twice-yearly fairs, he had opportunities for wider general culture than other regions might have provided, and this may account for the variety of his not-too-accurate geographical references. There is, in fact, little beyond the works clearly attributed to Chrétien that can provide evidence, and that only of artistic skill, of this author of at least five influential "courtly" romances.

ANALYSIS

Love, chivalry, *mesure* (moderation or balance), and irony are the primary elements of the romances of Chrétien de Troyes. His protagonist must, to be worthy of love, seek adventures by means of which he can display his prowess in knightly combat; at the same time, he cannot neglect the demands of love for the sake of adventure.

EREC ET ENIDE

Chrétien addresses the former problem in his earliest romance, *Erec et Enide*, his first Arthurian romance. Erec wins Enide as his bride and is so enamored of her that he ceases to enter tourneys or seek adventures. He accidentally hears Enide's soliloquy of concern that he is being mocked for his uxoriousness and commands her to dress in her best garments, to ride before him as he goes out to prove his skill, and to remain silent under all circumstances. Enide, riding ahead, sees ambushes prepared for Erec and breaks his command by warning him. He rebukes her each time and defeats his would-be attackers. The lovers are reconciled after an extended series of adventures; Erec is convinced of his wife's faithfulness and respect and Enide is convinced of his worth.

Erec et Enide demonstrates the pattern of swift rise (the winning of Enide), sudden fall (the blow to Erec's pride), and slow recovery (the adventure sequence) characteristic of many of Chrétien's romances. It is not Erec alone who must be corrected, although his lack of balance, his *démesure*, is greater than Enide's. Enide, whose words alert Erec to his faults, appears also to be submitting to correction as she endures Erec's harshness. She needs to speak and he to hear, but the result of the revelation is Erec's anger and distrust. Although it seems that she is being punished for no reason, earlier circumstances suggest that her concern for Erec's reputation is, in part, concern for her own status, since her marriage to Erec resulted in her being elevated from the daughter of a poor knight to being the wife of the heir to a kingdom. When, commanded to silence, she speaks to protect Erec, and Erec, to preserve them both, must perforce listen; the difference from the initial incident lies in the appropriateness of motivation and response. Once real reconciliation and understanding are achieved, the lovers return to their kingdom, Erec's prowess having been confirmed by his adventures.

YVAIN

Yvain presents the opposite problem from that of *Erec et Enide:* Yvain, a young knight of King Arthur's court, is so involved in knightly adventure that he neglects his duty as a lover, with disastrous results. Yvain leaves Arthur's court in order to be the first to attempt a new adventure—to find a spring whose water will cause a storm when it is poured over a magical rock beside it. The storm summons a knight whom Yvain defeats and pursues into the knight's city. Yvain, trapped in the city, is aided by Lunete, handmaiden to Laudine, the slain defender's widow. Yvain has fallen in love with Laudine and, through Lunete's machinations, the two are wed. Although he is passionately in love with Laudine, he is reminded by Gawain not to neglect adventure. Yvain receives Laudine's permission to seek adventures, but she sets a definite term on that permission—a year—after which her love will turn to hate. Yvain forgets, learns of Laudine's rejection from a messenger before all of the court, leaves the court, and goes mad. He abandons his clothing (signs of his rank), the court (his proper milieu), and his reason in an attempted flight from himself. After a long period of insanity, he is cured and starts on a long series of adventures, in the course of which he is befriended by a lion. All of his adventures necessitate rendering service, the proper use of his skills as a knight. With Lunete's help he conquers the last obstacle, Laudine's determined refusal to forgive him, and the lovers are reconciled.

Chrétien employs the same general structure in *Yvain* as he does in *Erec et Enide*, but the narrative is denser and the characterization more deft. From the beginning, Yvain's youthful self-centeredness and touchy pride prepare the reader for both his lack of understanding of what a lover's fidelity must be and his emotional devastation when his failure is made public. Laudine, whom Lunete manipulates into accepting Yvain as her new husband, is intensely concerned with her reputation—only feudal necessity obviates the potential ugliness of this new courtship—and her own pride is much injured by Yvain's negligence. This same concern with honor plays into Lunete's hands as she entraps Laudine in an oath to do all in her power to reunite the Knight with the Lion with his lady. Lunete's perspicacity contrasts with the prideful blindness of the two lovers, and even the Lion, in a scene of rich comedy and seriousness, demonstrates his faithfulness to Yvain, whom he believes to be dead, by attempting to commit suicide with Yvain's sword.

It is not simply the content of Yvain's adventures but their place in the narrative sequence that is meaningful in the romance. The same Yvain who could not get enough adventure finds himself required by his sworn word to perform two rescues nearly at one time, one of which is rescuing Lunete from the stake to which Laudine has condemned her for the "treason" of having aided Yvain. Yvain learns from his adventures that promises are neither to be made nor to be broken lightly and that he is not to be one such as Chrétien describes at the beginning of the romance, one who hears but does not understand: "for speech is completely wasted if not understood by the heart." At the end, however, Chrétien tempers Yvain's triumph with irony, causing one to wonder how perceptive Yvain really is when one reads of Laudine's less than gracious acquiescence—she has sworn an oath and will not be forsworn even if this means accepting Yvain—and Yvain's delight at their being reunited. In any event, a vital balance has been achieved between love and chivalry, and the Knight with the Lion has progressed in understanding beyond the Yvain of the beginning of the romance.

GUILLAUME D'ANGLETERRE

Although the love conventions Chrétien uses in his romances are usually, and inaccurately, described as those of "courtly love," the protagonists of *Erec et Enide* and *Yvain* are married as are Guillaume and Gratiien his wife in *Guillaume d'Angleterre*. Chrétien's much-contested third romance is the story of a family separated by adversity and rejoined after twenty years, during which both Guillaume and Gratiien have maintained their fidelity and the twin sons of their marriage have remained true to their noble birth despite bourgeois fostering. It is a tale in the romance mode although not strictly within the conventions of medieval romantic, that is courtly, love.

LANCELOT

Chrétien does deal with the extramarital passion

that characterized the Provençal love lyric in two of his romances, *Cligés* and *Lancelot*. In the latter, Chrétien is credited with being the creator of the story of the love between Lancelot and Guinevere, although he claims to have written the story at the behest of his patroness Marie de Champagne, daughter of Eleanor of Aquitaine. However reluctant Chrétien may seem—he turned over completion of the tale to one Godefroi de Leigny—this reluctance did not keep him from creating a complexly structured sequence of adventures each functioning not so much as instructive but as demonstrative of the lover's state. That Chrétien did not complete the romance himself may argue less for reluctance to write a romance of this kind than for the demands of writing the *Yvain*, generally believed to be contemporaneous. All that was significant in the *Lancelot* was completed by Chrétien; only the denouement remained for Godefroi.

In *Lancelot*, love and reason are set in opposition, and love triumphs. Lancelot, in quest of the queen, who has been abducted by Meleagant, prince of Gorre, is made to look almost foolish as he venerates a lock of Guinevere's hair as if it were a holy relic, or becomes so involved in a reverie that he is unhorsed when he does not respond to a challenge, yet he never fails in any of his adventures. Those who taunt him for his unavoidable although unknightly ride in a cart when he has no horse cannot touch him with their mockery. Lancelot's reasonable hesitation before riding in the cart leads to his being rejected by Guinevere, but his lover's folly of absolute obedience to Guinevere's commands to "do his worst" at a tournament is accounted to his glory. Chrétien is clear-sighted enough to portray this glorious folly, ironically, as folly still, and Guinevere, for all her imperiousness, mourns when a false report of Lancelot's death leads her to believe that her harshness is the true reason for his demise.

Once Lancelot and Guinevere meet in love, Chrétien shifts his emphasis to the conflict between Lancelot and Meleagant; Lancelot, by virtue of knightly prowess, maintains the necessary balance between love and chivalry as he champions Arthur's queen against her abductor's accusation of adultery.

Chrétien remains silent with regard to the truth of the accusation against Guinevere, and the tension between truth and protestation remains implicit as he focuses on the contrast between Lancelot and Meleagant as types of the lover: Meleagant, the abductor whose accusation is true, falls before Lancelot, the chivalrous lover, whose protestation is false. Chrétien narrates the story requested of him while making his own ironic observations by means of the dramatic and ironic tensions present in the narrative.

CLIGÉS

Cligés has been considered by some to be Chrétien's commentary on the Tristan legend. The general structure of the romance, the love story first of the parents and then of their son, Cligés, duplicates that of the Tristan tales. Later, Fenice, lover of Cligés, uses an elaborate stratagem to remain true to Cligés despite her marriage to his uncle, saying that she does wish to be a second Iseult. The lovers Fenice and Cligés are exemplary in their faithfulness to each other, but their derelictions otherwise are glaringly obvious. The romance ends with their being wed, but the closing comments attribute to Fenice's success in deceiving her husband the Eastern practice of using eunuchs as harem guards. Chrétien is never blatantly sarcastic, but one senses that the artist relishes giving *his* version of a very popular story.

PERCEVAL

Chrétien's career of innovation culminates in the unfinished *Perceval*. The romance, which in Chrétien's version is not overtly the Christian spiritual quest it was to become, is built around the theme of the Wasteland whose ruler, the wounded Fisher-King, can only be healed by certain questions asked by the chosen hero. This hero, Perceval, whose character is a compendium of the traits of Chrétien's earlier heroes, is brought up in ignorance and isolation by his mother and is so intent upon observing his conception of knightly decorum in the Fisher-King's presence that, fearing to seem uncouth, he fails to ask the necessary questions. Publicly denounced at Arthur's court, he sets out on a long, uncompleted series of adventures to redress his offense. The romance breaks off in the middle of a series of Gawain's adventures which form a parallel to Perceval's. There is controversy among scholars as to whether the romance would end with Perceval's triumphant return to ask the questions (a denouement used in later retellings of the tale) or with some ending that goes beyond the relatively simple pattern of Chrétien's other romances. The lack of resolution in *Perceval* led to several *Continuations* and one later medieval masterpiece, the *Parzival* of Wolfram von Eschenbach. Almost immediately, Chrétien's story was Christianized; that is, explicit links were made between the Grail and the chalice of the Last Supper and the lance of the Grail-ritual with the lance of the Crucifixion, by Robert de Boron. Later retellings of this version such as the Old French *Quest of the Holy Grail* (1225-1230) linked the grail-quest ever more firmly with the tragic downfall of Arthur's court; these versions led to the grail-story as retold in Middle English by Sir Thomas Malory.

Chrétien's contributions—the quest for adventure, the Lancelot-Guinevere affair, and the Grail-legend—provide the framework, lacking only the downfall of the Arthurian milieu, of the later Arthurian cycle of romances. Conventions that are present, it is true, in other romances of his time are crystallized in his works. It is unfair to his contemporaries and his literary descendants to term them mere imitators, but the medieval romance of chivalry received from Chrétien de Troyes a form ample and flexible enough to accommodate the variations, embellishments, and departures of those who came after him.

BIBLIOGRAPHY

Cazelles, Brigitte. *The Unholy Grail: A Social Reading of Chrétien de Troyes's Conte du Graal*. Stanford, Calif.: Stanford University Press, 1996. Attempts to situate *Conte du Graal* in its sociocultural context. Argues that Grail society is not the embodiment of a regenerated chivalry, but rather the illustration of Chrétien's awareness of the failure of traditional chivalry. Claims that chivalry in the work promotes violence and aggression.

Frappier, Jean. *Chrétien de Troyes: The Man and His Work*. Translated by Raymond J. Cormier. Athens: Ohio University Press, 1982. The best general introduction to Chrétien de Troyes and an excellent analysis of his works. Contains information on Chrétien's background and his literary form. Analyzes each of his major works. A good place for the general reader to begin. Also includes an extensive bibliography, categorized according to Chrétien's individual poems, his background, general studies about the author, the influence of classical antiquity, and Chrétien's literary style.

Guerin, M. Victoria. *The Fall of Kings and Princes: Structure and Destruction in Arthurian Tragedy*. Stanford, Calif.: Stanford University Press, 1995. Discusses how Chrétien draws from the relationship between Arthurian incest and Arthurian tragedy in *Le Chevalier de la Charrete* and *Le Conte du Graal*. Examines Mordred's incestuous origin and his illicit incestuous desire for his father's wife. Argues that Chrétien's two most enigmatic texts must be read side by side in order to understand their development of the relationship between incest and tragedy.

Guyer, Foster Erwin. *Chrétien de Troyes: Inventor of the Modern Novel*. New York: Bookman Associates, 1957. Explores the impact of Chrétien on later fiction. Argues that Chrétien's work had no immediate models, although it adapted something of the form and structure of Vergil's *Aeneid* and Ovid's love poetry. Concludes that Chrétien stands at the very beginning of the modern novelistic tradition.

_____. *Romance in the Making: Chrétien de Troyes and the Earliest French Romances*. New York: S. F. Vanni, 1954. Argues that Chrétien's style is inspired by Vergil and Ovid, his view of love by Ovid, and many of his plot elements by Geoffrey of Monmouth. None of Chrétien's sources, Guyer concludes, was French.

Lewis, Charles Bertram. *Classical Mythology and Arthurian Romance*. Geneva: Slatkine, 1974. Advances the interesting thesis that the plots of Chrétien's short fiction were largely derived from Greek mythology. Lewis believes that corrupt French versions of stories brought northward from Rome about Theseus and Helen of Troy provided the inspiration for *Yvain, Lancelot*, and *Erec et Enide*. Includes an extensive bibliography.

Loomis, Roger Sherman. *Arthurian Tradition and Chrétien de Troyes*. New York: Columbia University Press, 1949. A detailed study of Chrétien's immediate sources and his treatment of those works. Examines the author's literary art, his relationship to the rest of the Arthurian cycle, and his use of Celtic, Irish, and Welsh legends.

Luttrell, Claude. *The Creation of the First Arthurian Romance: A Quest*. Evanston, Ill.: Northwestern University Press, 1974. A detailed examination of Chrétien's stories in terms of the folklore patterns that they contain. Luttrell argues that the Celtic influence upon Chrétien was minimal.

Maddox, Donald. *The Arthurian Romances of Chrétien de Troyes: Once and Future Fictions*. Cambridge, England: Cambridge University Press, 1991. A good study of the tales. Includes bibliographical references and an index.

Amelia A. Rutledge, updated by Jeffrey L. Buller

AGATHA CHRISTIE

Born: Torquay, England; September 15, 1890
Died: Wallingford, England; January 12, 1976

PRINCIPAL SHORT FICTION

Poirot Investigates, 1924
Partners in Crime, 1929
The Mysterious Mr. Quin, 1930
The Thirteen Problems, 1932 (pb. in U.S. as *The Tuesday Club Murders*, 1933)
The Hound of Death and Other Stories, 1933
The Listerdale Mystery and Other Stories, 1934
Parker Pyne Investigates, 1934 (pb. in U.S. as *Mr. Parker Pyne, Detective*)
Murder in the Mews and Other Stories, 1937 (pb. in U.S. as *Dead Man's Mirror and Other Stories*)
The Regatta Mystery and Other Stories, 1939
The Labours of Hercules: Short Stories, 1947 (pb. in U.S. as *Labors of Hercules: New Adventures in Crime by Hercule Poirot*)
Witness for the Prosecution and Other Stories, 1948
Three Blind Mice and Other Stories, 1950
The Under Dog and Other Stories, 1951
The Adventures of the Christmas Pudding, and Selection of Entrées, 1960
Double Sin and Other Stories, 1961
Thirteen for Luck: A Selection of Mystery Stories for Young Readers, 1961
Star over Bethlehem and Other Stories, 1965 (as A. C. Mallowan)
Surprize! Surprize! A Collection of Mystery Stories with Unexpected Endings, 1965
Thirteen Clues for Miss Marple: A Collection of Mystery Stories, 1965
The Golden Ball and Other Stories, 1971
Hercule Poirot's Early Cases, 1974
Miss Marple's Final Cases, 1979

OTHER LITERARY FORMS

Agatha Christie is acknowledged as one of the world's most prolific writers. In addition to her shorter works, she is the author of more than fifty detective novels, including the famous Hercule Poirot and Miss Marple stories such as *Curtain: Hercule Poirot's Last Case* (1975) and *A Murder Is Announced* (1950). Christie wrote not only fifteen plays—one of which, *The Mousetrap* (pr. 1952), set a world record for the longest continuous run of performances—but also romance novels, poems, autobiographical works, and a children's book. She also published several books under the pseudonym Mary Westmacott. Immensely popular, many of her works have been adapted for stage, screen, and television.

The sales of her works have been unsurpassed by any other popular author.

ACHIEVEMENTS

As the most popular mystery writer of all time, Agatha Christie stands alone in the annals of detective fiction. As such, she has set the standards for others of this genre to follow. Her words have been translated into every modern European language. While her autobiographical works, plays, and romantic works are certainly successful, it is with her detective novels that she excels. During the fifty-odd years that she wrote these books, her skill with plot, character, and dialogue never wavered.

Following the dicta of plot development for whodunits, Christie nevertheless created myriad variations on a theme by manipulating the settings, characters, and developments in her stories. Part of her popularity is derived from this amazing ability to change format in so many ways—all familiar in tone to the avid Christie reader yet always fresh to the most jaded reader of detective fiction. Christie's strength, however, lies in her ability to create dialogue. Her characters' speeches are neither stilted nor long-winded, yet they reveal much about the plot, theme, and the characters themselves. Christie's works never rely on fantastic manipulation, on the kind of *deus ex machina* devices that others bring into their books. All is revealed simply and readily through her simple and elegant speeches and descriptions. She must be declared a master of the craft.

BIOGRAPHY

Dame Agatha Mary Clarissa (Miller) Christie was born into an upper-middle-class Victorian family on September 15, 1890, in Torquay, a refined English seaside town. Her mother (Clara), grandmothers, and a companion-teacher educated young Agatha at home. While this may sound stifling, her parents maintained an active salon and frequently entertained the likes of Rudyard Kipling and Henry James. Agatha learned to read at an early age and availed herself of her parents' library.

The first unhappy event in Christie's life occurred in 1901, when her father, Fredrick, died, leaving the

Agatha Christie (Library of Congress)

family with an uncertain financial future. Her mother rallied, however, spurred by the desire to provide her youngest daughter with the same opportunities that her sister and brother had had. Consequently, Christie was sent to the Continent (perhaps encountering there the prototype of the Belgian Hercule Poirot) and to Cairo for the social season. With the outbreak of World War I, Christie worked at a hospital, initially as a surgical nurse but then in the dispensary, an experience that would come in handy later as she killed unlucky victims in her stories with cyanide and arsenic. She had, by this time, been writing poems and short stories with a modicum of success, but this practice temporarily ended when she met and married young flying ace Archibald Christie in 1914. In fact, she did not write again until 1916, when she dashed off *The Mysterious Affair at Styles* (1920) in a matter of weeks. The manuscript was shunted from one publisher to another; in fact, it was four years until the book went into print. By then, Christie was busy with a new house and a new baby, so her writing again took second place.

In 1925, Christie published *The Secret of Chimneys*, and the next year she witnessed the highly acclaimed publication of *The Murder of Roger Ackroyd* (1926). The couple bought a new house, and all went well until the late fall, when Christie's mother died and her husband revealed that he was in love with another woman. All this proved to be too much for Christie; on December 6, she simply disappeared, to turn up eleven days later in a hotel under an assumed name. While much speculation has been given to this hiatus, no real evidence has so far been discovered of Christie's whereabouts. The author herself declined to comment on it at the time or in *An Autobiography* (1977).

After her return, the Christies lived apart until their divorce in 1928. Faced with the burden of earning a living for herself and for Rosalind, Christie began to examine her writing with a new attitude, which evidenced itself in one novel with which she was pleased, *The Big Four* (1927), and one that she professed to hate, *The Mystery of the Blue Train* (1928), but which she forced herself to write for the income it provided. This marked Christie's emergence as a professional. As impressive as this sounds, Christie was prone to make light of it, as in her portrayal of an author with writer's block in "The Mystery of the Spanish Shawl."

With a steady source of income established and her daughter in boarding school, Christie decided to vacation in the Middle East. There, she met archaeologist Max Mallowan, and they were married on September 11, 1930. The Mallowans divided their time between digs in various regions and England. Christie found that she could write a few books a year despite this nomadic life; indeed, many of her works incorporate this sense of travel and their faraway settings. One of her characters, Mr. Parker Pyne, was prone to sending clients to foreign places in search of adventure.

World War II upset the Mallowans' placid routine. Max joined the Royal Air Force, and Rosalind married. Christie was horrified by the war and found relief in her writing. Her works do not reflect her outer life—working again in a hospital dispensary—but rather her inner feelings of despair over the death of her young son-in-law and her husband's dangerous assignment in North Africa. She wrote no short stories during this period; she did, however, continue with longer works, including a Mary Westmacott romance and a semiautobiographical novel.

After the war, the Mallowans tried to resume their careers fully and found that they were showered with many honors. Christie, notably, was named a commander of the British Empire in 1956 and a Dame of the British Empire in 1971. She was highly productive during this later period of her life. In addition, many of her novels were made into films, her plays were produced, and her short stories were serialized on television. Unfortunately, by 1975, Christie's health had deteriorated, and she died on January 12, 1976.

ANALYSIS

Agatha Christie's enormous popularity must rest on some sort of measurable talent. While no one would disagree that she had a faculty for witty—if at times overly homely—dialogue, and that she could contrive numerous amusing plot twists, surely her singular ability was in her talent for creating memorable and unique characters to inhabit her stories. When any avid Christie reader is asked to name a favorite story, the reply must invariably contain the name of a favorite character as well. The answer will never be "The Eymanthian Boar" but stories of Hercule Poirot, or stories with Tommy and Tuppence in them. The devotion of the reader settles on a hero rather than on certain types of stories or even on the author herself. Christie's plots pale perforce to the cunning, charm, and cleverness of her characters.

"THE MYSTERY OF THE BLUE JAR" AND "THE RED SIGNAL"

Admittedly, however, some of her short stories do not have well-known protagonists in them. In fact, some focus on the source of evil instead of good. In "The Mystery of the Blue Jar," a pair of thieves utilize the current fad of occultism to perpetrate a clever ruse on a gullible young man. Jack Hartington persuades himself that he hears cries of help—presumably from a future crime—emanating from a pretty French lodger. She and her accomplice, who poses as a "Doctor of the Soul," convince Jack to hand over his uncle's priceless, and recently acquired, Ming vase. Christie pokes fun here at those who are quick to believe what they wish to be true. The reader is taken in neither by the obvious attraction that Jack has for the girl nor by the trust that he has in the false authority. Christie, however, is determined to teach a lesson to those easily duped by con artists and spiritualists, human forces working for evil ends.

A very pedantic and accurate medium appears, however, in "The Red Signal." Mrs. Thompson gives a horrific warning to one of several people during a séance, then, shrugging and yawning, trudges off into the night "dead beat." She is a most unconvincing spiritualist, yet she warns the victim truthfully of impending danger, which is narrowly averted.

The two stories serve as foils for each other, creating a kind of awareness of evil as a person or palpable existence to be taken into consideration. It is not to be thought that Christie either believed or disbelieved in communication with spirits. She did, however, infuse her stories with the ideas of wrongness as a guiding force, and it seems that her characters were moved to use this sinister ability to their advantage or to their defeat. This was clearly shown in "Where There's a Will," which was originally published as "Wireless." Here, the nephew needlessly engineers his wealthy aunt's death only to have her accidentally destroy the will made in his favor. In most less heroic tales of the occult, Christie points out that manipulation of fate with intent to harm results in moral disaster.

"In a Glass Darkly"

She takes a different tack with "In a Glass Darkly." Fate reveals itself in a mirrored act of murder to the narrator. He uses this glimpse of the future to break up the engagement of a young woman who later becomes his wife. Years later, to his surprise, the premonition that he had received turns out to refer not to his wife's ex-lover but to himself, perhaps because he has allowed his feelings of love for her to fester into murderous jealousy, into something evil.

Clearly, Christie's characters were not to be left to their own devices. They needed a firm hand to show them the path to righteousness: enter the Christie sleuth/hero. Not the first but certainly the most provocative of these is Mr. Harley Quin. After nearly two decades of writing Harlequin and Pierrot, it should come as no surprise that Christie would name her detectives after her favorite characters—*poirot* roughly translates as "buffoon."

HARLEY QUIN STORIES

Most of the Harley Quin stories appear in *The Mysterious Mr. Quin*, a title that is no doubt meant to lend an air of the supernatural to the detective and to his familiar, Mr. Satterthwaite. While initially appearing to be a normal human, Mr. Quin is thrown into odd lights by sunlight through stained glass windows or lamps with colored shades. The reader comes to look for—and becomes affected by—Mr. Quin's transformations because they indicate not only a magical solution to the crime at hand but also a magical resolution: Everyone lives happily ever after. Eventually, Satterthwaite absorbs some of his friend's abilities and attempts to solve crimes on his own. This is encouraged by Mr. Quin as, perhaps, his overriding mission is not simply to return the world (or at least Europe) to a happier, pre-Fall state but to teach its inhabitants how to do so also.

This probably reflects Christie's own astonishment at the outbreak of World War I and her desire to return her life to its prewar state. Prior to the war, Christie had been living the carefree life of a much-sought-after British belle. She had had many suitors and had spent her time going from one house party to the next, from Great Britain to the rest of Europe. The war marked the end of her happy youth and her unhappy marriage to Archibald Christie. The Harley Quin stories came at a time when her mother had passed away and her husband had left her for another woman. Christie must have felt as though only magic could set her life to rights, and she seemed to resolve her personal problems in these short stories, making them her admitted favorites.

PARKER PYNE STORIES

In contrast to this dark detective, cheerful little Parker Pyne never fails to provide a happy ending when none is available. He pines to bring happiness into the world, and very often he is extremely successful; other times, he fails. Pyne is not, technically speaking, a detective, but in some stories he does serve in this capacity. Primarily, his vocation is to replace sadness with joy, a kind of watered-down form of the labors of Poirot, who challenges evil with goodness or justice. Sometimes, Pyne's mission is to provide this happiness by finding a lost object or person, but for the most part, his stories involve contrived adventures for his clients that provide an outlet for their craving for excitement. In "The Case of the Discontented Soldier," Pyne casts two clients as hero and heroine in one of his little melodramas, thus raising his level of productivity. This victory is offset, however, by a very expensive failure in "The Case of the Discontented Husband." Here, when Pyne employs his regular vamp to spur jealousy in a languid marriage, the husband contracts a fatal case of "Madeleine-itis" for Pyne's femme fatale and actually leaves his wife. The reader must assume that—in this case at least—a refund was provided.

TOMMY AND TUPPENCE BERESFORD STORIES

Another pair of characters who cannot be classified as detectives are Tommy and Tuppence Beresford. They are so delightful and provide so much entertainment, however, that they must not be ignored. They are evidence of Christie's mastery of bantering dialogue as well as her otherwise subtle ability to poke fun at not only herself but also other mystery writers. The most recognizable example of this is the short-story anthology *Partners in Crime*, in which Tommy and Tuppence deliberately set out to solve mysteries in the style of well-known sleuths of the day. Sherlock Holmes, Father Brown, and even Christie's own Hercule Poirot all appear for their turn in the dunking booth of Christie's wit. While these stories are accused of being shallow, they do demonstrate her unflagging ability to see with a fresh eye and to rewrite a tired plot. In addition, the dialogue between the two heroes is extremely amusing. They are more like two sides of the same coin than a married couple who might normally display a sense of sexual tension in their speech patterns. In "The Case of the Missing Lady," Tuppence demands that Tommy—like Holmes—"leave that violin alone," hardly loving spousal words.

MISS MARPLE STORIES

Many other minor heroes appear in Christie's works, including the semiautobiographical Ariadne

Oliver, but among the more famous are Jane Marple and Hercule Poirot. Jane Marple is an ever-aging spinster who sits as an oracle in mythic St. Mary Mead, waiting, for the most part, for crimes to come to her. (A criticism of Christie's works is that given the age of some characters in original works, they must die at double their three score and ten. The only excuse might be that Christie did not expect such long-lived popularity for them.) Like Poirot, Miss Marple has an unerring eye for what is truly evil in people and keeps files on them by constant comparison to natives in her village as well as flowers in her garden. She is most at home in her flower-strewn sitting room, with maids whose given names (for example, Cherry) and states of mind are vegetative, or in her (or other people's) gardens, ruthlessly pulling up bindweed, choke weed, and other destructive vines. Miss Marple is also often observed knitting for infants; perhaps she is trying to protect them from harm with woolen chain mail, or perhaps she is merely trying to knit up the raveled sleeve of mystery. The reader is never quite sure.

Jane Marple is a very human character, often drawing on great inner strength to carry out her missions. She is very successful at convincing people of her authority. Unlike Poirot, she stops a crime from being committed in "The Affair at the Bungalow." While usually busy training servant girls, Miss Marple often stops to solve a crime through the use of her infallible logic and prodigious memory. The reader often stops and remembers with Miss Marple the details from childhood of sprinkles or jimmies called hundreds and thousands or of disappearing ink made from kitchen chemicals. It is this believable association with her that lends credence to mysteries solved by what can only be attributed to comparisons to known criminal types or to intuition, although the latter may be defended by Miss Marple's long experience with the evil side of people.

POIROT STORIES

Earlier, Christie had completed a series of stories featuring a rotund Belgian detective, Hercule Poirot, for *Sketch* magazine. He proved to be her most popular figure, and she brought him into her writings for the rest of her life. Unlike Mr. Quin, Poirot does not try to entrap the wrongdoer but lets him or her advance carefully watched, until the villain finally stumbles. In "Triangle at Rhodes," one of the characters demands why Poirot did not act to prevent a murder. He replies that to warn the police without physical evidence would be futile. He does warn the murderer to leave the scene before the crime is committed, but Poirot's advice is ignored.

Even Poirot's friends often ignore his advice, relying instead on their own faulty intuition. This is the case with Captain Arthur Hastings. Hastings does not appear in all the Poirot stories, but when he does, he becomes an integral part of the plot. He is a general dogsbody for Poirot, consistently pointing out the obvious—but wrong—conclusion to the mystery at hand. Poirot's task is to put him and the reader to rights by carefully examining the crime for evidence of evil. It is this element that is overlooked by Hastings, and it is the nearly faultless ability of Poirot to recognize wickedness instantly that leads to an accurate solution to the crime. In "The Second Gong," Poirot diagnoses an apparent suicide as murder even though almost all the physical evidence has been destroyed by the murderer.

This singular ability to spot the genuine article was something Christie loaned her characters from her own store of skills. She had a good eye for furniture, houses, clothing, and people. Since most of her characters were compilations of people she had heard about, known, or observed, the reader must surmise that the evil as well as the good were all apparent to Christie. She saw the petty jealousies and envies that could fester into larger sins and wrote about them in a very believable and entertaining manner. This was the crux of Christie's talent, and this is what led to her greatness.

OTHER MAJOR WORKS

LONG FICTION: *The Mysterious Affair at Styles: A Detective Story*, 1920; *The Secret Adversary*, 1922; *The Murder on the Links*, 1923; *The Man in the Brown Suit*, 1924; *The Secret of Chimneys*, 1925; *The Murder of Roger Ackroyd*, 1926; *The Big Four*, 1927; *The Mystery of the Blue Train*, 1928; *The Seven Dials Mystery*, 1929; *The Murder at the Vicarage*, 1930;

Giants' Bread, 1930 (as Mary Westmacott); *The Sittaford Mystery*, 1931 (pb. in U.S. as *The Murder at Hazelmoor*); *The Floating Admiral*, 1932 (with others); *Peril at End House*, 1932; *Lord Edgware Dies*, 1933 (pb. in U.S. as *Thirteen at Dinner*); *Murder on the Orient Express*, 1934 (pb. in U.S. as *Murder on the Calais Coach*); *Murder in Three Acts*, 1934; *Why Didn't They Ask Evans?*, 1934 (pb. in U.S. as *Boomerang Clue*, 1935); *Unfinished Portrait*, 1934 (as Westmacott); *Death in the Clouds*, 1935 (pb. in U.S. as *Death in the Air*); *The A. B. C. Murders: A New Poirot Mystery*, 1936; *Cards on the Table*, 1936; *Murder in Mesopotamia*, 1936; *Death on the Nile*, 1937; *Dumb Witness*, 1937 (pb. in U.S. as *Poirot Loses a Client*); *Appointment with Death: A Poirot Mystery*, 1938; *Hercule Poirot's Christmas*, 1938 (pb. in U.S. as *Murder for Christmas: A Poirot Story*); *Murder Is Easy*, 1939 (pb. in U.S. as *Easy to Kill*); *Ten Little Niggers*, 1939 (pb. in U.S. as *And Then There Were None*, 1940); *One, Two, Buckle My Shoe*, 1940 (pb. in U.S. as *The Patriotic Murders*, 1941); *Sad Cypress*, 1940; *Evil Under the Sun*, 1941; *N or M? The New Mystery*, 1941; *The Body in the Library*, 1942; *Five Little Pigs*, 1942 (pb. in U.S. as *Murder in Retrospect*); *The Moving Finger*, 1942; *Death Comes in the End*, 1944; *Towards Zero*, 1944; *Absent in the Spring*, 1944 (as Westmacott); *Sparkling Cyanide*, 1945 (pb. in U.S. as *Remembered Death*); *The Hollow: A Hercule Poirot Mystery*, 1946; *Murder Medley*, 1948; *Taken at the Flood*, 1948 (pb. in U.S. as *There Is a Tide . . .*); *The Rose and the Yew Tree*, 1948 (as Westmacott); *Crooked House*, 1949; *A Murder Is Announced*, 1950; *Blood Will Tell*, 1951; *They Came to Baghdad*, 1951; *They Do It with Mirrors*, 1952 (pb. in U.S. as *Murder with Mirrors*); *Mrs. McGinty's Dead*, 1952; *A Daughter's a Daughter*, 1952 (as Westmacott); *After the Funeral*, 1953 (pb. in U.S. as *Funerals Are Fatal*); *A Pocket Full of Rye*, 1953; *Destination Unknown*, 1954 (pb. in U.S. as *So Many Steps to Death*, 1955); *Hickory, Dickory, Dock*, 1955 (pb. in U.S. as *Hickory, Dickory, Death*); *Dead Man's Folly*, 1956; *The Burden*, 1956 (as Westmacott); *4:50 from Paddington*, 1957 (pb. in U.S. as *What Mrs. McGillicuddy Saw!*); *Ordeal by Innocence*, 1958; *Cat Among the Pigeons*, 1959; *The Pale Horse*, 1961;

The Mirror Crack'd from Side to Side, 1962 (pb. in U.S. as *The Mirror Crack'd*, 1963); *The Clocks*, 1963; *A Caribbean Mystery*, 1964; *At Bertram's Hotel*, 1965; *Third Girl*, 1966; *Endless Night*, 1967; *By the Pricking of My Thumb*, 1968; *Hallowe'en Party*, 1969; *Passenger to Frankfurt*, 1970; *Nemesis*, 1971; *Elephants Can Remember*, 1972; *Postern of Fate*, 1973; *Curtain: Hercule Poirot's Last Case*, 1975; *Sleeping Murder*, 1976 (posthumous).

PLAYS: *Black Coffee*, pr. 1930; *Ten Little Niggers*, pr. 1943 (pb. in U.S. as *Ten Little Indians*, pr. 1944); *Appointment with Death*, pr., pb. 1945; *Murder on the Nile*, pr., pb. 1946; *The Hollow*, pr. 1951; *The Mousetrap*, pr. 1952; *Witness for the Prosecution*, pr. 1953; *Spider's Web*, pr. 1954; *Towards Zero*, pr. 1956 (with Gerald Verner); *The Unexpected Guest*, pr., pb. 1958; *Verdict*, pr., pb. 1958; *Go Back for Murder*, pr., pb. 1960; *Afternoon at the Seaside*, pr. 1962; *The Patient*, pr. 1962; *The Rats*, pr. 1962; *Akhnaton*, pb. 1973 (also known as *Akhnaton and Nefertiti*).

POETRY: *The Road of Dreams*, 1925; *Poems*, 1973.

NONFICTION: *Come Tell Me How You Live*, 1946; *An Autobiography*, 1977.

BIBLIOGRAPHY

Bargainner, Earl F. *The Gentle Art of Murder*. Bowling Green, Ohio: Bowling Green State University Popular Press, 1980. With an extensive bibliography and two indices of characters and short-story titles, this book is a boon to those searching for an elusive reference. Bargainner analyzes Christie's works as separate achievements, each a pearl on an exquisite necklace, and he praises her ability to experiment with detective fiction "by employing elements not generally considered compatible with it."

Barnard, Robert. *A Talent to Deceive*. New York: Dodd, Mead, 1980. Intended to inform and entertain the casual Christie reader, this book follows Christie's writings as they developed in theme and plot throughout her lifetime. While there are good analyses of novels and detectives, the truly admirable features of this book are the exhaustive indices and annotated lists—including films—compiled by Barnard's wife.

Gill, Gillian. *Agatha Christie: The Woman and Her Mysteries*. New York: The Free Press, 1990. This short and highly readable biography is definitely of the popular, rather than critical, variety, employing as chapter titles seven different names used at one time or another by the mystery writer (including the assumed name Christie used during her infamous disappearance in 1926). Still, Gill goes out of her way to emphasize Christie's dedication to her art and the discipline of her life.

Ibarguengoitia, Jorge. "Agatha Christie: An Unlikely Obituary," translated by F. Soicher. *The Literary Review* 38 (Fall, 1994): 45-46. Claims he finds Christie's detective fiction unreadable because he either uncovers the murderer early on or else is unable to understand the detective's explanation.

Irons, Glenwood, and Joan Warthling Roberts. "From Spinster to Hipster: The 'Suitability' of Miss Marple and Anna Lee." In *Feminism in Women's Detective Fiction*, edited by Glenwood Irons. Toronto: University of Toronto Press, 1995. Discusses Christie's creation of Miss Marple as the archetypal British sinister detective figure in stories and novels. Analyzes Marple's basic methodology in *The Tuesday Club Murders*.

Maida, Patricia, and Nicholas B. Spornick. *Murder She Wrote*. Bowling Green, Ohio: Bowling Green State University Press, 1982. Divided neatly into sections by detective, this book allows its reader to go right to a necessary section without paging through much unneeded information. The authors confirm that Christie's characters and their "creative puzzles" gave the world a lasting gift.

Paul, Robert S. *Whatever Happened to Sherlock Holmes? Detective Fiction, Popular Theology, and Society*. Carbondale: Southern Illinois University Press, 1991. A study of detective fiction based on the general premise that detective stories mirror the morals and theological assumptions of their time. The chapter on Agatha Christie explores how her stories reflect what happens in a society when compassion is lacking.

Shenker, Israel. "The Past Master of Mysteries, She Built a Better Mousetrap." *Smithsonian* 21, no. 6 (1990): 86-95. For those who have neither the time nor the patience to wade through Christie's *An Autobiography*, this article provides a concise portrait of the author. Completed in honor of the one hundredth anniversary of her birthday, this carefully written biographical article lays the necessary groundwork for any Christie researcher.

Wagoner, Mary S. *Agatha Christie*. Boston: Twayne, 1986. While it is difficult, if not impossible, to find a book dedicated to Christie's short stories alone, this edition does manage to touch on almost all of them, although briefly. After an entire chapter devoted to these, it proceeds chronologically through the rest of Christie's work, ending with a brief bibliography. Wagoner deftly wraps the facets of Christie's life around her writing, defining Christie's style as both conventional and self-stylized.

Jennifer L. Wyatt

SANDRA CISNEROS

Born: Chicago, Illinois; December 20, 1954

PRINCIPAL SHORT FICTION

The House on Mango Street, 1984
Woman Hollering Creek and Other Stories, 1991

OTHER LITERARY FORMS

Sandra Cisneros is known for her poetry as well as her short fiction. She has published several collections of poems, including *Bad Boys* (1980), *My Wicked, Wicked Ways* (1987), and *Loose Woman* (1994); much of her poetry remains uncollected and unpublished, according to the author's wishes. She has also published a series of essays explaining her own creative processes as a writer in *The Americas Review*. In addition, she published *Hairs = Pelitos* (1984), a children's book illustrated by Terry Ybanez which expands on the chapter "Hairs" featured in *The House on Mango Street*.

ACHIEVEMENTS

Together with authors such as Ana Castillo, Denise Chávez, and Alma Villanueva, Sandra Cisneros is one of the literary voices that emerged in the 1980's and was responsible for securing for Chicana fiction a place in mainstream American literature. Her collection of short stories *Woman Hollering Creek and Other Stories* was the first work by and about Chicanas—that is, Mexican American women— to receive a contract with a major publishing house (Random House). Cisneros was awarded the Before Columbus American Book Award and the PEN Center West Award for her first collection of short fiction, *The House on Mango Street*. She is a two-time recipient of a National Endowment for the Arts Fellowship for Creative Writers for her poetry and fiction. In 1985, Cisneros received a Dobie-Paisano Fellowship. She was granted a MacArthur Fellowship in 1995.

BIOGRAPHY

Sandra Cisneros was born in 1954 into a working-class family in Chicago, Illinois. With a Mexican American mother, a Mexican father, and six brothers, she described her circumstances as being similar to having seven fathers. Because of close familial and cultural ties with Mexico, the Cisneros family moved back and forth between a series of cramped apartments in Chicago and the paternal grandmother's home in Mexico City. The concept of home or the lack of one would later weigh heavily in Cisneros's writing. The combination of an uprooted lifestyle and an ever-changing circle of friends, schools, and neighborhoods, as well as the isolation that resulted from her brothers' unwillingness to let a girl join in their play, led Cisneros to turn inward to a life of books. That time spent alone allowed an observant, creative voice to take root in the author.

Cisneros considered her career as a professional writer to have begun in 1974—the year in which she enrolled in a writing class as a junior at Loyola Uni-

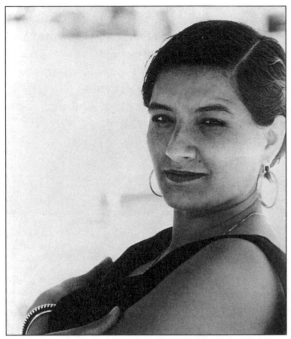

Sandra Cisneros (Rubén Guzmàn)

versity of Chicago, where she would later receive her bachelor of arts degree in English. It was her tenure at the University of Iowa's Writers' Workshop, from which she took a master of fine arts degree, however, that proved an invaluable aid in the formation of her own literary voice. During a discussion of Gaston Bachelard's *La Bétique de l'espace* (1957; *The Poetics of Space*, 1964), in which her classmates spoke of the house as a literary symbol complete with attics, stairways, and cellars of imagination and childhood, Cisneros realized that her experience was different from that of her college classmates. Her background was that of a multiethnic, working-class neighborhood complete with drunken bums, families sleeping on crowded floors, and rats. She ceased trying to make her style fit that of the perfect, white, and mostly male image that was foreign to her and, instead, undertook writing about that to which her classmates could not relate but was familiar to her.

Cisneros has used her education to foster change within the Chicano community. She taught high school dropouts for three years in a Chicano barrio. She has also worked as an administrative assistant at Loyola University, where she was involved in the re-cruitment of minority and disadvantaged students. In 1984, she was the literature director of the Guadalupe Cultural Arts Center of San Antonio, the city which she made her home. Cisneros served as writer-in-residence at the Michael Karolyi Artists Foundation in Vence, France, the University of Michigan in Ann Arbor, the University of California at Irvine, and the University of New Mexico in Albuquerque.

ANALYSIS

Sandra Cisneros said that she writes about the memories that will not let her sleep at night—about the stories that are waiting to be told. Drawing on the memories of her childhood and her cultural identity—the run-down, crowded apartment, the double-edged sword of being American yet not being considered American, the sight of women in her community closed in behind apartment windows—Cisneros's fiction avoids any romantic clichés of life in the barrio. Despite the sobering themes upon which Cisneros touches—poverty, sexism, and racism—she tells her stories with a voice that is at the same time strong, playful, and deceptively simple. Cisneros's distinctive style is marked by the grace with which Spanish words and phrases are woven into her stories. Central to her stories is a preoccupation with the house, the community, and the condition of women. Her images are vivid and lyrical. She acknowledges that she was influenced in style by the mix of poetry and fiction in Jorge Luis Borges's *El hacedor* (1960; *Dreamtigers*, 1964). Indeed, while Cisneros herself classifies her fiction as stories that read like poems, critics have not reached an agreement, labeling her works *The House on Mango Street* and *Woman Hollering Creek and Other Stories* alternatively as novels, short-story collections, series of vignettes, and prose poems.

THE HOUSE ON MANGO STREET

The series of sketches in *The House on Mango Street* offers a bittersweet view of life in a Chicago barrio. Readers follow the young adolescent narrator Esperanza—whose name (as explained in the story "My Name") means "hope" in Spanish and also implies too many letters, sadness, and waiting—as she makes the discoveries associated with maturing. She introduces the reader to her neighbors and her neighborhood, making them as familiar to the reader as they are to her. In the title story, Esperanza explains how her family came to live on Mango Street. The family had hoped that the house on Mango Street would be like the ones they had always dreamed of—with real stairs and several washrooms and a great big yard with trees and grass.

Esperanza sadly explains, however, that their house does not fulfill this wish at all. She is ashamed of her red brick house, as she has been of all of her family's previous dwellings. She succinctly describes the embarrassment that she felt when the family was living on Loomis and she had to show her apartment to a nun from her school. She pointed to the family's third-floor flat, located above a boarded-up laundry, and suffered the blow of the nun's disbelieving response, *"there?"* From that moment, Esperanza knew that she had to have a house—one that she could show with pride to people as if it were a reflection of herself. She was sure the family would have such a house soon. Yet the house on Mango Street is not that house.

Because Esperanza remarks that she wants a house "all my own. With my porch and my pillow, my pretty purple petunias. My books and my stories," Cisneros has been read as creating a grasping and selfish protagonist. Yet the section titled "Bums in the Attic" dispels this notion of untoward individualism. In this sketch—which resembles one of Cisneros's favorite children's stories, Virginia Lee Burton's *The Little House* (1978), in which the owners of a house on a country hill promise the house never to sell it—Esperanza speculates about the grand home on a hill that she will have someday. As much as she wants to leave Mango Street, however, she stresses that even in her country home she will not forget from where she came. She will not make her house a secured palace that locks out the world; she will instead offer her attic to the homeless so that they too will have a home.

In "Those Who Don't," the young Esperanza discusses in a matter-of-fact tone the concept of being the "other" in society. She knows that people who happen into her neighborhood think that her community is dangerous, but she knows her neighbors by

name and knows their backgrounds. Among her Latino friends she feels safe. Yet Esperanza can understand the stranger's apprehension, for when she and her family venture out of the security of their neighborhood, their bodies get tense and their eyes look straight ahead.

Cisneros's concern for the place women hold in Latino society is evident in the powerful story "Alicia Who Sees Mice." Alicia, Esperanza's friend, must rise early every morning "with the tortilla star" and the mice in the kitchen to make her father's lunch-box tortillas. Alicia's mother has died, and, Esperanza remarks, young Alicia has inherited her mother's duty as the family caregiver along with her "rolling pin and sleepiness." Alicia has dreams of escaping this life of confinement and sacrifice, however, with a university education. She studies hard all night with the mice that her father says do not exist. With its precise imagery, "Alicia Who Sees Mice" is at once a criticism of patriarchal oppression of women and a beacon for those women who would struggle to break away from that oppression.

The theme of education and writing as a means whereby women can escape from the barrio is also found in "Minerva Writes Poems." Minerva is only a bit older than Esperanza, "but already she has two kids and a husband who left . . . and keeps leaving." Minerva's husband reappears sporadically, but their reunion usually ends in violence and abuse. Minerva cries every day over her bad situation and writes poems at night. In an act of artistic and sisterly solidarity, she and Esperanza read their poems to each other, yet at this point, Esperanza feels helpless, unable to stop the beatings. In her reply, "There is nothing *I* can do," there is a sense that Esperanza is inciting Minerva to take action for herself as well as implying that society itself must change its attitudes.

This sisterly support for fulfillment through learning is echoed in "Edna's Ruthie." The title character is a talented but damaged woman who returns to her mother's home when she can no longer care for herself. Her own fondness for books—for hearing and telling a good story—inspires Esperanza in her own creative endeavors. Ruthie is moved to tears by Esperanza's recitation of children's stories, a response that conveys to the young girl the power of the word.

Esperanza's passage into adulthood is not without setbacks. In "Red Clowns," she goes to the amusement park with her friend Sally. When the sexually precocious Sally abandons Esperanza to slip away with a boy, Esperanza is molested and possibly raped by an older boy who tells her, "I love you Spanish girl, I love you." She is angry and sad and confused over the loss of her innocence. She cannot understand why everyone told her that sex would be so wonderful when, in fact, she found nothing pleasant about the perpetrator's dirty fingernails and sour breath. She wants to forget that degrading experience; she does not want to speak its horror. She yells at her friend Sally for leaving her, but she also directs her anger at a society that is partner to such an awful lie.

The fundamental conflict that besets Esperanza is resolved in "The Three Sisters." While Esperanza has repeatedly voiced her desire to escape the barrio and its double bind of racism and sexism which snares many women, she nevertheless loves her community and cannot come to terms with deserting it. Then three wise, eccentric, and decidedly feminist sisters settle the issue. Young Esperanza is strong, talented, and destined to "go very far," they tell her. Their encouraging words sanction her flight, yet the sisters remind her as well of the need for loyalty:

> When you leave you must remember to come back for the others. A circle, understand? You will always be Esperanza. You will always be Mango Street. You can't erase what you know. You can't forget who you are.

Young Esperanza can finally look to a life beyond the confines of her repressive environment.

WOMAN HOLLERING CREEK AND OTHER STORIES

Likewise, *Woman Hollering Creek and Other Stories* offers a glimpse into the lives of Chicanas who must confront daily the triple bind of not being considered Mexican, not being considered American, and not being male. Cisneros said that while the pieces of *Woman Hollering Creek and Other Stories* function individually, there is a single, unifying

thread of vision and experience that runs throughout the collection of twenty-two narratives. While the names of the narrators change with each work, each narrator retains a strong, determined, rebellious voice.

"ELEVEN"

In "Eleven," eleven-year-old Rachel's birthday prompts her to consider what it means to grow older. The wisdom of her eleven years has taught her that the years "underneath" the birthday, like the rings inside a tree trunk, make one a certain age. When people want to cry, she reasons, it is the part of them that is three that brings on tears; when they are scared, it is the part in them that is five that registers fear. For this reason, Rachel explains, she was not able to act eleven years old today in school when her teacher wrongly accused her of forgetting an ugly red sweater that had been in the coatroom for a month. All the years were welling up inside her, preventing Rachel from telling everyone that it was not her sweater. Instead, she was silent. She tries to be happy and remember that today she is eleven and that her mother will have a cake for her when she goes home. The part of Rachel that is three, however, comes out in front of the class instead. She wishes she were anything but eleven.

The narrator of the chilling "One Holy Night" is an adolescent girl who sells fruits and vegetables from her grandmother's pushcart. She meets a wanderer named Chaq who tells her that he is a descendant of a long line of Mayan kings. Intrigued by his story, the young woman begins to follow Chaq to his little room behind an automobile garage after she has sold each day's produce. Chaq spins mystic tales of the past and future greatness of his family's lineage as he entices the girl into her first sexual experience. She returns home to her grandmother and uncle a changed woman, barely able to contain her excitement. The young woman's secret, however, is soon discovered: She is pregnant. The family, in total disgrace, attempts to locate Chaq, who has since left town. Her uncle writes a letter in hope of finding the man who could correct his niece's ruined life. A response arrives from Chaq's sister. She explains that her brother's name is actually Chato, which means "fat-face"; he is thirty-seven, not at all Mayan, and not at all royal. The girl's family sends her to Mexico to give birth and to avoid disgrace. It is later learned that Chato has been captured and charged with the deaths of eleven women. The girl appears unfazed by the news, however, and continues to plan her dreams of children. She becomes indifferent to love.

"NEVER MARRY A MEXICAN"

The title "Never Marry a Mexican" sums up the advice that the protagonist Clemencia was told as a young girl by her Chicana mother who regretted marrying a Mexican. Her mother's words ultimately consign Clemencia to cultural and social marginality. Clemencia scorns the working-class Latino men in her life and refuses to consider any of them as potential husbands. However, ironically, the white men whom she favors follow the same advice her mother has instilled in her: They will become sexually involved with a Chicana, but they will not marry outside of their own race.

Caught uncomfortably between cultures, Clemencia attempts to make the most of her difficult status. She prides herself on remaining unattached, a seductress who beds white, married men while their wives are in the throes of childbirth. Yet her pain and loneliness are palpable. She nurses affection for one white married lover for eighteen years, eventually gaining revenge on him by entering into a sexual relationship with his son. For Clemencia, the unhealthy relationship yields and yet perverts what she ostensibly disavows: marriage and motherhood. Sexual intercourse with the young man, she believes, links her to his father and mother's marital relations, of which he is the product, and her lover's relative youth allows her to "mother" him.

"WOMAN HOLLERING CREEK"

The collection's title story is one of its strongest. It is a story of Cleófilas, a woman reared in a small town in Mexico not far from the Texas border. Cleófilas dreams of the romance and passion of the soap operas that she watches at her girlfriend's house. She believes her fantasy is realized when she meets Juan Pedro, a Texan who wants to marry her right away, "without a long engagement since he can't take off too much time from work." Cleófilas is whisked away across the border to Seguin, Texas, a town like so many others, with nothing of interest to walk to, "built so that you have to depend on husbands."

Life on "the other side" is, at first, a blessing for Cleófilas. Texas is the land of laundromats and dream homes. Running behind their new house is a creek that all call Woman Hollering. Cleófilas wonders if the odd name is connected to tales of La Llorona, the tragic mythical figure known to wail after drowning her children. Her enthusiasm for her new life ends quickly, however, with a slap to her face by Juan Pedro. That slap will start a long line of abuse and cause Cleófilas to think flatly, "This is the man I have waited my whole life for." Although she had always promised herself that she would not allow any man to hit her, Cleófilas, isolated at home, not allowed to correspond with her family, hindered by not knowing English, and afraid of Juan Pedro's rage, stays with him. When she begins to suspect that Juan Pedro is unfaithful, she thinks about returning to her native town but fears disgrace and does not act. Cleófilas had always thought that her life would be like a soap opera, "only now the episodes got sadder and sadder. And there were no commercials in between for comic relief." She becomes pregnant with their second child but is almost too afraid to ask Juan Pedro to take her to the clinic for prenatal care. Once at the clinic, Cleófilas breaks down and tells her plight to a sympathetic doctor who arranges a ride for her and her son to the bus station in San Antonio. The morning of their escape, Cleófilas is tense and frightened. As they pass over Woman Hollering Creek in a pickup truck, their spirited female driver lets out a Tarzan-like yell that startles her two passengers. On her way back to her father's home, Cleófilas catches a glimpse of what it is to be an autonomous woman.

OTHER MAJOR WORKS

POETRY: *Bad Boys*, 1980; *My Wicked, Wicked Ways*, 1987; *Loose Woman*, 1994.

CHILDREN'S LITERATURE: *Hairs = Pelitos*, 1984.

BIBLIOGRAPHY

Brady, Mary Pat. "The Contrapuntal Geographies of *Woman Hollering Creek and Other Stories*."

American Literature 71 (March, 1999): 117-150. Shows how Cisneros's narrative techniques challenge various spatial representations and lay bare hidden stories. Claims that Cisneros explores the various subtleties of violence of changing spatial relations.

Cisneros, Sandra. "On the Solitary Fate of Being Mexican, Female, Wicked, and Thirty-three: An Interview with Writer Sandra Cisneros." Interview by Pilar E. Rodríguez Aranda. *The Americas Review* 18, no. 1 (1990): 64-80. In an enlightening interview, Cisneros discusses her identity as a Chicana, her development as a writer, and her use of poetry and modern myth in her fiction. The interview focuses on the collections *My Wicked, Wicked Ways* and *The House on Mango Street*.

Doyle, Jacqueline. "More Room of Her Own: Sandra Cisneros' *The House on Mango Street*." *MELUS* 19 (Winter, 1994): 5-35. Discusses *The House on Mango Street* as a transformation of the terms of Virginia Woolf's vision in *A Room of One's Own* (1929). Asserts Cisneros's work provides a rich reconsideration of the contemporary feminist inheritance as influenced by Woolf.

Griffin, Susan E. "Resistance and Reinvention in Sandra Cisneros' *Woman Hollering Creek*." In *Ethnicity and the American Short Story*, edited by Julie Brown. New York: Garland Publishing, 1997. Discusses the role that Mexican popular culture and traditional Mexican narratives play in limiting women's sense of identity. Focuses primarily on the negative effects of popular romances in Mexico and televised soap operas.

Matchie, Thomas. "Literary Continuity in Sandra Cisneros's *The House on Mango Street*." *The Midwest Quarterly* 37 (Autumn, 1995): 67-79. Discusses how *The House on Mango Street* uses Mark Twain's *Adventures of Huckleberry Finn* (1884) and J. D. Salinger's *The Catcher in the Rye* (1951) as literary models of adolescents growing up in a culturally oppressive world. Like Huck and Holden, Cisneros's protagonist is innocent, sensitive, and vulnerable, and she grows mentally in the process of the narrative.

Mullen, Harryette. "'A Silence Between Us Like a Language': The Untranslatability of Experience in Sandra Cisneros's *Woman Hollering Creek*." *MELUS* 21 (Summer, 1996): 3-20. Argues that Spanish as a code comprehensible to an inside group and as a repressed language subordinate to English are central issues in *Woman Hollering Creek*.

Olivares, Julian. "Sandra Cisneros' *The House on Mango Street*, and the Poetics of Space." *The Americas Review* 15, nos. 3/4 (1987): 160-170. This essay is an in-depth analysis of the stories of *The House on Mango Street* in terms of Cisneros's distinctive use of the metaphor of a house situated in a Latino neighborhood. Contains bibliographical references pertinent to *The House on Mango Street*.

Sagel, Jim. "Sandra Cisneros: Conveying the Riches of the Latin American Culture Is the Author's Literary Goal." *Publishers Weekly* 238 (March 29, 1991): 74-75. In this informative interview, Cisneros speaks about the influence that her childhood had on her writing. The interview touches upon the personal side of the writer and includes a brief description of the genesis of the collection *Woman Hollering Creek and Other Stories*.

Thompson, Jeff. "'What Is Called Heaven?' Identity in Sandra Cisneros's *Woman Hollering Creek*." *Studies in Short Fiction* 31 (Summer, 1994): 415-424. States that the overall theme of the stories is the vulnerability of the female narrators. The vignettes should be read as symptomatic of a social structure that allows little cultural movement and little possibility for the creation of an identity outside the boundaries of the barrio.

Wyatt, Jean. "On Not Being *La Malinche*: Border Negotiations of Gender in Sandra Cisneros's 'Never Marry a Mexican' and 'Woman Hollering Creek.'" *Tulsa Studies in Women's Literature* 14 (Fall, 1995): 243-271. Discusses how the stories describe the difficulties of living on the border between Anglo-American and Mexican cultures and how the female protagonists of the stories struggle with sexuality and motherhood as icons that limit their identity.

Mary F. Yudin, updated by Theresa Kanoza

WALTER VAN TILBURG CLARK

Born: East Orland, Maine; August 3, 1909
Died: Reno, Nevada; November 10, 1971

PRINCIPAL SHORT FICTION

The Watchful Gods and Other Stories, 1950

OTHER LITERARY FORMS

In addition to his short stories, Walter Van Tilburg Clark wrote three novels—*The Ox-Bow Incident* (1940), *The City of Trembling Leaves* (1945), and *The Track of the Cat* (1949). The first and last of these were made into motion pictures. *Tim Hazard* (1951) is the enlarged version of *The City of Trembling Leaves*. Clark also produced an early book of poems, *Ten Women in Gale's House and Shorter Poems* (1932).

ACHIEVEMENTS

Although Walter Van Tilburg Clark is known primarily for his novels, his one volume of stories, as well as his uncollected short stories, have established him as a fine writer of short stories. In fact, his "The Wind and the Snow of Winter" received the O. Henry Award in 1945. In their Western settings, their ambiguous depiction of the American dream, their concern about personal identity and oneness with nature, and their essentially tragic vision, the short stories are of a piece with his three novels. Unlike some "Western" writers, Clark used his landscape as both subject and backdrop for his own philosophical themes. Less concerned with characters—one story virtually omits them, concentrating instead on animals as "characters"—than with ideas, Clark used his characters, many of whom seem stereotypical, to embody and actualize his notions about the possibility of defining self and position in the cosmos.

BIOGRAPHY

Walter Van Tilburg Clark was born on August 3, 1909, in East Orland, Maine, the first child of Walter Ernest and Euphemia Abrams Clark. In 1917, his father, a distinguished economics professor, became president of the University of Nevada at Reno. Therefore, the family had to move when Clark was only eight. In Reno, Clark attended public schools and later received his B.A. and M.A. degrees in English from the University of Nevada. Clark married Barbara Morse in 1933, and they became the parents of two children, Barbara Ann and Robert Morse. The couple settled in Cazenovia, New York, where Clark began a career in high school and college teaching as well as creative writing. In the next several years, Clark continued writing and taught at several schools, including the University of Montana, Reed College, and the University of Nevada, where he resigned after protesting the autocratic tendencies of the administration. He eventually returned there, however, to teach creative writing. Clark was also director of creative writing at San Francisco State College from 1956 to 1962. He died of cancer on November 10, 1971, at the age of sixty-two.

ANALYSIS

Walter Van Tilburg Clark once wrote that the primary impulse of the arts has been religious and ritualistic—with the central hope of "propitiating or enlisting Nature, the Gods, God, or whatever name one wishes to give the encompassing and still mysterious whole." Certainly Clark's fiction attests to such a view. In a world in which thought is often confused and fragmented, he advocates for humanity a stance of intellectual honesty, an acceptance of instinctive values, and a belief in love. The key is human experience. As Max Westbrook so aptly put it in his study of Clark, "Clark's literary credo, then, is based on the capacity of the unconscious mind to discover and to give shape to objective knowledge about the human experience."

"THE BUCK IN THE HILLS"

"The Buck in the Hills" may be Clark's clearest reflection in his stories of the literary credo mentioned above. Writing more or less in the terse, almost brittle, style of Ernest Hemingway, Clark opens the story with vividly descriptive passages of mountain scenery. The narrator, whose name the reader never learns, has returned to this setting after five years. It is really more than a return for him; it is a pilgrimage to a sacred place. Like Hemingway's heroes, he feels a deep need to replenish his spirit, to reattach himself to things solid and lasting. The clear sky, the strong mountains, and the cold wind all serve as a natural backdrop for the spiritual ritual of his pilgrimage. As he climbs toward the peak of a mountain, he recalls with pleasure an earlier climb with a dark girl "who knew all the flowers, and who, when I bet her she couldn't find more than thirty kinds, found more than fifty." On that day, as on this, the narrator felt a clear sense of the majesty of the mountains and the "big arch of the world we looked at," and he recalls spending two hours another time watching a hawk, "feeling myself lift magnificently when he swooped up toward me on the current up the col, and then balanced and turned above."

When he returns to his campsite by a shallow snow-water lake, he swims, naked, and as he floats in this cleansing ritual, looking up at the first stars showing above the ridge, he sings out "an operatic sounding something." At this point, just when his spiritual rejuvenation is nearly complete, the ritual is broken by the appearance of Tom Williams, one of the two men whom he had accompanied on this trip to the mountains. The plan had been for Williams and the other man, Chet McKenny, to spend a few days hunting, leaving the narrator alone. As he watches Williams approach, the narrator unhappily expects to see McKenny also, a man he dislikes not because of his stupidity but because of something deeper than that. Williams, however, is alone.

After a while Williams tells the narrator of the experience he has just had with McKenny, whom he calls a "first-rate bastard." During their hunt McKenny had purposely shot a deer in the leg so that he could herd it back to their camp rather than carry it. When they arrived at the camp, he slit the deer's throat, saying, "I never take more than one shot." Sickened by this brutal act, Williams drove off in his car, leaving McKenny to get out of the mountains as best he could. After Williams's story, both men agree that McKenny deserves to be left behind for what he

Walter Van Tilburg Clark (Library of Congress)

did. In another cleansing ritual, they both take a swim, becoming cheerful later as they sit by their fire drinking beer. The next morning, however, it is snowing, and as they silently head back down the mountain, the narrator feels that there is "something listening behind each tree and rock we passed, and something waiting among the taller trees down slope, blue through the falling snow. They wouldn't stop us, but they didn't like us either. The snow was their ally."

Thus there are two contrasting moods in "The Buck in the Hills": that of harmony and that of dissonance. At the beginning of the story, the narrator has succeeded after five years in reestablishing a right relationship with nature and thus with himself, but at the end, this relationship has been destroyed by the cruel actions of McKenny. The narrator's ritual of acceptance of the primordial in human beings has been overshadowed by McKenny's ritual of acceptance that human beings are somehow above nature. Ernest Hemingway's belief that morality is what one feels good after is in one sense reversed here to the idea that immorality is what one feels bad after; certainly the narrator and Williams, on their way down the mountain, feel bad. Human beings and nature in a right relationship is not a mere romantic notion to Clark. It is reality—indeed, perhaps man's only reality.

"THE PORTABLE PHONOGRAPH"

In "The Portable Phonograph" Clark ventures, if not into science fiction, at least into a kind of speculative fiction as he sets his story in a world of the future, one marked by the "toothed impress of great tanks" and the "scars of gigantic bombs." It seems a world devoid of human existence; the only visible life is a flock of wild geese flying south to escape the cold of winter. Above the frozen creek in a cave dug into the bank, however, there is human life: four men—survivors of some undescribed Armageddon— huddle before a smoldering peat fire in an image of primitive existence. Clark provides little background of these four almost grotesque men. One, the reader learns, is a doctor, probably of philosophy rather than of medicine. One is a young musician, quite ill with a cough. The other two are middle-aged. All are obviously intelligent. The cave belongs to the doctor, whose name is Jenkins, and he has invited the others to hear him read from one of his four books—the Bible, *Moby Dick, The Divine Comedy*, and William Shakespeare. In selfish satisfaction he explains that when he saw what was happening to the world, "I told myself, 'It is the end. I cannot take much; I will take these.'" His justification is his love for the books and his belief that they represent the "soul of what was good in us here."

When Jenkins finishes his reading from *The Tempest*, the others wait expectantly, and the former finally says grudgingly, "You wish to hear the phonograph." This is obviously the moment for which they have been waiting. Jenkins tenderly and almost lovingly brings out his portable phonograph and places it on the dirt-packed floor where the firelight will fall on it. He comments that he has been using thorns as needles, but that in deference to the musician, he will use one of the three steel needles that he has left. Since Jenkins will play only one record a week, there is some discussion as to what they will hear. The musician selects a Debussy nocturne, and as Jenkins places the record on the phonograph, the others all rise to their knees "in an attitude of worship."

As the piercing and singularly sweet sounds of the nocturne flood the cave, the men are captivated. In all but the musician there occur "sequences of tragically heightened recollection"; the musician, clenching the fingers of one hand over his teeth, hears only the music. At the conclusion of the piece, the three guests leave—the musician by himself, the other two together. Jenkins peers anxiously after them, waiting. When he hears the cough of the musician some distance off, he drops his canvas door and hurries to hide his phonograph in a deep hole in the cave wall. Sealing up the hole, he prays and then gets under the covers of his grass bed, feeling with his hand the "comfortable piece of lead pipe."

Structurally a very simple story, "The Portable Phonograph" is rich in its implications. In a devastated world four men represent what Jenkins refers to as "the doddering remnant of a race of mechanical fools." The books that he has saved symbolize the beauty of man's artistic creativity as opposed to the destructiveness of his mechanical creativity. Again, Clark portrays two sides of human nature, that which aspires to the heights of human spiritual and moral vision and that which drives him on to his own destruction. The cruel and bitter irony is that essentially man's imagination is at once his glory and his undoing. As the men kneel in expectation before the mechanical wonder of the phonograph, they worship it as a symbol of human ingenuity. The music that comes from the record provides for at least three of the men a temporary escape from their grim reality. Thus, man's drive for mechanical accomplishment— the same drive that has destroyed a world—now has also preserved the beauty of his musical accomplishment. This may well be what the musician understands as he lets his head "fall back in agony" while listening to the music. Human beings are forever blessed to create and doomed to destroy. That is why the piece of lead pipe is such a protective comfort to Jenkins as he closes "his smoke-smarting eyes." In order to protect what is left of art, he must rely on the very methods that have brought about its demise.

"THE INDIAN WELL"

In his excellent novel *The Track of the Cat*, Clark takes the reader into the realm of human unconscious as Curt Bridges, the protagonist, is driven to his own death while tracking both a real and an imagined cougar. In the short story "The Indian Well," set in the desert in 1940, Jim Suttler also seeks to kill a cougar, and although the mythological and psychological implications are not developed as fully as they are in the novel, the story is still powerful in its total effect. In what must be one of the best word pictures of the desert and the creatures that inhabit it, Clark devotes a half-dozen pages to the stark drama of life and death that takes place around a desert well; rattle-snakes, road runners, jackrabbits, hawks, lizards, coyotes, and a cow and her calf all play parts.

The story's only character is Jim Suttler, a grizzled old prospector who, with his mule Jenny, still seeks gold in abandoned and long-forgotten mines. Suttler is a man well-attuned to life in the desert wilderness. Armed with a rifle, an old six-shooter, and primitive mining tools, he is not merely a stereotyped prospector; his red beard and shoulder-length red hair might lead some to see in him a resemblance to Christ, but Suttler is unlike Christ in several ways. Early in the story, Suttler and Jenny arrive at Indian Well. The history of Indian Well is recorded on the walls of the rundown cabin nearby; names and dates go back to the previous century. All had used the well, and all had given vent to some expression, ranging from "God guide us" to "Giv it back to the injuns" to a more familiar libel: "Fifty miles from water, a hundred miles from wood, a million miles from God, and three feet from hell." Before Suttler leaves, he too will leave a message.

Finding some traces of gold in an abandoned mine near the well, Suttler decides to stay for a while to see if he can make it pay off. It is a comfortable time, and both he and Jenny regain some of the weight lost during their recent travels. Two events, however, change the idyllic mood of their stay. The first occurs when Suttler kills a range calf that, along with its mother, has strayed close to the well. While he has some qualms about killing the calf, Suttler, enjoying the sensation of providence, soon puts them out of his mind. Next, a cougar kills Jenny. This event inflames Suttler with the desire for revenge—even if "it takes a year"—so throughout the winter he sits up nights waiting for the cat to return. When he eventually kills it, he skins it and, uncovering Jenny's grave, places the skin over her carcass. His revenge complete, he cleanses himself at the well and leaves as a "starved but revived and volatile spirit." Thus, one more pass-erby has contributed to the history of Indian Well, and the life around the well goes on.

The basic element in "The Indian Well" is the ironic contrast between the beginning and the ending of the story, just as it is in "The Buck in the Hills." When they come upon Indian Well, Suttler and Jenny enter into a natural world that has its own ordered life and death, and they blend easily into it. Suttler appears to be a man at one with nature, yet at the end of the story, the death that he has inflicted upon the cougar stands as something apart from the ordered world of the well. It is a death that was motivated by the desire for revenge, a very human emotion. The reader might be suspicious when Suttler kills the calf, but he justifies such a killing on the basis of the meat that the calf provides. Killing the cougar, on the other hand, cannot be justified in any external way. The deep satisfaction that it brings to Suttler stands in opposition to any right relationship between human beings and nature; it is solely a part of Suttler's inner self. When the deed is done, Suttler can blend back into the natural world around him. For that one winter, however, as he lies in wait for the cougar, he exhibits man's all-too-common flaw of putting himself above the natural world. Still, because he knows what he has done and, moreover, accepts it, he is able once more to establish his relationship with the cosmic forces.

"HOOK"

In a very real sense, this establishing of a relationship with the cosmic forces is the goal of many of Clark's characters. Caught in the ambiguities of good and evil, of morality and immorality, they struggle to maintain a faith in humanity and to bring moral law into accordance with natural law, for only in that way can human beings be saved from their own destructive tendencies. Some critics, such as Chester Eisinger, see Clark as being rather pessimistic regarding the success of such a human attempt at unity and attribute to him a desire to retreat from other human beings. If this view is correct, then perhaps the story "Hook" is the best expression of what Clark wants to say. The main character in this story is a hawk who fulfills himself in flight, in battle, and in sex, until he is killed by a dog. His is a life cycle of instinct, and, as he lives it, he can easily enough be seen as an antihuman symbol. If Eisinger's view is wrong however, then it is possible to see Clark as a writer who seeks not a retreat from other human beings, but an explanation of humanity. For, like the hawks that appear so often in Clark's stories, human beings are also a part of nature and because he is, it is possible to see his task as one of defining himself in the context of the natural order of things. Whatever the outcome, Clark's characters do make the attempt.

OTHER MAJOR WORKS

LONG FICTION: *The Ox-Bow Incident*, 1940; *The City of Trembling Leaves*, 1945; *The Track of the Cat*, 1949; *Tim Hazard*, 1951.

POETRY: *Ten Women in Gale's House and Shorter Poems*, 1932.

NONFICTION: *The Journals of Alfred Doten, 1849-1903*, 1973 (3 volumes).

BIBLIOGRAPHY

Court, Franklin E. "Clark's 'The Wind and the Snow of Winter' and Celtic Oisin." *Studies in Short Fiction* 33 (Spring, 1996): 219-228. Examines the mythic pattern of Clark's most famous story against the background of the Celtic legend of wandering Oisin.

Eisinger, Chester E. *Fiction of the Forties*. Chicago: University of Chicago Press, 1963. Eisinger regards Clark's short stories as similar in theme (search for identity, desire to merge with nature, and rejection by nature) to the novels. While several short stories are mentioned in passing, Ei-

singer includes lengthy analyses of "The Buck in the Hills," "Hook," and "The Watchful Gods."

Kich, Martin. *Western American Novelists*. Vol. 1. New York: Garland, 1995. After a brief account of Clark's career, Kich provides an extensive, annotated bibliography, providing detailed commentary on reviews of virtually every significant prose fiction. Kich also annotates reference works with entries on Clark and books with chapters on his fiction.

Laird, Charlton, ed. *Walter Van Tilburg Clark: Critiques*. Reno: University of Nevada Press, 1983. A collection of eighteen pieces, some by Clark himself, on Clark's life, his major published work, and his literary craftsmanship. The book is most valuable for the essays on "The Watchful Gods" and "The Pretender," essays that portray Clark as a reviser/craftsman, and for the autobiographical information and the detailed chronology provided by his son.

Lee, Lawrence L. *Walter Van Tilburg Clark*. Boise, Idaho: Boise State College Press, 1973. In his monograph, Lee devotes a separate chapter to the short stories, which he believes repeat the themes of the novels but with greater clarity and insight. "The Portable Phonograph" and "The Watchful Gods" are discussed in some detail. Supplemented by a helpful bibliography.

Ronald, Ann. "Walter Van Tilburg Clark's Brave Bird, 'Hook.'" *Studies in Short Fiction* 25 (Fall, 1988): 433-439. Discusses the complex irony of the story, arguing that critics have wrongfully ignored it as a simple fable or animal tale for children.

Westbrook, Max. *Walter Van Tilburg Clark*. New York: Twayne, 1969. Westbrook's book remains the best overall assessment of Clark's literary work; in addition to a chronology of Clark's life, a biographical chapter, and a select bibliography, Westbrook includes a chapter on Clark's novella, *The Watchful Gods and Other Stories*, and several paragraph-length discussions of Clark's best short stories.

_____. "Walter Van Tilburg Clark and the American Dream." In *A Literary History of the Ameri-*

can West, edited by J. Golden Taylor. Fort Worth: Texas Christian University Press, 1987. Westbrook blends biography with criticism as he analyzes Clark's fiction and defines Clark's place in literary history. Using characters from stories and

novels, Westbrook depicts the Clark "hero" as an idealistic dreamer incapable of practical action. As a result, the American dream, or its nightmarish counterpart, becomes a real concern for Clark.

Wilton Eckley, updated by Thomas L. Erskine

ARTHUR C. CLARKE

Born: Minehead, Somerset, England; December 16, 1917

PRINCIPAL SHORT FICTION

Expedition to Earth, 1953
Reach for Tomorrow, 1956
Tales from the White Hart, 1957
The Other Side for the Sky, 1958
Tales of Ten Worlds, 1962
The Nine Billion Names of God: The Best Short Stories of Arthur C. Clarke, 1967
Of Time and Stars: The Worlds of Arthur C. Clarke, 1972
The Wind from the Sun: Stories of the Space Age, 1972
The Best of Arthur C. Clarke, 1937-1971, 1973
The Sentinel: Masterworks of Science Fiction and Fantasy, 1983
Dilemmas: The Secret, 1989
Tales from the Planet Earth, 1989
More than One Universe: The Collected Stories of Arthur C. Clarke, 1991

OTHER LITERARY FORMS

Arthur C. Clarke is best known for novels that chronicle near-future space and sea exploration or suggest transcendence of human form and limitations. He published an autobiographical novel based on his experience with radar in World War II, and he adapted several of his novels for film: *2001: A Space Odyssey* (1968) for Stanley Kubrick, *2010: Odyssey Two* (1982), and *Cradle* (1988). In 1997, *3001: The*

Final Odyssey was published. He contributed numerous articles on science and speculation, edited various scientific and science-fiction magazines, and wrote more than twenty books of nonfiction, including *By Space Possessed* (1993) and *The Snows of Olympus: A Garden of Mars* (1994). Clarke recorded some of his fictional works, lectured widely on science, the sea, and futuristic technology, and authored a television series, *Arthur C. Clarke's World of Strange Powers*. His writing has appeared in popular magazines under the pseudonyms E. G. O'Brien and Charles Willis.

ACHIEVEMENTS

Arthur C. Clarke has received numerous awards. The most representative include Hugo Awards for science fiction in 1956, 1974, and 1980; UNESCO's Kalinga Prize in 1961, for science writing; the Stuart Ballantine Gold Medal in 1963, for originating the concept of communications satellites; an Academy Award nomination in 1969 for best screenplay; Nebula Awards for science fiction in 1972, 1973, and 1980; a GALAXY Award for science fiction in 1979; and the Centennial Medal in 1984, for scientific achievements. Other distinguished honors include the prestigious Grand Master Award from the Science Fiction Writers of America in 1986, the Charles A. Lindbergh Award in 1987, and his election to the Society of Satellite Professions Hall of Fame in 1987 and to the Aerospace Hall of Fame in 1988. In 1989 Clarke became a Commander of the British Empire, and he received a knighthood for "services to literature" in 1998.

BIOGRAPHY

Reared in the country, Arthur Charles Clarke worked as a government auditor (1936-1941) in London, where he became active in the British Interplanetary Society (eventually becoming Chairman, 1946-1947, 1950-1952). A Royal Air Force instructor in the infant technology of radar during World War II, he published the first speculations on "stationary" communications satellites in 1945. After earning his B.S. in physics and mathematics at King's College, London (1948), he became assistant editor of *Science Abstracts* (1949-1951) before turning to full-time writing. Introduced in 1953 to scuba diving, he moved to what was then Ceylon in 1956 and remained there for many years. Clarke married Marilyn Mayfield in 1954, but they were divorced in 1964.

Clarke has more than five hundred works attributed to him. He is known as one of the most influential writers in the science-fiction field, as well as a visionary seer on scientific speculation. Clarke was the first, for example, to propose the idea of communications satellites, in his article "Extraterrestrial Relays" in 1945. He is a mathematician and physicist as well as a novelist and commentator. His talent for peering into the future has involved him in advising governments on communication and on the human use of space. Clarke believes in and popularizes his belief in the total exploration of space and the sea. He became Chancellor of the University of Moratuwa in Sri Lanka and is founder of the Arthur C. Clarke Center for Advanced Technology.

ANALYSIS

Exposed in his childhood to both the pulp magazines of Hugo Gernsback and the English literary tradition of fantasy and science fiction, Arthur C. Clarke sometimes forges an uneasy alliance between the two in his own stories. The matter-of-fact description of the marvelous of H. G. Wells, the poetic evocation of unknown places of Lord Dunsany, and the immense vistas of space and time of the philosopher Olaf Stapledon lie cheek-by-jowl with artificial suspense devices, awkward sentimentality, schoolboy silliness, and melodramatic manipulation of such hoary motifs as the "stranded astronaut" or the "end of the world"

Arthur C. Clarke (©Washington Post; reprinted by permission of the D.C. Public Library)

in his less distinguished fiction. At its best, however, Clarke's work shows glimpses of man's rise to interplanetary civilization or evokes the wonder, in suitably subdued tones, of his confrontation with extraterrestrial intelligences.

His 1967 collection of his "favorites" represents many facets of his career, from the raconteur of tall tales and ghost stories to the fantasist, the sentimentalist, the realist, and the poet of wonder. Most of his best and best-known stories are included, from the haunting rite of passage of a young lunar exile getting his first glimpse of the unapproachably radioactive world of his ancestors ("'If I Forget Thee, Oh Earth . . . ,'") to such "alien fables" of technological complacency as "Superiority" and "Before Eden."

"RESCUE PARTY"

Among them, "Rescue Party," his second professionally published story, looks forward to other tales of human progress and alien contact, but it is unusual in its strong story line and alien viewpoint. Although it makes one of his rare claims for human superiority, a fetish of *Astounding Science Fiction* editor John W. Campbell, Jr., the story's humor, style, and forecasts are vintage Clarke.

"Who was to blame?," it opens, setting the context of a paternalistic "Galactic Federation," sending a ship to rescue a few hundred survivors from Earth before its sun turns into a nova. With a million years between visits, they had been taken by surprise by man's rise to civilization in two-fifths of that time, signaled by radio waves detected two hundred light years away. With little more than four hours to go, the ship arrives at a deserted planet, sends out two search parties, and barely escapes the cataclysm, burning out its "main generators" in the effort. Directing its course to the receiving point of a communications array on Earth, the mile-long spaceship, now needing rescue itself, approaches rendezvous with an unexpected fleet of ships from the planet. Unprecedented in size, this fleet of "primitive" rockets demonstrates an acceleration of man's technological development so astonishing that the captain, the tentacled Alveron, whose ancient people are "Lords of the Universe," teasingly suggests the vast Federation beware of these upstarts. This "little joke" is followed by the narrator's quiet punch line: "Twenty years afterward, the remark didn't seem funny."

Humor of situation is evident throughout the story, from the concept of "administering" a galaxy to the discovery of the humans' "handicap" of bipedalism from an abandoned portrait of a City Alderman. The incongruity of the rescuers' need for rescue is mirrored by the precision which allows the aliens an unflappable split-second escape but brings them there in the first place too late and with too little to do anything useful, then finds them baffled by relatively primitive communications devices and an automatic subway. Although the story creaks in places—contemporary theory says the sun cannot become a nova, vacuum tubes are outmoded, helicopters never did become the wave of the future—those details can be sacrificed for the sake of the fable. The primary forecasts of space travel and posturban civilization should not be discounted, at the risk of being as naïve and complacent as the aliens, without even their limited security in their own superiority.

More commonly, Clarke sees alien technology as older and better than humans', as in two stories in which *2001: A Space Odyssey* is rooted. In "Encounter at Dawn," ancient astronauts "in the last days of the Empire" give tools to primitives a hundred thousand years before Babylon.

"THE SENTINEL"

Even more understated, "The Sentinel" is allegedly told by an eyewitness who begins by directing the reader to locate on the Moon the Mare Crisium (Sea of Crises), where the discovery took place. Part of a large 1996 expedition, he recalls fixing breakfast when a glint of light in the mountains caught his eye; staring through a telescope so fascinated him that he burned the sausages. From such homey touches, he led the climb to "Wilson's Folly," a plateau artificially leveled for a twelve-foot crystal pyramid "machine." Its force field gave way, after twenty years of frustrated investigation, to an atomic assault which reduced the mystery to fragments. The rest of the story is speculation, successive stages of Wilson's inferences.

Not a relic of lunar civilization, the artifact, half the age of Earth, was left by visitors: Wilson imagines it saying "I'm a stranger here myself." After its destruction, he "guesses" it must have been a beacon; interrupting its signal has triggered a "fire alarm." Lacking explicit alien intent, the pyramid emblemizes the unknown. Although such a potentially multivalent symbol invites other interpretations, Wilson's is supported by *2001*, in which a *rectangular slab under* the lunar surface signals *after* being exposed to sunlight. The final savage attack on the pyramid also seems significant to the narrator, although the pyramid might have been programmed to self-destruct.

The quasi-religious awe, tinged with fear as well as positive expectation, with which Wilson awaits the aliens' return has echoes elsewhere in Clarke. This story, moreover, with its judgment of space travel as a first step toward an incalculable destiny, many readers see as an article of faith in a grand design of a creator god. Such a pattern may lie beneath some of his work, but Clarke has also taken pains to discourage conventional religious interpretations.

"THE NINE BILLION NAMES OF GOD"

His work is dotted with attacks on religious or "mystical" belief and behavior, with one exception: the Scottish-born head of worldwide Buddhism in *The Deep Range* (1957), whose opposition to butchering whales is based partly on the conviction that aliens may judge man on his behavior toward his fellow creatures. Certainly the surprise ending of "The Nine Billion Names of God" is no proof of Clarke's sharing the faith of his Tibetan lamas. Although the story attacks the complacency of Western computer technicians whose efficiency speeds up the counting of all of God's names, the ending ("Overhead, without any fuss, the stars were going out") is that of a joke or a ghost story.

"THE STAR"

Rather than simply trivializing God, Clarke's award-winning short story "The Star" makes God destructive and merciless. A Jesuit astrophysicist, slightly defensive about his combined callings, the narrator is at the point of quiet desperation. Beginning "It is three thousand light-years to the Vatican," he finds no solace in the crucifix near his computer or the engraving of Loyola, whose order is not all that will end when the expedition makes public its findings.

In a retrospective narration that distances the action, the narrator recounts the ship's approach to the inappropriately named "Phoenix" Nebula, the debris of a supernova that destroyed an interplanetary civilization. Different from Wells's story of the same name, this cataclysm did not spare a people and let them find a sense of community. From their remains in a vault on the star's most distant planet, the crew finds evidence that this "disturbingly human" civilization was at its peak when it died. The narrator's colleagues see no room in nature for God's wrath or mercy, and the narrator denies his own right to judge God. He is troubled, however, by the date of the disruption; given its direction and distance, this must have been the "Star of Bethlehem," hanging low in the East before sunrise. Explicitly rejecting keeping the information secret or tampering with the data, he

is troubled in his faith because he cannot refuse (or refute) the findings of science.

A masterpiece of compression, poetic in style, somber in tone, and totally devoid of action and dialogue (not even the two lines of "The Sentinel"), "The Star" does not even state its conclusion. The narrator must either conclude that his colleagues are right or accept a God who would destroy this culture to impress a few humans.

"A MEETING WITH MEDUSA"

Considerably at variance with these and most of Clarke's short fiction is "A Meeting with Medusa." Appearing four years after his retrospective collection, it is one of his longest stories not given book length, and a sharp improvement over most of his work in the 1960's. Allusive and subtly patterned, both a character study and a tale of adventure, it continues Clarke's interest in "first contact" and alien landscapes, but it also fictionalizes J. D. Bernal's suggestion in *The World, the Flesh, and the Devil* (1929) that space exploration is the proper province of a human mind in a posthuman body.

All but destroyed when a mismanaged robot camera platform sent his dirigible, the *Queen Elizabeth IV*, down in flames, Howard Falcon is restored to life as a cyborg, the physical form of which is not revealed until the last of eight chapters. Seven years later, stronger and more durable, he argues successfully to be sent on an expedition into the atmosphere of Jupiter. After another three years, the actual adventure takes place.

Almost a part of the "raft," *Kon-Tiki*, supported by a hot hydrogen balloon (with emergency ram-jet and rocket motors), the wingless Falcon is nevertheless at a disadvantage when it comes to making contact with native life forms. Expecting at most a kind of plankton, he comes upon creatures whose nearest Earth analogues, in miniature, are varieties of sea life. Manta rays a hundred yards across seem docile browsers of floating wax mountains until their natural enemies appear. Radio-sensitive jellyfish over a mile wide, they repel attacking mantas with electrical discharges that also function for communications. A dirigible pilot once again, Falcon has neither their maneuverability nor their familiarity with local conditions.

Wryly amused at his ambassadorial role, he is understandably reluctant to obey the "Prime Directive" requiring him to avoid attacking intelligent creatures, at the cost of his own life if need be. When tentacles descend around the *Kon-Tiki*, he descends still lower; when the "Medusa" begins to "pat" his craft tentatively with a single tentacle, he cuts loose with his auxiliary engines. The Great Red Spot, blizzards of wax, atmospheric maelstroms, and various other features of the "world of the gods" can wait until another time.

A hero who has reignited man's imagination, Falcon is slipping away from identity with the human race, we now discover, along with our first glimpse of his undercarriage, hydraulic lifts, balloon tires, and seven foot height, if not of his "leathery mask" (now seen in a different light). Like the panicky "super-chimp" on the *Queen Elizabeth* whose face he used to see in dreams, he is "between two worlds," the biological and the mechanical. Immortal, it may be, he represents at its extreme the "cosmic loneliness" of Clarke's heroes.

Falcon is at the center of the story, although the predominant interest may be more in what he sees than in what he does. Jupiter is the "hero," at least of the middle sections of the story, in which Clarke combines his undersea experience and astrophysical theory to draw plausible inferences about an unlikely place for "life as we know it." Although he is not an adequate "ambassador" to the Jovians—who could be?—because he is not quite human, Falcon is the best possible explorer. A "new breed," he is for some purposes "more than human," although our bias toward the "handicap" of bipedalism may blind us to it. He is also one more piece of evidence that the "transcendence" of human limitations widespread in Clarke's fiction may be at best a mixed blessing. Suspenseful yet satiric, adventuresome yet calmly paced, "A Meeting with Medusa," in its poetic evocation of first contact and its sophisticated variations on transcendence and the "stranded astronaut," is a culmination of the shorter fiction which came before it.

"THE HAMMER OF GOD"

Several years elapsed before Clarke agreed to write another short story, "The Hammer of God," for *Time* Magazine's special issue *Beyond the Year 2000*, published in the fall of 1992. In this tale, Clarke wryly combines paradoxes to shape his whimsical yet ironic version of efforts to deflect an asteroid's possible collision with Earth.

Clarke combines extreme religious polarities; ancient mythological deities; futuristic technological, political, and economic achievements; and a cast characterized by their opposing actions and reactions: an eccentric politician, a sentimental captain, a very logical computer, an asteroid, and religious saboteurs. Facts about two previous asteroids serve to punctuate and divide the story into three parts. The first cataclysm sixty-five million years ago brought destruction to dinosaurs, plants, and other animals. In contrast, the second, in 1972, cut through Earth's atmosphere for two minutes, causing no damage. The third asteroid enters the solar system in 2212. Named Kali after the Hindu goddess of death and destruction, this traveler is the menace facing Captain Robert Singh, commander of the ship *Goliath*; his central computer, David; and his one-hundred-person team, Operation *ATLAS*. The captain's team wants to move a small chunk of the asteroid into a new path away from Earth.

Clarke envisions sophisticated technological and scientific advances. A neural-input cap, the "portable Brainman," fitting directly over a bald skull, allows the century-old Captain Singh to relive an experience from twenty years ago with his young son, Toby. The oil age ends with the advent of successful cold fusion. With lens-corrective laser shaping, eyeglasses are abolished, choices of skin coloring allow individuals to vary skin color as frequently as they change clothing, and scientific data from a radio beacon/measuring rod anchored within Kali supply David with facts to report on what the actual probability of impact would be.

Logical thinking is not characteristic for the captain of the *Goliath*. He focuses on whether his future friendships will be on Mars or the moon and speculates about how he can arrange that all the many decades of his life will be on Mars. His mind is not on ship business. Conversely, David's logical thoughts provide an alternative solution to the loss of hydrogen the ship experiences. With the remainder of the ship's own propellant, originally reserved to rendezvous with *Titan*, *Goliath* itself can push Kali into a new course that will bypass Earth. Unfortunately, no one explores Kali further before accepting David's maneuver.

This asteroid has a fatal hidden feature, a weak outer crust. When *Goliath* pushes with all its force against Kali, it breaks through this crust and is stuck. Despite all attempts to reverse and pull free, the effort is useless. Using the remainder of its fuel, the ship makes one final push on Kali, strong enough to slightly alter the asteroid's path and to permanently lock them into the asteroid's surface. Contrary to the ancient Hindu goddess Kali's almost endless blood sacrifices, this Kali's destructive sacrifices as she cuts through Earth's atmosphere for two minutes are trivial—only the ship's crew, ten thousand lives and one trillion dollars in damages. With skilled understatement, numerous paradoxes, and wry humor, Clarke again demonstrates in "The Hammer of God" his ability to craft an entertaining tale about Earth's potential collision with a stray asteroid from outer space. As a poet of the infinite, whose fables judge man from an "alien" point of view, Clarke stands alone.

OTHER MAJOR WORKS

LONG FICTION: *Prelude to Space*, 1951; *The Sands of Mars*, 1951; *Against the Fall of Night*, 1953, 1956 (revised as *The City and the Stars*); *Childhood's End*, 1953; *Earthlight*, 1955; *The Deep Range*, 1957; *Across the Sea of Stars*, 1959; *A Fall of Moondust*, 1961; *From the Ocean, from the Stars*, 1962; *Glide Path*, 1963; *Prelude to Mars*, 1965; *"The Lion of Comarre" and "Against the Fall of Night,"* 1968; *2001: A Space Odyssey*, 1968; *Rendezvous with Rama*, 1973; *Imperial Earth*, 1975; *The Fountains of Paradise*, 1979; *2010; Odyssey Two*, 1982; *The Songs of Distant Earth*, 1986; *2061: Odyssey Three*, 1987; *Cradle*, 1988 (with Gentry Lee); *Rama II*, 1989 (with Lee); *Beyond the Fall of Night*, 1990 (with Gregory Benford); *The Ghost from the Grand Banks*, 1990; *The Garden of Rama*, 1991 (with Lee); *The Hammer of God*, 1993; *Rama Revealed*, 1993

(with Lee); *Richter 10*, 1996 (with Mike McQuay); *3001: The Final Odyssey*, 1997; *The Light and Other Days*, 2000 (with Stephen Baxter).

NONFICTION: *Interplanetary Flight*, 1950; *The Exploration of Space*, 1951 (revised 1959); *Going into Space*, 1954; *The Exploration of the Moon*, 1954; *The Coast of Coral*, 1956; *The Making of a Moon*, 1957; *The Reefs of Taprobane*, 1957; *Voice Across the Sea*, 1958; *The Challenge of the Spaceship*, 1959; *The Challenge of the Sea*, 1960; *The First Five Fathoms*, 1960; *Indian Ocean Adventure*, 1961 (with Mike Wilson); *Profiles of the Future*, 1962; *Man and Space*, 1964 (with others); *Indian Ocean Treasure*, 1964 (with Wilson); *The Treasure of the Great Reef*, 1964; *Voices from the Sky*, 1965; *The Promise of Space*, 1968; *First on the Moon*, 1970 (with others); *Into Space*, 1971 (with Robert Silverberg); *Report on Planet Three and Other Speculations*, 1972; *Beyond Jupiter*, 1972 (with Chesley Bonestall); *The Lost Worlds of 2001*, 1972 (including canceled alternative chapters); *The View from Serendip*, 1977; *Ascent to Orbit: A Scientific Autobiography*, 1984; *1984, Spring: A Choice of Futures*, 1984; *Arthur C. Clarke's July 20, 2019: Life in the Twenty-first Century*, 1986; *The Odyssey File*, 1985 (with Peter Hyams); *Arthur C. Clarke's Chronicles of the Strange and Mysterious*, 1987; *Astounding Days: A Science Fictional Autobiography*, 1989; *How the World Was One: Beyond the Global Village*, 1992; *By Space Possessed*, 1993; *The Snows of Olympus: A Garden of Mars*, 1994; *Greetings, Carbon-based Bipeds! Collected Essays, 1934-1998*, 1999.

CHILDREN'S LITERATURE: *Islands in the Sky*, 1952; *Dolphin Island*, 1963.

BIBLIOGRAPHY

Brull, Steven, and Neil Gross. "The Next World According to Clarke." *Business Week*, February 24, 1997, 123-124. Notes that scientists take Clarke's musings about the future seriously, for Clarke has always blurred the lines between what people dream and what engineers create; notes that many respected scientists, engineers, and writers praise Clarke for infusing science fiction with verisimilitude and helping inspire real-world scientists.

Clarke, Arthur C. *Astounding Days: A Science-Fictional Autobiography*. New York: Bantam Books, 1989. Although this volume is not really an autobiography, Clarke offers a brief memoir of his youth. He explains how writers and editors of *Astounding* magazine (later named *Analog*) first aroused his interest in science fiction and discusses his work on rocketry and radar. Provides a pleasant diversion on Clarke's background.

_____. *The View from Serendip*. New York: Random House, 1977. Clarke writes with interest of the three *s*'s in his life—space, serendipity, and the sea. The twenty-five chapters touch on the events in his life, the people he has met, and the technological advances of the present and the future. A good introduction to Clarke's wide-ranging interests.

Guterl, Frederick V. "An Odyssey of Sorts." *Discover* 18 (May, 1997): 68-69. In this interview, Clarke discusses, among other subjects, the cold-fusion energy revolution and the evidence for life on Mars.

Lehman-Wilzig, Sam N. "Science-Fiction as Futurist Prediction: Alternate Visions of Heinlein and Clarke." *The Literary Review* 20 (Winter, 1977) 133-151. The author contrasts the science-fiction works of Clarke and Robert A. Heinlein and asserts that Heinlein is the superior stylist but Clarke is the one who excels in ideas—both technological and philosophical—and futurist vision.

McAleer, Neil. *Arthur C. Clarke: The Authorized Biography*. Chicago: Contemporary Books, 1992. A definitive account of Clarke's career, written with Clarke's cooperation.

Meisenheimer, Donald K., Jr. "Machining the Man: From Neurasthenia to Psychasthenia in SF and the Genre Western." *Science-Fiction Studies* 24 (November, 1997): 441-458. Argues that although Clarke works within the tradition of Wellsian science fiction, he also makes heavy use of the genre-Western established by Owen Wister and Frederic Remington.

Olander, Joseph D., and Martin Harry Greenberg, eds. *Arthur C. Clarke*. New York: Taplinger, 1977. This collection of nine essays on Clarke examines his individual works and his science-fiction writings in general. The editors state that Clarke is a hard science-fiction author whose commitment is to the universe. Provides a good source of textual criticism. Supplemented by a select bibliography and a biographical note.

Rabkin, Eric S. *Arthur C. Clarke*. San Bernardino, Calif.: Borgo Press, 1980. A good short introduction to Clarke's important science-fiction work, with brief descriptions. Robkin has high praise for Clarke and considers him one of the best in the science-fiction genre. Complemented by a bio-critical introduction, an annotated bibliography, and a chronology.

Reid, Robin Anne. *Arthur C. Clarke*. Westport, Conn.: Greenwood Press, 1997. A general introduction to Clarke's life and work, with a chapter on each of his nine novels.

David N. Samuelson, updated by Terry Theodore

COLETTE

Sidonie-Gabrielle Colette

Born: Saint-Sauveur-en-Puisaye, France; January 28, 1873

Died: Paris, France; August 3, 1954

PRINCIPAL SHORT FICTION

Les Vrilles de la vigne, 1908 (*The Tendrils of the Vine*, 1983)

L'Envers du music-hall, 1913 (*Music-Hall Side-lights*, 1957)

La Chambre éclairée, 1920

La Femme cachée, 1924 (*The Other Woman*, 1971)

Bella-Vista, 1937

Chambre d'hôtel, 1940 (*Chance Acquaintances*, 1952)

Le Képi, 1943

Gigi et autres nouvelles, 1944

La Fleur de l'âge, 1949 (*In the Flower of the Age*, 1983)

Paysage et portraits, 1958

The Stories of Colette, 1958 (also known as *The Tender Shoot and Other Stories*)

Contes des mille et un matins, 1970 (*The Thousand and One Mornings*, 1973)

The Collected Stories of Colette, 1983

OTHER LITERARY FORMS

Colette, whose complete works fill sixteen large volumes, is best known for her novels. Her first success, *La Vagabonde* (1911; *The Vagabond*, 1955), was followed by its sequel, *L'Entrave* (1913; *The Shackle*, 1964), and in time by *Chéri* (1920; English translation, 1929), *La Maison de Claudine* (1922; *My Mother's House*, 1953, a novelized autobiography of her early years that followed four Claudine novels, published from 1900 through 1903 under her first husband's name), *La Fin de Chéri* (1926; *The Last of Chéri*, 1932), *Le Blé en herbe* (1923; *The Ripening Corn*, 1931; also known as *The Ripening Seed*), *La Seconde* (1929; *The Other One*, 1931), *La Chatte* (1933; *The Cat*, 1936), *Julie de Carneilhan* (1941; English translation, 1952), and *Gigi* (1944; English

translation, 1952). These and many others constitute a substantial body of internationally famous novels. Colette is also the author of numerous volumes of memoirs, plays, film scenarios, essays, reviews, sketches, and criticism. A centenary edition of her *Œuvres complètes de Colette* (complete works of Colette). *Short Novels of Colette* (1951), edited by Glenway Wescott, contains translations of six of her novels. Robert Phelps edited *The Collected Stories of Colette*, which includes translations, again by various hands, of one hundred works of short fiction.

ACHIEVEMENTS

The publication of Colette's first Claudine segment preceded by five years her first notable success under her own name, *Dialogue de bêtes* (1904; *Creature Conversations*, 1951), a group of "dialogues" between her bulldog and her Angora cat. *The Vagabond*, published shortly after *L'Ingénue libertine* (1909; *The Gentle Libertine*, 1931), was nominated for a Prix Goncourt. The publication of *Chéri*, when she was forty-seven years old, ensured her reputation as a literary giant in France. She had achieved fame in journalism, the theater, on lecture tours in Europe and Africa, and as a writer whose works were admired in English, German, and Italian translations. She began her consistently successful work in the cinema in 1931. André Gide's journal entry for February 11, 1941, includes enthusiastic praise for Colette's writing style and for two of her works in particular, one published in 1922 and the other in 1937. In 1936, Colette succeeded the countess Anna-Élisabeth Mathieu de Noailles to a chair in the Académie Royale de Langue et de Littérature Francaises de Belgique (the Belgian Royal Academy of French Language and Literature). She completed her last long novel, *Julie de Carneilhan*, in 1941. At the end of World War II, she won election to the Académie Goncourt. A fifteen-volume edition of her complete works appeared in 1949. W. Somerset Maugham had said in 1938 that "no one in France now writes more admirably than Colette," and Wescott, in his introduction to *Short Novels of Colette*, calls her "supreme rememberer." A biographer, Herbert Lottman, quotes *The New York Times* obituary of August 4, 1954, which states that Colette's "fifty-odd novels and scores of short stories were as popular with housewives, shop girls and laborers as they were with intellectuals."

BIOGRAPHY

The four stages in the life of Sidonie-Gabrielle Colette are marked by her close associations with, first, her mother and, subsequently, each of her three husbands. Her devotion to her mother, along with the tensions that existed between them, is recorded at length in *Sido* (1929; English translation, 1953), the title being the name by which Adèle-Eugénie-Sidonie Landoy Colette was known. Captain Jules-Joseph Colette was Sido's second husband and the father of Colette. He died in 1905, Sido in 1912. Sido was strong of will and firm in her convictions and preju-

Colette (Library of Congress)

dices. Colette recalls both her strong reactions to challenge and her gentle hand braiding her daughter's hair in a setting of peace and serenity. During her childhood and adolescence, Colette developed a poet's appreciation of her rural environment in Burgundy and her private garden. She was twenty years old in 1893 when she married a friend of the family, Henri Gauthier-Villars, known as "Willy" both professionally and personally. It was with Willy that her literary career began.

With Willy's guidance, Colette produced writings that were published under Willy's name. These included the four Claudine novels, which would appear as a single book in 1923, and two other books. Eventually, she achieved enough independence to publish under the name Colette Willy and, after her final divorce in 1907, under the single name Colette. Willy's dominance had contributed less to Colette's dissatisfaction with him, and divorce from him, than his infidelities and sexual excesses had. Following her separation from Willy, Colette lived for about six years with Mathilde de Morny, called "Missy," a woman of the aristocracy who had been the Marquise de Belbeuf. She and Missy enjoyed a homosexual relationship and a penchant for participation in theatrical mimes, in one of which Colette's near-nudity created a sensation.

Colette's work for *Le Matin*, a prominent newspaper, brought her into the company of its editor, Henri de Jouvenel, whom she married in December, 1912, and with whom she had a daughter, born in July, 1913. The daughter, Colette's only child, was named Colette and was affectionately called "Bel-Gazou." Colette's pet name for de Jouvenel was "Sidi the Pasha." It was while she was married to de Jouvenel that Colette gained renown, the result, in particular, of the novels *Chéri* and *The Ripening Seed*. The first of these novels is the story of a tragic love affair between a very young man and a middle-aged woman; *The Ripening Seed*, evoking the ancient Greek romance by Longus, *Daphnis and Chloë*, relates the sexual education of an adolescent boy by an experienced older woman. Colette's second marriage disintegrated in 1923, the year *The Ripening Seed* was published.

In 1925, when Colette was fifty-two years old, she met Maurice Goudeket, a journalist sixteen years her junior, who was to become her third husband. The formal marriage took place on April 3, 1935, about six months before the death of Henri de Jouvenel. Her marriage to de Jouvenel had been marred by the infidelities of both partners, including Colette's alleged affair with her stepson Bertrand de Jouvenel, with whom she vacationed in Switzerland after the divorce. In Goudeket, by contrast, Colette found a partner whose compatibility with her artistic disposition and her need for independence provided precisely the kind of love and constant friendship that sustained her literary productivity in later life. Among her important works during this period are *The Cat, Bella-Vista, Julie de Carneilhan*, "Le Képi" ("The Kepi"), and *Gigi*.

During the World War II years of 1939-1945, Colette wrote a weekly account of living in Paris during the German occupation. On December 12, 1941, the Gestapo arrested her husband because he was Jewish and placed him in a prison camp in Compiègne for two months. After the liberation of Paris in August, 1944, and following the great commercial success of *Gigi*, Colette won election to the prestigious and very influential Académie Goncourt; five years later, she became its president.

The last decade of Colette's life was one of continued literary activity despite the pains of sciatica and severe arthritis. In addition to her other honors, Colette was named as Chevalier of the Legion of Honor in 1920; she became an officer in 1928, a commander in 1936, and a *grand officier* in 1953, also, the American ambassador to France presented her with a citation in honor of her election to the National Institute of Arts and Letters of America. She named Goudeket, who had initiated the publication of her complete works, as her literary executor. Immobilized by her illness, she died on August 3, 1954, and received a state funeral.

ANALYSIS

Colette drew only a hazy line, or area, of demarcation between her fiction and her reflections. Many of her short fictional pieces are indistinguishable from lyrical autobiography, which is the case with her Claudine novels. It is not really possible, or advisable, to differentiate, or try to differentiate, with precision her "short fiction" from her novellas, her reminiscences, her lyrical descriptions, and her accounts of persons and places. She has a primitivist tendency—many would call it a gift—for experiencing gardens, flowers, pets, and even objects as extensions of both herself and the vital aura of her physical existence. She took no pains to distance herself from her narratives and expositions, and she has been compared to Marcel Proust in her projection of her own person and persona into her fiction. Often in her work, Colette assumes the position of her reader's confidant, speaking in such a way that the reader becomes party to her activities, fictional or otherwise. Her milieu is regularly the ambience of private places and native haunts. She does not translate philosophy, economics, politics, or religion into fictional prose. Her concern is the profound complexity of simple human relationships—parents and children, lonely individuals, lovers, entertainers, and friends.

"CLOUK"

An early set of sketches forms the story of "Clouk" (identified as "Clouk/Chéri" by Colette in her 1941 set of papers) and describes the lovesickness and loneliness of a wealthy young man whose adenoidal condition results in a nasal sound that becomes his nickname. His love for Lulu, a seamstress's assistant who becomes a popular entertainer, persists after she has left him and as he gradually loses his small circle of friends, to whom he and his reactions become increasingly tedious. His self-deception and growing introversion produce for him a chrysalis of security within which he encloses himself. From this cocoon, no less than Chéri, the very handsome young hero of two novels will fly off in beauty. Colette speaks of this metamorphosis in the imagery of the pale small slough of a skin from which a resplendent and diabolic snake emerges. There is in this imagery a vestige of Colette's own ophidian and entomological nature. Molting, she passed from dependence upon her husband Willy to the clever and self-sufficient sophisticate who wrote the Chéri novels and *The Ripening Seed*. The beauty that she found in life, however, was in some way the beauty that she, as a delicate butterfly, had embryonized. Maurice Goudeket describes one of her last gestures as a winglike fluttering of her hands, and her last word, "Look," embraced the room in which she lay dying, with all of its contents, including a box of butterflies. To read Colette is to see her constantly in all that she describes, especially in her description of Clouk.

Colette gives to the spoken word an organic life that removes the genetic boundary between human and animal, as well as that between narrator and character. Her early short fiction includes a number of dialogues, many with one voice suppressed, others with narration that combines stream-of-consciousness progression with direct discourse, and still others recording the conversation of animals. Human characters in these dialogues have such mundane identities as masseuse, godchild, hairstylist, or saleslady.

THE LETTERS

A "letter" to her friend Valentine is signed "Colette Willy" and takes up the matter of Colette's appearances in mime drama with "Missy." The "letter" recapitulates Valentine's disapproval of Colette's nudity on stage. The incidents are part of the author's actual history, but the letter is a work of fiction. Where other writers produce autobiographical fiction, Colette may be said to produce fictive autobiography. There are at least ten other short works addressed to, or focused upon, "my friend Valentine," and they pulsate with gossip. One work begins with quotations from an unsigned letter to Valentine and gets caught up in the events of a harvesting of grapes. Another describes Valentine's undressing, applying makeup, and dressing in front of Colette; the rites of fashion are infused with an air of homosexuality that is implicit with both calm intimacy and incipient dissatisfaction, a kind of jealousy on Colette's part. One very short story opens with Valentine's comments upon her recent haircut and goes on to encompass a dialogic disquisition on hairstyles and hair; it is concise, devoid of any suggestion of plot, and, in its patent mundanity, a work of fiction resonant with the dimensions of vanity. Colette's specialty is an appreciation of the profundity of mundane femininity.

"THE TENDRILS OF THE VINE"

Colette's fable about the tendrils of the vine was first published in *Le Mercure musical* on May 15, 1905. It would much later be included with, and provide the title of, her 1908 collection of short stories, *The Tendrils of the Vine*. The tale begins with a third-person narration about a nightingale that sings to stay awake in order not to be caught and bound by the tendrils of a vine. Colette then speaks in the first person as an observer of the nightingale. She concludes with an identification of herself as the nightingale, whose song is her self-confession. Just like the nightingale, Colette loses happiness and pleasant sleep, along with the fear of the tendrils of the vine, which in Colette's case stands for Willy's dominance. The story reflects the inception of Colette's move away from dependence upon Willy.

"THE TENDER SHOOT"

In this allegory of a vine, a plant is personified. In two later works, *The Ripening Seed* and the short story "Le Tendron" ("The Tender Shoot"), humans may be said to be "plantified." The "tender shoot" is a sensually uninhibited country girl of fifteen and a half years who responds to the eroticism of a man almost fifty-two years of age; she fears only the ill will of her mother, and, when she and her lover are surprised by her mother, she joins her mother in an attack upon the man. The story antedates Vladimir Nabokov's *Lolita* (1955) by at least a dozen years, and it differs from *Lolita* in length, in the girl's retention of her virginity, and in having been written by a woman; the theme, however, is identical for each work. The statement inherent in Colette's personification of plants and plantification of humans is that the pliancy and tenderness of life can persist only as traces in the toughness and coarseness upon which survival depends. Something of this statement obtains as well in the two dialogues between Toby-Chien, Colette's bulldog, and Kiki-la-Doucette, her Angora cat, which are included in *The Tendrils of the Vine* and which remove the barriers between the animal and human worlds.

"LOVE"

"Amour" ("Love"), one of the stories in *Music-Hall Sidelights*, offers a characteristic relationship in

Colette's work: Gloria, an English dancer, and Marcel, a stage-door Johnny, fall in love; Gloria wants to prolong the idyllic movement toward intimacy, and Marcel wants to abbreviate it; when finally Gloria is ready to terminate the flirtation by capitulating, Marcel has terminated it by departing. Here, again, Colette rehearses a very ordinary relationship by presenting its surface in such a way as to furnish the reader with an experience of the profound dimensions of averseness that inform every attraction of one human being to another.

This is carried on in a story such as "Matinée" to reflect the attitudes of performers to each other, one performer's (the narrator's) distance from her colleagues, and the extrapolated distance of the matinée audience from the performers. "Lola" is a story about a performing dog, the titular character, whose concession to the narrator ranges from reserved approach, as the narrator seeks to feed her, to resentful capitulation, as the narrator purchases her. Lola, the dog herself, expresses the nature of her capitulation in the concluding paragraph. "Le Laissé-pour-compte" ("The Misfit") is a moderately longer story than others in the volume and outlines in unsentimental narrative the loneliness of a young song-and-dance woman, billed as Roussalka, who is contemned and avoided by her family (eight acrobats) and her fellow performers; she asserts her integrity by eating plums alone in a stifling boardinghouse room and shooting the pits at the grave markers and chapel of a neighboring cemetery. In "La Fenice," the narrator becomes depressed as she watches the women performers in a small Neapolitan café (called La Fenice, that is, "The Phoenix"); she envisages the return of the women to their grimy lodgings and, although there is a raging storm outside, leaves the café to brave the elements in a carriage. The fabulous bird that gives the café its name and the story its title is reduced to the brief glow of a candle in an entertainer's fireless room and the monotonous repetition of the acts from day to day. Yet this very repetition ensures the renewed vitality of the burned-out entertainers who know a constant renaissance from the ashes of weariness. *Music-Hall Sidelights* also provides more of Colette's dialogues-for-one: for example, "L'Accompagnatrice" ("The Accompanist"), which is a telephone message by a woman whose aspirations for the stage have been defeated by out-of-wedlock maternity, and "Nostalgie" ("Nostalgia"), the telephone tale of a woman whom the theater has passed by.

"MONSIEUR MAURICE"

A story entitled "Monsieur Maurice," published well before Colette met Maurice Goudeket and in no way suggestive of him, appears in her 1924 collection *The Other Woman*. It exemplifies her handling of narration from the male perspective: Maurice Houssiaux, attempting to dispose of two women candidates for an unneeded stenographic position, hires the elder candidate after she recalls his activities and mien as a young man. The recollection by the little gray-haired lady works upon Monsieur Maurice more effectively than the deference shown by the very attractive younger candidate. All the stories in *The Other Woman* are quite short.

Most of the stories that are representative of Colette's mature years are, like "The Tender Shoot," comparatively long, stories such as "Bella-Vista," "The Kepi," "L'Enfant malade" ("The Sick Child"), and *Gigi*, which is properly a novella, a brilliant celebration of the world that Colette knew during her twenties. Gigi is an ingenue who comes of age during the *fin de siécle*, the last decade of the nineteenth century. Gigi's real name, Gilberte, sounds an echo of Proust's Gilberte Swann. There is as well in Gigi some strain of the tender shoot that captivates mature men. Where *Gigi*, however, is delightfully atavistic, "Bella-Vista," the title story of her 1937 collection, is truer to the depths of Colette's thought.

"BELLA-VISTA"

"Bella-Vista" dramatizes the tension that informs "les mystérieux attraits de ce que nous n'aimons pas" (the mysterious drawing-power of what we do not like). Colette writes here in first-person narrative, using her own name, about her early springtime stay at a villa on the French Riviera while she awaits the construction of the villa that will be hers. Two women, Madame Suzanne and her American partner, Madame Ruby, run the Bella-Vista, where a mysterious Monsieur Daste is also a guest. M. Daste's strange but unadmitted antipathy to animals is sensed by Colette's dog Pati and culminates in his murder of first one and then nineteen parakeets. M. Daste is in every respect the antithesis of Colette, yet Colette knows that she must in some way incorporate her antithesis, her dark side. The strange relationship of Suzanne and Ruby, the alternation of beautiful and bad weather, and the malevolence of M. Daste work a kind of spell upon Colette, who decides to leave Bella-Vista, however, only when she realizes that she is no longer enjoying herself. Just prior to her departure, she learns that Madame Ruby is a man named Richard, who is being shielded from police arrest by his consort, Madame Suzanne, and who has impregnated Lucie, one of the maids. The ending is not so much a surprise as a fitting resolution of the visiting Colette's uneasiness and suspicion.

"THE KEPI"

"The Kepi," again a title story (this time of a 1943 collection), also involves the young Colette as a character and as still married to Willy. She meets a middle-aged writer, one Madame Marco, who is having an affair with a younger man, Lieutenant Alexis Trallard. During a session of love, Marco, in wrinkled chemise, puts the lieutenant's kepi on her head and gives it a provocative tilt. She is suddenly startled at the expression on Alexis's face. Although he says nothing, the lieutenant makes it clear that the affair has ended. The separation is gradual but definite, and Marco ceases to have a lover. It is the complex dimensionality of this apparently superficial and trivial bit of play that illustrates the tension beneath the surface of every individual's living existence. Colette captures it by having herself assume the role of her reader and encapsulating a reader's reaction to Marco's story, for Marco tells her story to Colette. Robert Phelps adjudges "The Kepi" as "probably the least sentimental love story ever told."

"APRIL"

Phelps adds that "Avril" ("April"), which is included in *In the Flower of the Age* but originally was a chapter excluded from *The Ripening Seed*, is probably "the truest" love story ever told. The adolescents, Vinca and Philippe, who have grown up together and take for granted a mutual commitment to love, are on the point of consummating their affection when, in the wooded area in which they find themselves, they come upon a mature couple in the act of love. Philippe suffers a wave of shame, which propels him into removing Vinca from the scene so that they may rejoin the bicycle caravan from which they have been briefly separated and regain the security of innocence, although they can no longer possess their own innocence.

"THE SICK CHILD"

"The Sick Child" is the last story that Colette wrote, and it is one of the most magical of her works of short fiction. In it, a dying boy achieves glorious experiences through feats of imagination, all of which cease to be tenable by him once his illness is reversed and he is returned to the prospect of living. The association of the unhindered imagination with the world of death and the recognition of the bleakness incumbent upon the obligations of living constitute Colette's most affecting theme.

In all of her short fiction, as in her novellas and novels, Colette probes, with a deftness that seems effortless and inevitable, the subtlest and, at the same time, the most profound synapses of human affection.

OTHER MAJOR WORKS

LONG FICTION: *Claudine à l'école*, 1900 (*Claudine at School*, 1956); *Claudine à Paris*, 1901 (*Claudine in Paris*, 1958); *Claudine en ménage*, 1902 (*The Indulgent Husband*, 1935; also known as *Claudine Married*); *Claudine s'en va*, 1903 (*The Innocent Wife*, 1934; also known as *Claudine and Annie*); *La Retraite sentimentale*, 1907 (*Retreat from Love*, 1974); *L'Ingénue Libertine*, 1909 (*The Gentle Libertine*, 1931; also known as *The Innocent Libertine*); *La Vagabonde*, 1911 (*The Vagabond*, 1954); *L'Entrave*, 1913 (*Recaptured*, 1932; better known as *The Shackle*); *Mitsou: Ou, Comment l'esprit vient aux filles*, 1919 (*Mitsou: Or, How Girls Grow Wise*, 1930); *Chéri*, 1920 (English translation, 1929); *Le Blé en herbe*, 1923 (*The Ripening Corn*, 1931; also known as *The Ripening Seed*); *La Fin de Chéri*, 1926 (*The Last of Chéri*, 1932); *La Naissance du jour*, 1928 (*A Lesson in Love*, 1932; also known as *Break of Day*); *La Seconde*, 1929 (*The Other One*, 1931); *La Chatte*, 1933 (*The Cat*, 1936); *Duo*, 1934 (*Duo*,

1935; also known as *The Married Lover*); *Julie de Carneilhan*, 1941 (English translation, 1952); *Gigi*, 1944 (English translation, 1952); *Seven by Colette*, 1955 (includes short fiction).

PLAYS: *Chéri*, pb. 1922 (with Léopold Marchand; English adaptation, 1959); *L'Enfant et les sortilèges*, pb. 1925 (opera; music by Maurice Ravel; *The Boy and the Magic*, 1964); *Gigi*, pr., pb. 1952 (adaptation of her novel, with Anita Loos).

NONFICTION: *Les Heures longues, 1914-1917*, 1917; *Dans la foule*, 1918; *Le Voyage egoïste*, 1922 (*Journey for Myself: Selfish Memoires*, 1971); *La Maison de Claudine*, 1922 (*My Mother's House*, 1953); *Sido*, 1929 (English translation, 1953); *Histoires pour Bel-Gazou*, 1930; *Ces Plaisirs*, 1932 (better known as *Le Pur et l'impur*, 1941; *The Pure and the Impure*, 1967); *Paradis terrestres*, 1932; *Prisons et paradis*, 1932; *La Jumelle noire*, 1934-1938; *Mes apprentissages*, 1936 (*My Apprentice-ships*, 1957); *Mes Cahiers*, 1941; *Journal à rebours*, 1941, and *De ma fenêtre*, 1942 (translated together as *Looking Backwards*, 1975); *Flore et Pomone*, 1943; *Nudité*, 1943; *Trois . . . Six . . . Neuf*, 1944; *Belles saisons*, 1945; *Une Amitié inattendue: Corres-pondance de Colette et de Francis Jammes*, 1945; *L'Étoile vesper*, 1946 (*The Evening Star*, 1973); *Pour un herbier*, 1948 (*For a Flower Album*, 1959); *Le Fanal bleu*, 1949 (*The Blue Lantern*, 1963); *Places*, 1970 (in English; includes short sketches unavailable in a French collection); *Letters from Colette*, 1980.

ANIMAL VIGNETTES AND DIALOGUES: *Dialogues de bêtes*, 1904 (*Creature Conversations*, 1951); *Sept dialogues de bêtes*, 1905 (*Barks and Purrs*, 1913); *Prrou, Poucette, et quelques autres*, 1913 (*Other Creatures*, 1951); *La paix chez les bêtes*, 1916 (rev. of *Prrou, Poucette, et quelques autres*; *Cats, Dogs, and I*, 1924); *Douze dialogues de bêtes*, 1930 (*Crea-tures Great and Small*, 1951); *Chats*, 1936; *Splen-deur des papillons*, 1937; *Chats de Colette*, 1949.

MISCELLANEOUS: *Œuvres complètes de Colette*, 1948-1950 (15 volumes); *The Works*, 1951-1964 (17 volumes).

BIBLIOGRAPHY
Cummins, Laurel. "Reading in Colette: Domination, Resistance, Autonomy." *Studies in Twentieth Cen-tury Literature* 20 (Summer, 1996): 451-465. Ar-gues that when Colette's characters engage in reading, a dynamic of domination and resistance is established; the father's censoring intervention debilitates, but the mother's model of reading as dialogue and resistance empowers.

Holmes, Diana. *Colette*. New York: St. Martin's Press, 1991. Notes how Colette's fiction deals with female sexuality, domestic life, and the prob-lem of working women in a man's world. Argues that Colette's stories need to be judged by female critics. Claims that Colette's stories are open-ended and thus innovative for their time.

Huffer, Lynne. *Another Colette: The Question of Gendered Writing*. Ann Arbor: University of Michigan Press, 1992. Chapters on Colette's ma-ternal model, her use of fictions and "phallacies," her handling of sexual performance, and her role as writer. Includes notes and bibliography. Rec-ommended for advanced students only.

Ladenson, Elisabeth. "Colette for Export Only." *Yale French Studies*, no. 90 (1996): 25-46. Discusses lesbian desire in Colette's fiction; argues that les-bian episodes in Colette's work have been dis-torted by American critics who have suggested lesbianism where bisexuality would have been more appropriate.

Lottman, Herbert. *Colette: A Life*. Boston: Little, Brown, 1991. The twenty-four photographs in-cluded in this text help to bring to life the pursuits and notoriety of Colette. Particularly valuable as complements to this reliable but rather matter-of-fact and sketchy biography are the photographs of Colette and Willy at table, Colette and her bulldog Toby-Chien, Colette in her *Egyptian Dream* theat-rical costume, Sido at sixty, Henri de Jouvenel, Bel-Gazou, and two views of Colette with Mau-rice Goudeket. Lottman's list of Colette's works in the chronology of their publication is useful, but he omits the posthumous publications.

Phelps, Robert. *Colette: Earthly Paradise*. New York: Farrar, Straus & Giroux, 1966. Phelps, who has elsewhere compiled the best collection of Co-lette's short fiction in English translation, has in this collection put together an autobiography of Colette "drawn from the writings of her lifetime." The eighteen pages of his foreword and chronology contain a superb introduction to Colette's career. The materials of the text are judiciously selected and arranged; they include translations of segments of *Belles saisons* and *Les Heures longues*.

Rogers, Juliette M. "The 'Counter-Public Sphere': Colette's Gendered Collective." *Modern Language Notes* 111 (September, 1996): 734-746. Argues that although Colette claimed she was apolitical, her works are often grounded in social practices and familial relationships of French everyday life in the time in which she wrote. Argues that Colette incorporates feminist notions of the development of identity through a concept of community, a gendered collective that defines itself against society as a whole.

Sarde, Michèle. *Colette: Free and Fettered*. Translated from the French by Richard Miller. New York: William Morrow, 1980. Sarde's study of Colette's life and work is the most informative book on Colette available. It has not been superseded by subsequent studies, such as Richardson's and Lottman's (above), and profits from a Gallic stamp and mood that non-French commentators have not yet begun to match. The research is superior to that of all existing biographies, and the bibliographical appendices are thoroughly practical, including posthumous publications and Richard Miller's additions, with considerable assistance from the Gibbard chronology, of available English translations. The forty-three photographs included in this volume exceed the Lottman collection in quantity and range but not in quality.

Strand, Dana. *Colette: A Study of the Short Fiction*. New York: Twayne, 1995. Explores Colette's treatment of mothers and daughters, women and men, gender role playing, old age, morality, reality, and the artist. A separate section explores her view of herself as a writer, and a third section includes commentary by her important critics. A chronology and bibliography make this a very useful research tool.

_____. "The 'Third Woman' in Colette's 'Chance Acquaintances.'" *Studies in Short Fiction* 29 (Fall, 1992): 499-508. Argues that in "Chance Acquaintances" Colette fashions a story that, despite a male plot structure, veers significantly from the masculine model. The writer who becomes the reluctant confidant of the wayward husband in the story is Colette herself, whose perspective reveals the inadequacies of generally accepted gender differences.

Wescott, Glenway. *Images of Truth: Remembrances and Criticism*. New York: Harper & Row, 1962. Chapter 4, "An Introduction to Colette," is reprinted from *Short Novels of Colette* (1951) and from Wescott's introduction to *Break of Day*. Chapter 5, "A Call on Colette and Goudeket," and chapter 4 provide valuable observations of the methods and person of Colette. Chapter 5 is quite moving in its details of the reception that Wescott received from a very ill Colette only two years before her death. During the visit, Colette said that *The Pure and the Impure* was her best book.

Roy Arthur Swanson

JOHN COLLIER

Born: London, England; May 3, 1901
Died: Pacific Palisades, California; April 6, 1980

PRINCIPAL SHORT FICTION

Epistle to a Friend, 1931
No Traveller Returns, 1931
Green Thoughts, 1932
The Devil and All, 1934
Variations on a Theme, 1935
Presenting Moonshine, 1941
A Touch of Nutmeg and More Unlikely Stories,
    1943
Fancies and Goodnights, 1951
Pictures in the Fire, 1958
The John Collier Reader, 1972
The Best of John Collier, 1975

OTHER LITERARY FORMS

In addition to his short fiction, John Collier wrote poetry, novels, and screenplays, as well as edited collections. Many of his works are fantasies, mysteries, parodies, or social satires. Collier joined Sandy Wilson to make Collier's most popular novel, *His Monkey Wife: Or, Married to a Chimp* (1930), into a musical of the same title; *Wet Saturday* appeared as a one-act play in 1941, first in New York City; and "Evening Primrose" (with music by Stephen Sondheim) was produced by ABC television. *John Milton's "Paradise Lost": Screenplay for Cinema of the Mind* (1973) reexamined that literary classic as a "screenplay for the cinema mind." Collier's motion-picture scripts were performed by cinema greats such as Bette Davis, Katharine Hepburn, and Charlton Heston.

ACHIEVEMENTS

A versatile writer, John Collier is best remembered for his witty and macabre short fantasies and mysteries and for his shocking and satiric novel of manners, *His Monkey Wife: Or, Married to a Chimp*, a story of the love and marriage of a man and a chimpanzee. Though largely ignored by scholars, Collier

has achieved wide popular fame, particularly in the United States, for his cheerful, tongue-in-cheek treatment of human foibles and pretensions. His understatement can be devastating and his cynicism incorrigible. He received four awards for his poetry from *This Quarter*, all in 1922. He also received the 1952 Edgar Allan Poe Award from Mystery Writers of America for *Fancies and Goodnights*, which Ellery Queen had earlier selected for the "Queen's Quorum," a definitive list of outstanding mystery short-story collections, and which later won the International Fantasy Award. The best of his short stories have been compared to those of Saki (H. H. Munro), Ambrose Bierce, and Roald Dahl because they are imaginative, offbeat, and difficult to classify.

BIOGRAPHY

Born in London to a once-well-to-do family, the son of John George and Emily Mary Noyes Collier, John Collier was educated privately. His uncle Vincent, author of a single novel, guided his education, beginning with readings of Hans Christian Andersen and continuing with the major Victorians, including Charles Darwin, Edward Gibbon, and John Stuart Mill. Having begun writing poetry at age nineteen, Collier, despite parental opposition, went on to become the poetry editor of *Time and Tide* during the 1920's and 1930's. He was a determined writer, an avant-garde intellectual, who managed to survive on an income of two pounds a week, supplemented with money earned writing regular book reviews and acting as foreign correspondent in London for a Japanese newspaper. Eventually, tired of city "squalor," he moved to the country, where he continued writing regularly in a variety of forms. Then in 1935, he moved to Cassis, France, but his novels and short stories had already earned for him a literary reputation for wit and whimsy that led to a contract with RKO Pictures Corporation in the United States. There, he wrote screenplays and became active in television production for a thirty-year period. A number of his important stories were written between 1937 and

1939, many, he claimed, to help alleviate his financial problems. During that period, he lived in a variety of places, including Oxfordshire and London (1937), Cassis, France (1938), Paris, Ireland, and Manhattan (1939-1940), and Hollywood (1942-1953), whose extravagant lifestyle fascinated him but whose inhabitants aroused his contempt. He published a series of stories in a flurry of effort in the 1950's. He married Harriet Hess in Mexico, on May 25, 1954, and then, finding himself gray-listed by the Federal Bureau of Investigation (FBI), settled in France, where he devoted time to horticulture. His son, John G. S. Collier, was born in Nice. In 1979, Collier returned to California, where he lived first in Santa Monica and then in Pacific Palisades. He died of a stroke in Pacific Palisades on April 6, 1980.

ANALYSIS

At their best, John Collier's works are lightly satiric, elegantly styled pieces, ironic, sardonic and bizarre, though occasionally unexpectedly grim. Their dialogue is deft, their style economical and clever, their plots subtle, swift, and memorable, their outcomes surprising. They expose the shallow vanities of contemporary manners, mores, and sentimentality. They involve sharply observed studies of the inanities, conflicts, and power plays involved in male-female relationships, and the greed, hypocrisy, and pretensions of professionals, tradesmen, Hollywood types, and even gentlemen. His doctors promote absurd cures (one even disembowels a patient for personal gain); his dentists rationalize pulling every tooth in one's head for the right fee; his psychiatrists explain away the Devil; his industrialists are hardened sadists and his gentlemen profligate dandies; and his artists pander to prevailing tastes or find themselves victims of the system. The scientist in "Man Overboard" pursues a sea monster and then flying saucers, while the one in "Youth from Vienna" seeks the fountain of youth. Sometimes Collier's language debunks, as in the description of one character's ideals as "as lofty as the bridge of his nose" or of a girl "who lives chastely with her Lee-Enfield, her Ballard, her light Winchester." Often Collier will interject a formal and brilliantly contrived sentence with a Victorian tone, sometimes to call attention to the dichotomy between true elegance and vulgar pretense, sometimes to underscore the false face behind which ill-will hides. Whatever his approach, Collier's genius for understatement and for deft characterization creates a world of magic and power in which human disaster, sexual attraction, and everyday vice are subjects of black humor, irony, and satire.

A number of Collier's stories juxtapose the ordinary and the supernatural and in particular involve deliberate or chance encounters between people and diabolical tempters or fallen angels. Many of these tales, like others in Collier's canon, set in opposition the logical and the emotional or psychological, with logic being the mainstay of the Devil and his cohorts ("I have *reason* on my side," sneers the Devil) and emotion an unfathomable but dependable motivator of human action. Collier's hell seems very familiar and is even mistaken for Buenos Aires in one tale. His universe, according to another story, is really a pint of beer, whose bubbles contain separate worlds.

THE DEVIL AND ALL

The collection *The Devil and All* contains some of the best of the Devil stories. "The Possession of Angela Bradshaw," a light spoof on the "new morality," tells of a respectable and a rather ordinary young lady of unquestionably superior upbringing, a Miss Bradshaw, who inexplicably begins to "swear like a trooper" and recite scurrilous doggerel verses, which horrify her parents and repel her fiancé. An attempted exorcism fails and only an agreement to allow the young lady to marry a presentable young poet will persuade him to give up possession of her. Gazing into her eyes had resulted in his literally "possessing" her body—and heart. "The Right Side" and "Halfway to Hell" both begin with suicides. In the first, a young man contemplating a plunge off a bridge is stopped by a helpful devil who provides a vision of fiends enjoying the lewd pleasures of Totenham Court Road and souls trapped in the circles of hell. A damp and chilly dance hall proves a most cunning condemnation: an eternity of boredom. In the second, the suicide has chosen to taste all the little pleasures of life before making a grand farewell in response to a jilting, but when provided a view of hell through its

Piccadilly Circus underground entrance, he schemes to tempt his demon escort with a powerful drink described as "liquid fire" and to keep his soul from hell.

In "After the Ball," a hulking, brutish demon, desperate to join hell's "Infernal" football league, must capture a soul for his would-be team to kick around; he goes after an upright bachelor whose rectitude leads the Devil in a hellish dance until the would-be victim's marriage; then the wife's greed and infidelity do what the fiend never could alone: damn his soul.

PICTURES IN THE FIRE

The title story in *Pictures in the Fire*, depicts Hollywood as the center of contractual arrangements with the Devil, a Hollywood agent selling the souls of his clients in film options, and a finicky actress so distracting that the Devil himself fails to renew an option for a soul. In "Bird of Prey," the Devil is a monstrous bird who spawns an equally monstrous offspring, whose vocal imitations lead to domestic malice and damnation. "Hell Hath No Fury" depicts what happens when a fallen angel and a humanized fiend become roommates and what types of men they attract. "Fallen Angel," in turn, demonstrates the power of psychological jargon and Freudian analysis to transform angel to housewife and the foulest fiend into a "tailless" boring Wall Street success. Such stories call attention to the number of Devil/hell/fire related expressions, such as "damn and blast you," "a devilish situation," "hellishly dull," "carry you to Hell for tuppence," "fought like a demon," and "getting on like a house on fire."

The last two tales in the Devil set fit in with another common Collier concern: the effects of women on innocent mankind. Many (but not all) of Collier's women are obsessive, selfish tyrants or greedy, sexually driven manipulators, whom *The New York Times* critic Thomas Lask describes as "predatory, bloodsucking, life-throttling and generally plain nasty." Even when they are more positive figures, they have disturbing, disruptive effects on poor males. In other words, there is a misogynistic edge to many of the stories. "Sleeping Beauty" is among the most negative of the lot. In it, an educated young man of erudite diction, charmed by a beautiful but sleeping young lady in a carnival act, spends a fortune to buy the act,

pay off despicable relatives, and hire a medical specialist to revive her. Her awakened persona, however, is that of a rude and vulgar slut, whose every word grates on sensitive ears and who is only ravishing when returned to silent slumber. Mrs. Beaseley, of "Incident on a Lake," is a domineering tyrant who destroys her husband's happiness at every opportunity but who is finally done in by an even more beastly creature than she. The innocent-seeming beauty of "If Youth Knew If Age Could" is really the corrupted plaything of a rich old man.

"DE MORTUIS"

Collier's husbands murder wives or vice versa. In "De Mortuis," a doctor repairing his basement floor learns of his young wife's lascivious behavior from sympathetic male visitors who think he has murdered her and approve; when her return seems to confirm his newly aroused suspicions, he cements her corpse in the cellar. Readers hear only his sweet invitation for her to see his handiwork in the cellar; all the rest is implied. The horror of the tale comes from the speed with which an educated and presumably human doctor accepts the hearsay evidence of rude, bragging bumpkins and acts on it, without even providing his wife a chance at rebuttal or defense. In "Back for Christmas," a henpecked Dr. Carpenter miscalculates his wife's fanatical obsession with control and efficiency and finds his carefully contrived and seemingly perfect murder exposed, while the husband in "Three Bears Cottage," angered by his wife's seemingly selfish choice of the better eggs for herself, plots to poison her with deadly mushrooms only to discover that her "generosity" makes his plan backfire (and frees her to run off with a man waiting in the wings). In "Over Insurance," a negative version of O'Henry's "Gift of the Magi," two lovebirds find that the costly purchase of insurance to benefit the one or the other in case of sudden demise leads to poverty, unhappiness, selfish obsession, and double poisoning.

"A MATTER OF TASTE," "THE CHASER," "LITTLE MOMENTO"

"A Matter of Taste" follows a traditional detective format as members of the Medusa Club discuss exotic means of murder and a consulting pathologist to the Home Office relates a famous murder case in which a husband, suspected of having given his wife poisoned chocolates, has actually made chocolates so appetizing that she ate herself to death. The short classics "The Chaser" and "Little Momento" are masterpieces of understatement. In "The Chaser," a murder *in potencia* depends on the naïveté of the young lover who expects romance to endure statically forever and to remain pleasurable, in contrast to the knowing cynicism of the apothecary who understands that change is essential and that unchanging, overpowering love can lead to boredom and hatred. In "Little Momento," a seemingly kindly old man, showing off his peculiar mementos reminiscent of past romantic indiscretions and domestic crimes in his neighborhood, actually provides his listener a motive and a plan for murder and himself a new memento to show off to future visitors.

"THE LADY ON THE GREY"

"The Lady on the Grey" is a bit of a turnaround for Collier, for its males are Anglo-Irish womanizers who, together with their ancestors, have deflowered the peasants of their county for more than three centuries and who finally get their comeuppance from a queenly ghost who transforms them into wretched curs. In "Without Benefit of Galsworthy," a foolish retired major, a *pukka sahib*, gives up everything, his wife and children, his club and job and reputation, for a servant girl, who, upon finally being informed of his passion, refuses to have anything to do with him (he blames her refusal on the "bloody Bolsheviks"), while in "Think No Evil" an unreasonably jealous husband keeps throwing his wife and best friend together, hoping to find evidence of her infidelity, until, after a number of years of such forced encounters, they do finally succumb, but, just as he is ready to murder them for their suspected acts, innocently reveal the unexpected recentness of their passion.

FANCIES AND GOODNIGHTS

Collier describes his *Fancies and Goodnights* as "a continuing blunder toward an arbitrary, surrealist way of expressing things," and some of his grimmer fantasies are indeed surreal. Most memorable is his "Green Thoughts," in which a hybrid orchid, among the effects of a friend who died mysteriously while

on expedition, proves a deadly carnivore, consuming first the family cat and then family member after family member. A profligate young nephew, however, who recognizes his family's faces amid the strange new buds of this rapidly growing plant, proves even deadlier, for the plant simply acts out of its nature in a passive, plantlike way, whereas the nephew's animal instincts make him nasty and vengeful. The final line of this tale is vintage Collier:

> Among fish, the dory, they say, screams when it is seized upon by man; among insects, the caterpillar of the death's-head moth is capable of a still, small shriek of terror; in the vegetable world, only the mandrake could voice its agony—till now.

"EVENING PRIMROSE"

Another surreal tale is "Evening Primrose," an odd account of the secret and monstrous world of department store mannequins and the dropouts from the real world who move among them and are ultimately destroyed by them. Told by a poet who seeks sanctuary from urban headaches and finds the love of another longtime dropout, the story has the flavor of the film *Invasion of the Body Snatchers* in that it exposes the conformist attitudes of such department store creatures of the night, their distrust of social dissent, and their reliance on "Dark Men" to transform human outsiders into manageable mannequins.

"GAVIN O'LEARY"

On a lighter yet equally fantastic note, "Gavin O'Leary" traces the career of a sensitive flea, who absorbs into his nature the characteristics and personality of whatever person's blood he imbibes. As long as he is down on the farm, he is a well-adjusted creature, simple and content, but when the blood mixture becomes too heady during a romantic film, Gavin, the flea, imbued by his host's passion for a glamorous screenstar, becomes devoured by love for the actress and is not content until he reaches Hollywood and rests in her bosom. Her obsession with an egocentric male star, however, induces the same obsession in Gavin, who, now a performing Hollywood flea star, begins to reflect the decadence, egotism, and homosexuality of his new host (affecting "violet evening suits," "epicene underwear," and scandalously "strange parties" in Bel Air). Only a leap to the breast of a successful actress whose self-love assures his contentment saves him from the perversions of most Hollywood elite.

CRUELTY, VANITY, GREED

Stories about human cruelty, vanity, greed, indifference, and the strange obsessions associated with these characteristics abound. Particularly disturbing is "The Steel Cat," in which an inventor develops a silly contraption which he believes is a superior mousetrap and relies on a pet mouse of whom he has become very fond to demonstrate its virtues; however, the sadistic industrialist whom he tries to interest in marketing the invention plays on his greed to force him to let his pet die in the trap and then leaves with no intention of marketing such a product. In like manner, the bullheaded American businessman in "The Invisible Dove Dancer of Strathpheen Island" becomes obsessed with possessing what he thinks is an elusive beauty who is rejecting his suit and ends up wringing the neck of the creature he pursues. In "Midnight Blue," a wife previously dominated by her husband and children assumes the family power when she helps her husband cover up a murder he has committed. Then in "Wet Saturday," an entire family conspires to cover up a lumpish daughter's murder of a wished-for suitor and to place the blame entirely on an innocent and close family friend, who accidentally walks in on the crime. In "Ah, the University!" a stingy father who forces his son to study to be a cardsharp instead of a university student bets his fortune in hopes of a big win but leaves his winnings when he misunderstands his son's winning ploy, a ploy that will finance the son's university education.

THE SUPERNATURAL

Sometimes in Collier's fiction, the supernatural or the absurd infuses a common vice with extra pique. In "Old Acquaintance," a jealous husband is obsessed with his belief that his wife, who has in reality just died of pneumonia, is running around town with an old rival, whom he finally learns died months before. In "The Frog Prince," when a young lady's fiancé announces that he plans to marry an overweight moron instead because of the value of her dowry, the jilted lady disguises herself as a man and courts and mar-

ries the moron herself. Later a medical miracle dispels the fat to reveal "a lean, agile, witty, and very handsome man" with whom, after a necessary role reversal, she lives quite happily. "Seasons of Mists" concerns bigamy, deception, and betrayal. In it, a young man falls in love with identical twins and, deciding he must have both, marries them both under the guise of being himself a set of identical twins. Then, when marriage brings boredom, he becomes his own rival and persuades each of his wives to cheat with his supposed brother; their imagined betrayal stirs his jealousy and destroys his marriages.

Collier attacks Hemingway-style artists in "Variation on a Theme" and "Collaboration." The writer in "Variation on a Theme" adopts a gorilla to help him instill the primitive in his efforts. Ironically, the gorilla, impressed by the author's clever stylistics, secretly trades novels, only to find his own a literary success and the true artist's work rejected as obscene, seditious libel. "Collaboration" focuses on a stylist who requires an infusion of he-man life experiences to make his books salable but who must pay the price of his wife's infidelity for his artistic success.

SURPRISE ENDINGS

Collier takes pleasure in surprise endings or unique, unexpected twists. His stories often end with an amusing moral, such as that of "Halfway to Hell," which concludes that girls who "play fast and loose with the affections of small men with blue eyes" may "find themselves left in the lurch," a disturbing transformation (the would-be arsonist in "Great Possibilities" becomes head of a fire brigade), or a stinging truth (the lifelike dummy created for a ventriloquist act in "Spring Fever" seems more real than its creator). At other times, the reader is left to imagine the horrors to come, as at the end of "Bottle Party," when a rowdy, sex-starved ship's crew "unstopper" a genie bottle at sea and find a duped male instead of a beautiful female genie: "Their disappointment knew no bounds, and they used him with the utmost barbarity." Sometimes there is an expected reversal, as in "Are You Too Late or Was I Too Early." In this story, a man who falls in love with a spirit who moves on the edge of his consciousness discovers that perhaps he is the spirit who haunts her. At other times there is a telling revelation. "The Touch of Nutmeg Makes It," which first appeared in *A Touch of Nutmeg and More Unlikely Stories*, for example, concerns a man acquitted for murder because of a lack of evidence, but more particularly, a lack of motive; the story ends with a final statement that reveals to his kindhearted listeners, the readers, and the speaker himself the obsessive and unexpected motive which compelled his hideous deed.

A number of Collier's tales hinge on a confusion between animate and inanimate, human and inhuman, with mannequins being taken for humans and humans for mannequins, with fleas, pigs, plants, cats, and gorillas behaving in human ways and humans behaving in subhuman ways. Sexual conquest, infidelity, and narcissism lead to comedy, obsession, and murder. Lovers hide in trunks, pose as stuffed trophies, and reduce themselves to absurdity in a variety of ways. Humans struggle for eternal youth, while sickness, old age, and death catch them unawares. Vulgar commercialism replaces older values. Appearance belies reality, and reality fades into a hazy mist filled with apparitions; evil and good are difficult to separate; and life is an ironic joke with a trick ending. Only ordinary people with no pretentions win sympathy for their plight.

OTHER MAJOR WORKS

LONG FICTION: *His Monkey Wife: Or, Married to a Chimp*, 1930; *Tom's A-Cold*, 1933 (also as *Full Circle*, 1933); *Defy the Foul Fiend: Or, The Misadventures of a Heart*, 1934; *The Poacher*, 1935.

PLAYS: *Wet Saturday*, 1941; *John Milton's "Paradise Lost": Screenplay for Cinema of the Mind*, 1973.

SCREENPLAYS: *Sylvia Scarlett*, 1936 (with Gladys Unger and Mortimer Offner); *Elephant Boy*, 1937 (with Akos Tolnay and Marcia de Silva); *Her Cardboard Lover*, 1942; *Deception*, 1946 (with Joseph Than); *Roseanna McCoy*, 1949; *The African Queen*, 1951 (original screenplay); *The Story of Three Loves*, 1953 (with Jan Lustig and George Froeschel); *I Am a Camera*, 1955; *The War Lord*, 1965 (with Millard Kaufman).

POETRY: *Gemini: Poems*, 1931.

NONFICTION: *Just the Other Day: An Informal History of Great Britain Since the War*, 1932 (with Iain Lang).

EDITED TEXT: *The Scandal and Credulities of John Aubrey*, 1931.

BIBLIOGRAPHY

Kessel, John J. "John Collier." In *Supernatural Fiction Writers: Fantasy and Horror, 2: A. E. Coppard to Roger Zelazny*, edited by Everett Franklin Bleiler. New York: Scribner's, 1985. A brief introduction to Collier's fantasy fiction, commenting on selected works of fiction and placing him within a context of fantasy writers.

Lachman, Marvin S. "John Collier." In *British Mystery Writers, 1920-1939*. Vol. 77 in *Dictionary of Literary Biography*. Detroit: Gale Research, 1989. Lachman explores Collier's skill in writing about domestic murder and malice and praises his economical style, his clever turns of speech, and his "small miracles of characterization."

Milne, Tom. "The Elusive John Collier." *Sight and Sound* 45 (Spring, 1976): 104-108. Milne discusses Collier's career as a film writer and provides a brief analysis of his fiction.

Richardson, Betty. *John Collier*. Boston: Twayne, 1983. Richardson provides a comprehensive survey of Collier's life and milieu, poetry, novels, screenplays, and short fiction to argue that Collier was a radical, a craftsman, a visionary, and a clever and iconoclastic social satirist unappreciated in his time but worthy of revaluation today. Born into a world of Victorian values, he was skeptical of twentieth century dogmas and ideologies that he feared restricted human behavior and crippled human aspirations. Richardson concludes that Collier's "witty, jaunty, honest, and clear-sighted" writing will endure and blames his neglect on his unusual variety of literary forms, changing critical tastes, his publication in popular journals, and his own personal modesty.

Theroux, Paul. *Sunrise with Sea Monsters*. Boston: Houghton Mifflin, 1985. Theroux praises the heroine of *His Monkey Wife*, Emily the chimpanzee, as "sensitive, witty, resourceful," and personable, and he argues that humans pale beside her. He says that Collier attacks "the jaded twenties types" as "true apes" in need of a "simian redeemer." He finds the misogyny in Collier's tales "wickedly cheerful" and "irresistible" and Collier himself "one of the great literary unclassifiables . . . another synonym for genius."

Vanatta, Dennis. *The English Short Story: 1945-1980*. Boston: Twayne, 1985. Brief discussion of Collier's fantasies; including discussions of "Evening Primrose," "Witch's Money," and "Three Bears Cottage"; comments on Collier's precise style that is often marked by excessive cleverness.

Gina Macdonald

WILLIAM CONGREVE

Born: Bardsey, Yorkshire, England; January 24, 1670
Died: London, England; January 19, 1729

<small>PRINCIPAL SHORT FICTION</small>
Incognita: Or, Love and Duty Reconcil'd, 1692

<small>OTHER LITERARY FORMS</small>

William Congreve wrote four comedies and one quite financially successful tragedy (*The Mourning Bride*, 1697). He is best known for his play *The Way of the World* (1700), although *The Old Batchelor* (1693) was more popular during his lifetime. *The Double Dealer* (1693) is his darkest comedy, and *Love for Love* (1695) is currently favored by anthologists, who see it as both readable and playable. Congreve also wrote poetry, lyrics which were set by such famous musicians as Henry Purcell and John Eccles, and an opera, *Semele* (1710). He translated works of Ovid, Homer, Juvenal, and Persius and collaborated with William Walsh and Sir John Vanbrugh on a translation of Jean-Baptiste Poquelin Molière's *Monsieur de Pourceaugnac* (1669), known as *Squire Trelooby* (1704).

<small>ACHIEVEMENTS</small>

Better known for his plays than for his fiction, translations, and poetry, Congreve was one of the later writers of Restoration comedy and is generally credited with bringing that genre to its maturity. Acclaimed for his clever plotting, his gift for characterization, and his witty and elegant dialogue, Congreve

is considered one of the greatest playwrights of the Restoration. Following the phenomenal success of his first play, *The Old Batchelor*, Congreve enjoyed great popularity as a playwright, until the failure of what is considered to be his masterwork, *The Way of the World*. Discouraged by the failure and financially secure as a result of previous stage success and a series of lucrative government posts secured for him by a patron, Congreve eventually gave up writing for the stage.

<small>BIOGRAPHY</small>

Because William Congreve's father was in the army, the family moved several times, one of their longest tours being in Ireland. Congreve attended Kilkenny College (where he met Jonathan Swift), Trinity College in Dublin, and finally the Middle Temple in London. After he wrote *Incognita* and his five plays, Congreve at the age of thirty went into semiretirement as a writer. This action was partially a result of an accusation by the clergyman Jeremy Collier that his work was immoral and profane, and also because he was disappointed in public reaction toward his personal attempts to move toward a more aesthetic art form. Although Congreve never married, he was devoted to at least two women: the actress Anne Bracegirdle, for whom he devised most of his charming, independent, female roles; and Henrietta, the second Duchess of Marlborough, by whom he had a daughter, Mary. Congreve was in poor health during his later years, suffering from cataracts and poor eyesight, gout and recurring lameness, and obe-

William Congreve (Library of Congress)

sity. He died in London in 1729 and was buried in Westminster Abbey.

ANALYSIS

In the preface to *Incognita*, Congreve explains that the tale was written "in imitation of dramatic writing," and he boasts that he observes in it the three classic unities of time, place, and action (which he renames contrivance). The story resembles nothing so much as William Shakespeare's *Romeo and Juliet* (c. 1595) without a tragic ending. The two major male characters, Aurelian and his look-alike Hippolito, who have been schoolmates in Siena, arrive in Florence just in time to enter the festivities centering on the upcoming wedding of Donna Catharina, a kinswoman to the great Duke. The young men decide to participate in disguise, lest Aurelian's father restrain their merriment. At the masquerade ball that evening, both young men fall in love, Aurelian with a beautiful young lady who wishes to be known as Incognita, and Hippolito with Leonora, who mistakes him for her cousin Don

Lorenzo, whose costume he has bought. On the next day the two young students perform so admirably in the lists that they are granted the honor of the field. Recognizing his son, Don Fabio announces that the wedding of Aurelian and Juliana, which had been previously arranged by the parents, would take place the next day. As Aurelian and Hippolito had exchanged names upon entering Florence, Leonora thinks she is defying custom when she marries Aurelian (who is actually Hippolito). Incognita, who is really Juliana, swoons, runs away in male disguise, and suffers greatly because she feels that because of her love she must disobey her father and marry Hippolito (who proves to be Aurelian, after all). Two family feuds are settled by the marriage, which is approved by both generations after the mistaken identities are revealed.

Walter Allen in *The English Novel* says that "before 'Incognita' prose fiction had been artless in form; indeed, form can hardly be said to have existed at all." He adds that *Incognita* represents in miniature "the formal aspects" of the fiction later associated with Jane Austen, Henry James, and Ivy Compton-Burnett. The civilized, polished, skeptical, and humorous voice of the author gives *Incognita* its unity, but because fiction writing was as yet not a socially acceptable occupation for a gentleman, Congreve abandoned that art form to write drama.

The importance of *Incognita* lies not only in the fact that it is such an early example of short fiction but also in that its form is so unusual, yet perceptible. It is so dramatic that readers can almost visualize the puckish stage-manager-author standing just offstage and commenting wittily to the audience. The young author indeed intrudes upon this narrative frequently, utilizing the same sophisticated, elegant humor that he is later to allow the protagonists in *The Way of the World*. Congreve includes directions for lighting, sound, and costume, employs theatrical imagery, and permits the tale to fall into an almost visible five-act comedy division. Antecedent action is revealed early, and, at what would surely be the end of Act I, the audience learns that the purchase of Lorenzo's costume for Hippolito is going to cause the visitors some problems.

Just as Congreve the dramatist was later to with-hold the introduction of his ladies until Act II, he acquaints us with Leonora and Incognita at the ball only after the reader has become well acquainted with their two young men. The ball and the tilting (which occur in what would be Acts II and V of a drama) contribute to the symmetry of structure, as both are gatherings of society to which Aurelian and Hippolito are admitted in disguise. The beginning of the tale involves preparations for disguise and offers a balance to the conclusion, when all disguises are removed. Scenes complicated by mistaken identity abound, and after disclosures, discoveries, and recognition, the story ends in a comic celebration with the entire company awaiting the wedding of Aurelian and Juliana. Since *Incognita* begins with the wedding of Catherine and Ferdinand, the symmetry is complete. All "knots" are easily untied, but the spectator-reader will see that the action has not been as probable as Congreve has promised in his preface. The four major characters remain disguised, literally or figuratively, for most of the narrative's unfolding, affirming its artificiality and emphasizing the difference between appearance and reality, and illusion and life.

OTHER MAJOR WORKS

PLAYS: *The Old Batchelor*, pr., pb. 1693; *The Double Dealer*, pr. 1693; *Love for Love*, pr., pb. 1695; *The Mourning Bride*, pr., pb. 1697; *The Way of the World*, pr., pb. 1700; *The Judgement of Paris*, pr., pb. 1701 (masque); *Squire Trelooby*, pr., pb. 1704 (with Sir John Vanbrugh and William Walsh; adaptation of Molière's *Monsieur de Pourceaugnac)*; *Semele*, pb. 1710 (libretto); *The Complete Plays of William Congreve*, pb. 1967 (Herbert Davis, editor).

POETRY: *Poems upon Several Occasions*, 1710.

NONFICTION: *Amendments of Mr. Collier's False and Imperfect Citations*, 1698; *William Congreve: Letters and Documents*, 1964 (John C. Hodges, editor).

TRANSLATIONS: *Ovid's Art of Love, Book III*, 1709; *Ovid's Metamorphoses*, 1717 (with John Dryden and Joseph Addison).

MISCELLANEOUS: *Examen Poeticum*, 1693; *The Works of Mr. William Congreve*, 1710; *The Complete Works of William Congreve*, 1923 (4 volumes).

BIBLIOGRAPHY

Hodges, John C. *William Congreve: The Man*. New York: Modern Language Association of America, 1941. Though somewhat dated, this is still a good standard biography of Congreve. Hodges traces Congreve's youth in Ireland, his college years at Trinity College, Dublin, his life among the coffeehouses and theaters of London, and his relationships with the actress Annie Bracegirdle and the Duchess of Marlborough. A readable introduction to Congreve's life, this volume also briefly discusses his major works.

Lindsay, Alexander, and Howard Erskine-Hill, eds. *Congreve: The Critical Heritage*. London: Routledge, 1989. An anthology of critical material on Congreve, divided into three sections: "The Early Reception, 1691-1700," "The Eighteenth-Century Response, 1701-1793," and "The Nineteenth Century and After, 1802-1913." Included are many interesting pieces by contemporaries such as John Dryden and Joseph Addison, and a poem praising Congreve by his friend Jonathan Swift. Though no modern criticism is included, this volume is invaluable as a record of responses to Congreve's work in literary history.

Love, Harold. *Congreve*. Oxford, England: Basil Blackwell, 1974. Love begins with a brief biographical sketch of Congreve and a general discussion of his works, with an interesting focus on the theatrical milieu of the Restoration and the way Congreve's writing may have been affected by the actors and actresses he knew and had in mind as he wrote. Individual chapters on *The Old Batchelour, The Double Dealer, Love for Love*, and *The Way of the World* discuss these major works in detail. The final chapter, "Some Dissenters," outlines and then counters some common arguments against Congreve's greatness as a dramatist.

Morris, Brian, ed. *William Congreve*. London: Ernest & Benn, 1972. The nine essays in this record of the York Symposium of 1970 deal mainly with Congreve's four major comedies (*The Old Batchelour, The Double Dealer, Love for Love*, and *The Way of the World*). Critical examinations of the texts address areas such as "Wit and Convention in Congreve's Comedies," "Plot and Meaning in Congreve's Comedies," and "Passion, 'Poetical Justice,' and Dramatic Law." A few essays deal with the staging of Congreve's plays, including a piece by Kenneth Muir on modern revivals of the plays with fascinating accounts of Dame Edith Evans as Millamant, Sir John Gielgud as Mirable and Valentine, and Sir Laurence Olivier as Tattle.

Thomas, David. *William Congreve*. New York: St.

Martin's Press, 1992. A good introduction to the life and works of Congreve. Includes bibliographical references and an index.

Young, Douglas M. *The Feminist Voices in Restoration Comedy: The Virtuous Women in the Playworlds of Etherege, Wycherley, and Congreve.* Lanham, Md.: University Press of America, 1997. A thoughtful examination of the female characters in the fiction and drama of Congreve, Sir George Etherege, and William Wycherly.

Sue L. Kimball, updated by Catherine Swanson

EVAN S. CONNELL, JR.

Born: Kansas City, Missouri; August 17, 1924

PRINCIPAL SHORT FICTION

The Anatomy Lesson and Other Stories, 1957
At the Crossroads: Stories, 1965
Saint Augustine's Pigeon, 1980
The Collected Stories of Evan S. Connell, 1995

OTHER LITERARY FORMS

Evan S. Connell, Jr.'s literary career extends across all forms and genres. He wrote a number of highly successful and acclaimed short stories and novels, including *Mrs. Bridge* (1959) and *Mr. Bridge* (1969), which have been recognized as minor modern classics, and *The Alchymist's Journal* (1991). He also wrote book-length poems. In nonfiction, Connell produced studies of famous explorers in *A Long Desire* (1979) and a collection of essays on various subjects, *The White Lantern* (1980). One of his most popular works is *Son of the Morning Star: Custer and the Little Bighorn* (1984), an acute, penetrating, and poetic meditation on the often tragic relationship between white settlers and Native Americans.

ACHIEVEMENTS

Evan S. Connell, Jr.'s first novel, *Mrs. Bridge*, was a best-seller and was nominated for the National Book Award for Fiction in 1960. Connell's writing

earned him Saxton and John Simon Guggenheim Memorial Foundation Fellowships and a Rockefeller Foundation grant. *Son of the Morning Star* was a best-seller and won for Connell a National Book Critics Circle Award. In 1987 he was honored with an American Academy and Institute of Arts and Letters Award.

BIOGRAPHY

Evan Shelby Connell, Jr., was born in Kansas City, Missouri, the son and grandson of physicians. He attended Southwestern High School in Kansas City, and later Dartmouth College in Hanover, New Hampshire. Through his early college years, Connell intended to become a doctor; this ambition changed, however, after he left Dartmouth to serve in the United States armed forces during World War II. Leaving Dartmouth before he graduated, Connell joined the Navy, where he was assigned to flight school, becoming first a pilot and then, after completing his training, a flight instructor. During his time in the Navy, from 1943 through 1945, he saw no actual combat. When Connell completed his military service, he enrolled in the University of Kansas and finished his undergraduate education there with a degree in English. Further studies followed at Stanford University, Columbia University, and San Francisco City College (now San Francisco State University). In addition to enrolling in writing courses, Connell took courses in art, especially painting and sculpture.

Having embarked upon a literary career, Connell began publishing his short stories in various small and literary magazines. The quality of his work was recognized early, and writings soon appeared in anthologies. His work was chosen for *Prize Stories: The O. Henry Awards* in 1949 and again in 1951, and his works were published in *The Best American Short Stories* in 1955. His first collection of stories, *The Anatomy Lesson and Other Stories*, appeared in 1957, causing critics to take note of this new and strikingly different talent. Throughout most of Connell's career, his reputation among critics and other writers has been consistently higher than his recognition among the general public. Fairly early recognition of Connell's abilities also came in the form of grants, fellowships, and awards.

In addition to his own writing, Connell was active from 1959 through 1965 as the editor of *Contact*, a literary magazine published in California, where he made his home. One of Connell's earlier books, his novel *Mrs. Bridge*, was quickly recognized as a modern classic by a small but discerning band of readers. The companion work, *Mr. Bridge*, was also accorded the status of a cult classic. Connell's first real popular success was his 1984 study of Custer and the Indian wars, *Son of the Morning Star*. He spent four years researching for the book, reading firsthand accounts and visiting the battle site of the Little Bighorn four times. The 1991 *The Alchymist's Journal* also earned praise from critics as a "highly cerebral and wisdom-filled work." Connell eventually made his home in Santa Fe, New Mexico.

ANALYSIS

Evan S. Connell, Jr., is a careful and precise writer, whose fictions capture and reveal their meanings through detail, observation, and implication. Settings and descriptions of how his characters dress and appear offer subtle but unmistakable clues to the inner lives of the individuals in Connell's stories. Quite often these individuals appear to be conventional, even boring characters; Mr. and Mrs. Bridge, for example, seem at first to be almost numbingly normal. A closer

and more sympathetic examination, however, shows that even the mask of midwestern, middle American normality often covers passion, doubts, and dreams.

Connell is a master of the quotidian, the everyday or ordinary. Sometimes he uses the everyday settings in a satirical fashion, exposing the gap between modern culture's stated beliefs and its actions. This satire, however, is generally restrained, even muted, rather than being broad or forced. More open and pointed attacks are found not in Connell's prose fictions but in his long poems, especially *Points for a Compass Rose* (1973), which is overtly political.

Connell is most concerned with the people in his stories and in the baffling, mysterious fashions in which they fall in and out of love, rejoice over happy events, cry over sad ones, and, in essence, live their everyday but compellingly wonderful lives. Through an extensive but not obtrusive vocabulary and a lean, economical prose style, Connell reveals these everyday people and their lives as matters worth careful observation and consideration.

Each story by Connell creates, in the space of only a few pages, a world that is uniquely its own. This world may be, and often is, connected with the every-

Evan S. Connell, Jr. (Janet Fries)

day world of modern American life, but inevitably it also carries with it the hint of other ways, other views, and these provide insight into more varied experiences. Often these alternate lifestyles are introduced by a character who disturbs the tranquil flow of the ordinary and then fades from the story. There is something more possible than ordinary life, these characters suggest, and this suggestion and the reactions of other figures in the story to it are central to Connell's fictions.

"THE FISHERMAN FROM CHIHUAHUA"

Sometimes this sense of otherness is presented obliquely, as in "The Fisherman from Chihuahua." In this story, the ordinary restaurant known as Pendleton's is visited by a tall, mysterious Mexican who suddenly, and for no explicable reason, begins to sing a piercing, meaningless dirge. Although at first annoyed, the owner and his regular patrons begin to look forward to the man's visits and his unearthly singing, which reveal a glimpse of something that they cannot name. When the tall Mexican abruptly ceases his visits, those who remain are left with a sense of loss.

"THE WALLS OF AVILA"

This division between necessary but boring life and romantic adventures is explored more explicitly in a pair of stories featuring the character known only by his initials, J. D. In "The Walls of Avila," J. D. returns to his hometown after years of wandering throughout Europe, Africa, and Asia. J. D. spins eloquent and elaborate tales of his adventures, and his stories are packed with such vivid detail that they make distant places, such as the ancient village of Avila, in Spain, seem as real as New York or as tangible as a suburban house. J. D.'s tales leave his childhood friends depressed and angry because they are now older, more "mature," and established but feel they have missed the adventures of life. J. D. has given them a glimpse of a romantic life that is denied to them, perhaps because of their own failures or fears.

"THE PALACE OF THE MOORISH KINGS"

These themes are explored in even greater detail in "The Palace of the Moorish Kings." Again, J. D. spins his wonderful yarns, and apparently the man

has been everywhere: the Black Pagoda in Konorak, the islands of Micronesia, the painted caves of Altamira. Now, he wishes to return home, get married, and find a job. His friends are partly relieved by this decision, since it affirms that their choices and lives have been, after all, correct. At the same time, however, they sense that when J. D. settles down it will mark the end to their own dreams, even as lived through him. One of them attempts to explain their mixed feelings to J. D.: "It's simply that you have lived as the rest of us dreamed of living, which is not easy for us to accept."

"ARCTURUS"

One of Connell's most ambitious and fully realized flights in short fiction has been his series of stories about the Muhlbach family, who live across the river from Manhattan in a moderately exclusive New Jersey suburb. Like the Bridges, who appeared in short stories before receiving more extended treatment in novels, the Muhlbachs have appeared in both stories and novels, and one of the short stories, "The Mountains of Guatemala," later reappeared, revised, as the opening chapter of the novel *Double Honeymoon* (1976).

By returning to the same characters in successive stories, Connell is able to develop them more fully and completely. This gradual development is especially important for Karl Muhlbach, since his inner life and especially his emotional crises following the death of his wife are the central themes of all these stories. That death is signaled in typically indirect Connell fashion in the first of the Muhlbach stories, "Arcturus." This is a key story in the body of Connell's work for several reasons: First, it introduces the Muhlbach family; second, "Arcturus" is a high point in Connell's literary technique of presenting deeply emotional, disturbing events through oblique reference. In many ways, "Arcturus" is powerful precisely because of what is not said, what is left unexpressed. Finally, the story is one of the best pieces of American short fiction written during the second half of the twentieth century.

The plot of "Arcturus" is deceptively simple. Karl Muhlbach and his wife, Joyce, are expecting a guest, Sandy Kirk. Sandy is an old boyfriend of Joyce, and the reader learns through hints that he has been asked for a final visit because Joyce is dying. As the Muhlbachs wait, their children, Otto and Donna, drowse by the fireplace. Otto is aware that something is going to happen, that some tension pervades the room, but he cannot quite recognize it. Still, it troubles him throughout the evening, even after he is put to bed; later, when Sandy has left, Karl must reassure his son that everything will be well, but even as he says the words, he doubts them.

"Arcturus" is a story about perceptions. Connell structures his narrative so that the reader shares directly the thoughts of Karl and his son, and those of Sandy Kirk, but Joyce Muhlbach, the very center of the story, remains closed and unexplained. Her actions and remarks can be observed, but the reader must attempt to deduce their underlying causes with little assistance from the author. In a sense, this is the very position in which the men of the story find themselves, as they struggle to understand what Joyce is trying to tell them and to comprehend what she wants to hear.

Perceptions vary. Sandy, who at first seems to be so much more sophisticated and worldly than Karl, turns out to be the less imaginative and intuitive of the two men. Although he once thought that he was in love with Joyce, Sandy cannot understand her, and he leaves the Muhlbachs' house not only confused but also a little frightened. Karl, on the other hand, emerges as a much more generous and expansive soul, full of unexpected talents (such as speaking German) or knowledge (most notably of astronomy). Finally, Otto, being poised between childhood and adolescence, has the unique perspective which that precarious position brings; as noted, he recognizes the tension in the house but cannot comprehend its cause. "Are the stars falling?" he asks his father, his symbolic question for all disorder and confusion. In a sense, with the death of Joyce, the stars will fall for the family; still, Karl Muhlbach answers "no," and his son is reassured.

In this story, Connell deliberately echoes one of the great masterpieces of modern short fiction, James Joyce's "The Dead," an intention signaled even by the name of Mrs. Muhlbach, Joyce. The parallels be-

tween the two works are many and striking, and it seems clear that Connell is fashioning an answer to the earlier work. Both stories take place in winter, during a snowfall, and in each a husband must confront and react to his wife's earlier affections for another man. In "The Dead," the former lover is dead and buried, while in "Arcturus" it is the wife who will soon die. Even scenes are repeated, although with a twist, for in Joyce's story the husband stands at a second-story window looking out over a snow-covered landscape, while in Connell's it is Karl who stands on the ground, staring up at the windows of his own house. Despite these differences, both men experience a sense of loss and isolation and realize intuitively that it is not only death but also life itself that can make men and women as separate and distant as stars.

"SAINT AUGUSTINE'S PIGEON"

The next story about the Muhlbachs is "Saint Augustine's Pigeon," in which Karl Muhlbach attempts to adjust to the death of Joyce and construct a new life for himself and his two children. These attempts are fumbling, even slightly pathetic, as Karl's emotional needs are complicated by his sexual desires. In "Saint Augustine's Pigeon," Karl Muhlbach impulsively leaves his placid suburban home one evening to travel into New York, where he intends to find a mistress.

Muhlbach's efforts are both desperate and farcical. In Greenwich Village, he plays chess with a young bohemian girl who calls herself Rouge, but after Karl wins the game he finds himself forced into buying soup for Rouge and two of her friends. After the meal, the young people abruptly vanish, and Karl finds himself alone. He then takes a taxi to a tawdry night spot called Club Sahara. It is aptly named, for here Karl Muhlbach finds only sterile shows of sex and has his pocket picked. Later, he must call a sick friend out of bed to have a check cashed in order to spend the night, drunk, in a hotel. His trip into the city has been an unmitigated disaster, a descent into hell.

Unfulfilled desire is the essence of "Saint Augustine's Pigeon," and what is important in the story is not Karl Muhlbach's actions but his reasons for them and his emotional responses. The story gains its title, and opens with a quotation from, the early Church father Saint Augustine of Hippo, and throughout the story Karl Muhlbach's perceptions are filtered through Augustine's philosophy of humankind's inherently sinful and incomplete nature. Although he is not very sinful, except in intention, Karl Muhlbach is certainly incomplete.

"THE MOUNTAINS OF GUATEMALA"

This incomplete nature is further explored in the story "The Mountains of Guatemala," in which Muhlbach again fails to make the human connection that he so desperately needs. Once more, he meets a younger woman, named Lambeth. By coincidence, Karl and Lambeth arrive at a party together, and everyone assumes that they are a couple. The irony of this is not lost on Karl, and it makes his isolation more acute than ever. Throughout the story, he broods over a tourist brochure of Guatemala, which gives the story its title and functions as a symbol of Muhlbach's unrealized dreams.

"OTTO AND THE MAGI"

These dreams change to nightmares in the third story in the sequence, "Otto and the Magi," an exploration of the relationship between Karl Muhlbach and his son, Otto, whose own small failures and defeats are echoes of his father's. In the key central portion of the story, Karl and Otto look over a government pamphlet about fallout shelters. In fact, Karl has already constructed a shelter in his own yard, and later that night he sleeps there, having horrible dreams. He awakens to find that he is suffocating, because Otto has stuffed a potato into the shelter's air intake valve.

The shelter is a symbol of Karl's life since the death of his wife. He has withdrawn, psychologically and emotionally, and now he literally goes underground, sealing himself off from a world that he can neither understand nor control. What Otto does can be seen as an attempt, typically fumbled, to reestablish the fragile links between father and son. As the story ends, it is questionable whether these links can be reestablished, since Karl turns again to logic and reason, rather than emotion, to understand and resolve his dilemma. Logic and reason, the Muhlbach stories suggest, are bleak resources with which to manage tangled human relations.

The Muhlbach series displays Connell's mastery of short fiction. Actions are sparse, and everyday events fill the stage: People meet, talk, fail to connect, regret the past, plan vaguely for the future. The real actions in these stories, as in most of Connell's fiction, are internal, in the thoughts and emotions of his characters. These inner lives are deep and often philosophical, and even such a seemingly commonplace character as Karl reveals deep and unsuspected attributes, listening to Johann Sebastian Bach, speaking German, quoting Saint Augustine. In these masterful stories, the quotidian world is shown to be full of human beings' deepest fears and most enduring dreams.

THE COLLECTED STORIES OF EVAN S. CONNELL

The Collected Stories of Evan S. Connell features an assemblage of fifty-six short stories written by the author between 1946 and 1995, including fifteen older stories and thirteen later ones never before published in book form. Arranged by common theme, the entries reflect the acerbic yet compassionate view the author holds toward his protagonists. In "Madame Broulard," a hollow French landlady is described "as so much alone, trying to hold on to something, anything, that retains a shred of meaning," an observation that could be applied to any number of his characters. Connell is a master of measuring the impact of great events through the eyes of the bourgeoisie. Broulard herself is torn between playing the generous host to an American visitor and being a victim of occupational forces, from German troops to American tourists. In "The Cuban Missile Crisis," the international nuclear dance of death between the Soviet Union and the United States is played out in the mind of one individual as he passes time in a New York pool hall.

Interspersed throughout the stories are the random indignities suffered by individuals. In "Mademoiselle from Kansas City," a New York prostitute is connected by chance to a customer from her old hometown, an occasion that threatens to shatter her self-imposed state of detachment from the past. The comedic tone in a few of his stories can take on a dark tone, as in "The Short Happy Life of Henrietta," the tale of a naïve Nebraska tourist in Paris who, because of a language gap, meets a gruesome death as the result of a foolish misunderstanding.

Connell returns to the theme of a romantic life denied in "The Most Beautiful," the story of a young Hispanic man living in squalid surroundings, who copes with his condition by engaging in an imaginary love affair with a model whose picture he has lifted from a magazine. A similar theme is examined in "Succubus," when a distinguished elderly gentleman relates a tale of unrequited love during a shipboard romance, an incident that forever frames his view of love. In each case Connell instills in his characters a persona and passion unlike that of the typically sterile middle-class figures who populate his longer fictions. In so doing, he offers an ambiguity that gives full range to his entire body of work.

Altogether, the stories demonstrate Connell's skill in providing his narratives with precise points of view that allow the reader to easily identify with the author's protagonists as they struggle with the vagaries of life. A critic once commented that Connell's view of the world as reflected in his stories was that of a man who felt "like a refugee in a precarious place." It is a situation his characters invariably find themselves in and one they have little hope or capability of escaping with their dignity still intact.

OTHER MAJOR WORKS

LONG FICTION: *Mrs. Bridge*, 1959; *The Patriot*, 1960; *The Diary of a Rapist*, 1966; *Mr. Bridge*, 1969; *The Connoisseur*, 1974; *Double Honeymoon*, 1976; *The Alchymist's Journal*, 1991; *Deus lo Volt! Chronicle of the Crusades*, 2000.

POETRY: *Notes from a Bottle Found on the Beach at Carmel*, 1963; *Points for a Compass Rose*, 1973.

NONFICTION: *A Long Desire*, 1979; *The White Lantern*, 1980; *Son of the Morning Star: Custer and the Little Bighorn*, 1984.

BIBLIOGRAPHY

Blaisdell, Gus. "After Ground Zero: The Writings of Evan S. Connell, Jr." *New Mexico Quarterly* 36 (Summer, 1966): 181-207. Contains helpful and revealing insight into Connell's earlier works, which include many of his formative short stories.

Brooke, Allen. "Introverts and Emigres." *New Criterion* 14 (October, 1995): 58-63. Brooke finds an uneven quality to the short stories of Connell. He believes Connell reserves his best stories for conventional characters, while those which deal with fashionable types are narrow and pointless.

Connell, Evan S., Jr. "Evan S. Connell." Interview by Patricia Holt. *Publishers Weekly* 220 (November 20, 1981): 12-13. Connell speaks perceptively about his efforts and aims in his writing, with some interesting sidelights on his critical and popular reception.

_____. "Evan S. Connell, Jr." Interview by Dan Tooker and Roger Hofheins. In *Fiction: Interviews with Northern California Writers*. New York: Harcourt Brace Jovanovich, 1976. Connell is often cited by critics as the foremost of the Northern California writers, who created a literary movement that has had considerable impact on contemporary American fiction. Connell is articulate in presenting his views, especially on the themes and methods of his own writing.

Myers, Edward. "Notes from a Bottle Found on the Beach at Sausalito: An Interview with Evan S. Connell." *The Literary Review* 35 (Fall, 1991): 60-69. In this wide-ranging interview, Connell discusses his literary influences and his interest in alchemy, the early West, and pre-Columbian art.

Sipper, Ralph B. "The Great Helmsman." Review of *The Collected Stories of Evan S. Connell*, by Evan S. Connell, Jr. *Los Angeles Times Book Review*, February 11, 1996, 3. Comments on the stories' urban settings as more barbarous than primitive ones, their characters who deny history, and closed-in beings with subdued passions ready to explode.

Wanner, Irene. "A Collection of Gems by Connell." *The Seattle Times*, March 3, 1996, p. M2. A review of *The Collected Stories of Evan S. Connell*; explains the language and pace of his stories and his control of multiple conflicts; discusses a number of the stories as finely wrought studies of human nature.

Michael Witkoski, updated by William Hoffman

JOSEPH CONRAD
Jósef Teodor Konrad Nałęcz Korzeniowski

Born: Near Berdyczów, Poland; December 3, 1857
Died: Oswalds, Bishopsbourne, England; August 3, 1924

PRINCIPAL SHORT FICTION
Tales of Unrest, 1898
Youth: A Narrative, and Two Other Stories, 1902
Heart of Darkness, 1899, 1902 (book)
Typhoon, and Other Stories, 1903
A Set of Six, 1908
'Twixt Land and Sea, 1912
Within the Tides, 1915
Tales of Hearsay, 1925
The Sisters, 1928
The Complete Stories of Joseph Conrad, 1933

OTHER LITERARY FORMS
Joseph Conrad is best known for his powerful and psychologically penetrating novels, which, like his shorter fiction, are often set in exotic locales, frequently the Far East, at sea, or a combination of the two, as with his most famous work *Lord Jim: A Tale* (1900). Even when using a more conventional setting, such as London in *The Secret Agent: A Simple Tale* (1907), or Geneva, Switzerland, in *Under Western Eyes* (1911), Conrad maintains a sense of otherness because his characters live in a moral shadow world of revolutionaries and adventures.

In addition to three plays based on his stories, Conrad produced three volumes of autobiographical writings, which, however, often conceal more than they explain about his varied and often dramatic personal life. Following his death, several edited collections of Conrad's correspondence were published, and these letters offer some insight into his fiction.

ACHIEVEMENTS
Joseph Conrad is one of the outstanding writers in English literature and, because of his background and achievements, occupies a unique position. To a great degree, Conrad was the creator of the psychological story and modern spy novel. Because of his genius and insight, Conrad transformed the typical setting of the adventure romance—the mysterious Far East, the shadowy underworld of the secret agent—into an acceptable setting for the serious writer and greatly expanded the range of English literature.

Conrad avoided direct narrative, presenting his plots as a tale told by someone who either recounted the events from memory or passed along a story heard from someone else. The narrator in a Conrad story also gives events obliquely, partially revealing them, speculating on their cause and possible meaning, and then adding new and often essential information, so that the reader must participate in interpreting the unfolding story.

Conrad used this method because he felt that it accurately reflected the manner in which people understand actions in real life but also employed it because of his characters, who cannot be understood quickly, for they are not simple persons. Complicated and often contradictory figures, their actions, like their personalities, must be apprehended gradually and from different angles.

A writer who did not learn English until his twenties, Conrad brought a sense of newness and scrupulous care to the language. He uses an extensive vocabulary, particularly in his descriptive passages of settings, internal as well as external. His style produces in the reader the moral and psychological equivalent to the emotions and inner struggles felt by the characters.

These qualities of plot, character, and style were recognized by the noted American critic H. L. Mencken when he wrote about Conrad that "[t]here was something almost suggesting the vastness of a natural phenomenon. He transcended all the rules."

BIOGRAPHY
Joseph Conrad had one of the most unusual lives of any major writer in English literature. He was born in Berdyczów, Poland, on December 3, 1857, and

Joseph Conrad (Library of Congress)

was christened Jósef Teodor Konrad Nałęcz Korzeniowski. His father, Apollo Korzeniowski, was a Polish intellectual and writer whose works included original verse and translations of William Shakespeare. Apollo Korzeniowski was also a fervent Polish patriot, and his activities against Russian repression (Poland was at that time part of the Russian Empire) caused his arrest and exile in 1861. Apollo Korzeniowski, along with his wife, Ewelina Bobrowska, and his young son, Josef, was sent to Vologda, a dismal town northeast of Moscow.

The climate was severe, and living conditions were harsh. Ewelina died in April, 1865, when young Josef was only seven years old. A few years later, after Apollo had been released from exile because of ill health, he too died, and at eleven years old, Josef was placed in the care of his maternal uncle, a kindly man who provided for his education and supported him with funds for many years.

Because of these memories and his own intense patriotism, Josef found life in occupied Poland unbearable, and, when doctors recommended a seaside environment for his own frail health, he left for Mar-

seilles, France, in October, 1874. In Marseilles, he lived on funds from his uncle and engaged in a shadowy enterprise to smuggle weapons to royalist rebels in Spain. In 1877, Josef and some companions bought a ship for that purpose, but their plot was betrayed and their vessel, the *Tremolino*, was deliberately run aground to avoid capture. The spring of the following year, having lost all of his money gambling at Monte Carlo, Josef attempted suicide. The wound was minor, and within a month he was able to sign aboard his first English ship, the *Mavis*. On April 24, 1878, Jósef Korzeniowski, soon known as Joseph Conrad, became an English sailor; he would remain one for the next seventeen years, serving on eighteen different vessels but commanding only one, the *Otago*, in 1888.

During these voyages, Conrad traveled to the settings for his stories. In 1883, he was second mate on board the *Palestine*, which caught fire and later sank, leaving the crew to survive in open boats until they reached land. In 1890, Conrad was in the Belgian Congo as part of a trading company, but within a year he left, his health seriously weakened by malaria and his psychological and moral sense severely shaken by the ruthless, amoral exploitation of the natives by Europeans who were avid for ivory.

By this time, Conrad had concluded that his seafaring career was unsuccessful, and he had already started work, in 1889, on his first novel, *Almayer's Folly* (1895), and achieved English citizenship in 1886. In January, 1894, Conrad ended his naval career, determined to become a writer. *Almayer's Folly* gained favorable critical notice, primarily for its exotic setting and characters. Conrad's next work, *An Outcast of the Islands* (1896), seemed to mark him as a talented but perhaps limited author of exotic romances. With the appearance of *The Nigger of the "Narcissus"* (1898), however, the literary world was forced to take note of a new and strikingly original talent.

Having dedicated himself to writing, Conrad settled at Pent Farm, in Kent, with his wife Jessie George, to whom he was married on March 24, 1896. The Conrads had two sons, Alfred Borys, born in 1898, and John Alexander, born in 1906.

As an author, Conrad was critically acknowledged but was not very popular for many years. Even such powerful novels as *Lord Jim: A Tale* or *Nostromo: A Tale of the Seaboard* (1904) or *Under Western Eyes*, which have since been recognized as classics, had relatively modest sales. To supplement his income, Conrad wrote shorter fiction for popular magazines; these stories were collected in eight volumes during Conrad's lifetime. In 1913 came his first truly popular work, *Chance*. Having achieved financial stability, Conrad moved in 1919 to Oswalds, near Canterbury, where he spent the remaining years of his life. He was offered, but declined, a knighthood in 1924. That same year, after long bouts of frequent bad health, he died of a heart attack on August 3. He was buried at Canterbury.

ANALYSIS

Throughout his career, Joseph Conrad returned to a constellation of central themes that were expressed through the actions of his characters and, more important, through those characters' reactions to events around them. These themes can best be considered when they are grouped into two generally opposing categories. A sense of personal, moral heroism and honor is contrasted to betrayal and guilt. Typically, a Conradian character will discover, in the crucible of a dangerous situation, that he does or does not live up to the inner standards he has hoped to maintain. This realization may not come immediately, and often the true meanings of a character's actions are revealed only long afterward, through a retelling of his story.

The second grouping contrasts illusion with reality. Illusion is often a belief in "progress" or some grand political scheme. It is unmasked by reality, which, in Conrad, inevitably assumes the form and tone of pessimistic irony. Through the device of a narrator recounting the story, the truth gradually emerges, revealing the tragic difference between what characters believe themselves and the world to be, and what they actually are.

"AN OUTPOST OF PROGRESS"

The division between these two groupings is present even in Conrad's early story "An Outpost of Prog-

ress." Like many of his fictions, it is set in the tropics, specifically a desolate ivory trading station in the isolated reaches of the Congo. Two hapless Europeans, Kayerts and Carlier, arrive at the station, filled with dreams of riches and slogans of civilization. They quickly disintegrate, their original illusions giving way to true madness. Kayerts shoots his companion, then hangs himself from a cross in the station's unkempt graveyard. The outpost of progress has been overrun by the forces of savagery.

The story is fiercely ironic. Kayerts and Carlier are caricatures, the first fat, the second thin, both incredibly stupid. "Incapable of independent thought," as Conrad describes them, they are lost without society to dictate their thoughts and actions. Although they loudly repeat the hollow slogans of progress, the two white men are obviously greatly inferior to their native helper, who watches their decay with dark satisfaction. Using simple, unsympathetic characters and a violent, even melodramatic plot, Conrad presents his themes in the starkest possible fashion.

"THE LAGOON"

In the story "The Lagoon," written at almost the same time as "An Outpost of Progress," Conrad handles the conflict between betrayal and guilt, on the one hand, and guilt versus honor and heroism, on the other, with more subtlety. An unnamed white man spends the night in the house of Arsat, a young Malay, who is tending his dying wife. During the long tropical night, Arsat tells his friend the story of how he and his brother had fled with the woman from their local chief. The three had been pursued and, at the moment of their escape, Arsat's brother had fallen behind and cried out for help. Arsat had not responded, however, fleeing instead to safety with his lover. Now, when she is dead, he speaks of returning for revenge.

In a moment of crisis Arsat made a decision, and for years he has suffered the moral consequences of that action. Although Conrad refrains from judging his character, Arsat clearly believes that he has failed; his only hope is to perform some heroic action, such as seeking vengeance, that will restore his earlier sense of himself as an honorable, loyal person and brother. Implicit in the story, however, is the sense that Arsat cannot undo the past and that his hopes are only illusions. This sense is reinforced powerfully by Conrad's extensive descriptions of the Malaysian jungle, which seems to overwhelm the characters, rendering them incapable of action while mocking their vain hopes.

"YOUTH"

"Youth," Conrad's first indisputable masterpiece among his shorter fictions, introduces his famous narrator Marlow. In the story, Marlow, forty-two when he tells his tale, recounts events that happened twenty years before when he sailed on the *Judea*, laden with a cargo of coal for Bangkok. An ill-fated ship, the *Judea* is beset by an endless, almost comical series of calamities that climaxes when the coal catches fire and explodes, leaving the crew to reach land in open boats. The events are drawn largely from Conrad's own experiences as mate on the *Palestine* in 1881.

The contrasts between heroism and cowardice, between reality and illusion run throughout the story, but Conrad blends them in a fashion that reveals that the distinctions between them are not as simple as might be supposed. As Marlow recognizes, his earlier self was full of the illusions of youth, yet it was those very illusions that sustained him and allowed him to achieve the standards by which he wished to live and act. In that sense, illusion made heroism possible. Such a situation is obviously ironic, and throughout his story Marlow comments frequently on the tangled relationship between romanticism and practicality, illusion and reality. Unlike other Conrad tales, however, "Youth" does not treat this division with pessimism but with optimism, no doubt because it is a story of youth and because Marlow, for whatever reason, did uphold his personal standards of integrity and moral courage.

HEART OF DARKNESS

Heart of Darkness, perhaps Conrad's most famous work, is a novella based on his experience as mate on the riverboat *Roi des Belges* in the Congo during 1890. In this story, Conrad once again uses Marlow as his main character and narrator, and the events are a literal and symbolic journey by Marlow into that "immense heart of darkness" that is both the African jungle and the human soul. A powerful, searing work,

Heart of Darkness is one of the first masterpieces of symbolism in English literature and Conrad's most acutely penetrating psychological study.

The story itself is relatively simple. Marlow signs on with a Belgian company that exports ivory from the Congo; employed as a mate on the company's steamboat, he sails upriver to meet the renowned Kurtz, a trader who has become legendary for the success of his efforts and the force of his character. Marlow has heard, however, that Kurtz is more than an ivory trader and that he has evolved into a powerful force of civilization and progress. When Marlow arrives at Kurtz's station, he finds instead that the man has reverted to savagery, becoming a dreaded, almost supernatural figure to the natives. The site is ringed with posts decorated with human skulls, and Kurtz's presence casts an evil presence over the African jungle. Marlow carries the sick, delirious Kurtz back down the river, but the man dies during the journey as the riverboat narrowly escapes an ambush by the terrified and outraged natives.

The impact of *Heart of Darkness* comes from the nearly devastating effects of what Marlow sees and experiences. A naïve young man in the earlier "Youth," Marlow is still relatively innocent at the start of *Heart of Darkness*. By the end of the story, that innocence has been forever shattered, a loss shared by the attentive reader. The world of the story grows increasingly corrupted and corrupting. The adventures Marlow undergoes become stranger, and the characters whom he meets are increasingly odd, starting with the greedy traders whom Marlow ironically describes as "pilgrims," to an eccentric Russian who wanders in dress clothes through the jungle, to Kurtz himself, that figure of ultimate madness. The native Africans, whether cruelly abused workers, actually slaves, of the trading company or savages in awe of Kurtz, retain a sort of primeval dignity, but they, too, are beyond Marlow's experience and initial comprehension. The Congo of *Heart of Darkness* is a strange and terrifying world, a place where the normal order of civilized life has become not only inverted but also perverted.

To render this complex and disturbing moral vision, Conrad uses an intricate framing structure for his narrative. The story opens with Marlow and four friends talking about their experiences. One of the listeners, who is never named, in turn conveys to the reader the story told by Marlow. This story-within-a-story shuttles back and forth, as Marlow recounts part of his tale, then comments upon it, and then often makes an additional reflection upon his own observations. In a sense, by retelling the events, Marlow comes to understand them, a process that is shared by the reader. Instead of interrupting the flow of the story, Marlow's remarks become an essential part of the plot, and often the reader does not fully understand what has happened until Marlow's explanations reveal the extent and significance of the action.

Heart of Darkness gains immensely through Conrad's use of symbolism, because much of the meaning of the story is too terrifying and bleak to be expressed in plain prose; the inhumanity and savagery of the European exploiters, Kurtz in particular, are expressed more powerfully through a symbolic, rather than overt, presentation. Throughout the narrative, clusters of images occur at significant points to underscore the meaning of events as Marlow comes to understand them. Opposites are frequent: Brightness is contrasted with gloom, the lush growth of the jungle is juxtaposed to the sterility of the white traders, and the luxuriant, even alarming life of the wild is always connected with death and decomposition. Running throughout the story are images and metaphors of madness, especially the insanity caused by isolation. The dominant symbol for the entire work is found in its title and final words: All creation is a vast "heart of darkness." Since its publication, *Heart of Darkness* has been recognized as a masterpiece of English literature, and readers have responded to the work on several different levels. An attack on imperialism, a parable of moral and ethical growth and decline, a psychological study—*Heart of Darkness* is all these things and something more.

"TYPHOON"

With the writing of "Typhoon," Conrad suspended his customary moral and psychological complexities to present a fairly straightforward sea story. The *Nan-Shan*, a vessel filled with Chinese coolies returning home from Malaysia, runs headlong into a ferocious typhoon. As the crew struggles above decks to save the ship, an equally dangerous furor erupts below, as the sea's violent motions scatter the passengers' baggage, mixing their hard-earned silver coins in total confusion. The Chinese begin a desperate combat among themselves, each man intent upon regaining his own money. Captain MacWhirr and his first mate, Jukes, must battle these two storms, either of which could wreck the ship.

Captain MacWhirr and Jukes are total opposites. MacWhirr is a stolid, perhaps stupid man, so devoid of imagination that he experiences little self-doubt and few terrors. Even the looming typhoon does not frighten him, since he has never experienced such a storm and cannot comprehend its dangers. Jukes, on the other hand, is a more typical Conradian character, sensitive, anxious to prove worthy of his own inner moral code, and acutely conscious of the dangers that the sea can pose. As with so many other figures in Conrad's fictions, Jukes seems to believe in a sense that these dangers are somehow meant for him personally, as a trial of his own character. MacWhirr suffers from no such beliefs, since they are beyond his comprehension.

With the onset of the typhoon, the seeming limitations of Captain MacWhirr become strengths, while Jukes's supposedly higher qualities might, if left unchecked, paralyze him at the critical moment. Ironically, MacWhirr is Jukes's salvation. Since the Captain lacks the imagination to realize that he should be afraid, he is therefore not afraid and continues in his plodding but effective fashion. Jukes, in order to live up to his moral code, has no choice but to follow, acting more bravely and coolly than his inner doubts might otherwise allow. Together, the two men lead the crew in heroic efforts that save the *Nan-Shan*.

The only complexity that Conrad employs in "Typhoon" is in his narrative structure. The story shifts from third person to passages of letters from Captain MacWhirr, Jukes, and the ship's engineer to their families. This second layer is overlain by a third, in which the letters are read, sometimes with commentary, by the families in England. Through this method, Conrad allows the major characters to present the story as they experience and perceive it and adds a further contrast between the men who actually endure the storm and those who only read about it, and so cannot fully grasp its strength and danger.

"THE DUEL"

"The Duel," sometimes titled "The Duellists," is the story of two officers in Napoleon Bonaparte's army, who wage their own private war for sixteen years, while about them all Europe is plunged into a larger, much more deadly combat. Conrad was an avid student of the Napoleonic period, and he based his story on an actual rivalry. More than the story of two men, "The Duel" is Conrad's reflections upon the Napoleonic age.

The two progatonists are Feraud from Gascony in southern France—a region noted for its hot-blooded, impetuous natives—and D'Hubert, a Picard, with the reserved nature characteristic of that northern region. Through an accidental incident, the two become engaged in an affair of honor that can be settled only by a duel. Once begun, the duel is protracted to farcical lengths, extending from Paris to Moscow, from the time of Napoleon's greatest triumphs to his final defeat at Waterloo. Finally, D'Hubert falls in love and marries, finding life more worthwhile than this questionable affair of honor. In the final encounter, he emerges victorious and spares Feraud's life on the promise that the combat will now, finally, end.

The tale is briskly and even comically rendered, with Conrad's typical ironies in this case turned positive. The darker aspects of his vision are reserved for his wider view of the Napoleonic age: What might be seen as humorous when only two men are involved becomes tragic almost beyond comprehension when entire nations are the duelists. Feraud and D'Hubert fight only each other in their affair, while Napoleon engaged all the countries of Europe. At the end of that wider struggle, Conrad implies, there was no happy resolution, only the desolation that follows the exhausted silence of the battlefield. This bleaker vision, however, is not allowed to overwhelm the essentially humorous basis of the story.

The title of the work may contain a clue to one of its themes, the typical Conrad subject of the "double," the other person who is so like the hero yet somehow different. During the interminable encounters, D'Hubert comes to believe that he is linked, in some mysterious and unbreakable fashion, to Feraud. They are "secret sharers," in one sense literally so, because they cannot reveal that their duel began over a trivial misunderstanding and was prolonged out of fear of embarrassment. They are also "secret sharers" in a wider sense, because their lives have fullest meaning only when joined together. In this way, the "duellists" are indeed "dual," and their relationship is not only one of combat but also, in fact, one of union.

"GASPAR RUIZ"

"Gaspar Ruiz" was based upon actual events in the Chilean revolution against Spain of the 1830's. The title character, an immensely strong but rather simpleminded peasant, joins the army of the rebels. Captured during battle, he is forced to join the Loyalist army and is then once again made a prisoner, this time by his former comrades. Condemned as a traitor, Gaspar Ruiz escapes and is sheltered by a Loyalist family whose daughter, Erminia, he later marries. A series of misadventures leads Gaspar to become a general in the Loyalist army, although his political sense is almost nonexistent and he wishes, as much as he can comprehend the matter, to be a Chilean patriot. When Erminia and her daughter are captured by the rebels and held in a mountain fort, Gaspar has a cannon strapped to his huge back so it can batter open the gate and free them. The desperate tactic works, but Gaspar is mortally wounded, and Erminia kills herself, dying with her husband.

The story is told in typical Conrad fashion—that is, long after the events have occurred and by two different narrators. One of them is General Santierra, who, as a lieutenant in the rebel army, knew Gaspar Ruiz and is now the guardian of Gaspar's grown daughter. The second narrator, who opens the story in the third person but who is revealed, at the close, to be a guest of General Santierra, answers questions that Santierra raises. This narrator explains that revolutions are a distillation of human experience and that they bring some human beings to fame who otherwise would be resigned to oblivion. In revolutions, genuine social ideals, such as freedom or equality, may be passionately held in the abstract but are ferociously violated in actuality, just as Gaspar Ruiz, a true if bewildered patriot, was condemned and made a traitor by circumstances and false accusations. In a sense, the unnamed guest is reinforcing a constant Conrad theme, the difference between reality and illusion.

"THE SECRET SHARER"

Probably Conrad's most famous short story, "The Secret Sharer" is a deceptively simple tale that carries such deep, perhaps unfathomable moral and psychological undertones that since its publication readers and critics have remained puzzled and fascinated by its elusive, evocative power. In the story, a young captain, new to his first command, is startled to discover a naked man swimming by his ship's side. Once aboard, the swimmer, named Leggatt, confesses that he is fleeing from his own ship, the *Sephora*, because he murdered a fellow sailor. The act was justified, as the young captain quickly realizes, for the *Sephora* was in danger of foundering during a violent storm, and the murdered man, by failing to obey Leggatt's orders, had placed the ship and its crew in immediate danger. Now, however, Leggatt is a hunted man. The captain hides Leggatt in his own cabin, keeping him safely out of sight until he can sail his ship close enough to an island to allow Leggatt to escape.

By pledging and then keeping his word to the mysterious Leggatt, the young captain upholds his own moral code, even though it runs counter to conventional law and morality. In doing so, he proves that he is capable of living up to that "ideal conception of one's personality every man sets up for himself secretly." The fact that morality is established and maintained secretly—in this case, literally so—is a Conradian irony and a central paradox of this tale. Adding to the reader's bewilderment is the fact that the young captain's "ideal conception" is nowhere presented explicitly. The reader is able to see the captain's code in action and perhaps assess its consequences but must deduce from these tantalizing clues what must constitute the standards that the young officer so earnestly desires to uphold.

The captain's code is indeed a puzzling one, for not only does it require him to be faithful to a murderer, but also it causes him to risk his own ship. To give Leggatt the best possible chance to swim to safety, the captain steers dangerously close to shore, risking running aground or perhaps breaking up on the shoals. Naturally, he cannot tell his crew why he orders this difficult, dangerous maneuver, so another secret is layered upon those already present. When the captain is successful in his plan, for the first time he feels a sense of unity and closeness with his vessel, a mystical—and again, secret—bond.

The meanings of "The Secret Sharer" are hidden in its deceptively straightforward narrative. The work is full of ambiguity and possible double meanings, all presented in brisk, even prosaic fashion. Even the title is multiple: Since Leggatt is unknown to anyone but the captain, his presence is indeed a secret, but he and the young commander also share common secrets, both Leggatt's presence and the "ideal conception of one's personality," which seems to be their joint moral code. Since these meanings are complementary, rather than contradictory, they add to the resonance of the story.

Other touches add to the story's depth. The young captain and Leggatt are so similar that they seem to be doubles, and Conrad obviously intends this identification to be as much moral as physical. Both men feel themselves to be outcasts, Leggatt actually so, because of his crime; the captain, psychologically, because of his newness to the ship and its crew. In one sense, Leggatt can be seen as an alter ego of the narrator, perhaps even a projection of his darker, maybe criminal, side. It may even be possible, as some critics have suggested, that Leggatt does not actually exist but is only a figment of the young captain's imagination.

Such an unusual, even implausible interpretation indicates the perplexity that "The Secret Sharer" elicits in readers and underscores why this story, so famous in itself, is also emblematic of all Conrad's fiction. Under the guise of a simple sea tale, he has gathered the themes that constantly flowed through his works: the ideal sense of self that must be tested and proved under difficult situations; the conflict between loyalty and betrayal, reality and illusion; and, above all, the innate need for human beings to preserve, even in trying circumstances and against conventional pressures, a moral code whose only reward is a secret that may, perhaps, never be shared.

OTHER MAJOR WORKS

LONG FICTION: *Almayer's Folly*, 1895; *An Outcast of the Islands*, 1896; *The Children of the Sea: A Tale of the Forecastle*, 1897 (republished as *The Nigger of the "Narcissus": A Tale of the Sea*, 1898); *Lord Jim: A Tale*, 1900; *The Inheritors*, 1901 (with Ford Madox Ford); *Romance*, 1903 (with Ford Madox Ford); *Nostromo: A Tale of the Seaboard*, 1904; *The Secret Agent: A Simple Tale*, 1907; *The Nature of a Crime*, 1909 (serial), 1924 (book; with Ford Madox Ford); *Under Western Eyes*, 1911; *Chance*, 1913; *Victory: An Island Tale*, 1915; *The Shadow-Line: A Confession*, 1917; *The Arrow of Gold*, 1919; *The Rescue: A Romance of the Shadows*, 1920; *The Rover*, 1923; *Suspense: A Napoleonic Novel*, 1925 (incomplete).

PLAYS: *One Day More: A Play in One Act*, pr. 1905; *The Secret Agent: A Drama in Four Acts*, pb. 1921; *Laughing Anne: A Play*, pb. 1923.

NONFICTION: *The Mirror of the Sea*, 1906; *Some Reminiscences*, 1912 (published in the United States as *A Personal Record*); *Notes on Life and Letters*, 1921; *Joseph Conrad's Diary of His Journey Up the Valley of the Congo in 1890*, 1926; *Last Essays*, 1926; *Joseph Conrad: Life and Letters*, 1927 (Gérard Jean-Aubry, editor); *Joseph Conrad's Letters to His Wife*, 1927; *Conrad to a Friend*, 1928 (Richard Curle, editor); *Letters from Joseph Conrad, 1895-1924*, 1928 (Edward Garnett, editor); *Lettres françaises de Joseph Conrad*, 1929 (Gérard Jean-Aubry, editor); *Letters of Joseph Conrad to Marguerite Doradowska*, 1940 (John A. Gee and Paul J. Sturm, editors); *The Collected Letters of Joseph Conrad: Volume I, 1861-1897*, 1983; *The Collected Letters of Joseph Conrad: Volume II, 1898-1902*, 1986; *The Collected Letters of Joseph Conrad: Volume III, 1903-1907*, 1988.

BIBLIOGRAPHY

Billy, Ted. *A Wilderness of Words: Closure and Disclosure in Conrad's Short Fiction*. Lubbock: Texas Tech University Press, 1997. In this study of Conrad's linguistic skepticism, Billy empha-sizes endings in Conrad's short fiction and how they either harmonize or clash with other narrative elements in nineteen of Conrad's short novels and tales. Argues that Conrad presents knowledge of the world as fundamentally illusory.

DeKoven, Marianne. "Conrad's Unrest." *Journal of Modern Literature* 21 (Winter, 1997/1998): 241-249. Argues that in Conrad's *Tales of Unrest* the concept of unrest is linked to modes of spirituality at odds with Western reason. Claims that the Enlightenment rationalism that freed the West from superstition did so by repressing spiritual and psychic forces; contends that the force of unrest in Conrad's stories is the force of modernism.

Gillon, Adam. *Joseph Conrad*. Boston: Twayne, 1982. A solid introduction to Conrad's life and art, written by a native Pole. Provides relatively brief but insightful analysis of the more significant shorter works.

Graver, Lawrence. *Conrad's Short Fiction*. Berkeley: University of California Press, 1969. This study of Conrad's stories is grouped chronologically and displays the linkages between the shorter fictions and individual stories, and between them as a group and the novels. Since it covers the lesser-known stories as well as the more famous ones, it is essential for placing Conrad's development of themes and styles within a larger artistic context.

Johnson, A. James M. "Victorian Anthropology, Racism, and *Heart of Darkness*." *Ariel* 28 (October, 1997): 111-131. Argues that Conrad uncritically accepted racist assumptions of Victorian anthropology in *Heart of Darkness*.

Kingsbury, Celia M. "'Infinities of Absolution': Reason, Rumor, and Duty in Joseph Conrad's 'The Tale.'" *Modern Fiction Studies* 44 (Fall, 1998): 715-729. Argues that because the narrator is lost in the wild illogic of rumor he commits a reprehensible act he believes to be demanded by duty.

Leavis, F. R. *The Great Tradition*. London: Chatto & Windus, 1948. Leavis, one of the most distinguished of modern English literary critics, places Conrad within the scope of the English literary world, showing how he drew from, and added to, that heritage. An invaluable study for those trying to understand what Conrad might have been attempting in his writing and how he could have perceived his place within a wider literary context.

Lewis, Pericles. "'His Sympathies Were in the Right Place': *Heart of Darkness* and the Discourse of National Character." *Nineteenth-Century Literature* 53 (September, 1998): 211-244. Shows how Conrad contributed to modernist literary technique by structuring conflict between the "ethical" and the "sociological" in Marlow's decision to align himself with Kurtz over the Company.

Meyers, Jeffrey. *Joseph Conrad: A Bibliography.* New York: Charles Scribner's Sons, 1991. A briskly moving, no-nonsense biography that surveys the key points and themes of the major works. Very good at placing Conrad within the social and intellectual milieu of his day and offering good insights from other literary figures, such as Ford Madox Ford, who significantly influenced Conrad's literary career.

Najder, Zdzislaw. *Joseph Conrad: A Chronicle.* Translated by Halina Carroll-Najder. Cambridge, England: Cambridge University Press, 1983. A thorough and sympathetic biography of Conrad written by a countryman. The volume stresses the influence of Conrad's Polish heritage on his personality and art. Najder draws many telling and intriguing parallels between Conrad's life and his writing.

Stape, J. H. *The Cambridge Companion to Joseph Conrad.* Cambridge, England: Cambridge University Press, 1996. In this collection of essays on most of Conrad's major work by different critics, the most helpful for a study of his short fiction are the essays "Conradian Narrative" by Jakob Lothe, which surveys Conrad's narrative techniques and conventions, and "The Short Fiction" by Gail Fraser, which discusses Conrad's experimentation with short narrative.

Tennant, Roger. *Joseph Conrad: A Biography.* New York: Atheneum, 1987. Not a scholarly work, but a readable study that concentrates on Conrad's sea years and his later struggles with ill health and financial difficulties. Its main weakness is a lack of emphasis on Conrad's early and formative years in Poland, but, when used with Zdzislaw Najder's work (above), it can be helpful.

Michael Witkoski

FRANK CONROY

Born: New York, New York; January 15, 1936

PRINCIPAL SHORT FICTION

Midair, 1985

OTHER LITERARY FORMS

Reviewer Terrence Rafferty praised Frank Conroy's first book, *Stop-Time* (1967), as a "terrifically original contribution to the autobiography-of-a-young man genre." His first novel, *Body and Soul* (1993), is an old-fashioned, often refreshingly upbeat *Bildungsroman*, the history of a musical prodigy's development from humble beginnings to concert fame as a piano virtuoso.

ACHIEVEMENTS

Frank Conroy has received fellowships from the John Simon Guggenheim Memorial Foundation, the Rockefeller Foundation, the National Foundation for the Arts and Humanities, and the National Council for the Arts. *Stop-Time* was nominated for a National Book Award. He has taught writing at workshops and universities, including Massachusetts Institute of Technology, American University, Brandeis University, and George Mason University.

BIOGRAPHY

Frank Conroy was born in New York City in 1936 and attended Peter Stuyvesant High School. He won a scholarship to attend Haverford College, a small

Liberal Arts-oriented school in suburban Philadelphia. Upon being graduated in 1958 with a B.A. in English, he married the daughter of a socially prominent family. They met at a college soccer game. The couple divorced after a thirteen-year marriage that produced two sons, Danny and Will. Conroy dedicated *Midair* to "Maggie," his second wife. They have a teenage son, Tim.

In January, 1970, Conroy published his first story, "Car Games," in *The New Yorker*. That same year the magazine published "The Mysterious Case of R," and, in 1974 and 1984, respectively, "Celestial Events" and "Midair," the title story of his collection. Conroy considers himself primarily a teacher, a profession he entered at the renowned Writers' Workshop, University of Iowa, where he became the director early in the 1990's. Between his appointments there, he served as director of the Literature Program of the National Endowment of the Arts (NEA), 1981-1987, during which he insisted on teaching at least one class. For about four years, between college and his first teaching position, he worked full time as a jazz pianist in New York. While with the NEA, Frank Conroy, pianist, sat in with a group at Washington's Georgetown Fish House. He writes widely on the subject of jazz.

ANALYSIS

As a story writer and fictional memoirist, Frank Conroy is a disciple of the early James Joyce. The "showings-forth" of suddenly apprehended truths Joyce called "epiphanies." Writing of passages in "The Sense of the Meeting," Conroy conveys epiphanic moments when a father recognizes in the setting of his old college on whose basketball team the son plays, that, looking at his son in the double vision of his own past and his maturing son's present, he is overcome by "a great rush of bitterness, protective love, a desire to shelter the boy against some vague, unnamed threat." Seemingly unrelated, the stories in *Midair* make up a composite that the title reinforces. Their strategy is a variation on Joyce's *A Portrait of the Artist as a Young Man* (1916), in which young Stephen Dedalus builds to an assured sense of high purpose. The reader finds in story after story that what is literally airborne—as in the title story, where a child is held out a fifth-story window—must be perceived epiphanically. Anne Tyler puts it well: "We begin to associate with that suspended instant that precedes a new comprehension, or a radical swerve in one's life." Maggie Conroy once urged her husband, if asked about the long intervals between books—eighteen and eight years—to reply, "I've been doing errands." To Conroy himself, it was quite logical that he had written only three books to date. "I really never thought of writing as a career. Although *Stop-Time* was a critical success, I never got any signals that I could make a living as a writer. So I had to look elsewhere to figure out how I was going to support myself."

"MIDAIR"

Most introspective persons experience dramas even in the quotidian, rethink such catalytic moments, and find themselves fashioning out of them a circuitry of remembered links. At the end of perhaps Conroy's finest story, an elevator slightly malfunctions between the sixty-third and sixty-fourth floors. The only other occupant with the protagonist, Sean, is a young man whom he takes momentarily for his son, who is away at college. The

> two ideas overlap—the idea of [son] Philip and the idea of the young man—and in that moment time seems to slow down. It is as if Sean had seen his son across a supernatural barrier—as if he, Sean, were a ghost haunting the elevator, able to see the real body of his son but unable to be seen by him. An almost unbearable sadness comes over him.

That night, rethinking how he "saved" the frightened young man by assuring him he had experienced scares like this before (Sean had never been on that elevator before), he flashes back to an earlier time in the story when he was six and his improvident father, unexpectedly returned from a mental hospital, carried him out on the windowsill of their apartment five floors up. "Here, in the darkness, he can see the cracks in the sidewalk from more than forty years ago. He feels no fear—only a sense of astonishment." The story is told by the man, who was once the small boy, who directly or obliquely is at the center. Whether describing Sean the boy asking why Sean the father is crying ("he has never felt as close to another human being") or conveying the signs by which Sean senses that his marriage is coming apart, Conroy evokes the powerful influence that events from the past can exert on the present. For him, all things have double meanings.

"GOSSIP"

This is the only story in *Midair* dealing with what Conroy calls his main calling: teaching. It may be one of the few in which a creative-writing professor's evolving relationship with a promising and beautiful woman who is his student does not lead to the inevitable tryst. Anne Tyler gives "Gossip" faint praise in her *New Republic* review, finding it "less successful" because it is about "writing and writing teachers." Like "Midair," the story moves deftly, often unexpectedly, among different periods in George's life. He discovers in early middle age that he is an effective teacher of writing, a discovery made in relation to a gifted and dedicated female student named Joan to whom George gives all of his teaching self:

He spent week after week, month after month going after every weakness he could find in her prose, attacking from one direction after another, trying to tear the work apart in front of her eyes. She responded by writing better and better stuff, paradoxically with more and more confidence, until it became difficult for him to find any of the weaknesses she had originally exhibited.

The story builds to a tension that is a version of art-for-art's-sake. George must regard her writing as sacrosanct with a life of its own outside any other. When his wife suggests they invite some of his students, including Joan, to dinner, he awakens to the knowledge that Joan, though not his lover, has far transcended the tyro-tutor accommodation:

She was important to him, and the degree of importance was a secret which he must keep to himself. Their relationship was based on the tacit understanding that they would remain always in their respective roles of teacher and student, and he needed her enough to want to do nothing to threaten that arrangement. Dinner, small talk, socializing, were full of imponderables, and the prospect made him nervous.

What makes George uneasy can be said in the title of this story—gossip, the subtly threatening waves of words that deluge our lives with, as William H. Pritchard puts it, "power over the self and what others say about that self and its relationships." Gossip that enmeshes teacher and student—were they or were they not sleeping together?—takes its toll. Joan leaves school before the term ends; George is harassed by his wife, and yet Conroy can conclude: "Everyone was connected in a web, and yet despite it, people loved one another."

"THE SENSE OF THE MEETING"

In this father-son story Conroy takes a worn, often sentimentalized, donnée about a father returning to his alma mater to see his son play in the big game and, by staying inside the parent's head, endows the experience with a bittersweet flavor that few but this writer could bring off. Kirby, too thin and weak to play sports and medically excused from them in college, nevertheless introduced his son Alan to basketball early. At the moment of demonstrating successfully the hook shot, Kirby "saw a complex expression of pleasure, pride, and eagerness on the boy's face . . . at that precise moment . . . understood the force of his son's love." It is a Joycean/Conroyan epiphanic moment again. The reader is advised to remember it, for in the next paragraph the narrative flashes forward to Kirby's arrival by train in Philadelphia for the game in which his son will play. He is met by the six-foot-six Gus, his former roommate. Gus was captain of the basketball team, Kirby editor of the literary magazine. Conroy hints at an athlete-versus-aesthete tension that is leavened by the arrival at the club of the third of their coterie. Charley was thin, nervous, and self-conscious in college but is now self-possessed, well-spoken, handsome—a thriving Philadelphia lawyer. They reminisce over boilermakers until it is time for Kirby to be driven to Alan's dorm. By bringing the son on stage, Conroy generates more interest than has been provided by the men's bleak hindsight that they have settled for less. The reader infers that the father's concern for his capable and resourceful son may be a reflex of his own disappointments. The subtexts of one dorm scene and of two basketball games—wins—reveal Conroy at his best: "He was relieved to get out of the room. He didn't understand what came over him sometimes when he saw Alan on Alan's own turf, a great rush of bitter-sweet, protective love, a desire to shelter the boy against some vague, unnamed threat." After Alan's pass enables a teammate to hit a half-court shot just as time runs out, Alan's words, the last of the story, reinforce the father-son connection: "I'm glad you saw it. . . . There's no way I could have told you." In fiction and in life, showing/doing counts more than telling. For Terrence Rafferty, "the delicate texture of achieved expression can't always be willed—that sometimes, unpredictably, the patterns just coalesce around us."

OTHER MAJOR WORKS

LONG FICTION: *Body and Soul*, 1993.
NONFICTION: *Stop-Time*, 1967.

BIBLIOGRAPHY

Conroy, Frank. "Frank Conroy." Interview by Sybil S. Steinberg. *Publishers Weekly* (August 23, 1993): 44. Upholds *Publishers Weekly's tradition of high-quality interviews. Conroy discusses the difficulties of writing fiction in which music is central, why Stop-Time* came out at exactly the wrong time ("Everybody was taking drugs and making love, and here was this sort of neoclassical memoir"), and his meager output.

Pritchard, William H. Review of *Midair*, by Frank Conroy. *The New York Times Book Review* 98 (October 3, 1993): 12. While wondering "what Mr. Conroy has been up to as a writer" during nearly two decades of silence between *Stop-Time* and *Midair*, Pritchard connects the memoir and the stories by stressing this author's exceptional grasp of the pains of childhood, the relationship between sons and fathers, looked at, in the first and last stories, from the angle of each. Finds Conroy's "reliance on the actual" does not rule out the abstract.

Rafferty, Terrence. Review of *Midair*, by Frank Conroy. *The Nation* 242 (January 11, 1986): 23-24. Sees *Midair* as, in part, a completion of *Stop-Time* and the two works together as "the best record we have of the ups and downs of writing as if your life depended on it." Favors "Car Games," Conroy's *New Yorker* debut story as *Midair's* best, a vicious parody of *Stop-Time*.

Tyler, Anne. Review of *Midair*, by Frank Conroy. *The New Republic* 193 (November 18, 1985): 48-50. Easily the most imaginative of *Midair's* reviews. Noting that all the characters are men, novelist Tyler identifies the underlying concerns of the seven stories: "How to live in the world as an adult male. How men connect with their sons and fathers, their old college roommates, their squash opponents. How they cling to their drinking rituals and their driving rituals."

Richard Hauer Costa

ROBERT COOVER

Born: Charles City, Iowa; February 4, 1932

OTHER LITERARY FORMS

Besides the above-mentioned collections of short fiction and novellas and many uncollected short stories, Robert Coover's production includes the novels *The Origin of the Brunists* (1966), *The Universal Baseball Association, Inc., J. Henry Waugh, Prop.* (1968), *The Public Burning* (1977), *Gerald's Party* (1985), *Pinocchio in Venice* (1991), *John's Wife* (1996), and *Ghost Town* (1998); a collection of plays entitled *A Theological Position* (1972), which contains *The Kid*, *Love Scene*, *Rip Awake*, and the title play; the screenplay *After Lazarus* (1980); a play, *Bridge Hound* (1981); several poems, reviews, and translations published in journals; a screenplay/novella *Hair o' the Chine*; the film *On a Confrontation in Iowa City* (1969); and theater adaptations of "The Babysitter" and *Spanking the Maid*. Coover has also published a few essays on authors he admires, such as Samuel Beckett ("The Last Quixote," in *New American Review*, 1970) and Gabriel García Márquez ("The Master's Voice," in *New American Review*, 1977).

ACHIEVEMENTS

Robert Coover is one of the authors regularly mentioned in relation to that slippery term "postmodernism." As a result of the iconoclastic and experimental nature of his fiction, Coover's work does not enjoy a widespread audience; his reputation among academics, however, is well established, and the reviews of his works have been consistently positive. Although in the beginning of his career he had to resort to teaching in order to support his family, he soon began to gain recognition, receiving several prizes and fellowships: a William Faulkner Award for Best First Novel (1966), a Rockefeller Foundation grant (1969), two John Simon Guggenheim Memorial Foundation Fellowships (1971, 1974), an Academy of Arts and Letters award (1975), a National Book Award nomination for *The Public Burning*, a National Endowment for the Humanities Award (1985), a Rea Award (1987) for *A Night at the Movies*, a Rhode Island Governor's Arts Award (1988), and Deutscher Akademischer Austauschdienst Fellowship (1990). The publisher Alfred A. Knopf's rejection of *The Public Burning* after initial acceptance brought some notoriety to Coover. Since the novel deals with the trial of Ethel and Julius Rosenberg and presents former president Richard M. Nixon as its central narrator, the publisher thought it would be too controversial. Eventually, *The Public Burning* was published by Viking Press and became a Book-of-the-Month Club selection. Critical studies about Coover started in the late 1970's. Still, in spite of the critical acclaim and the considerable amount of scholarship about his work, Coover's work remains relatively unknown to the public, and some of his early novels are now out of print.

BIOGRAPHY

Robert Lowell Coover was born in Charles City, Iowa. His family soon moved to Indiana and then to Herrin, Illinois. His father managed the local newspa-

Robert Coover (National Archives)

per, the *Herrin Daily Journal*, which prompted Coover's interest in journalism. His college education began at Southern Illinois University (1949-1951), but he transferred to Indiana University, where he received a B.A., with a major in Slavic studies, in 1953. After graduation, Coover was drafted and joined the United States Naval Reserve.

While in Spain, he met Maria del Pilar Sans-Mallafré, who became his wife on June 13, 1959. During these years, his interest in fiction began. His first published story, "Blackdamp," was the seed of his first novel, *The Origin of the Brunists*. He received an M.A. from the University of Chicago in 1965. During the following years, Coover and his family alternated stays in Europe with periods in the United States. The several awards he received during the 1970's made him financially secure and allowed him to continue writing.

Coover has held appointments at Bard College, the University of Iowa, Columbia University, Prince-

ton University, the Virginia Military Institute, and he has been a distinguished professor at Brown University since 1979. He has also been writer-in-residence at Wisconsin State University. In spite of a large amount of time spent abroad (in Europe and in South America) and his outspoken need to take distance from his own country, Coover's production is very "American," since he often bases his fiction on American events, persons, and national myths. Coover often manipulates historical events for artistic purposes, but he has a solid knowledge of the facts.

In the late 1980's, Coover began teaching writing on computers. With the rise of the World Wide Web in the 1990's, he made significant progress in the use of hyperfiction. Hyperfiction, also referred to as hypertext fiction, tree fiction, nonlinear fiction, or electronic fiction, is fiction written with the capabilities of hypertext. Hyperfiction is truly nonlinear since it cannot be represented on a printed page. The reader takes an active role in hyperfiction, choosing which links to click on and which paths to follow. Thus, the narrative may be very different from one reading to the next, depending on the choices made by the reader. Readers can follow different characters, or points of view, or skip back and forth between different time zones. By clicking on an interesting name, place, event, or idea, the reader can be taken to a new page connected to that name, place, event, or idea.

Coover reads, writes, and reviews hyperfiction. He teaches hyperfiction workshops at Brown University. The Hypertext Hotel is a collaborative hyperfiction that grew out of Coover's workshops. During the 1990's, students, authors, and scholars have added to the fictional hotel text. Coover developed a course at Brown that introduces students to the possibilities of hyperfiction. He also been known to encourage the use of hyperfiction and the software that makes it possible. Coover is the author of the now classic "The End of the Book," an article in which he explains hyperfiction and his general optimism that it will someday replace books.

ANALYSIS

Robert Coover's central concern is the human being's need for fiction. Because of the complexity of human existence, people are constantly inventing patterns that give them an illusion of order in a chaotic world. For Coover, any effort to explain the world involves some kind of fiction-making process. History, religion, culture, and scientific explanations are fictional at their core; they are invented narratives through which human beings try to explain the world to themselves. The problem, Coover would say, is that people tend to forget the fictional nature of the fictional systems they create and become trapped by them, making dogmas out of the fictions. The artist's function, then, is to reexamine these fictions, tear them down, and offer new perspectives on the same material, in order to make the reader aware of the arbitrariness of the construct.

Coover's fiction often has been labeled "metafiction"—that is, fiction about fiction—and indeed most of his works are comments on previously existing fictional constructs. If in his longer works he examines the bigger metaphoric narratives such as religion, history, or politics (that one of the theorists of postmodernism, Jean-François Lyotard, has called "metanarratives"), in his shorter works Coover turns to smaller constructs, usually literary fictions.

In the prologue to the "Seven Exemplary Fictions" contained in *Pricksongs and Descants*, Coover addresses Miguel de Cervantes as follows:

> But, don Miguel, the optimism, the innocence, the aura of possibility you experienced have been largely drained away, and the universe is closing in on us again. Like you, we, too, seem to be standing at the end of one age and on the threshold of another.

Just as Cervantes stood at the end of a tradition and managed to open a door for a new type of fiction, contemporary authors confront a changing world in need of new fictional forms that can reflect this world's nature better. Just as Cervantes tried to stress the difference between romance and the real world through the mishaps of Don Quixote, Coover wants to stress the fictionality and arbitrariness of some fictions that hold a tight grip on the reader's consciousness. Like Cervantes, Coover wants to free readers from an uncritical acceptance of untrue or oversimplified ideas that limit and falsify their outlook on life. Fictions, Coover and Cervantes would say, are not there to provide an escape by creating fantasies for the reader. When they do so, Coover continues writing in his prologue, the artist "must conduct the reader to the real, away from mystification to clarification, away from magic to maturity, away from mystery to revelations."

This quotation, coming from an author whose work is usually considered "difficult," might seem somehow odd. How does Coover's fiction clarify, or what does it reveal? His work often presents constantly metamorphosing worlds, which mimic the state of constant change in the real world. Just as the world is continuously changing, Coover's fictions also refuse to present stable, easily describable characters or scenarios. Coover also calls attention to the fictionality of fiction by focusing on the process and the means of creation rather than on the product. As he states in the prologue, the novelist turns to the familiar material and "defamiliarizes" it in order to liberate readers' imagination from arbitrary constraints and in order to make them reevaluate their reactions to those constraints. These are the main strategies of Coover's two collections of stories, *Pricksongs and Descants* and *A Night at the Movies*.

PRICKSONGS AND DESCANTS

The title of the first collection refers to musical terms, variations played against a basic line (the basic line of the familiar narrative). As one character in one of the stories says, however, they are also "death-c— and prick-songs," which prepares the reader for the sometimes shocking motifs of death and sex scattered throughout the stories. In *Pricksongs and Descants*, Coover turns to the familiar material of folktales and biblical stories. Using this material offers him the possibility of manipulating the reader's expectations. One of the ways in which Coover forces the reader to look at familiar stories from new perspectives is by retelling them from an unfamiliar point of view. For example, the story "The Brother" is Coover's version of the biblical flood told from the point of view of Noah's brother, who, after helping Noah to build the ark, is left to drown. "J's Marriage" describes how Joseph tries to come to terms with his marriage to the Virgin Mary and his alternating moods of amazement, frustration, and desperation. Some of the stories of the same collection are based on traditional folktales: "The Door" evokes "Little Red Riding Hood," "The Gingerbread House," reminds one of "Hanzel and Gretel," "The Milkmaid of Samaniego" is based on the Spanish folktale of the same title; and *Hair o' the Chine*, a novella, mocks the tale of the "Three Little Pigs and the Wolf." Coover subverts, however, the original narratives by stressing the cruelty and the motifs of sex, violence, and death underlying most folktales. Revealing the darker side of familiar stories is in fact one of Coover's recurrent techniques.

In other stories of *Pricksongs and Descants*, Coover experiments with the formal aspects of fiction-making. He reminds the reader of the artificiality of fiction by presenting stories that are repertoires of narrative possibilities. Often, Coover juxtaposes several different beginnings, or potential stories, but leaves them undeveloped. He interweaves the different story lines, some of which are complementary and some of which might be contradictory, as is the case in "Quenby and Ola, Swede and Carl" and in "The Magic Poker." In the "Sentient Lens" section and in "Klee's Dead," Coover explores the possibilities and the limitations of the narrational voice: In the first set of stories, Coover denies the possibility of an objective narrative voice by portraying a camera that constantly interferes with the events of the story; in "Klee's Dead," the supposedly "omniscient" narrator is unable to explain the reasons for Paul Klee's suicide.

In most of the stories of *Pricksongs and Descants*, the figures are types described with a flaunted lack of depth of characterization, which prevents the reader from identifying with them in any possible way. This contributes to the critical distance that Coover thinks it is necessary to maintain toward fiction. As critic Cristina Bacchilega says in her article about Coover's use of the *Märchen* (folktales) in this collection, while "the *Märchen* is symbolic of development, of a passage from immaturity to maturity, Coover's fictions present rather static characters . . . the only dynamic process allowed is in the reader's new awareness of the world as a construct of fictions." The

function of the artist in contemporary society is one of Coover's recurring concerns, which surfaces in "Panel Game," "Romance of Thin Man and Fat Lady," and "The Hat Act," all of which portray cruel and insatiable audiences who, in their thirst for entertainment, do not hesitate to exterminate the artists if their performance does not stand up to their expectations.

A NIGHT AT THE MOVIES

In *A Night at the Movies*, Coover probes the nature of filmic fictions, which present a greater danger of being taken for "real" because of the immediacy of filmic images. Coover approaches film from three perspectives. In the stories "Shootout at Gentry's Junction," "Charlie in the House of Rue," "Gilda's Dream," and "You Must Remember This," Coover demythologizes specific films and offers his own version of the story, usually baring the ideology of the original version. In "After Lazarus" and "Inside the Frame," he explores the conventions through which these fictions create an illusion of an independent world on the screen. In "The Phantom of the Movie Palace" and "Intermission," he challenges the ontological status of reality and film by making the characters cross the boundaries that separate these two realms.

"Shootout at Gentry's Junction" is a parody of the ideology and of the form of the Western film *High Noon* (1952). Coover parodies the narrative line and the easy identification of good and evil typical of most Westerns. The film celebrates the code of honor and personal integrity typical of the Western hero; abandoned by everybody, the sheriff of the film, played by Gary Cooper, has to fight alone with the villain and his gang. In the story, however, the protagonist is a fastidious, neurotic sheriff who is obsessed with fulfilling the role imposed on him. The villain is Don Pedro, the Mexican bandit, whose major talent is expressing himself by expelling intestinal gas. As in the film, the narrative progresses toward the confrontation of the villain and the sheriff. The tight structure of the film, however, is disrupted in the story by giving both characters a different kind of discourse. The sheriff's discourse has a traditional narrative line. It is narrated in the past tense and refers to formulas taken directly from the visual tradition of the Western. The Mexican's discourse is in the present tense and in broken English, influenced by Spanish. Furthermore, Coover makes the Mexican ubiquitous. Readers never really know where he is—he seems everywhere at the same time, raping the schoolmarm at the local school, cheating at cards in the saloon, and burning papers at the sheriff's office. After shooting the sheriff, the Mexican sets the town on fire and rides into the sunset.

The irreverence of Coover's version of *Casablanca* (1942) is even greater. *Casablanca* has become the epitome of the romantic melodrama, drawing like the Western upon codes of honor and heroic behavior. In "You Must Remember This," Coover gives his version of what might have happened between frames. Quite literally, Rick and Ilsa fall between frames and make furious love several times. The love story becomes a pornographic movie. The disruption of the moral code of the film creates an avalanche of disruptions in other categories: Rick and Ilsa begin to sense that their senses of time and place are fading, and their identities become increasingly diffused. At the end of the story, the characters melt into nothingness after several desperate attempts to return to the mythic movie.

Other stories in the collection *A Night at the Movies* aim at exposing the artificiality of the technical conventions of film. Written in the form of a screenplay, "After Lazarus" parodies the notion of the camera as the ultimately objective narrator. In the story, the camera "hesitates," "pauses," "follows back at a discreet distance," and rapidly moves back when frightened. "Inside the Frame" refers in its very title to film-related terms. If films construct a narrative through the sum of frames that all have a reason and a function in the global construct of the story, this story presents several possible beginnings of stories in one single frame. In "Inside the Frame," the reader gets glimpses of what could be potential stories: a woman stepping off a bus, an Indian with a knife between his teeth, a man praying at a grave, a singing couple, a sleepwalker. There is no development, no explanation of the images. "Lap Dissolves" is a literary imitation of the film technique. The story fades from one film-related situation to the next, with the words giving the cues to the transformation of the scenario.

Coover disrupts the ontological boundaries between "reality" and fiction by making the protagonists of "The Phantom of the Movie Palace" and "Intermission" move between them. The mad projectionist of the first story lives in an abandoned movie palace and plays with the reels of film, constructing films by cutting and pasting images of other films. Somehow, his experiments go awry, and he becomes trapped in the fictions he has been creating. The girl of "Intermission" enters a film-related fantasy when the film in the story ends and she steps into the lobby of the movie theater to buy a snack. Outside the theater, she is thrown into a series of situations directly drawn from Hollywood films: She moves from a car race with gangsters, to a tent with Rudolph Valentino, to the sea surrounded by sharks. In what is supposed to be "reality," she becomes a dynamic individual, but back in the cinema she returns to the passivity that Hollywood fictions seem to invite.

BRIAR ROSE

In *Briar Rose*, a novella and a retelling of the fable of Sleeping Beauty, Coover travels deeply into the dreams of the sleeping princess and into the forest of briars and brambles that plague the prince as he tries to rescue her. The story centers on the powers of the human imagination and escalates to an erotic pace as sex and storytelling fuse together. As the prince fights his way to the princess's bed chamber to awaken her from a deathly enchanted sleep, Coover involves the reader by dangling numerous interpretative possibilities just below the surface of this brief narrative.

Coover's genius is displayed in his use of words, drifting back and forth between reality and dreams. His speculations about what makes a prince forge through the briars and what a princess dreams about while magically asleep for one hundred years are thought-provoking, mysterious, compelling, and at times hilarious. As the tale unwinds, Coover exposes the masculine desire to prey on female beauty. In addition, he leads the reader to contemplate the necessity that women resist male yearnings that are projected onto them. The tale is a bit dull in places and lacks a definite ending with some culminating metaphor, but Coover constructs an intriguing story that is well known, turned in on itself, and explored to reveal different levels of human consciousness.

In his major collections of stories, Coover elaborates on his fundamental concern, namely the necessity for the individual to distinguish between reality and fiction and to be liberated from dogmatic thinking. In order to do so, Coover emphasizes the self-reflexive, antirealistic elements of his fiction. The result is original, highly engaging, and energetic stories that probe human beings' relationships to the myths that shape their lives.

OTHER MAJOR WORKS

LONG FICTION: *The Origin of the Brunists*, 1966; *The Universal Baseball Association, Inc., J. Henry Waugh, Prop.*, 1968; *The Public Burning*, 1977; *Gerald's Party*, 1985; *Pinocchio in Venice*, 1991; *John's Wife*, 1996; *Ghost Town*, 1998.

PLAYS: *The Kid*, pr., pb. 1972; *Love Scene*, pb. 1972; *Rip Awake*, pr. 1972; *Bridge Hound*, pr. 1981; *A Theological Position*, pb. 1972 (collection).

SCREENPLAY: *On a Confrontation in Iowa City*, 1969; *After Lazarus*, 1980.

NONFICTION: "The Last Quixote," 1970; "The Master's Voice," 1977.

BIBLIOGRAPHY

Andersen, Richard. *Robert Coover*. Boston: Twayne, 1981. A useful and very accessible introduction to Coover's production up to 1981. Andersen combines plot summary with commentary, helping the reader to make an initial acquaintance with Coover's work. Notes, select bibliography, and index.

Coover, Robert. "Interview." *Short Story*, n.s. 1 (Fall, 1993): 89-94. Coover comments on the difference between the short story and the novel, the writing of *Pricksongs and Descants*, his use of sexuality in his fiction, his iconoclastic streak, postmodernism, and his use of the short story to test narrative forms.

_____. Interview by Amanda Smith. *Publishers Weekly* 230 (December 26, 1986): 44-45. Coover discusses the motivations that lie behind his ex-
perimental fiction; states he believes that the artist finds his metaphors for the world in the most vulnerable areas of human outreach; he insists that he is in pursuit of the mainstream. What many people consider experimental, Coover argues, is actually traditional in the sense that it has gone back to old forms to find its new form.

Cope, Jackson. *Robert Coover's Fictions*. Baltimore: The Johns Hopkins University Press, 1986. More sophisticated than Richard Andersen's book. Cope supposes that readers know Coover's work and uses several approaches to it, analyzing his techniques, his subject matter, and the critical theories that cast light on his work. Contains an index.

Gordon, Lois. *Robert Coover: The Universal Fiction-making Process*. Carbondale: Southern Illinois University Press, 1983. Like Richard Andersen's book, this volume provides a friendly introduction and overview of Coover's work, placing him in the context of metafictional or postmodernist literature. Notes, select bibliography, and index.

Kennedy, Thomas E. *Robert Coover: A Study of the Short Fiction*. New York: Twayne, 1992. An introduction to Coover's short fiction. Discusses the postmodernist trend in fiction in the 1960's and Coover's place in that tradition. Provides summary analyses of Coover's stories, as well as discussions of critical reception of Coover's fiction. Also includes interviews with Coover, as well as previously published criticism, including William H. Gass's review of *Pricksongs and Descants*.

McCaffery, Larry. *The Metafictional Muse: The Works of Robert Coover, Donald Barthelme, and William H. Gass*. Pittsburgh: University of Pittsburgh Press, 1982. After describing what he considers a major current in contemporary American fiction, McCaffery discusses the metafictional traits of Coover's work and relates him to other important contemporary American writers.

_____. "Robert Coover on His Own and Other Fictions." *Genre* 14 (Spring, 1981): 45-84. A lively discussion in which Coover examines, among other things, the importance of stories about storytelling, the function of the writer in a world threatened by nuclear apocalypse, the fiction that has influenced his work, and popular culture.

Maltby, Paul. *Dissident Postmodernists: Barthelme, Coover, Pynchon*. Philadelphia: University of Pennsylvania Press, 1991. A comparative look at these three writers and their fictions. Includes a bibliography and an index.

"The Pleasures of the (Hyper)text." *The New Yorker* 70 (June/July, 1994): 43-44. Discusses Coover's Hypertext Hotel, the country's first online writing space dedicated to the computer-generated mode of literature known as hypertext; describes

Coover's writing class at Brown University and its use of hypertext.

Scholes, Robert. "Metafiction." *The Iowa Review* 1, no. 3 (Fall, 1970): 100-115. Initially theoretical, then descriptive, this article discusses four major metafictional writers: Coover, William H. Gass, Donald Barthelme, and John Barth. Scholes categorizes the different types of metafictional writing and classifies Coover's *Pricksongs and Descants* as "structural" metafiction, since it is concerned with the order of fiction rather than with the conditions of being.

Carlota Larrea, updated by Alvin K. Benson

A. E. COPPARD

Born: Folkestone, Kent, England; January 4, 1878
Died: Dunmow, England; January 18, 1957

PRINCIPAL SHORT FICTION

Adam and Eve and Pinch Me, 1921
Clorinda Walks in Heaven, 1922
The Black Dog, 1923
Fishmonger's Fiddle, 1925
The Field of Mustard, 1926
Count Stephan, 1928
Silver Circus, 1928
The Gollan, 1929
The Higgler, 1930
The Man from Kilsheelan, 1930
Easter Day, 1931
The Hundredth Story of A. E. Coppard, 1931
Nixey's Harlequin, 1931
Crotty Shinkwin, and the Beauty Spot, 1932
Ring the Bells of Heaven, 1933
Dunky Fitlow, 1933
Emergency Exit, 1934
Polly Oliver, 1935
Ninepenny Flute, 1937
These Hopes of Heaven, 1937
Tapster's Tapestry, 1938
You Never Know, Do You?, 1939

Ugly Anna and Other Tales, 1944
Fearful Pleasures, 1946
Selected Tales from His Twelve Volumes Published Between the Wars, 1946
The Dark-Eyed Lady: Fourteen Tales, 1947
The Collected Tales of A. E. Coppard, 1948
Lucy in Her Pink Jacket, 1954
Simple Day, 1978

OTHER LITERARY FORMS

A. E. Coppard published three slender volumes of poetry, *Hips and Haws* (1922), *Pelagea and Other Poems* (1926), and *Cherry Ripe* (1935), and two collections, *Yokohama Garland* (1926) and *Collected Poems* (1928). In 1957, he published his autobiography, *It's Me, O Lord!*

ACHIEVEMENTS

Though not widely known among general readers, Coppard has experienced a resurgence of popularity as a result of the adaptation of several of his stories for *Masterpiece Theatre* on public television. For both his mastery of the short-story form and his sensitive portrayal of English rural life, Coppard is an important figure in the development of the short story as a serious literary form. From a background of poverty and with no formal education, Coppard advanced through a number of clerical and accounting jobs in Oxford, reading and associating with the students there. Becoming increasingly active in political activities and writing for journals, Coppard eventually decided to write professionally. In the 1920's and 1930's, he was considered one of the foremost short-story writers in England. Coppard's stories are frequently compared to those of Anton Chekhov and Thomas Hardy, whose influence Coppard acknowledged, and also to those of his contemporaries H. E. Bates and D. H. Lawrence. Although his poetry has not generated much acclaim, Coppard's prose is eloquently lyrical, its evocation of mood and portrayal of emotion particularly noteworthy.

BIOGRAPHY

Alfred Edgar Coppard's remarkable life contributed to his early success. To such an influential editor-writer as Ford Madox Ford, he was a rustic wise man or gypsy, a character out of one of his own dark country stories. Coppard was born into poverty and attended only four years of elementary school in Brighton. His father was a tailor, his mother a housemaid; when his father died young, Coppard had to help the family survive by taking a series of menial jobs. At age twenty-one, he became a clerk in an engineering firm in Brighton, where he remained for seven years, advancing to cashier. As a teenager and young man he walked the English countryside, absorbing its landscapes and the language of country folk he met in roadside taverns, a favorite setting for many of his later tales. He was a fine athlete and even supplemented his income as a successful professional sprinter. He married in 1906 and a year later took a better position as an accountant for an ironworks in Oxford, a position he held for twelve years. During his years in Oxford he read, often in the Bodleian, associated with students, heard and sometimes met such luminaries as Vachel Lindsay, Aldous Huxley, and William Butler Yeats, and, finally, began to write. He also became involved in Socialist politics and joined the Women's Social and Political Union. Finally, in 1919, having published seven or eight tales in journals such as the *Manchester Guardian* and a

few poems in journals such as *The Egoist* (edited by T. S. Eliot), he decided to leave his position at the foundry and become a professional writer. On April 1, 1919, at age forty-one, he moved to a small cottage outside Oxford at Shepherd's Pit, where he lived alone in the woods, becoming aware of "the ignoring docility of the earth" and, finally, publishing his first collection of tales on the second anniversary (*Adam and Eve and Pinch Me*, 1921) of his new career. His first book was well-received and thrust him into prominence as one of the leading English short-story writers. Over the next thirty years his production of tales, poems, and reviews was steady and of high quality. A second marriage, to Winifred May de Kok in 1931, endured, but his reputation as a short-story writer began to wane in the mid-1930's; his last collection of tales (1954) was not even reviewed by the *Times Literary Supplement*. *The Collected Tales*, however, was a clear success, and the autobiography he completed on the eve of his fatal illness in 1957 is a delight.

ANALYSIS

The unique quality of A. E. Coppard's short fiction derives from his powers as a lyrical writer, his sympathetic understanding of the rural, lower-class folk who organically inhabit the English countryside so memorably evoked in his tales, and his "uncanny perception," as Frank O'Connor remarked, "of a woman's secretiveness and mystery." Coppard's earliest reviewers and critics emphasized the poetic quality of his tales. The title story from *The Field of Mustard* is one of the great stories in English, and it suggests the full range of Coppard's creative genius, including his lyric portrayal of the English countryside and its folk, especially its women, whose language and life-consciousness seem wedded to the landscape.

"THE FIELD OF MUSTARD"

Like other lyric short stories, "The Field of Mustard" is nearly plotless. It opens with the suggestion that everything has already happened to the main characters, "three sere disvirgined women from Pollock's Cross." What remains for Coppard is to evoke the quality of these lives and the countryside of which they are a part; the tale proceeds as a kind of lyric meditation on life and death in nature. The women have come to "the Black Wood" in order to gather "dead branches" from the living trees, and on their way home, two of them, Dinah Lock and Rose Olliver, become involved in an intimate conversation that reveals the hopelessness of their lives. Rose, wishing she had children but knowing she never will, cannot understand why Dinah is not happy with her four children. Dinah complains that "a family's a torment. I never wanted mine." Dinah's "corpulence dispossessed her of tragedy," and perhaps because she has had the burden as well as the fulfillment of motherhood, she expressed the bitterness of life in what serves almost as a refrain: "Oh God, cradle and grave is all for we." They are old but their hearts are young, and the truth of Dinah's complaint, "that's the cussedness of nature, it makes a mock of you," is reflected in the world around them: The depleted women are associated with the mustard field and the "sour scent rising faintly from its yellow blooms." Against this natural order, Dinah and Rose wish that "this world was all a garden"; but "the wind blew strongly athwart the yellow field, and the odour of mustard rushed upon the brooding women."

As Dinah and Rose continue their conversation, they complain of their feeble husbands and discover a mutual loss: Each had been a lover of Rufus Blackthorn, a local gamekeeper. He was "a pretty man," "handsome," "black as coal and bold as a fox"; and although "he was good to women," he was "a perfect devil," "deep as the sea." Gradually Coppard's pattern of imagery reveals the source of these women's loss to be the very wellspring of life—their love and sexual vitality. The suggestion is explicit in their lover's name, "Blackthorn," who had brought them most in life yet left them now with "old grief or new rancour." This grim reality is suggested earlier when the women meet an old man in the Black Wood; he shows them a timepiece given him by "a noble Christian man," but is met only with Dinah's profane taunt, "Ah! I suppose he slept wid Jesus?" Outraged, the old man calls Dinah "a great fat thing," shouts an obscenity, and leaving them, puts "his fingers to his nose." Dinah's bitter mockery of Christian love gradually

merges with the sour scent of mustard and surfaces transformed in Rose's recollection of how Blackthorn once joked of having slept with a dead man. These women, gathered in "the Black Wood" to collect dead wood from the living trees, have in effect slept with death. The yellow mustard blooms quiver in the wind, yet they are sour. The same "wind hustled the two women close together," and they touch; but, bereft of their sexual vitality, they are left only with Dinah's earlier observation that "it's such a mercy to have a friend at all" and her repeated appeal, "I like you, Rose, I wish you was a man." The tale ends with the women "quiet and voiceless,"

> in fading light they came to their homes. But how windy, dispossessed, and ravaged roved the darkening world! Clouds were borne frantically across the heavens, as if in a rout of battle, and the lovely earth seemed to sigh in grief at some calamity all unknown to men.

Coppard's lyric tales celebrate the oral tradition. His stories are often tales of tales being told, perhaps in a country tavern (as in "Alas, Poor Bollington!"). In some tales an oral narrator addresses the reader directly, and in others the rural settings, the characters, and the events—often of love ending in violence—draw obviously upon the materials of traditional folk ballads. Coppard himself loved to sing ballads and Elizabethan folk songs, and the main characters in these stories are sometimes singers, or their tales are "balladed about." In many tales, Coppard used rhythmic language, poetically inverted constructions, and repeated expressions that function as refrains in ballads. The most explicit example of a tale intended to resound with balladic qualities is "A Broadsheet Ballad," a tale of two laborers waiting in a tavern for the rain to pass. They begin to talk of a local murder trial, and one is moved by the thought of a hanging: "Hanging's a dreadful thing," he exclaims; and at length, with "almost a sigh," he repeats. "Hanging's a dreadful thing." His sigh serves as the tale's refrain and causes his fellow to tell within the tale a longer tale of a love triangle that ended in a murder and an unjust hanging. Finally, the sigh-refrain and the strange narration coalesce in the laborer's language:

Ah, when things make a turn against you it's as certain as twelve o'clock, when they take a turn; you get no more chance than a rabbit from a weasel. It's like dropping your matches into a stream, you needn't waste the bending of your back to pick them out—they're no good on, they'll never strike again.

Coppard's lyric mode is perfectly suited to his grand theme: the darkness of love, its fleeting loveliness and inevitable entanglements and treacheries. He writes of triangles, entrapping circumstances, and betrayals in which, as often as not, a lover betrays himself or herself out of foolishness, timidity, or blind adherence to custom. Some of his best tales, like "Dusky Ruth" and "The Higgler," dwell on the mysterious elusiveness of love, often as this involves an alluring but ungraspable woman. Men and women are drawn together by circumstances and deep undercurrents of unarticulated feeling but are separated before they consummate their love.

"THE HIGGLER"

Because of its portrayal of unconsummated love, its treatment of the rural poor, and its poetic atmosphere that arises from the countryside itself, "The Higgler" (the first story in *The Collected Tales*) is fully characteristic of Coppard's best work. It is not simply a tale of unconsummated love, for its main character comes to absorb and reflect the eternal forces of conflict in nature. For Coppard this involves more than man's economic struggle to wrest his living from nature; it involves man's conflict with man in war, his conflict with his lover, his conflict with himself, and ultimately, with his own life source, the mother.

Harvey Witlow is the higgler, a man whose business it is to travel the countryside in a horse-drawn wagon, buying produce from small farms. The story opens with the higgler making his way across Shag Moor, a desolate place where "solitude . . . now . . . shivered and looked sinister." Witlow is shrewd and crafty, "but the season was backward, eggs were scarce, trade was bad"; and he stands to lose the meager business he has struggled to establish for himself since returning from the war, as well as his opportunity to marry. "That's what war does for you," he

says. "I was better off working for farmers; much; but it's no good chattering about it, it's the trick of life; when you get so far, then you can go and order your funeral." After this dismal beginning, Witlow is presented with an unexpected opportunity to improve his life in every way; but he is destined to outwit himself, as his name suggests, and to know more fully the "trick of life." As the tale develops, then, the reader watches him miss his opportunity and resume his descent into general desolation.

His chance comes when he stops at the farm of a Mrs. Sadgrove. Here the higgler finds plenty of produce as well as the intriguing possibility of a relationship with Mrs. Sadgrove's daughter, Mary, another of Coppard's alluring, secretive women. Mary's quiet beauty attracts Witlow, but he imagines her to be too "well-up" and "highly cultivated" for him. She shows no interest in him, so he is unprepared when, after several trips to the farm and an invitation to dinner, Mrs. Sadgrove tells him of her poor health and her desire that he should wed Mary and take over the farm. The higgler leaves bewildered. Here is his life's opportunity: The farm is prosperous, and he is far more attracted to Mary than to Sophy, the poor girl he eventually marries; besides, Mary will inherit five hundred pounds on her twenty-fifth birthday. It is simply too good to believe, and after consulting with his mother about his opportunity, Witlow grows increasingly suspicious. The reader has already been told that "mothers are inscrutable beings to their sons, always"; and Witlow is confused by his mother's enthusiasm over his opportunity. Even the natural world somehow conspires to frighten him: "Autumn was advancing, and the apples were down, the bracken dying, the furze out of bloom, and the farm on the moor looked more and more lonely. . . ."

So Witlow begins to avoid the Sadgrove farm and suddenly marries Sophy. Within months, his "affairs had again taken a rude turn. Marriage, alas, was not all it might be; his wife and his mother quarrelled unendingly," and his business fails badly. His only chance seems to be to return to the Sadgrove farm, where he might obtain a loan; but he does so reluctantly, for he knows Mrs. Sadgrove to be a hard woman. She exploits her help and "was reputed to be a 'grinder'"; and he has betrayed her confidence. In an increasingly dark atmosphere of loss, Witlow returns across Shag Moor to the Sadgrove farm, where Mary meets him with the news of her mother's death that day. Now a prolonged, eerie, and utterly powerful scene develops as the higgler agrees to help Mary prepare her mother's body, which lies alone upstairs in a state of rigor mortis. He sends Mary away and confronts the dead mother, whose stiff outstretched arm had been impossible for Mary to manage.

Moments later, in their intimacy near the dead mother, Witlow blurts out, "Did you know as she once asked me to marry you?" Finally Mary reveals that her mother actually opposed the marriage: "The girl bowed her head, lovely in her grief and modesty. 'She was against it, but I made her ask you. . . . I was fond of you—then.'" To his distress and confusion, Mary insists that he leave at once, and he drives "away in deep darkness, the wind howling, his thoughts strange and bitter."

"ARABESQUE: THE MOUSE"

Coppard's vision of life caught in a struggle against itself, of the violence in nature and its mockery of morality, of the deceit among humans and of humans' denial of their true nature—all this is marvelously represented in one of his first and finest tales, "Arabesque: The Mouse." It is a psychological horror story of a middle-aged man who sits alone one night reading Russian novels until he thinks he is mad. He is an idealist who was obsessed by the incompatibilities of property and virtue, justice and sin. He looks at a "print by Utamaro of a suckling child caressing its mother's breasts" and his mind drifts to recall his own mother and then a brief experience with a lover. These recollections merge in a compelling pattern of images that unite finally, and horribly, with an actual experience this night with a mouse. As a child horrified by the sight of some dead larks that had been intended for supper, he sought comfort from his mother and found her sitting by the fire with her bodice open, "squeezing her breasts; long thin streams of milk spurted into the fire with a little plunging noise." Telling him that she was weaning his little sister, she draws him to her breast and presses his face "against the delicate warmth of her

bosom." She allows him to do it; "so he discovered the throb of the heart in his mother's breast. Wonderful it was for him to experience it, although she could not explain it to him." They feel his own beat, and his mother assures him his heart is "good if it beats truly. Let it always beat truly, Filip." The child kisses "her bosom in his ecstasy and whisper[s] soothingly: 'Little mother! little mother.'"

The boy forgets the horror of the dead larks bundled by their feet, but the next day his mother is run over by a heavy cart, and before she dies her mutilated hands are amputated. For years the image of his mother's bleeding stumps of arms had haunted his dreams. Into his mind, however, now floats the recollection of an experience with a lovely country girl he had met and accompanied home. It was "dark, dark . . . , the night an obsidian net"; finally in their intimacy she had unbuttoned his coat, and with her hands on his breast asked, "Oh, how your heart beats! Does it beat truly?" In a "little fury of love" he cried "Little mother, little mother!" and confused the girl. At that moment footsteps and the clack of a bolt cause them to part forever.

The sound of the bolt hurls him into the present, where, frightened, he opens his cupboard to find a mouse sitting on its haunches before a snapped trap. "Its head was bowed, but its beadlike eyes were full of brightness, and it sat blinking, it did not flee." Then to his horror he sees that the trap had caught only the feet, "and the thing crouched there holding out its two bleeding stumps humanly, too stricken to stir." He throws the mouse from his window into the darkness, then sits stunned, "limp with pity too deep for tears" before running down into the street in a vain search for the "little philosopher." Later he drops the tiny feet into the fire, resets the trap, and carefully replaces it. "Arabesque: The Mouse" is a masterwork of interwoven imagery whose unity is caught in such details as the mother's heartbeat, the mother's milk streaming with a plunging noise into the fire, the mouse's eyes, and the "obsidian net" of night.

Coppard's characters are sometimes shattered by such thoughts and experiences, but the author never lost his own sense of the natural magnificence and fleeting loveliness in life. It is true that many of his late tales pursue in a more thoughtful and comic manner the natural and psychological forces in life that were simply, but organically and poetically, present in such earlier tales as "The Higgler"; that is, in some of his later stories the reader can too easily see him playing with thoughts about Alfred Adler, Sigmund Freud, and, repeatedly, Charles Darwin (whose prose he admired). Yet the last tale (the title story) of his final volume is one of his best. "Lucy in Her Pink Jacket" is almost a hymn to nature, a song of acceptance in which lovers meet accidentally in a magnificent mountain setting. Their lovemaking is beautiful, natural, and relaxed, and they accept the web of circumstances causing them to part. Coppard's description of his last parting character might serve as our own image of himself: "Stepping out into the bright eager morning it was not long before [he] was whistling softly as he went his way, a sort of thoughtful, plaintive, museful air."

OTHER MAJOR WORKS

POETRY: *Hips and Haws*, 1922; *Pelagea and Other Poems*, 1926; *Yokohama Garland*, 1926; *Collected Poems*, 1928; *Cherry Ripe*, 1935.

NONFICTION: *Rummy: That Noble Game Expounded*, 1933; *It's Me, O Lord!*, 1957.

CHILDREN'S LITERATURE: *Pink Furniture*, 1930.

BIBLIOGRAPHY

Allen, Walter. *The Short Story in English*. New York: Oxford University Press, 1981. Includes a brief analysis of Coppard's "The Higgler," suggesting that the story is as unpredictable as life itself, with nothing seemingly arranged or contrived by Coppard.

Bates, H. E. "Katherine Mansfield and A. E. Coppard." In *The Modern Short Story: A Critical Survey*. London: Evensford Productions, 1972. Coppard's contemporary and fellow author of short stories discusses Coppard's role in the development of the modern English short story. Bates discerns an unfortunate influence of Henry James on Coppard's work, which is remarkable in its Elizabethan lyricism and its homage to the oral tradition. Includes an index.

Beachcroft, T. O. *The Modest Art: A Survey of the Short Story in English*. New York: Oxford University Press, 1968. Discusses Coppard's two basic generic veins—the highly fantastic in such stories as "Adam and Eve and Pinch Me," and the naturalistic in stories such as "The Higgler" and "The Water Cress Girl."

Cowley, Malcolm. "Book Reviews: *Adam and Eve and Pinch Me*." *The Dial* 71, no. 1 (July, 1921): 93-95. Describes Coppard's careful workmanship, his skillful narration, and his artful blend of fantasy and realism. Cowley notes Coppard's emotional unity, his insight into characters, his animated landscapes, and his role in keeping the short-story form vital.

Ginden, James. "A. E. Coppard and H. E. Bates." In *The English Short Story, 1880-1945: A Critical History*, edited by Joseph M. Flora. Boston: Twayne, 1985. Compares Coppard's and H. E. Bates's treatment of rural life as well as their dedication to the short story as distinguished from other literary forms. Although both authors employed the techniques of the modern short story, Ginden does not consider them "modernists," arguing that their work lacks the reliance on symbol or metaphor and instead stresses anecdote and description.

Kalasky, Drew, ed. *Short Story Criticism: Excerpts from Criticism of the Works of Short Fiction Writers*. Vol. 21. Detroit, Mich.: Gale Research, Inc., 1996. A thoughtful collection of criticism of works by Coppard, Jean Rhys, William Sansom, William Saroyan, Giovanni Verga, and others.

Lessing, Doris. Introduction to *Selected Stories by A. E. Coppard*. London: Jonathan Cape, 1972. Lessing attributes the general appeal of Coppard's fiction to his exceptional talent for storytelling. Coppard was an expert craftsman, but it is the authentic growth of characters and events that involves the reader.

O'Connor, Frank. *The Lonely Voice: A Study of the Short Story*. New York: World Publishing, 1962. O'Connor examines Coppard's themes of poverty, personal freedom, and women in the context of other modern short fiction by Irish, English,

American, and Russian writers. The two great English storytellers, according to O'Connor, are Coppard and D. H. Lawrence. Though both authors share workingclass backgrounds, Coppard is a more deliberate, self-conscious artist, and he betrays feelings of social inadequacy.

Bert Bender, updated by Lou Thompson

JULIO CORTÁZAR

Born: Brussels, Belgium; August 26, 1914
Died: Paris, France; February 12, 1984

PRINCIPAL SHORT FICTION

Bestiario, 1951
Final de juego, 1956
Las armas secretas, 1959
Historias de cronopios y de famas, 1962
    (*Cronopios and Famas*, 1969)
End of the Game and Other Stories, 1963 (also as
    Blow-Up and Other Stories, 1967)
Todos los fuegos el fuego, 1966 (*All Fires the Fire
    and Other Stories*, 1973)
Octaedro, 1974 (included in *A Change of Light and
    Other Stories*, 1980)
Alguien que anda por ahí y otros relatos, 1977 (in-
    cluded in *A Change of Light and Other Stories*,
    1980)
Un tal Lucas, 1979 (*A Certain Lucas*, 1984)
Queremos tanto a Glenda y otros relatos, 1980 (*We
    Love Glenda So Much and Other Tales*, 1983)
Deshoras, 1982

OTHER LITERARY FORMS

Julio Cortázar's literary career, which lasted almost forty years, includes—besides his short stories—novels, plays, poetry, translations, and essays of literary criticism. In his essay on short fiction entitled "Algunos aspectos del cuento" ("Some Aspects of the Short Story"), Cortázar studies the varying role of the reader with regard to different literary forms. Cortázar's first book, *Presencia* (1938), was a collection of poetry that he published under the pseudonym Julio Denís. He translated authors as diverse as Louisa May Alcott and Edgar Allan Poe into Spanish and considered French Symbolist poetry to be of enormous influence on his prose writing. He experimented with a form of collage in his later works of short fiction.

ACHIEVEMENTS

An antirealist, Cortázar is often grouped with Gabriel García Márquez as one of the foremost proponents of the Magical Realism movement and, during his lifetime, one of the most articulate spokespersons on the subject of Latin American fiction.

Although Cortázar is most admired for his short stories (his short story "Las babas del diablo" was made into a classic film in 1966 called *Blow-Up* by director Michelangelo Antonioni), it was the publication of the novel *Rayuela* (1963; *Hopscotch*, 1966) that placed the author among the twentieth century's greatest writers. *The Times Literary Supplement* called *Hopscotch* the "first great novel of Spanish America."

BIOGRAPHY

Julio Cortázar was born in Brussels, Belgium, in 1914, during the German occupation. His Argentine parents were stationed there while his father was on the staff of a commercial mission. Cortázar's antecedents came from the Basque region of Spain, as well as France and Germany, and they had settled in Argentina. When Cortázar was four years old, his parents returned to Argentina, where he would grow up in Banfield, a suburb of Buenos Aires. His father abandoned the family, and he was reared by his mother and an aunt.

Cortázar attended the Escuela Norman Mariano Acosta in Buenos Aires and earned a degree as a public-school teacher in 1932. In 1937, he accepted a high school teaching post and shortly thereafter published *Presencia*, a collection of poems, under the pseudonym Julio Denís. In 1940, he published an essay on Arthur Rimbaud, under the same pseudonym, and began to teach a class on the French Symbolist movement at the University of Cuyo in Mendoza. In 1946, Jorge Luis Borges, at that time the editor of the literary journal *Anales de Buenos Aires*, published "Casa tomada" ("House Taken Over")—the first work that Julio Cortázar penned under his own name.

A writer with outspoken political beliefs, Cortázar was defiantly anti-Peronist. He was arrested and as a result was forced to relinquish his academic career in Argentina. Instead, however, he became a translator and, in 1951, went to Paris, where he soon established permanent residency. Much of his best short fiction, including "Bestiary" and "End of the Game," was published in the 1950's and reveals his experience as an expatriate—a Latin American living in Paris.

In Paris, Cortázar got a job as a translator for UNESCO, which he kept for the rest of his life despite his international success as an author. In 1953, he married Aurora Bernandez, with whom he translated Poe's prose works into Spanish, while they lived briefly in Rome. In 1963, he published *Hopscotch* and, after a visit to Cuba, became a powerful figure on both the literary and the political scenes.

His audience grew wider during the 1960's and 1970's with the translation of *Rayuela* into dozens of languages and the appearance of the film *Blow-Up*. He also traveled extensively to such diverse places as Chile, New York, and Oklahoma to attend conferences, receive awards, and participate in political tribunals. In 1981, he finally became a French citizen. He died in Paris in February, 1984, of leukemia and heart disease. He is buried in the Montparnasse cemetery in Paris.

ANALYSIS

Influenced by the European movements of nineteenth century Symbolism and twentieth century Sur-

Julio Cortázar (Library of Congress)

realism, Julio Cortázar combines symbols, dreams, and the fantastic with what seems to be an ordinary, realistic situation in order to expose a different kind of reality that exists in the innermost heart and mind of modern human beings. Like Poe, Cortázar is fascinated by terror. He uses human beings' worst nightmares to explore which fears control them and how phobias and dreams coexist with seemingly rational thought. Using symbols and metaphors for subconscious obsessions, Cortázar's short fictions, unlike those of the Surrealists, are carefully constructed. His journey into the irrational is not a free-flowing adventure; rather, it is a study of a particular corner of the mind that is common to all people.

"BESTIARY"

"Bestiary," an early story published in 1951, contains many of the elements of poesy and mystery that are characteristic of the nineteenth century Symbolists so admired by Cortázar. The story is told by a child whose scope of understanding and point of view are limited, thereby leaving certain details vague and confusing. Isabel is sent to the country for the summer to stay in a home inhabited by another child, Nino, and three adults: Luis, Nino's father; Rema, who may or may not be Nino's mother, Luis' wife or sister, Nino's sister, or the housekeeper; and the Kid, who is not a kid but Luis' brother. The information given about the family is not specific in those terms, but it is quite specific in Isabel's feelings about each person. The over whelming oddity about this summer home is that a tiger is allowed to roam freely about the house and grounds. The people are advised as to the location of the tiger each day, and they go about their business as usual by simply avoiding the room or part of the fields in which the tiger happens to be.

Life seems to be filled with very typical activities: Luis works in his study; the children gather an ant collection; and Rema supervises meals. Isabel is especially fond of Rema but not of the Kid. Events are relayed that expose Isabel's true feelings about the Kid and the kind of person she believes him to be. He is surly at the dinner table. Once, after Nino has hit a ball through the window leading to the Kid's room, the Kid hits Nino; the most disturbing moment, however, is a scene between Rema and the Kid during which Isabel acts as a voyeur, revealing some sort of sexual abuse on the part of the Kid toward Rema. Because of Isabel's admiration for Rema, she decides to take revenge on the Kid. The culmination of the story is that Isabel lies to the family about the whereabouts of the tiger, sending the Kid into the room where the animal is. Screams are heard, and it is clear that the Kid has been mauled to death. Isabel notices that Rema squeezes her hand with what the child believes to be gratitude.

Many critics have speculated about the meaning of the tiger. Cortázar, in true Symbolist fashion, has himself said that the reader receives a richer experience if no specific symbol is attributed to the animal in this story. As in the works of Poe, constant tension and terror pervade the work, and the tiger's meaning becomes a relative one—a personal nightmare for each character and each reader.

"LETTER TO A YOUNG LADY IN PARIS"

"Letter to a Young Lady in Paris" begins on a charming note. It is a letter from a young man to his girlfriend, who is visiting Paris. She has asked him to move into her apartment, and, through very delicate language, he tries to convince her that he would disrupt her very orderly and truly elegant apartment. He succumbs to her wishes, however, and moves his belongings, but on the way up in the elevator he begins to feel sick. Panic ensues when he vomits a bunny rabbit, and, while living in the apartment, each wave of anxiety produces another. Soon, he is sequestering ten bunny rabbits in an armoire. The rabbits sleep in the daytime and are awakened at night; he manages to keep his secret from his girlfriend's nosy maid. The nocturnal insomnia and the constant production of bunny rabbits drive him to jump out the window along with the last one regurgitated. The charming letter is really a suicide note, and the seemingly eccentric but sweet story becomes a horrific account of phobia and insanity.

"AXOLOTL"

Cortázar seems particularly fascinated with the unusual placement of animals in these stories. In "Bestiary" and "Letter to a Young Lady in Paris," animals take over the lives of people. In another short story, "Axolotl," the man who visits the aquarium every day to see the axolotl swim becomes the axolotl. The narrative point of view switches back and forth between the man and the sea creature, telling the story from both points of view, but since there is no regular pattern or warning when the point of view changes, it is often difficult to determine inside whose skin readers are. The nightmare of being trapped inside the body of a beast is the human's experience, and the panic of being abandoned by the man is the axolotl's final cry. The only hope, as noted by the axolotl, is the creation of art where the writer can become another and communicate on behalf of all creatures—expressing the feelings of all creatures so that none may feel the terror of isolation and imprisonment.

"ALL FIRES THE FIRE"

The shifting of narrative point of view as well as the alternation of time and place is a technique that

Cortázar developed during his career as an author. A later story, "All Fires the Fire," revolves around two unhappy love triangles. One takes place in modern times and one during a gladiator fight in an ancient coliseum. Again, Cortázar uses animals to provide a menacing tone to what seem to be ordinary failures in romance. In both cases, raging blazes burn the lovers to death. No clear delineation is made when the story shifts scenes. The reader begins to sense these changes as the story unfolds; the scenes are different, but the tension never desists. The author creates deliberate ambiguity so that the reader, who is being intentionally confused by the author, nevertheless receives signals at the same time. Like the Symbolist writers whom he admired, Cortázar, in "All Fires the Fire," understands the power of the suggestive image and insists that readers use their own senses to feel the intensity of hate, lust, and love in both triangles. Through smell, sound, and sight, the reader gets two complete and distinct pictures that have similar endings. Like the Surrealist writers who unraveled the varying layers of the mind, Cortázar here projects two events that occur at two different times in two different places yet at the same moment in the reader's consciousness.

"BLOW-UP"

Through fractured narration, Cortázar is able to examine how the mind can appropriate different personalities and points of view. The games of the mind are a constant theme in the works of Cortázar, and it is for that reason that a journey into his fictive world is an opportunity to explore the relationship between what seems to be real and what seems to be illogical. Cortázar confounds the reader's system of beliefs with his manipulation of discourse. He begins the story "Blow-Up," for example, by stating: "It'll never be known how this has to be told, in the first person or in the second, using the third person plural or continually inventing modes that will serve for nothing." He continues by telling readers how he writes—by typewriter—making them absolutely aware of the fact that they are going to enter the world of fiction. Although "Blow-Up" begins on this self-conscious trial, which seems to draw an obvious distinction between art and life, its actual theme is the inter-

changeability of the two. The narrator introduces the reader to the story's hero, a French-Chilean photographer named Robert Michel, and then becomes him. The story is narrated alternatively in first-person "I" and third-person "he" and becomes a collage of identities.

Out for a stroll on a pleasant November day, the photographer happens by chance upon a scene that disturbs him. Chance is an essential component of the world of magic, the fantastic and the illogical in Cortázar's short fiction. Chance rearranges preexisting order and creates a new future, past, and present for Cortázar's characters. The photographer/narrator witnesses a brief moment between a young man, a woman, and an older man sitting in a car—another love triangle with menacing undertones—and creates a history of what might have brought all three to the quai near the Seine. After the particular episode, he creates a future for them of what might happen to each of them afterward. Later, when he himself reflects on the episode, he studies his photographs as if the moments were frozen in time. Strangely, the more he studies his enlargements the more his memory alters. Because he creates a fiction about each of the people involved, the photo and his involvement in their little dramas become fiction as well, and he is not at all certain of what he has witnessed. The whole episode develops into a dream, a game of the mind.

The photographs that he had taken, which were supposed to reproduce reality with exactitude, become a collage of suggestions. Magnified, the photographs reveal even less about what he thought had occurred. The photographer believes that his camera is empowered with precision and with accuracy; he discovers, however, that the artwork has a life of its own that is constantly re-creating itself.

The search for truth in art is the pervading theme in Julio Cortázar's short fiction. He attempts to break with realist attitudes to force the reader to look beyond that which is ordinary and comfortable in order to explore the realms that seem, on the surface, incomprehensible and fearful. Cortázar believes that as human beings, people must recognize the inexplicable as just that and must admit that they do not have control over everything. The characters in "Bestiary" do not have control over the tiger. The young man in "Letter to a Young Lady in Paris" does not have control over the rabbits that he regurgitates. "All Fires the Fire" depicts the characters involved in passionate love triangles whose emotions are out of control. Finally, in "Blow-Up," the artist's work has a life of its own.

It was the Symbolist movement that gave Cortázar his stylistic signature and the Surrealists who divulged the irrational to later artists. Cortázar combined his appreciation for both movements and consolidated them with his own voice to create exciting and challenging short fiction.

OTHER MAJOR WORKS

LONG FICTION: *Los premios*, 1960 (*The Winners*, 1965); *Rayuela*, 1963 (*Hopscotch*, 1966); *62; Modelo para armar*, 1968 (*62: A Model Kit*, 1972); *Libro de Manuel*, 1973 (*A Manual for Manuel*, 1978).

POETRY: *Presencia*, 1938 (as Julio Denís); *Los reyes*, 1949; *Pameos y meopas*, 1971; *Salvo el crepúsculo*, 1984.

NONFICTION: *Buenos Aires Buenos Aires*, 1968 (English translation, 1968); *Último round*, 1969; *Viaje alrededor de una mesa*, 1970; *Prosa del observatorio*, 1972 (with Antonio Galvez); *Fantomas contra los vampiros multinacionales: Una utopía realizable*, 1975; *Literatura en la revolución y revolución en la literatura*, 1976 (with Mario Vargas Llosa and Oscar Collazos); *Paris: The Essence of Image*, 1981; *Los autonautas de la cosmopista*, 1983; *Nicaragua, tan violentamente dulce*, 1983 (*Nicaraguan Sketches*, 1989).

TRANSLATIONS: *Robinson Crusoe*, 1945 (of Daniel Defoe's *Robinson Crusoe*); *El inmoralista*, 1947 (of André Gide's *L'Immoraliste*); *El hombre que sabía demasiado*, c. 1948-1951 (of G. K. Chesterton's *The Man Who Knew Too Much*); *Vida y Cartas de John Keats*, c. 1948-1951 (of Lord Houghton's *Life and Letters of John Keats*); *Filosofía de la risa y del llanto*, 1950 (of Alfred Stern's *Philosophie du rire et des pleurs*); *La filosofia de Sartre y el psicoanálisis existentialista*, 1951 (of Alfred Stern's *Sartre, His Philosophy and Psychoanalysis*).

MISCELLANEOUS: *La vuelta al día en ochenta mundos*, 1967 (*Around the Day in Eighty Worlds*, 1986); *Último round*, 1969; *Divertimiento*, 1986; *El examen*, 1986.

BIBLIOGRAPHY

Alazraki, Jaime, and Ivan Ivask, eds. *The Final Island*. Norman: University of Oklahoma Press, 1978. *The Final Island* is a collection of essays, including two by Cortázar himself, about the role of magic or the marvelous as it works alongside what appears to be realism in Cortázar's fiction. In a more general way, the history of fiction is approached with the theory that the fabulous is itself more revealing about human truth than is the so-called realism. Contains a chronology and an extensive bibliography that offers data on Cortázar's publications in several languages.

Alonso, Carlos J., ed. *Julio Cortázar: New Readings*. New York: Cambridge University Press, 1998. Part of the Cambridge Studies in Latin American and Iberian Literature series. Includes bibliographical references and an index.

Garfield, Evelyn Picon. *Julio Cortázar*. New York: Frederick Ungar, 1975. Garfield begins and ends her study with personal interviews that she obtained with Cortázar at his home in Provence, France. She studies the neurotic obsession of the characters in Cortázar's fiction and offers first-hand commentary by Cortázar on his methods of writing and his own experiences that helped create his work. Cortázar's philosophies, his preferences, and even his own personal nightmares are expounded upon, illuminating much of the symbolism found in his work. Chronology, analysis, complete bibliography, and index.

Hernandez del Castillo, Ana. *Keats, Poe, and the Shaping of Cortázar's Mythopoesis*. Amsterdam: John Benjamins, 1981. Studies the influence of John Keats and Edgar Allan Poe on the work of Cortázar. The author states that of these two poets, whose works Cortázar translated, Poe had the greater influence on Cortázar. Studies the role of the archetypes in mythology and psychology and how they have been used in the works of all three writers. Contains an excellent index, which includes references that have had an enormous impact on trends in the twentieth century.

Peavler, Terry J. *Julio Cortázar*. Boston: Twayne, 1990. Peavler divides Cortázar's short fiction into four categories—the fantastic, the mysterious, the psychological, and the realistic—in order to show how Cortázar used these genres as games to study discourse. He argues that studying any of Cortázar's works as merely "psychological" or "political" is a superficial understanding of Cortázar's intent, which is really to study the nature of fiction itself. That is why Cortázar's narrative often changes voice, undermines itself, and even offers a choice of endings. Includes a chronology and a through bibliography, and offers intelligent analysis.

Stavans, Ilan. *Julio Cortázar: A Study of the Short Fiction*. New York: Twayne, 1996. A study of Cortázar's short fiction that shows how his art reflects his life and his life is affected by his art. Stavans calls his book an "autobiography" of Cortázar's short fiction that attempts to trace the sources of his short stories in biographical information. Divides Cortázar's work into two creative periods of his life: 1945 to 1966 and 1967 to 1983.

Sugano, Marian Zwerling. "Beyond What Meets the Eye: The Photographic Analogy in Cortázar's Short Stories." *Style* 27 (Fall, 1993): 332-351. Summarizes and critiques Cortazar's analogy between the short story and photography in his essays, "Some Aspects of the Short Story" and "On the Short Story and Its Environs"; explains how Cortázar dramatizes the analogy in "Blow-Up" and "Apocalypse at Solentiname."

Susan Nayel

JAMES GOULD COZZENS

Born: Chicago, Illinois; August 19, 1903
Died: Stuart, Florida; August 9, 1978

PRINCIPAL SHORT FICTION
Child's Play, 1958
Children and Others, 1964
A Flower in Her Hair, 1975

OTHER LITERARY FORMS

Of James Gould Cozzens's fourteen published books, thirteen are novels. Two won special acclaim; *Guard of Honor* (1948; Pulitzer Prize in fiction, 1949) is widely regarded as one of the best American novels of World War II, and *By Love Possessed* (1957; Howells Medal of the American Society of Arts and Letters, 1960) was a major best-seller. Cozzens's only volume of short fiction, *Children and Others*, contains seventeen of his twenty-nine published stories. It was a Book-of-the-Month Club selection, as were five of his novels.

ACHIEVEMENTS

James Gould Cozzens has consistently been neglected by the serious critics during his fifty-five-year writing career. He never received the proper recognition and honors accorded to his contemporaries, including Theodore Dreiser, William Faulkner, F. Scott Fitzgerald, Ernest Hemingway, and Sinclair Lewis. Cozzens is partly to blame because he lived such a reclusive life, avoiding close contact with people and devoting himself totally to the craft of writing. Another reason may also be that his work fits no definite category in American fiction. He has become the least read and least taught of the major American writers enjoying the status of "cult author." Cozzens launched his writing career at age twenty-one and did not involve himself in self-promotion. He always felt that the first objective of writers should be to perfect and master their art. Despite six Book-of-the-Month Club selections and a Pulitzer Prize, Cozzens's work remains largely unknown to the general readership.

James Gould Cozzens (Library of Congress)

With the exception of *By Love Possessed*, his books have never circulated widely as paperbacks and none was ever adopted as a classroom text. Critics have long regarded Cozzens as too highly intellectual a novelist, too detached in his writings, and lacking involvement with his characters. Cozzens is at his best creating traditional social novels with believable characters exhibiting a variety of weaknesses and strengths. Two important themes run throughout his work. He believes in the ultimate dignity of humans and in a moral order imposed on what seems to be a chaotic, meaningless world.

BIOGRAPHY

Born in Chicago, James Gould Cozzens grew up on Staten Island, New York, attended the Kent School in Connecticut, and then went to Harvard University in 1922, where he remained for two years. During the mid-1920's he served as a tutor of American children in Cuba and Europe. In 1927, he married Bernice Baumgarten, a New York literary agent; they had no children. In 1938, Cozzens was briefly a guest editor at *Fortune*. With the outbreak of World War II, he en-

tered the U.S. Army Air Force, worked on various classified stateside assignments, and was discharged as a major in 1945. Cozzens was a member of the National Institute of Arts and Letters, received two O. Henry Awards for short fiction in 1931 and 1936, the Pulitzer Prize for Fiction in 1949, and the Howells Medal of the American Society of Arts and Letters in 1960.

ANALYSIS

Although most of the stories collected in *Children and Others* were originally published between 1930 and 1937, three of them—including James Gould Cozzens's best, "Eyes to See"—were first published as late as 1964. This fact suggests that his continuing interest in and developing mastery of the short-story form complements and illuminates his career-long devotion to the novel.

Of the five sections into which the collection is divided, the first two, "Child's Play" and "Away at School," containing ten stories between them, are perceptive recollections of childhood experiences. Although Cozzens is rigorously impersonal in his fiction, readers may be pardoned for imagining that one of the children of his title is the young Cozzens. We see a little boy turned in on his own imaginative self, and later a student at Durham (modeled on the Kent School, which Cozzens attended)—precocious, self-conscious, and at times frightened. The third section, "War Between the States," is composed of two Civil War stories. In the late 1930's, Cozzens assembled material for a Civil War novel but found that he could not write it, and perhaps in the stories the reader sees something of what that novel might have been. The fourth section, "Love and Kisses," with four stories, examines the complexity of inexorably changing relations between men and women. The seventeenth, last, and longest story, "Eyes to See," written in 1963, is Cozzens at his distilled best and hence deserves somewhat more extended consideration than its predecessors.

"TOTAL STRANGER"

"Total Stranger," from part 1, which received the O. Henry Memorial Award for the best story of 1936, develops—with typical indirection and understated humor—the process by which a boy begins to see his father in an entirely new light. John is being driven back to his New England prep school by his father, who is distinctly dissatisfied with his son's undistinguished academic performance there, and who does not accept the boy's self-serving explanations and ill-constructed defenses. John has never had trouble getting around his mother; with his father, however, who is authoritative, competent, and always right, it is a different matter.

They stop for the night at a bad but conveniently located hotel and there encounter, by chance, a "total stranger," a Mrs. Prentice. John finds her notably attractive and shortly discovers that the two adults know each other well from years before. John is curious and confused; Mrs. Prentice seems to know or remember an altogether different man, yet she says to his father, "Will, you haven't changed a bit!" Words such as "strange," "bewildering," and "astonishment" register the boy's evolving perception of his father and realization, finally, that before he himself had been born, before his father had known his mother, before Mrs. Prentice had met Mr. Prentice, the two of them had been in love. Leaving the next morning, John says, "Somehow it all fitted together. I could feel that."

In literal fact, it is Mrs. Prentice who is to the boy a "total stranger"; metaphorically and more important, however, it is his father—or much of his father's life—which John has never before glimpsed. What John sees and hears and intuits of his father and Mrs. Prentice might have evoked alarm, contempt, amusement, or jealousy. That the chance meeting with the stranger in fact strengthens the boy's love and admiration for his father is apparent in the story's last line, in which John confesses that he never did do much better at school, but that "that year and the year following, I would occasionally try to, for I thought it would please my father."

"FAREWELL TO CUBA"

"Farewell to Cuba," a second prize O. Henry Award winner in 1931, is set in Havana and focuses on Martin Gibbs, an American bank employee who is planning to leave the island the next day with Celia after twenty-two years' residence. Cozzens, who lived in Cuba in the 1920's, makes the island atmosphere an almost tangible force in the drama, with its heat, humidity, smells, noise, and the loneliness. Life there has worn Martin out and he is getting old, yet—much as he wants to—he is afraid to leave. He has always been a resident alien, and now, he feels, he is about to desert into the unknown. He wonders both how he can do it and how he can not do it.

Up in their hot, airless hotel room, Martin tries to comfort Celia. At least they have some money, he tells her. She is haggard, sick, drenched with sweat, and unable to eat. She is trying to rest, perhaps to sleep. Tomorrow, he assures her, they will be gone, heading North. At Celia's urging, and over his protestation that he will stay with her, Martin spends his last night with three old friends—Joe Carriker, a car dealer, George Biehl, a banker, and Homer Loran, a newspaper publisher. He has always had a good time with them, Martin reflects, even though he cannot really see much point in it, since he expects never to see them again, but where else can he go? Through the four friends' conversation Cozzens delineates the life Martin has led for too long. His friends offer advice, warnings, endless drinks, horror stories, even a loan if that will help. Why must he leave? Martin cryptically explains, "As it happens, I'm not alone. That's all."

That is not all, as we discover shortly. Despite initial appearances, Celia is the wife of another man, a very powerful man from whom she has run away. On the stairs up to their room, with his friend George comatose in the lobby below, Martin wonders how his scheme can possibly work—it all seems a terrible mistake. He finds Celia as he left her, quiet on the bed, but there is an empty Veronal bottle on the bureau. Celia has taken an overdose; she could not live with her sickness and fear or with her knowledge that Martin had taken ninety thousand dollars from the bank. All that remains is his confession and a call to the police. Martin has come suddenly and inescapably to the end of the road.

By withholding significant information—Celia's true identity, Martin's theft from the bank—Cozzens makes "Farewell to Cuba" in its conclusion a more overtly dramatic story than "Total Stranger," with its benign vision of familial relations. Almost from the beginning of "Farewell to Cuba," however, we have known—or at least strongly suspected—that Martin's escape attempt will fail, that he will not live happily ever after with Celia. How—not whether—he will be thwarted and finally entrapped is the question. Martin, an intelligent, experienced man, does his best. He has planned and schemed for freedom for himself and the woman he loves, and we are never allowed to regard him as a criminal; but in the end, for reasons he could not have anticipated, he is left bereaved, penniless, and facing a long prison sentence.

"EYES TO SEE"

"Eyes to See," a subtle and ambitious narrative forty-two pages long, is another story of parents and children, love and death, and a boy's coming of age. Cozzens's multiplex development of the first-person retrospective point of view is not only intimately related to but also a manifestation of theme. The story follows four days in the life of Dick Maitland, age fifteen, son of Dr. and Mrs. Charles Maitland, who on a football Saturday is summoned home from prep school owing to the wholly unexpected death of his mother, who—in the words of the title—he "never had eyes to see," as other than his mother, that is. Plans are made; telegrams, flowers, and family members (expected and unexpected) arrive; the funeral and subsequent gatherings occur; conversations are listened to and overheard; and Dick is sent back to school. The narrator's retrospective inflections on Mrs. Maitland's extramaternal identities shortly expose his more essential concern: those difficult discoveries of self and others that will form the ground of his postadolescent identity.

In parts 1 and 2 of this thirteen-part story, Cozzens juxtaposes two worlds, the old and the new, waiting to be born, the terrible, paradoxical simultaneous existence with which young Maitland will soon have to grapple. In part 1, bad luck is followed by worse (or is it better?) as Dick's mother dies, her hopeless case aggravated by specialists. In part 2, at the school football game, bad luck (the star quarterback fumbles) is followed by a successful trick play which brings a touchdown. What these details collectively suggest is that the patterns and assumptions of the

protagonist's sheltered, predictable childhood are breaking down. What is good, what is bad, what is usual, all require redefinition.

The new Maitland, as Cozzens first observes in part 3, feels more than he understands but not a great deal more. "That which was to be demonstrated lay beyond the then-grasp of my awareness; but only a little beyond." This is the essence of Cozzens's management of point of view: fully delineating the obliquities and never overtly violating the integrity of the "then-grasp" of his fifteen-year-old protagonist. The adult retrospective narrator easily coexists with his younger self, providing facts and cultural and other history, but, most important, reflecting upon and illustrating his younger self's growing but uneven powers of awareness and assimilation.

Two relatives on whom the latter half of the story focuses are Cousin Eben and Cousin Lois, strikingly handsome and beautiful, respectively, nominally son and daughter-in-law of Dick's great-aunt Margaret, who had, a generation before, scandalized the Maitlands and other respectable people by running off to join the Perfectionists of Oneida (New York) Colony, and whose practice of "complex marriage" (polygamy) places Cousin Eben's ancestry almost beyond young Dick's "then-grasp."

What is within his understanding by the end of the story has much to do with love (or sex) and death, his awareness that "henceforth anything could happen to anyone." From an early point in the story, from his construction of the facts of his mother's biography, the narrator notes his younger self's squeamishness about sex, his refusal of reason's syllogistic instruction that "All children are a result of sexual commerce. A child was begotten on my mother. Therefore. . . ." Before the story ends, young Dick not only receives that fact but also vicariously enacts it through the unknowing agency of Cousin Eben and Cousin Lois.

They, who have hitherto embodied mysteries of familial relations and antipathies and, obliquely, parentage, greatly embarrass their priggish young relative, himself now and forever an only child, by having produced three children in three years. As Dick is finally drifting off to sleep on the night of his mother's funeral, various words and phrases rise to consciousness. One is "Theophilus Pell," founder of the Oneida Colony; others are "complex marriage" and "bastard," which Cousin Eben has blithely admitted he is in the eyes of the law. Another is "exceptional children," first heard in Cousin Eben's discussion of the teaching of retarded children. Then Dick hears, shortly visualizes, and—despite prayerful forbearance—is excited to ejaculation by those exotic two in the next room making love: "I also, in extremis, had to give way. . . ."

"Eyes to See," in its lucid though formal prose, its self-assured handling of complex form, and its subtle and moving evocation of adolescent self-discovery, is Cozzens at his best in the short story. Although Cozzens once observed that he stopped writing short fiction when he no longer needed the money, and although he was more at ease and more impressive as a novelist, *Children and Others* is a memorable if uneven collection.

From the beginning of his career in the 1920's, Cozzens's stories and novels evoked sharply conflicting responses. By some critics he was set down as a literary and social conservative, narrow in interests and sympathies, orthodox in technique, increasingly pedantic in style, and too often given to melodrama and pathos. Admirers, equally vigorous, found him unquestionably a major novelist, a master craftsman, and a superb social historian, whose hallmarks were his irony, worldly wisdom, and deadly penetration into individual character and the social environment. Adjudication of such critical extremes must await the passage of time, but Samuel Johnson's dictum—that "Nothing can please many, and please long, but just representation of general nature"—appears to be the aesthetic principle by which Cozzens would be content to be judged.

OTHER MAJOR WORKS

LONG FICTION: *Confusion*, 1924; *Michael Scarlett*, 1925; *Cock Pit*, 1928; *The Son of Perdition*, 1929; *S. S. San Pedro*, 1931; *The Last Adam*, 1933; *Castaway*, 1934; *Men and Brethren*, 1936; *Ask Me Tomorrow*, 1940; *The Just and the Unjust*, 1942; *Guard of Honor*, 1948; *By Love Possessed*, 1957;

Morning, Noon, and Night, 1968.

MISCELLANEOUS: *Just Representations*, 1978 (Matthew Bruccoli, editor).

BIBLIOGRAPHY

Bruccoli, Matthew J. *James Gould Cozzens: A Descriptive Bibliography*. Pittsburgh, Pa.: University of Pittsburgh Press, 1981. A thorough and scholarly listing of Cozzens's works that is indispensable to both the student and the scholar.

_____. *James Gould Cozzens: A Life Apart*. New York: Harvest/HBJ, 1983. Bruccoli has emerged as Cozzens's most ardent literary champion. His biography of the reclusive writer is a highly readable and interesting account of Cozzens's remarkable career. The writer, working with limited cooperation from Cozzens, has critically examined the author's letters, diaries, and notebooks. The biography contains several appendices, notes, and an index.

Bruccoli, Matthew J., ed. *James Gould Cozzens: New Acquist of True Experience*. Carbondale: Southern Illinois University Press, 1979. This collection by Bruccoli of ten varied essays on Cozzens examines his work in general and in specific novels. The editor also included a variety of short statements by well-known writers such as Malcolm Cowley, James Dickey, and C. P. Snow among others, who praise Cozzens's literary achievements. Includes a complete list of publications by Cozzens.

Cozzens, James Gould. *Just Representations: A James Gould Cozzens Reader*. Edited by Matthew J. Bruccoli. New York: Harcourt Brace Jovanovich, 1978. Bruccoli has compiled a representative collection of Cozzens's writings over the decades from his short stories, novels, essays, letters, and a complete novella. The pieces provide the best example of Cozzens's autobiographical comments on his private life. A brief biography and notes from Cozzens are used to introduce the study.

Hicks, Granville. *James Gould Cozzens*. Minneapolis: University of Minnesota Press, 1966. A short study on Cozzens's literary career with primary emphasis on his major novels. Recommended for its brevity on the subject, but the study is very limited and highly selective in its overall critical appraisal. Hicks fails to examine Cozzens's short stories and nonfictional writings. Includes a select bibliography.

Michel, Pierre. *James Gould Cozzens*. Boston: Twayne, 1974. A good literary study of Cozzens that examines his short stories, early novels, transitional novels, and major work. It excludes the poetry, essays, other nonfiction, and biographical detail. Michel demonstrates a continuity and evolution of themes by Cozzens over the decades as well as a ripening mastery of his craft. A good introduction to the writer. Includes a chronology and a select bibliography.

Mooney, Harry John, Jr. *James Gould Cozzens: Nov-*

elist of Intellect. Pittsburgh: University of Pittsburgh Press, 1963. Mooney is an admirer of Cozzens and believes him to be a novelist equal to the best. After closely examining eight of Cozzens's novels, he defends the writer against the critics. Mooney speaks highly of Cozzens's growing literary mastery and his working well within the mainstream framework of the American novel. His final summation is that Cozzens is a deliberate and complicated artist.

Sterne, Richard Clark. *Dark Mirror: The Sense of Injustice in Modern European and American Literature*. New York: Fordham University Press, 1994. Contains a detailed discussion of the novel *The Just and the Unjust* (1942).

Allen Shepherd, updated by Terry Theodore

STEPHEN CRANE

Born: Newark, New Jersey; November 1, 1871
Died: Badenweiler, Germany; June 5, 1900

PRINCIPAL SHORT FICTION

The Little Regiment and Other Episodes of the American Civil War, 1896
The Open Boat and Other Tales of Adventure, 1898
The Monster and Other Stories, 1899
Whilomville Stories, 1900
Wounds in the Rain, 1900
Last Words, 1902

OTHER LITERARY FORMS

Stephen Crane began his brief writing life as a journalist, and he continued writing for newspapers, notably as a war correspondent, throughout his career, sometimes basing his short stories on events that he had first narrated in press reports. He also wrote raw-edged, realistic novels in which he employed journalistic techniques, most significantly in *Maggie: A Girl of the Streets* (1893) and *The Red Badge of*

Courage: An Episode of the American Civil War (1895). By contrast, he composed wry, evocative, often cryptic poems, published in *The Black Riders and Other Lines* (1895) and *War Is Kind* (1899), that seemed to reveal the philosophy behind the world created in his fiction.

ACHIEVEMENTS

Stephen Crane's fiction has proved hard to classify—not, however, because he defies categorization, but because he worked in two nearly incompatible literary styles at once, while being a groundbreaker in both.

On one hand, he founded the American branch of literary naturalism (this style had originated in France) in his early novels. These works emphasized the sordid aspects of modern life, noted the overpowering shaping influence of environment on human destiny, and scandalously discounted the importance of morality as an effective factor touching on his characters' behavior. In this style, he was followed by writers such as Theodore Dreiser and Frank Norris.

On the other hand, in these same early novels he developed a descriptive style that made him a founder of American impressionism. While the naturalist component of his writing stressed how subjectivity was dominated by social forces, the impressionist component, through coloristic effects and vivid metaphors, stressed the heightened perceptions of individual characters from whose perspectives the story was presented. The man closest to Crane in his own time in developing this impressionist style was Joseph Conrad, though, it will be recognized, this method of drawing from a character's viewpoint became a central tool of twentieth century literature and was prominently employed by authors such as William Faulkner, Virginia Woolf, and Henry James.

Crane took the unusual tack of both playing up his characters' points of view in presenting the world and downplaying the characters' abilities to influence that world. Although this combination of strategies could be made to work satisfactorily, later authors who have taken Crane's path have tended to develop only one of these strands. Moreover, many critics have found Crane's dual emphases to be jarring and incompletely thought through, particularly in his novels. In fact, many have felt that it is only in his short stories that he seemed thoroughly to blend the two manners.

BIOGRAPHY

To some degree, Stephen Crane's life followed a perverse pattern. He was acclaimed for the authenticity of his writings about events that he had never experienced and then spent the remainder of his few years experiencing the events that he had described in prose—often with disastrous consequences.

Born on November 1, 1871, in Newark, New Jersey, Crane was the last child in the large family of a Methodist minister, Jonathan Townley Crane. The family moved frequently from parish to parish and, in 1878, came to Port Jervis, New York, in forested Sullivan County, where Crane would set most of his early stories. Two years later, his father died, and his mother had to begin struggling to support the family, doing church work and writing for religious publications.

Crane determined to be a writer early in his life, and though he attended a few semesters at Lafayette College and then Syracuse University, his real interest in his college years was in soaking up the atmosphere of New York City lowlife and writing freelance articles for newspapers. In 1892, he completed his first novel, *Maggie: A Girl of the Streets*, the story of a young girl driven into streetwalking by a Bowery Romeo. This first novel was so shocking in tone and full of obscenity (in those days, this meant that it contained words such as "hell") that it was rejected by respectable publishers. Borrowing money, Crane printed the book himself, and though it went unread and unsold, it garnered the appreciation of two of the outstanding literary figures of the day, Hamlin Garland and William Dean Howells.

His next book, *The Red Badge of Courage*, a novel about the Civil War, brought him universal acclaim and celebrity status. In the year of the book's publication, however, as if living out his fiction, he defended an unjustly accused prostitute against the corrupt New York City police, just as he had defended the

Stephen Crane (Library of Congress)

poor prostitute Maggie in prose, and found undeserved blight attached to his name. From then on, life would be made difficult for him in New York City by the angered police force.

He more or less abandoned New York at this point, easily enough since the authority of his army novel had placed him in much demand as a war correspondent. Going to Florida to wait for a ship to Cuba, where a rebellion against the Spanish colonialists was taking place, Crane met Cora Taylor, the madame of a house of ill repute who was to become his common-law wife. The ill-fated ship that he eventually boarded sank, and Crane barely escaped with his life, though, on the positive side, he produced from the experience what many consider his greatest short story, "The Open Boat."

As if to show that he could describe real wars as well as he could imagine them, he began shuttling from battle to battle as a reporter, first going to the Greco-Turkish War and then back to view the Spanish-American War, ruining his health in the process. Between wars, he stayed in the manorial Brede Place in England, where he became acquainted with a number of other expatriates who lived in the area, including Joseph Conrad, Harold Frederic, and Henry James.

His problems with the police and the irregularity of his liaison with Cora Taylor—she could not get a divorce from her long-estranged husband—would have made it difficult for Crane to live in his homeland, so in 1899, he settled at the manor for good. Sick and beset with financial woes brought on by extravagant living and an openhanded generosity to visitors, he wrote feverishly but unavailingly to clear his debts. He died the next year from tuberculosis, after having traveled to the Continent to seek a cure.

ANALYSIS

Perhaps because his writing career was so short, critics have devoted much space to Stephen Crane's slight, decidedly apprentice series of sketches collectively entitled *The Sullivan County Tales*. One trait that the sketches do have in their favor is that they contain all the facets of style and theme that Crane was to utilize as his writing developed. The reader finds the overbearing power of the environment, the vivid descriptions, the premise that these descriptions reflect the heightened consciousness of a character or characters, and the idea that this very heightening involves a distortion of perception that needs to be overcome for the characters' adequate adjustment to, and comprehension of, reality. Also of significance is that these stories are generally concerned with the actions of four campers and hence reflect not only on individual psychology but also on the psychology of group dynamics. This was also to become a focus of Crane's writing.

"FOUR MEN IN A CAVE"

In one of the better pieces from this series, "Four Men in a Cave," a quartet of campers decides to explore a cave in order to have something to brag about when they return to the city. Their scarcely concealed fears about the expedition are rendered by Crane's enlivening of stalactites that jab down at them and stalagmites that shoot up at them from crevices. At the end of their path, they find a hermit who invites them to a game of poker, but their fear-stoked imaginations visualize the gamester as a ghoul or Aztec priest. Only later after escaping the cave, in a comic denouement, do they learn of the cave dweller's true identity, that of a mad farmer who took to solitude when he lost his land and wife through gambling. By this time, there seems to be little to brag about, since what has happened has exposed their cowardice and credulity.

The story provides an early example of the rough-and-ready combination of impressionist subjectivity, in how the descriptions in the piece are tinged by the campers' fears, and naturalist objectivity, in how the overwhelming environment of the cave, for part of the story, controls the men's action while dwarfing them. Further, the piece indicates the way, as Crane sees it, emotions can be constructed collectively, as when each camper tells the others how he has misidentified the hermit, adding to the growing hysteria.

"AN EXPERIMENT IN MISERY"

In 1894, Crane published a maturer story, "An Experiment in Misery," in which he transposed the narrative of a cave journey into a serious study of urban social conditions. In the originally printed version of the piece, two middle-class men observe tramps and speculate about their motives and feelings. On impulse, the younger man decides to dress as a tramp in order to penetrate into their secrets. (Such a tactic, of disguising oneself to uncover hidden areas of society, was a common practice of crusading reporters at that time.)

In the later, revised version of this story, the one that is more commonly known, Crane removed the beginning and ending that reveal the protagonist to be slumming; yet, though his social origins are obscured, the story still concerns a neophyte who knows nothing of the life of the underclass and who is being initiated into the ways of the Bowery slums. The high point of the tale, corresponding to the cave exploration, is the hero's entrance into an evil-smelling flophouse. He has trouble sleeping in the noisome room, for his keyed-up fancy sees morbid, highly romanticized symbols everywhere. He understands the shriek of a nightmare-tossed sleeper as a metaphoric protest of the downtrodden.

Awakening the next morning, the protagonist barely remarks on the stench, and this seems to indicate that, merely through familiarity, some of the falsely romantic pictures that he has entertained about the life of the city's poorest have begun to rub off. Exactly what positive things he has learned and of what value such learning will be to him are never clear and, indeed, as Crane grew, while his stories still turned on the loss of illusions, they began to lose the dogmatic assurance that such a change is necessarily for the good.

The last scene of the sketch, though, does make a more definite point, this one about the nature of groups. The hero has begun to associate with a fellow tramp called the assassin and now, after his initiatory night, seems both adjusted to his new station and accepted by the tramp world, at least insofar as the assassin is willing to regale him with his life story. By abandoning his preconceptions about poverty, the protagonist has quite seamlessly fitted himself into the alien milieu, yet this joining of one community has a negative side effect of distancing him from another. The last tableau has the assassin and the hero lounging on park benches as the morning rush-hour crowd streams by them. Here, soon after the hero has had the comfortable feeling of being accepted in one society, he has the poignant realization that, as a bum, he no longer belongs to the larger American working world. There is even a sly hint, given by the fact that the youth begins employing the same grandiose, romanticized terms in depicting his separation from the business world that he had earlier used to depict the flophouse, that he has embarked on a new course of building delusions. In other words, his loss of illusions about the reality of tramp life has been counteracted (as if a vacuum needed to be filled) by the imbibing of a new set of illusions about the vast gulf between the classes. Each community one may join seems to have its own supply of false perspectives.

"THE OPEN BOAT"

In 1897, after his near death at sea, Crane produced what most name his greatest short story and what some even rank as his supreme achievement, placing it above his novels. This is "The Open Boat." Again there are four men. They are in a small boat, a dinghy, escapees from a sunken vessel, desperately trying to row to shore in heavy seas.

The famed first sentence establishes both the parameters of the fictional world and a new chastening of Crane's style. It reads, "None of them knew the color of the sky." Literally, they are too intent on staying afloat to notice the heavens; figuratively, in this godless universe the men cannot look to the sky for help but must rely on their own muscles and wits, which, against the elements, are little enough. Furthermore, the opening's very dismissal of color descriptions, given that much of Crane's earlier work, such as *The Red Badge of Courage*, depends heavily on color imagery, can be seen as the author's pledge to restrain some of the flashiness of his style.

This restraint is evident not only in a more tempered use of language here but also in the nature of the protagonists' delusions. In works such as the slum experiment, the romanticized preconceptions that determine the protagonist's viewpoint can be seen as trivial products of a shallow culture—that is, as marginal concerns—whereas in the sea story, the men's illusions are necessities of life. The men in the boat want to believe that they must survive, since they have been fighting so hard. If they do not believe this, how can they continue rowing? The point is put wrenchingly at one moment when the men refuse to accept that they will drown, as it seems they will, in the breakers near the shore. Such illusions (about the meaningfulness of valor and effort) obviously have more universal relevance than others with which Crane has dealt, and that is why the story strikes so deep; the illusions also, ingeniously, tie in with the reader's expectations. As much as the reader begins to identify with the four men (and they are sympathetically portrayed), he or she will want them to survive and thus will be on the verge of agreeing to their illusions. Thus, Crane engineers a remarkable and subtle interlocking of readers' and characters' beliefs.

Furthermore, the functionality of the possibly delusive beliefs of the struggling men—that is, the fact that they need to believe that they will make it ashore to keep up the arduous fight for life—helps Crane to a fuller, more positive view of human community. The men in the cave were merely partners in error, but these toilers share a belief system that sustains them in their mutually supportive labor, which the characters themselves recognize as "a subtle brotherhood of men." The men's shared recognition of the supportive structure of human groups gives weight to the story's last phrase, which says, of the three survivors who have reached land, "and they felt that they could then be interpreters."

The story, written in the third person, is given largely from the viewpoint of one of the four, a newspaper correspondent. This is not evident at once, however, since the narrative begins by simply objectively reporting the details of the men's struggle to stay afloat and reproducing their laconic comments. In this way, the group is put first and only later, when the correspondent's thoughts are revealed, does the reader learn of his centrality as the story begins to be slightly colored by his position. What the focus on his consciousness reveals, aiding Crane in deepening his presentation, is how the subtle brotherhood is felt individually.

After rowing near to the shore but not being able to attract anyone's attention, the crew settle down for a night at sea. While whoever is rowing stays awake,

the others sleep like the dead they may soon become, and at this point, the story dwells more intently on the correspondent's outlook as he takes his turn at the oars. The newspaperman reconsiders the beliefs that have been keeping them afloat, seeing the weakness in them and accepting, now that he is alone, the possibility of an ironic death—that is, one coming in sight of shore after their courageous struggle. Yet his existential angst, an acknowledgment that there is no special heavenly providence, neither stops him from his muscle-torturing rowing nor diminishes his revived illusions on the morrow, when they again all breast the waves together.

If this line of reasoning shows him mentally divorcing himself from the collective ideology, another night thought implies that, in another direction, he is gaining a deeper sense of solidarity. He remembers a verse that he had learned in school about a legionnaire dying far from home with only a comrade to share his last moments. The correspondent had thought little of the poem, both because he had never been in extremis (and so saw little to the pathos of the case) and, as Crane notes, had formerly looked cynically at his fellows (and so had found unpalatable or unbelievable the care of one soldier for another). A day's experience in the dinghy has made him keenly aware of the two aspects of experience that he had overlooked or undervalued, and thus has given him a clear understanding of the networks (those of democratic brotherhood) and circumstances (a no-holds-barred fight against an indifferent universe) that underlie the human social world. This understanding can be applied in many ways, not only toward a grasp of group interaction but also toward an interpretation of honest art.

Still, the most telling incident of his lonely watch is not so much any of his thoughts as an action. The boat, the correspondent finds, has become the magnet to a huge shark. Achingly, he wishes that one of his fellow sailors were awake to share his fidgety vigil; yet, he resists any impulse he has to rouse them or even to question aloud whether any of them is conscious for fear that he should waken a sleeper. Even if alone he cannot continue with the group illusion, he can, though alone, effortlessly maintain the group's implicit morality, which holds that each should un-complainingly shoulder as much of the burden as possible, while never revealing irritation or fear. Much later, the newspaperman learns that another of the four, the captain, was awake and aware of the predator's presence during what had been taken to be the correspondent's moment of isolated anguish. The hidden coexistent alertness of the captain suggests the ongoing mutuality of the group that undergirds even seemingly isolated times of subjectivity.

To bring this story in line with the last one mentioned, it is worth noting that the small group in the boat is contrasted to a group on shore just as, in "An Experiment in Misery," the hoboes were contrasted to the society of the gainfully employed. When the rowers are near the coast on the first day, they vainly hope to attract the ministering attentions of people on land. They do attract their attention, but the people, tourists from a hotel, merrily wave at them, thinking that the men in the dinghy are fishermen. The heedlessness, inanity, and seeming stupidity of the group on shore compare unfavorably with the hard-won, brave alertness of the boatmen, pointing to the fact that the small group's ethical solidarity is not of a type with the weaker unity found in the larger society. The men's deep harmony rather—beautiful as it is— is something that can be found only in pockets. The depicting of the community on the land foreshadows elements of Crane's later, darker pictures of community, as in "The Blue Hotel," where what sustains a group is not a life-enhancing though flimsy hope but a tacitly accepted lie.

"THE BRIDE COMES TO YELLOW SKY"

In the year that he wrote "The Open Boat" and the next year, Crane was to compose three other brilliant stories, two of which dealt with myths of the Old West. Both these Western tales were written in his mature, unadorned style, and both continued his focus on the belief systems of communities. What is new to them is a greater flexibility in the handling of plot. Previously, he had simply followed his characters through a continuous chronological sequence from start to finish; now, however, he began shifting between differently located character groups and jumping around in time.

In "The Bride Comes to Yellow Sky," the action begins on a train moving through Texas, carrying Yellow Sky's sheriff, Jack Potter, and his new wife back to town. Potter is apprehensive about his reception, since he has married out of town in a whirlwind courtship and none of the townspeople knows of his new status. The scene shifts to the interior of a Yellow Sky saloon, where the gathered, barricaded patrons have other things to be apprehensive about than Potter's marriage. Scratchy Wilson, the local ruffian, has gotten drunk and is shooting in the main street, while, as the bar's occupants admit, the only man able to cow him is the absent sheriff. Scratchy Wilson himself, as the reader learns in another scene shift, not aware of Potter's trip, is truculently looking for the sheriff so that they can engage in a showdown. In truth, the reader, knowing of Potter's imminence, will probably share Wilson's expectation of a gun battle, which is not an unreasonable forecast of the plot's unfolding. Yet, this expectation is founded on a deeper belief, that the West will always be an uncivilized place of outlaws and pistols. A chagrined Scratchy recognizes that this belief is invalid and that an era has passed when he finds that the sheriff has taken a wife. After meeting the couple, he holsters his guns and stalks off toward the horizon.

"THE BLUE HOTEL"

A tragic variation on similar themes of violence and community beliefs appears in "The Blue Hotel," a story that a few critics rank in importance above "The Open Boat." The tale concerns a fatalistic traveler, the Swede, who stops for the night in a hotel in Nebraska. (This protagonist's name will be picked up by Ernest Hemingway, a Crane admirer, for an equally fatalistic character in his short-story masterpiece "The Killers.") Through the Swede's conversation with the hotel owner, Scully, and other stoppers, it appears that, based perhaps on an immersion in dime novels, the Swede thinks that this town—or, for that matter, any town in the West—is a hotbed of bloodshed and mayhem. After his fears seem to be allayed by the officious owner, who assures him that he is mistaken, the Swede overreacts by becoming boisterous and familiar. This mood of his eventually dissipates when, involved in a game of cards, he accuses the owner's son of cheating. The upshot is that the pair engage in a fistfight, which the Swede wins. He is now triumphant but can no longer find any welcome at the hotel; so he wanders off to a nearby saloon, in which his even more high-strung and aggressive demonstrations lead to his death at the hands of an icy but violent gambler he had been prodding to drink with him.

At this point, the story seems a grim meditation on the truth or falsity of myths. What seemed to be the manifestly absurd belief of the Swede has been proven partially true by his own death. Yet, it appears this truth would never have been exposed except for the Swede's own pushy production of the proper circumstances for Western violence to emerge. There is, however, another turn of the cards. A final scene is described in which, months later, two of the hotel's card players, witnesses of the dispute between the Swede and Scully's son, discuss events of that fateful evening. One of them, the Easterner, claims that the whole group collected at the hotel that night is responsible for what led to the death since they all knew that the owner's son was cheating but did not back up the Swede when he accused the youth.

In one way, this final episode indicates that perhaps the Swede's suspicions were accurate in yet another sense; the whole town is made up, metaphorically, of killers in that the community is willing to sacrifice an outsider to maintain its own dubious harmony. From this angle, though, this Western town's particular violence merely crystallizes and externalizes any hypocritical town's underlying psychic economy. (Crane depicted this economy more explicitly in his novella *The Monster*.) In another way—and here the increasing complexity of Crane's thought on community is evident—even after the final episode, it still appears that the Swede's murder has some justification.

There are two points to be made in this connection. For one, throughout the story, Crane represents the frailty of human existence as it is established on the prairies in the depths of winter. The story begins by underlining the presumptuousness of Scully's hotel's bright blue color, not so much as it may be an affront to the other, staider buildings in town, but in its

assertiveness against the grimness of the white wastes of nature surrounding and swamping the little burg. The insignificance of human beings measured against the universe is explicitly stated by Crane in an oft-quoted passage. He speaks of humans clinging to a "whirling, fire-smitten, icelocked, disease-stricken, space-lost bulb." He goes on to say that the "conceit of man" in striving to prevail in such conditions is "the very engine of life." It is true that they all killed the Swede in some sense, but the fragility of the human community, it may be surmised, demands that its members all practice respect and forbearance toward one another so that a common front can be presented against uncaring nature. If anyone consistently violates this unwritten code, as the Swede does, he must be eliminated for group self-preservation. It is significant in this light that the Swede, who demands a grudge match with the owner's son, would take the men away from the large, red-hot stove (symbol of the warmth of peaceful intercourse and home comfort) outside to fight in subzero weather. To restate this, for his own egotistical purposes, the Swede would drag everyone into a much greater exposure to a harsh environment than life in the community, were it running harmoniously, would ever make necessary.

The second point to be made is that Crane's portrait of the gambler, which interrupts the narrative at a high point and which, thus, seems at first sight a cumbersome miscalculation by the author, allows the reader a fuller understanding of the place of an outsider in this Western society. If the reader had been given only the Swede's treatment to go by, he or she would be forced to conclude that, whatever the necessity of the visitor's expulsion, this town has little tolerance for aberrant personalities. Yet, such a position has to be modified after Crane's presentation of the gambler, whose disreputable calling excludes him from the city's better social functions but whose behavior in other areas—he bows to the restrictions put on him with good grace and is a charitable family man who will not prey on the better citizens—conforms enough to standards to allow him to be generally accepted. Intervening at this point, Crane's portrayal of this second (relative) outsider is used to indicate that the community will permit in its midst a character who has not followed all of its rules, provided such a character does not, as the Swede does, insistently and continuously breach the accepted norms.

All this taken together does not, certainly, excuse a murder. What it does show is that Crane's understanding of how a community sustains itself has expanded beyond the understanding that he had at the time of the sea story. He indicates that the guiding principle of mutual support found in the dinghy has remained operative, even in a far less threatened situation, while adding that violations of this principle can lead to less happy consequences than might have been foreseen in the earlier story.

"DEATH AND THE CHILD"

Finally, in "Death and the Child," Crane produced an excellent story about war, the topic which had been both the most consistent and the least successful subject of his short pieces. The intertwined themes of the effect of illusions and the ways that an individual can be integrated into, or excluded from, a community, the most important themes of Crane's work, are again central. In this piece, the character who nurses illusions is Peza, a journalist who has decided to join the Greek side during the Greco-Turkish War, motivated by unrealistic ideas about the glories of classical Greece and the adventure of fighting. Once he reaches the battle lines, however, he finds it impossible to join the other combatants.

He is displeased by the nonchalance of the troops, who refuse to strike heroic poses, but what actually ends up turning him away from solidarity is his realization that to become part of the group he must accept not only a largely humdrum life but also the possibility of a prosaic death. In other words, it is not coming down to earth with the common men that ultimately scares him but the understanding that he may have to come down under the earth (into a grave) with them.

The story exhibits what had become the traits of Crane's mature style. He writes with a terse, crisp, subdued prose that is occasionally shot through with startling or picturesque imagery, this imagery being the residue of his initial, more flowery style. Crane also exhibits a mastery of plotting. This is brought out by the careful joining of Peza's emotional states to his gyrations around the battle camp as well as by the story's final encounter, where Peza comes upon an abandoned child, who, too young to comprehend war, still has a clearer view of reality than the distraught journalist. This skill at plotting is not something that Crane possessed from the beginning, which brings up a last point.

It might be said that there is a chronological distinction between Crane's interests and his method of narration. While his thematic concerns were constant throughout his career, though as he grew older his attention to how a community was created and sustained grew in weight, his ability to construct complex plots is one that he picked up during the course of his creative life. There are authors who advance little after their first books, but in Crane's case, it can definitely be said that there was a promise for the future that his short life never redeemed.

OTHER MAJOR WORKS

LONG FICTION: *Maggie: A Girl of the Streets*, 1893, 1896; *The Red Badge of Courage: An Episode of the American Civil War*, 1895; *George's Mother*, 1896; *The Third Violet*, 1897; *Active Service*, 1899; *The Monster*, 1898 (serial), 1899 (novella, pb. in *The Monster and Other Stories*); *The O'Ruddy: A Romance*, 1903 (with Robert Barr).

PLAYS: *The Ghost*, pr. 1899 (fragment; with Henry James); *The Blood of the Martyr*, pb. 1940.

POETRY: *The Black Riders and Other Lines*, 1895; *A Souvenir and a Medley*, 1896; *War Is Kind*, 1899; *The University Press of Virginia Edition of the Works of Stephen Crane*, 1970 (Vol. X).

NONFICTION: *The Great Battles of the World*, 1901; *The War Dispatches of Stephen Crane*, 1964.

BIBLIOGRAPHY

Benfey, Christopher. *The Double Life of Stephen Crane*. New York: Alfred A. Knopf, 1992. This brief (294-page) biography of Crane makes a virtue out of necessity by translating the dearth of biographical information about Crane—who died at the age of twenty-eight—into the key to his character. For Benfey, Crane is "a man who . . .

vanished into his own fictions," a writer who planned his life by writing about experiences before living them. Thus, for Benfey, Crane's life is not so much mysterious as it is "duplicate."

Berryman, John. *Stephen Crane*. New York: William Sloane Associates, 1950. This combined biography and interpretation has been superseded as a biography, but it continues to be an absorbing Freudian reading of Crane's life and work. Berryman, himself a major American poet, eloquently explains the patterns of family conflict that appear in Crane's fiction. Furthermore, Berryman's wide-ranging interests allow him to tackle such large topics as Crane's influence on the birth of the short story, a form which, though existing earlier, came to prominence only in the 1890's. Includes notes and index.

Colvert, James B. *Stephen Crane*. New York: Harcourt Brace Jovanovich, 1984. This short biography by a notable Crane scholar has as one of its emphases the inclusion of many photographs and illustrations. These not only show Crane and his friends but also depict some of the scenes that Crane described in his writing. Chronology, notes.

_____. "Stephen Crane and Postmodern Theory." *American Literary Realism* 28 (Fall, 1995): 4-22. A survey of postmodern approaches to Crane's fiction. Summarizes the basic premises of postmodern interpretation, examining how these premises have been applied to such Crane stories as "The Open Boat," "The Upturned Face," and "Maggie"; balances such interpretive strategies against critics who affirm more traditional, humanistic approaches.

Davis, Linda H. *Badge of Courage: The Life of Stephen Crane*. Boston: Houghton Mifflin, 1998. Makes use of research to separate the real Crane from the legends, myths, and rumors about his life; discusses his pioneering a new way of writing about war in *The Red Badge of Courage* and his short stories.

Halliburton, David. *The Color of the Sky: A Study of Stephen Crane*. Cambridge, England: Cambridge University Press, 1989. Though somewhat thematically disorganized, the author's philosophical

grounding and ability to look at Crane's works from unusual angles make for many provocative readings. In his discussion of "The Blue Hotel," for example, he finds much more aggression directed against the Swede than may at first appear, coming not only from seemingly benign characters but also from the layout of the town. Notes, index.

Metress, Christopher. "From Indifference to Anxiety: Knowledge and the Reader in 'The Open Boat.'" *Studies in Short Fiction* 28 (Winter, 1991): 47-53. Shows how the structure of "The Open Boat" (made up of four key moments) creates an epistemological dilemma for readers, moving them from a position of indifference to a state of epistemological anxiety. By suggesting that the survivors have become interpreters, Crane implies that we must get rid of indifference to the difficulty of gaining knowledge and embrace the inevitable anxiety of that failure.

Nagel, James. *Stephen Crane and Literary Impressionism*. University Park: Pennsylvania State University Press, 1980. Nagel carefully delineates what he considers Crane's application of impressionist concepts of painting to fiction, which involved Crane's "awareness that the apprehension of reality is limited to empirical data interpreted by a single human intelligence." This led the writer to a stress on the flawed visions of men and women and a depiction of the dangers of this natural one-sidedness in works such as *Maggie: A Girl of the Streets*, as well as depictions of characters who transcended this weakness through an acceptance of human inadequacies in such works as "The Open Boat." Notes, index.

Robertson, Michael. *Stephen Crane: Journalism and the Making of Modern American Literature*. New York: Columbia University Press, 1997. Argues that Crane's success inspired later journalists to think of their work as preparatory for writing fiction; claims the blurring of fact and fiction in newspapers during Crane's life suited his own narrative experiments.

Stallman, R. W. *Stephen Crane: A Biography*. New York: George Braziller, 1968. This definitive biography involves a thorough sifting of all the circumstances surrounding Crane's major fiction, a sifting that is especially impressive in the case of "The Open Boat." Stallman also gives the reader a feeling for Crane's times. Contains a meticulous bibliography (Stallman later composed a book-length bibliography), extensive notes, an index, and appendices that include contemporary reviews of Crane's work and obituaries.

Wertheim, Stanley, and Paul Sorrentino. *The Crane Log: A Documentary Life of Stephen Crane 1871-1900*. New York: G. K. Hall, 1994. Stanley and Sorrentino, editors of *The Correspondence of Stephen Crane* (1988), have attempted to counter many of the falsehoods that have bedeviled analyses of Crane's life and work by providing a documentary record of the author's life. Opening with biographical notes on persons mentioned in the text and lavishly sourced, *The Crane Log* is divided into seven chapters, beginning with the no-

tation in Crane's father's diary of the birth of his fourteenth child, Stephen, and ending with a newspaper report of Crane's funeral, written by Wallace Stevens.

Wolford, Chester L. *Stephen Crane: A Study of the Short Fiction*. Boston: Twayne, 1989. This overly brief but useful look at Crane's short fiction provides Wolford's sensitive readings as well as commentary on the major points that have been raised in critical discussions of the Crane pieces. In describing "The Bride Comes to Yellow Sky," for example, Wolford explains his view of how the story fits into the archetypical patterns of the passing of the West narratives, while also exploring why other critics have seen Crane's story as a simple parody. About half of the book is given over to selected Crane letters and extractions from other critics' writings on Crane's short pieces. Includes a chronology, bibliography, and index.

James Feast

D

ROALD DAHL

Born: Llandaff, South Wales; September 13, 1916
Died: Oxford, England; November 23, 1990

OTHER LITERARY FORMS

In addition to his numerous short stories, Roald Dahl is well known for his children's novels and collections of verse. Several of his children's books have been made into films, including *Charlie and the Chocolate Factory* (1964), for which he wrote the screenplay, and *The Witches* (1983). Dahl also co-wrote the screenplays for the films *You Only Live Twice* (1967) and *Chitty-Chitty Bang-Bang* (1968), as well as several others. In the 1980's, Dahl published two volumes of autobiography, *Boy: Tales of Childhood* (1984) and *Going Solo* (1986), about his work with the Shell Oil Company and his days with the Royal Air Force during World War II.

ACHIEVEMENTS

In addition to an early collection of stories about pilots and their experiences in war and peacetime, Dahl produced a variety of modern gothic stories, which include grotesque fantasies, murder mysteries, and bizarre gamesmanship. Ironic reversals and surprise endings are major devices used to create effects ranging from comedy to terror.

Dahl's books have been translated into more than fifteen languages and have been best sellers in many countries. Popular in Great Britain and the United States, his stories appeared in well-known magazines such as *Town and Country, The New Yorker, The Atlantic Monthly, Esquire*, and *Playboy*. His work won for him three Edgar Allan Poe awards, in 1953, 1959, and 1980, and the Whitbread and Federation of Children's Books Group awards in 1983 for *The Witches*. Dahl's stories have been adapted for British television, and his children's books are both popular and controversial, because they often share the macabre sensibility of his work for adults.

BIOGRAPHY

Roald Dahl was born in Llandaff, near Cardiff, in South Wales, in 1916, to Norwegian-born parents. He was the only boy in his father's second family. Dahl's father and uncle had left Norway to seek their fortunes, and Dahl's father found it in equipping ships sailing out of the busy Cardiff docks. By the time Dahl was born, his father, who died when Dahl was four, had become wealthy. Dahl attended an Anglican public school in Llandaff before going to a prepatory school in Weston-Super-Mare, across the Severn Estuary from Cardiff, and then to the Repton School in Yorkshire. Dahl hated the public school atmosphere and the separation from his family; he was prevented from becoming a prefect at the Repton School because of his lack of seriousness about school discipline.

After he was graduated from the Repton School in 1932, Dahl went on a school-sponsored exploration of the interior of Newfoundland before joining the Shell Oil Company. He spent several years working in London before being sent to Dar-es-Salaam as a Shell Oil representative. In 1938, he joined the Royal Air Force, and, despite his unusual height, he was trained as a pilot. Though he was wounded once, he served as a fighter pilot in Africa, Greece, and Syria. He also served in intelligence units and was made a wing commander. His stories collected in *Over to You: Ten Stories of Flyers and Flying* are based on these experiences.

In 1953, Dahl married actress Patricia Neal, and they had five children, one of whom died of the measles at age seven. Dahl began writing stories for children after making up bedtime tales for his own children. In the late 1960's, Neal suffered an incapacitating illness, and Dahl helped her through a slow recovery. In 1983, they divorced, and Dahl remarried. He died in November, 1990.

ANALYSIS

In stories ranging from the macabre to the hilarious, Roald Dahl enriched the modern gothic tale through the indirection and subtlety of a narrative method loaded with surprises for the unsuspecting reader. His most famous works include "Lamb to the Slaughter," "Royal Jelly," "Man from the South," "The Landlady," and "Neck." In situations which include both domestic life and high adventure, Dahl creates suspense and humor of a highly sophisticated nature. Beyond the simple surface of the stories lie the psychological complexities that fascinate his readers. In many of the stories, for example, a hidden sexual theme controls the violence of the plot. Jealousy, hatred, lust, and greed dominate the characters of Dahl's stories.

"LAMB TO THE SLAUGHTER"

In "Lamb to the Slaughter," a woman murders her husband and succeeds in serving the murder weapon, a large leg of lamb (deadly when frozen, delicious when cooked), to the police officers who investigate his death. An ironic tour de force, the story is typical of Dahl's ability to develop an effect both chilling

and wryly humorous. The story begins as Mrs. Maloney, a highly domestic, apparently devoted wife, awaits her husband's arrival home. His drink is prepared for him, but no dinner is waiting because on Thursdays they always dine out. Six months pregnant, Mrs. Maloney is especially eager to have company in the house since she now remains at home all day. Her husband's behavior when he arrives, however, is much different from the usual friendliness and tenderness she expects. He drinks more than usual and rejects her sympathetic inquiries about his work as a detective. When he bluntly informs her that

Roald Dahl (Library of Congress)

he is divorcing her, she is stunned and can think only of somehow maintaining their daily routine by preparing supper. Automatically, she descends to the cellar, where she reaches into the freezer and retrieves the first thing she touches, a large leg of lamb. After lugging the heavy package upstairs, she observes her husband standing with his back to her. When he angrily announces that he will go out for supper, she unhesitatingly swings the leg of lamb high in the air and brings it down hard on the back of his head.

Instantly killed, the detective falls to the floor with a crash that brings Mrs. Maloney out of her state of shock, and she begins immediately to fear the consequences for herself and her unborn child. She quickly plans a maneuver which will supply her with an alibi and which prepares the way for Dahl's ironic denouement. She puts the lamb into the oven to cook, tidies her hair, and rehearses an anticipated conversation with the grocer who will sell her the vegetables lacking for her husband's dinner. She manages to chat pleasantly with the grocer, and when she returns home, she unleashes her emotions in an expression of sincere shock and grief at the sight of her husband's crumpled body. Nearly hysterical, she telephones the police, who have all been friends of her husband and who treat her with sympathy and understanding when they arrive. Still, they check her alibi, and, finding it satisfactory, they begin to search the house for the murder weapon, which may provide clues to the identity of the murderer. When Mrs. Maloney begs them, as friends deserving hospitality, to eat the meal she cannot bear to eat now, they hesitate but finally agree. While they are devouring the juicy lamb, their dining conversation reflects the irony of their unwitting ignorance: Surely, they say, the murder weapon must be somewhere in the house, even right under their noses. In the next room Mrs. Maloney giggles as they finish off the main dish. A simple prose narrative turning on a single major irony, the tale has been transferred to film, and, in either medium, it effectively demonstrates the author's characteristically ironic denouement, which has been likened in effect to the appearance of a grinning skull.

"ROYAL JELLY"

Another story which depends on a pattern of ironies is "Royal Jelly," one of Dahl's famous tales of the grotesque. The plot concerns a baby born to a beekeeper who experiments with the products of his hives. Almost from birth, the beekeeper's new daughter loses weight because she cannot tolerate the formula his wife prepares. When the anxious mother becomes exhausted from worry and sleepless nights, the father calmly takes over the schedule of feedings. Noticing in one of his apiculture journals that bees nurtured on royal jelly, one of the richest food substances

known to humans, gain many times their birth weight, the concerned father secretly decides to add some royal jelly to the baby's formula.

At first the effect of the new food seems favorable, for the baby begins to eat eagerly and to sleep peacefully between feedings. When the beekeeper adds more and more royal jelly to the formula, the child gains weight and becomes cherublike in appearance. Within a short time, however, the baby demands such huge quantities of the food that the pleased father can no longer hide his secret. His wife is angry when she learns of his casual experimentation with their precious child. In his efforts to reassure her, he makes a still more startling revelation. He himself has been consuming tremendous amounts of the potent substance ever since he read that it helped overcome infertility in men. Their beautiful new baby is the result of his desperate attempt.

For the first time in months the anxious wife looks closely at her husband. To her horror, she finds his appearance much altered. He has not merely gained weight, but the contours of his body seem very strange. His neck has nearly disappeared, and tufts of stiff black body hair point upward to his head. The child in the crib, too, is surprisingly beelike in appearance. Like a queen bee, however, she has begun developing her digestive and reproductive organs at the expense of her tiny limbs. Her belly is swollen and glossy; her arms and legs lie motionless on the sides of the bed. The story concludes with the father's final ironic reference to his daughter as their "little queen." In his concern for her nurture, he has assumed the role of a worker bee; indeed, his capacity for emotional exchange is seriously diminished. The final scene depicts the horror and the helplessness of the mother estranged from her husband and her child by a bizarre turn of nature that she cannot comprehend.

"MAN FROM THE SOUTH"

Another of Dahl's most famous tales of the grotesque is "Man from the South," a story of macabre gamesmanship at a fashionable Jamaican resort hotel. The narrator of this story becomes the reluctant referee in a bizarre gambling arrangement between a wealthy, middle-aged South American businessman and a handsome young British soldier. Casually observing the satisfactory regularity with which the soldier's cigarette lighter operates, the South American bets that it will not light ten times in succession. The soldier accepts the bet eagerly, partly in an effort to counteract the boredom of the long summer afternoon and partly to impress an attractive young lady relaxing near the pool. The narrator observes the conversation with only mild interest until he notices the arrogance of the ugly South American, dwarfish yet somehow given to the gestures of a much more powerful man. The stakes he proposes are shocking: The South American offers his Cadillac against the little finger of the soldier's left hand, a situation at first refused by the soldier, then accepted by him in order to avoid losing face. The gamblers, the young lady, and the narrator-referee adjourn from their pool-side setting to an upstairs hotel room, where a maid rather questioningly supplies the objects the South American requests. A cutting board, a sharp meat knife, string, and pegs are provided; the soldier's left hand is tied to the board; the South American places his car keys on the table. All the while the narrator ponders the chilling efficiency with which the older man performs the task.

Despite the anxiety of the narrator and the young lady, the soldier begins nervously to test the lighter. The suspense grows as once, twice, as many as eight times the lighter functions perfectly, but a sudden interruption ends the gambling. The South American's wife enters and begins to shake her husband back and forth so rapidly that he resembles a cigarette lighter himself. Then the woman releases him and apologizes at length for her husband's disgusting gambling practices: He has already taken thirty-seven fingers and lost eleven cars. Moreover, the car he has been using this time belongs to her. In this characteristic reversal, she appears, at least to the narrator and the relieved soldier, a comfortingly normal deliverer, and her husband appears the embodiment of the morally grotesque. The narrator relaxes as he watches her walk across the room to retrieve her car keys. Yet his glimpse of her hand on the table provides the final ironic twist. Only a thumb and finger remain on the claw-shaped hand, a grotesque suggestion of what

she has won and lost from her husband. A study in the grotesque, the story demonstrates Dahl's surprising reversals and frequent use of an observer-narrator who serves as an intermediate figure between fantasy and reality.

"NECK"

A narrator of the intermediate type also provides the filtering consciousness in the story "Neck," which offers another ironic view of the hidden violence of domestic life. Comparable to "Lamb to the Slaughter," the story concerns Sir Basil and his wife, Lady Turton, proprietors of a major British publishing firm. The setting is Wooton House, one of the great stone houses of the English Renaissance, and it is the atmosphere of wealth, beauty, and ease that attracts the narrator, an ambitious newspaper columnist who visits Sir Basil.

In the manner of relating inner-circle gossip, the journalist begins by describing the wealthy Turton family and Sir Basil's forty peaceful years of bachelor life, marked only by his consuming interest in a collection of paintings and sculpture. After the death of Basil's father, insiders on Fleet Street begin laying bets as to the number of bachelor days remaining to Sir Basil before one of the many ambitious London women succeeds in managing him and his fortune. The insiders are surprised, however, when Natalia, a haughty beauty from the Continent, triumphs over the resentful Englishwomen, and within six years she assumes control of the Turton Press. Having once been seated next to her at a party, the narrator observes that she is a lovely opportunist with the "air of a wild mustang," a rebellious spirit particularly contrary to the mild civility of Sir Basil.

All this information, the narrator insists, is merely background for his experiences at the Turton home, where he discovers an unusually eclectic environment created by the display of modern sculpture in the elegant gardens of the past. Sculptured topiary, pools, fountains, and lovely flowers provide the backdrop for the work of Sir Jacob Epstein, Constantin Brancusi, and Augustus Saint-Gaudens, to name only a few of the artists included in Basil's collection. Certainly the narrator anticipates an enchanting weekend there while he gathers fascinating details about the

Turtons for his column. Once in the house, however, he perceives that something is wrong, and he prides himself on his heightened sensitivity, the result of having spent much time in the homes of others.

The almost stereotyped situation of spending the weekend in a great house where mischief seems imminent gives succeeding events the quality of a gothic burlesque. The journalist's anxiety is multiplied, for example, by the strange behavior of the butler, who requests that he receive in place of tips one-third of the guest's card winnings during the visit. The butler also betrays his dislike for the lady of the house and offers the tip that she almost always overbids her hand, an important detail of characterization which will be fully realized in the climax of the story. First, however, the narrator's suspicions are confirmed when, at dinner with the other guests, he observes a quite obvious triangular love relationship between Lady Turton, Major Haddock, a handsome retired serviceman, and Carmen La Rosa, a wealthy horsewoman visiting the Turtons. Sir Basil seems so distracted by the whole affair that the narrator feels quite embarrassed for him and hopes to leave as soon as possible.

The butler also displays great sympathy for Sir Basil and obvious hatred for Lady Turton, whom the butler regards as a mere usurper and source of pain to his beloved master. The evening concludes most awkwardly when the lady abruptly dismisses the guests, the butler, and even Sir Basil so that she can have a quiet chat alone with Major Haddock. Naturally, the narrator's suspicions mount to tremendous proportions. Indeed, the next morning the household seems more troubled than ever, and Basil behaves so strangely that the concerned narrator suggests they take a stroll around the grounds.

As they discuss the sculptures, Basil's only pleasant distraction, they cannot help noticing in the distance some intruders on the grounds. Near one of the sculptures done by Henry Moore, a man and woman seem to be behaving flirtatiously. The woman playfully sticks her head and arms through the various openings in the huge statue; her companion laughs uproariously and draws close to her, perhaps to kiss her. As the gentlemen draw nearer, they realize with embarrassment that the pair below are not intruders but Lady Turton and Major Haddock, amusing themselves with Basil's prized collection. Suddenly the lady begins to struggle, however; her head is caught fast in the sculpture, and her partner cannot help her. While she waves her arms frantically, Basil becomes increasingly nonchalant as he slows his pace and resumes casual conversation with the narrator. Certainly Lady Turton has overbid her hand this time.

The climactic scene occurs when Basil and the narrator reach the anxious pair. Natalia furiously demands that Basil cut her free from the sculpture, and the butler soon appears with an ax and saw for his master to use. Basil pauses briefly, however, to admire the sculpture, which is one of his favorites. In the interim, the narrator observes that for some reason the butler seems to want Basil to select the ax, by far the more dangerous of the implements. Then Basil, with startling speed, reaches for the ax and without hesitation prepares to swing at his wife's neck. The terrified narrator shuts his eyes in anticipation of her death. When he opens his eyes, however, the ax appears still upraised, and the lady seems only gurgling with hysteria. Basil, acknowledging that the ax is much too dangerous for this job, exchanges it for the saw. For the narrator, however, the change of implements is insignificant now: In his imagination, the lady's execution has taken place, and, after that terrifying moment, nothing will ever be the same. In contrast, Basil's eyes begin to twinkle secretly as he begins sawing through the heavy wood.

Readers are left with a puzzle at the end of the story, for from the description of the lady's head in the last scene, they cannot be absolutely sure that the blow has not landed. For them, as for the narrator, the event is realized in the imagination. On another level, the lady has only been threatened with a punishment that fits her crime of overreaching. What passes for justice in her case adds to the comic effect generated by the stereotyped situation and such characters as the aspiring journalist, the passionate usurper, the sinister butler, the major named for a fish, and the overweight horsewoman named Carmen. The mild-mannered Basil enjoys a triumph uncommon to most henpecked husbands.

Typical of Dahl, the story "Neck" has several sides: It is an entertaining anecdote offered by an easily impressed narrator, a modern gothic tale with comic elements, and finally, perhaps, an examination of what constitutes reality. For readers cannot help identifying momentarily with the narrator when he closes his eyes to avoid watching the ax fall; what happens to the lady in the ambiguous final scene is, after all, what readers believe about it. Perhaps a major reason for the success and popularity of Dahl's work and of mystery stories in general is their essentially Romantic attitude, an insistence on a world of possibilities beyond humdrum daily existence. The vision such stories create provocatively mingles the extremes of joy and pain, laughs and shrieks of terror, in offering a singularly pleasing, if brief, sensation of the realities beyond typical human experience.

OTHER MAJOR WORKS

LONG FICTION: *Sometime Never: A Fable for Supermen*, 1948; *My Uncle Oswald*, 1979.

PLAYS: *The Honeys*, 1955.

SCREENPLAYS: *You Only Live Twice*, 1967 (with Harry Jack Bloom); *Chitty-Chitty Bang-Bang*, 1968 (with Ken Hughes); *The Night-Digger*, 1970; *The Lightning Bug*, 1971; *Willy Wonka and the Chocolate Factory*, 1971.

NONFICTION: *Boy: Tales of Childhood*, 1984; *Going Solo*, 1986.

CHILDREN'S LITERATURE: *The Gremlins*, 1943; *James and the Giant Peach*, 1961; *Charlie and the Chocolate Factory*, 1964; *The Magic Finger*, 1966; *Fantastic Mr. Fox*, 1970; *Charlie and the Great Glass Elevator*, 1972; *Danny, The Champion of the World*, 1975; *The Wonderful World of Henry Sugar*, 1977 (British title, *The Wonderful Story of Henry Sugar and Six More*, 1977); *The Complete Adventures of Charlie and Mr. Willy Wonka*, 1978 (omnibus edition); *The Enormous Crocodile*, 1978; *The Twits*, 1980; *George's Marvelous Medicine*, 1981; *The BFG*, 1982; *Revolting Rhymes*, 1982; *Dirty Beasts*, 1983; *The Witches*, 1983; *The Giraffe and the Pelly and Me*,

1985; *Matilda*, 1988; *Rhyme Stew*, 1989; *Esio Trot*, 1990; *The Vicar of Nibbleswicke*, 1990; *The Minpins*, 1991.

BIBLIOGRAPHY

Dahl, Roald. *Boy: Tales of Childhood*. New York: Farrar, Straus & Girous, 1984. The first volume of Dahl's autobiography tells of his childhood in Wales, his visits to Norway to see relatives, and his schooling.

_____. *Going Solo*. New York: Farrar, Straus & Giroux, 1986. The second volume of Dahl's autobiography provides information on his work for the Shell Oil Company, in London and in Africa, and on his years in the Royal Air Force during World War II.

Salwak, Dale, and Daryl F. Mallet, eds. *Roald Dahl: From the Gremlins to the Chocolate Factory*, by Alan Warren. Rev. ed. San Bernardino, Calif.: Borgo Press, 1994. A thorough study of Dahl and the evolution of his fiction. Includes bibliographical references and an index.

Treglown, Jeremy. *Roald Dahl: A Biography*. New York: Farrar, Straus and Giroux, 1994. Treglown uncovers a Dahl more complex than his largely self-created public persona has previously suggested. Alternates discussions of Dahl's fiction with biographical narrative; claims that in his ambition to be a successful public figure Dahl never really grew up.

West, Mark L. *Roald Dahl*. New York: Twayne, 1992. A general introduction to Dahl's life and art. Discusses Dahl as a caricaturist who exaggerates certain character traits to focus the reader's attention on behavior patterns that might otherwise go unnoticed. Argues that, in his collection *Kiss Kiss*, Dahl focuses primarily on tensions between men and women, which, though not realistic, are drawn from real life.

Chapel Louise Petty, updated by
Karen M. Cleveland Marwick

DANTE

Born: Florence, Italy; May or June, 1265
Died: Ravenna, Italy; September 13 or 14, 1321

PRINCIPAL SHORT FICTION

La divina commedia, c. 1320 (*The Divine Comedy*, 1802, 3 volumes)

OTHER LITERARY FORMS

Other than his *The Divine Comedy*, Dante left a volume of works in poetic and prose forms. Around 1292, his *La vita nuova* (c. 1292; *Vita Nuova*, 1861; better known as *The New Life*, 1867), a collection of love lyrics linked by prose commentaries that tell the history of Dante's love for Beatrice, was published. *Il convivio* (c. 1307; *The Banquet*, 1903) was intended to be a commentary on fourteen of Dante's *canzoni*; the philosophical work was left unfinished. A theoretical work on the common language, *De vulgari eloquentia* (c. 1306; English translation, 1890) is a treatise on philology. *De monarchia* (c. 1313; English translation, 1890) is a treatise on monarchy and its relation to the church. Thirteen surviving letters written in Latin and poetic essays exchanged with Giovanni del Virgilio are contained in *Epistolae* (c. 1300-1321; English translation, 1902) and *Eclogae* (1319; *Eclogues*, 1902). A Latin dissertation on natural philosophy, *Quaestio de aqua et terra* (1320; English translation, 1902) is the text of a lecture Dante gave in Verona at the invitation of Cangrande della Scala.

ACHIEVEMENTS

Dante is the most famous Italian author and perhaps the most widely read of all medieval writers. His works are the foundation for all Italian literature, and his stature was instrumental in establishing the Florentine dialect as the basis for the modern Italian language. *The Divine Comedy* has been translated into virtually all languages, and it has been the source of inspiration for famous and diverse authors such as William Shakespeare, Miguel de Cervantes, T. S. Eliot, Albert Camus, and William Faulkner. This monumental work is recognized as a compendium of all medieval learning; it is an erudite and masterful presentation of the philosophical, theological, astronomical, lyrical, and cultural ideas of the times, while on a narrative level it weaves together myriad fascinating tales. Throughout Italy and the entire civilized world there are schools, cultural organizations, benevolent societies, literary journals, medals of achievement, and even city streets and other landmarks named in his honor. Dante's *The Divine Comedy* is a classic and a magnificent tribute to the human spirit.

BIOGRAPHY

In the spring of 1265, it is believed, Dante was born to a Florentine family of the lesser nobility called Alighieri. Bella, his mother, died within a few years of his birth, and his father remarried shortly thereafter. As a result Dante had at least three half-brothers. In 1274, at age nine, he first met Beatrice, and he considered this the most significant event of his childhood. Daughter of Folco Portinari, Beatrice was to become "the glorious lady of my mind," the very essence of the literary mistress in the courtly tradition. As far as is known, Dante saw her only once more, during his eighteenth year. During his youth he probably studied with the Franciscans in Florence. Much he learned on his own, and he may have studied rhetoric with Brunetto Latini. He began to write around age eighteen and was befriended by the older poet Guido Cavalcanti.

Shortly after his father's death (c. 1283), Dante entered into a prearranged marriage with Gemma Donati. They had at least two sons and a daughter. On June 11, 1289, Dante first became involved in public life, for he took part in the Battle of Campaldino against Arezzo. During the same year he fought in the conquest of the Castle of Caprona from the Pisans. On June 8, 1290, Beatrice died, and Dante began to study philosophy in order "to console himself." In 1295, he first entered political life. Since it was a time of such great political strife, his reasons for doing so are not known or understood. From 1295 to

Dante (Library of Congress)

1297, Dante was part of the People's Special Council and a member of the Council of One Hundred. He served as an ambassador to San Gimignano and was elected Prior for two months in 1300, the Jubilee Year proclaimed by Pope Boniface VIII. In 1301, at the approach of Charles of Valois, Dante and two others were sent on an embassy to the Pope. The Pontiff retained Dante after the others had left, recognizing, no doubt, that Dante was a formidable adversary.

The first sentence of exile against Dante reached him in Siena on January 27, 1302. He was fined five thousand florins, sentenced to two years in prison, and prohibited from holding any public office. When he failed to return to Florence to clear his name, he was condemned to be burned at the stake. That sentence was delivered on March 10, 1302, and Dante never again returned to Florence. In 1310, Henry VII of Luxemburg came to Italy and aroused Dante's hopes for a pacification and unification under one rule of the Italian city states. Because of Henry's complete failure, however, his hopes were dashed. In 1315, Florence offered to repeal Dante's sentence provided that he acknowledge his past errors. He re-

fused. His remaining years were spent in wandering from court to court, city to city. He may have been in Romagna and Ravenna during 1315-1316. In 1320, he lectured in Verona. He fell ill in 1321 as he returned to Ravenna from an ambassadorial mission to Venice. He died on either the thirteenth or fourteenth of September, 1321.

ANALYSIS

Viewed as a whole, *The Divine Comedy* is a poem of such grandeur that it defies any simple classification. While being related to the great epic journeys of Homer and Vergil, it is like many medieval works relating journeys beyond the limits of this world for the edification and instruction of a sinner. It surpasses those spiritual journeys in that it ranges over the entire culture of the Middle Ages. Simultaneously it is a work of doctrine, science, philosophy, theology, vision, autobiography, praise of women, and allegory. In fact, *The Divine Comedy* is an encyclopedic compendium of practically all medieval learning. Some have called it the single most significant document inherited from the Middle Ages.

Dante called it a "comedy" both because of its happy ending and its style, which lies between that of the tragedy and that of the elegy. He chose to write it in the Italian of Florence, incorporating into it many Latinisms. From the all-pervading misery, adversity, avariciousness, and corruption surrounding him, he wished to show the path to goodness, the salvation of the human soul guided both by reason and divine grace. Dante intended the work to be read on four levels: the literal, allegorical, moral, and anagogical. Structurally, he wrote the poem in hendecasyllabic lines (eleven syllables) which are grouped in threes to make interlocking tercets; this form is called terza rima (*aba*, *bcb*, *cdc*, and so on). The tercets are grouped together into conceptual units or strophes of approximately 150 lines each and called "cantos." The entire poem has one hundred cantos consisting of an introductory canto and three principal divisions or *canticles* of thirty-three cantos each: the *Inferno* (*Hell*), the *Purgatorio* (*Purgatory*), and the *Paradiso* (*Paradise*). Each of these divisions corresponds to Dante's conception of cosmology.

Dante's cosmology is essentially that of ancient Ptolemic astronomy. The earth has Jerusalem at its center and is the fixed center of the universe. Hell is shaped like a vast funnel, a cone-shaped pit beginning near the earth's surface and extending to its center. The sides of the funnel form a series of diminishing concentric rounds in which various types of impenitents receive their punishment; the severity of punishment increases with each level of the descent. This abyss was created by the fall of Lucifer, and it is he who is punished at earth's center, that point farthest removed from God. In the Southern Hemisphere and on the opposite side of the earth from Jerusalem, there is a conical-shaped mountain presumably formed by the ground displaced by Satan's fall. This is the Mount of Purgatory where souls find themselves on seven ledges carved into the mountain. The ledges correspond to the seven capital sins: pride, envy, wrath, sloth, avarice, gluttony, and lust. Added to the ante-Purgatory at the base and the garden of earthly paradise at the summit, they form nine divisions on the mount. Paradise is composed of the nine heavenly spheres which revolve ever more rapidly and in ever wider orbits around earth. Crowning all creation is the Empyrean, where God is surrounded by the spirits of the triumphant blessed.

For good or for ill, readers have tended to single out individual portions of *The Divine Comedy* and to view them as brief fictional narratives. Such selecting is not new. Because of the interesting nature and dramatic intensity of certain episodes, they seem particularly worthy of special, critical reading; individual readers tend to identify with and to select certain episodes from the rest. Among those episodes most frequently chosen for explication are those of Francesca (*Inferno*, canto 5), Brunetto Latini (*Inf.* 15), Farinata and Cavalcante (*Inf.* 10), Piero delle Vigne (*Inf.* 13), Vanni Fucci (*Inf.* 24), Ulysses (*Inf.* 26), and Satan (*Inf.* 34). To these one might also add Cato of Utica (*Purgatorio* 1) and La Pia (*Purg.* 5). The *Inferno* contains most of the frequently cited episodes; of these, the stories of Francesca, Ulysses, and Ugolino offer especially interesting examples of Dante's narrative art and technique. They will be examined here because of their high drama, which

approaches tragedy, and their striking similarities.

Dante's real Hell begins only in the second circle, where the lustful are forever borne about on the warm winds of tempest. It is there that Francesca da Rimini tells Dante her sadly tragic tale. As if thinking aloud, she tells of how she and her brother-in-law, Paolo, were reading together the romance of Lancelot. They were particularly drawn to that part describing how Lancelot was overpowered by his violent passion for Guinevere. Francesca and Paolo were alone, never fearing their weakness. "We were reading one day for delight of Lancelot, how love seized him: We were alone and unsuspecting." The immediate characteristics of this narrative are concision, speed, directness, and energy. She continues by saying that the story made them lift their eyes several times and blush. It was the climax of the story that conquered them; when Lancelot kissed his lady, Paolo kissed Francesca. The romance, she says, and its author were both panderers. That day they read no further. During the narration of this tale Paolo weeps, and out of pity Dante "swooned as if in death and dropped like a dead body."

Whereas Lancelot's kiss had fallen on his lady's "smile" (*riso*), Paolo's fell on his beloved's "mouth" (*bocca*) and hence is delineated a transformation of the spiritual into the physiological, a descent from idealized courtly love to realistic physical love, from the romanticism of an imagined "ideal" to the realism of the *salatia amoris*. Courtly love is replaced by eros, lust, and adultery, and that replacement is clear in the two words *riso* and *bocca*. While reading a tale of the ideology of courtly love, Francesca and Paolo were seduced and forgot the ugliness of sin and its inevitable consequence. That Dante swoons on hearing this tale must be seen to represent more than an act of compassion. On one level, his physical fall represents their fall. On a more complex level, he must have identified himself with the seductive nature of courtly love, for he began his literary career as a poet of the *dolce stil nuovo* (sweet new style) and sang the praises of courtly love.

Most modern readers would probably agree that Francesca's story is not a great tragedy but rather a melodramatic *Liebestod*, a romantic drama. Of great interest is the fact that Paolo, eternally bound to Franccsca, nevei ullers a word during the canto; of equal interest is the fact that Dante places this sympathetic, moving couple in Hell. His great compassion and sympathy for sinners condemned to Hell can be explained by the recognition of one of the most salient characteristics of the entire *The Divine Comedy*. Dante writes with a double point of view: He is simultaneously the poem's author and a character in it. Hence, while Dante the earth-bound pilgrim can show interest, sympathy, and compassion, Dante the moral and theological poet can justify condemning the lovers to Hell. His double point of view permits him both to express romantic love and to condemn the participants in it for impenitence.

Duality of viewpoint is nowhere more apparent than in the episode of Ulysses and his final voyage. In the twenty-sixth canto, Dante and Vergil, his guide, are in hell's eighth circle, an assemblage of ten ditches collectively called Malebolge. As they look down from the bridge leading from the seventh to the eighth ditch, Dante says that he experiences great grief sufficiently intense to cause him to want to curb his poetic gifts; yet he writes lyric, idyllic poetry as he describes all the small lights he sees below—to him they seem like the fireflies seen by the peasant resting on a hill on a summer eve. Suddenly he is reminded of Elisha, whose eyes could not distinguish anything but the flame as Elijah rose to heaven in his fiery chariot. The pilgrim Dante is so intent on the sight below that he almost falls; he entreats his guide to identify the approaching double-crested flame which reminds him of the funeral pyre of Eteocles and Polynices. Vergil identifies the sinners therein as Ulysses and Diomed, and he states the triple treachery of which they are guilty: the ambush of the Trojan horse, the deception of Deidamia to lure away her Achilles, and the theft of the sacred Palladium, the image of Pallas Athene. Dante is so insistent on meeting Ulysses that the reader is prepared for a meeting with a special character.

After complimenting Dante on his lively interest, Vergil asks Ulysses to relate the events of his final voyage. What follows is a pure invention by Dante, who had never read Homer. He says that from the greater part of the double flame came details of Ulysses's death. Having left the sorceress Circe, he was still overcome by the passion to "gain experience of the world and of the vices and worth of men." Not fondness for his son, not duty to his father, not love for his wife could calm his passion. He put forth on the open sea with his old and winded crew. When they arrived at Gibraltar, the "pillars of Hercules" across whose face was printed the warning to sailors not to venture beyond (*"Nec plus ultra"*), Ulysses easily persuaded his men to sail on. He counseled them not to deny experience and told them they "were not born to live as animals, but to follow virtue and knowledge." Off they sailed toward the Southwest in a mad flight ("folle volo") and continued for five days. Suddenly they came in the Southern Hemisphere within sight of a high brown mountain which is held to be the mount of Purgatory. Before they could reach its shores, which, as pagans, they had no right to see, a huge water spout surged from the sea. It whirled the ship about three times, and the fourth time plunged it to the bottom.

The narration of Ulysses's final voyage is so engrossing that some readers have viewed him as a tragic hero rather than as a sinner in Hell for the sin of false counseling; but this view loses sight of Dante's double point of view. Ulysses is in the eighth *bolgia* because that is where false counselors are punished by being enclosed in flame. He is bound in the same flame with Diomed his accomplice because their burning eloquence was used to conceal their real mind. Just as the peasant in the lovely simile introducing the episode might be seen as the lover of honesty, home, and family, Ulysses can be seen as the opposite—the arrogant one who scorns all such homely virtues. Vergil clearly states Ulysses' triple treachery, and the ancient hero himself confesses that he has no regard for his love or duty to son, wife, and father. He also is impenitent as he brags about how effective his flattering words were in leading his sailors: "My companions I made so eager for the road with these brief words that then I could hardly have held them back." He clearly deserves his spot in Hell, and one might easily wonder why then Dante treats him with such tragic grandeur.

John D. Sinclair has written: "It is the greatness of Ulysses that makes his doom so overwhelming, and such greatness and such doom together give to this canto more than any other in the *Inferno* the quality and power of high tragedy." One can only explain the seeming contradiction between Ulysses the condemned sinner and the exalted tragic hero by recalling Dante's double point of view. Dante the pilgrim-character admires Ulysses for his "insatiable human hunger and quest after knowledge of the world"; the ancient hero's motivation is not unlike Dante's own in his pilgrimage. At the same time, however, Dante the poet and creator of the episode feels justified in condemning the ancient sailor for sin. To admire Ulysses as does Dante the pilgrim is to forget the sin for which he is condemned. To understand Dante the poet-creator is both to refuse involvement in the intense drama of the character's tragic situation and to accept the rightness of divine judgment.

The dilemma posed by the Ulysses episode is also evident in that of Count Ugolino. Ugolina della Gherardesca, count of Donoratico, was a noble Pisan politician who was often forced by expedience to change political party or allegiance. Dante discovers him in Hell's lowest circle, Antenora, where the treacherous to country or to cause are punished. There is no fire or tormented screaming in this region, for it is at the point in the universe which is farthest removed from the sun and God. Everything is frozen. Imprisoned in the frozen Lake of Cocytus, the traitor Ugolino gnaws with bestial hatred on the skull of his bitter enemy and rival, Archbishop Ruggiero Ubaldini. Dante begs the count to tell of how he died and not, significantly, of his sin. That which causes the count to comply is the desire that perhaps his words will "be seed that may bear fruit of infamy" to the archbishop.

The Ugolino episode is the longest in the *Inferno*. Ugolino tells of how he was with four of his sons in a Pisan tower for several months. One night he had a dream which revealed the future to him—in it a father and his sons were torn apart by hunters' dogs, "hounds lean, trained and eager." When he awoke he heard his sleeping children crying from hunger. Then, at the hour they were usually fed, they heard the

tower door being nailed shut. For a day and night Ugolino remained speechless and without tears. When he bit his hand from grief the following day, one of his sons thinking that he was hungry offered his father the flesh of his children to eat. Four more days they remained in silence. The son Gaddo begged his father for help and died. During the fifth and sixth days the other three sons died. Ugolino grieved for two more days and "then fasting had more power than grief." This means that he died of starvation rather than of grief and not, as some have held, because he ate of his sons' flesh. When he finishes telling his tale, Ugolino throws himself again into the furious task of gnawing the archbishop's skull with his teeth. Dante is so moved that he inveighs against Pisa and calls for its destruction. Even though Ugolino had betrayed his political parties, his city's strongholds, and his grandson and rival, Nino Visconti, the evil archbishop had no right to make his sons suffer and die of starvation. Theirs is the "most horrible tragedy" of the *Inferno*.

There is a certain quality of tragic grandeur in Ugolino. He says nothing of his treacherous political dealings, he accuses nobody, he indulges in no recriminations, and he does not attempt to justify himself. He asks for no pity. In comparison with the tragedy of which he was the protagonist, his past seems insignificant to him. He was forced to stand by impotently and observe the agony of his sons. His tragic situation is summed up in the cry of his son: "Father why do you not help me?" That plea must continue to torment him and cause much of the bestial rage he vents on the silent archbishop.

In the Ugolino episode, as in those of Francesca and Ulysses, one is tempted to forget the sin of the character in the face of his tragedy and inner appeal. In all three one must recognize Dante's admiration of the character and condemning judgment of the sinner. All three episodes are characterized by a succinct rapidity of narration uncontaminated by useless detail or editorial commentary. All three sinners tell their own tales, and each is condemned for eternity to be bound with his accomplice in sin. It is Dante's viewpoint as pilgrim and Everyman that establishes the tragic stature of the three narrators; and it is Dante's viewpoint as the poet trained in theology, scholastic philosophy, and morality which justifies placing all three in hell.

OTHER MAJOR WORKS

POETRY: *La vita nuova*, c. 1292 (*Vita Nuova*, 1861; better known as *The New Life*, 1867).

NONFICTION: *Epistolae*, c. 1300-1321 (English translation, 1902); *De vulgari eloquentia*, c. 1306 (English translation, 1890); *Il convivio*, c. 1307 (*The Banquet*, 1903); *De monarchia*, c. 1313 (English translation, 1890; also known as *Monarchy*, 1954, better known as *On World Government*, 1957); "Epistola X," c. 1316 (English translation, 1902); *Eclogae*, 1319 (*Eclogues*, 1902); *Quaestio de aqua et terra*, 1320 (English translation, 1902); *Translation of the Latin Works of Dante Alighieri*, 1904; *Literary Criticism of Dante Alighieri*, 1973.

BIBLIOGRAPHY

Barbi, Michele. *Life of Dante*. Translated and edited by Paul G. Ruggiers. Berkeley: University of California Press, 1960. The definitive biography of Dante. Divided into three parts: the life, minor works, and *The Divine Comedy*. Contains a lengthy and thorough bibliography of English works on Dante and English translations of his works. Although somewhat dated, this book is a very interesting resource.

Barolini, Teodolinda. *Dante's Poets*. Princeton, N.J.: Princeton University Press, 1984. An extensive study of the poets that appear in *The Divine Comedy* and their influence on Dante's thought and literary style. The first chapter examines references to Dante's own early poetic works, while the second analyzes major figures such as Guido Cavalcanti, Guittone d'Arezzo, and Bertran de Born. The final chapter deals with the influence of the epic poets such as Vergil and Statius and Dante's resolution of classical thought with medieval philosophy.

Bergin, Thomas. *Dante*. Boston: Houghton Mifflin, 1965. Perhaps the best concise study of Dante and his times available in English. Sets the foundation for an understanding of Dante's works, with an introduction to the social and intellectual life in Europe and Florence during the Middle Ages, and then proceeds to discuss Dante's early formation. Analyzes all the major works and concludes with an extensive discussion of *The Divine Comedy*. Includes a bibliography, notes, and an index of names.

Gallagher, Joseph. *To Hell and Back with Dante: A Modern Reader's Guide to "The Divine Comedy."* Liguori, Mo.: Triumph Books, 1996. An indispensable tool for any student of the work.

Hollander, Robert. *Studies in Dante*. Ravenna, Italy: Longo Editore, 1980. A collection of essays from a noted scholar dealing with various aspects of Dante scholarship. The topics range from a discussion of *The New Life*, which traces Dante's conception of Beatrice, to a lengthy study on the influence of contemporary poets and the doctrine of the Church Fathers, to a subtle reading of individual cantos.

Iannucci, Amilcare A., ed. *Dante: Contemporary Perspectives*. Toronto: University of Toronto Press, 1997. Offers excellent criticism of Dante's work from fresh points of view. Includes bibliographical references and an index.

Quinones, Ricardo J. *Dante Alighieri*. New York: Twayne, 1998. A good introduction to the life and works of Dante. For the beginning student.

Vossler, Karl. *Mediaeval Culture: An Introduction to Dante and His Times*. 2 vols. New York: Frederick Ungar, 1958. An excellent introduction to the history of the culture from which Dante's poetry arises. Volume 1 discusses the background of the poet on religion, philosophy, ethical and political thought, and the contemporary literature of the Middle Ages. In volume 2, Dante's work alone is analyzed. A very detailed work covering topics such as "Dante and Aristotle," "Dante and Augustine," "Dante's Personality," and "The Church in the Middle Ages." Includes a detailed and extensive index of names and important concepts.

James D. Tedder, updated by Victor A. Santi

ALPHONSE DAUDET

Born: Nîmes, France; May 13, 1840
Died: Paris, France; December 16, 1897

PRINCIPAL SHORT FICTION

Lettres de mon moulin, 1869 (*Letters from My Mill*, 1880)
Contes du lundi, 1873, 1876 (*Monday Tales*, 1927)
Les Femmes d'artistes, 1874 (*Artists' Wives*, 1890)
La Fédor, 1896
Le Trésor d'Arlatan, 1897

OTHER LITERARY FORMS

Alphonse Daudet began his career—as did most aspiring writers in nineteenth century France—with a small volume of poems; then he turned to writing short essays and stories (called *chroniques*) for newspapers as a means of livelihood. He also tried his hand at writing for the theater in those early years, sometimes in collaboration, sometimes alone. He felt his true vocation, however, was in the novel, and he began his career as a novelist with a fictionalized account of his own youth, written when he was twenty-eight years old. Thereafter he published some fifteen novels, one every other year on the average until his death. Until he was forty, some of his time was occupied by journalism, consisting of *chroniques*, short stories, and drama criticism, most of it collected in volumes during his lifetime. He wrote half a dozen full-length plays during his mature years, without ever really achieving a great public success. After his death, the interesting diary of his fatal illness was published, as were some fragmentary personal reminiscences, but he never wrote a formal autobiography.

ACHIEVEMENTS

Although Alphonse Daudet was one of the most popular writers of his era, the bulk of his literary work has fallen into obscurity. Some of his works, such as *Lettres de mon moulin, Adventures prodigieuses de Tartarin de Tarascon* (1872; *The New Don Quixote*, 1875), and, to a lesser degree, *Le Petit Chose* (1868; *The Little Good-for-Nothing*, 1878) and *Contes du lundi* have been reprinted, adapted to film, and anthologized; stories such as "La Chèvre de M. Seguin" ("M. Seguin's Goat") have joined the corpus of household tales, and his musical drama *L'Arlésienne* (1872; the lady from Arles), with its accompaniment by Georges Bizet, is still performed. His present-day reputation as a storyteller, however, overshadows his nineteenth century acclaim as a novelist, just as a focus on his Provençal writings has obscured the cosmopolitan nature of his works. The diversity of genre and subjects, indeed, makes Daudet unclassifiable as a writer. His works combine elements of Romanticism, realism, and naturalism, but they evade any attempts to link him definitively with any one major movement of his time. Widely translated and read in the English-speaking world of the later nineteenth century as well as in the French, he was saluted as the "French Dickens." His work, apart from its intrinsic literary value, reveals an ongoing awareness of the controversies and concerns of his time and thus serves as an invaluable document of the life and concerns of the nineteenth century. Although Daudet's novel *Fromont jeune et Risler aîné* (1874; *Fromont the Younger and Risler the Elder*, 1880) was crowned by the French Academy, Daudet never submitted his name for membership in this prestigious body, seeing it as a threat to his independence. As the initial executor of the will of his friend Edmond Goncourt, he had a hand in the establishment of the famed Goncourt Academy. His true "award" came, however, from the Parisian crowds that turned out to salute his memory as his casket was borne to the cemetery.

BIOGRAPHY

Nothing had more effect on Alphonse Daudet's rather uneventful life than the fact that he was born and brought up in southern France, the Midi. Throughout his life, Daudet maintained that the meridional temperament, which was his heritage, made him profoundly different from Northerners and accounted for his facile volubility and intense emotionalism. Although he was a Parisian by adoption for most of his life, it is a fact that his identity as a southerner, including the distinctive accent of the Midi, never faded, and his great gifts as a spellbinding talker in social situations is widely attested.

For the first eight years of his life, Daudet lived in Nîmes, with its strong flavor of ancient Roman civilization. The family then moved to Lyons, where Alphonse experienced both a less prosperous family life and a more "northern" culture and atmosphere

Alphonse Daudet (Library of Congress)

than Nîmes had afforded, although it was still distinctly part of the Midi. His studies were interrupted at age sixteen so he could take on the post of class assistant in a school in the southern town of Alès, thus relieving his family of a financial burden.

He lasted only a few months in that post, however, and at the age of seventeen he went to Paris and moved in with his older brother Ernest. He had been writing since his early teens, and within a year of his

arrival in Paris he was able to arrange publication of a small volume of his poems and even had some success reciting his poems in a few literary salons of the day. With the help of his brother, he obtained a sinecure as secretary to the Duc de Morny, and he supplemented his income with occasional journalism and work for the theater, so he could enjoy the bohemian existence of the spirited young man-about-Paris with literary aspirations.

Health problems and an unhappy relationship with a mistress marked those bohemian years. Marriage in 1867 and the birth of a child a year later confirmed the start of a serious literary career and a very bourgeois family existence. Fame did not come quickly—there were several failures, especially in the theater, and his novels and short stories were only modest successes at first. He still needed the income from journalism, but significant sums of money accrued for the first time with the publication in 1874 of his first attempt at a realistic novel, set in Paris. That novel, *Fromont jeune et Risler aîné*, was the book that revealed to him his vocation as a popular novelist, and he enjoyed success and prosperity in that role for the next fifteen years.

By 1890, however, his health had deteriorated from the effects of the late stage of the syphilis he had contracted in his bohemian youth. It began to be difficult for him to walk and even to hold a pen since all his joints were afflicted. The unremitting pain inevitably slowed down his work pace, although, his brain being completely unaffected, he remained determined to continue working every day. His last works seemed uninspired and excessively didactic and sentimental, except for two remarkable short stories composed in 1896 and 1897, in which he movingly evoked, in fictional disguise, details of his youthful literary beginnings. When death came, in December of 1897, he had just completed a novel and a dramatization of an earlier novel, both of which were published posthumously and represent the final acts of a literary career spanning nearly forty years.

ANALYSIS

Storytelling was probably Alphonse Daudet's most fundamental talent as a writer. His first writings, in verse, told a story more often than not, and his early newspaper work was largely anecdotal in nature. So ingrained was the storytelling impulse, indeed, that his first novels were either episodic in structure—*The Little Good-for-Nothing* and *The New Don Quixote*—or were composed of several interwoven but plainly separate plots, tenuously and artificially linked to one another. Throughout the 1870's, while his popularity began to grow, the critics insistently pointed out that Daudet seemed to be too "short-winded" to write a full-length novel of adequately unified conception, calling him, with pejorative intent, a talented *conteur* who was out of his depth in the novel. Daudet did not really lay the ghost of this criticism to rest until the 1880's, when his novels—especially *Sapho* (1884; *Sappho*, 1886)—won acclaim for their sustained formal excellence.

In retrospect, critical opinion seems not to have been far wrong, for it is primarily Daudet's short-story output of the 1860's and 1870's which still survives as literature rather than the awkwardly constructed novels of that period. In the long run, indeed, the survival of Daudet's total literary reputation may ultimately rest on his achievement in the short story alone. Certainly it is when telling a story that Daudet is at his most typical and at his best as a writer.

The heart of Alphonse Daudet's claim to fame as a short-story writer is to be found in a handful of the best stories from two collections. *Letters from My Mill* and *Monday Tales*, plus two longer compositions unexpectedly produced at the very end of his career when he momentarily returned to the long-neglected literary form of his beginnings.

LETTERS FROM MY MILL

As the title indicates, all the twenty-five stories in *Letters from My Mill* are cast in the form of letters; this enabled Daudet to provide each tale with a framework and an intimate, personal tone suggesting that narrator and reader are close friends. Much of the charm of these stories derives from this conversational narrative tone.

In perhaps the best-known of these stories, "M. Seguin's Goat," the tale of the goat who wanted freedom, is told as an exemplary tale by the narrator to a fellow writer who is being urged to give up his free-

lance status in favor of the regular income of a staff journalist. The narrative itself is therefore constantly interrupted by asides to the presumed audience of one, exhorting him to recognize the dangers of freedom and the advantages of security, as demonstrated by the case of the goat. By means of a subtly controlled irony, however, Daudet is able to undercut his own narrator's voice, making the account of the goat's escape from M. Seguin's tether to the mountain so delightful an experience and the goat's battle with the wolf so bravely heroic that the lesson the ending should carry ("And in the morning, the wolf devoured the poor goat") must ring hollow to the reader. The narrator's personality thus directly affects the impact of the story—indeed, the narrator, who is unaware that his own choice of words is undermining his purpose, becomes the main character in the story and the ultimate focus of our amused interest. The story creates an unusually inventive role for the narrator and makes a quite original use of the device of irony.

A parallel technique accounts for the delightful effect of another story in the collection, "L'Elixir de Révérend Père Gaucher" ("The Reverend Father Gaucher's Elixir"), which recounts the mock-tragic plight of a monk who has created a *liqueur* which has made his monastery prosperous but who cannot prepare the beverage without committing the sin of drunkenness because he must keep tasting the product to be sure it is exactly right. In this instance, the narrator is a priest, who means his story to be a solemn account of a pious soul inadvertently brought to damnation but who cannot keep from making the story comic and even ribald. The ironic gap between the narrator's intention and his effect is here, as in "M. Seguin's Goat," the principal pleasure afforded the reader.

The various narrators of *Letters from My Mill* can be spellbinding in quite different ways from this device of comic irony. In one of the finest stories, "L'Arlésienne," for example, the narrator is almost completely self-effacing. The narration of this stark tale of unrequited love, ending in desperation and suicide, proceeds by means of the simplest words and direct, unadorned sentences. Nothing calls attention to the voice or personality of the narrator. Instead, the tightly restrained narrative style suggests the emotional impact the story is having on the narrator, with the result that the power of the tale is brought home to the reader with swift and unexpected immediacy.

In quite another vein, Daudet affects the tone of the sententious moralist to underline the import of his melancholy "La Légende de l'homme à la cervelle d'or" ("The Legend of the Man with the Golden Brain"), a fable which uses a horrifying image to characterize the inevitable fate of the creative artist in society. In the famous tale of medieval Avignon, "La Mule du Pape" ("The Pope's Mule"), Daudet creates a narrator whose gleeful relish of this tale of the patient revenge of a mule on his tormentor is made apparent in every sentence. The note of joyful celebration is struck at the very outset ("Anyone who has not seen Avignon at the time of the Popes hasn't seen anything") and is sustained until the moment of the mule's triumph, buoying up the reader on waves of infectious gaiety. The technical range of this device—making the voice and personality of the narrator integral to the tone and meaning of the story—is stunning in *Letters from My Mill* and constitutes the principal contribution this collection makes to the evolution of short-story technique in France. Moreover, as Daudet understood quite well, the device was the essential secret of the "charm" his stories were said to have when *Letters from My Mill* was published in 1869.

MONDAY TALES

The stories Daudet published in the 1870's naturally continued to make use of the carefully developed narrative voice as a principal ingredient, although the subject matter he chose to treat underwent a major shift. In place of the meridional environment of his youth, Daudet began to write about the Paris in and near which he was living. His experiences as a member of the national guard during the Franco-Prussian War provided him with much material as the decade began, and the atmosphere of Parisian literary life, in cafés and salons, quickly became a major source of observations and inspiration when peace returned. For a considerable period in the early 1870's, Daudet contributed a story a week to one of the best-known newspapers in Paris, and, because those stories appeared regularly in the Monday edition, they had the rubric "Contes de lundi." The pressure of a weekly obligation inevitable resulted in very uneven quality, but Daudet was rigorously conscientious about artistic standards when he arranged for book publication of those stories. Only a small fraction of them was reprinted, and the rest were consigned to oblivion. Moreover, the collection which appeared in 1873 under the title *Monday Tales* was thoroughly revised, and winnowed, later in the decade for a definitive edition which came out in 1879, with a number of the former items missing and some new ones added.

In its definitive form, *Monday Tales* affords the cream of Daudet's short-story production in the 1870's. Its best-known story is certainly "La Dernière Classe" ("The Last Class"), the touching account of the last day on which the French language would be permitted in an Alsatian school during the Franco-Prussian War. For this tale, Daudet's choice of a narrator was one of the schoolboys, perhaps symbolically named Frantz. As seen through Frantz's youthful eyes, the day's events are naturally awash in sentimentality and pathos, and the style and tone of the narration are suitably emotion-choked. Yet the effect is neither cloying nor facile but profoundly moving, in part because Daudet plays off the teacher, M. Hamel, who is quietly dignified and solemn, against the childish narrator, Frantz, who is innocent and frivolous at the start but is gradually affected by the unusual demeanor of his teacher. The powerful emotion inherent in the story's theme is fully realized and earned by the author's careful, gradual unfolding of the drama and his precise depiction of the subtle interplay of emotions in the classroom.

Another frequently anthologized story from *Monday Tales* is "Le Siège de Berlin" ("The Siege of Berlin"), which dramatizes the self-deception the French tended to engage in as an escape from the insistently depressing bulletins from the front during the Franco-Prussian War. The best of the nonwar stories in *Monday Tales* harks back in tone, technique, and setting to the manner of *Letters from My Mill*. "Les Trois Messes basses" ("The Three Low Masses") is a merry Christmas tale about a priest succumbing to the sin of gluttony by racing shamelessly through the required three masses on Christmas night so he will get to the traditional holiday feast as quickly as possible. A tone of gentle mockery, as of a vastly amused outside observer, characterizes the narrative voice throughout the tale.

LA FÉDOR *and* LE TRÉSOR D'ARLATAN

By the end of the 1870's, Daudet had become financially secure; he no longer needed the income from journalism since he was firmly established in his career as a novelist. The writing of short stories virtually ceased for him at that point, until 1896, when, for reasons unknown, he interrupted work on a novel to write *La Fédor*, a short story about the death and funeral of a famous actress and the emotions that event awakened in a middle-aged writer who had once been her lover. The writing in this story is delicately controlled, the psychological nuances are subtle and entirely convincing, and the narrative never even risks descending to the easy tug at the heart strings which the theme naturally invites.

A similarly disciplined performance, and on an obviously parallel subject, was produced by Daudet several months later. This was his longest short story ever, the kind the French call a *nouvelle*, and it was entitled *Le Trésor d'Arlatan* (Arlatan's treasure). This story recounts the efforts of a young writer to forget an actress with whom he had been having a painfully unhappy relationship. The writer abandons Paris and goes to live in an isolated cabin in the woods, near his birthplace in southern France, but he finds that his memory is still haunted by the image of his former mistress. He is cured of his sick obsession only when he succumbs to curiosity about a local quack named Arlatan and his "treasure" of assorted nostrums, curios, mementoes, and even pornographic pictures, all of it reputed to have magic curative powers. He pays to see the "treasure" and finds therein a nude photograph of his former mistress. The disgust that fills him is enough to exorcize her image forever, and he returns to Paris. The outstanding feature of this work is the profound and sophisticated handling of the psychology of obsession and the dark side of human emotions.

These last two stories, miraculously salvaged from the wreckage of a once great talent, display some of Daudet's finest writing. Although not technically innovative and suffused with their author's bubbling personality, as were the best stories of *Letters from My Mill*, *La Fédor*, and *Le Trésor d'Arlatan*, they demonstrate that the serious and mature gifts Daudet brought to his best novels, such as *Sappho*, could be applied to the short-story form as well. That he was able to achieve these fine compositions in spite of his failing health and declining literary power at the time can perhaps be attributed to the intensely felt personal meaning the two stories had for him, since they are barely disguised reminiscences of his own past. Whatever the explanation, the two final tales join with the best of *Letters from My Mill* and *Monday Tales* to form a distinguished and durable body of achievement in the genre, which occupies a position of honor in the history of the French short story.

OTHER MAJOR WORKS

LONG FICTION: *Le Petit Chose*, 1868 (*My Brother Jack*, 1877; also as *The Little Good-for-Nothing*, 1878); *Adventures prodigieuses de Tartarin de Tarascon*, 1872 (*The New Don Quixote*, 1875; also as *Tartarin of Tarascon*, 1910); *Fromont jeune et Risler aîné*, 1874 (*Fromont the Younger and Risler the Elder*, 1880); *Jack*, 1876 (English translation, 1877); *Le Nabab*, 1877 (*The Nabob*, 1878); *Les Rois en exil*, 1879 (*Kings in Exile*, 1880); *Numa Roumestan*, 1881 (English translation, 1882); *L'Évangéliste*, 1883 (English translation, 1883; also as *Port Salvation*, 1883); *Sapho*, 1884 (*Sappho*, 1886); *L'Immortel*, 1888 (*One of the Forty*, 1888).

PLAYS: *La Dernière Idole*, pr., pb. 1862 (with Ernest Lépine); *L'Oeillet blanc*, pr. 1865 (with Ernest Manuell); *The Last Lily*, 1870; *L'Arlésienne*, pr. 1872; *Lise Tavernier*, pr. 1872 (English translation, 1890).

POETRY: *Les Amoureuses*, 1858, 1873.

NONFICTION: *Souvenirs d'un homme de lettres*, 1888 (*Recollections of a Literary Man*, 1889); *Trente Ans de Paris*, 1888 (*Thirty Years of Paris and of My Literary Life*, 1888).

MISCELLANEOUS: *The Works*, 1898-1900 (24 volumes).

BIBLIOGRAPHY

Dobie, Grace Vera. *Alphonse Daudet*. London: Nelson, 1949. This literary biography is a reliable source of facts on the writer's life from a traditional viewpoint. Provides, however, little assessment of his works.

Hamilton, James F. "The Recovery of Psychic Center in Daudet's *lettres de mon moulin*." *Nineteenth-Century French Studies* 5 (Fall/Winter, 1995/1996): 133-143. Argues that the book's bipolar structure reflects a struggle in the male ego for and against the integration of the feminine; suggests that the windmill and the lighthouse reflect the feminine versus the masculine side of the self.

Hare, Geoffrey E. *Alphonse Daudet: A Critical Bibliography*. 2 vols. London: Grant & Cutler, 1978. A painstakingly compiled bibliography of the author's works by genre, along with listings of French and international studies; astute critical commentary on critical works.

MacConmara, Maitiú. "Provincial Culture in the Work of Two French Writers." *Studies* 53 (Summer, 1974): 167-176. An analysis of Guy de Maupassant and Daudet's treatments of minority cultures. Claims that Daudet's Provençal works reveal the crisis of an old civilization invaded by dominant French social and cultural forces.

Roche, Alphonse Victor. *Alphonse Daudet*. Boston: Twayne, 1976. A biographical approach that summarizes Daudet's major works: Contains, however, a number of proofreading blunders.

Sachs, Murray. *The Career of Alphonse Daudet: A Critical Study*. Cambridge, Mass.: Harvard University Press, 1965. An excellent, reliable study of the author and his works.

Murray Sachs, updated by Anna M. Wittman

GUY DAVENPORT

Born: Anderson, South Carolina; November 23, 1927

PRINCIPAL SHORT FICTION

Tatlin!, 1974
Da Vinci's Bicycle: Ten Stories, 1979
Eclogues: Eight Stories, 1981
Apples and Pears and Other Stories, 1984
The Jules Verne Steam Balloon, 1987
The Drummer of the Eleventh North Devonshire Fusiliers, 1990
A Table of Green Fields: Ten Stories, 1993
The Cardiff Team, 1996
Twelve Stories, 1997

OTHER LITERARY FORMS

Guy Davenport occupies a rare position in American letters, since he is renowned in so many diverse areas. Not only is he one of contemporary American literature's most complex short-story writers, but also he is one of its most influential literary critics, translators, and classical scholars. He has published more than seventy stories in several collections. In the first four collections, he has supplied his own distinctive black-and-white illustrations. He has also published a collection of poems and translations, entitled *Thasos and Ohio: Poems and Translations* (1986), and an early volume of poems, *Flowers and Leaves* (1966).

Besides his collections of short fiction and poetry, Davenport has published highly acclaimed translations of Heraklitus, Diogenes, and the poets Sappho and Archilochus. He has also published a number of critically praised nonfiction works: *The Geography of the Imagination* (1981), *Every Force Evolves a Form* (1987), *The Hunter Gracchus, and Other Papers on*

Literature and Art (1996), and *Objects on a Table: Harmonious Disarray in Art and Literature* (1998). These volumes contain essays which cover such challenging thinkers as James Joyce, Ezra Pound, Charles Olson, Ludwig Wittgenstein, and the late work of Samuel Beckett, to mention but a few. He has also edited a selection of writings on Swiss naturalist Louis Agassiz.

ACHIEVEMENTS

Among Guy Davenport's honors are a Blumenthal-Leviton Prize (1967), a Kentucky Research Award (1976), a University of Kentucky Arts and Sciences Distinguished Professor citation (1977), a Morton Dauwen Zabel Award (1981), American Book Award nominations (1981 and 1982), a National Book Critics Circle Award nomination (1982), a University of Kentucky Alumni Distinguished Professor citation (1983), and a Thomas Carter Award for literary criticism (1987).

BIOGRAPHY

Guy Mattison Davenport, Jr., was born on November 23, 1927, in Anderson, South Carolina, to Guy Mattison, an express agent, and Marie (Fant) Davenport. He earned a B.A. from Duke University in 1948. He then attended the University of Oxford, Merton College, on a Rhodes scholarship, receiving a B.Litt. in 1950. After spending two years in the military (1950-1952), he taught for several years at Washington University in St. Louis. Having finished his Ph.D. at Harvard University in 1961 in classical literature, he taught at Haverford College in Philadelphia until 1963. He then accepted a position in the English department at the University of Kentucky, where he taught until 1992.

ANALYSIS

First and foremost, Guy Davenport is a practicing modernist in a postmodernist literary world. In much of his fiction, he employs standard modernist techniques, still called "experimental" by more conservative critics. By using methods usually associated with the visual art of collage, he juxtaposes images of the past with the present, hoping to demonstrate the per-

sistent efficacious energies of the archaic and how they can still be used to redeem humankind from the relentless onslaught of mechanization. These energies reside in the human imagination as it intersects and interacts with the local environment in much the same way that Pound, one of Davenport's major influences, and William Carlos Williams present the fragmentation that takes place when human beings are separated from their geographical, cultural, and spiritual origins. He calls his literary techniques, especially in his more experimental stories, "assemblages of history and necessary fiction," thus combining Wallace Stevens's notion of a "supreme fiction" with Pound's and Williams's reliance on a historical tradition grounded in a specific geographical location. He has stated that "my stories are lessons in history."

Most important, however, is that much of Davenport's fiction is obsessed with an attempt to regenerate an Edenic innocence that "civilization" has destroyed by its incessant rationality. The "Fall" into experience, time, and knowledge becomes a major subject matter of most of his fictions. His greatest work is the trilogy detailing the highly intellectual and erotic adventures of Adriaan van Hovendaal, a Dutch philosopher, and his attempt to create a utopian community based on the teachings of the French philosopher Charles Fourier. The work of Fourier can be read as a virtual blueprint of this trilogy, which consists of the bulk of *Apples and Pears and Other Stories*, most of *The Jules Verne Steam Balloon*, and the longest story in *The Drummer of the Eleventh North Devonshire Fusiliers* (which can also be called a novella), *Wo es war, soll ich werden*. A number of other stories, while not containing the identical characters as does the trilogy, treat the theme of the damage done to the instinctual life by so-called civilization and its persistent need to thwart the human desire for affection. The "apples and pears" Davenport frequently mentions in his fictions constitute a fractal motif which establishes his extreme allusiveness, for such trees are what Odysseus returns to at the end of his epic wandering. These orchards also echo the purity of the Garden of Eden, in which healthy human desires are permitted full prelapsarian expression.

Davenport's earliest short stories appeared in his first collection, entitled *Tatlin!* He readily admits that he was forty-three years old when he first began writing short stories and unashamedly labels his writing "primitive and contrived." His stories are much closer to the openly inventive fictions of the ancient Roman writer Lucius Apuleius, the medieval tales of Sir Thomas Malory, and the sensual celebrations of François Rabelais. Davenport also lists those writers who have had the greatest influence on him as a fiction writer: Joyce, Franz Kafka, Eudora Welty, and Gustave Flaubert. He also identifies other artists, not necessarily writers, who have helped form his creative sensibilities. His admiration of the techniques of ideogram used in the poetry of Pound, Williams, and Olson, along with the enormous range of their poetic projects, has entered the highly original imagination of Davenport. He attributes, as an important influence on his unique way of envisioning reality, the architectonic arrangement of images of the experimental filmmaker Stan Brakhage. He has also adopted a number of Brakhage's methods for his own fiction making, specifically the replacement of narrative and documentation by a series of images that formulate a structure of their own as they emerge. As he himself has stated: "I trust the image; my business is to get it onto the page." As example of such is one of the ten "stories" in *The Cardiff Team*, a quarter-page prose image reminiscent of haiku, entitled "Veranda Hung with Wisteria."

Davenport's fictions are virtually impossible to decipher if one attempts to analyze them according to standard literary techniques such as plot, character, theme, and setting. There is rarely a clearly outlined plot in which a protagonist journeys somewhere, confronts overwhelming difficulties, and, by overcoming them, learns something new about his inner self. Readers stand a much better chance of understanding Davenport's work if they stop trying to analyze them as conventional short stories. What interests Davenport is that his readers experience the creative process along with him, much in the way one experiences a tour of a museum of modern art accompanied by an all-knowing guide who points out important structural elements in what looks chaotic on first viewing.

Davenport is a declared modernist and as such must be examined with the same methods that one would apply to Max Ernst, Pablo Picasso, Georges Braque, or Paul Klee: collage and montage. What the viewer brings to collage and montage is the ability to detect multilayered structures in terms of juxtaposition and parataxis—that is, the way certain similar elements begin to formulate parallels of their own and how they play off each other to create new combinations and, therefore, new forms.

"THE AEROPLANES AT BRESCIA"

Davenport's first story, "The Aeroplanes at Brescia," illustrates clearly the way he uses montage and juxtaposition to engender a field of fictive possibilities that creates its own kind of information and entertainment. What becomes most compelling about the story is not its narrative structure but rather the process of its own creation. Watching the way that Davenport permits his imagination to work on certain facts about a famous air show that took place in Brescia in 1909, featuring archaic flying machines, takes precedence over the actual event. The subject matter of the story is not what happened at that air show but, more important, who saw it and what they wrote about it. Davenport is much more interested in versions of what happened because that is how he envisions history. What he finds fascinating, and bases his fiction on, is the version that Kafka described in a newspaper article that he wrote about the event and that subsequently became his first published writing. Davenport placed next to it (the literal meaning of "parataxis") a version of the same event by Kafka's biographer Max Brod, who was also there with Kafka. Other important people were also present, such as Giacomo Puccini and Gabriele D'Annunzio, and Davenport offers his version of what he imagined they observed, a version that becomes as plausible as Kafka's and Brod's. There is also some conjecture that the linguistic philosopher Wittgenstein *may* also have been there since he was obsessed with flight and archaic flying machines from his early youth. The author therefore includes what Wittgenstein *might have seen* as an alternate possibility that adds to the richness of multiple fictive possibilities of a single event in 1909. Other critics have labeled these literary techniques "fictive approximations of reality" that rest on "as-if" propositions about history rather than so-called objective documentation.

"TATLIN!" AND "ROBOT"

Davenport, a painterly writer, envisions a page as a picture or a texture of images and uses pictures themselves as integral parts of the text. In the stories "Tatlin!" and "Robot," he uses actual drawings that he did to illustrate important elements, in these cases images of both Vladimir Ilich Lenin and Joseph Stalin as iconographic presences, and abstract sculptures that Tatlin created and that Davenport copied from fading photographs. In the charming narrative called "Robot," telling of the serendipitous discovery of the Caves of Lascaux by French teenage boys in 1941 and the awesome entry of the great French anthropologist priest-scholar Abbé Henri Breuil into the caves, Davenport uses his own drawings of the images found in the cave. While his drawings virtually replicate those magnificent prehistorical images, they also become an additional text, another version of the historical event and, therefore, form a collage rather than a flat, linear report of an important discovery. By fabricating layers of perception, paratactically, he creates multiple perspectives that resemble Picasso's cubist vision. Since Robot is the name of the dog that leads the boys to the caves while chasing a rabbit, the reader gets a dog's-eye view of the event, a version as significant as the human, since the title of the story is "Robot."

"THE DAWN IN EREWHON"

The most important story in the collection *Tatlin!*, however, is the concluding one, entitled "The Dawn in Erewhon," which takes up exactly one half of the entire book. Davenport expands enormously the range of his allusions, rivaling Pound at his densest in the *Cantos LII-LXXI* (1940) and Olson at his most allusive in *The Maximus Poems* (1960). He admits to evoking the names of ninety-three historical personages in the story "The Aeroplanes at Brescia" alone. In "The Dawn in Erewhon," the allusions and perspectives accelerate prodigiously. While an omniscient voice narrates most of the story, a few pages are taken from the notebooks of the Dutch philosopher Adriaan van Hovendaal, whom Davenport

thinks he saw in Amsterdam fifteen years earlier, although no actual biography or notebooks are known to exist. The title evolved from Samuel Butler's satiric, pastoral utopia called *Erewhon* (1872), an anagram of "nowhere."

Davenport's "The Dawn in Erewhon" is his version of an Edenic pastoral utopia modeled on Butler's *Erewhon* to the extent that they both mutually criticize the damage that modern civilization does to the life of instinct. Butler's satire attacks the Victorian fear of sexuality and Christianity's persistent condemnation of the body, while traditionally favoring the needs of the intellect over those of the body. Consistent with Davenport's recurrent theme, that of the fall from a childhood innocence into the experience of self-consciousness, he attempts in this story to regenerate an Edenic childlike vision through which experience can be redeemed on both spiritual and physical levels. The intellectual genius of van Hovendaal is always put to the service of the desires of the body; his life is the opposite of the overly cerebral thinker lost in the life-denying abstractions of philosophical inquiry. Though Davenport documents in spectacular detail the cognitive sources of van Hovendaal's intellectual background by using a Joycean stream-of-consciousness technique of juxtaposing hundreds of quotations, in at least six languages, running through his mind, he demonstrates in much greater detail the endless sexual activities that vivify his affective life and transform it into forms of ecstatic consciousness, which are multiplied many times over with each succeeding chapter.

The major characters Bruno and Kaatje, who reappear in many later works, first appear in "The Dawn in Erewhon." They revel in each other's and Adriaan's company. They also enjoy each other sexually in couples and trios without guilt or jealousy. They have become the first group that Davenport consciously forms into a unit, best described by the French sociological philosopher Charles Fourier as "Little Hordes," whose primary duty is to fulfill their instinctual desires for pleasure. Much of the action throughout "The Dawn in Erewhon" consists of camping trips to idyllic forests, elaborate assignment of duties in establishing campsites, careful division of labor, and a strict parceling out of time spent alone doing whatever they wish. The day concludes with multiple sexual activities in which everyone must be satisfied. All erotic exercises, while delineated in the most specific sexual language, are presented as elaborate rituals of innocence and childlike joy. Since control and aggression, elements that prevent healthy sexual expression, have been removed from this little but highly structured society, Davenport's fictions become rituals of regenerative innocence.

Certain standard literary and philosophical dichotomies, such as the Dionysian versus the Apollonian, or the mind-body struggle, and other typical Freudian battlefields that produce neurosis and anxiety, are notably absent from Davenport's fiction. Fourier, who predated Sigmund Freud by a hundred years, proposed that people could be truly happy if they were permitted to construct lives that would cooperate with the instincts rather than denigrating and deploring them. Fourier has been called the only true philosopher of happiness. Indeed, he wrote twelve volumes in which he outlined exactly how such a society might come about. All Davenport's major fictions from "The Dawn in Erewhon" to *Wo es war, soll ich werden* can be read as philosophical parables illustrating the possibility of regenerating innocent happiness when characters live according to their deepest instinctual desires but only, however, within rather highly structured Fourierist parameters. Though the white-hot sexual rhetoric may appear to promote sexual anarchy, nothing could be further from the author's intention. Sex is healthy only if it is practiced in a healthy society; there is no possibility that a "sexual outlaw" would ever be permitted within Davenport's Fourierist society.

What Davenport has accomplished within much of his utopian fiction is to exclude any figure that even slightly resembles the typical hero—that is, a charismatic male who by the force of his individuality and aggressive power becomes the director and, in essence, owner of a specific locale and group. Adriaan van Hovendaal is respected by the younger and indefatigably sexual Bruno and Kaatje not because of his ability to control situations but rather because he permits himself to participate in their passionate at-

traction, a key concept in Fourier. They also see him as an intellectual whose mind and body work in consonance and as one whose intuition and perception have led him back to a primal imagination that understands the continuity of life and death. He, first and last, lives a life of balance and harmony. Most important, however, is that the society created by the mutual trust, love, and care between and among Adriaan, Bruno, and Kaatje demonstrates the concept of harmony by embodying it. As long as they are assisting one another in enjoying the desires of the body, they are helping to enact what Fourier called "Sessions of the Court of Love," which will eventually regenerate a new Eden or the Fourierist "New Amorous World."

DA VINCI'S BICYCLE

Davenport's next collection of stories is entitled *Da Vinci's Bicycle*. Four of the stories deal with classical Greek and Roman locations and characters, though "Ithaka" details an awkward meeting with Ezra Pound and his mistress, Olga Rudge, in Rapallo, Italy. In the story "The Antiquities of Elis," the place, Elis, site of the ancient Olympic Games, becomes the principal character, while ancient voices supply historical information to the reader. In "The Invention of Photography in Toledo," Davenport plays with quasi-surrealist montage, juxtaposing the glorious Toledo of Spain with its American counterpart, Toledo, Ohio. The most effective and humorous piece in the collection, however, is the first story, called "The Richard Nixon Freischutz Rag," in which Davenport juxtaposes the oracular utterings of Chairman Mao Tse-tung to the documented banality of Richard Nixon's responses on his visit to China in 1972.

The most important assemblage in this collection is "Au Tombeau de Charles Fourier" (at the tomb of Charles Fourier), a French expression which also means paying homage to a great person. There are thirty chapters, or cantos, composed of nine paragraphs, or stanzas, each, and each paragraph is made up of four lines. The exceptions are the tenth section, which is two lines, and the thirtieth paragraph, which consists of two paragraphs: the first containing the usual four lines while the second contains three. The scene of the meditation on the tomb of Charles Fourier in the famous cemetery of Montmartre is an example of a meditation on ruins, one of the literary forms in which Davenport has maintained an interest throughout his career. One of Davenport's most famous literary essays is his brilliant explication of Olson's densely constructed poem "The Kingfishers." Davenport found Olson's "The Kingfishers," along with Percy Bysshe Shelley's "Ozymandias" and John Keats's "Ode on a Grecian Urn," to be involved in the same poetic process—that is, an observer laments the destructive ravages that time has on all material objects, even those of great religious or political significance. The point that Davenport is making, along with Shelley, Keats, and Olson, is that, even though Time has destroyed the physical body of Charles Fourier and the others, the body of their work, the essence of their aesthetic beliefs, still exists and affects people to this very day.

The principal message that runs throughout this dense and complicated assemblage is that reality comes into existence only through words and the ability of the poet or priest or shaman to construct worlds through the efficacy of verbal power. Davenport celebrates other linguistic saints in the story, such as Gertrude Stein, whose presence at the beginning and the end of the work establishes the verbal as the iconographic medium through which other saints become visible. The hero to whom Davenport compares Fourier is the great Dogon metaphysician and wise man Ogotemmêli. After the French anthropologist Marcel Griaule spent fifteen years, off and on, with the West African Dogon tribe, the elders decided to trust him with the deep information concerning the cosmology on which their reality was built. The blind Ogotemmêli invited Griaule to sit with him for thirty-three days, during which he revealed to him, in massive detail and from memory (since Dogon society had no written language), the Dogon cosmology. As Davenport puts it: "He teaches him the structure and meaning of the world." The entire Dogon cosmological structure is based on the model of a loom, in which all things are stitched together to create a harmonious world, very much in the way Fourier stitched together an equally coherent utopian society, which he called the "New Harmonious World." The book that Griaule published subsequently influenced

another contemporary American writer, Robert Kelly, who is often compared to Davenport not only because of the erudite scholarship embedded in his work but also because of his long poem "The Loom" (1975), which is also built on Dogon cosmology.

The point that Davenport wants to make is that the spiritual realities that these great cosmological geniuses proposed are not really dead, because their words exist and are felt today. Language is key in that it alone escapes the ravages of time and it alone preserves the numinous power of the sacred. In paying homage to Fourier, Davenport also pays homage to the other priests of the word, modernists such as Beckett, Joyce, and Picasso, whose high modernism evolved from their recognition of the persistent recurrence of the energies of the archaic, which reestablishes a sense of order in the world.

ECLOGUES

Davenport's third collection of short fiction, *Eclogues*, continues his interest in, and exploration of, ancient and modern Edenic narratives. The title of the collection comes from a literary form used by many classical Greek and Roman poets such as Vergil and Theocritus and is synonymous with the term "pastoral." Important practitioners of the form in English literature were Edmund Spenser, William Shakespeare, Christopher Marlowe, John Milton, Shelley, and Matthew Arnold. Davenport, being a classical scholar, wants to expand the application of the term to include lives lived under ideal conditions. The ideal that Davenport pursues evolves from the word's etymological root: idyll. His models are the *Idylls* of Theocritus, the Greek poet and inventor of the pastoral form in which he presents the happy rustic lives of shepherds and farmers in Sicily. The Greek root of the word means "form" or "picture," which applies accurately to Davenport's precise drawings of the idealized figures of adolescent boys throughout the text.

Two stories stand out as further elaborations of Davenport's parables of innocence. "The Death of Picasso" consists of thirty-nine excerpts from the notebooks of the major character from the "The Dawn in Erewhon," Adriaan van Hovendaal. A new and even more precociously sexual teenager named Sander appears; he becomes a kind of ephebe, or student, of van Hovendaal. Both of them exchange information and insights focused on the death of Picasso and the mutual meditations they share on Picasso's significance as an artistic synthesizer of the ancient and the modern world, which resulted in modernism, a movement that Picasso virtually invented. By pursuing art's chaotic boundaries, he rediscovered the archaic imagination, which then enabled him to ground his aesthetic energies in an unbounded primordial source. His work removed any residual negative implications that the word "primitivism" may have previously acquired. Indeed, modernism finds its order in the pre-Socratic, process-oriented imagination of Herakleitos rather than the life-denying categories of Aristotelian abstractions. Though the story records the death of Picasso, it also dramatizes his revolutionary restoration of the archaic to its proper place in what Davenport calls the "history of attention."

In one of the shorter stories in *Eclogues*, called "Mesoroposthonippidon," Davenport narrates humorous anecdotes about the ancient Greek philosopher Diogenes, who spent his life disarming people of high rank with the simplicity of his life. Because he had no possessions, he felt perfectly free to speak his mind to anyone, including Plato and Alexander the Great, whom he chided for blocking his sunlight. Five of the eight stories in this collection deal with classical settings and characters, with the purpose of pointing out their relevance to modern times.

The longest and most complex story in the collection is the pastoral romance entitled "On Some Lines of Virgil." The piece is carefully structured, consisting of 135 sections of five stanzas or paragraphs each; every stanza is four lines long. The allusion to Vergil immediately alerts the reader to the possibility that the narrative may reveal Davenport's habitual theme of the regeneration of an Edenic or, in this case, Arcadian community. Indeed, Vergil's *Bucolics, Georgics,* and *Eclogues* were presentations of such idealized settings.

In this romance, the setting is Bordeaux, an ancient, southwestern French city and the birthplace of such famous painters and writers as Rosa Bonheur, Odilon Redon, François Mauriac, Charles de Montes-

quieu, and most important, Michel Eyquem de Montaigne. The painter Francisco de Goya, though not native to Bordeaux, painted some of his greatest works there. Davenport is careful to point out that Bonheur's *The Horse Fair* and Goya's *The Bulls of Bordeaux* are unconscious continuations of the horses and bulls found in the Caves of Lascaux, another example of how the modern imagination is grounded in the archaic. Tullio, the professorial scholar, exhorts his little horde of four that true history, which is the history of attention, consists of developing the ability to detect these patterns and that his deepest desire is "to write a history of the imagination in our time. . . . All these need to be reseen [in the light of the archaic]. The new modifies everything before, and even finds a tradition for the first time." Davenport's aesthetic theory resembles T. S. Eliot's classic statement in "Tradition and the Individual Talent" but lacks the Calvinist undertones that would not permit Eliot to use the word "imagination."

The Little Horde in this highly erotic Arcadia consists of four French teenagers: Jonquille, Jolivet, Michel, and the barely adolescent Victor. In the midst of their frequent erotic games, they travel to one of the ancient caves near Bordeaux, taking with them the young, legless Marc Aurel but accompanied by Tullio, a mature and responsible married adult. Davenport, though giving his adolescents full sexual freedom, positions an older scholar nearby to place their orgies in some sort of context. Tullio, the shepherd in this eclogue and whose name obviously derives from Marcus Tullius Cicero (known throughout the ancient world as "Tully"), serves as their intellectual guide and helps them understand the nature of their friendship, much in the same way that Cicero wrote the definitive essays on friendship (*Laelius de amicitia,* 44 B.C.E.) and old age (*Cato maior de senectute,* 44 B.C.E.), which became handbooks on Stoic philosophy. Again, youth and friendship are better understood if they are viewed against the background of old age, just as the prelogical tableaux in the caves of Lascaux become subtextual foundations of the great works of Picasso, Klee, and Goya.

APPLES AND PEARS AND OTHER STORIES

There can be little doubt that Davenport's fourth

collection of stories, *Apples and Pears and Other Stories*, is his masterpiece. The 233-page novella *Apples and Pears* constitutes a fine work of fiction. This novella revels in its richness, diversity, and brilliance and demonstrates the enormous scope of his intellectual terrain. The style recalls James Joyce's *Ulysses* (1922) at its most lucid; its four parts are firmly grounded in Davenport's most successful use of Fourier's utopian vision.

The three stories preceding *Apples and Pears* are also some of Davenport's most convincing fictions. All three are journeys of one kind or another. "The Bowmen of Shu" is constructed out of the battlefield diaries of the sculptor Henri Gaudier-Brzeska, while "Fifty-seven Views of Fujiyama" paratactically narrates the seventeenth century poet Matsuo Bashō's mountain journey alongside a modern couple's camping trip in New Hampshire. One of the most delightful and humorous stories in all Davenport's work is "The Chair," which finds Kafka accompanying the Rebbe of Belz on a tour of the Czechoslovakian spa at Marienbad in 1916.

In the novella *Apples and Pears*, Davenport uses the same techniques that he used in "The Death of Picasso" and "The Dawn in Erewhon"—that is, notebooks, diaries, and memoirs. The major consciousness throughout most of the text is the same Dutch philosopher and essayist in Butler's *Erewhon*, Adriaan van Hovendaal. New members swell the Fourierist "horde" into eight participants, including van Hovendaal. There are characters from previous works, Sander, Bruno, and Kaatje, and new adolescents, Jan, Hans, Saartje, and Sander's sister, Grietje.

The work is also structured along rather firm Fourierist lines in that there are four major sections that follow his four-part structure of an ideal society, which he called "The Harmony of the Four Movements"; he divides them into categories of the social, the animal, the organic, and the material. The four chapters of Davenport's work generally follow that scheme but not necessarily in that order. Van Hovendaal labels the first section "An Erewhonian Sketchbook" and uses a Napoleonic rather than a Gregorian calendar, calling the months Messidor (July), Thermidor (August), and Fructidor (September). The changes of the names of the months signified the arrival of the New Harmonious World, which was expected to follow the French Revolution.

Davenport translates the major line from Fourier's twelve-volume work that summarizes his entire philosophy of social happiness: "The series distributes the harmonies. The attractions are proportionate to our destinies." The series, to Fourier and Davenport, are groups that operate democratically and are drawn together by mutual attractions. As long as each member of the group is permitted to act on his mutually passional attraction toward others, an order and balance is established, and harmony reigns. These harmonious conjunctions take place continuously throughout *Apples and Pears*, as the group, gently directed by van Hovendaal, combine in every conceivable sexual coupling. Most important, however, is that this work becomes Davenport's "history of affection."

THE JULES VERNE STEAM BALLOON

The fifth volume is a collection of nine short stories entitled *The Jules Verne Steam Balloon*. Four of the nine stories are connected within the collection, since some of the same characters appear in all four, and some of those characters were participants in the novella *Apples and Pears*. The setting has moved from The Netherlands to Denmark, but youthful beauty and charm dictate the action. "The Meadow," "The Bicycle Rider," "The Jules Verne Steam Balloon," and the concluding story, "The Ringdove Sign," are all parables of innocence involving basically the same Fourierist ritual camping trips to idyllic forests, where they enjoy one another's bodies in clean, childlike sexual celebration. New adolescents join the "little horde," such as Pascal, Hugo, Franklin, Mariana, Kim, and Anders, but the project remains the same—that is, the more sexually comfortable enable those fearful of letting go to become more relaxed in their bodies. Only in "The Bicycle Rider" does a negative presence enter the highly organized promiscuity of the group. One of the most attractive and strongest of the young men has become addicted to drugs and has fallen into the condition of not being able to focus on life around him; most important, he has become incapable of any sexual response. Since the dynamics of the community are predicated on the passional attraction among the members of the group, he becomes the outcast and eventually dies.

THE DRUMMER OF THE ELEVENTH NORTH DEVONSHIRE FUSILIERS

The sixth volume of short fiction, which contains four stories and a novella, is entitled *The Drummer of the Eleventh North Devonshire Fusiliers*. While "Colin Maillard" and "Badger" both deal with the early passional attraction between preadolescent boys, the novella *Wo es war, soll ich werden* continues the activities of the expanding Fourierist group. Davenport also makes major philosophical and critical statements that help the reader understand some of his theoretical background. Davenport's style is so packed with multiphasic allusions, Joycean puns and conundrums, and phenomenological scene-shifting that an occasional glance at his sources and influences usually helps. He does inform his reader that *Wo es war, soll ich werden* is the conclusion of a trilogy that also includes *Apples and Pears* and *The Jules Verne Steam Balloon*.

The activity remains the same, as do some of the characters, but a deeper philosophical note enters both the dialogue and general discussion of the group. A superb Joycean, Davenport describes for the reader some of his own literary methods through a character named Allen in the story "Badger." He first explains the fall that takes place when one enters adolescence: "What you see, you know, Allen said, you own. You take it in. Everything's an essence . . . at twelve you understand everything. Afterward, you have to give it up and specialize." He then further elucidates:

> The film of essences, one photon thick, is continuous. Everything apprehended is in the continuum of this film. So all correspondences, the relation of information to other information, are first of all differences. Colors, shapes, textures.

If a reader of Davenport applied these "ways" of reading and observing to Davenport's work, a number of confusing elements might become clear.

Hugo explains that the title of the novella *Wo es war, soll ich werden* is a phrase from Freud. Jacques Lacan, the eminent French psychoanalyst, said that the phrase contains "pre-Socratic eloquence." Hugo translates it as "where it was, there must I begin to be," and Holger then sees it as another proof that "genius is a disease: Mann's paradox," with Thomas Mann's great *Der Tod in Venedig* (1912; *Death in Venice*, 1925) and *Doktor Faustus* (1947; *Doctor Faustus*, 1948) being notable examples of German romantic agony. Hugo quickly points out Freud's meaning: "No no, Hugo said. Freud meant that a wound, healing, can command the organism's whole attention, and thus becomes the beginning of a larger health." Hugo's explication summarizes Davenport's entire fictive enterprise in that all of his Fourierest parables of innocence attempt to move the joyfully "erotic" away from the German Romantic death wish. Western civilization need not end in apocalyptic self-immolation.

THE CARDIFF TEAM

In crafting *The Cardiff Team* collection, Davenport relies on many of the props he used in previous works. The first story in the collection places Kafka in a nudist colony. Whereas he used Stein in *Da Vinci's Bicycle*, in "Boys Smell Like Oranges" he evokes the presence of two perambulatory philosophers: Professor Lucien Levy-Bruhl and Pastor Maurice Leenhardt. These older men, on walking through the Bois de Boulogne, encounter the lawn-strewn bodies of a team of footballers. Two of these later remark that the old men were either shocked or infatuated by their adolescent forms, and the boys constitute part of yet another "Little Horde" of sexual utopians. In the last work of the collection, "The Cardiff Team," they also arrive at the same philosophical speculation the philosophers had been discussing in the Bois—the power of language to enact religion, as witnessed by the New Caledonians in their reverence for math multiplication tables, a litany of which concludes the story. This story clarifies an opposition of friendship, in its imagination-driven pan-sexual diversity ("what's in books and the world and feeling great in my pants were cooperative"), to tyranny and war and all manner of oppression.

Davenport reveres Fourier for the same reasons that André Breton, the founder of Surrealism, honored him with an ode. All three men attempt to regenerate forms of prelapsarian innocence that envision the world with a childlike sense of the marvelous and celebrate life in all of its ecstatic physicality. The purpose of the sexual exercises as opposed to the spiritual exercises of Saint Ignatius of Loyola, for example, is to recuperate the endless capacities of the imagination, with pleasure as the primary motivating force, to eradicate the life-denying abstractions of logical positivism, and to celebrate again and again the renaissance of the archaic.

OTHER MAJOR WORKS

POETRY: *Flowers and Leaves*, 1966; *Thasos and Ohio: Poems and Translations*, 1986.

NONFICTION: *Pennant Key-Indexed Study Guide to Homer's "Iliad,"* 1967; *Pennant Key-Indexed Study Guide to Homer's "Odyssey,"* 1967; *The Geography of the Imagination*, 1981; *Every Force Evolves a Form*, 1987; *The Hunter Gracchus, and Other Papers on Literature and Art*, 1996; *Objects on a Table: Harmonious Disarray in Art and Literature*, 1998.

TRANSLATIONS: *Anakreon*, 1991; *Seven Greeks*, 1995.

EDITED TEXT: *The Intelligence of Louis Agassiz: A Specimen Book of Scientific Writings*, 1963.

BIBLIOGRAPHY

Arias-Misson, Alain. "Erotic Ear, Amoral Eye." *Chicago Review* 35 (Spring, 1986): 66-71. Arias-Misson proposes that *Apples and Pears* constitutes Davenport's mythmaking as an alternative to the demythologizing that most contemporary fiction exemplifies. He genuinely wants his storytelling to aspire to the condition of myth and, as such, revivify the reader's sense of the world as a physically satisfying place.

Bawer, Bruce. "The Stories of Guy Davenport's Fiction à la Fourier." *The New Criterion* 3 (December, 1984): 8-14. One of the most intelligent and perceptive analyses of Davenport's work. Bawer labels Davenport a foursquare modernist and a devout Poundian. He admires greatly his enormously esoteric imagination but is worried about where the affectionate stops and the merely sexual

begins. He praises Davenport for reminding readers of their humanity and the importance of affection.

Blake, Nancy. "'An Exact Precession': Leonardo, Gertrude, and Guy Davenport's *Da Vinci's Bicycle*." In *Critical Angles: European Views of Contemporary Literature*, edited by Marc Chénetier. Carbondale: Southern Illinois University Press, 1986. Blake suggests that Davenport can be best understood if one views his work as rendering homage to his predecessors and, thus, renewing their vital force and the reader's.

Crane, Joan St. C. *Guy Davenport: A Descriptive Bibliography 1947-1995*. Haverford, Pa.: Green Shade, 1996. A good source for the student of Davenport.

Davenport, Guy. *Fifty Drawings*. New York: Dim Gray Bar Press, 1996. A collection of the writer's drawings.

Jarman, Mark. "The Hunter Davenport." *Hudson Review* 50, no. 2 (Summer, 1997): 333. Discusses Davenport's adherence to modernist techniques despite his postmodernist mileau. He focuses on nineteenth and twentieth century subjects, drawing comparisons between past events and present occurrences.

_____. *The Hunter Gracchus: And Other Papers on Literature and Art*. Washington, D.C.: Counterpoint, 1996. This collection of essays written by Davenport during the 1980's and 1990's on a variety of literary and cultural subjects reflects the extensive reading and erudition so evident in his short fiction.

Klinkowitz, Jerome. Review of *Apple and Pears and Other Stories*. *The Review of Contemporary Fiction* (Spring, 1986): 216-218. Klinkowitz proposes *Apples and Pears* as not only Davenport's strongest work but also the work in which he pulls all his influences together, from Wallace Stevens's necessary fictions to Pound's reverence of the archaic. He has kept philosophy, sexuality, and history in an ideal balance. A genuinely helpful and intelligent essay.

Madden, David W. "Stories Told in Collage." *San Francisco Chronicle*, January 9, 1994, p. 4. A review of Davenport's collection of stories *A Table of Green Fields* by a well-known short-story writer, critic, and novelist; claims that the stories recall Ernest Hemingway and Sherwood Anderson but have most in common with Raymond Carver; argues that many of the stories are difficult postmodern experiments in themes of the illusion of time and the relationship between artists and their models.

Olsen, Lance. "A Guidebook to the Last Modernist: Davenport on Davenport and *Da Vinci's Bicycle*." *Journal of Narrative Technique* 16 (Spring, 1986): 148-161. The single most brilliant and insightful essay written on Davenport, even though it covers only *Da Vinci's Bicycle*. Olsen traces the origin of Davenport's modernism in the "renaissance of the archaic" and places him alongside classic modernists such as Joyce, T. S. Eliot, and Pound. Davenport is the last modernist because he still believes in the omnipotence of language and its ability to humanize an increasingly dehumanizing world.

Patrick Meanor, updated by Scott D. Vander Ploeg

PETER HO DAVIES

Born: Coventry, England; August 30, 1966

PRINCIPAL SHORT FICTION

The Ugliest House in the World, 1997
Equal Love, 2000

OTHER LITERARY FORMS

Peter Ho Davies is known primarily as a short-story writer.

ACHIEVEMENTS

Peter Ho Davies' work was selected for *The Best American Short Stories* in 1995 and 1996. He won an O. Henry Award in 1998. A recipient of a fellowship from the National Endowment for the Arts, he has also been awarded the John Llewelyn Rhys and PEN/Macmillan Prizes in the United Kingdom and the H. L. Davis Oregon Book Award in the United States.

BIOGRAPHY

Peter Ho Davies was born in Coventry, England, on August 30, 1966, to a Welsh father and a Chinese mother. In 1987, he earned a B.S. in physics and in the history of philosophy and science from the University of Manchester, England. In 1989, he received a B.A. in English from Cambridge University. In 1992, he moved to the United States, where he received an M.A. in creative writing from Boston University in 1993. His first published story was "The Ugliest House in the World," which appeared in *The Antioch Review* in 1995. Subsequent stories appeared in magazines including *The Atlantic Monthly*, *Harper's*, *The Paris Review*, *Ploughshares*, and *Story*.

Davies was a lecturer at Emory University from 1996 to 1997, and he became assistant professor in the creative writing program at the University of Oregon in 1997. In 1999, he took up a similar position at the University of Michigan at Ann Arbor. He married Lynne Anne Raugley in 1994.

ANALYSIS

Peter Ho Davies' first collection is notable for the variety of times and places in which the stories are set. "The Ugliest House in the World" and *A Union* take place in Wales, in different time periods. "Buoyancy"—about a man's obsession with diving to the bottom of an old mining pool—and "The Silver Screen"—about a group of Malayan communists who fight the British—are set in Southeast Asia. "Relief" takes place in South Africa, among veterans of Rourke's Drift, which was where British troops defeated the Zulus. Other stories take place in Patagonia and England.

In such a wide-ranging collection, many themes emerge. Some stories are shaped by tragedy, such as the death of a child or a suicide. Deception, both of self and others, underlies "Coventry" as well as "I Don't Know, What Do You Think?" Happy endings are rare; optimism, where it occurs, is hard won and never absolute. Occasionally there is humor, especially in the hilarious "The Silver Screen," which also has its moments of horror, cruelty, and betrayal.

The dominant theme of Davies' second collection is family relationships, particularly, as Davies put it, "the relationships between grown children and aging parents." "Today Is Sunday" explores the antagonistic but affectionate relationship between a man and his father as they visit the father's senile mother. In "Cakes for Baby," a couple decide to support the wife's divorced mother financially, even though it may mean postponing having children. In "Brave Girl," a young girl has to cope with the separation of her parents; "On the Terraces" shows a mother and her elder son facing the death of a younger son from acquired immunodeficiency syndrome (AIDS), although they are never able to comprehend his homosexuality.

The tone of Davies' stories is often detached, tending to the unemotional. His writing is crisp and lucid, and the images are precisely observed. The stories are quietly compassionate; Davies is reluctant to judge human foibles, preferring instead to delineate the complexity, the inconclusiveness of life, with its painful defeats and occasional small victories.

"THE UGLIEST HOUSE IN THE WORLD"

Guilt and social resentments surface when a young physician visits his Welsh father, who has retired to a village in North Wales after forty years in England. The purpose of the son's visit is to attend the funeral of Gareth, a neighborhood boy who was killed when a stone gatepost on the father's property fell on him.

At the funeral, local people accuse the father of negligence, a charge that adds to his feelings of guilt. Underlying the hostility is the feeling that the father is an outsider, even though he was born in the village. The next day, Welsh nationalist slogans are daubed on the father's house. The son, however, believes no one was to blame for the boy's death, and he appears to understand neither the local resentments nor the depth of his father's feelings. The latter are revealed

when, in the emotional climax of the story, the father goes to great lengths to catch a fish that he had promised to Gareth and presents it to the boy's mother instead.

In an ironic conclusion, the son whitewashes his father's cottage. When he has finished, it shines brightly in the morning sun. The reader suspects that the feelings of guilt that the tragic incident has caused, and the social strife it has aroused, will not be so easily healed.

A UNION

This novella about a strike at a Welsh quarry in 1899 explores the themes of shame and responsibility. To whom is a man responsible when he goes on strike—his fellow workers or his wife and family? Davies explores this theme in the subtly drawn tensions that surface in the marriage of Thomas and Catrin Jones. The tension is apparent on the day the strike begins, when they take delivery of a grandfather clock for which they had been saving. Catrin has set her heart on it, and Thomas pretends that it is still all right for her to have it. The irony is that the clock it too big to fit in their small parlor, and Thomas must saw it down to make room for it.

As the strike drags on, tensions between husband and wife become apparent in the wife's offhanded remarks that convey her resentment. There are hints that Catrin has become pregnant, but since the couple earlier agreed they could not afford a third child, neither mentions it. After some months, the union money runs out and workers begin to straggle back to the quarry; Thomas clings to his pride until he gazes on his newborn baby, after which he, too, returns to work. In a nice irony, Catrin expresses her new pride in him. The episode parallels and contrasts the incident with the clock, which also, like the baby, was more than the couple could afford. This time, however, the newcomer, a living thing not an inanimate object, produces reconciliation rather than conflict.

In addition to the light it shines on the different attitudes of the men and the women to the strike, the story presents a sympathetic portrait of the striking quarrymen in their bitter struggle with the ruthless quarry owners. It has humor too, concerning the fanatical, bald clergyman Price, who urges the strikers on and is the only character who gains from the dispute. As his power and influence increase, he develops a full head of hair and a black beard. As the strike collapses, he falls into the quarry and is killed. There is little mourning; it is time for a new beginning.

"THE HULL CASE"

In this calmly told story, a harmonious marriage is gradually destroyed by a couple's differing responses to an unidentified-flying-object (UFO) sighting. The story takes place in the early 1960's in New Hampshire. An African American man, Henry Hull, and his white wife Helen are being interviewed about their strange experience by an Air Force colonel.

Through flashbacks, the difficulties the interracial couple has had to endure in white New England are made clear. Henry is constantly reminded that he has transgressed a social code: People stare as the couple enter a diner, and a motel, pretending to be full, turns them away. Helen dismisses such slights as imaginary, and, although Henry feels them keenly, he does not become embittered, and the marriage thrives. How ironic it is, then, that a successful interracial marriage should founder at the intrusion of a supposed encounter with aliens.

During the interview with the colonel, Henry is embarrassed; he does not expect to be believed (another incident that reveals the black man's perspective). Helen claims to remember being abducted by aliens who performed experiments on her; Henry has no memory of this and resents the way she insists on mentioning it. Helen believes the aliens have taken one of her eggs; she remembers being shown strange children. Henry suspects the dreams may be unconscious compensations for the fact that Helen has miscarried twice. This conflict suggests that it is Helen's anxiety about her inability to produce children that may be at the heart of the chasm that opens between the couple, even though ostensibly the cause is their disagreement over the UFO. The fact that Henry finally, under hypnosis, recalls being abducted does nothing to improve the marriage. The final image, of Henry dreaming that he sees his wife levitating from the bed surrounded by a blue light, is an ample metaphor for their estrangement: She is apart from him now, the dream seems to say, unreachable, alien.

"SMALL WORLD"

Wilson, a married man in early middle age, returns to Boston alone on a business trip, near where he grew up. He thinks back to when he was fifteen and his parents divorced. He remembers the guilt he felt when his father told him that he and his wife realized they did not love each other at the time Wilson was born, since the love they felt for the baby was so much more real and intense. Wilson concluded he was to blame for their divorce. The guilt has dominated his life. Pointedly, he is referred to only by his family name, Wilson—he cannot escape his family past.

Wilson encounters Joyce, his high school sweetheart, prompting reminiscences of how, in his confusion, he had "adopted" her parents as surrogates, which made him feel guilty yet again for "cheating" on his own parents. Then Joyce informs him that her own parents are now divorcing. Like the young Wilson, she too feels guilt.

Davies weaves many variations and crosscurrents into this finely wrought story about parental love and the long shadow cast by parents' relations with their children. The effect is like a complex dance in which love and trust are lost but then recovered, if only precariously, as the children seek their own life and loves. The fact that Wilson's wife is pregnant with their first child is a telling detail; the cycle of interlocking family destinies is about to spring up again. Although Wilson betrays his wife by making love to Joyce, the story ends on an optimistic note. Somehow his act of adultery rekindles his love for his wife, a sign of the many detours, none of them predictable, that love may take on its meandering course through human life.

BIBLIOGRAPHY

Eder, Richard. "'Equal Love': When Children Become Parents of Their Parents." Review of *Equal Love*, by Peter Ho Davies. *The New York Times*, February 2, 2000, p. E9. Eder comments that Davies writes with considerable skill but sometimes at the expense of "conveyed feeling." Not all the stories are successful; the best are on the wild side. These include "The Next Life" and "The

Hull Case." The latter is the most "moving and suggestive" story in the collection.

Kirkus Reviews. Review of *The Ugliest House in the World*, by Peter Ho Davies (July 15, 1997). This review finds the collection "ingenious, moving, and exasperating in turn." The reviewer praises Davies' insightful view of human nature and his skill in plotting, especially in the title story. Also singled out for praise are Davies' originality and his affection for his characters in *A Union*. "Relief" and "Safe" are found to be the weaker stories.

Reynolds, Susan Salter. "Equal Love." Review of *Equal Love*, by Peter Ho Davies. *The Los Angeles Times*, February 6, 2000, p. 11. Brief review that selects "The Hull Case" as one of the best stories in the collection and in general praises the "digni-fied precision" with which Davies describes the inner lives of his characters.

Steinberg, Sybil S. Review of *Equal Love*, by Peter Ho Davies. *Publishers Weekly* 246, no. 47 (November 22, 1999): 41. Davies' stories use "resonant, precise images to pave the way to intimate truths." The reviewer also praises Davies' craftsmanship, complexity, and his "compassionate voice."

_____. Review of *The Ugliest House in the World*, by Peter Ho Davies. *Publishers Weekly* 244, no. 33 (August 11, 1997): 384. Davies' first collection is hailed for its "spare style, taut prose and arresting images," the only weak point being the "melodramatic" *A Union*.

Bryan Aubrey

RHYS DAVIES

Born: Blaenclydach in the Rhondda Fawr Valley, Wales; November 9, 1901 or 1903
Died: London, England; August 21, 1978

PRINCIPAL SHORT FICTION
Aaron, 1927
The Song of Songs, and Other Stories, 1927
The Bed of Feathers, 1929
The Stars, the World, and Women, 1930
Tale, 1930
Arfon, 1931
A Pig in a Poke, 1931
A Woman, 1931
Daisy Matthews and Three Other Tales, 1932
Love Provoked, 1933
One of Norah's Early Days, 1935
The Things Men Do, 1936
A Finger in Every Pie, 1942
Selected Stories, 1945
The Trip to London, 1946

Boy with a Trumpet, 1949 (pb. in U.S. as *Boy with a Trumpet and Other Selected Stories*, 1951)
The Collected Stories of Rhys Davies, 1955
The Darling of Her Heart and Other Stories, 1958
The Chosen One and Other Stories, 1967
The Best of Rhys Davies, 1979
Rhys Davies: Collected Stories, 1996

OTHER LITERARY FORMS

Rhys Davies' *Ram with Red Horns* (1996) has stimulated reader interest and prompted requests for reprints of some of his other novels. In chronological order, Davies' novels include *The Withered Root* (1927); *Rings on Her Fingers* (1930); *Count Your Blessings* (1932); *The Red Hills* (1932); *Honey and Bread* (1935); *A Time to Laugh* (1937); *Jubilee Blues* (1938); *Tomorrow to Fresh Woods* (1941); *The Black Venus* (1944); *The Dark Daughters* (1947), based on William Shakespeare's *King Lear*; *The Perishable Quality* (1957), which includes an affectionate portrait of Dylan Thomas; *Girl Waiting in the Shade* (1960); and *Nobody Answered the Bell* (1971). Davies' plays include *The Ripening Wheat* (1937); its revised version, *The Maid of Cefn Ydlfa* (pb. 1938); and *No Escape* (pb. 1955), a three-act play based on Davies' novel, *Under the Rose* (1940). His nonfiction includes a travelogue, *My Wales* (1937); a biography, *Sea Urchin: Adventures of Jorgen Jorgensen* (1940); *The Story of Wales* (1943); and *Print of a Hare's Foot: An Autobiographical Beginning* (1969). Adaptations of Davies' novels and short stories have been produced for radio and television.

ACHIEVEMENTS

During World War II, Rhys Davies worked in the British War Office (1941-1942). He was honored as an Officer of the Order of the British Empire (1968). He received the Welsh Arts Council prize (1971). Mystery Writers of America presented him with the Edgar Allan Poe Award for "The Chosen One" (1966). His stories and articles appeared regularly in magazines. He is listed in *The Author's and Writer's Who's Who* (1971), *Who's Who in America* (1978), and *Who's Who* (1978).

BIOGRAPHY

Rhys Davies was born Rees Vivian Davies and spent his youth in Clydach, a Welsh coal-mining village, where, according to his autobiography, "wages and God were grim." Davies' easygoing father and thrifty mother owned a grocery shop, the Royal Stores. The parents, five children, and a servant lived in rooms behind and above the store.

Life was restrictive for young Davies. He disliked wearing an itchy wool shirt to church and hearing the *hwyl* (impassioned preaching) of a Nonconformist minister every Sunday, so in adolescence he joined the Anglican church. After dropping out of school at fourteen, Davies educated himself by observing people, listening to gossip, absorbing Celtic legends, and reading Homer's *Odyssey* (c. 800 B.C.E.; English translation, 1616) and books by Gustave Flaubert, Guy de Maupassant, and Anton Chekhov.

In 1920, Davies traveled to London, where he roomed in boardinghouses. He supported himself as a

Rhys Davies (Library of Congress)

salesman of men's clothing and lived frugally, except for the purchase of a pair of spats and a malacca cane. He began writing poetry and plays but soon discovered that short stories were his forte. In London, he associated with avant-garde artists such as H. E. Bates, Liam O'Flaherty, Hugh McDiarmid, Nina Hamnett, and Anna Kavan.

In 1926, Charles Lahr, owner of the Progressive Bookshop, published six of Davies' short stories in *The New Coterie* magazine. With an advance on a novel from an American publisher, Davies traveled to France. Through Lahr, he met D. H. Lawrence and his wife at Bandol. Lawrence greatly influenced Davies' writing.

Residence in London allowed Davies personal freedom, where his sexual ambivalence was accepted. Many acquaintances believed he was homosexual; however, he later maintained a close and devoted relationship with Anna Kavan, another writer. None of his writing, including his autobiography, reveals his sexual orientation.

Only when Davies was short of money did he ever return to Wales, where he lived in his parents' home and wrote prolifically. Quiet and mild-mannered, he followed a rigorous, disciplined writing schedule. He wrote a first draft on lined tablets, revised, and then recopied on another lined tablet. A heavy smoker, Davies died of lung cancer in 1978.

ANALYSIS

In the preface to *The Collected Stories of Rhys Davies*, Rhys Davies says that short-story writers write for love, not money. A short story gives "the release of a day off," while novels are "noisy and dense." Davies says he "dives" into a story's elements in the first paragraph. Middle episodes move quickly and conclude with either a surprise ending or an uncertain resolution.

Wales in the years between 1920 and 1970 is the setting for most of Davies' naturalistic stories; a few have settings in London or on the Continent. However, universal themes emerge: the struggle of the individual for self-determination; youthful idealism followed by disillusionment; frustrated sexual relationships between men and women; greed and guilt that erode the spirit; economic and social restrictions that lock women into poverty, abuse, or outmoded traditions; the realistic, occasionally humorous, effects of death on the living; the power of secrets; and the need for revenge.

Character-driven, many of Davies' stories have real-life connections. He skillfully characterizes coal miners emerging from collieries deep in the earth, their "bodies black with coal dust, their eyes white as marble, and their lips glistening red"; their wives and mothers, harassed by meal preparation and ritual baths; lonely travelers on trains in England and France; women who have "stepped over the line" of propriety and duty; and vengeful women.

Davies' early stories have a somber tone. Later, he interjects wry humor into ordinarily somber situations, such as death and its rituals. For example, in "Resurrection," a woman who is properly "laid out" in her coffin sits up and asks for a drink of water. Her angry sister, who has spent time and money in preparation for the funeral says, "Lie back, thee, lie back.

Dead you are." Davies got this idea from "laying out" rituals in Clydach. A few of Davies' stories, such as "The Farm" and "The Revelation," are lighthearted romances.

"THE NIGHTGOWN"

During Davies' boyhood in the early 1900's, he observed a woman who bought large quantities of groceries on credit at his parents' Royal Stores in the mining village of Clydach. In "The Nightgown," a fictionalized true story, Davies evokes sympathy for this hardworking Welsh woman, locked into her role as servant for her burly husband and five strapping adult sons. Mrs. Rees suppresses her femininity and wears baggy clothing and her son's cast-off cap. Without benefit of praise or affection, she spends her days dutifully cooking and laundering. After laboring in the coal mines, her husband and sons return home to bathe in the kitchen tub, dress in freshly ironed clothing, and consume a huge meal. Then they leave for soccer games or the tavern.

Gradually Mrs. Rees' health declines, but the men never notice as long as good food and clean clothing are prompt. By saving a few pennies each week from household money, she secretly buys a lovely white silk nightgown and instructs her neighbor to "lay her out" in it someday. The end of the story fully reveals the Rees men's callousness. When she dies, they are shocked to see her dressed "like an angel" in the lacy gown, but with their typical lack of empathy they wonder if insurance will cover the gown's extra expense. Then, without shedding a tear, Mr. Rees asks the neighbor if she knows any respectable widows or spinsters who might replace his dead wife.

"THE TRIP TO LONDON"

Davies observed travelers on frequent train trips between London and Wales and also on the Continent. His observations prompted several stories with train settings, such as this suspenseful three-part story about a "black widow" who lures male travelers to their deaths. Davies' description of the woman's expensive clothing and jewelry, her sensual body language, her comment about why women like to shop, and her reaction to a London news story are clues that indicate her motives for murder. Like many of Davies' stories, "The Trip to London" ends without resolution.

The first segment of the story begins in London, where a handsome, well-dressed, fortyish woman with glittering black eyes enters a train compartment and engages two male commuters in friendly conversation. A third man enters the compartment. He does not join their conversation, but he is fascinated by the woman's sensual body language as she eats candy and fruit, smokes, and turns magazine pages. The two commuters complain that their wives spend all their money on shopping trips to London. She laughs and explains that most women shop to compensate for unhappy relations with men. However, that is not her problem, she says, because she is a widow and lives alone. When she leaves the train, the third man follows her to return a lace handkerchief she has dropped. They share a drink and agree to meet the next evening in a secluded place—to prevent gossip and guard her reputation. Later, he follows her to a dark and lonely Victorian house on the outskirts of town, surrounded by deep ponds. Then Davies abruptly leaves the reader in suspense about what happens.

The story segues into a second segment, in which the handsome woman seduces another traveler in a London restaurant and repeats the scenario. Suspense builds. Then, on a third train trip from London, the woman, now dressed in expensive fur and jewels, shares a compartment with two women and the husband of one, who furtively admires her. His wife and her friend read aloud a story in the London paper about the recent disappearance of two men who were carrying large amounts of money. Suddenly, with dark eyes "snapping like a whip," the "black widow" scolds the man for smoking in the compartment. His wife protectively clutches his arm, and the story ends with an uncertain resolution.

"THE DILEMMA OF CATHERINE FUCHSIAS"

In this ironic story, Davies indicates that women are held to a higher moral standard than men. The protagonist, Catherine, faces a dilemma: how to preserve her reputation after she has stepped over the line of propriety. Davies characterizes Catherine as a thrifty, capable, and morally upright spinster, who has kept house for her father until his death. She lives in a secluded cottage surrounded by colorful purple fuchsias, perhaps symbolic of her passionate heart. Lonely and longing for love, she becomes the secret mistress of a retired merchant, who has returned to Banog with his coldhearted English wife. He visits Catherine after church every Sunday evening. When he dies in her bed, Catherine is faced with telling his widow, while trying to save her own reputation.

Discovery of her moral lapse will mean social ostracism in the village. At first, she panics, but then she coolly concocts clever lies to cover up her secret affair. Frantically, she dresses the corpse before his body grows cold and lays him out. Then she runs to the wife's home and tells her to call a doctor. She claims the man was walking past her cottage, admiring her fuchsias, when he had a heart attack. The wife is angry and suspicious and asks how he got upstairs and into Catherine's bed. Catherine fakes a sprained back from carrying him upstairs, and the doctor believes her. Catherine convinces the townspeople, even the minister, that she is a chaste woman.

Just when she thinks she has convinced everyone of her innocence, the truth is revealed. A lawyer sends Catherine a notice that her lover has left her a large sum of money in his will. The minister "casts her out of church," and the women of Banog shun her. Haughtily, Catherine tells former friends that she will take her money and move to Aberystwyth to start a new life. The postmistress, however, informs Catherine that she will write a cousin in Aberystwyth and tell all.

"REVELATION"

Davies' wry sense of humor is evident in this amusing story, which reveals how a woman's sexual inhibitions, combined with a man's ignorance, can ruin a marriage and how a bit of romance can change their attitudes. Gomer and Blodwen have been married less than a year, but they are incompatible and quarrel constantly. After work in the collieries, Gomer takes a message to his boss's house that Montague will be late. When he knocks on the door, Montague's English wife opens it, stark naked. Gomer is stunned by her beauty. He has never seen a naked woman before. Without embarrassment, she laughs and says that she expected Montague when she answered the door—no harm done.

Gomer's eyes are opened as to what a sexually enriched marriage might be. He plucks a rose from the Montague's garden and takes it to Blodwen, who greets him with a frown and harsh words. Instead of reacting in anger, he speaks gently, gives her the rose, and whispers an erotic suggestion in her ear. Her virago of a mother arrives to "straighten him out," but Gomer asserts himself and sends her home. Then Gomer and Blodwen shyly embrace, implying that a satisfying sexual relationship has begun.

OTHER MAJOR WORKS

LONG FICTION: *The Withered Root*, 1927; *Rings on Her Fingers*, 1930; *Count Your Blessings*, 1932; *The Red Hills*, 1932; *Honey and Bread*, 1935; *A Time to Laugh*, 1937; *Jubilee Blues*, 1938; *Under the Rose*, 1940; *Tomorrow to Fresh Woods*, 1941; *The Black Venus*, 1944; *The Dark Daughters*, 1947; *The Perishable Quality*, 1957; *Girl Waiting in the Shade*, 1960; *Nobody Answered the Bell*, 1971; *Ram with Red Horns*, 1996 (posthumous).

PLAYS: *The Ripening Wheat*, pr. 1937 (revised as *The Maid of Cefn Ydlfa*, pb. 1938); *No Escape*, pb. 1955 (with Archibald Batty).

NONFICTION: *My Wales*, 1937; *Sea Urchin: Adventures of Jorgen Jorgensen*, 1940; *The Story of Wales*, 1943; *Print of a Hare's Foot: An Autobiographical Beginning*, 1969.

BIBLIOGRAPHY

Adam, G. F. "Rhys Davies." *Three Contemporary Anglo-Welsh Novelists: Jack Jones, Rhys Davies, and Hilda Vaughan*. Bern: Franke, 1950. Analysis discusses Davies' childhood impressions of religion, the influence of D. H. Lawrence's erotic philosophy, sociological conflicts in Wales brought about by industrialization, recurring themes in Davies' short stories, Davies' characterizations (especially of strong women), and Davies' sense of humor.

Davies, Philippa. Introduction to *Ram with Red Horns*. Chester Springs, Pa.: Dufor Editions, 1996. A professor at the University of Wales, Philippa Davies has explored Rhys Davies' fiction as it relates to history. She predicts that revived interest in his realistic work will result in a new biography, a new short-story anthology, and adaptations for television. She discusses ways in which Davies' was contradictory on social and political issues, in his ethnicity, and in his personal life.

Davies, Rhys. Preface to *The Collected Stories of Rhys Davies*. London: Heinemann, 1955. Davies explains that he chose the forty-three stories in the anthology because they are his favorites. He has organized them to avoid monotony. Comic stories follow tragic, and Welsh settings follow London. In metaphorical terms he compares the short story to a small garden, while a novel is like a littered public park. He compares humor to "a rascal that must be kept in control." Humor should "steal on a reader, unsuspected." Davies prefers "dark funereal tales, though not always."

_____. *Print of a Hare's Foot*. London: Heinemann, 1969, 1997. Davies' memoir gives insight into his boyhood experiences in Clydach Vale. Especially interesting are his conversations with D. H. Lawrence. Includes entertaining anecdotes and descriptions of various women friends, like Nina Hamnett, and landladies, whom he calls "keyhole spies." However, Davies is evasive about much of his personal life.

Rees, David. *Rhys Davies*. Cardiff: University of Wales Press, 1975. Analyses of novels written between 1954 and 1970: characterizations, settings and moods, the theme of the struggle for sexual and social dominance, assessment of Davies' portrayal of Welsh life, personal style as a creative writer, characterizations, regional settings, and universal themes.

Martha E. Rhynes

OSAMU DAZAI
Shūji Tsushima

Born: Kanagi, Japan; June 19, 1909
Died: Tokyo, Japan; June 13, 1948

PRINCIPAL SHORT FICTION

Bannen, 1936
Tokyo hakkei, 1941
Kajitsu, 1944
Otogizōshi, 1945
Shinshaku shokoku banashi, 1945
Fuyu no hanabi, 1947
Dazai Osamu: Selected Stories and Sketches, 1983
Run, Melos! and Other Stories, 1988
Crackling Mountain and Other Stories, 1989
Self Portraits, 1991
Blue Bamboo: Tales of Fantasy and Romance,
    1993

OTHER LITERARY FORMS

Osamu Dazai's international fame is based largely on a short novel, *Shayō* (1947; *The Setting Sun*, 1956). Translations also exist of a defensive fictional autobiography, *Ningen shikkaku* (1948; *No Longer Human*, 1958), and an equally personal travelogue, *Tsugaru* (1944; English translation, 1985; also as *Return to Tsugaru: Travels of a Purple Tramp*, 1985). Dazai published two plays as well as a number of essays, and like all Japanese authors, he experimented with the haiku. His total literary output is, with regard to genre, almost as versatile as it is prolific.

ACHIEVEMENTS

During his life, Osamu Dazai was much more of a cult figure than an institutional model, and for this reason he did not receive the major awards available in his milieu. After his death, however, he was accorded widespread homage. A literary journal has instituted an annual Osamu Dazai prize, televised memorial services at Dazai's graveside take place annually, and at least three memorial sites have been established throughout Japan.

BIOGRAPHY

All forms of autobiographical fiction are popular in Japan, especially the "I" novel, and Osamu Dazai's fictional reenactment of his own life has become the hallmark of his style. Indeed, his personal entourage, including his wives, mistresses, intimate friends, and members of his immediate family, repeatedly turn up in his fiction under their own names or thinly disguised pseudonyms. A bare chronology of the principal events in Dazai's life would be a somewhat sordid account of sexual encounters, family disputes, drugs, drinking, and attempted suicides. Only when accompanied by introspective analysis, artistic reflections, and literary parallels, as they are in the author's fiction, do these events become material of universal human interest.

Dazai was a poor little rich boy born Shūji Tsushima in the northernmost district of the main island of Japan. At the age of nineteen, shortly after meeting a geisha, Hatsuyo, he unsuccessfully attempted suicide. Four months later, he began the study of French literature at Tokyo University. In the same year, he made a joint suicide attempt with a waitress; he recovered, but she died. In the following month, he married Hatsuyo. Along with magazine editing and short-story writing, he engaged in leftist political activities. In 1933, he used for the first time his pen name, Osamu Dazai, with a story that won a newspaper prize. Three years later, he published his first collection of stories and entered a mental hospital. In 1937, he again unsuccessfully attempted suicide, this time with Hatsuyo; shortly thereafter, their union was dissolved, and he entered into an arranged marriage with a woman from his own social class. During the war, he was disqualified by ill health from active military service, but he engaged in various noncombatant activities while continuing to write. For some time, he carried on a correspondence with a young woman, Ota Shizuko, on literary subjects, and, shortly after their initial meeting in 1941, she became his mistress. In 1947, while writing *The Setting Sun*, he established a liaison with a beautician, Yamazaki Tomie, while still involved with and living with his wife. Shortly after completing *No Longer Human*, the most explicit of his confessional fiction, Dazai committed suicide with Tomie by drowning, leaving behind several notes, including one to his wife.

ANALYSIS

Osamu Dazai's longer narratives are easier than his stories for Western readers to approach. In the blending of autobiography and fiction, he resembles Marcel Proust and Thomas Wolfe. The protagonist of most of his fiction is perennially the same character, a loser in society who, nevertheless, wins the sympathy of the reader. As such, he has been compared to Tom Sawyer and Holden Caulfield. He has equal resemblance to a stock character in classical Russian fiction, the useless man. Since Dazai knew the work of Ivan Goncharov, who portrayed this type in the novel *Oblomov* (1859; English translation, 1915), it would not be farfetched to describe Dazai's perennial persona as a decadent Oblomov. He is, however, a greater misfit in society, and he never succeeds in solving his problems. In *No Longer Human*, Dazai describes himself as a man "who dreads human beings," and in reference to city crowds in "Tokyo Hakkei" ("Eight Views of Tokyo"), he is reminded of the question posed by a Western author, "What is love?" and the answer, "To dream of beautiful things and do dirty ones." He is placed by critic Phyllis I. Lyons in "the school of irresponsibility and decadence." All this makes him appeal to youth both in Japan and elsewhere. As a rebel against convention, he highlights the antagonism between rich and poor and the clash between parents and children. In his youth, he had frequently acted the part of a buffoon, and he sometimes portrays this aspect of his personality in his fiction. His tone varies between self-dramatization and self-satire. In two of his works based on plots from William Shakespeare and Friedrich Schiller, however, he radically departs from his ostensible autobiographical mold. Although various episodes in Dazai's fiction treat human debasement, there is nothing prurient in his descriptions, which are frequently laconic or subtle. Occasionally,

he resembles Honoré de Balzac with endless references to crude and minor details of life, debts, expenditures, and financial waste.

"AN ALMANAC OF PAIN" *and* RETURN TO TSUGARU

In one of his stories, "Kuno no nenkan" ("An Almanac of Pain"), he suggests that he does not have thoughts, only likes and dislikes, and that he wants "to record in fragmentary form just those realities I cannot forget." Because of writing these personal fragments instead of formal history or philosophy, he describes himself in the same work as "a writer of the marketplace." In *Return to Tsugaru*, he remarks that "the gods spare no love for a man who goes burdened under the bad karma of having to sell manuscripts filled with details of his family in order to make a living." One of his themes is the problems of family life, but he frequently maintains that only individuals count. Edward Seidensticker regards Dazai as "a superb comic writer," but little of this comic genius is apparent in translation. It consists in caricature of himself as well as others and the portrayal of absurd situations rather than satire. Dazai is perhaps the outstanding example in any literature of solipsistic intertextuality or the constant quotation of previous works from his own pen. In *Return to Tsugaru*, for example, he quotes frequently and extensively from his own stories as well as from histories and guidebooks by other authors. Indeed, key passages from his early stories reappear over and over in his later works.

Despite the wide variety of style and subject matter in Dazai's short stories, they may be divided into two main categories, fantasy and autobiography. The latter group belongs to a special Japanese genre, *shishōsetsu*, or personal fiction. In stories about his own physical and psychological development, Dazai adheres closely to historical fact but arranges details to suit his aesthetic purpose. Among his recurring themes are the individual and the family, friendship, the search for identity, class barriers and distinctions, and the ambivalence of personality. "Omoide" ("Recollections") embodies all these themes in a Proust-like, somewhat lugubrious reminiscence of childhood. Blending the tones of irony and confession, he describes such episodes as sexual initiation and the trading of books for bird eggs and such feelings as loneliness and longing for parental love. A later story, "Gangu" ("Toys"), concerns his return home after a long absence. Here, he uses a narrative artifice of taking the reader into his confidence while assuming that the action takes place at the moment he is speaking or thinking. He goes back to the early stages of infancy and introduces one of his common scatological motifs of making water. His fantasies seem more real than his actual surroundings. In "Anitachi" ("My Older Brothers"), he portrays his histrionic involvement with French satanism and the role of a dandy, which he defines as a handsome, accomplished man loved by more than one woman. This and other narratives of his behavior with women do not measure up to the level of rakishness associated with contemporary France or even with the known details of his own activities. He portrays himself as bashful, inept, and inadequate in his sexual relationships, nearly all of which are with women of a lower social class.

"PUTTING GRANNY OUT TO DIE" AND "EIGHT VIEWS OF TOKYO"

Dazai several times describes his abortive suicide attempts. The title of the translation of "Ubasute" ("Putting Granny Out to Die"), refers to an ancient custom of exposing old people to the elements when they are no longer able to cope with life, but the story itself concerns his attempted suicide with Hatsuyo. En route to a mountain inn, he rehashes various derogatory terms that have been applied to him, "liar, swellhead, lecher, idler, squanderer," and then makes a sincere prayer in the toilet, a typical combination of incongruous elements. Dazai suggests that, although he represents a composite of unsavory qualities, he is still superior to the common lot. The reader wonders, however, whether Dazai's life story would have been worthy of attention if he had not belonged to a wealthy and influential family and whether a proletarian would have written it in the same style. His "Eight Views of Tokyo" is another example of a title not descriptive of the contents. Although it promises an account of urban life in the manner of Charles Dickens or Balzac, the work itself consists of further true confessions. It mentions only casually a project

to write about Tokyo that was never carried out. Dazai includes an epigraph, "For one who has suffered," and introduces the marketplace theme by referring to his ten volumes of "mediocre writings" already published. He bids farewell to his youth, denies the accusation that he has joined the ranks of the philistines, and vaguely alludes to his radical political activities. Most important, he announces a spiritual crisis in the form of a "serious aspiration to become a writer." He affirms that his autobiographical style is inseparable from his art, an unambiguous declaration that the first-person narrator in most of his works is indeed himself. Striking a pose like Balzac, he observes that he himself has become one of the sights of Tokyo.

In the realm of fantasy, Dazai draws on native classical sources. "Gyofukuki" ("Transformation") combines the thoughts of a young girl about the death of a young man in a mountain pool with a folktale about a man who turned into a serpent after eating several trout. After her drunken father attempts to rape her, the girl commits suicide in the pool, fantasizing in the process that she has been transformed into a carp. The story has no connection with Franz Kafka's *Die Verwandlung* (1915; *The Metamorphosis*, 1936) but has some resemblance to Ovid's retelling of classical legends. "Sarugashima" ("The Island of Monkeys") is more like Kafka and has an outlook less gloomy. The narrator engages in dialogue with a group of monkeys after a sea voyage. Looking back on his own childhood, he seems to interpret his present incarnation as a sign of immortality or transmigration. Suddenly he realizes that people are coming to gape at him. He agrees with the most compatible of the monkeys that it is better to choose unknown dangers over boring regularity. The story concludes with a news item that two monkeys have escaped from the London Zoo. Another simian tale, "Saruzuka" ("The Mound of the Monkey's Grave"), resembles a Voltairean *conte philosophique*. A young couple flee from their parents because religious differences in the two households have kept them from marrying. They are accompanied by a monkey who acts as their servant. When a child is born, the monkey demonstrates an affection equal to that of the father and mother.

One day, in the absence of the parents, the monkey, in giving the child a bath, immerses it in boiling water, not realizing the fatal consequences of the deed. He later commits suicide at the child's grave, and the parents abandon the world for religion. Dazai, intervening in the narrative, asks which sect they have chosen. The tragic story loses its point, he observes, if the original faith of either parent must be adopted by the other.

"Currency" and "Taking the Wen Away"

"Kohei" ("Currency") conforms to an extensive Western genre, the thingaresque, a form of narrative in which the protagonist, either an animal or inanimate object, provides an intensely realistic portrayal of the social conditions in which it exists. The genre derives from Lucius Apuleius's *The Golden Ass* (second century C.E.) and was also used by Dazai's forerunner Natsume Sōseki in his *Wagahai wa Neko de aru* (1905-1906; *I Am a Cat*, 1961). Dazai's story concerns the experiences of a one-hundred-yen note as it is passed from hand to hand in Tokyo in the aftermath of World War II. The story is exceptional in having absolutely nothing to do with the personal life of the author, but it does illustrate an aspect of Dazai's style described by James O'Brien as ironic reversal: Much of the story illustrates a woman's greed, but it concludes with the noble sacrifice of a prostitute. "Kobutori" ("Taking the Wen Away"), based on an ancient tale, describes a Rip Van Winkle situation in which an old man with a large wen climbs a hill at night in a drunken condition and encounters ten red demons, contentedly drunk like himself. As the old man joins them in a delirious dance, they insist that he return another time and let them take his wen with them as a pledge. A rich old man also with a wen, hearing this story, goes to the same place, but his measured cadences displease the demons and they prepare to leave. He catches one of them, entreating that his wen be removed, but they think he is asking for its return. They give him that of the first man, and he then has two. Dazai concludes that the story has no moral except to point up the currents of comedy and tragedy in life.

"Das Gemeine"

Dazai's two streams of autobiography and fantasy are brought together in "Das Gemeine" ("Das Gemeine"), whose title is the German word for "vulgarity"; however, the strands are interwoven in such a way that no coherent plot structure can be discerned. For this reason, the story, one of Dazai's most difficult, is sometimes considered as an example of Dadaism or deliberate mystification. It is both a pastiche of Western literature and an account of the efforts of Dazai and his collaborators to establish a literary journal. It begins humorously with the narrator, Sanojiro, contemplating a double suicide until jilted by his paramour. He then becomes involved with a waitress at a sake stand. As a means of expressing spring joy, he composes a poem opposite in tone to the *ubi sunt* theme of French Renaissance poetry. Later, Dazai himself, as a character in the story, intones, "The rain falls on the town," paraphrasing a famous line by Arthur Rimbaud. He asks his fellow editors whether they prefer strawberries prepared for the market or purely natural ones, an allegory for literary works as well as a reflection of his theme of the marketplace. At the end of the story, the narrator, while questioning his identity, is run over by a train and records his death in the manner of the protagonist of "Transformation." Here, as in the rest of Dazai's works, the emphasis is on the individual rather than society. His stories as well as his longer fiction use his own personality to portray various contradictions in the human condition.

Other major works

LONG FICTION: *Shin Hamuretto*, 1941; *Seigi to bishō*, 1942; *Udaijin Sanetomo*, 1943; *Pandora no hako*, 1945 (originally titled "Hibari no koe"); *Sekibetsu*, 1945; *Shayō*, 1947 (*The Setting Sun*, 1956); *Ningen shikkaku*, 1948 (*No Longer Human*, 1958).

PLAYS: *Fuyu no hanabi*, pb. 1946; *Haru no kaeha*, pb. 1946.

NONFICTION: *Tsugaru*, 1944 (English translation, 1985; also as *Return to Tsugaru: Travels of a Purple Tramp*, 1985).

MISCELLANEOUS: *Dazai Osamu zenshū*, 1967-1968 (thirteen volumes).

BIBLIOGRAPHY

Cohn, Joel R. *Studies in the Comic Spirit in Modern Japanese Fiction.* Cambridge, Mass.: Harvard University Press, 1998. Examines humor in the works of Dazai, Masuji Ibuse, and Hisashi Inoue. Includes bibliographical references and an index.

Keene, Donald. *Landscapes and Portraits: Appreciations of Japanese Culture.* Tokyo: Kodansha International, 1971. Of particular relevance is the section on Osamu Dazai in chapter 4, "Three Modern Novelists," which focuses on the difference between Western and Japanese responses to Dazai's fiction, the strongly autobiographical elements in his works, and the style and major themes of his narrative. Supplemented by illustrations and a short reading list.

Kirkup, James. "Now Out of Japan Something New." *The Times,* December 13, 1990. A brief biographical sketch, followed by comments on Dazai's short stories and autobiographical essays; focuses on Dazai's collection *Crackling Mountains*; discusses Dazai's variations on the title story, one of the best-known folktales in Japan.

Motofùji, Frank T. "Dazai Osamu." In *Approaches to the Modern Japanese Short Story*, edited by Thomas E. Swann and Kinya Tsuruta. Totsuka: Waseda University Press, 1982. Provides analyses of two short stories, "Villon's Wife" and "A Sound of Hammering," written in 1947, one year before the author's suicide. The two stories are seen as reflections of the dilemma of the writer in postwar Japan, overwhelmed by the chaos of a ruined past.

Lyon, Phyllis I. *The Saga of Dazai Osamu: A Critical Study with Translations.* Stanford, Calif.: Stanford University Press, 1985. Various critical perspectives; includes a bibliography and index.

O'Brien, James. *Dazai Osamu.* Boston: Twayne, 1975. An introductory story that combines a biography with a chronologically based study of Dazai's creative output. Preceded by a chronological summary and followed by a select bibliography.

Rimer, J. Rhomas. "Dazai Osamu: The Death of the Past, *The Setting Sun.*" In *Modern Japanese Fiction and Its Traditions: An Introduction.* Princeton, N.J.: Princeton University Press, 1978. Views the novel *The Setting Sun* as a reflection of the tensions in Japan before, during, and after the war years. The characters and situations relentlessly probe the realities of a transitional period.

Ueda, Makoto. "Dazai Osamu." In *Modern Japanese Writers and the Nature of Literature.* Stanford, Calif.: Stanford University Press, 1976. Focuses on the literary concepts of Dazai as revealed within his fiction. Underlying his "expansive, emotional, and spontaneous" prose style, with its seeming artlessness, is a view of literature as a "food for losers." Includes references to the Japanese originals of the texts discussed and a bibliography focusing on Dazai.

Vachon, John. "An Overly Sensitive Heart." *The Daily Yomiuri,* November 25, 1990, p. 7. A review of Dazai's *Self-Portraits: Tales from Life of Japan's Great Decadent Romantic*; provides a brief biographical sketch and comments on Dazai's style in the eighteen pieces of this early work; notes that he is better in the short story than the novel.

Westerhoven, James, trans. Preface to *Return to Tsugaru: Travels of a Purple Tramp.* Tokyo: Kodansha International, 1985. An overview of the developments of the novel, viewing it as the journal of a quest for love, founded on the premise that acceptance and love require the shedding of all affection. Includes a brief biography with background material to the novel (a family tree and a map of Dazai's journey through the Tsugaru peninsula).

Wolfe, Alan Stephen. *Suicidal Narrative in Modern Japan: The Case of Dazai Osamu.* Princeton, N.J.: Princeton University Press, 1990. An insightful study. Includes bibliographical references and an index.

A. Owen Aldridge, updated by Anna M. Wittman

WALTER DE LA MARE

Born: Charlton, Kent, England; April 25, 1873
Died: Twickenham, Middlesex, England; June 22, 1956

PRINCIPAL SHORT FICTION

Story and Rhyme: A Selection, 1921
The Riddle and Other Stories, 1923
Ding Dong Bell, 1924
Broomsticks and Other Tales, 1925
Miss Jemima, 1925
Readings, 1925-1926 (2 volumes)
The Connoisseur and Other Tales, 1926
Told Again: Traditional Tales, 1927
Old Joe, 1927
On the Edge, 1930
Seven Short Stories, 1931
The Lord Fish, 1933
The Nap and Other Stories, 1936
The Wind Blows Over, 1936
Animal Stories, 1939
The Picnic, 1941
The Best Stories of Walter de la Mare, 1942
The Old Lion and Other Stories, 1942
The Magic Jacket and Other Stories, 1943
The Scarecrow and Other Stories, 1945
The Dutch Cheese and Other Stories, 1946
Collected Stories for Children, 1947
A Beginning and Other Stories, 1955
Ghost Stories, 1956

OTHER LITERARY FORMS

In addition to his numerous volumes of short fiction, Walter de la Mare published poetry, novels, anthologies of various kinds, collections of essays, one play, and scores of essays, reviews, and articles published separately. In the United States, de la Mare is better known as a children's writer than he is for the other genres in which he worked.

ACHIEVEMENTS

De la Mare's remarkable literary career spans more than five decades. The English novelist, poet, dramatist, short-story writer, critic, essayist, and anthropologist is best known today as a writer infused with a Romantic imagination. He has often been compared to William Blake and Thomas Hardy because of similarities in thematic development of mortality and visionary illumination. Often labeled as an escapist because of his retreat from reality, de la Mare's work touches on dreams, fantasy worlds, emotional states, and transcendent pursuits. Best known in the United States for his children's literature, he has produced numerous volumes of prose and verse in the genre. All his work is suffused by a childlike quality of imagination. De la Mare's writings have still not received the attention they deserve. He lived a quiet, uneventful life, always reluctant to impart information about himself. Throughout his life de la Mare wrote poetry. It is this work that represents his truest and most lasting literary achievement. In 1948, de la Mare received the Companion of Honour and in 1953, the Order of Merit. During the next three years he also received honorary degrees from five colleges, including Oxford and Cambridge.

BIOGRAPHY

Walter de la Mare was born on April 25, 1873, in Charlton, Kent, the son of well-to-do parents, James Edward de la Mare and Lucy Sophia Browning de la Mare. In her book *Walter de la Mare* (1966), Doris Ross McCrosson said that de la Mare's life "was singularly and refreshingly uneventful." De la Mare was educated at St. Paul's Cathedral Choir School in London, where he was the founder and editor of the school magazine, *The Choristers' Journal*. In 1890, at the age of seventeen, de la Mare began working as a bookkeeper at the Anglo-American Oil Company in London, a position he held for almost twenty years. While working as a bookkeeper, de la Mare began writing stories, essays, and poetry, many of which were published in various magazines. For a while, de la Mare wrote under the pseudonym "Walter Ramal." Soon after the publication of his first books, he was granted a civil list pension by the British government amounting to one hundred pounds a year. Thereafter, he devoted himself entirely to literature and writing. De la Mare died at home on June 22, 1956, at the age of eighty-three. He is buried at St. Paul's Cathedral.

ANALYSIS

Walter de la Mare's stories take the form both of wish fulfillment and nightmare projections. Believing that the everyday world of mundane experience is a veil hiding a "real" world, de la Mare used dream forms as a means of piercing the veil as well as a means of suggesting that between dream and reality looms, as de la Mare said, "no impassable abyss." Because of their hallucinatory character, dreams merge with states of madness, travel to mysterious realms, childhood visions. The surfaces of de la Mare's stories belie an underlying reality; rendering the texture of everyday experience with exquisite detail, he built his surfaces with such lucidity that a reader is often surprised to find a horror beneath that which is apparently placid or a joy beneath that which is apparently mundane.

"THE RIDDLE"

"The Riddle" starts like a fairy tale with such lightness and grace that one might expect a "happy ever after" ending. Soon, however, it becomes apparent that the quavering voice of the grandmother betokens something more than age, and the gifts she presents to her seven grandchildren become something more than sugar plums. Although it is never made explicit, one may assume that the grandchildren have come to live with their grandmother because of the death of their parents. The aged woman says to the children, ". . . bring me smiling faces that call back to my mind my own son Harry." The children are told they may come in the presence of their grandmother twice a day—in the morning and in the evening. The rest of the time they have the run of the house with the exception of the large spare bedroom where there stands in a corner an old oak chest, older than the aged woman's own grandmother.

The chest represents death. It is later revealed to be decorated as a coffin, and it attracts the children one by one. Harry is first. Opening the chest, he finds something strangely seductive that reminds him of

his mother, so he climbs in and the lid miraculously closes. When the other children tell their grandmother of Harry's disappearance, she responds, "Then he must be gone away for a time. . . . But remember, all of you, do not meddle with the oak chest."

Now it becomes apparent that the grandmother, herself so close to death that she seems more feeble every day, is also to be identified with the oak chest and that rather than a good fairy dispensing sugarplums she is a wicked witch seducing the children to their death. Ann is the last child to be called to the chest, and she walks as if in a dream and as if she were being guided by the hand. One paragraph more ends the story. With the children all gone, the grandmother enters the spare room, but her eyesight is too dim for her to see, and her mind is a tangled skein of memories which include memories of little children.

"THE ORGY"

"The Orgy: An Idyll" seems an entirely different kind of story. Rather than being set in a house with myriad rooms suggesting something of the gothic, "The Orgy" is set mainly in a large and elegant de-

Walter de la Mare (Library of Congress)

partment store in London; rather than beginning with a "once upon a time" element, it opens on a bright May morning, crisp, brisk, scintillating. Details of the great packed street down which Philip walks leave readers no doubt that here is the world of their own experience. Before the action is ended, however, it becomes clear that the story is an extravaganza. Philip is engaged in a buying orgy, charging everything that strikes his fancy to the account of his uncle who has just disinherited him, and the orgy is a fanciful idyll of the wish fulfillment variety. Philip's desire for revenge projected into bright, hallucinatory images is carried into action in exactly the way the uncle will understand—to the tune of "a couple of hundred thousand pounds," a considerable amount of money in 1931, the year the story was published.

"IN THE FOREST"

"In the Forest" is a brilliant exercise in point of view restricted to the mind of a small boy in such a way that the childlike behavior and lack of perception characteristic of the very young take on the aura of nightmare. At no time does de la Mare vary the focus; no words are used that a child could not know; no insight is offered that a child could not understand. Although the child occasionally feels a twinge of guilt because he has not obeyed his mother, he is completely impervious to the horror of the action going on around him.

The story opens when the boy's father is leaving to go to war. The boy is half asleep and is moving in and out of consciousness. It is the advent of the fall of the year, and a storm has brought down leaves that are still green from the trees. Although the leaves are still green, it is getting cold. The boy asks his father to bring him a gun back from the war and notices without comment that his father, instead of leaving immediately, keeps coming back to say good-bye. Unaware of the anguish being suffered by his father and mother, the boy asks his mother if she is glad his father is going to the war. The mother does not answer, but the boy's simple statement makes the point. "But she was crying over the baby, so I went out into the forest till dinner."

Later the boy chops wood, an activity that causes him to be hot and excited, and then he brings the logs into the house. The wind is roaring as if it is angry, more leaves are falling, and the weather is cold and misty. The boy finds his mother asleep with the baby in her arms, and the baby, too, is asleep, although, as the boy notices, the baby scarcely seems to be breathing. The boy falls asleep by the warm hearth and stays there all night. In the morning he rushes out, glad that his father is gone, because now he can do just as he pleases. Visiting the snares, he finds a young rabbit caught by one leg and, imitating his father, kills the hare with a crack on the neck and carries it to the house by the hind legs. Later he wonders how "they would carry back" his father's body "if he was killed in the war."

Because the baby is crying, the boy chooses to spend his days in the forest until one day when he tells his mother he is going to "bring her some fish for dinner!" The dialogue that follows is the first that occurs in the story. The mother tells the boy that the baby is very ill and tries to get him to touch and hold his baby brother, asking: "Do you love it?" The boy shakes his head and persists: "I think I should *like* to go fishing mother . . . and I promise you shall have the biggest I catch." Then, denying the mother's plea that he go for the doctor, the boy runs out saying, "It's only crying."

He catches no fish and believes the fish would not bite because he has been wicked, so he goes home, and now for the first time he hears cannons on the other side of the forest. When he gets home, he finds his mother angry, calling him a coward, and the baby dead. The next day he consents to his mother's request that he go for the sexton, but as he is on his way he hears a rifle sound and "a scream like a rabbit," and he is frightened and runs home. Since his mother has already called him a coward, however, he lies to her, telling her the sexton was gone. Now the mother decides she must take the dead baby to the graveyard herself, and once again she addresses her son: "Won't you kiss your little brother, Robbie?"

Alone, the boy eats more than he should and builds the fire up so high that its noise drowns out any outside noises. Alone, he believes he is in a dream "that would never come to an end." He does not cry, but he feels angry at being left alone, and he is afraid.

He also feels guilty about the amount of food he has consumed. He fears his mother's return and yet longs for her, feeling that he loves her and is sorry for his wickedness.

The next thing he knows, it is broad daylight. His mother has still not returned, but he hears a groan at the doorway. It is his father with a "small hole" at the back of his shoulder; dark, thick blood covers the withered leaves on which he lies. The boy tries to give his father water and tells him about the baby, "but he didn't show that he could hear anything." Then the boy hears his mother coming back and runs out to tell her "that it was father." The story ends as abruptly as it begins, but the point of view so neatly restricted and the image patterns masterfully arranged create the tenor and vehicle of an Everyman's Freudian nightmare. The subtly stated but powerfully conveyed theme delineates an Oedipal pattern that raises the story from an isolated and factual experience to an overwhelming and communal dream having mythic proportions.

"AN IDEAL CRAFTSMAN"

"An Ideal Craftsman" is just as powerful. Although the story makes use of a young boy as protagonist, point of view is different from that found in "In the Forest." This time de la Mare allows an omniscient narrator to move in and out of the consciousness of the two major characters. Once again, however, a horror is present, foreshadowed from the beginning of the story; once again the aura of dream is cast over the entire story; and once again death, this time murder, is the focal point of the story.

For a short-story writer of such consummate skill, de la Mare has attracted almost no critical attention, and what books have been written about him concentrate more on his other writings than on his pieces of short fiction. This lack of attention is a great pity. In her book *Walter de la Mare*, McCrosson devotes only one chapter of some twenty pages to de la Mare's short-story craft, but her summary of his achievement is accurate:

> His preoccupation with good and evil puts him on a level with Hawthorne and Conrad; his mastery of suspense and terror is equal to Poe's; the subtlety of his

characterizations occasionally rivals James's. And the range of his portrayals is impressive: children, old maids, the demented, old idealists and young pessimists, artists, business men, dandys, young women in love—all of whom share in the mysterious and sometimes maddening business called living.

OTHER MAJOR WORKS

LONG FICTION: *Henry Brocken*, 1904; *The Return*, 1910; *The Three Mulla-Mulgars*, 1910 (reprinted as *The Three Royal Monkeys: Or, The Three Mulla-Mulgars*, 1935); *Memoirs of a Midget*, 1921; *At First Sight: A Novel*, 1928.

PLAYS: *Crossings: A Fairy Play*, pr. 1919.

POETRY: *Songs of Childhood*, 1902; *Poems*, 1906; *The Listeners and Other Poems*, 1912; *A Child's Day: A Book of Rhymes*, 1912; *Peacock Pie: A Book of Rhymes*, 1913; *The Sunken Garden and Other Poems*, 1917; *Motley and Other Poems*, 1918; *Flora: A Book of Drawings*, 1919; *Poems 1901 to 1918*, 1920; *Story and Rhyme*, 1921; *The Veil and Other Poems*, 1921; *Down-Adown-Derry: A Book of Fairy Poems*, 1922; *Thus Her Tale*, 1923; *A Ballad of Christmas*, 1924; *Stuff and Nonsense and So On*, 1927; *Self to Self*, 1928; *The Snowdrop*, 1929; *News*, 1930; *Poems for Children*, 1930; *Lucy*, 1931; *Old Rhymes and New*, 1932; *The Fleeting and Other Poems*, 1933; *Poems 1919 to 1934*, 1935; *This Year, Next Year*, 1937; *Memory and Other Poems*, 1938; *Haunted*, 1939; *Bells and Grass*, 1941; *Collected Poems*, 1941; *Collected Rhymes and Verses*, 1944; *The Burning-Glass and Other Poems*, 1945; *The Traveller*, 1946; *Rhymes and Verses: Collected Poems for Young People*, 1947; *Inward Companion*, 1950; *Winged Chariot*, 1951; *O Lovely England and Other Poems*, 1953; *The Complete Poems*, 1969.

NONFICTION: *Rupert Brooke and the Intellectual Imagination*, 1919; *The Printing of Poetry*, 1931; *Lewis Carroll*, 1932; *Poetry in Prose*, 1936; *Pleasures and Speculations*, 1940; *Chardin, J.B.S. 1699-1779*, 1948; *Private View*, 1953.

EDITED TEXTS: *Come Hither*, 1923; *The Shakespeare Songs*, 1929; *Christina Rossetti's Poems*, 1930; *Desert Islands and Robinson Crusoe*, 1930; *Stories from the Bible*, 1930; *Early One Morning in the Spring*, 1935; *Animal Stories*, 1939; *Behold, This Dreamer!*, 1939; *Love*, 1943.

BIBLIOGRAPHY

Allen, Walter. *The Short Story in English*. New York: Oxford University Press, 1981. Argues that, as a short-story writer, de la Mare closely resembles Henry James in his supernatural stories, for his stories are rooted in mundane reality.

Atkins, John. *Walter de la Mare: An Exploration*. London: C & J Temple, 1947. A slim volume of appreciation by Atkins, who concentrates on de la Mare's stories and on two of the novels, neglecting the verse, which he considers inferior. The study is a rambling discourse without a solid structure and is not recommended for newcomers to de la Mare.

Duffin, Henry Charles. *Walter de la Mare: A Study of His Poetry*. London: Sidgwick & Jackson, 1949. The author focuses on de la Mare's verse. He considers him a sublime visionary poet of exceptional lucidity whose excessive creative energies are diminished in the prose stories, which he also considers delightful. His main thesis is that de la Mare's poetry neither criticizes nor escapes life, but rather heightens it.

Hopkins, Kenneth. *Walter de la Mare*. 1953. Rev. ed. London: Longmans, Green, 1957. This slim volume touches on de la Mare's life and his prose and verse writings. The author, who is an ardent admirer of de la Mare, briefly examines all of his major writings. A useful but limited introduction to de la Mare. Supplemented by a select bibliography.

McCrosson, Doris Ross. *Walter de la Mare*. New York: Twayne, 1966. A good critical introduction to de la Mare. McCrosson examines at length the author's total literary output, concentrating particularly on the novels, which she feels not only have been neglected but also contain the clearest statement of his vision of life. The writer points out that de la Mare's fascinating quest into the mysteries of life never coalesced into a coherent vision. Complemented by a chronology and a select bibliography.

Manwaring, Randle. "Memories of Walter de la Mare." *Contemporary Review* 264 (March, 1994): 148-152. A reminiscence of a longtime acquaintance of de la Mare that comments on his style and his influence. Reflects de la Mare's childish delight in simple things that is so often reflected in his stories.

Megroz, R. L. *Walter de la Mare: A Biographical and Critical Study*. London: Hodder & Stoughton, 1924. Megroz conducted the first study of de la Mare's work, "treading what is almost virgin soil," as he phrased it. The author professes his deep admiration for de la Mare, sketches a brief biography, comments on personal impressions, and then devotes his study to the poetry. His book is less a critical examination of de la Mare and more an appreciation.

Wagenknecht, Edward. *Seven Masters of Supernatural Fiction*. New York: Greenwood Press, 1991. See the chapter on Walter de la Mare, which includes a brief biographical sketch and discusses his fiction in the context of the English literary tradition. Wagenknecht deals with both the short and the long fiction, providing a succinct overview of de la Mare's body of work in prose.

Whistler, Theresa. *Imagination of the Heart: The Life of Walter de la Mare*. London: Duckworth, 1993. A good biography of de la Mare. Includes bibliographical references and an index.

Mary Rohrberger, updated by Terry Theodore

SAMUEL R. DELANY

Born: New York, New York; April 1, 1942

PRINCIPAL SHORT FICTION

"The Star Pit," 1966

"Aye, and Gomorrah," 1967

We, in Some Strange Power's Employ, Move on a Rigorous Line, 1968 (novella; also known as *Lines of Power*)

"Time Considered as a Helix of Semiprecious Stones," 1969

Driftglass: Ten Tales of Speculative Fiction, 1971

Prismatica, 1977 (novella)

Tales of Nevèrÿon, 1979

Distant Stars, 1981

Atlantis: Three Tales, 1995

OTHER LITERARY FORMS

Samuel R. Delany has produced more than a dozen novels, including *Hogg* (1993), *They Fly at Çiron* (1993), and *The Mad Man* (1994), and a relatively small body of highly acclaimed short fiction. He has worked primarily in science fiction and fantasy, but all his fiction is known for its intricate literary qualities. His work has been translated into many languages and is internationally renowned. Delany's memoirs, especially *The Motion of Light in Water: Sex and Science Fiction Writing in the East Village, 1957-1965* (1988), provide insight into his formative writing years. His nonfiction works include *Shorter Views: Queer Thoughts and the Politics of the Paraliterary* (1999) and *Times Square Red, Times Square Blue* (1999).

ACHIEVEMENTS

Throughout Samuel R. Delany's career, his work has been recognized as far above the level of "pulp" science fiction. Many of his novels and short stories have been nominated for Nebula or Hugo awards, including *The Ballad of Beta-2* (1965), "The Star Pit" (1966), "Driftglass" (1971), *Nova* (1968), *Dhalgren* (1975), *Triton* (1976), and *Prismatica* (1977). *The Einstein Intersection* (1967), "Aye, and Gomorrah"

(1967), and "Time Considered as a Helix of Semiprecious Stones" (1969) won the Nebula Award. "Time Considered as a Helix of Semiprecious Stones" also won a Hugo Award. In 1980, Delany was honored with an American Book Award nomination for his *Tales of Nevèrÿon*, and he was given the Science Fiction Research Association's Pilgrim Award in 1985. *The Motion of Light in Water* was awarded a Hugo Award for Nonfiction in 1989, and in 1996 he received the Lambda Literary Award in Science Fiction and Fantasy for *Atlantis*. In 1993, Delany received the William Whitehead Memorial Award for a Lifetime Contribution to Gay and Lesbian Literature.

BIOGRAPHY

Samuel Ray Delany, Jr., was born April 1, 1942, into a middle-class, professional family (two uncles were well-known judges in New York City) in Harlem, New York. His father, Samuel Ray Delany, Sr., was a funeral director, and his mother, Margaret Carey Delaney (née Boyd), was a clerk in a local library. At summer camp one year, he chose the nickname "Chip" for himself and has been called that ever since.

Delany's early education took place at Dalton, an exclusive, primarily white school on the East Side. He then attended the Bronx High School of Science, where the average intelligence quotient of the students was 140. Although his scores in most subjects were excellent (particularly in math), Delaney's school career was often made more difficult by what would much later be diagnosed as dyslexia. His parents had forced him to become right-handed, and, partially as a result, Delany had immense difficulty with spelling, with a particular propensity for writing words backward. A broken and jumbled mishmash of misspellings, his writing was opaque even to him once he had forgotten the intended meaning of the words. His parents always encouraged him to write, however, because they had been told by a tutor that if Delany wrote as much as possible his spelling would have to improve. His mother read to him constantly, and his father even read aloud Mark Twain's *The Adventures of Huckleberry Finn* (1884), chapter by chapter.

On August 24, 1961, Delany married Marilyn Hacker. A first pregnancy for Marilyn ended in a miscarriage in 1961, but in 1974 the couple had a daughter, Iva Alyxander. Delany and Hacker were divorced in 1980, after an unconventional marriage about which he wrote in *The Motion of Light in Water.*

Delany attended City College in New York City (now City University of New York) in 1960 and again from 1962 to 1963, but dropped out to finish *Babel-17* (1966). Despite his lack of a formal degree, however, Delany has held several prestigious academic posts. He was Butler Professor of English at State University of New York at Buffalo, in 1975, and senior fellow at the Center for Twentieth Century Studies at the University of Wisconsin, Milwaukee, in 1977. He also held the posts of senior fellow at the Society for the Humanities at Cornell University, in 1987, and professor of comparative literature at the University of Massachusetts, Amherst, in 1988. In 1995, Delaney was a visiting writer at the universities of Minnesota and Idaho, and in 1997 he was a visiting professor at Michigan State University. In January of 2000, he joined the faculty in the English department at the State University of New York at Buffalo.

ANALYSIS

In *The Motion of Light in Water*, Delany spoke of himself as: "A black man. A gay man. A writer." Though these three truths do not "explain" Delany's life, they are the primary roots from which his writings have sprung. Delany's work often features marginalized characters, people outside society's mainstream, such as slaves or those who have been biologically modified (through tattooing or piercing, for example).

Delany himself—in his lifestyle, chosen profession, and chosen genre—is outside the American mainstream. Yet, he has found a way, through writing, to express and empower himself. This has not been easy, and many of the characters in his early short stories, whose tales were often narrated in first person, were as full of longing—or more so—at the

end of the story as at the beginning. In Delany's later stories, particularly in *Tales of Nevèrÿon*, the characters often do find a place and a purpose for themselves.

Delany's first published novels, while grand in scope and rich with allusion, metaphor, and lyricism, still fit easily within science fiction's traditions. In 1975, however, Delany changed everyone's perspective of him with *Dhalgren*, his longest book at over eight-hundred pages and his best known and most controversial work. *Dhalgren* has been Delany's most commercially successful work, but, despite being nominated for a Nebula, most of the book's critical acclaim has come from outside the science-fiction community. In fact, many within that community, both fans and other writers, disliked the book, perhaps because it met few of the expectations that had been established within science fiction.

Some fans and critics hailed *Triton* (1976) as a return to science fiction, but a careful reading of the book will show the same underlying complex of ideas at work. With *The Mad Man* (1994), Delany departed completely from science fiction and moved into realism with a tale of murder, New York, and homosexuality in the age of acquired immunodeficiency syndrome (AIDS).

"AYE, AND GOMORRAH"

Though Delany is primarily known for his novels, his short stories form a critical body of work that must be considered. One of his best-known stories is "Aye, and Gomorrah," which was written in September, 1966, while Delany was at the Milford Science Fiction Writers Conference in Connecticut. It was immediately bought by Harlan Ellison for an influential anthology called *Dangerous Visions*, published in 1967. It was the story that, as Delany himself noted, helped him to make the transition from "an unknown to a known entity."

This very brief story takes place mainly in Istanbul, Turkey, but its setting is clearly secondary to its subject: the neutering of people who work in space and those who, because of a syndrome called free-fall-sexual-displacement complex, worship them sexually. The former, known as spacers, are attracted to the latter, called frelks, only for the money that the frelks will give them to perform acts that are not specified in the story but that have clearly sexual undertones. Yet, the androgynous nature of the frelks prevents any real sexual relationship.

While on the spacer equivalent of "shore leave," the young protagonist of "Aye, and Gomorrah" meets a Turkish girl, who wants to seduce the spacer but does not have the money necessary to bribe him. She is open about her obsession with spacers, although she does not like being a frelk—she believes that she is a "pervert" in the sense that a "pervert substitutes something unattainable for 'normal' love: the homosexual, a mirror, the fetishist, a shoe or a watch or a girdle."

The idea of being a sexual outcast is a frequent theme in Delany's work, perhaps stemming from his coming to terms with his homosexuality. In *Triton*, for example, the main character, Bron, undergoes a sex change, ostensibly to be able to understand women better, but instead becomes even more confused about his (or her) own sexuality. "Aye, and Gomorrah" focuses on the retarded sexuality of the spacers and the futile sexual longings of the frelks. In "The Tale of the Small Sarg" the character of Gorgik, a former slave who has become "civilized," reveals that he cannot function sexually unless either he or his partner is wearing some physical sign of ownership, such as a slave collar.

Yet, Delany often applies a light touch to these issues in his stories. In "Aye, and Gomorrah," the young spacer is constantly being corrected because of his tendency to assign the wrong gender of the word "frelk" in different languages. "*Une* frelk," he is told by a Frenchman, and he learns from a Latina that it is *frelko* in Spanish.

WE, IN SOME STRANGE POWER'S EMPLOY, MOVE ON A RIGOROUS LINE

We, in Some Strange Power's Employ, Move on a Rigorous Line tells the story of a power-cable layer, or "line demon," who is promoted to "line devil" and faces his first tough decisions while in command. The power company group stumbles across a band of "angels" who live up on a cliff with their "pteracycles," which seem to be flying motorcycles. Bringing power to this wild gang is seen by its members as a chal-

lenge to their lifestyle, but the power company must abide by the law, which states that power must be made available to each individual.

The irony of the story lies in its conclusion. Having defeated the head angel's attempt to drive them off, the power company employees go up to the gang's retreat, called High Haven. On finding that it has been deserted by the angels, however, the head devil decides that: "If there's nobody living up here, there's no reason to run power up here—by law." In essence, the power workers have destroyed what they set out to help with their civilizing gift of electricity. The story's narrator, at least, regrets it.

"TIME CONSIDERED AS A HELIX OF SEMIPRECIOUS STONES"

"Time Considered as a Helix of Semiprecious Stones," which was written in Milford in July of 1968 and published in 1969, also presents a mocking approach to modern society. The main character, who changes his identity almost with each page, comments, often bitingly (in parentheses within the text) on the world as it passes by: "A very tanned, very blond man . . . came down the rocks (artificial) between the ferns (real) growing along the stream (real water; phony current)." Later, he notes that "automation has become the upper crust's way of flaunting the labor surplus."

The subject of the story is the behavior of a criminal once it has been predicted that he will commit a specific crime. Interwoven with this theme is that of the Singers, who are "people who look at things, then go and tell people what they've seen. What makes them Singers is their ability to make people listen." One Singer, a youth named Hawk, is a familiar Delany character all the way down to his deeply bitten fingernails. Unable to love in a "normal" way, he prefers pain to pleasure, much to the protagonist's dismay. The protagonist, meanwhile, characterizes his own aberration, the "will" to steal, as "an impulse toward the absurd and the tasteless. . . ," but it is a *want*, a *need*—like the need for love—and it cannot be forever denied.

"DRIFTGLASS"

"Driftglass" bears some similarity to "Aye, and Gomorrah," particularly in its description of adolescents sent off for surgical alteration so that they can perform certain tasks better. In this case, however, the youths, rather than having body parts removed, have them added. Marine work for the Aquatic Corp. requires "a week of operations [to] make an amphibious creature that can exist for a month on either side of the sea's foam-fraught surface." The resulting "amphimen," a term that includes females, lay huge power cables to run oil wells and chemical distillation plants and to provide for herds of whales as well as to supply underwater farms and mines.

The main character, however, has had his life ruined in an undersea volcanic accident. Living his lonely life on a Brazilian beach, Cal Svenson hunts for what he calls driftglass in the surf—unlikely treasures in the form of Coca-Cola bottles and discarded glass pounded by the sea into *objets d'art*. Cal has no regrets about his choice of career; in fact, he persuades his friend to allow his children (Cal's godchildren) to go into service with "the Corp" and be made into "amphimen."

TALES OF NEVÈRŸON

Not all Delany's stories are science-fiction tales set in the future. For example, the loosely related stories found in the *Tales of Nevèrÿon* collection are set in a mythical past. These stories owe much to the genre of swashbuckling fantasy fiction called sword-and-sorcery, though they depart as radically from the conventions of that genre as *Dhalgren* does from science fiction.

Sword-and-sorcery is, itself, a marginalized literature. It has received little respect from mainstream critics, even those willing to admit, grudgingly, that science fiction has something to offer. However, in the hands of some writers (Robert E. Howard, Fritz Leiber, Karl Edward Wagner) sword-and-sorcery has achieved notable commercial success and generated enough small press scholarship to deserve broader critical consideration.

Delany is, according to James Sallis in *Ash of Stars: On the Writing of Samuel R. Delany* (1996), "the man who would intellectualize" sword-and-sorcery. Certainly, Delany's *Nevèrÿon* stories have contributed two things to the genre. First, while sword-and-sorcery must develop a historical "feel," most

writers achieve this with descriptions of walled cities, ruins, and sword fights. The focus is on large-scale, dramatic events—war being a favorite. A common criticism here is that readers seldom see how armies are fed or how cities survive in the absence of an economy other than trade.

Delany's *Nevèrÿon* stories, in contrast, develop a sense of history by focusing on exactly those details that other writers neglect. In "The Tale of Gorgik," the first *Nevèrÿon* story, the reader learns of docks and warehouses, of sailors and slaves. The main trade item described is not jewels or exotic furs but little rubber balls.

"The Tale of Old Venn" shows readers the ship builders and fishing boats. The astrolabe's invention is part of the story's background, and the development of an early writing system leads one character, Norema, to thoughts on origins and philosophy.

Although sword-and-sorcery is generally set at a time when cultures are moving from barter to monetary economies and from rural to urban societies, most writers use these facts only to force characters into motion. Delany makes the change to a monetary economy a major focus of such stories as "The Tale of Potters and Dragons," where attempts to control the rubber-ball trade and the change from three-legged to four-legged pots are important plot developments. Is it coincidence that one character is named Madam Keyne (reminiscent of John Maynard Keynes, the economist)?

Delany's second contribution to sword-and-sorcery is his far greater emphasis on character than on the plot and action that drives most work in the genre. In fact, there is little plot at all in the *Nevèrÿon* stories. There are certainly no larger-than-life characters. Gorgik, who appears in most of the tales and is the closest Delany comes to a barbarian warrior, is, in fact, a "civilized" man and has the psychological scars to prove it. Only "The Tale of Dragons and Dreamers" has much fighting, and it is not an imprisoned Gorgik who does it. It is Small Sarg, a youth, who handles the killing.

Many characters in the *Nevèrÿon* stories are women, but not in the usual roles of princess, harlot, or woman warrior (the only woman warrior is named

Raven). Instead, women are merchants, inventors, and fishers. There is a part-time prostitute whose story is told in "The Tale of Rumor and Desire"; this is Clodon, a man.

OTHER MAJOR WORKS

LONG FICTION: *The Jewels of Aptor*, 1962, 1968; *Captives of the Flame*, 1963; *The Towers of Toron*, 1964, 1966; *City of a Thousand Suns*, 1965, 1966; *The Ballad of Beta-2*, 1965; *Empire Star*, 1966; *Babel-17*, 1966; *The Einstein Intersection*, 1967; *Nova*, 1968; *Out of the Dead City*, 1968; *The Fall of the Towers*, 1970; *The Tides of Lust*, 1973 (originally entitled *Equinox*); *Dhalgren*, 1975; *Triton*, 1976 (originally entitled *Trouble on Triton*); *Empire*, 1978 (a graphics novel); *Neveryóna: Or, The Tale of Signs and Cities*, 1983; *Stars in My Pocket Like Grains of Sand*, 1984; *Flight from Nevèrÿon*, 1985; *The Bridge of Lost Desire*, 1987; *Hogg*, 1993; *They Fly at Çiron*, 1993; *The Mad Man*, 1994.

NONFICTION: *The Jewel-Hinged Jaw*, 1977; *The American Shore: Meditations on a Tale of Science Fiction by Thomas M. Disch*, 1978; *Heavenly Breakfast: An Essay on the Winter of Love*, 1979; *Starboard Wine: More Notes on the Language of Science Fiction*, 1984; *The Straits of Messina*, 1987; *The Motion of Light in Water: Sex and Science-Fiction Writing in the East Village, 1957-1965*, 1988 (memoir); *Silent Interviews*, 1994; *Longer Views*, 1996; *Bread and Wine: An Erotic Tale of New York City, an Autobiographical Account*, 1998; *Shorter Views: Queer Thoughts and the Politics of the Paraliterary*, 1999; *Times Square Red, Times Square Blue*, 1999; *1984: Selected Letters*, 2000.

MISCELLANEOUS: *Quark: A Quarterly of Speculative Fiction*, 1970-1971 (edited with Marilyn Hacker).

BIBLIOGRAPHY

Barbour, Douglas. *Worlds Out of Words: The SF Novels of Samuel R. Delany*. London: Bran's Head Books, 1979. This fairly early critique of Delany's works gives a brief biography of Delany and a general discussion of his works, before concentrating on different aspects such as cultural, literary, and mythological allusions and some individual works. Includes notes and primary bibliography.

Dery, Mark. "Black to the Future: Interviews with Samuel R. Delany, Greg Tate, and Tricia Rose." *The South Atlantic Quarterly* 92 (Fall, 1993): 735-778. Examines why so few African Americans write science fiction, since it is a genre in which encounters with the Other are central; discusses these matters with Delany and others.

Fox, Robert Elliot. *Conscientious Sorcerers: The Black Postmodernist Fiction of LeRoi Jones/Amiri Baraka, Ishmael Reed, and Samuel R. Delany*. New York: Greenwood Press, 1987. Fox's text is useful for comparing and contrasting Delany's writing with that of his contemporaries in black fiction. Despite the gulf between their genres, Fox manages to find some similarity in the styles and subjects of these writers. Contains bibliographical information and an index.

Kelso, Sylvia. "'Across Never': Postmodern Theory and Narrative Praxis in Samuel R. Delany's Nevèrÿon Cycle." *Science-Fiction Studies* 24 (July, 1997): 289-301. Argues that Derridean theory supplies the "Symbolic Order" of the blurred margins and centerless structure of Delany's *Nevèrÿon* cycle and that Michel Foucault's use of sadomasochistic experience is imaged in the cycle's "homoerotic Imaginary."

McEvoy, Seth. *Samuel R. Delany*. New York: Frederick Ungar, 1984. Much of the information in this text comes from personal interviews that McEvoy did with Delany. The book covers biographical information and interpretation of individual works, including short fiction as well as long fiction. Complemented by notes to the chapters and an index.

Reid-Pharr, Robert F. "Disseminating Heterotopia" *African American Review* 28 (Fall, 1994): 347-357. Discusses how Delany confronts traditional ideas of proper identity and community politics, deconstructing lines between black and white communities and homosexual and heterosexual communities.

Review of Contemporary Fiction 16 (Fall, 1996).

Special issue on Delany with essays on his novels and his science-fiction theory and criticism. Features an essay on his tales and an interview with Delany in which he discusses his theory of science fiction and his ideas about science fiction as a genre and a way of reading.

Sallis, James, ed. *Ash of Stars: On the Writing of Samuel R. Delany.* Jackson: University Press of Mississippi, 1996. An excellent source for information on Delany's life and work. Includes a bibliography and an index.

Slusser, George Edgar. *The Delany Intersection: Samuel R. Delany Considered as a Writer of Semi-Precious Words.* San Bernardino, Calif.: Borgo Press, 1977. This text sets out the structuralist interpretation of Delany's works, using Delany's lit-erary criticism pieces to judge his own writing. Also traces the evolution of Delany's work from heroic epics to psychological fiction and beyond. Brief biographical and bibliographical notes.

Weedman, Jane. *Samuel R. Delany.* Mercer Island, Wash.: Starmont House, 1982. Weedman discusses a wide range of subjects, including influences on Delany's writing, biographical events, stylistic and critical concepts, and Delany's development as a writer. A detailed chronology can be found at the beginning of the book, and annotated primary and secondary bibliographies have been included at its end. Also includes an index.

Jo-Ellen Lipman Boon, updated by
Charles A. Gramlich

AUGUST DERLETH

Born: Sauk City, Wisconsin; February 24, 1909
Died: Sauk City, Wisconsin; July 4, 1971

PRINCIPAL SHORT FICTION

In re, Sherlock Holmes: The Adventures of Solar Pons, 1945
Sac Prairie People, 1948
The Memoirs of Solar Pons, 1951
Three Problems for Solar Pons, 1952
The Return of Solar Pons, 1958
The Reminiscences of Solar Pons, 1961
The Casebook of Solar Pons, 1965
The Adventure of the Orient Express, 1965
Praed Street Papers, 1965
A Praed Street Dossier, 1968
The Chronicles of Solar Pons, 1973

OTHER LITERARY FORMS

A tremendously prolific writer, August Derleth produced an amazing number of novels, poems, and essays, in addition to short fiction. Included among these are mystery and horror tales, children's books, and histories. He wrote a series of novels, nonfiction, and poetry called the Sac Prairie Saga, five books in his Wisconsin Saga, ten novels in the Judge Peck mystery series (1934-1953), biographies of Henry David Thoreau, Ralph Waldo Emerson, Zona Gale, and H. P. Lovecraft, and a memoir of Sinclair Lewis, Sherwood Anderson, and Edgar Lee Masters. In addition, he wrote about and collected comic books, edited many anthologies of science fiction, and made several studies of homicide.

ACHIEVEMENTS

Although Derleth was certainly one of the most versatile and prolific American writers of the twentieth century, he is also relatively unknown, and little has been written about him and his work. He became a professional writer while in his teens and received a John Simon Guggenheim Memorial Foundation Fellowship in 1938. Among the honors he received are the Award of Merit given by the State Historical Society (for children's books based on Wisconsin's history) in 1954, the Scholastic Award in 1958, the Midland Authors Award (for poetry) in 1965, the Ann Radcliffe Award in 1967, and the Best Nonfiction Award from the Council for Wisconsin Writers for *Return to Walden West* (1970) in 1971. His greatest literary achievement may well be his Sac Prairie Saga.

In the area of short fiction, his contributions are most notable in mystery-detective fiction and horror stories. As editor and publisher, he is credited with preserving and bringing to the reading public the tales of the major horror fiction writer H. P. Lovecraft. His major contribution to mystery-detective fiction is his Solar Pons series (1945-1973), which kept alive the spirit and style of Sir Arthur Conan Doyle's work after he had ceased writing new adventures.

BIOGRAPHY

Born in Sauk City, Wisconsin, on February 24, 1909, August William Derleth was the son of William Julius and Rose Louise Volk Derleth. He attended St. Aloysius School and Sauk City High School and received his B.A. from the University of Wisconsin at Madison in 1930. His career in writing began early, when he sold his first story, "Bat's Belfry," at age fifteen, and his interest in horror stories continued throughout his life. Some of his later tales are written on themes reminiscent of H. P. Lovecraft, whose work Derleth admired.

During his youth, Derleth also enjoyed Doyle's Sherlock Holmes stories. After writing to Doyle to ask if he would write any more adventures and receiving no promise that he would do so, Derleth decided to continue the tradition himself. Thus, in 1928, while still a student, he created the Solar Pons character, patterned after Holmes. His story "The Adventures of the Black Narcissus" appeared in *Dragnet* magazine in February, 1929. With this success, he quickly wrote new adventures. Unfortunately, the 1929 stock market crash wiped out *Dragnet*, and these stories remained unpublished until years later.

Derleth worked as an editor of *Mystic Magazine* for Fawcett Publications in Minneapolis in 1930-1931, leaving when the magazine was discontinued to edit *The Midwesterner* in Madison. In 1933, he contracted with the publishers Loring and Mussey for

a series of mystery novels, and in 1934 the first Judge Peck novel, *Murder Stalks the Wakely Family*, was published.

In 1939 Derleth bought property near Sauk City, where he built his home, "Place of Hawks." From 1939 to 1943 he was a lecturer in American Regional Literature at the University of Wisconsin. With David

August Derleth (AP/Wide World Photos)

Wandrei, he founded Arkham House Publishers in 1939. As owner and cofounder from 1939 to 1971, he made some of his greatest contributions, including the preservation of H. P. Lovecraft's fiction in book form after the original collections went out of print in the late 1940's and 1950's.

After his early successes, Derleth never achieved much national recognition. After the late 1930's and early 1940's, his work was no longer reviewed in the major publications. Since he wrote quickly and rarely revised his work, he has been criticized for failing to develop and polish his craft. Indeed, much of his writing was done for magazines and commercial books in an attempt to supplement his income, but even his "serious" work, such as his Sac Prairie Saga, seemed to flow easily and was not critically revised.

In 1941, he was appointed literary editor of the Madison *Capital-Times*, and he remained at that post for most of the rest of his life. He married Sandra Winters in 1953, and they had two children. They were divorced in 1959. From 1960 to 1963, he edited the poetry magazine *Hawk and Whippoorwill*, and from 1967 to 1971, he edited and published *The Arkham Collector*. He died in Sauk City, Wisconsin, on July 4, 1971, after a heart attack.

ANALYSIS

Although it has been said that the "true and most original Derleth" is not to be found in his fiction, August Derleth's short stories have also won him admirers. His horror stories, many in the tradition of H. P. Lovecraft, have appeared in magazines for popular reading. His most skilled work in the area of short fiction, however, is probably his Solar Pons series. Clearly undertaken as an imitation, these stories recall for Sherlock Holmes fans the wonderful adventures of Baker Street, with Solar Pons as the new master detective. Each of these stories is constructed along a line of deductive reasoning that is very Holmesian in character. The three examples that follow will serve to illustrate Derleth's skill in creating adventures of this type.

"THE ADVENTURE OF THE RUDBERG NUMBERS"

"The Adventure of the Rudberg Numbers" is an ingenious speculation on the invention of the atomic bomb as a tangential result of one of Solar Pons's elegant solutions to a crime. It is related by his Dr. Watson-like associate, Parker, who is the detective's foil. Bancroft Pons, a high official in the Foreign Office and brother to the detective, introduces the plot. A young woman with defective eyesight named Lillian Pargeter has consulted him, by mistake, about the abduction of her brother, a thirty-five-year-old physicist employed by the government in research. A double has been substituted in his place who goes to his of-fice at the regular times. Lillian detects the substitution only by the calluses on his right hand. The imposter is able to mimic her brother's gait, speech, and appearance but not his left-handedness.

Pons consults his reference book on physics and studies the scientist's papers assiduously. After an entire night's concentration he concludes that the formulae are Rudberg numbers which refer to the radiation of heat and light, and he speculates that Pargeter has discovered the law of the fissionability of the atom. He puts together the information he has gotten from the sister, that their social life is quite constricted because her brother insists on boring everyone with his theories, since no one at work takes him seriously, with the fact that one of the people he had recently expatiated to is a close associate of the German ambassador, who is a friend of an espionage agent, von Grafenstein.

Pons summons Alfred Peake, who is head of a gang of boys, the Praed Street Irregulars, who will do anything for a guinea. Pons gives them money to buy Halloween costumes and instructs them to storm into Grafenstein's house as if they were trick-or-treating. They are to search through the mansion until they find the scientist, and Pons gives them a photograph so they will recognize him. Just as he suspected, the physicist's face has been bandaged and he has been confined to bed. The twenty boys manage to get him to the waiting limousine. Pargeter is sent to America, and his double is charged with giving information to foreign agents and put under detention pending trial. Subsequent events prove that the Americans were not as skeptical as the British about Pargeter's radical theories. Not only is the plot line of this story elegantly maneuvered, with an extraordinary amount of highly technical information used in its solution, but also the minor characters, such as the landlady and the boys in the street gang, are amusingly handled. Everything falls perfectly into place, like a masterly chess game without a single wasted move.

"THE ADVENTURE OF THE REMARKABLE WORM"

"The Adventure of the Remarkable Worm" turns on a cryptic postcard and an etymological specimen. It begins on a summer afternoon in the 1930's as a heavy woman in a housedress and a shawl with a florid face and a provincial accent enters, quite agitated. Her employer is an expatriate American of Spanish background named Idomeno Persano, who lives alone, collects insects, and is always ready to give the neighborhood children a shilling for an interesting bug to add to his collection. A month ago he received a postcard which frightened him so intensely that he has not since left the house. On the front of the card was a sketch of a fat man running away from a dog. That very day he had gotten a worm, mailed inside a matchbox. He became paralyzed as he inspected it; his last words were, "the dog."

As Pons and Parker arrive with the cleaning woman, they see immediately that Mr. Persano, seated in front of a horrible caterpillar in a small box, is dead. Scattered on the table are etymology books in which, apparently, he had been attempting to identify the insect. Pons finds the discarded wrapping and notes that the return address does not coincide with the postmark. The caterpillar is furry and has four horns; from the head uncoils a slender, threadlike tongue; it has four rows of centipede feet; and it is four inches long and two inches wide, with double antennae. Pons deduces that it has been artificially assembled: The head is a sphinx moth, the torso is a centipede, one set of antennae are from a Luna moth, the other from a katydid. He squeezes it with a tweezers and fangs spurting venom shoot forth from the horns. He has noted the gash with a swollen area around it on the victim's finger and deduces that he had been poisoned. Pons excuses himself and returns at midnight to announce that he has found the murderer: "a short, dark-skinned man" who is named Angelo Perro, which is Spanish for *dog*.

Parker is totally bewildered, so Pons shows him a clipping from a Chicago paper announcing that on June 29 Angelo Perro was paroled from Fort Leavenworth; he was convicted in 1914 for transporting and delivering narcotics and served eleven years. Evidence against him had been furnished by a former member of his gang named "Big Id" Persano, who had been given a suspended sentence in return for his assistance in obtaining the conviction. The postcard had been the announcement that "the little dog" was

now free to chase the fat man, and Persano had been corpulent. Pons congratulates his own neat solution in the concluding sentence: "an ingenious little puzzle, Parker, however elementary in final analysis."

"THE ADVENTURE OF THE CAMBERWELL BEAUTY"

"The Adventure of the Camberwell Beauty" is about the disappearance of the lovely ward of a millionaire, an ancient Chinese who lives underground, through dusty, cobwebbed corridors and sliding passages in a slum neighborhood of London. Set on a May evening in the early 1930's shortly after Parker's marriage, the solution takes Pons only a single day. Karah, the beautiful girl who has been abducted, is supposed to have been taken by Baron Corvus, who has one wooden leg. Three sets of footprints at the foot of Corvus's boat landing are shown to Pons. Pons notices that both the peg-legged prints and the woman's high-heeled prints are uneven, deeper on one side than the other. He puts this fact together with the fact that Peters, the Oriental's servant, limps. It does not take him long to establish the fact that Peters and Karah met at Oxford, that Peters's leg was wounded in the war, that their marriage has been opposed by his employer, that Peters himself has hidden his fiancé on a boat and taken her shoes with which to make the fake footprints, and that they plan to elope. He helps the lovers to make their getaway and then reports back to his Asian client, who says contentedly, "So I shall lose both of them. They should be happy with each other."

Derleth creates likable characters with credible motivations; even his villains are not totally unsympathetic. Pons is modeled on Sherlock Holmes down to the last detail, even to his violin-playing and the deerstalker. Derleth's public was apparently as insatiable as Arthur Conan Doyle's; he said in his foreword to *Three Problems for Solar Pons* that his detective "managed to attract a solid core of followers; it is for these devotees of the Sacred Writings that this little book is offered in, as it were, the last bow of the Sherlock Holmes of Praed Street." He went on, however, at his public's insistence, to write a number of encores. Pons took, as a matter of fact, several more "last bows."

OTHER MAJOR WORKS

LONG FICTION: *Murder Stalks the Wakely Family*, 1934; *The Man on All Fours*, 1934; *Sign of Fear*, 1935; *Three Who Died*, 1935; *Still Is the Summer Night*, 1937; *Wind over Wisconsin*, 1938; *Restless Is the River*, 1939; *Sentence Deferred*, 1939; *Bright Journey*, 1940; *The Narracong Riddle*, 1940; *Evening in Spring*, 1941; *Sweet Genevieve*, 1942; *Shadow of Night*, 1943; *The Seven Who Waited*, 1943; *Mischief in the Lane*, 1944; *No Future for Luana*, 1945; *The Shield of the Valiant*, 1945; *Fell Purpose*, 1953; *Death by Design*, 1953; *House on the Mound*, 1958; *The Hills Stand Watch*, 1960; *The Shadow in the Glass*, 1963; *Mr. Fairlie's Final Journey*, 1968; *The Wind Leans West*, 1969.

POETRY: *Hawk on the Wind*, 1938; *Man Track Here*, 1939; *Here on a Darkling Plain*, 1940; *Wind in the Elms*, 1941; *Rind of Earth*, 1942; *Selected Poems*, 1944; *And You, Thoreau!*, 1944; *The Edge of Night*, 1945; *Habitant of Dusk: A Garland for Cassandra*, 1946; *Rendezvous in a Landscape*, 1952; *Psyche*, 1953; *Country Poems*, 1956; *West of Morning*, 1960; *This Wound*, 1962; *Country Places*, 1965; *The Only Place We Live*, 1966; *By Owl Light*, 1967; *Collected Poems, 1937-1967*, 1967; *Caitlin*, 1969; *The Landscape of the Heart*, 1970; *Last Light*, 1978.

NONFICTION: *Still Small Voice: The Biography of Zona Gale*, 1940; *Village Year: A Sac Prairie Journal*, 1941; *The Wisconsin: River of a Thousand Isles*, 1942; *H. P. L.: A Memoir*, 1945; *Writing Fiction*, 1946; *Village Daybook: A Sac Prairie Journal*, 1947; *The Milwaukee Road: Its First Hundred Years*, 1948; *Sauk County: A Centennial History*, 1948; *Some Notes on H. P. Lovecraft*, 1959; *Walden West*, 1961; *Concord Rebel: A Life of Henry David Thoreau*, 1962; *Three Literary Men: A Memoir of Sinclair Lewis, Sherwood Anderson, Edgar Lee Masters*, 1963; *Countryman's Journal*, 1963; *Wisconsin County: A Sac Prairie Journal*, 1965; *Vincennes: Portal to the West*, 1968; *Return to Walden West*, 1970; *Emerson, Our Contemporary*, 1970.

CHILDREN'S LITERATURE: *Oliver, the Wayward Owl*, 1945; *The Captive Island*, 1952; *The Country of the Hawk*, 1952; *Empire of Fur*, 1953; *Land of Gray Gold*, 1954; *Father Marquette and the Great Rivers*, 1955; *Land of Sky-Blue Waters*, 1955; *St. Ignatius and the Company of Jesus*, 1956; *Columbus and the New World*, 1957; *The Moon Tenders*, 1958; *The Mill Creek Irregulars*, 1959; *Wilbur, the Trusting Whippoorwill*, 1959; *The Pinkertons Ride Again*, 1960; *The Ghost of Black Hawk Island*, 1961; *Sweet Land of Michigan*, 1962; *The Tent Show Summer*, 1963; *The Irregulars Strike Again*, 1964; *The House by the River*, 1965; *The Watcher on the Heights*, 1966; *Wisconsin*, 1967; *The Beast in Holgar's Woods*, 1968; *The Prince Goes West*, 1968; *Three Straw Men*, 1970.

BIBLIOGRAPHY

Bishop, Zealia. "A Wisconsin Balzac: A Profile of August Derleth." In *The Curse of Yig*. Sauk City, Wis.: Arkham House, 1953. One of the few articles of any length on the life and career of August Derleth.

Blei, Norbert. "August Derleth: Storyteller of Sac Prairie." *Chicago Tribune Magazine*, August 15, 1971. A very informative and interesting article based on an interview with Derleth. Derleth's opinions and point of view are presented in a sympathetic manner. A good quality short study on Derleth and his work.

Muckian, Michael, and Dan Benson. "One of the State's Great Writers Is Nearly Forgotten." *Milwaukee Journal Sentinel Magazine*, August 13, 1995, p. 8. A biographical sketch, accompanied by an account of efforts by Derleth's children and admirers to reissue his work and create new interest in him; also includes an interview with Derleth's son, who talks about his father's death wish in the last years of his life.

Schroth, Evelyn M. *The Derleth Saga*. Appleton, Wis.: Quintain Press, 1979. The only available study of Derleth's Sac Prairie Saga. The body of work is interpreted from Schroth's personal point of view, but the discussion does give the reader an overview of this important series of works, rated by some as Derleth's finest literary achievement.

Starrett, Vincent. Introduction to *The Adventures of Solar Pons*. London: Robson Books, 1975. A short introduction to Derleth and his Solar Pons creation. Since so little is available on Derleth, students who wish additional information on the Solar Pons series could also consult introductions in these collections: *The Reminiscences of Solar Pons* (1961; an introduction by Anthony Boucher and "A Chronology of Solar Pons," by Robert Patrick), and *The Return of Solar Pons* (1958; introduction by Edgar W. Smith).

Wilson, Alison W. *August Derleth: A Bibliography.* Metuchen, N.J.: Scarecrow Press, 1983. The best full-length source available for information on the life and works of August Derleth and an indispensable volume for sorting through his amazing literary production. The book begins with a preface, an introduction, and a chronology, including interesting details on his activities and literary reputation. Lists and explains briefly all of his works, divided into "Fantasy World" and "Sac Prairie and the Real World." Contains a helpful index by title.

Zell, Fran. "August Derleth's Gus Elker Stories in One Volume." *Milwaukee Journal Sentinel Cue,* November 10, 1996, p. 13. A review of *Country Matters,* arguing that the Gus Elker stories are formulaic and predictable, but that they have preserved a bucolic world and way of life prior to television.

Ruth Rosenberg, updated by Susan L. Piepke

PHILIP K. DICK

Born: Chicago, Illinois; December 16, 1928
Died: Santa Ana, California; March 2, 1982

PRINCIPAL SHORT FICTION
A Handful of Darkness, 1955
The Variable Man and Other Stories, 1957
The Preserving Machine and Other Stories, 1969
The Book of Philip K. Dick, 1973 (British title, *The Turning Wheel and Other Stories,* 1977)
The Best of Philip K. Dick, 1977
The Golden Man, 1980
Robots, Androids, and Mechanical Oddities: The Science Fiction of Philip K. Dick, 1985
I Hope I Shall Arrive Soon, 1985
Beyond Lies the Wub: Volume 1, The Collected Stories of Philip K. Dick, 1987
Second Variety: Volume 2, The Collected Stories of Philip K. Dick, 1987
The Father-Thing: Volume 3, The Collected Stories of Philip K. Dick, 1987
The Days of Perky Pat: Volume 4, The Collected Stories of Philip K. Dick, 1987
The Little Black Box: Volume 5, The Collected Stories of Philip K. Dick, 1987
The Collected Stories of Philip K. Dick, 1987

OTHER LITERARY FORMS
Philip K. Dick's large body of science-fiction stories (he published more than one hundred stories in science-fiction magazines) is matched by his large number of science-fiction novels (he published more than thirty). Most of his short stories were first published in the 1950's, whereas he concentrated on the novel form in the 1960's and 1970's.

ACHIEVEMENTS
Philip K. Dick's work received little critical attention during the early part of his career, but he later became regarded as one of the most important writers of science fiction. Dick concentrates less on the technical aspects of science fiction than he does on character and theme, though his stories and novels do involve such things as time travel, space flight to distant galaxies, robots, and androids. In 1963, his

Philip K. Dick in 1974 (Courtesy of the Philip K. Dick Society)

novel *The Man in the High Castle* (1962) won science-fiction's Hugo Award as the best novel of the year, and in 1975, he was given the John W. Campbell Memorial Award for *Flow My Tears, the Policeman Said* (1974). The Campbell award may seem somewhat ironic, since Dick has written that Campbell, who edited *Astounding*, considered his work "not only worthless but also, as he put it, 'Nuts.'"

BIOGRAPHY

Philip K. Dick was born in Chicago in 1928; his twin sister died at a few months of age. While Dick was still very young, his parents moved to Berkeley, California, and Dick grew up there. Dick's parents were divorced when he was four years old, and he did not see his father for many years after that. Dick attended Berkeley High School and was graduated in 1945. He then went to the University of California at Berkeley but dropped out after a year in order to escape compulsory service in the campus Reserve Officers' Training Corps (ROTC). In 1947, he took a job as a radio announcer for a classical music station in Berkeley, and from 1948 to 1952, he worked as a record store manager.

In 1951, Dick sold his first story, "Roog," to Anthony Boucher at *Fantasy and Science Fiction*, but the story did not appear until 1953. Dick had attended an informal writing class that Boucher taught in Berkeley and considered Boucher a good friend and editorial adviser. Dick's first story to be published was "Beyond Lies the Wub" (1952), in the science-fiction magazine *Planet Stories*.

Most of Dick's short stories were written in the 1950's and 1960's. He published seventy-three short stories between 1952 and 1955, while the last years of his life saw only a few stories. As his output of short stories diminished, however, his production of novels grew, some of them based on material from the stories. For example, his novel *The Penultimate Truth* (1964) draws on the story "The Mold of Yancy." His first published novel was *Solar Lottery* (1955). Many of Dick's novels were published first only in paperback, and it was not until later in his career that his work began to receive critical acclaim.

In 1970, Dick's fourth wife left him, and he plunged into despair. He apparently had experimented with drugs, including LSD, during the 1960's, but he began using them heavily and finally attempted suicide in 1972. He later gave lectures for antidrug organizations. In 1973, Dick married again and had a son in addition to his two daughters from previous marriages. Sometime during this period, he moved from the San Francisco area to Southern California. Dick also had a series of religious experiences in the 1970's, and these influenced his later work, particularly the trilogy consisting of *The Divine Invasion* (1981), *Valis* (1981), and *The Transmigration of Timothy Archer* (1982). Dick's novel *Do Androids Dream of Electric Sheep?* (1968) was made into the film *Blade Runner* in 1982, and his story "We Can Remember It for You Wholesale" was adapted for the screen as *Total Recall* (1990).

Dick died in 1982. After his death, the Philip K. Dick Award was established to recognize the best science-fiction novel published in paperback each year.

ANALYSIS

Philip K. Dick often commented that "the two basic topics which fascinate me are 'What is reality?' and 'What constitutes the authentic human being?'" Science-fiction writers are naturally questioners of reality, since they are constantly asking "What if?" Despite his robots and androids, time travel and spaceships, Dick is not a writer of technical science fiction. He is concerned with human values, and his speculative "what ifs" aim to answer his two main questions, if they can be answered. Reality in Dick's stories is fluid; just when readers think that they understand what is real and what is not, Dick moves the goalposts. Fakes, deceptions, misunderstandings, and differing points of view all cloud the issue of what is real. In each story, the answer might be somewhat different. Ultimately, reality seems to be something defined on personal terms, something slightly different for each individual. Dick's exploration of "what constitutes the authentic human being," however, does yield a fairly clear-cut answer: It is "*caritas* (or *agape*)," unselfish brotherly love or empathy, the "esteem of good people for one another." Many of Dick's stories portray the exact opposite in the form of political or corporate evil, a desire for power, a selfish lack of concern for others. The underlying theme of love, however, is still there, in the little human being who fights for his or her individualism, for his or her own decisions and not someone else's. In some stories *caritas* is overt; in others it either is simply hinted at or is conspicuous in its absence. Despite the importance of Dick's main themes, the stories are not just metaphysical tracts: They are enjoyable, often amusing, sometimes horrifying excursions.

"ROOG"

"Roog," Dick's first story to be accepted for publication, already displays his concern for point of view, his idea that for different people, or in this story, dogs, reality is different. "Roog" concerns a dog that is firmly convinced that the garbagemen who pick up his master's trash each week are taking an offering or sacrifice, which prevents them from taking his master, as they would like to do. In commenting on this story, Dick wrote, "I began to develop the idea that each creature lives in a world somewhat different from all the other creatures and their worlds." Obviously, the dog's reality is different from the master's. To the dog's master, the garbagemen are there to take the trash away, and the dog's howls of warning, despair, and fear are simply annoying and likely to bring on the complaints of neighbors. The dog, however, locked in his view of reality, exemplifies *caritas:* He loves his master, and he unselfishly confronts these fearsome beings each week in order to protect him. The story smoothly switches back and forth from the points of view of the dog, his master, and even the Roogs, as the dog calls the evil garbagemen.

"RAUTAVAARA'S CASE"

One of Dick's last stories, "Rautavaara's Case," published in 1980, also contrasts several opposing points of view, none of which can firmly be said to have the true picture. The narrator of "Rautavaara's Case" is a being from the Proxima Centaurus system who has no body but is "plasma." This entity and his colleagues are monitoring the thoughts of Agneta Rautavaara, whose brain, but not her body, has been kept alive after an accident that killed her co-workers. Rautavaara's thoughts seem to reveal the presence of Christ with those killed and the promise of an afterlife, but is it a "genuine window on the next world" or "a presentation of Rautavaara's own cultural racial propensities?" The plasma beings introduce to Rautavaara's thoughts their version of the Savior, and the result horrifies Rautavaara and the Earth people who are also monitoring her case. Rautavaara's brain is taken off its support and the "window" is closed.

"Rautavaara's Case" twists reality in all sorts of ways. Christians have long believed in an afterlife; this story suggests that what kind of an afterlife a person has depends on that person's beliefs. There is also the possibility that all Rautavaara's thoughts have been hallucinations, that her mind was driven mad by complete sensory deprivation. Is what Rautavaara is experiencing real in any way, or has her mind created some sort of reality for her, since she has no other inputs? Reality differs for the Earth people and the beings from Proxima Centaurus as well: Because they cannot understand each other, cannot even agree on right and wrong, because their points of view are so different, there is no consensual reality—nothing that they agree on as being true. The only thing that is sure is what actions were taken, and there are even disagreements about whether those actions were right.

"PROJECT: EARTH"

Many of Philip Dick's stories meditate directly or obliquely on the existence of God. "Project: Earth" concerns a boy, Tommy, who discovers that the boarder at his friend's house is keeping an enormous file on Earth and has a cage with nine tiny people in it. He steals the people, lets them explore his room, and gets a friend to make clothes for them. When the boarder gets them back, they attack him and escape.

There are a number of biblical references in "Project: Earth" which make the story a comment on the nature of human beings. The boarder tells Tommy about the failure of Project A, which he describes as consisting of beings like humans but with wings. Pride brought Project A down. Project B, men, the boarder considers to have failed because it was influenced by Project A. Project C, the little people, has in turn been influenced by Project B: When the boarder gets the little people back, "They had clothes on. Little suits of clothing. Like the others, a long time before," like Adam and Eve. In this story, there is no confidence in the excellence of God's plan. With each project, it is the creature's individuality and desire for self-determination that make the plan a failure, yet the story seems quietly to approve of this. The boarder seems rather like a scientist who experiments on animals; he does not seem particularly interested in the little people or in men except as they fit into his experiment.

"THE TROUBLE WITH BUBBLES" AND "SMALL TOWN"

In "The Trouble with Bubbles" and "Small Town," human beings themselves are the experimenters. Bubbles are a kind of advanced terrarium: "Sub-atomic worlds, in controlled containers. We start life

going on a sub-atomic world, feed it problems to make it evolve, try to raise it higher and higher." Creating these worlds is a popular pastime, but now people are taking their worlds and wantonly destroying them. The story treats the moral issues of humans playing God. The world builders do not allow the cultures they create to determine their own futures, and the cultures can even be destroyed on a whim. Again, Dick supports humans' desire for free will and questions the excellence of God's will: The story ends with an earthquake that kills thousands of people—an "act of God" analogous to the smashing of bubbles. Is it, however, an act of God, or are the characters in the story a bubble civilization themselves?

"Small Town" also portrays human beings creating their own world. Verne Haskel is a henpecked, cuckolded husband who retreats to his basement to work on his electric train layout. The layout re-creates Haskel's hometown, and, one day, when his life becomes unbearable, he starts to change the town, removing the places that he does not like and adding places that he thinks would make the town better. It is a way of regaining power and control, of creating his own reality. Finally, though, Verne's reality becomes everyone's reality: When his wife and her lover go to the police station to report him missing, assuming that he has somehow disappeared into his substitute reality of the train layout, they find that the whole town has changed in accord with Verne's vision, and they realize that they will soon feel Verne's revenge. In Dick's stories, it is often the downtrodden but persevering little guy who is the hero, who is fighting for individualism and self-determination, but in "Small Town," Haskel wants to determine not only his own life but also everyone else's. He is a wrathful god, punishing those who go against him, desiring total control.

"THE MOLD OF YANCY"

"The Mold of Yancy" also describes an attempt to control a population. Yancy is a father figure created by a group of advertising executives to mold the thoughts and opinions of the population of the moon Callisto. Yancy pronounces on everything from garlic in cooking to war; the purpose of the campaign is to get the citizens of Callisto to accept anything he says—"Yancy does all their thinking for them." One of the advertising executives rebels, however, and tells a representative from Earth the reason behind the campaign: The trading syndicates that operate on Callisto want to expand their territory to Ganymede, which would mean a war. They want the public to accept a war that Yancy will condone. Once the Earth representative, who has been sent to investigate Callisto's drift toward totalitarianism, understands its cause, he calls in the police to arrest the heads of the trading syndicates and develops a plan to have the Yancy campaign start promoting individualistic thought.

"The Mold of Yancy" concerns a manipulation of reality intended to take away a population's individualism. Again, Dick promotes thinking for oneself, making one's own moral judgments. As in many of Dick's stories, here he sees evil in large corporations; in Dick's view, business enterprises are usually looking out for their own good and no one else's. "The Mold of Yancy" is also one of the stories in which the reader can hear Dick speaking out "loud and clear *against* the prevailing hysterias of the times," in Norman Spinrad's words. The story was written in the 1950's, the era of McCarthyism, when anyone who considered questioning the government's policies was suspected of disloyalty to the country. "The Mold of Yancy" is Dick's protest against this kind of thinking.

"SECOND VARIETY"

"Second Variety" also comments on "the prevailing hysterias of the times" in its portrayal of a suicidal end to the Cold War. It is set toward the end of a massive war between United Nations troops (which in this story means the United States and its allies) and the Soviet Union. The end of the war is near because the Americans have devised a kind of robot—a "claw"—that kills soldiers or anyone else not wearing an identification tab. The claws, which are made by automatic machinery below the Earth's surface, have been designed to repair themselves and, most important, to learn. They are, in that sense, alive. When Major Hendricks agrees to meet the Russians on their lines for a conference, he learns that the claws have developed an android—a robot that looks like a human—that pays no attention to the radioactive identification tabs. These robots come in several varieties designed to play on the sympathies of the soldiers: a little boy clutching a teddy bear, a wounded one-legged soldier. The Russians believe that there may be more than only these two types. At the end of the story, Hendricks realizes that the woman he has trusted to go to the moon base and send help back to him is yet another variety of these murderous robots.

Dick commented that in this story "my grand theme—who is human and who only appears (masquerades) as human?—emerges most fully." What defines a human being? Is it the ability to learn, to adapt oneself to the situation? The androids are certainly intelligent. One could say that they are no more murderous than the humans who started the war. Dick suggests, however, that compassion makes the difference; the androids know that they can achieve their aims by appealing to the soldiers' pity. The story also elucidates Dick's antiwar stance: War is an act of suicide.

"THE LITTLE BLACK BOX"

In the afterword to *The Golden Man*, Dick wrote that "The Little Black Box" is "closer to being my credo than any of the other stories here." The story makes Dick's belief in *caritas* explicit in a reworking of the Christ story. The United States and other countries are worried about a new religion sweeping the planet. They treat it as a political movement, believing that it threatens their power. Followers of Wilbur Mercer, the story's Christ figure, are a threat to the political system because they follow different rules: When one of the government's employees becomes a Mercerite, he loses his job after telling them that their persecution of the new religion is morally wrong. Mercerites enter into empathy with their leader by grasping the handles of an "empathy box." They then feel what Mercer feels, suffer what he suffers. It is a voluntary act of caring, and the end of the story makes it clear that the government cannot defeat it.

Dick's two main themes—what is real and what is human—run through virtually every story that he has written. He is never didactic, though; the stories are not boring tracts on his own particular worldview.

Dick's vision is not always a cheerful one: Governments are perfidious, human beings can be evil, corporate greed is rampant. As he has written, however, "I trust . . . that you will not misread me and see dislike and anger only; please reach out to me at the core below that, the core of love." The core of love defines what is real and what is human.

OTHER MAJOR WORKS

LONG FICTION: *Solar Lottery*, 1955 (British title, *World of Chance*, 1956); *The World Jones Made*, 1956; *The Man Who Japed*, 1956; *Eye in the Sky*, 1957; *The Cosmic Puppets*, 1957; *Time out of Joint*, 1959; *Dr. Futurity*, 1960; *Vulcan's Hammer*, 1960; *The Man in the High Castle*, 1962; *The Game-Players of Titan*, 1963; *Martian Time-Slip*, 1964; *Clans of the Alphane Moon*, 1964; *The Penultimate Truth*, 1964; *The Simulacra*, 1964; *The Three Stigmata of Palmer Eldritch*, 1964; *The Simulacra*, 1964; *The Penultimate Truth*, 1964; *Clans of the Alphane Moon*, 1964; *Dr. Bloodmoney: Or, How We Got Along After the Bomb*, 1965; *The Crack in Space (Cantata 140)*, 1966; *Now Wait for Last Year*, 1966; *The Unteleported Man*, 1966 (British title, *Lies, Inc.*, 1984); *Counter-Clock World*, 1967; *The Zap Gun*, 1967; *The Ganymede Takeover*, 1967 (with Ray Nelson); *Do Androids Dream of Electric Sheep?*, 1968 (reissued as *Blade Runner*, 1982); *Ubik*, 1969; *Galactic Pot-Healer*, 1969; *The Philip K. Dick Omnibus*, 1970; *A Maze of Death*, 1970; *Our Friends from Frolix 8*, 1970; *We Can Build You*, 1972; *Flow My Tears, the Policeman Said*, 1974; *Confessions of a Crap Artist*, 1975; *Deus Irae*, 1976 (with Roger Zelazny); *A Scanner Darkly*, 1977; *Valis*, 1981; *The Divine Invasion*, 1981; *The Transmigration of Timothy Archer*, 1982; *The Man Whose Teeth Were All Exactly Alike*, 1984; *Radio Free Albemuth*, 1985; *Humpty Dumpty in Oakland*, 1986; *In Milton Lumky Territory*, 1985; *Puttering About in a Small Land*, 1985; *Mary and the Giant*, 1987; *The Broken Bubble*, 1988.

NONFICTION: *Philip K. Dick: In His Own Words*, 1984; *In Pursuit of Valis: Selections from the Exegesis*, 1991 (Lawrence Sutin, editor); *The Selected Letters of Philip K. Dick*, 1991-1993 (Don Herron, editor); *The Shifting Realities of Philip K. Dick: Selected Literary and Philosophical Writings*, 1995 (Lawrence Sutin, editor).

MISCELLANEOUS: *The Dark Haired Girl*, 1988.

BIBLIOGRAPHY

Aldiss, Brian W., and David Wingrove. *Trillion Year Spree: The History of Science Fiction*. London: Victor Gollancz, 1986. Aldiss's work is useful as an overall survey of themes and writers of science fiction, and he allots several pages to Dick's work. His focus is on Dick's novels, but his comments are useful for looking at the short stories as well.

Dick, Anne R. *Search for Philip K. Dick, 1928-1982: A Memoir and Biography of the Science Fiction Writer*. Lewiston: Edwin Mellen Press, 1995. An important documentation of Dick's life, told in candid detail by his wife.

DiTommaso, Lorenzo. "Redemption in Philip K. Dick's *The Man in the High Castle*." *Science-Fiction Studies* 26 (March, 1999): 91-119. Discusses the role of Christian theology in Dick's fiction, particularly gnostic Christian dualism and fundamental Pauline theology. Discusses *The Man in the High Castle* as an important stage in the development of Dick's thought.

Gillespie, Bruce, ed. *Philip K. Dick: Electric Shepherd*. Melbourne: Norstrilia Press, 1975. This collection of essays on Dick's work includes an article by Dick himself called "The Android and the Human."

Golumbia, David. "Resisting 'The World': Philip K. Dick, Cultural Studies, and Metaphysical Realism." *Science-Fiction Studies* 23 (March, 1996): 83-102. A discussion of reality and appearance and metaphysics and politics in Dick's work and thought; comments on the relationship of his thought to culture studies.

Lee Zoreda, Margaret. "Bakhtin, Blobels and Philip Dick." *Journal of Popular Culture* 28 (Winter, 1994): 55-61. A discussion of the story "Oh, to Be a Blobel" from a Bakhtinian perspective; argues the story demonstrates the complexities in the presence/absence of dialogism. Discusses how the story demonstrates the misery, suffering, and irreversible injury created by the military-capitalist complex.

Science-Fiction Studies 2, no. 1 (March, 1975). This issue of the journal is devoted to the work of Dick and contains essays by writers eminent in the field of science-fiction criticism.

Sutin, Lawrence. *Divine Invasions: A Life of Philip K. Dick*. New York: Harmony Books, 1989. Sutin has written a well-researched biography that includes some discussion of Dick's work.

Suvin, Darko. "Philip K. Dick's Opus: Artifice as Refuge and World View." In *Positions and Presuppositions in Science Fiction*. London: Mac-millan, 1988. Suvin's essay focuses mainly on Dick's novel *The Man in the High Castle*, but many of his observations are useful in examining the short stories.

Umland, Samuel J., ed. *Philip K. Dick: Contemporary Critical Interpretations*. Westport, Conn.: Greenwood Press, 1995. An indispensable collection of essays on Dick's varied body of work. Umland has compiled extremely valuable primary and second bibliographies. Like Umland's introduction, the essays take careful note of the body of critical literature already published on Dick.

Karen M. Cleveland Marwick

CHARLES DICKENS

Born: Portsmouth, England; February 7, 1812
Died: Gad's Hill, near Rochester, England; June 9, 1870

PRINCIPAL SHORT FICTION

Sketches by Boz, 1836
A Christmas Carol, 1843
The Chimes, 1844
The Cricket on the Hearth, 1845
The Battle of Life, 1846
The Haunted Man, 1848
Reprinted Pieces, 1858
The Uncommercial Traveller, 1860
George Silverman's Explanation, 1868
Christmas Stories, 1871

OTHER LITERARY FORMS

Although he wrote stories, essays, and theatricals, Charles Dickens is chiefly remembered for his many novels.

ACHIEVEMENTS

In the nineteenth century, Charles Dickens dominated the literary world like few writers before or since. His career coincided with the first half of the reign of Queen Victoria, before Charles Darwin and Karl Marx had eroded that century's liberal consensus. Although best known for his novels, his shorter works, particularly his Christmas stories, also gained lasting fame; largely because of his influence, fiction became the property of an increasingly democratic and literate society on both sides of the Atlantic Ocean. Dickens mastered the serial novel, producing most of his major works in parts that were published monthly. His exaggerated humor and sentimentality touched a deep chord in the reading public of the day, and his cast of legendary characters is legion. A social commentator of both private and public evils, he criticized his age for the destructive nature of the new factory system in *Hard Times* (1854), the utilitarian philosophy of Jeremy Bentham in *Oliver Twist* (1837-1839), the dehumanizing greed exhibited by Ebenezer Scrooge in *A Christmas Carol*, and legal corruption in *Bleak House* (1852-1853). Not only did Dickens entertain, but also his moral concerns helped shape the public conscience of his own and later times.

BIOGRAPHY

Born into a large, lower-middle-class family whose fortunes were perennially unsettled, Charles Dickens grew up amid the scenes of his novels, in

Charles Dickens (Library of Congress)

America; participated in amateur theatricals; and played the Victorian *paterfamilias* to a large household. However successful Dickens the public man may have seemed, his personal life was often troubled. In 1858, his marriage to Catherine Hogarth, never an entirely compatible union, failed, and he turned to a considerably younger woman, the actress Ellen Ternan, for affection and companionship. In 1870, while working on *The Mystery of Edwin Drood*, which to all appearances would have been the gloomiest of his novels, Dickens suffered a fatal stroke. The one-time apprentice died an eminent Victorian, mourned by the world.

ANALYSIS

Although most readers associate his name with novels rather than short pieces, Charles Dickens began his literary career with short fiction, and he never entirely grew away from it. In *Sketches by Boz*, the collection of his first literary work, readers find sketches and short stories that braid together the realism and fancy that mingle more naturally in *Hard Times, Little Dorrit* (1855-1857), and *Great Expectations* (1860-1861). The sketches, such as "Seven Dials," "The Election for Beadle," and "A Visit to Newgate," offer a subjectively perceived picture of real people, places, and events: As Dickens informs his reader in the last of these three pieces, "We took no notes, made no memoranda, measured none of the yards. . . ." Instead, "We saw the prison, and saw the prisoners, and what we did see, and what we thought, we will tell at once in our own way." Thus, the sketches offer readers reality filtered through a consciousness that a reader of the novels will identify at once as distinctively Dickensian. In contrast, the short stories, such as the melodramatic "A Black Veil," are imitations and read like what they are, an apprentice writer's attempt to purvey the gothic eeriness and jailyard gloom that proved eminently marketable in the 1820's and 1830's.

When the astonishing success of the *Pickwick Papers* (1836-1837) launched Dickens as a novelist, he was still relying heavily on the tactics of short fiction. The adventures of Mr. Pickwick and his friends might almost be seen as a loosely joined series of short sto-

London and various provincial towns in southeastern England. Two traumatic events of his youth, his father's imprisonment for debt and his own humiliating apprenticeship at a shoe-blacking factory, gave Dickens a lifelong sympathy for the poor and a fear of poverty. When the family finances improved, Dickens went to school and eventually became a reporter of court proceedings and parliamentary debates. His superior reporting soon won for him a job with the *Morning Chronicle*. A collection of his journalistic pieces, *Sketches by Boz*, soon gained favorable attention, and the publishers Chapman and Hall engaged him to write an accompaniment for a series of sporting sketches. In his own words, Dickens "thought of Mr. Pickwick," and with this inspired creation won the wide and devoted readership he was not to relinquish throughout his long writing career.

Although he completed fourteen novels and many short pieces, Dickens did not exhaust his great energies in writing. He campaigned actively for social reform; edited journals; traveled widely, frequently, and profitably on public reading tours in England and ries; and Dickens repeatedly interrupts the main action of the novel with "interpolated tales," most of them somber or supernatural such as those found in *Sketches by Boz*. In the *Pickwick Papers*, however, the tales of melancholy, deprivation, and loneliness do more than accommodate the tastes of the audience; they counterpoise the generally cheerful, comfortable, sociable climate of Mr. Pickwick's world.

"QUEER CLIENT"

For example, the story of the "Queer Client," related by an old frequenter of the Inns of Court, connects the worlds of innocence and guilt by showing the naïve Mr. Pickwick how little he knows of the sorrows these ancient legal chambers have witnessed: "the waiting—the hope—the disappointment—the fear—the misery—the poverty." The tale begins in the Marshalsea, where Heyling, a young man cruelly forsaken by his prosperous father and yet more cruelly prosecuted by his father-in-law, has been imprisoned for debt, as Dickens's father had been. In the dark, unwholesome prison, Heyling watches first his infant son and then his wife weaken and die. When, through ironic fate, he inherits the paternal fortune that has been withheld during his father's lifetime, Heyling leaves the prison, but the prison does not leave him. Prematurely aged and consumed from within by a passion for revenge, he devotes all his energies to making his father-in-law pay for his former brutality. Chance brings Heyling to a deserted beach where the old man's son is drowning, and, by withholding aid, Heyling achieves half his revenge. Then, with the help of an attorney "well known as a man of no great nicety in his professional dealings," Heyling gradually buys up the loans his father-in-law has taken out and at last confronts the old man with the same fate his daughter had suffered: "Tonight I consign you to the living death to which you devoted her—a hopeless prison." This vengeance, however, loses some of its sweetness when the victim, hounded beyond endurance, dies on the spot.

The tale of the Queer Client is in a number of ways typical of its author. In the story we see Dickens's characteristic dislike for the legal system, which he repeatedly portrayed as a pernicious and parasitic institution that corrupted lawyers while it ruined cli-

ents, and his indignation at the inhumanity of the prisons, of debtors' prisons in particular. Like so many of Dickens's short pieces, the story of the Queer Client involves improbable if not downright supernatural happenings, and, like the other tales in the *Pickwick Papers*, it serves as a kind of gloss to the comic action in the main plot. Heyling, imprisoned and warped by his imprisonment, both resembles and differs from Pickwick, who is unfairly jailed for breach of promise but does not permit himself the perverse self-indulgence of revenging himself on those who have wronged him. Both the parallels and the contrasts prove significant here. By including the tale of the Queer Client in his novel, Dickens shows that the Pickwickian idyll is precarious—a subtle shift of circumstances could easily swing Mr. Pickwick's plight from comedy to tragedy—but, by making the short tale extraneous to the main plot, he undercuts this very point. Pickwick and Heyling, although they endure the same wrong, inhabit different worlds.

Thus, *Pickwick Papers* contains short tales at least in part because the young Dickens found in them an ingenious if obviously mechanical means of bringing the darker realities into the charmed lives of his characters. With experience he learned to weave darkness more naturally into the texture of the worlds he fashioned; in *Little Dorrit*, written some twenty years after *Pickwick Papers*, he uses the interpolated tale in a more sophisticated way. The caustic Miss Wade's autobiographical manuscript, "The History of a Self-Tormentor," gains a measure of sympathy for a previously unsympathetic character by letting the reader see how the embittered woman views herself and others and hence understand, though not excuse, her actions.

Although Dickens used first-person narration only occasionally in his novels, many of his short pieces are related from this point of view. In the collaborative sequences of tales that make up the special Christmas numbers of *Household Words* (1850-1859) and *All the Year Round* (1859-1870), the comments of individuated narrators such as Charley at the Holly Tree Inn, Dr. Marigold, Mrs. Lirriper, and the Boy at Mugby Junction frame and connect the tales. In many of the independent short pieces, the first-person narration proves yet more important, for it permits Dickens to offer his reader, as he does in "The History of a Self-Tormentor," a glimpse into an unconventional consciousness. Perhaps the most subtle of these psychological experiments, and the piece of short fiction that has most intrigued Dickens's critics, is *George Silverman's Explanation*.

GEORGE SILVERMAN'S EXPLANATION

George Silverman begins his tale as many a storyteller has done: "It happened in this wise," but he breaks off directly, as if unsure whether he has hit on the right words to explain his explanation. He resumes with the same phrase and again pauses, tentative, tongue-tied—a clumsy start, the reader might conclude, but after finishing the narrative he may be more likely to see the opening passage as an artful affectation of artlessness. For once George Silverman launches in earnest into his narrative, he uses language shrewdly and skillfully to gain sympathy and approval for a code of behavior that is more than a little curious.

Born in abject poverty, George is from infancy abused as a "worldly little devil" for desiring and demanding the necessities of life: food, drink, warmth. Bent by his early experience, he goes through life continually trying to demonstrate his unworldliness but continually failing to do so. Convalescing at a farmhouse, the recently orphaned George shrinks away from the young girl who lives there. His motives, as he presents them, are noble—he fears that he will infect young Sylvia with the disease that killed his parents—but his actions make the household consider him sullen and solitary.

Later in his career, George exonerates the pious hypocrite of a guardian who has very clearly swindled him out of his inheritance. His reward is to be denounced as a worldly sinner by the old fraud he has shielded and his whole Evangelical congregation. Having gained a university education, George accepts a meager post as clergyman from the tightfisted Lady Fareway, who shamelessly takes advantage of his unworldliness by making him her unpaid secretary and her daughter's unpaid tutor. Miss Fareway, who turns out to be beautiful, good, and intelligent, comes to love her tutor, who cherishes a secret love for her.

Rather than accept the gift that fortune has presented, however, Silverman high-mindedly contrives to transfer Miss Fareway's love to a "more worthy" object, his student, Mr. Wharton. Silverman, as self-denying as William Makepeace Thackeray's Captain Dobbin or Edmond Rostand's Cyrano, marries the woman he loves to the man he has caused her to love, and, for his disinterestedness, loses his job and his reputation since the vindictive Lady Fareway charges him with accepting a bribe to snare her daughter for Wharton.

On first reading, *George Silverman's Explanation* seems a plausible account. We accept Silverman as what he claims to be, a selfless, unworldly soul victimized by others. It is well to remember, however, that the story we have before us is of Silverman's own telling. When we separate the actual events from the subjective interpretations accorded them by the narrator, Silverman's merits seem less certain. Might not his perennial self-sacrifice be an inverted form of selfishness? In keeping the world at arm's length and in refusing the blessing of love, wealth, and companionship, is not Silverman showing himself to be more concerned with his private code than with his fellow men? Can we admire such a sterile ethic? Ultimately *George Silverman's Explanation* makes very little clear. The narrator's plight is undeniably pathetic, but his true character remains an enigma.

THE CHRISTMAS BOOKS

If Dickens's reasons for writing *George Silverman's Explanation* are uncertain, he left no doubt as to his objectives for his five Christmas books, which appeared between 1843 and 1848. "My purpose," Dickens wrote of these short books, "was, in a whimsical kind of masque which the good humor of the season justified, to waken some loving and forbearing thoughts, never out of season in a Christian land." Christmas as Dickens describes it, with its feasting and dancing, its cozy firesides and frosty landscapes, is more a secular than a religious celebration. The message that his Christmas books convey is likewise a human rather than a divine one: good will to humans.

This recurrent moral is stated at its simplest in a Christmas tale from the *Pickwick Papers*, "The Story of the Goblins Who Stole a Sexton," in which Gabriel Grub, a morose gravedigger who scoffs at humanity, is carried off by the Goblins on Christmas Eve, shown many a scene of mortal joy and sorrow, and thus taught to sympathize with his fellow humans. The most sophisticated rendition of the idea occurs in the last of the Christmas books, *The Haunted Man*, in which Redlaw the chemist, a memory-plagued solitary with much wisdom of the head but little of the heart, gains the power to take away people's remembrances but renounces it when he learns the Christmas lesson that recollection of good and bad experiences alike is what binds humans to humans. However, the best-loved variation on the theme is *A Christmas Carol*, the short piece that is probably Dickens's most widely known work.

A CHRISTMAS CAROL

A Christmas Carol begins, naturally enough, on Christmas Eve, as the miserly misanthrope Ebenezer Scrooge repeatedly demonstrates to his nephew, his poor clerk Bob Crachit, and other holiday-makers that Yuletide cheer is, to him, "humbug." At home in his gloomy chambers, Scrooge is visited by the ghost of his former business partner Jacob Marley, who has been dead seven years to the very day. Encumbered by a chain of cash boxes, padlocks, keys, and purses, Marley explains to Scrooge that he wears a chain he had forged in his own lifetime and that he now walks abroad because in life his soul had never ventured beyond the limits of their counting house. Before departing, Marley urges Scrooge to avoid the same sort of fate and tells him that for his future good he will be haunted by three spirits.

The first of these, the Ghost of Christmas Past, takes Scrooge back to earlier Christmases in his life. The miser's leathery old heart begins to soften as he feels the sadness of being a small boy left behind at school, the conviviality of a holiday dance at old Fezziwig's, where the young Scrooge had been an apprentice, and the shame of being set free by the gentle girl who knew that her suitor's heart had come to have room for but one ideal—"the master-passion, Gain." The lusty Ghost of Christmas Present escorts Scrooge through London and shows him the domestic felicity that Yuletide celebrations confer on humble

households and prosperous ones, on the Crachits and his nephew's family. Finally, the shrouded specter of Christmas Yet To Come presents the future that lies ahead if Scrooge fails to open his heart and mend his ways. The Crachits will grow yet poorer, and their lame Tiny Tim will die; Scrooge himself will pass unlamented from the scene, and the charwoman, the laundress, and the undertaker's man will divide his possessions.

The story ends on Christmas Day, when Scrooge ventures forth a changed man. Having learned to look beyond himself, Scrooge now understands how to keep Christmas. He gives generously of his wealth and himself to his fellow men. This conversion story, a timely one for the smug and prosperous Victorian middle class, has continued to speak to Dickens's readers, who find in *A Christmas Carol* a very clear version of a point that Dickens makes in most of his writings. Perhaps the one great gift that his fiction offers people is the encouragement not to conform to any particular standard to perfect themselves but to savor the diverse spectacle of humanity and to play their own parts in the pageant with compassion and good cheer.

OTHER MAJOR WORKS

LONG FICTION: *Pickwick Papers*, 1836-1837 (originally pb. as *The Posthumous Papers of the Pickwick Club*); *Oliver Twist*, 1837-1839 (originally published as *The Adventures of Oliver Twist*); *Nicholas Nickleby*, 1838-1839 (originally pb. as *The Life and Adventures of Nicholas Nickleby*); *The Old Curiosity Shop*, 1840-1841; *Barnaby Rudge: A Tale of the Riots of '80*, 1841; *Martin Chuzzlewit*, 1843-1844 (originally pb. as *The Life and Adventures of Martin Chuzzlewit*); *Dombey and Son*, 1846-1848 (originally pb. as *Dealings with the Firm of Dombey and Son, Wholesale, Retail, and for Exportation*); *David Copperfield*, 1849-1850 (originally pb. as *The Personal History of David Copperfield*); *Bleak House*, 1852-1853; *Hard Times*, 1854 (originally pb. as *Hard Times for These Times*); *Little Dorrit*, 1855-1857; *A Tale of Two Cities*, 1859; *Great Expectations*, 1860-1861; *Our Mutual Friend*, 1864-1865; *The Mystery of Edwin Drood*, 1870 (unfinished).

PLAYS: *The Strange Gentleman*, pr. 1836; *The Village Coquettes*, pr., pb. 1836; *Mr. Nightingale's Diary*, pr., pb. 1851 (with Mark Lemon); *No Thoroughfare*, pr., pb. 1867 (with Wilkie Collins).

NONFICTION: *American Notes*, 1842; *Pictures from Italy*, 1846.

CHILDREN'S LITERATURE: *A Child's History of England*, 1852-1854; *The Life of Our Lord*, 1934.

EDITED PERIODICALS: *Master Humphrey's Clock*, 1840-1841; *Household Words*, 1850-1859; *All the Year Round*, 1859-1870.

BIBLIOGRAPHY

Ackroyd, Peter. *Dickens*. London: Sinclair-Stevenson, 1990. The author, a major English novelist, writes a biography of Dickens that warrants the characterization of being Dickensian both in its length and in the quality of its portrayal of the nineteenth century writer and his times. In re-creating that past, Ackroyd has produced a brilliant work of historical imagination.

Butterword, R. D. "*A Christmas Carol* and the Masque." *Studies in Short Fiction* 30 (Winter, 1993): 63-69. Discusses how Dickens's famous Christmas story embodies many of the characteristics of the masque tradition. Considers some of the implications of this tradition for the story, such as the foreshortening of character development.

Carey, John. *The Violent Effigy: A Study of Dickens' Imagination*. London: Faber & Faber, 1979. The number of works about Dickens and the various aspects of his career is enormous. Carey, in one insightful Dickens study, focuses on Dickens's fascination with various human oddities as a spur to his artistic inspiration.

Davis, Paul B. *Charles Dickens A to Z: The Essential Reference to His Life and Work*. New York: Facts on File, 1998. An excellent handbook for the student of Dickens.

Erickson, Lee. "The Primitive Keynesianism of Dickens's *A Christmas Carol*." *Studies in the Literary Imagination* 30 (Spring, 1997): 51-66. A Keynesian reading of Dickens's story that shows how Scrooge is an economic hoarder because of his fear of the financial future and his need for complete financial liquidity. Claims that Dickens correctly diagnoses the economic depression of Christmas, 1843.

Ford, George H., and Lauriat Lane, Jr., eds. *The Dickens Critics*. Ithaca, N. Y.: Cornell University Press, 1961. This collection consists of more than thirty essays concerned with various aspects of Dickens's literary life. Represented are notables such as Edgar Allan Poe, Henry James, Anthony Trollope, George Bernard Shaw, T. S. Eliot, Aldous Huxley, George Orwell, Graham Greene, and Edgar Johnson.

Hobsbaum, Philip. *A Reader's Guide to Charles Dickens*. Syracuse, N.Y.: Syracuse University Press, 1998. Part of the Reader's Guide series, this is a good manual for beginning students.

Johnson, Edgar. *Charles Dickens*. 2 vols. New York: Simon & Schuster, 1952. Subtitled "His Tragedy and Triumph," this work was perhaps the first major scholarly biography of Dickens. The author integrates into his study an excellent discussion and analysis of Dickens's writings. It remains a classic.

Kaplan, Fred. *Dickens: A Biography*. New York: William Morrow, 1988. Published a generation later than Edgar Johnson's study of Dickens, Kaplan's biography is more forthright about Dickens's family life and personal qualities, especially his relationship with the actress Ellen Ternan. An interesting and well-written work.

Newton, Ruth, and Naomi Lebowitz. *The Impossible Romance: Dickens, Manzoni, Zola, and James*. Columbia: University of Missouri Press, 1990. Discusses the impact of religious sensibility on literary form and ideology in Dickens's fiction.

Reed, John Robert. *Dickens and Thackeray*. Athens: Ohio University Press, 1995. Discusses how beliefs about punishment and forgiveness affect how Dickens and William Makepeace Thackeray told their stories. Discusses Dickens's major fiction in terms of moral and narrative issues.

Tytler, Graeme. "Dickens's 'The Signalman.'" *The Explicator* 53 (Fall, 1994): 26-29. Argues that the story is about a man suffering from a type of insanity known in the nineteenth century as lypemania or monomania; discusses the symptoms of the signalman.

Wilson, Angus. *The World of Charles Dickens*. New York: *Viking Press*, 1970. The author, an Englishman, has been a professor of literature, has pub-

lished a major work on Rudyard Kipling, and has written several novels. This relatively brief study is enriched by many period illustrations ranging from George Cruikshank to Gustave Doré.

Peter W. Graham, updated by Eugene S. Larson

DENIS DIDEROT

Born: Langres, France; October 5, 1713
Died: Paris, France; July 31, 1784

PRINCIPAL SHORT FICTION

"L'Oiseau blanc," 1748

"Les Deux Amis de Bourbonne," 1773 ("The Two Friends from Bourbonne," 1964)

Supplément au voyage de Bougainville, 1796 (*Supplement to Bougainville's Voyage*, 1926)

"Ceci n'est pas un conte," 1798 ("This Is Not a Story," 1960)

"Madame de la Carlière: Ou, Sur l'inconséquence du jugement public de nos actions particulières," 1798

Rameau's Nephew and Other Works, 1964

OTHER LITERARY FORMS

Denis Diderot was an inveterate experimenter with literary forms, creating new variations on traditional forms in his several novels and plays and inventing wholly new forms for his essays, philosophical discourses, and satirical dialogues. He was a pioneer in the writing of art criticism and was the author of some of the most brilliant personal letters in the French language. He contributed a widely varied group of articles—on scientific, historical, and philosophical subjects—to the *Encyclopédie: Ou, Dictionnaire raisonné des sciences, des arts, et des métiers* (1751-1772; *Encyclopedia*, 1965), of which he was also coeditor. His first publications were translations from English, a language he knew well; and, as a result of his youthful interest in mathemat-

ics, he published early in his career a volume of mathematical studies. He even published a small amount of not very distinguished verse. In general, Diderot tried his hand at just about every literary form then known and invented a few hybrids—especially the ingenious combination of narrative, dialogue, and essay used in *Rameau's Nephew and Other Works*—which had not previously existed.

ACHIEVEMENTS

Critical reactions to Diderot have varied greatly over the years. His contemporaries admired him as a dramatist of sentimental plays and a social critic, who had edited with Jean Le Rond D'Alembert the *Encyclopedia*. When Diderot died in 1784, most people did not know that his contributions to literature were as significant as those of his eminent contemporaries Voltaire and Jean-Jacques Rousseau. With the posthumous publication of his masterpieces, which include his dramatic dialogue *Rameau's Nephew and Other Works*, his novels *La Religieuse* (1796; *The Nun*, 1797) and *Jacques le fataliste et son maître* (1796; *Jacques the Fatalist and His Master*, 1797), and especially his art criticism, readers could finally appreciate his mastery of the art of dialogue, his ability to make people reflect on the complex motivations for their moral choices, the originality of his reflections on painting, and his importance in the evolution of eighteenth century French novels. *The Nun* is a powerful denunciation of the exploitation of women. In this novel, the main character is forced to stay in a convent against her will. In *Jacques the Fatalist and*

His Master, Diderot experimented with many narrative techniques to make readers see from several different perspectives the interconnected themes of freedom and fatalism.

BIOGRAPHY

Denis Diderot's father was not only a reputed craftsman, a maker of cutlery, but also a respected and educated citizen who provided enlightened upbringing for his children. Denis was first educated by the Jesuits in his native Langres, and, when he

Denis Diderot (Library of Congress)

showed precocious abilities, he was sent by his father to study at the Jesuit college in Paris. Moreover, when he developed doubts about his faith, he was permitted to abandon his preparations for the priesthood in favor of the study of law. The law, however, failed to attract young Diderot for long, and he spent the period of his twenties leading a rather bohemian existence, studying on his own, spending time in the cafés where intellectuals gathered, and earning his living by tutoring and literary hack work such as ghostwriting sermons or making translations of technical documents for publishers. After he married at the age

of thirty, he began to write seriously, publishing a set of philosophical reflections and some mathematical papers.

In 1745, at the age of thirty-two, the central turning point in his life occurred: A publisher asked him to make a French translation of the famous encyclopedia of Ephraim Chambers, published in England in 1728. Diderot managed to persuade the publisher to undertake a brand new, much more comprehensive work in place of a mere translation, and, for the next twenty-five years, Diderot's life was centered on the creation of the *Encyclopédie*, the largest single publishing venture of the age. Nevertheless, he found time throughout that period for literary work of his own: novels, plays, essays, and art criticism all appeared at intervals, together with philosophical essays of a materialist and skeptical cast which attracted the dangerous attention of the censors.

For a short time in 1749, Diderot actually found himself imprisoned, because the ideas expressed in his *Lettre sur les aveugles* (1749; *An Essay on Blindness*, 1750) were considered sacrilegious. With the successful conclusion of *L'Encyclopédie*, Diderot, in need of regular income, was rescued by a royal admirer, Catherine of Russia. She generously purchased Diderot's personal library, while allowing him to remain in possession of the books during his lifetime, adding to the purchase price an annual stipend as Diderot's salary for serving as curator of the collection. This arrangement gave Diderot the financial security to devote his last years to the completion of several projects which included the novel *Jacques the Fatalist and His Master*, the small but significant group of short stories, a new play, and several philosophical and historical essays. Much of that work remained unpublished when he died of a coronary thrombosis at the age of seventy.

ANALYSIS

Denis Diderot's first venture into fiction was a mildly spicy fantasy called *Les Bijoux indiscrets* (1748; *The Indiscreet Toys*, 1749), which he published anonymously in 1748 in hope of alleviating his financial problems. At about the same time, and probably for the same pecuniary reason, he wrote his first short story. It was in similar naughty-fantastic vein and was called "L'Oiseau blanc" (the white bird). That story was not published in his lifetime, and it is too superficial and derivative in both content and technique to reveal anything about Diderot's development as a short-story writer. It is only worth mentioning as a reminder that, for Diderot, telling stories was a constant literary impulse and that he made no real distinction between novels and short stories. Indeed, it is notable that, in all of his novel-length fictions and in a number of his personal letters, there are digressive passages in which a complete tale of some kind is told; some of these tales have been detached from their original source and published separately as short stories. Quite a substantial volume could be composed of such digressions and labeled Diderot's short stories, but, in fact, there are only five texts, all composed between 1770 and 1773, which were never intended to be part of anything else and which constitute Diderot's contribution to the art of the short story.

"THE TWO FRIENDS FROM BOURBONNE"

The first of the five, "The Two Friends from Bourbonne," is a tale about the nature of friendship, set in a small town near Diderot's birthplace. In its earliest version, set down in 1769 or 1770, it was a brief exemplary tale intended as a criticism of a story set in America, which idealized friendship by means of an exotic fable about the Iroquois and which was written by a contemporary of his, Jean-Francois, Marquis de Saint-Lambert. Diderot pointedly detailed a case of friendship between two very ordinary people, living simple lives in a familiar setting and in present time, as a contrast to Saint-Lambert's remote fantasy. The early version ended with the death of one of the friends, but eventually an account of what happened thereafter to the other friend was added, together with a sort of epilogue on the poetics of the short story which has made "The Two Friends from Bourbonne" a particularly celebrated and influential text. The story itself is simple and directly told: The two friends are actually cousins, Olivier and Félix, born the same day, in the same house, to two sisters. One sister dies in childbirth, and the two boys are reared together by the other sister, so that their close

relationship is a matter of daily routine, unmarked by self-conscious heroics and constituting a part of their nature. They do everything together and even fall in love at the same time with the same girl. To resolve that problem, Félix withdraws in favor of Olivier and, without quite understanding his own emotions, chooses to leave respectable society and becomes a smuggler. Arrested and on the point of being hanged for his crimes, Félix is rescued in a daring gesture by Olivier and escapes to freedom, although Olivier is mortally wounded in the event. The adventures of Félix, as a hunted criminal after his friend's death, are varied and harrowing, but their constant focus is Félix's unremitting effort to give financial aid to Olivier's widow and children. At the story's conclusion, the narrator informs the reader that Félix is still alive at the time of writing but living in exile, serving in the Prussian military. The narrative style is remarkable for its spareness and rapidity. No physical descriptions of people or of places interrupt the account of events, which is given in short, precise, and generally unadorned sentences. The direct and unemotional style is intended to underline both the drama of the events and their authentic immediacy, based as they are on real events and people known to Diderot.

The famous epilogue on poetics, abruptly intruded into "The Two Friends from Bourbonne" after the narrative concludes, makes two main points: First, if one distinguishes three main types of tale (larger-than-life, wholly fantastic, and historical), then this one belongs to the historical category; and second, the historical type can only succeed if it overcomes the central contradiction of its requirements, which are that it be credibly true-to-life and at the same time emotionally captivating. Diderot suggests that the best means of overcoming this contradiction is for the artist to lard his narrative, at every step, with small circumstantial details which are exactly observed and which therefore blend the note of authenticity into the very texture of the narrator's rhetorical art designed to captivate. This device of the systematic accumulation of realistic details is, indeed, the fundamental technique at work in "The Two Friends from Bourbonne" and accounts for the reader's impression that he is not dealing with a "tale," that is, an invented yarn, but with a faithful account of actual happenings.

"THIS IS NOT A STORY"

The same technique is even more pointedly employed in a story Diderot wrote a short time later about the moral perplexities which occur in the relations between the sexes in our society. This time his very title proclaimed his method: "Ceci n'est pas un conte" ("This Is Not a Story") plays on the double meaning attached to the French word *conte* (both "narrative" and "made-up story") to suggest that the narrative which follows is no invention or lie, but a true story. In fact it is two stories, one describing an apparent instance of the cruel exploitation of a man's love by a woman, the other describing the cruel exploitation of a woman's love by a man; and both stories are based on actual events known to Diderot. Even the names used are not fictitious but the real ones. Diderot's purpose in thus underlining the reality of the stories was to emphasize that the exploitation of each sex by the other is verifiably natural human behavior, however, morally repugnant to some, and that it is not susceptible of rational explanation. Modern laws and mores demand that love, once given, be constant; yet it is unfortunately in human nature that love can be as suddenly and as inexplicably withdrawn as given. Diderot's two stories thus jointly illustrate the lamentable gap between moral principles and true nature. The reader is left, at the narrative's conclusion, not with a confident moral judgment about the relations between the sexes, but with a perplexing moral dilemma.

What is of even greater interest in "This Is Not a Story," however, is the additional contribution it makes to the poetics of the short story. Besides the accumulation of realistic detail, Diderot this time casts the tale in the form of a dialogue in order to attain even greater authenticity, for, as the author notes in his opening paragraph, when one tells any story, it is always *to* an audience of at least one, and that audience will normally react, interrupt, comment, or question, rather than simply listen in silence. To reproduce the storytelling situation truthfully, Diderot has equipped "This Is Not a Story" with both a narrator and an interlocutor, and the narrative unfolds from the dialogue between the two. The dialogue device adds more than realism to a short story, as Diderot well knew from having used it in other kinds of writing: It also adds a note of dramatic tension to the narrative, allows for the creation of a distinctive "voice" for both narrator and interlocutor, and, above all, permits the presentation of more than one perspective on what the narrative may signify. This last advantage was particularly dear to Diderot because he was not given, by temperament, to preaching a personal point of view but used fiction to render the complex and unresolvable moral ambiguity he saw everywhere in the world, and for that purpose dialogue was admirably suited.

Logically enough, the three other texts of that period (1770-1773) which belong in the category of the short story are all composed in dialogue form. One purports to be the simple transcription of a talk that took place in his father's house in Langres, among the father, his three children (including Denis Diderot himself), and several neighbors who chance to drop in during the conversation. The focus of the conversation is the moral question of whether it is ever permissible to act outside the law even in the interest of greater justice. Several exemplary cases are discussed, the central one being the case cited by the father who, having once been called on to distribute an inheritance, was tempted to destroy an unjust will he discovered in order to be free to distribute the inheritance in a more just fashion. No clear resolution emerges from the dialogue, only the sense of a moral question too complex to admit to a satisfactory single answer.

"MADAME DE LA CARLIÈRE"

Another story, "Madame de la Carlière," uses the dialogue form to recount and comment on the tale of a woman who tries to use the power of public opinion to guarantee her marriage against the disaster of infidelity. Madame de la Carlière does this by exacting from her future husband a pledge of fidelity witnessed by an assembly of all their friends, with the understanding that, if either partner subsequently broke the pledge, that partner would be publicly denounced before the same assembly of witnesses. The idea is that public vows will have greater force than the traditional private religious or legal vows of marriage; but the device fails, the marriage breaks up, Madame de la Carlière dies of a broken heart, and her husband is made into a social pariah by the condemnation of public opinion. As the dialogue makes clear, however, the husband's act of "infidelity" was veiled in ambiguities and had no element of the deliberate and conscious betrayal about it. Madame de la Carlière's extreme reaction can be interpreted as unreasonable, and the severity of the public's judgment of the husband appears quite unjustified. Diderot's point in this story, as in "This Is Not a Story," is that the relations between the sexes are too unpredictable to be controlled by laws, religion, or even public opinion.

SUPPLEMENT TO BOUGAINVILLE'S VOYAGE

A similar conception informs the last of this group of stories in dialogue, the shocking *Supplément au voyage de Bougainville* (*Supplement to Bougainville's Voyage*), in which Diderot invents a "supplement" to Louis-Antoine de Bougainville's 1771 account of his journey around the world, which details the uninhibited sexual mores of the inhabitants of Tahiti. The dialogue treats the "supplement" as the occasion for comparing sexual mores in Europe and in Tahiti and for weighing the relative wisdom and moral values in the two disparate cultures. Again, the only firm conclusion reached is that European laws and religious principles governing the relations between the sexes are well intentioned but culpably blind to the realities of human nature.

Diderot's stories are never models of disciplined and unified composition. In their sometimes erratic movement, sudden changes of direction, tone or perspective, and absence of discernible form, the stories reflect their author's restless and probing mind, curious about everything and certain of nothing. Only occasionally do they offer examples of sustained narrative art, as in "The Two Friends from Bourbonne," the plot of which is recounted in an admirably taut, nervous, and dramatic prose. Mostly they are not stories at all, in any strict sense of the word, but brilliant and animated discourses about moral issues. If they are memorable, it is because each story creates in the reader's mind the vivid and profoundly analyzed image of a major dilemma. Historically, Diderot's stories are important because they laid the theoretical groundwork for the modern short story, which blossomed as a recognized art form a generation after his death.

OTHER MAJOR WORKS

LONG FICTION: *Les Bijoux indiscrets*, 1748 (*The Indiscreet Toys*, 1749); *Jacques le fataliste et son maître*, 1796 (wr. c. 1771; *Jacques the Fatalist and His Master*, 1797); *La Religieuse*, 1796 (*The Nun*, 1797); *Le Neveu de Rameau*, 1821, 1891 (*Rameau's Nephew*, 1897). Although the official complete edition of Diderot's novels is found in the twenty-volume *Œuvres compltes* (1875-1877), edited by Jean Asszat and Maurice Tourneax, they are readily available in the Classiques Garnier, edited by Henri Bnac (1962). An edition of *Œuvres complètes* has been updated under the editorship of Herbert Dieckmann, Jean Fabre, and Jacques Proust (1975-1995). All the novels are available in English in various popular editions.

PLAYS: *Le Fils naturel*, pb. 1757 (*Dorval: Or, The Test of Virtue*, 1767); *Le Père de famille*, pb. 1758 (*The Father of the Family*, 1770; also as *The Family Picture*, 1871); *Est'il bon? Est'il méchant?*, pr. 1781.

NONFICTION: *Pensées philosophiques*, 1746 (English translation, 1819; also as *Philosophical Thoughts*, 1916); *Lettre sur les aveugles*, 1749 (*An Essay on Blindness*, 1750; also as *Letter on the Blind*, 1916); *Notes et commentaires*, 1749; *Lettre sur les sourds et muets*, 1751 (*Letter on the Deaf and Dumb*, 1916); *Pensées sur l'interprétation de la nature*, 1754; *Entretiens sur "Le Fils naturel,"* 1757; *Discours sur la poésie dramatique*, 1758 (English translation of chapters 1-5 in *Dramatic Essays of the Neo-Classical Age*, 1950); *Les Salons*, 1759-1781 (serial; 9 volumes), 1845, 1857 (book); *De la suffisance de la religion naturelle*, 1770 (wr. 1747); *Entretien d'un père avec ses enfants*, 1773 (*A Conversations Between a Father and His Children*, 1964); *Essai sur Sénèque*, 1778 (revised and expanded as *Essai sur les règnes de Claude et Néron*, 1782); *Essais sur la peinture*, 1796 (wr. c. 1765); *Pensées détachées sur la peinture*,

1798; *Plan d'une université pour le gouvernement de Russie*, 1813-1814 (wr. c. 1775-1776); *Paradoxe sur le comédien*, 1830 (wr. 1773; *The Paradox of Acting*, 1883); *La promenade du sceptique*, 1830 (wr. 1747); *Le Rêve de d'Alembert*, 1830 (wr. 1769; *D'Alembert's Dream*, 1927); *Diderot's Early Philosophical Works*, 1916 (includes *Letter on the Blind, Letter on the Deaf and Dumb, Philosophical Thoughts*); *Concerning the Education of a Prince*, 1941 (wr. 1758); *Correspondance*, 1955-1970 (16 volumes); *Œuvres philosophiques*, 1956; *Œuvres esthétiques*, 1959; *Œuvres politiques*, 1962.

TRANSLATIONS: *L'Histoire de Grèce*, 1743 (of Temple Stanyan's *Grecian History*); *Principes de la philosophie morale: Ou, Essai de M. S.*** sur le mérite et la vertu, avec reflexions*, 1745 (of the Earl of Shaftesbury's *An Inquiry Concerning Virtue and Merit*); *Dictionnaire universel de médecine*, 1746-1748 (of Robert James's *A Medical Dictionary*).

EDITED TEXT: *Encyclopédie: Ou, Dictionnaire raisonné des sciences, des arts, et des métiers*, 1751-1772 (17 volumes of text, 11 volumes of plates; partial translation *Selected Essays from the Encyclopedy*, 1772; complete translation, *Encyclopedia*, 1965).

MISCELLANEOUS: *Œuvres*, 1798 (15 volumes); *Œuvres complètes*, 1875-1877 (20 volumes); *Diderot, Interpreter of Nature: Selected Writings*, 1937 (includes short fiction); *Selected Writings*, 1966.

BIBLIOGRAPHY

Creech, James. *Diderot: Thresholds of Representation*. Columbus: Ohio State University Press, 1986. This very clear explanation of Diderot's aesthetics enables readers to appreciate the originality of Diderot's art criticism. Creech also shows how Diderot utilized these theories in order to represent social reality in the fiction.

Cronk, Nicholas. "Reading Expectations: The Narration of Hume in *Jacques le fataliste*." *The Modern Language Review* 91 (April, 1996): 330-341. Argues that David Hume's ideas of causation and determinism influenced Diderot's philosophic voice and narrative structure. Claims that Diderot exemplifies the compatibility of the apparently contradictory positions of "reader-freedom" and "reader-direction."

Fellows, Otis. *Diderot*. Rev. ed. Boston: Twayne, 1989. This volume is an excellent short introduction to the works of Diderot. Fellows describes very well Diderot's evolution as a writer despite the fact that censorship prevented him from publishing his major works during his lifetime. Contains a good annotated bibliography.

France, Peter. *Diderot*. Oxford, England: Oxford University Press, 1983. In this relatively short book, France explains very clearly Diderot's originality as a free thinker, an art critic, and a social critic. France's chapters on *Rameau's Nephew* and Diderot's aesthetics are especially thought-provoking. This book complements very nicely Otis Fellows's book (above) on Diderot.

Furbank, Philip Nicholas. *Diderot: A Critical Biography*. New York: Alfred A. Knopf, 1992. An excellent biography of the philosopher-writer.

Hampshire, Stuart. "The Cast Charmer." *The New York Review of Books* 40 (March 4, 1993): 15-18. Notes that Diderot made natural emotions the center of his morality; Diderot argued that the soul is in constant flux and that any conventional morality entails ambiguities; he did not believe in perfectibility or acknowledge the idea of the good, and he was amused by his own inconsistencies and weaknesses.

Loy, Robert J. *Diderot's Determined Fatalist*. New York: King's Crown Press, 1950. Although this study deals directly with *Jacques the Fatalist and His Master*, Loy argues persuasively that Diderot's experimentation with various narrative techniques in this novel enables readers to understand his originality as a writer of both short and long fiction.

Rex, Walter E. *Diderot's Counterpoints: The Dynamics of Contrariety in His Major Works*. Oxford: Voltaire Foundation, 1998. Examines Diderot's works in relation to his era. Includes bibliographical references and an index.

Wilson, Arthur M. *Diderot*. New York: Oxford University Press, 1972. This essential and well-researched biography of Diderot also includes insightful analyses of his major works. Wilson defines Diderot's importance in the development of the French Enlightenment and the critical reception of his works since the eighteenth century. The notes and bibliography are essential for all Diderot scholars.

Murray Sachs,
updated by Edmund J. Campion

ISAK DINESEN
Baroness Karen Blixen-Finecke

Born: Rungstedlund, Denmark; April 17, 1885
Died: Rungstedlund, Denmark; September 7, 1962

PRINCIPAL SHORT FICTION

Seven Gothic Tales, 1934

Vinter-Eventyr, 1942 (*Winter's Tales*, 1942)

Sidste Fortællinger, 1957 (*Last Tales*, 1957)

Skæbne-Anekdoter, 1958 (*Anecdotes of Destiny*, 1958)

Ehrengard, 1963

Efterladte Fortællinger, 1975 (*Carnival: Entertainments and Posthumous Tales*, 1977)

OTHER LITERARY FORMS

In addition to her numerous tales and stories, Isak Dinesen wrote many letters and essays. She is particularly well known, however, for her narrative *Den afrikanske Farm* (1937; *Out of Africa*, 1937), which tells of her years in Kenya (a sequel was published in 1960). After her death, two volumes of letters, written while in Africa, were published, as were her essays.

ACHIEVEMENTS

Isak Dinesen has a special position in modern literature in that she is a major author in two languages. Although a native of Denmark, she wrote in both English and Danish, creating her tales as original works in both tongues. Popular with the critics as well as the general public, she was appointed an honorary member of the American Academy of Arts and Letters in 1957 and was repeatedly mentioned as a candidate for the Nobel Prize in Literature. Her initial success came in the English-speaking world. With time, however, she became successful also at home, where her magnetic personality and storytelling gifts gradually captivated the public. Aided by the medium of radio, she became a veritable cultural institution in Denmark. Since her death, her critical reputation has steadily grown both at home and abroad, and she has come to be considered a modern master of short fiction.

BIOGRAPHY

Isak Dinesen's life may be divided into three parts, namely her childhood and youth, her time in Africa, and her years as a recognized writer. Her parents came from very different social backgrounds. From her father, Wilhelm Dinesen, a landed proprietor, she inherited a love of adventure, nature, and storytelling. Her mother, in contrast, came from a bourgeois family of merchants and attempted to foster a sense of duty, obligation, and guilt in her three daughters. Karen Christenze (Isak is a pseudonym that she assumed at the beginning of her writing career) was her father's favorite daughter and thereby was able to avoid some of her mother's puritanical manacles. At the age of ten, however, her father's suicide turned her youth into a period of mostly joyless desperation. Early she began writing stories and short plays, for which she had been prepared by an unsystematic private education. She also studied art and traveled abroad with her mother, sisters, and aunt.

The second period in Dinesen's life began in 1914, when she married her first cousin, the Baron Bror Blixen-Finecke, and with him settled down to manage a coffee plantation outside Nairobi, in British East Africa. Her husband infected her with syphilis

Isak Dinesen (Library of Congress)

and proved himself a poor manager of the plantation; the couple was separated in 1921 and divorced four years later. Living in what was then known as Kenya as the manager of a different, and larger, coffee farm, Dinesen cultivated a friendship with Denys Finch Hatton, whom she had met in 1918. A confirmed bachelor, Finch Hatton had no desire to marry Dinesen, which grieved her. Dinesen's African life came to an end in 1931, when the coffee farm had to be sold and Finch died in the crash of his private plane.

Dinesen returned to Denmark in a state of abject poverty. Supported by her family and inspired by the success of a few stories, which years earlier had been published under the pen name Oceola, she set out to create a new life for herself as a writer. Other stories, written during her African sojourn, existed in draft form, and some of these gradually became perfected and included in *Seven Gothic Tales*, the English-language edition of which became both a critical and a popular success. Her autobiographical narrative *Out of Africa* established her as a major presence on the

literary scene both in Denmark and in the English-language world, and subsequent books were also enthusiastically received. An indication of Dinesen's popularity in the United States is the fact that five of her titles were chosen as Book-of-the-Month Club selections. Living at her birthplace, Rungstedlund, north of Copenhagen, Denmark, she gathered her admirers around her and tended her literary reputation.

During most of her adult life, Dinesen was plagued by illness, which was exacerbated by much strenuous travel abroad and the entertainment of numerous guests at home. After a particularly taxing summer, she died at her home on September 7, 1962.

ANALYSIS

Isak Dinesen reacted against the psychological and social realism of contemporary Danish literature and looked back to the Romantic storytellers for inspiration. Like them, she preferred the longer, drawn-out tale to the short story proper, and authorial narration, often with overtly present narrators, is a hallmark of her narratives. Her chosen form therefore often struck her contemporaries as old-fashioned. This was also the case with her thematic concerns, for her stories take place mostly in the century between 1770 and 1870 and express the ethos of a bygone age. She speaks in favor of such aristocratic values as duty, honor, and justice, but she also rejects the Christian dulistic worldview and questions the role of religion and the place of women in contemporary bourgeois society. Above all, however, the role of art in human life constitutes a central theme of her authorship. Through art, a unified vision is possible, and such a monistic perception of reality is, for Dinesen, a primary source of meaning in general and of comfort in difficult times.

"THE MONKEY"

"Aben" ("The Monkey"), a long story from *Seven Gothic Tales*, is a good example of Dinesen's "gothic" or fantastic narratives that also exhibits many of her thematic concerns. Its setting is a noble milieu in northern Germany in the 1830's; its theme is the nature of love. Boris, a young lieutenant in the Prussian Royal Guards, has become involved in a homosexual scandal in the capital and is seeking the aid of his maiden aunt, Cathinka, the Prioress of Cloister Seven, a convent for spinsters of noble blood. In order to escape dishonor and almost certain death, Boris has resolved to marry, thus hoping to lay to rest the rumors of his homosexual involvement with other members of his regiment. His aunt, who is well acquainted with the various noble families of the land, is being asked to select a suitable mate for him. The fantastic element of the story is found in the relationship between the Prioress and her little gray monkey, to which she has a mysterious bond and with which she, from time to time and in accordance with traditional Scandinavian folk belief in shape-shifting, exchanges her identity. The monkey is connected with the idea of love through the love goddess of an ancient Baltic people, the Wends. The goddess looks like a beautiful woman from the front and like a monkey from the back. Through this image, Dinesen argues against the Judeo-Christian distinction between the heteroerotic, which is acceptable to society, and the homoerotic, which is not. Speaking in favor of a monistic outlook on human sexuality, Dinesen, through the similarity between the Wendish love-goddess and the Janus face, problematizes the distinction between normal and abnormal sexuality. The text actually foregrounds the question of how it can be determined which side is the front and which is the back of the goddess, and the implied answer is that no such determination can be made on objective grounds.

There is, nevertheless, a recognition on Dinesen's part that people have to live up to the expectations of their society if they are to get along in life. Boris has certain duties to his family, and, despite his sexual difference from the norm, he is obligated to repress his desires and to force himself to marry. The Prioress, who at this time and in a mysterious way is possessed by aspects of her monkey's personality, chooses as his bride the only daughter of a neighbor, a tall and strong young woman named Athena, whom Boris has known since childhood. Her father welcomes Boris as a suitor and says that he would delight in seeing the young man's features in the faces of his grandchildren. Athena rejects him, however, and states unequivocally that she will never marry; she will not, in other words, yield to her duty to her family. There is a strong implication in the text that Athena is as troubled by her gender role as Boris is by his.

Athena's rejection infuriates the Prioress, who arranges a supper of seduction during which Athena gets drunk. As the girl goes to her room, the Prioress gives Boris an aphrodisiac to help him complete his conquest, and he struggles with Athena, who knocks out two of his teeth. Boris interprets this as a symbolic castration and feels that he has been freed from his obligation to have a normal conjugal relationship with her, should they get married. She has won his battle with traditional sexuality for him, and he therefore triumphantly kisses her with his bloody mouth. The significance of this perverted and ironic image of defloration is not lost on Athena, who, in horror and disgust, loses consciousness. Boris does not touch her further.

The next morning, Athena is told by the Prioress that she is now most likely pregnant and that her only hope of avoiding dishonor is to marry Boris. Together, they then watch as the Prioress, who all along has been in the grip of the personality of the monkey, reasserts her own true self through an intense struggle with the little animal. This astonishing event affects Athena deeply, and she resigns herself to marrying Boris, with the proviso, however, that she is to have dominion in their relationship. Athena's and Boris's union is thus marked by the back side of the love goddess in several ways. Erotically, they are misfits in that they both look on heterosexuality with revulsion. Psychologically and emotionally, their union is a result of a power struggle, touched by the fantastic, rather than a consequence of the usual process of falling in love. Morally, their marriage represents a surrender to the expectations of their families, but it is unlikely that they will do their real duty and have children. Socially, their marriage will also be out of the ordinary, because, in opposition to the patriarchal norm of their time and place, the wife will rule the roost with the consent of her husband. Dinesen thus problematizes one of the fundamental oppositions of human life, namely that between male and female, and offers a critique of both sex roles and Christian dualism.

"THE YOUNG MAN WITH THE CARNATION"

While the stories in Dinesen's *Seven Gothic Tales* touch on the fantastic and frequently present challenges to the readers, those of *Winter's Tales* are more traditional, and therefore also more readily accessible, narratives. Written during the German occupation of Denmark, they are tales for difficult times, in which the possibility of reconciliation and restoration is held dear.

"Den unge mand med nelliken" ("The Young Man with the Carnation"), which introduces the English-language edition of the collection, is a powerful expression of Dinesen's theory of art. Its protagonist, Charlie Despard, is a young English writer who, while born and reared in circumstances of great poverty, has transmuted the pain of his childhood experiences into his first novel, with which he has had tremendous success. Because of his newfound reputation as a writer, he has been able to marry a beautiful young woman from a family of means, and outwardly he has every reason to be happy, which indeed, for a time, he has been. As Dinesen indicates through his name, however, he is now in despair, for he has found that art has failed him. He has nothing more to say as a writer, while at the same time he feels that life holds no joys for him. His is not simply a bad case of writer's block, though, but a case of someone who, because of his erstwhile happiness, has lost his ability to create. The story tells about how Charlie comes to terms with his situation and regains his creativity.

While traveling on the Continent, Charlie and his wife have been separated for a few days but have planned to meet at a hotel in Amsterdam. Charlie arrives last and goes to his wife's room, where he finds her asleep with her door unlocked. Shortly after his arrival, someone else tries to open the door, and, when Charlie gets out of bed to investigate, he finds a young man who, wearing a carnation, is obviously on his way to a rendezvous. Charlie's first reaction is envy, for he believes the young man to have found the happiness which he, himself, is lacking. He then experiences a shock at his wife's infidelity, feels sorry for himself, writes her a brief note, and leaves in search of that happiness which he sensed in the face of the young man with the carnation.

During the next few hours, his mind is in turmoil, and he walks along the waterfront, contemplating his situation. He is then found by some sailors who believe him to be thinking of suicide and who therefore invite him to come with them to a tavern. The men spend the night telling one another stories, and Charlie's tales indicate that he now suffers from no loss of creativity; the experience of the night has given him the pain which is needed by the artist. His regained creativity gives him the strength to face his wife, and he returns to the hotel only to find that he, the previous night, had entered the wrong room. Dinesen's imagery shows that Charlie the fiction writer interprets his experience as a kind of resurrection, which is followed by a dialogue with God. Charlie is told by God that he had been created in order to write and that it is God who wants him to tell his stories and who therefore gave him the pain of the previous evening. He is promised, however, that God will not measure out any more distress to him than what is needed for his art. Charlie accepts the idea that pain is a necessary condition of creativity and realizes that it is the young man with the carnation who is to be pitied, rather than himself.

Dinesen's theory of art is thus basically a romantic one, in which the joys of life are viewed as inferior to art and therefore fundamentally incompatible with creative endeavor. The artist is required to sacrifice normal human happiness for the privilege of being able to commune with the divine, which is the essence of artistic creation.

"SORROW-ACRE"

Another significant aspect of "The Young Man with the Carnation" is the concept of duty, which manifests itself as Charlie's obligation to God to be a writer of stories. In "Sorg-agre" ("Sorrow-Acre"), the next story in *Winter's Tales*, duty is a central motif that contributes much to the story's theme. "Sorrow-Acre" tells about a young Dane named Adam who has spent several years in England, but who, at the beginning of the story, has just returned home to his ancestral estate only to find himself in conflict with his uncle, the ruler of the manor. Adam represents the beginnings of a new social order and serves as the embodiment of the ideas of the French Revolution, while his uncle advocates a traditional, aristocratic view of life. The three intertwined plots of the story are played out against the backdrop of life on this semifeudal Danish country estate in the late 1700's.

The first plot concerns the uncle's dealings with Anne-Marie, the mother of a young man who has been accused of a crime. There is little proof in the case, and the uncle admits that he has no basis for making a judgment about the man's guilt or innocence. When Anne-Marie begs for the freedom of her son, however, he offers her a bargain: If she can cut a certain rye field in the course of one day, her son will receive his freedom. The outward drama of the story concerns Anne-Marie's superhuman attempt at harvesting the field, which is normally three days' work for a man. She succeeds but at the end dies from exhaustion.

The second plot line concerns the relationship between Adam and his uncle. Adam finds his uncle's action barbarous and threatens to leave because of his sense of outrage. The uncle defends himself by referring to the divine principle of arbitrary power, saying that because he is essentially like a god in his relationship to his serflike farm workers, his actions should not be questioned. While the drama in the rye field may seem like a tragedy to most mortals, the unresolved question of the young man's innocence or guilt adds a divinely comic flavor to Anne-Marie's attempt to buy his freedom. A nobleman may approach the divine by accepting and appreciating the comic aspects of human life. The uncle would himself, he says, like nothing better than to be in a position where he might be able to buy himself a son at the cost of his own life, thus ensuring the succession of the family line. He has lost his only son and has recently, in his rather advanced age, married the young lady who was intended to be his son's bride.

The third strand of the plot involves the relationship between Adam and his uncle's young wife. It is very much against Adam's interests that his uncle should receive an heir, for if the uncle were to die childless, Adam would inherit the estate. It has been prophesied by a gypsy, however, that Adam's posterity is to possess the estate, and it is becoming clear to Adam that he has a duty to the family to give his un-

cle a legal heir. The young wife's attitude toward Adam would clearly facilitate such an unspoken arrangement.

All the main characters in this tale thus exemplify the principle of duty, particularly as it concerns the continuation of a family line. Adam recognizes that he has been brought back to Denmark by fate and that he must play his part in the drama of his family. He is reconciled to his uncle, who begs him to stay; the uncle surely knows that Adam is essential to the success of his project. The uncle's young wife knows that she has been brought into the family expressly for the purpose of providing an heir. Anne-Marie, whose death is a powerful reminder of a person's duty to his or her descendants, sets a powerful example of commitment to one's family.

"THE SAILOR-BOY'S TALE"

Dinesen sees a connection between duty and the concept of justice, for it is a paramount duty of human beings to strive to be just. Her idea of justice is clearly expressed in "Skibsdrængens fortælling" ("The Sailor-Boy's Tale"), a rather simple story that is also found in *Winter's Tales*. Like "The Monkey," "The Sailor-Boy's Tale" presupposes that the reader is familiar with folk beliefs related to shape-shifting, the idea that a human being may temporarily take on the form of an animal. The story tells about a young sailor boy named Simon, who, during a storm in the Mediterranean, climbs the mainmast of his ship to free a peregrine falcon that has become caught in the rigging. Before Simon sets it free, the falcon pecks his thumb sufficiently hard to draw blood, and Simon retaliates by hitting it on the head. This incident proves to be significant to Dinesen's portrait of justice and its operation.

Two years later, Simon's ship has come to the herring markets in the town of Bodø in northern Norway, where Simon meets and falls in love with a young girl named Nora. One evening, when he is on his way to a meeting with the girl, he runs into an overly friendly Russian sailor, whose behavior has homosexual overtones. Simon, who does not want to be late for his meeting with the girl, stabs and kills the Russian, after which he is pursued by the dead man's shipmates. While he is hiding in the crowd at a dance, an old pagan Lapp woman named Sunniva shows up, says that Simon is her son, and tells him to come home with her. Sunniva wipes off his bloody knife on her skirt and, while hiding Simon when the Russian sailors come looking for him, cuts her thumb to explain the presence of blood. She then arranges for safe passage for him back to his ship, at which point she reveals that she is the falcon that Simon released during the storm in the Mediterranean. She has rescued him both because she likes him and because of her sense of justice, for he deserves to be paid back for helping her. To completely settle her accounts with him, she then boxes his ear in return for his blow to her head while she was in the shape of the falcon.

Sunniva also explains to Simon that she admires his devotion to the girl Nora and that the females of the earth hold together. Referring to men as their sons, she indicates that the world is really run by women, who are bound together with a matriarchal compact. Sunniva's pagan matriarchy gestures at Dinesen's questioning of both traditional sex roles and the Christian religion.

"The Heroine"

Dinesen's rather gentle critique of Christianity in "The Sailor-Boy's Tale" becomes relentlessly satirical in "Heloise" ("The Heroine"), in which she casts a woman stripper in the role of the Christian savior. A young Englishman named Frederick Lamond, together with a company of French travelers, is caught in a German border town at the time of the Franco-Prussian war. A student of religious philosophy, Frederick is at the time writing a treatise on the doctrine of the Atonement. When the German army marches into town, he and the other stranded travelers are accused of espionage. A famous messianic prophecy from the Book of Isaiah, which is quoted in Frederick's manuscript, is read as a code by the Germans and forms the main proof of their accusation.

One of the travelers is a woman named Heloise, whose rare beauty greatly impresses one of the German officers. Realizing that the accusation of espionage may not have much merit, he offers the travelers a bargain: If Heloise will appear before him in the nude, they will be permitted to continue to France; otherwise, they will be shot. Heloise turns to the

company and leaves the decision in their hands, and they all vote to refuse the German's demand. The officer, who respects the courage of both Heloise and her companions, then decides to let them go after all, and he apologizes to Heloise, whom he terms a heroine, by sending her a big bouquet of roses.

Six years later, Frederick is in Paris to attend some lectures in his field. Entertained by a friend, he is taken to a music hall, where the most beautiful woman in Paris is appearing nude in a show. It turns out that the woman is Heloise, whom Frederick still remembers well. They meet and reminisce after the show, and Heloise explains what in her opinion was at stake in the dramatic incident six years earlier. It was not only the lives of the travelers, she says, which hung in the balance but also their ability to live with their consciences. It would have cost her very little to comply with the German's demand; for her, it would have been a professional matter, not one of conscience. The other travelers, however, would have never gotten over it if Heloise were to have bought their freedom at the cost of exposing her body. Frederick now understands that her heroism did not consist in standing up to the German officer's demands but in looking after the welfare of her companions' souls. Heloise, who through the imagery in the story has been carefully presented as a kind of Christ-figure, now appears, to both Frederick and the reader, as a full-blown savior.

Portraying a stripper as someone who saves people from guilt constitutes a truly ironic comment on traditional Christian religion. Casting a woman in such a position undercuts the traditional conception of women's roles as well. "The Heroine," through its overt questioning of central religious and social norms, therefore becomes one of Dinesen's most radical stories.

"Babette's Feast"

Heloise's parting comment to Frederick is that she wishes that he might have seen her perform six years earlier, when her beauty was at its fullest. Heloise has the temperament of an artist in that art, in her case the beauty of her body, gives meaning to her life. A similar commitment is held by the title character in "Babettes gæstebud" ("Babette's Feast") from *Anec-*

dotes of Destiny, who, like Heloise, is French. Babette is a famous Parisian chef who had to flee her country at the time of the Paris Commune. She finds her way to a small Norwegian fishing village, where she, for the next fourteen years, lives as a maid in the home of two spinsters. These two sisters are the daughters of a minister who founded a pietistic religious society and who, because of his asceticism, rejected his daughters' suitors. Years after his death, his daughters live solely for their father's memory and religious ideals.

Babette regularly plays the French lottery and chances to win ten thousand francs, which she wishes to spend on a French dinner at the centenary of the minister's birth. The various foreign dishes are disconcerting to the guests, who are all members of the minister's sect; only one of them, the former suitor of one of the daughters, is able to appreciate Babette's culinary artistry. When, at the end of the dinner, the two sisters learn that the utterly exhausted Babette has spent all her money on the project, they cannot understand her motivation, but Babette states that she has done it for her own sake: She is an artist who craves excellence in her field of endeavor.

Like Babette, Dinesen placed high demands on herself. She felt a strong sense of duty and loyalty to the artist within her, thus her tales are exquisitely crafted but not numerous. She relentlessly pursued her unitary vision, subtly criticizing those aspects of life which went against the grain of her thought, such as the dualism of received religion and traditional sex roles. Through her authorship she prepared a literary feast that continues to be enjoyed by numerous readers.

OTHER MAJOR WORKS

LONG FICTION: *Gengældelsens Veje*, 1944 (*The Angelic Avengers*, 1946; written under the pseudonym Pierre Andrézel).

NONFICTION: *Den afrikanske Farm*, 1937 (*Out of Africa*, 1937); *Skygger paa Græsset*, 1960 (*Shadows on the Grass*, 1960); *Essays*, 1965; *Breve fra Afrika 1914-1931*, 1978 (*Letters from Africa 1914-1931*, 1981); *Daguerreotypes, and Other Essays*, 1979; *Samlede essays*, 1985.

BIBLIOGRAPHY

Aiken, Susan Hardy. *Isak Dinesen and the Engendering of Narrative*. Chicago: University of Chicago Press, 1990. Offers thoughtful critical interpretation of Dinesen's works. Includes bibliographical references and an index.

Bassoff, Bruce. "Babette Can Cook: Life and Art in Three Stories by Isak Dinesen." *Studies in Short Fiction* 27 (Summer, 1990): 385-389. Discusses the plot elements of desire for transcendence, a fall caused by confrontation with the real world, and new knowledge or resignation in "The Ring," "The Diver," and "Babette's Feast."

Bjørnvig, Thorkild. *The Pact: My Friendship with Isak Dinesen*. Translated from the Danish by Ingvar Schousboe and William Jay Smith. Baton Rouge: Louisiana State University Press, 1983. This short book offers Bjørnvig's account of his friendship with Dinesen, from their first meeting in 1948 to their definitive parting in 1954. Written by an accomplished poet, the volume is interesting in its own right as well as for the insight into Dinesen which it provides.

Donelson, Linda. *Out of Isak Dinesen in Africa: The Untold Story*. Iowa City, Iowa: Coulsong List, 1995. A good, updated biography of Dinesen. Includes bibliographical references and an index.

Hannah, Donald. *"Isak Dinesen" and Karen Blixen: The Mask and the Reality*. London: Putnam and Company, 1971. The biographical sections are particularly valuable in charting the development also of Dinesen's aesthetic, especially Dinesen's emphasis on the nature of story, her masklike impersonality, and the nature of her characters. The second half of the book, devoted to Dinesen's art, focuses on her process of writing and the general characteristics of her stories, and it analyzes several of the most important.

Henriksen, Aage. "The Empty Space Between Art and Church." In *Out of Denmark*, edited by Bodil Warmberg. Copenhagen: Danish Cultural Institute, 1985. Henriksen asserts that the underlying principle of all Dinesen's tales is the discovery that reality is transformed into a dream. Contends that Dinesen's stories are based on the complicated nature of human love.

Johannesson, Eric O. *The World of Isak Dinesen*. Seattle: University of Washington Press, 1961. From the theoretical perspective of the New Criticism, Johannesson offers brief but close analyses of Dinesen's tales, concluding that the art of storytelling is the author's central theme and the basis for her worldview. The book serves as an excellent introduction to Dinesen's work. Contains a good bibliography as well as an index.

Juhl, Marianne, and Bo Hakon Jørgensen. *Diana's Revenge: Two Lines in Isak Dinesen's Authorship*. Translated from the Danish by Anne Born. Odense, Denmark: Odense University Press, 1985. This volume contains two sophisticated scholarly and critical essays of considerable length. Juhl's contribution, "Sex and Consciousness," is informed by feminist theory. Jørgensen, in "The Ways of Art," discusses the relationship between Dinesen's sensuality and her art. Their book, which includes a good bibliography, is particularly strong in its discussion of Dinesen's use of classical symbols.

Langbaum, Robert Woodrow. *The Gayety of Vision: A Study of Isak Dinesen's Art*. New York: Random House, 1964. In an extensive study that will serve as a suitable introduction to Dinesen for the experienced reader, Langbaum places her within the Western literary tradition. A major claim is that, by dissolving the distinction between fact and value, Dinesen is able to achieve a unified vision of the beauty, sadness, and gaiety of life. Good bibliography, index.

Migel, Parmenia. *Titania: The Biography of Isak Dinesen*. New York: Random House, 1967. The work of a writer rather than that of a scholar, Migel's biography truly represents a labor of love. Migel, a friend of Dinesen, promised Dinesen that she would be her biographer once Dinesen had died. The resulting volume is aimed at an audience of Dinesen devotees but will be of interest to others as well. Bibliography, index.

Mullins, Maire. "Home, Community, and the Gift That Gives in Isak Dinesen's 'Babette's Feast.'" *Women's Studies* 23 (1994): 217-228. Argues that the meal Babette prepares is not a gift but a demonstration of her own aesthetic powers. Argues that Babette subverts the phallo-logocentric society in which she finds herself and transforms home and community through her presence.

Rashkin, Esther. "A Recipe for Mourning: Isak Dinesen's 'Babette's Feast.'" *Style* 29 (Fall, 1995): 356-374. Claims the story is a psychoanalytic reflection on the process involved in overcoming an inability to mourn, for which it writes a recipe for transcendence of that inability through the preparation and consumption of food.

Stambaugh, Sara. *The Witch and the Goddess in the Stories of Isak Dinesen: A Feminist Reading*. Ann Arbor: UMI Research Press, 1988. Stambaugh offers a feminist-inspired examination of the portraits of women which are found in Dinesen's texts. The strength of her brief study is the recognition of the centrality of gender for an understanding of Dinesen's work; its weakness is its lack of theoretical sophistication. The book has a complete scholarly apparatus.

Thurman, Judith. *Isak Dinesen: The Life of a Storyteller*. New York: St. Martin's Press, 1982. Thurman's biography constitutes the fullest treatment of Dinesen's life and work in any language. Meticulously researched and highly readable, it provides an account of the writer's life, brief analyses of her works, and extensive discussion of the relationship between her life and works. Addressed to both scholars and an educated nonspecialist audience, it contains scholarly notes, a select bibliography, and a useful index.

Yacobi, Tamar. "Pictorial Models and Narrative Ekphrasis." *Poetics Today* 16 (Winter, 1995): 599-649. Discusses interrelations between pictorial models and narrative ekphrasis in which the two join forces to bring a visual image into literary play. Illustrates interplays between the ekphrastic model and narrativity through the poetics of Dinesen.

Jan Sjåvik

THOMAS M. DISCH

Born: Des Moines, Iowa; February 2, 1940

PRINCIPAL SHORT FICTION

One Hundred and Two H-Bombs, and Other Science Fiction Stories, 1966

Fun with Your New Head, 1968 (also as *Under Compulsion*)

Getting into Death, 1973

The Early Science Fiction Stories of Thomas M. Disch, 1977

The Brave Little Toaster, 1980

Fundamental Disch, 1980

The Man Who Had No Idea, 1982

Ringtime, 1983

Torturing Mr. Amberwell, 1985

The Silver Pillow: A Tale of Witchcraft, 1987 (children's story)

The Brave Little Toaster Goes to Mars, 1988 (children's story)

OTHER LITERARY FORMS

Thomas M. Disch is as versatile as he is prolific, having published, in addition to his short fiction, novels, poetry, and children's books. Among his nonfiction works is *The Dreams Our Stuff Is Made Of: How Science Fiction Conquered the World* (1998). He has written theater criticism, lectured at various universities, and created a computer-interactive novel entitled *Amnesia* (1985). His other novels include *On Wings of Song* (1979) and *The M.D.* (1991), a fable about a boy's use of supernatural powers to accomplish good deeds and punish evil.

ACHIEVEMENTS

Though known primarily as a science-fiction writer, Thomas M. Disch is hard to categorize. He was part of the New Wave science-fiction writers of the 1960's, many of whose works appeared in the English magazine *New Worlds*, under the editorship of Michael Moorcock and might be said to belong to an "absurdist" tradition within science fiction. With three titles included among editor David Pringle's list of the one hundred best science-fiction novels—*Camp Concentration* (1968), *334* (1972), and *On Wings of Song*—Disch is one of the serious writers who have brought science fiction a little of the intellectual respectability long denied works of popular culture. Two stories won Disch the O. Henry Prize, in 1975 and 1979. The novella *The Brave Little Toaster* won nominations for both the Hugo and Nebula Awards in 1980 and won a British Science-Fiction Award in 1981. In 1999 Disch won the Michael J. Braude Award for light verse.

BIOGRAPHY

Thomas Michael Disch was born in Des Moines, Iowa, the son of Felix Henry and Helen (Gilbertson) Disch. He went to Cooper Union and New York University but never graduated. After working in an advertising agency and a bank, he started writing full time in the mid-1960's. His travels in England, Turkey, Italy, and Mexico provided settings for some of his stories. Disch has worked with Charles Naylor, his longtime companion, on various anthologies and the novel *Neighboring Lives* (1981). He also collaborated with John Sladek on *Black Alice* (1968), a thriller about a kidnapping in the South, and a gothic romance published under the pseudonym Cassandra Knye. Disch was a theater critic for *The Nation* from 1987 to 1991 and a theater critic for the *New York Daily News* beginning in 1993. He became artist-in-residence at the College of William and Mary in 1996.

ANALYSIS

Two themes recur frequently in Thomas M. Disch's short fiction and dominate his best work: the desperateness of the battle to establish and sustain a meaningful identity in a hostile and mercurial world, and the uneasy metaphorical relationship between sex and death. The former theme has various manifestations in his work, motivating both sober and nightmarish stories such as "Descending" and "The Asian Shore" and more delicately satirical, sometimes even playful, stories such as "Displaying the Flag" and "The Man Who Had No Idea." The second theme, however, is restricted to the display of a narrower spectrum of ironic unease, characteristic of such stories as "Death and the Single Girl" and "Let Us Quickly Hasten to the Gate of Ivory."

"GETTING INTO DEATH"

Disch's two main themes are merged and presented most explicitly in "Getting into Death," in which a female writer tries to reconcile herself to her impending death from an incurable illness. She reflects on the various roles she has played as wife, mother, and writer while she studies more closely and critically than ever before the daughter and sister who visit her in the hospital. She is also attended in her death-watch by a series of religious officers, having checked all the available categories under the heading "religion" on her admission form. She finds the solace which they offer almost useless, and they refuse to satisfy her curiosity about the strategies which their other charges use in facing their final hours. Now that she is about to die, she finds herself curiously uncertain as to who she is and has been; even as a writer she has been both B. C. Millar, author of rigorous and rather esoteric detective stories, and Cassandra Knye, author of highly popular and emotionally lurid gothic romances.

Cassandra comes to see new significance in both these kinds of literary endeavor. Her detective novels come to be images of a reified world in which death is the central feature of a puzzle to be solved. (She begins work on a new B. C. Millar novel, a murder mystery told from the viewpoint of the corpse.) Her gothics, meanwhile, become parables in which the threat of sexual violation is symbolic of the threat of mortality. Her eventual reconciliation with the idea of death emerges from a strange inversion of this symbology, when she comes to see death in the same terms as sex, as a "medium in which relationships may exist."

"LET US QUICKLY HASTEN TO THE GATE OF IVORY"

The relationship between sex and death is further explored in the story which follows "Getting into Death" in the collection of that name: "Let Us

Thomas M. Disch (©Miriam Berkely)

Quickly Hasten to the Gate of Ivory." In this story a brother and sister unconsciously subject to incestuous desires go in search of their parents' graves and find themselves lost in an infinite cemetery, alone with each other in an ocean of *memento mori*.

"DEATH AND THE SINGLE GIRL"

Death is the ultimate loss of identity, but it is far from being the only threat to the integrity and security of consciousness. In "Death and the Single Girl" the demoralized heroine calls Death on the telephone and asks that he should visit her with his fatal orgasm. Unfortunately, Death can no longer cope with the demands placed upon him by modern America, and he proves to be impotent. After several unsuccessful attempts to arouse him she settles for "the next best thing" and becomes his receptionist and switchboard operator.

"THE ASIAN SHORE"

In "The Asian Shore," perhaps Disch's most powerful story, it is not death but alienation of a fearfully literal kind which threatens the protagonist. He is an American tourist wintering in Turkey who finds himself haunted by a miserable woman and a young starveling, who call out a name when he passes them by. Despite the length of his stay his suitcases remain unpacked, and he cannot tear down the emblems of personality abandoned by the previous occupant of his room. Gradually he allows himself to be spiritually absorbed into his environment, unable to assert himself sufficiently to maintain his own identity against a subtle but relentless pressure. He simply does not have the psychic strength to sustain himself against a new personality that possesses him—a personality whose need to exist is, it seems, far stronger than his own. In the end he is claimed by the alien shore that waits on the far side of the Bosporus and by the woman and her child.

"THE JOYCELIN SHRAGER STORY"

The attempt to discover in life a meaning which it does not possess, and the futility of trying to impose spurious meanings, are the themes of "The Joycelin Shrager Story," in which an aging member of the avant-garde film community becomes infatuated with a girl who is making her awkward and unremarkable existence the subject of an endless, continuing film called *The Dance of Life*. To woo her he praises her endeavor and exerts pressure on his friends and acquaintances to back up his pandering with fake appreciation and applause. At first this is merely a ploy intended to maintain the sexual relationship between them, but he gradually becomes fascinated by the film as he assumes a leading part in it. In the end he has to face a crisis induced by the prospect of a wedding night surrounded by lights and cameras, when his pretenses are tested to destruction. If a genuinely realistic account of everyday existence does not constitute art, and if in the end everyday life cannot bear the strain of such exposure, what justification is there for either the way one lives or the ways in which one tries to transmute experience into art?

"THE MAN WHO HAD NO IDEA"

Disch's later work recovers something of the iconoclastic enthusiasm of his earlier works. "The Man Who Had No Idea," first published in 1978, is set in a magnificently absurd future America in which free speech—even casual conversation—is a privilege that has to be earned. Licenses to communicate must be won, initially, by passing examinations geared to test adolescents for articulateness. Having been provisionally awarded, they must win two endorsements from established talkers in order to be made permanent. The hero of the story is a marginal case whose struggle to win his full license is a difficult one. His conversational skills seem adequate enough, but he is cursed by the fact that he has nothing to say—he simply is not very interesting to talk to. The world would hardly be impoverished if he were condemned to eternal silence, but his own social prestige and self-esteem are entirely bound up with being licensed.

THE BRAVE LITTLE TOASTER *and* THE BRAVE LITTLE TOASTER GOES TO MARS

Disch's short fiction of the 1980's continued in the same relaxed satirical vein as "The Man Who Had No Idea." *The Brave Little Toaster* is a subtle parody which gently extrapolated the anthropomorphic method of moralistic children's animated movies to an absurd extreme. The substitution of household appliances for animals was presumably supposed to highlight the fact that cinema audiences were ridiculously eager to have their responsive buttons pushed, but it proved that the threshold of skepticism was even lower than many people had supposed. This was not the first of Disch's parodies to be so straight-faced and so accurately targeted as to be mistakable for the genuine article, but it eventually proved to be the most successful, finally published in book form in 1986, when it was made into an animated film by Disney, as if it were no more and no less than an earnestly cute heroic fantasy. Disch delightedly sallied forth into even more remote hinterlands of parodic excess in a sequel, *The Brave Little Toaster Goes to Mars*, although a projected third story, *The Brave Little Toaster Splits the Atom*, never materialized.

THE 1990'S

Much of Disch's short fiction of the 1990's reverted to a more caustic vein of satire in which he scathingly lampooned and lambasted various individuals and collectives who excited his ire. "Abduction of Bunny Steiner: Or, A Shameless Lie" (1992) pulls no punches in parodying the best-selling accounts of the alleged abduction by aliens of horror writer Whitley Strieber and his son. Other fashionable targets on which Disch zeroed in during this critical phase included television-based personality cults, which are subjected to mockery in "Celebrity Love" (1990); millenarian cultists joyously looking forward to the end of the world, whose wishes are ironically granted in "A Family of the Post-Apocalypse" (1993); and emotive fundraising campaigns, whose exploitative tactics are spoofed in "The Children's Fund to Save the Dinosaurs: A Charity Appeal" (1997). Such sharply pointed tales serve to underline the fact that Disch gradually moved in the course of his career from being a writer of offbeat fantasies and surreal science fiction to becoming one of the leading Swiftian satirists of the twentieth century's close.

OTHER MAJOR WORKS

LONG FICTION: *The Genocides*, 1965; *Mankind Under the Leash*, 1966 (also as *The Puppies of Terra*, 1978); *The House That Fear Built*, 1966 (with John Sladek, both as Cassandra Knye); *Echo 'Round His Bones*, 1967; *Black Alice*, 1968 (with John Sladek, both as Thom Demijohn); *Camp Concentration*, 1968; *The Prisoner*, 1969; *334*, 1972; *Clara Reeve*, 1975 (as Leonie Hargrave); *On Wings of Song*, 1979; *Neighboring Lives*, 1981 (with Charles Naylor); *The Businessman: A Tale of Terror*, 1984; *Amnesia*, 1985 (computer-interactive novel); *The M.D.*, 1991; *The Priest: A Gothic Romance*, 1994; *The Sub: A Study in Witchcraft*, 1999.

POETRY: *The Right Way to Figure Plumbing*, 1972; *ABCDEFG HIJKLM NOPQRST UVWXYZ*, 1981; *Orders of the Retina*, 1982; *Burn This*, 1982; *Here I Am, There You Are, Where Were We*, 1984; *Dark Verses and Light*, 1991; *The Dark Old House*, 1996.

NONFICTION: *The Castle of Indolence: On Poetry, Poets, and Poetasters*, 1995; *The Dreams Our Stuff Is Made Of: How Science Fiction Conquered the World*, 1998.

CHILDREN'S LITERATURE: *The Tale of Dan De Lion*, 1986.

EDITED TEXTS: *The Ruins of Earth*, 1971; *Bad Moon Rising*, 1975; *The New Improved Sun*, 1975; *New Constellations*, 1976 (with Charles Naylor); *Strangeness*, 1977 (with Naylor).

BIBLIOGRAPHY

Ash, Brian. *The Visual Encyclopedia of Science Fiction*. London: Trewin Copplestone, 1977. Despite its title, this compendium of science-fiction information contains brief essays by well-known science-fiction writers on themes and concepts in the genre. Disch is mentioned several times, though this volume is more useful as a general introduction to science fiction. Illustrations.

Clemons, Walter. "The Joyously Versatile Thomas Disch." *Newsweek* 112 (July 11, 1988): 66-67. A biographical account that claims Disch is one of America's most gifted writers whose work is hard to categorize.

Crowley, John. "Fiction in Review." *The Yale Review* 83 (April, 1995): 134-146. A summary survey of Disch's work in various genres, including his short stories; suggests that Disch was wearying of the constraints of the horror genre.

Delany, Samuel R. *The American Shore: Meditations on a Tale of Science Fiction by Thomas M. Disch*. Elizabethtown, N.Y. : Dragon Press, 1978. The renowned science-fiction author writes about "The Asian Shore."

_____. Introduction to *Fundamental Disch*. New York: Bantam Books, 1980. A master of science fiction introduces his own selection of eighteen Disch stories, with brief commentaries on "Slaves" and "The Asian Shore." This volume also contains several appendices.

Finkle, David. *Publishers Weekly* 238 (April 19, 1991): 48-49. A sketch of Disch's literary career and an informal interview in which Disch talks about his horror fiction and his plans for work in the future.

Stableford, Brian. "Thomas Disch." In *Science Fiction Writers: Critical Studies of the Major Authors from the Early Nineteenth Century to the Present Day*, edited by Richard Bleiler. 2d ed. New York: Charles Scribner's Sons, 1999. An overview of Disch's life and writings, updated from the first edition (1982). Of particular interest are brief selections of Disch's commentaries on science fiction. Bibliography.

Wolfe, Gary K. *The Known and the Unknown: The Iconography of Science Fiction.* Kent, Ohio: The Kent State University Press, 1979. This study explores the images that have developed into the icons of science fiction. The book is divided into three major sections. References to Disch are limited to the novel *334* in the chapter titled "Icon of the City." Supplemented by a preface, an afterword, notes, and an index.

Brian Stableford

STEPHEN DIXON

Born: Brooklyn, New York; June 6, 1936

PRINCIPAL SHORT FICTION

No Relief, 1976

Quite Contrary: The Mary and Newt Story, 1979

Fourteen Stories, 1980

Movies, 1983

Time to Go, 1984

The Play and Other Stories, 1988

Love and Will, 1989

All Gone, 1990

Friends: More Will and Magna Stories, 1990

Moon, 1993

Long Made Short, 1994

The Stories of Stephen Dixon, 1994

Man on Stage: Play Stories, 1996

Sleep: Stories, 1999

OTHER LITERARY FORMS

Stephen Dixon has published the following novels: *Work* (1977), *Too Late* (1978), *Fall and Rise* (1985), *Garbage* (1988), *Frog* (1991), *Interstate* (1995), *Gould: A Novel in Two Novels* (1997), and *Thirty: Pieces of a Novel* (1999).

ACHIEVEMENTS

In 1974-1975, Stephen Dixon received a grant from the National Endowment for the Arts, and in 1977, both an O. Henry Award and a Pushcart Prize. He won an American Academy of Arts and Letters prize in 1983 and was awarded a John Simon Guggenheim Memorial Foundation Fellowship in 1984. In 1986, Dixon won the John Train Humor Prize awarded by *The Paris Review*. His novel/stories *Frog* was a finalist for the National Book Award in 1991 and for the PEN/Faulkner Award in 1992; his novel *Interstate* was a finalist for the National Book Award in 1995. Dixon has had stories appear in *Prize Stories: The O. Henry Awards* and *The Best American Short Stories*.

BIOGRAPHY

Stephen Dixon was born Stephen Ditchik in Brooklyn, New York, on June 6, 1936, the son of a dentist and an interior decorator. After going to public school in Manhattan, where his father set up a dental practice, he attended New York City College and received a B.A. degree in 1958. Following a short stint as a newsman in Washington, D.C., he returned to New York in 1961 to work as a news editor for Columbia Broadcasting System and as an editor for two detective magazines. During 1964-1965, he attended Stanford University on a Wallace Stegner Fellowship and began publishing stories in *The Paris Review*, *The Atlantic Monthly*, and numerous smaller magazines.

In 1979, Dixon began teaching creative writing at New York University's School of Continuing Education, and in the following fall he was hired as an assistant professor at Johns Hopkins University, where he became a professor and the chair of the university's Writing Seminars program. In 1982, he married

Anne Frydman, a teacher of Russian literature, with whom he had two daughters.

ANALYSIS

Stephen Dixon's short fiction is almost always characterized as being "experimental," "fabulous," or "quirky" in the tradition of Franz Kafka and Samuel Beckett. However, although Dixon has experimented with a wide range of narrative devices and fictional techniques, many of his stories, as imaginative and inventive as they may be, largely seem to be just that—bloodless experiments with devices and techniques rather than stories about real human events.

Dixon's favorite technique—what some critics have called "experimental realism"—is to create stories that seem grounded in solid, everyday reality and at the same time completely fantastic in their plots and character configurations. This narrative method was made famous in the early twentieth century by Franz Kafka in such stories as *Die Verwandlung* (1915; *The Metamorphosis*, 1936)—a fiction which seems absolutely realistic in its most minute details once the reader accepts the fantastic initial premise that the central character is a giant dung beetle. The technique is also similar to what has been called Magical Realism as practiced by South American writer Gabriel García Márquez, in which fantastic and fabulous events are described as if they were taking place in a specific real world instead of in the "once-upon-a-time" world of fairy tales or in the purely imaginative world of folktales and parables.

"MAN OF LETTERS"

Many of Dixon's stories are experiments with traditional narrative structures. For example, "Man of Letters" makes use of the epistolary form, in which a man named Newt, who features in a number of Dixon's stories, writes a series of letters to a woman he has been dating. Although he begins the first letter with the sentence, "I don't want to see you anymore," by the time he has verbally examined the relationship and justified his decision by writing a whole stack of letters, he ends by saying, "No matter what I'll be seeing you Friday night." It is as if the very act of

writing has so self-consciously engaged the protagonist that he cannot state his feelings; he is too busy trying to impress instead of saying simply what he wants to express. Many of Dixon's stories convey this sense of becoming bogged down in verbal and narrative cleverness, thus never quite expressing a truly human experience.

"THE SIGNING"

In a number of Dixon's stories, characters try to avoid coming to terms with tragedy. In "The Signing," for example, a man's wife dies, and as he leaves the hospital room, a nurse asks him about arrangements for the body. He tells her to burn it or to give it to science, for he wants only to get away from the hospital as quickly as he can. As the man catches a bus to escape, a security guard follows him to try to get him to sign the necessary papers. He not only refuses to return to the hospital but also throws away the wristwatch his wife gave him, says he is going to let their car rot in the street, and even takes off the clothes she bought for him and throws them out the bus window. By wanting to destroy everything connected with his wife, the protagonist seems both to be expressing a grief that goes beyond ordinary responses and to be rejecting grief by completely obliterating its source. Often characters in Dixon's stories act as if they do not care about the relationships in which they are involved.

"LAST MAY"

A number of male protagonists in Dixon's stories move in and out of relationships in such passive ways that their relationships seem to be tentative and transitory. In "Last May," a character named Bud, another recurring Dixon male protagonist, meets a woman while visiting his dying father in a hospital, where the woman's mother is also a patient. A scene in which the two make love in Bud's father's hospital room is described in the same unfeeling way that Bud's care for his father is described. After the death of the two parents, Bud visits the woman at her home, but he does not feel the same way about her and never calls her again. When she visits and asks for an explanation of his failure to call, he says he has none. In the last sentence of the story, she says, "All right, then that's it, then I'm leaving." With no response from Bud, who somehow cannot continue with the relationship outside the context of hospitals and death, she leaves.

"THE INTRUDER"

Dixon can narrate the most shocking and horrifying events in such a flat, deadpan style that the events become transformed into a kind of surrealistic and highly stylized set of gestures that the reader accepts, only to become appalled by their acceptance. "The Intruder," perhaps the most extreme example of this technique, begins with a man entering his apartment to find his girlfriend being raped by an intruder who is threatening her with a knife. The story describes in graphic detail the intruder's forcing both the woman and the man to engage in sex acts with him. However, it is the stripped-down and matter-of-fact style with which the acts are described that creates the strange, surreal effect of the story. As horrifying as the events are, they seem to take place in a world without emotional response.

FROG

A number of stories, such as "Frog's Nanny," "Frog Dances," "Frog Made Free," "Frog Takes a Swim," and "Frog's Mom," are included in Dixon's 1991 novel entitled *Frog*. Howard, the recurring character in these stories, is more human and vulnerable than earlier Dixon characters, such as Newt and Bud. In "Frog Dances," for example, Howard sees a man dancing with a baby to a slow, tragic movement from a symphony by Gustav Mahler in an apartment window. The man seems so enraptured that Howard thinks he must get married and have a child because he wants to have the same experience. Although, like other Dixon protagonists, Howard seems caught in the trap of transitory relationships, it is a trap that he wishes to escape. The story ends with Howard, after some abortive relationships, getting married, having a baby, and dancing with his baby to Mahler's symphonies.

Poignancy changes to pathos in "Frog Takes a Swim," in which Howard, while on the beach with his daughter, takes a quick swim. When he returns, she has disappeared, and the rest of the story charts his heartbroken search for her. Although Dixon's earlier stories are told in a flat indifferent style, this one is filled with anguish. The story ends with Howard sitting in the snow on the beach where he last saw his

daughter begging her to materialize, crying that he is heartbroken and that he will never ask her where she has been if she will, by some miracle, reappear.

"MAN, WOMAN AND BOY"

"Man, Woman and Boy," chosen for the annual publication *The Best American Short Stories* in 1993, is one of Dixon's most human and affecting stories. It is a straightforward examination of a couple who have reached a point in their relationship in which they are both together and separate at once. Although they care for each other, they are indifferent to each other. Although they still want each other, they repel each other. They love each other but often hiss, "I hate you." It is a situation familiar to many couples, and Dixon tells it in a sensitive and unembellished way. The husband continually says to himself that he loves his wife and goes to bed thinking he cannot wait until she comes to bed so he can hold her. At the same time, there is a sense of loss, loneliness, and hopelessness. The story communicates in a carefully controlled way the complex realization that both love and hate can exist simultaneously and that most male/female relationships exist as just such an inextricable mix of opposite emotions.

OTHER MAJOR WORKS

LONG FICTION: *Work*, 1977; *Too Late*, 1978; *Fall and Rise*, 1985; *Garbage*, 1988; *Frog*, 1991; *Interstate*, 1995; *Gould: A Novel in Two Novels*, 1997; *Thirty: Pieces of a Novel*, 1999.

BIBLIOGRAPHY

Boyd, Greg. "The Story's Stories: A Letter to Stephen Dixon." In *Balzac's Dolls, and Other Essays, Studies, and Literary Sketches*. Dalphne, Ala.: Légèreté Press, 1987. An essay that discusses Dixon's short-fiction themes and techniques in the form of a letter to him; argues that Dixon's fiction is unique for its conversational intimacy and its rhythms of seemingly unmediated thought. Discusses themes and narrative devices in several stories; comments on how his books hold together as unified collections.

Ferguson, William. "Which Version Do You Prefer?" *Los Angeles Times*, September 4, 1994, p. 12. A review of *The Stories of Stephen Dixon*; comments on Dixon's themes of the relations between the sexes, the plight of the individual in a hostile society, the unstable nature of truth. Argues that Dixon's characters reinvent themselves in language that is often more substantial than they are; notes that many of his male characters become compulsive talkers when rejected by women.

Klinkowitz, Jerome. "Experimental Realism." In *Postmodern Fiction*, edited by Larry McCaffery. New York: Greenwood Press, 1986. Comments on Dixon as an example of superrealism, which sees the limitations of its form as positive aids; briefly discusses Dixon's story "Said," which takes the redundant convention of identifying each line of a speaker and makes it a self-apparently opaque sign.

Klinkowitz, Jerome. *The Self-Apparent Word: Fiction as Language/Language as Fiction*. Carbondale: Southern Illinois University Press, 1984. Claims that Dixon is able to take the most familiar narrative conventions and reinvest them with a sense of novelty new to contemporary realism; discusses these tactics in several stories, focusing on such self-reflexive devices as how stories need reshaping and how fictions are generated.

Passaro, Vince. "S.A.S.E." *The New York Times*, Mary 16, 1999, p. 7. A review of *Thirty: Pieces of a Novel* and the collection of stories *Sleep*. Suggests that Dixon's stories are strongly autobiographical and that his strength lies in the quick revelation of a rushing and exhibitionist prose. Discusses Dixon's treatment of sexuality in his stories.

Salzman, Arthur. "To See a World in a Grain of Sand: Expanding Literary Minimalism." *Contemporary Literature* 31 (1990): 423-433. Discusses Dixon as a writer who redefines minimalism as a set of ways of asking questions about the contemporary world; argues that, in Dixon's fiction, what charges otherwise anonymous, menial jobs with interest is language—urban lingoes, inside dope, and coded cryptics.

Charles E. May

HARRIET DOERR

Born: Pasadena, California; April 8, 1910

PRINCIPAL SHORT FICTION

"Edie: A Life," 1989

The Tiger in the Grass: Stories and Other Inventions, 1995

OTHER LITERARY FORMS

Harriet Doerr is best known for her 1984 autobiographical novel *Stones for Ibarra*, about a woman who moves to Mexico with her husband and lives in a small village. It is a book, Doerr has said, about how "memories are like corks left out of bottles. They swell. They no longer fit." She also is the author of a another novel about Mexico, *Consider This, Senora*, published in 1993.

ACHIEVEMENTS

The fact that Harriet Doerr was seventy-five when her first novel *Stones for Ibarra* was published was a source of fascination and even wonder for reviewers and interviewers. However, when the novel won the American Book Award the following year, critics were forced to admit that the most significant thing about Doerr was not her age but her talent. The book was a best-seller and has since become a twentieth century classic. Her novel *Consider This, Senora* also was a national best-seller. Her story "Edie: A Life" was included in *The Best American Short Stories 1989*.

BIOGRAPHY

Harriet Doerr was born in Pasadena, California, in 1910; her grandfather was Henry Edwards Huntington, the railroad tycoon, whose reputation as both a philanthropist and a robber baron would always haunt Doerr. Doerr's father was Howard Huntington, Henry Huntington's only son; she has five brothers and sisters. During her childhood, her grandfather's estate, now the Huntington Library, Art Collections, and Botanical Gardens in San Marino, California, was a playground for her and her brothers and sisters. She also remembers Christmas parties at her Uncle Fred's place in Long Beach, the Bixby Ranch, center of the historic twenty-eight-thousand-acre Rancho Los Alamitos.

Doerr had a tutor when she was a child but entered Polytechnic Elementary School in Pasadena in the fourth grade. She went to Smith College in Northhampton, Massachusetts, in 1927 but returned to Pasadena the following year. She then traveled to Palo Alto, where Albert Doerr, whom she would marry in 1930, was attending Stanford University. Their first child, Mike, was born in 1931, and their daughter Martha was born in 1935. Beginning in the 1930's, Doerr and her husband made several extended trips to Mexico to oversee her husband's family mining business there; much of her fiction derives from the times she lived in Mexico, particularly a year-long sojourn in 1950.

After her husband's death in 1972, on a dare from her children, Doerr went back to school, taking courses at Scripps College and then attending Stanford University on a Wallace Stegner Fellowship, during which time she received encouragement from Stegner and John L'Heureux to write Stones for Ibarra.

ANALYSIS

Called by one reviewer the "mother of spare prose, a patron saint of life's enduring details," Harriet Doerr has published a small body of fiction that has been highly praised for its classically spare style and its ability to evoke the personal past. All of Doerr's fiction is based on her own long life, most of it focusing on the times she and her husband lived in Mexico as the only Americans in a small village.

Doerr's short stories, like all her fiction, are so thoroughly enmeshed with autobiography that the question of whether events she describes actually occurred matters little. Referred to by reviewers as essays, recollections, stories, and sketches, her short fictional pieces in *The Tiger in the Grass*, which she subtitles *Stories and Other Inventions*, derive their power from the unassuming voice of their narrator, who delights in language's ability to stimulate discovery. Doerr's short fiction admirably reflects what she once told an interviewer: that everything and everyone you meet rubs off on you and is never lost. "That's what's eternal," Doerr says, "these little specks of experience in a great, enormous river that has no end."

"EDIE: A LIFE"

Although like many of the short fictions in her collection *The Tiger in the Grass* "Edie: A Life" is highly autobiographical, it is the most popular choice of short-story anthology editors primarily because it has the kind of well-made unity that critics expect of the modern short story. As the title suggests, the story is an account of the life of one person, Edith Fisk, governess to the five half-orphaned children of the Ransom family. However, unlike book-length biographical accounts, this "life" of Edie narrowly focuses on the governess's relationship to the family, a stylistic limitation that, typical of the short story, transforms her into a significant symbolic character rather than a well-rounded realistic individual.

Brought over from England to California after the mother has died during the birth of twins, Edie immediately transforms the grieving family, becoming as much a part of their lives as food and water. In a twelve-year period, while the father brings three different wives into the home, Edie is the "mast" the children cling to in a "squall of stepmothers." While mysterious adult affairs disrupt the house, Edie creates an alternate world of sheltering security.

When Edie is sixty years old and the children have all left, she moves to a beach cottage with a pension for the rest of her life. The story ends in the late 1940's when Edie is dying of cancer and the children imagine the two little girls she once cared for in England, Alice and Anne, living in a tower, still seven and eight years old, writing to express their sorrow at her illness. "Edie: A Life" is an interesting example of how Doerr uses familiar literary conventions and a crystalline prose style to transform mere reality into a magical realm. There is a curious old-fashioned nineteenth century feel to the story, even though it is told in the modern economic style for which Doerr is famous.

Although the story is ostensibly about the "life" of Edie, she is little more in the story than a stable center, a fantasy fulfillment in the fashion of Mary Poppins, an adult who is able to respond to children as if they were adults even as she is willing effortlessly to enter into their childlike experience. The events of this autobiographical recollection may be based on real life, but the story itself is a highly stylized literary convention.

"THE TIGER IN THE GRASS"

The title piece of Doerr's short fiction collection is largely a reminiscence motivated by the fact that the narrator's son, who has lung and brain cancer, has given her a stuffed tiger for her eighty-fifth birthday to remind her to write an account of her life. The tiger motif is further emphasized by her glaucoma doctor, who tells her that peripheral vision is how "we see the tiger in the grass," adding, "It's also how the tiger sees us." These two tiger references provide the structural link for the recollections, which reflect both opportunities for experience as well as the inevitable dangers always lurking in one's life.

The sketch focuses primarily on three different flawless periods of the narrator's life: the summers in the 1930's which she and her husband and two children spent at a beach house, the times she and her husband spent in Mexico (much more detailed in Doerr's two novels), and the time she went back to school in 1975 and took writing classes. The accounts are separated by brief anecdotal paragraphs about her ailing son.

The series of reminiscences ends with Doerr's rumination about the pleasure of writing as a discovery of things she did not know she had lost. Echoing the "tiger in the grass" metaphor that introduced the sketch, Doerr concludes, "Let us celebrate our vision, clear or clouded, central or peripheral." Sidelong she sees the tiger in the grass as half threat and half

friend, accepting the fact that, "We are still in step after all this time, my tiger in the grass and I."

"MEXICO"

The longest section of fictionalized reminiscences in Doerr's short-fiction collection focuses on, as might be expected by those familiar with Doerr's novels, her experiences in Mexico. Although some of these pieces, such as "The Seasons," are brief lyrical descriptions, others are longer narrative accounts. "Sun, Pure Air, and a View," for example, focuses on a widow named Morgan Sloane who comes to live among the dozen exiles in the Mexican town of Santa Felicia. As Morgan tries to deal with her loneliness after the death of her husband, she settles into the rhythmic routine of village life.

When her daughter, who has come for a brief visit, leaves, the Mexican caretaker who has helped her adjust reminds her of the pleasures of a simple life in the words of Doerr's second novel. "Consider this, senora," he says, "On a day like today you can tell from here what kind of ice cream the vendor is selling." With full acceptance of her age and her solitary life, she glances without mercy into her mirror and then crosses to the window to "consider the view."

OTHER MAJOR WORKS

LONG FICTION: *Stones for Ibarra* 1984; *Consider This, Senora*, 1993.

BIBLIOGRAPHY

Doerr, Harriet. "Enough About Age." Interview by Pamela Warrick. *The Los Angeles Times*, August 27, 1993, p. E1. An interview with Doerr on the publication of *Consider This, Senora*. Doerr talks about her decision to get her college degree after her husband's death in 1972 and her experience in the creative writing program at Stanford University. She talks about the importance of memory, saying that no experience one has had is ever lost.

_____. "Harriet Doerr: When All of Life Is Important, the Search for the Right Word Is Endless." Interview by Steve Profitt. *The Los Angeles Times*, December 31, 1999, p. 31. In this interview, Doerr talks about the lessons she learned from her life in Mexico, her matter-of-fact style, the importance of memory in her work, and her attitude toward mortality. Doerr says she sees no harm in the fact that the older one gets the more memory and imagination become the same.

————. Interview by Lisa See. *Publishers Weekly* 240 (August 9, 1993): 420. Doerr discusses her youth, family history, and marriage to Albert Doerr; she talks about how she turned to writing after her husband's death, her love of Mexico, and the differences between her two novels.

Lacy, Robert. "Harriet Doerr Discloses She Has Few Regrets." Review of *The Tiger in the Grass*, by Harriet Doerr. *Minneapolis Star Tribune*, January 18, 1996, p. 16F. Comments on the importance of Mexico to Doerr's work. Argues that "Edie: A Life" is the best story in the collection, for it shows the wealthy being instructed by the poor while Doerr's prose shows wit and keenness of observation.

Reynolds, Susan Salter. "Haunted by Memory." *The Los Angeles Times Magazine*, February 8, 1998, 12. In this extensive article, based on an interview, Reynolds provides a biographical sketch supplemented by Doerr's memories of her childhood. Doerr talks about her nurse Edie Pink, the subject of her best-known story, "Edie," and other autobiographical sources of her work. She explains her use of detail by noting that a great deal comes from a small thing if "you see it in a certain light and you leave yourself open."

————. "Memories of Pleasure and Pain." Review of *The Tiger in the Grass*, by Harriet Doerr. *The Los Angeles Times*, December 15, 1995, p. E4. Focuses on the importance of memory in the stories. Reynolds says Doerr has one of those sly memories that is sharpest and clearest when focusing on life's best times; notes that her memories of childhood are fragmented, but her memories of Mexico are the source of metaphors and connecting tissue in the work.

Silko, Leslie Marmon. "Pablo, Domingo, Richard, and Sara." Review of *Stones for Ibarra*, by Harriet Doerr. *The New York Times Book Review*, January 8, 1984, 8. Silko argues that the village of Ibarra takes over as the central interest in the story and the American couple serve only as a point of departure for the reader. Calls the work a poet's novel and a tribute to the native culture and the basic human impulse to tell a story.

Streitfield, David. "The Strength of Age." *The Washington Post*, September 26, 1993, p. X15. In this interview/review, Streitfield provides biographical background and comments on Doerr's focus on expatriates in Mexico. Doerr says she does not try to understand mysterious things and that what she loves about Mexico is that it is a mysterious country.

Charles E. May

JOSÉ DONOSO

Born: Santiago, Chile; October 5, 1924
Died: Santiago, Chile; December 7, 1996

PRINCIPAL SHORT FICTION

Veraneo y otros cuentos, 1955
Dos cuentos, 1956
El Charlestón, 1960 (*Charleston and Other
    Stories*, 1977)
Los mejores cuentos de José Donoso, 1965
Cuentos, 1971
Tres novelitas burguesas, 1973 (*Sacred Families*,
    1977)
Cuatro para Delfina, 1982
Seis cuentos para ganar, 1985
Taratuta; Naturaleza muerta con cachimba, 1990
    (novellas; *"Taratuta" and "Still Life with
    Pipe,"* 1993)

OTHER LITERARY FORMS

José Donoso's major literary reputation is as a
novelist; among his novels, *El obsceno pájaro de la
noche* (1970; *The Obscene Bird of Night*, 1973)
stands out internationally as his signature masterpiece. In the 1990's he published *Donde van a morir
los elefantes* (1995) and *El mocho* (1997). He has
written a number of autobiographical works, one of
which is the significant *Historia personal del
"boom"* (1972; *The Boom in Spanish American Literature: A Personal History*, 1977), a play based on
one of the novellas in *Cuatro para Delfina*, and a volume of poetry.

ACHIEVEMENTS

Receiving his B.A. at Princeton University with
the aid of a Doherty Foundation Fellowship, José
Donoso went on to win the Santiago Municipal
Short-Story Prize for *Veraneo y otros cuentos*, the
William Faulkner Foundation Prize for his first novel,
Coronación (1957; *Coronation*, 1965), two John Simon Guggenheim Memorial Foundation Fellowships
(1968, 1973), and a Woodrow Wilson Fellowship
(1992). His other awards include the Chile-Italia

Prize for journalism, the National Prize for Literature
(Chile), the Prize for Criticism (Spain), the Mondello
Prize (Italy), the Roger Caillois Prize (France), and,
in 1990, the Grand Cross of Civilian Merit, granted
by Spain's Cabinet of Ministers.

BIOGRAPHY

José Donoso Yañez was born in Santiago, Chile,
on October 5, 1924. He specialized in English during
his early education and majored in English literature
at Princeton University, where he published his first
two short stories, both written in English: "The Blue
Woman" (1950) and "The Poisoned Pastries" (1951).
Returning to Chile, he published "China," his first
short story written in Spanish, in 1954. The seven stories of his prizewinning first volume of short stories,
published at his own expense, include the outstanding
"El Güero" ("The Güero") and "Una señora" ("A
Lady"). During a biennium in Buenos Aires (1958-
1960) he met an artist, also from Chile, María del
Pilar Serrano, whom he married in 1961. His travels
subsequently took him to Mexico, to the University
of Iowa, where he lectured for the Writers' Workshop, to Mallorca, where he and his wife adopted an
infant girl, to Colorado State University for a lecture-
ship terminated by illness, to Spain again in 1973, to
a post at Princeton University in 1975, back to Spain
in 1976, and, finally, home to Chile in 1981.

Literary history identifies Donoso with the "boom"
in Spanish American literature that occurred during
the 1960's and 1970's, comprising such notable writers as Julio Cortázar, Carlos Fuentes, Gabriel García
Márquez, Juan Rulfo, and Mario Vargas Llosa.
Donoso's critical contribution to this movement is his
The Boom in Spanish American Literature.

His last years in Chile, following the global fame
he had received for *The Obscene Bird of Night* and
his other novels, were clouded by political opposition
to his antigovernment writings. Along with many
Spanish American artists, intellectuals, and writers,
he was bitterly opposed to the military overthrow of
President Salvador Allende and the installation of the

dictator Augusto Pinochet. Donoso died on December 7, 1996, at the age of seventy-two.

ANALYSIS

José Donoso, like Marcel Proust, William Faulkner, and the stream-of-consciousness writers, gave literary testament to the belief that ultimate human reality is disclosed not in rational observation, historicity, or scientific proof but in the workings of human emotion and imagination. For Donoso, as for Proust, the reality of an event is not its actual occurrence but the subjective recollection and reexperience of it. This view of reality is shared, in general, by writers of the Spanish American "boom," whose fiction tends to be cyclic, discontinuous, intertextual, and indiscriminately narrated, as opposed to conventionally linear, plot-oriented, and fixedly narrated.

If a story by Donoso starts with conventional narration of sequential and explicable actions, it will eventually challenge the reader with either a narrator who exposes him/herself as androgynous or an undemarcated plurality of narrators and with events that defy rational explication or analysis. In his novels *El lugar sin límites* (1966; *Hell Has No Limits*, 1972) and *The Obscene Bird of Night*, for example, a male narrator experiences life as a woman; in his short stories "The Güero" and "Santelices" a creative imagination vitally exceeds ordinary existence and then fatally exceeds itself: The güero (fair-haired male) follows a sorceress's path of jungle mystery in preference to the normal activities of his European heritage and meets a magical death; Santelices, an office worker, deprived of the pictures that have provided him with a life of fully imagined bestial ambience, feeds his subsequently uncontrolled imagination to the point of leaping to his death from his office window to rescue an imaginary female from an imaginary horde of beasts.

Three characteristic elements of Donoso's fiction are surrealism (his presentation of the superrealism of imagination), existentialism (in his major characters' unrelenting exercise of personal and authentic choice), and a kind of deconstructionist or introverted semiotics (by which language appears to speak about itself).

José Donoso in 1993 (©Layle Silbert)

"A LADY"

One of the shortest of Donoso's short stories is also one of his most typical. "A Lady" seems to be quite straightforward in its simple first-person narration of a man who catches sight of a fiftyish lady, ordinary but not unattractive, and continues to see her around town, always from a distance. His imagination details her way of life and her role in life, until, after her appearances cease, he culls her name from an obituary and attends her funeral. The story has the quality of a Joycean epiphany, except for the narrator's confession of feeling a "special tranquillity" after his walk home from the funeral. The satisfying calm, instead of sadness or sympathy, translates the burden of the story from incidence and coincidence to concerted hunting, finding, and disposing—the result of his perversely creative imagination.

The narrator's first, and perhaps only, proximity to the lady is on a streetcar, where he sees her "knee covered with a green raincoat" next to his knee and then glances at her figure. All that follows is the narrator's construction of a satisfied desire to destroy a female, the psychological transference having resulted, possibly, from either hatred of his mother or loss of a potential (or actual) mate, or both. The streetcar, the obituary, and the funeral are real; all else is in the narrator's imagination, which is not necessarily false, because it is the narrator's own reality. Such reality, because it inheres in the narrator, constitutes the narrator: It is not self-deception.

GASPARD DE LA NUIT

Orchestration of the various aspects of imagination, as the development and projection of one's individual reality, is perfected in the novella *Gaspard de la nuit*. The novella concludes a trilogy made up of the novella and two short stories, so called because of recurrent themes and characters. In the first of the stories, "Chattanooga Choo-Choo," characters control their lovers and partners by disassembling and reassembling their body parts; the second story concerns the reality of art. Each story begins prosaically and quickly develops into a phantasm.

In this, the third story, Mauricio, a sixteen-year-old reared by his paternal grandmother after his parents' separation, is to spend a trimester with his mother and her current consort. Mauricio's eerily unconventional behavior disturbs and offends his mother. He has no interest in food, sports, record players, motor scooters, rock music, or any of the usual preoccupations of teenagers. He spends his time walking and whistling the three movements—*Ondine* (water nymph), *Le Gibet* (the gallows), and *Scarbo* (scarab, or Punch and Judy clown)—of Maurice Ravel's *Gaspard de la nuit* (1908), the title of which ("casper of the night") is an epithet of Satan. Existentialistically, Mauricio refuses to find his essence in material possessions or bourgeois mentality.

The first three sections of the novella correspond to the three movements of Ravel's composition, which Mauricio whistles flawlessly, following the interpretation of Ravel's friend, the pianist Robert Casadesus. In the fourth section, Mauricio loses his ability to impeccably whistle the composition as he finds his essence by transferring himself into the life and freedom of a raggedly dressed vagrant coeval, the vagrant thereby taking on the life, whistling talent,

and bourgeois accoutrements of Mauricio. Having become Mauricio, the former vagrant delights the mother by eating upon invitation, asking for a motor scooter, and readily agreeing to go on a trip with the mother and her consort. Having become a vagrant, Mauricio, refusing to be identified by those among whom he might remain for too long, walks off "toward other things." The walk away from the constrictions and identity determinations of middle-class life are also strikingly dramatized in his short story "The Walk."

"THE WALK"

Like *Gaspard de la nuit*, "Paseo" ("The Walk") consists of five sections, or movements, in the last two of which occur pronounced changes of situation and personal identity.

In the first section, a mature narrator recalls from his childhood the saddened mien of his father and two uncles. In the next two sections, the narrator describes the household of his widowed father, himself, his two uncles, and his unmarried aunt, Matilde. The members of the household follow a comfortable but inflexible routine, presided over by Aunt Matilde, who keeps house, takes care of clothing, supervises the servants and cooks, and directs the evening billiard games, telling each of her brothers when to shoot. The routine continues even after a sick, runty white dog appears as the narrator and his aunt are returning from church, and his "aunt's and the dog's eyes" meet.

In the concluding sections, the dog becomes part of the household. Matilde nurses it to health, cares for it, and regularly walks it. Her attention shifts from the males of the house to the white dog; and one day she takes the dog for a walk and is never seen again. The narrator supposes that Aunt Matilde "got lost in the city, or in death, or in a place more mysterious than both." The reader familiar with Donoso's fiction may understand that whatever Matilde's course may have been, it was indisputably her own.

"THE CLOSED DOOR"

If there is any heaven or bliss of pure blessedness in human existence, it is to be discovered, outside religious faith, only at the supremely tenuous intersection of dreams and death. The dream is the vital imagination, uninhibited and uncontrolled by physical objectivity, and sleep is a minor mode of death. This is the notion developed by Donoso in "La puerta cerrada" ("The Closed Door"). Sebastián Rengifo spends most of his time sleeping to the consternation of his mother and the irritation of his employer. His dreams take him to a world of light and of ineffable happiness, which an oneiric closed door will not permit him to bring into his waking state. He is so certain that he will one day breach the door that he makes a bet with his employer: If he dies with an expression of bliss on his face, it will be proof of his success, and the employer will provide a proper funeral for him; if not, the employer will inter him in a pauper's grave. The bet continues, even after Sebastián resigns his position to devote himself to sleep. He becomes a vagrant, sleeping at will, and eventually returns to his employer's home, where he dies with such an expression of joy on his face that the employer concedes and provides the proper funeral. The story contains the qualification that one has to be alive in order to dream and the suggestion that the reality of life is fatally explicit in the passage of the unfettered imagination through the door of death.

GREEN ATOM NUMBER FIVE *and* STILL LIFE WITH PIPE

The distance between the falseness of material life and the reality of the dream is measured in these two novellas, published, respectively, in 1973 and 1990, as the distance between art as material possession and art as living imagination. The earlier novella, the second story of the Sacred Families trilogy, shows the disintegration of a married couple whose mass of trendy possessions disappears through theft and mysterious loss. Their concern with the husband's painting *Green Atom Number Five* is not a matter of its inherent value but of its value as a gift to his wife. When the painting disappears, they search for it, taking the painting's material weight designation, "Pound-Ounces 204" (that is, 12¾ pounds), to be the address of its location. Their futile search culminates in their tearing off each other's clothing.

Donoso's last novella, *Still Life with Pipe*, is the obverse of *Green Atom Number Five*. The still life is

a painting which Marcos Ruiz Gallardo comes more and more to experience rather than to understand. The deepening experience is directly proportional to his coming to love Hilda Botto, to whom his incapacity for love had hitherto rendered him indifferent. The fully developed situation incorporates the lovers, as Marcos sees Hilda and himself, into the painting, which is newly entitled *The Gentleman Marcos Ruiz Gallardo and His Lady*. Marcos learns that art, unpossessed by and alien to rational comprehension, substantiates those viewers who see it outside the contexts of monetary value or semantic interpretation.

OTHER MAJOR WORKS

LONG FICTION: *Coronación*, 1957 (*Coronation*, 1965); *Este domingo*, 1966 (*This Sunday*, 1967); *El Lugar sin límites*, 1966 (*Hell Has No Limits*, 1972); *El obsceno pájaro de la noche*, 1970 (*The Obscene Bird of Night*, 1973); *Casa de campo*, 1978 (*A House in the Country*, 1984); *La misteriosa desaparición de la Marquesita de Loria*, 1980; *El jardín de al lado*, 1981 (*The Garden Next Door*, 1992); *La desesperanza*, 1986 (*Curfew*, 1988); *Donde van a morir los elefantes*, 1995; *El mocho*, 1997.

PLAYS: *Sueños de mala muerte*, pb. 1985; *Este domingo: Versión teatral de la novela homónima*, pb. 1990 (with Carlos Cerda).

POETRY: *Poemas de un novelista*, 1981.

NONFICTION: *Historia personal del "boom,"* 1972 (*The Boom in Spanish American Literature: A Personal History*, 1977).

BIBLIOGRAPHY

González Mandri, Flora. *José Donoso's House of Fiction: A Dramatic Construction of Time and Place*. Detroit, Mich.: Wayne State University Press, 1995. Focuses on Donoso's incorporation of masks and houses in his fiction, the latter implicating allusions to Henry James. Although the study is chiefly of the novels, it includes searching attention to the short story "Santelices" and the novella *Taratuta*.

King, Sarah E. *The Magical and the Monstrous: Two Faces of the Child-Figure in the Fiction of Julio*

Cortázar and José Donoso. New York: Garland, 1992. Pages 63-73 examine Donoso's short fiction, including "The Walk." Informative, although the short citations in Spanish are not translated into English, and the "white dog" (*perra blanca*) in "The Walk" is identified as "the human-like yellow dog." Despite the minor obstacles for the non-Spanish reader, this comparative study of two figures of the Spanish American "boom" is valuable.

Magnarelli, Sharon. *Understanding José Donoso*. Columbia, S.C.: University of South Carolina Press, 1993. Thoroughgoing study of Donoso's works. The second chapter is given over to the short stories, with lengthy analyses of "The Walk" ("one of Donoso's most superbly crafted stories") and "Santeliccs," a story leading the writer to consider that artistic imagination may be the original sin. Chapter 7 analyzes the novellas of *Sacred Families*, calling special attention to the semiotics of the trilogy.

McMurray, George R. *José Donoso*. Boston: Twayne, 1979. Very readable and informative account of the life and work of Donoso, especially the chapters entitled "The Short Stories" and "*Sacred Families:* Middle-Class Reality and Fantasy." Unmatched in its depth of insight. McMurray, a prominent expert on Spanish American literature, was personally acquainted with Donoso and gained much firsthand knowledge about the author's work. His analyses of the existentialism, surrealism, and Freudianism that inform the fiction are valid and edifying.

Roy Arthur Swanson

FYODOR DOSTOEVSKI

Born: Moscow, Russia; November 11, 1821
Died: St. Petersburg, Russia; February 9, 1881

PRINCIPAL SHORT FICTION

Sochineniya, 1860 (2 volumes)
Polnoye sobraniye sochineniy, 1865-1870 (4 volumes)
Povesti i rasskazy, 1882
A Christmas Tree and a Wedding, and an Honest Thief, 1917
White Nights and Other Stories, 1918
An Honest Thief and Other Stories, 1919
The Short Novels of Dostoevsky, 1945

OTHER LITERARY FORMS

In addition to short fiction, Fyodor Dostoevski wrote novels, nonfiction, criticism, and *Yevgeniya Grande* (1844), a translation of Honoré de Balzac's novel *Eugénie Grandet* (1833). In his own time, Dostoevski was exceptionally influential, especially through *Dnevnik pisatelya* (1876-1877, 1800-1881; *The Diary of a Writer*, 1949), a series of miscellaneous writings that he published occasionally in St. Petersburg. Dostoevski also wrote a series of essays on Russian literature, some *feuilletons*, and the well-known travelogue "Zimniye zametki o letnikh vpechatleniyakh" (1863; "Winter Notes on Summer Impressions," 1955). His most famous contribution in his own time was his speech in Alexander Pushkin's honor, given on the occasion of the dedication of a monument to Pushkin in 1880.

ACHIEVEMENTS

In the world literature of the nineteenth century, Fyodor Dostoevski has few rivals. Some of his characters have penetrated literary consciousness and produced a new generation in the works of prominent twentieth century authors such as Jean-Paul Sartre and Jorge Luis Borges. He initiated psychological realism, inspiring both Friedrich Wilhelm Nietzsche and Sigmund Freud. His novels are read in translation in twenty-six languages. Dostoevski was originally suppressed in the Soviet Union, only to reemerge as even more influential in the second half of the twentieth century, finding a whole new generation of admirers in his transformed homeland. Even though his style is markedly nineteenth century, Dostoevski still seems quite modern even in the twentieth century.

BIOGRAPHY

Fyodor Mikhailovich Dostoevski was born on November 11, 1821, in a small Moscow public hospital, where his father, Dr. Mikhail Andreevich Dostoevski, worked. He was the second son to the doctor and Marya Fyodorovna (née Nechaeva). One year after his mother's death, in 1837, Fyodor enrolled in the St. Petersburg Academy for Military Engineers. He completed his studies at the academy even after his father had died of a stroke in 1839, thanks to the inheritance of the Dostoevski estate.

Like so many writers' attempts, Dostoevski's first foray into the literary world was through translation—in his case, of Balzac's *Eugénie Grandet*, appearing in print in 1844. His first original work was a novel in letters, *Bednye lyudi* (1846; *Poor Folk*, 1887), which met with immediate success, creating quite a literary sensation even before its publication. The great critic Vissarion Belinsky hailed it with such enthusiasm that the novice writer was propelled into early fame.

Dostoevski followed this initial success with *Dvoynik* (1846; *The Double*, 1917). It was met more coolly, was considered an artistic failure, and was generally unpopular. The failure of *The Double*, as seen in the twentieth century, is quite ironic, since it contains many of the thematic occupations that eventually made Dostoevski famous. His next novel, *Netochka Nezvanova* (1849; English translation, 1920), was fated never to be completed. Most novels then appeared in journals and were serialized; this was the case with all Dostoevski's novels. After the first three installments of *Netochka Nezvanova* (English translation, 1920) appeared in 1849, Dostoevski was arrested for participating in a secret anticzarist society, the Petrashevsky Circle. He and thirty-two of

Fyodor Dostoevski (Library of Congress)

his associates were arrested, imprisoned for eight months, and sentenced to death. At precisely the moment that his comrades were facing the firing squad, the sentence was commuted to hard labor. Dostoevski spent four years in hard labor at Omsk, followed by three years of exile from the capital.

He married Marya Isaeva in 1857, while still in Siberia. He was beginning to suffer from epilepsy, however, and she was also sickly. They returned to St. Petersburg in 1859, and shortly thereafter his works began again to appear in print. Life, however, did not return to normal. In 1864, his brother died, leaving him a second family to support. His wife, too, died the same year. Strapped financially, Dostoevski accepted an advance payment, agreeing to deliver a novel to a publisher that same year—or else forfeit the profits from all his subsequent works. He succeeded in completing *Igrok* (1866; *The Gambler*, 1887), satisfying this publisher thanks to his stenographer, Anna Snitkina, whom he married in 1867. They left Russia for a few years, returning in 1871. The novels that he wrote while abroad established him as an important writer but not as a popular or successful one. In fact, during his life, he met with very little recognition.

The one shining exception to this neglect came at the dedication of a monument to Pushkin, in 1880. Thousands of people greeted his speech enthusiastically. He died only a few months later, in 1881, when an even larger crowd attended his funeral.

ANALYSIS

Fyodor Dostoevski's works fall into two periods that coincide with the time before his imprisonment and following it. The seven-year hiatus in his creative output between 1849 and 1857 corresponds to the four years that he spent in prison and the three subsequent years during which he was banished in Siberia. The first period produced primarily shorter novels and short stories, many of which have never been translated into English; the latter period is represented more by the great novels, the epithet denoting both significance and size, as well as by *Dnevnik pisatelya*, 1876-1877, 1880-1881 (2 volumes, partial translation as *Pages from the Journal of an Author*, 1916; complete translation as *The Diary of a Writer*, 1949), which also contains several new short stories.

In Dostoevski's works, complex structures are created that introduce fundamentally antipodal constructs and that produce, among other effects, a mythologization of the antagonistic elements. Thus, the city, often the St. Petersburg of Dostoevski's present, contrasts with the countryside. The squalor of poverty permeates St. Petersburg with sounds and smells in Dickensian realistic fashion, as opposed to the quaint, provincial quiet of the country. Usually, problems or actual troublemakers come from the city, or, if one leaves the provinces for the city, one may become "infected" with urban discontent and return to plague the countryside. In another prevalent dichotomy, the "man of the forties" (that is, the optimistic believer in the Enlightenment) often clashes with the "man of the sixties" (that is, the atheistic and/or nihilistic revolutionary). This conflict often is positioned generationally, and it is seldom clear whether the representative of either generation should prevail.

Often throughout Dostoevski's works, men of a higher social class, although not necessarily a very high class, interact most significantly with women who are socially inferior, usually powerless or "compromised." The relationship takes on many different attitudes in the various works, but, in almost every case, the woman turns out to be of greater virtue or higher moral and spiritual constitution than the man who, nevertheless, from his privileged position in society, usually fares better than the woman.

Perhaps most important of all the themes in his work is the belief in God versus atheism. If there is no God, many of Dostoevski's characters realize, then either every human being is a God or every human being is nothing at all. This conflict can, and sometimes does, take place within a single person as well as between two characters. Atheism usually appears in its most extreme state—that is, in the belief that, since there is no God, the human being must be God. While Dostoevski's proponents of atheism are strong-willed, disciplined, and morbidly dedicated, in Dostoevski's world they need to accept the existence of God as their only chance for peace or, in the final analysis, for existing in the world at all. While free will is interpreted by these radical proponents as the ability to become gods, the submission to the will of the divine God is the only means toward happiness. Those who fail to redeem themselves through God either perish or are subject to enormous spiritual and psychological torment. Such conflict forms the crux of more than one novel in Dostoevski's latter period, and it will be the treatment of this element in Dostoevski's work that will earn for him recognition as the founder of existentialism in literature. Ironically from the point of view of Dostoevski's beliefs, it is his existential writings rather than his metaphysical ones that constitute his most profound influence on world literature in the twentieth century.

Most of Dostoevski's short stories are simpler works than the novels, both in terms of the psychology of the characters and in terms of structure.

"WHITE NIGHTS"

One of his best-known short stories, "Belye nochi" ("White Nights"), is subtitled "A Sentimental Story from the Diary of a Dreamer." The unnamed protagonist of this work meets a young woman, Nastenka, by chance one evening along the embankment. When they have the opportunity to speak to each other, they find that they have much in common: Neither of them is able to enjoy a life of his or her own, and both of them, because of varying circumstances, are confined to their own abodes, occupied most of the time in daydreaming. Nastenka is physically restrained by her grandmother by being pinned to her skirt; the male protagonist is confined by his abject poverty and the inertia of unsociability to his quarters, with the green wallpaper and the spiderwebs. At the end of the story, Nastenka, nevertheless, is able to escape her fate thanks to the offices of the young boarder, who has taken pity on her, but she has had to wait an entire year; it is precisely at the end of this year that she meets the protagonist, whom, she claims, she would certainly love, and does in fact love, but as she truly still loves the other, she must relinquish. Nastenka leaves, imploring the protagonist not to blame her, knowing that he cannot blame her because he loves her. The protagonist feels that, somehow, this "moment" that they have shared is enough love to sustain him for a lifetime of dreaming. This story, unusual in the oeuvre of Dostoevski, does not involve the motif of the abused young woman, and the rejected young man seems quite content with his fate. Unlike most of Dostoevski's women, Nastenka has succeeded in meeting an honorable man who seemingly keeps his word, making her a singular female in the works of Dostoevski.

"A CHRISTMAS TREE AND A WEDDING"

More in keeping with Dostoevski's image of the abused, victimized woman is the young girl in "Elka i svad'ba" ("A Christmas Tree and a Wedding"). The first-person narrator relates how he notices the indecent attention of a "great man" of society toward an eleven-year-old girl playing with dolls, who has been promised a huge dowry during one family's Christmas party. The "great man" is interested only in the fabulous dowry and bides his time. Five years later, the narrator notices a wedding taking place in the church and focuses on the face of the very young bride, "pale and melancholy," her eyes perhaps even red from "recent weeping" and her look of "childish

innocence," where could be detected "something indescribably naive . . . mutely begging for mercy." He recognizes the young girl of a few years before and also the "great man," who is now the groom. The narrator concludes that it was a "good stroke of business." In this story, the theme of the helpless woman completely at the mercy of rapacious, evil men plays a major role, and the fate of the young girl in "A Christmas Tree and a Wedding," for all her money, bodes much worse than that of the impoverished Nastenka.

"THE DREAM OF A RIDICULOUS MAN"

Perhaps Dostoevski's best-known short story, "Son smeshnogo cheloveha" ("The Dream of a Ridiculous Man") presents more of the most typical Dostoevskian philosophy of any short story. In it, a petty clerk who has realized that he has no reason to live believes that he should commit suicide to put an end to his ridiculous existence. Just when he decides to do so, a young girl accosts him and seemingly tries to engage his assistance. He pushes her aside, but his action causes him great shame, and he feels deep pity for the young girl. The experience of these two emotions causes him to postpone his suicide, if only for a few hours. Meanwhile, he falls asleep, and in his dream he shoots himself. Then, after he is dead and buried, he is transported to an Earth-like planet inhabited by people who only love. Unfortunately, he corrupts the entire population, causing wars, antipathies, and alienation. Upon awakening, the man feels that he has undergone a revelation and must preach his new religion, trying to convince people that it is possible to live in harmony together and to love sincerely people other than oneself.

In "The Dream of a Ridiculous Man," many themes from Dostoevski's mature novels appear: whether one is a zero or a human, whether there is an afterlife, suffering as the only condition for the possibility of love, and suicide as a means of investing significance to human action, as well as many more. It is in the great novels that the complex world wherein the actions of all Dostoevski's creations take place, including the short works. To read a short story without a fundamental background in other seminal works—for example *Zapiski iz podpolya* (1864;

Notes from the Underground, 1918)—would very likely lead to a trap that could trivialize what are, by themselves, minor works such as the short stories. If, however, the short stories are contextualized within the entire oeuvre of Dostoevski over both his major periods, they form several interesting transitional points between many of his philosophical designs.

The young girls, usually victimized by poverty and evil men, seem to be an outgrowth of an early novel, *Poor Folk*, and a continuing motif throughout the later period. Here, an orphan serf girl is pressured into a marriage that will doubtless cause her endless degradation and possibly physical harm. The paradoxical "spiteful man" of *Notes from the Underground* is the model of the "little clerk" who, nevertheless, has been influenced by German romantic philosophy and against logical positivism. His voice and "spite" reverberate almost palpably in the short stories as well as in the great novels. The theme of life as suffering and love or compassion as life's greatest suffering is developed throughout the great novels, which, when used as a backdrop for the short works, provides a glimpse into the motivations of many of the protagonists.

Dostoevski's short stories clearly have a place of their own in Russian literature. Together, they form a miniature portrait of the most compelling people in Dostoevski's world. Reading them, along with the longer works, gives the discriminating reader an insight into one of the most powerful and intricate minds of the nineteenth century.

OTHER MAJOR WORKS

LONG FICTION: *Bednye lyudi*, 1846 (*Poor Folk*, 1887); *Dvoynik*, 1846 (*The Double*, 1917); *Netochka Nezvanova*, 1849 (English translation, 1920); *Unizhennye i oskorblyonnye*, 1861 (*Injury and Insult*, 1886; better known as *The Insulted and Injured*, 1887); *Zapiski iz myortvogo doma*, 1861-1862 (*Buried Alive: Or, Ten Years of Penal Servitude in Siberia*, 1881; better known as *The House of the Dead*, 1915); *Zapiski iz podpolya*, 1864 (*Letters from the Underworld*, 1913; better known as *Notes from the Underground*, 1918); *Igrok*, 1866 (*The Gambler*, 1887); *Prestupleniye i nakazaniye*, 1866 (*Crime and*

Punishment, 1886); *Idiot*, 1868 (*The Idiot*, 1887); *Vechny muzh*, 1870 (*The Permanent Husband*, 1888; better known as *The Eternal Husband*, 1917); *Besy*, 1871-1872 (*The Possessed*, 1913; also as *The Devils*, 1953); *Podrostok*, 1875 (*A Raw Youth*, 1916); *Bratya Karamazovy*, 1879-1880 (*The Brothers Karamazov*, 1912); *The Novels*, 1912 (12 volumes).

NONFICTION: "Zimniye zametki o letnikh vpechatleniyakh," 1863 ("Winter Notes on Summer Impressions," 1955); *Dnevnik pisatelya*, 1876-1877, 1880-1881 (2 volumes, partial translation as *Pages from the Journal of an Author*, 1916; complete translation as *The Diary of a Writer*, 1949); *Pisma*, 1928-1959 (4 volumes); *Iz arkhiva F. M. Dostoyevskogo: "Prestupleniye i nakazaniye,"* 1931 (*The Notebooks for "Crime and Punishment,"* 1967); *Iz arkhiva F. M. Dostoyevskogo: "Idiot,"* 1931 (*The Notebooks for "The Idiot,"* 1967); *Zapisnyye tetradi, F. M. Dostoyevskogo*, 1935 (*The Notebooks for "The Possessed,"* 1968); *F. M. Dostoyevsky: Materialy i issledovaniya*, 1935 (*The Notebooks for "The Brothers Karamazov,"* 1971); *Dostoevsky's Occasional Writings*, 1963; *F. M. Dostoyevsky v rabote nad romanom "Podrostok,"* 1965 (*The Notebooks for "A Raw Youth,"* 1969); *Neizdannyy Dostoevsky: Zapisnyye knizhki i tetradi 1860-1881 gg.*, 1971 (3 volumes; *The Unpublished Dostoevsky: Diaries and Notebooks, 1860-1881*, 1973-1976); *F. M. Dostoyevsky ob iskusstve*, 1973; *Selected Letters of Fyodor Dostoyevsky*, 1987.

TRANSLATION: *Yevgeniya Grande*, 1844 (of Honoré de Balzac's novel *Eugénie Grandet*).

MISCELLANEOUS: *Polnoe sobranie sochinenii v tridtsati tomakh*, 1972-   (30 volumes).

BIBLIOGRAPHY

Catteau, Jacques. *Dostoevsky and the Process of Literary Creation*. Translated by Audrey Littlewood. Cambridge, England: Cambridge University Press, 1989. This excellent book offers detailed textual analysis and factual information on Dostoevski. The categories that form the subheadings range from "Time and Space in the World of the Novels" to ones such as "Money." Catteau provides a thematic overview of the pressures and inspirations that motivated Dostoevski. The volume includes ninety-five pages of notes and bibliography, as well as an index.

Frank, Joseph. *Dostoevsky: The Miraculous Years, 1865-1871.* Princeton, N.J.: Princeton University Press, 1995. The fourth volume in Frank's series on the life and works of Dostoevksi. Includes an extended discussion of Dostoeski's novella *The Gambler* from an ethnic-psychological perspective as a commentary on the Russian national character and an extended discussion of the classical construction of the novella *The Eternal Husband*, which Frank sees as Dostoeski's most perfect shorter work.

Grossman, Leonid. *Dostoevsky: A Biography.* Translated by Mary Mackler. New York: Bobbs-Merrill, 1975. Grossman was himself a good writer, and his critical work reads very well. There are moments of suspense and drama, but most of all, one senses the care and consideration taken by the author on Dostoevski's behalf. Generally. Grossman's volume covers Dostoevski's life and works, creative product, and critical reception. Includes detailed notes and an index.

Jackson, Robert Louis, ed. *Dialogues with Dostoevsky: The Overwhelming Questions.* Stanford, Calif.: Stanford University Press, 1993. Chapters on the writer's relationships with Ivan Turgenev, Leo Tolstoy, Anton Chekhov, Maxim Gorky, Nikolai Gogol, William Shakespeare, and Friedrich Nietzsche.

Kjetsaa, Geir. *Fyodor Dostoevsky: A Writer's Life.* Translated by Siri Hustvedt and David McDuff. New York: Viking, 1987. By far the best work on Dostoevski's life: very through and very interesting. Kjetsaa debunks the myth of Dostoevski's father's murder definitively; his access to archives closed to previous scholars provides him the unambiguous evidence. His viewpoint is, appropriately, to shed light on the creation of Dostoevski's fiction, citing letters and notes as artistic points of departure for Dostoevski. The thorough, up-to-date bibliography of thirty pages will direct future

scholars to his resources. Some illustrations, index.

Mochulsky, K. V. *Dostoevsky: His Life and Work.* Translated by Michael Minihan. Princeton, N.J.: Princeton University Press, 1967. This book's title may slightly mislead the reader into thinking that the author is somehow isolating Dostoevski's life from his work. Mochulsky, however, informs the reader in his preface that "the life and work of Dostoevsky are inseparable. He lived in literature." Thus, rather than making a large work consisting of two major parts, Mochulsky interweaves biography and literary analysis brilliantly. His style is engaging and very accessible. This book is regularly recommended for undergraduates by many teachers of courses on Dostoevski.

Straus, Nina Pelikan. *Dostoevsky and the Woman Question: Rereadings at the End of a Century.* New York: St. Martin's Press, 1994. Although, like most books on Dostoeski, this study centers on the novels, it is helpful in understanding his work generally; it argues that Dostoeski's compulsion to depict men's cruelties to women is a constitutive part of his vision and his metaphysics. Claims that Dostoeski attacks masculine notions of autonomy and that his works evolve toward "the death of the patriarchy."

Wasiolek, Edward. *Dostoevsky: The Major Fiction.* Cambridge: Massachussetts Institute of Technology Press, 1964. In this interesting and comprehensive work, Wasiolek not only addresses virtually all Dostoevski's fiction but also introduces much of the contemporary political polemics. He also includes a well-balanced assessment of many important subsequent literary critical opinions, which is interwoven in his analysis of the individual works. Includes notes about the first publication of Dostoevski's works as well as a detailed bibliography presenting both general subject headings (for example, a work's reception in the West) and writing apropos an individual work.

Christine Tomei

ELLEN DOUGLAS
Josephine Ayres Haxton

Born: Natchez, Mississippi; July 12, 1921

PRINCIPAL SHORT FICTION

Black Cloud, White Cloud, 1963 (revised as *Black Cloud, White Cloud: Two Novellas and Two Stories*, 1989)

Truth: Four Stories I Am Finally Old Enough to Tell, 1998

OTHER LITERARY FORMS

Between 1962 and 1988, Ellen Douglas produced six novels. She also published a children's book, *"The Magic Carpet" and Other Tales*, in which she retold familiar fairy tales. Her nonfiction works include a critical study, *Walker Percy's "The Last Gentleman"* (1969) and numerous essays published in periodicals, journals, and edited collections.

ACHIEVEMENTS

In 1961, Ellen Douglas received a Houghton Mifflin Literary Fellowship, and *A Family's Affairs* (1962) was awarded a citation for best novel of the year by *The New York Times*. In 1963, *Black Cloud, White Cloud* was named one of the year's five best fiction works by *The New York Times*. Her short story "On the Lake" was included in *Prize Stories: The O. Henry Awards* in 1961, and "Grant" was included in the 1996 collection. "Grant" also appeared in *New Stories from the South: The Year's Best* in 1996, and "Julia and Nellie" was selected for the annual publication the following year. She has received a National Endowment for the Humanities grant, a Mississippi Institute of Arts and Letters Award for Literature, and grants from the National Education Association. In 1989, Douglas was honored by the Fellowship of Southern Writers.

BIOGRAPHY

Josephine Ayres was born in Natchez, Mississippi, on July 12, 1921. She attended school in Hope, Arkansas, and Alexandria, Louisiana, but spent summers with her many relatives in Natchez. After a year at Randolph Macon Women's College, she transferred to the University of Mississippi, receiving her B.A. in 1942. In 1945, she married Kenneth Haxton and went to live in his hometown, Greenville, Mississippi. They had three children, Richard, Ayres, and Brooks. After their divorce in 1983, Josephine moved to Jackson, Mississippi.

Although she has always worked on her writing, Josephine Ayres Haxton did not decide on a literary career until she was thirty-four, and it was several years after that before her fiction appeared in print. Her first efforts were short stories, like "On the Lake," which *The New Yorker* published in 1961; later she transformed several of her stories into a novel, *A Family's Affairs* (1962). Because some of her characters were modeled on family members, she chose to use the pseudonym Ellen Douglas.

During the next three and a half decades, Douglas produced a book approximately every five years, lectured frequently, and taught at Northeast Louisiana University, Hollins College, the University of Mississippi, the University of Virginia, and Millsaps College. In her seventies she gave up teaching, although she continued to write, publishing a second collection of short fiction in 1998.

ANALYSIS

Although Ellen Douglas addresses such twentieth century problems as racism, alienation, and cultural breakdown, her approach is unlike that of most contemporary writers. Her characters may be confused about the direction their lives should take, but the author herself is not in doubt; her works reflect her unswerving adherence to Judeo-Christian ethics. Like the great moralists of the eighteenth and nineteenth centuries, such as Jane Austen and Charles Dickens, Douglas believes that such happiness as this world can provide is achieved only by putting principles above selfish considerations, by placing the needs of others ahead of own's own.

This preoccupation with the way people behave toward one another is evident throughout Douglas's short fiction. "The House on the Bluff," from *Black Cloud, White Cloud*, examines the relationships between a number of characters, primarily members of two white families, who have lived in the same community for generations, and the blacks who were so much a part of their lives. With so many possibilities for kindness, compassion, and pure spitefulness, it is not surprising that a child like Anna McGovern often finds this world quite puzzling.

Whether they are told by first-person narrators or in the third person, Douglas's short stories and novellas generally have a single point of view. Almost always the protagonist is both sincere and sympathetic. "I Just Love Carrie Lee" is an exception; in that story, the reader is expected to see beyond what the unreliable narrator says. Most of the time, however, the reader and the protagonist move together toward the recognition of some truth about human nature or about life. While Douglas is too much of a realist to minimize the difficulties inherent in human relationships, she always holds out hope that, despite their differences, her characters can become more tolerant and more empathetic.

"I JUST LOVE CARRIE LEE"

One of the pervasive themes in *Black Cloud, White Cloud* is how difficult it is for even the best-intentioned whites and blacks to surmount the racial barriers erected by time and tradition. In the satirical monologue "I Just Love Carrie Lee," Emma, the white narrator, thinks of herself as a model employer. She points out an obvious truth: that, unlike transplanted Yankees, Southerners take responsibility for their black employees—for instance, making sure that they have an income even when they cannot do their usual work. However, despite her protestations, Emma does not really "love" Carrie Lee. Though the two women do know each other intimately, they are not friends, for while Emma admits she depends on Carrie Lee, she does not respect her. She quotes Carrie Lee's homey truths in order to laugh at them, and even when she allows Carrie Lee to enter the white church for family weddings and funerals, she does so primarily so that Emma can admire her gen-

Ellen Douglas (©Miriam Berkley)

erosity. Ironically, it is not Emma but Carrie Lee who knows the real meaning of life and love. The very comments that Emma finds so amusing prove how much wiser the servant is than the mistress.

HOLD ON

The novella *Hold On*, from *Black Cloud, White Cloud*, is told from the perspective of Anna McGovern Glover, who appeared as a child in *A Family's Affairs* but who appears here an adult, living in Philippi, West Virginia, with her husband Richard and their children. The central incident of this novella was first related in "On the Lake." Anna invites a black woman, Estella Moseby, to go fishing with her. During the afternoon, Anna becomes aware of the differences between them; for example, Estella fearlessly kills a cottonmouth, a type of water snake, but she is superstitious about being "marked" during pregnancy and has a profound terror of water. When they start back, the lake becomes rough, and Estella panics, causing the boat to capsize, but Anna manages to hold on to Estella until help arrives, and she survives. The short story ends here, whereas the novella is much more complex. In it, though Estella believes that Anna saved her life, Anna believes she failed her. Not only did she fail to give Estella a life preserver or even to make sure she could swim but also she kicked Estella away so that she herself would not drown. Her search for the truth takes Anna to one of the rescuers, Carl Jensen, who, because of an incident in his own past, can see that Anna's feelings are born out of a pervasive sense of guilt about the past treatment of African Americans. The novella ends with Anna determined to "hold on" to Estella, even if their relationship remains less than perfect.

"ABOUT LOVING WOMEN"

The impact of the past on the present is also the subject of "About Loving Women," which was written for *That's What I Like (About the South) and Other New Southern Stories for the Nineties* (1993). The narrator is a high school boy, who is desperately in love with a girl named Roseanne. Just when their romance seems to be flourishing, Roseanne's former boyfriend, Henry, moves to town, and Roseanne begins avoiding the narrator. During the inevitable fight between the rivals, Henry begins to cry for Roseanne, and suddenly the narrator remembers his own tears when he was just five and had to say goodbye to an uncle's girlfriend, who had made a pet of him. What he learned then and what Henry has just found out is that once a man has been betrayed by the woman he loves, he can never regain his lost innocence.

TRUTH

Reviewers are divided as to whether *Truth* should be classified as fiction or as nonfiction. However, in her 1977 interview with Charline R. McCord, Douglas referred to the works in the collection as short stories. Douglas has made no secret of the fact that she sets her fiction in actual places and bases her characters on people she knows. Thus in *Black Cloud, White Cloud*, Homochitto can be read as Natchez, and Philippi, as Greenville. In Douglas's first novel, two of her aunts were so thinly disguised that at their request she published the book under a pseudonym. In *Truth*, Douglas describes real events and uses real names for people and places. However, the point of the book is that truth is elusive and that what is called history is essentially indistinguishable from fiction.

In all four stories in *Truth*, Douglas has two roles:

She is an observer or investigator, on one hand, and a storyteller, on the other. In "Grant," she looks back on the final months of her husband's uncle's life, which he spent in her home; in "Julia and Nellie," she reports the speculations of family members and friends about a scandalous relationship; in "Hampton," she reconstructs the life of a black chauffeur she knows; and in "On Second Creek," she looks into the executions of slaves in 1861 and also discovers some long-concealed secrets. In every case, the author's investigations provide her with more questions than answers, for, even when she is sure of facts, she has to guess or invent the reasons why people felt and thought as they did. Because both history and fiction are mixtures of truth and lies, Douglas suggests, one should focus less on supposed facts and more on moral choices. Those are the real truths that give both fiction and history a lasting significance.

OTHER MAJOR WORKS

LONG FICTION: *A Family's Affairs*, 1962; *Where the Dreams Cross*, 1968; *Apostles of Light*, 1973; *The Rock Cried Out*, 1979; *A Lifetime Burning*, 1982; *Can't Quit You, Baby*, 1988.

NONFICTION: *Walker Percy's "The Last Gentleman,"* 1969.

CHILDREN'S LITERATURE: *"The Magic Carpet" and Other Tales*, 1987.

BIBLIOGRAPHY

Broughton, Panthea Reid, and Susan Millar Williams. "Ellen Douglas." In *Southern Women Writers: The New Generation*, edited by Tonette Bond Inge. Tuscaloosa: University of Alabama Press, 1990. Focuses on Douglas's development as an artist from her early works to *Can't Quit You, Baby. Black Cloud, White Cloud* is discussed in detail.

Chappell, Fred. "The Good Songs Behind Us: Southern Fiction of the 1990's." In *That's What I Like (About the South) and Other New Southern Stories for the Nineties*, edited by George Garrett and Paul Ruffin. Columbia: University of South Carolina Press, 1993. Another important southern writer uses Ellen Douglas's story "About Loving Women," which appears in the volume, to exemplify the importance of memory and history in southern fiction.

Douglas, Ellen. Afterword to *Black Cloud, White Cloud*. Rev. ed. Jackson: University Press of Mississippi, 1989. The author identifies the themes and symbolic patterns she now sees dominate this book. She also emphasizes the importance of storytelling in a rapidly changing world.

_____. "Interview with Ellen Douglas: February 25, 1997." Interview by Charlene R. McCord. *Mississippi Quarterly: The Journal of Southern Culture* 51 (Spring, 1998): 291-321. Deals primarily with the writing process and the teaching of writing. Douglas comments on the short stories in her second collection.

Feddersen, Rick. "An Interview with Ellen Douglas." In *Speaking of the Short Story: Interviews with Contemporary Writers*, edited by Farhat Iftekharuddin, Mary Rohrberger, and Maurice Lee. Jackson: University Press of Mississippi, 1997. Douglas speaks about her experiences with short fiction and also comments on story sequences and novels written in that form.

Jones, John Griffin. "Ellen Douglas." In *Mississippi Writers Talking*, edited by John Griffin Jones. Vol. 2. Jackson: University Press of Mississippi, 1983.

The author reflects on how her family, her southern heritage, and her awareness of racial injustice have influenced her work.

McHaney, Thomas L., and Noel Polk, eds. "Ellen Douglas." *The Southern Quarterly: A Journal of the Arts in the South* 33 (Summer, 1995). This special issue contains essays on the author and her works, two interviews, and extensive bibliographies. Also includes the text of Douglas's speech "I Have Found It."

Manning, Carol S. "Ellen Douglas: Moralist and Realist." In *Women Writers of the Contemporary South*, edited by Peggy Whitman Prenshaw. Jackson: University Press of Mississippi, 1984. Contends that while, as a realist, Douglas understands yearnings for total freedom, as a moralist she believes human beings should take responsibility for their actions.

Stockwell, Joe. *Ellen Douglas*. Jackson: Mississippi Library Commission, 1977. The author is seen as a traditional moralist and satirist. Includes an indepth analysis of *Black Cloud, White Cloud*.

Rosemary M. Canfield Reisman

SERGEI DOVLATOV

Born: Ufa, U.S.S.R.; September 3, 1941
Died: Brooklyn, New York; August 24, 1990

PRINCIPAL SHORT FICTION

Solo na Undervude: Zapisnye knizhki, 1980
Kompromiss, 1981 (*The Compromise*, 1983)
Zona: Zapiski nadziratelia, 1982 (*The Zone: A Prison Camp Guard's Story*, 1985)
Nashi, 1983 (*Ours: A Russian Family Album*, 1989)
Zapovednik: Povest', 1983 (novella)

Remeslo: Povest' v dvukh chastiakh, 1985 (novella)
Chemodan, 1986 (*The Suitcase*, 1990)
Inostranka, 1986 (novella; *A Foreign Woman*, 1991)
Filial, 1987 (novella)
Predstavlenie, 1987

OTHER LITERARY FORMS

Sergei Dovlatov was a respected journalist in his native country before being forced to emigrate. He also published in several Soviet underground journals. His major works are all entitled "novels," although they read much more like short-story collections. His "considerable talent" is cited by *The Christian Science Monitor* as "best suited to the short story and the sketch." Dovlatov was also an editor, a contributor, and a cofounder of *New American*, a newspaper expressly for Russian émigrés.

ACHIEVEMENTS

Dovlatov is primarily recognized as one voice among a bevy of Soviet emigrant writers that includes Joseph Brodsky, Edward Limonov, Vassily Aksyonov, Yuz Aleshkovsky, Vladimir Voinovich, and Dmitri Savitsky, compatriots in the fact that they either were not published in their native homeland or were defamed in Soviet Russia as potential enemies of the state. In addition to cofounding *New American*, Dovlatov focused his attention on the intrinsic problem of the Soviet writer: the forced choice between country and intellectual freedom. *Contemporary Authors* quotes Dovlatov as stating, "I can live in freedom without my native land, but I'm physically incapable of living without freedom." He was a member of the International Association of Poets, Playwrights, Editors, Essayists, and Novelists (PEN).

BIOGRAPHY

Sergei Dovlatov was born to Donat Mechik, a theater director, and Nora Dovlatov, a proofreader. He attended the University of Leningrad for two years, dropped out, and was ultimately drafted into the Soviet army, where he served as a guard for high-security prison camps. This latter experience was the basis for *Zona: Zapiski nadziratelia* (1982; *The Zone: A Prison Camp Guard's Story*, 1985), which purports to be the written documents of an inmate that have been smuggled out to the Western world. In 1963, Dovlatov married Elena Ritman, a union that produced two children, Katherine and Nicholas.

Dovlatov began to work as a journalist in 1965, initially in Leningrad, then in Tallinn, Estonia. During this period and until 1978, he was the subject of intense governmental harassment. Despite his position as a respected journalist, he was unable to obtain publication for his fictional works via official means.

Undaunted, he began to publish in unauthorized and underground sources, including the Russian-language edition of *Kontinent*. He also involved himself in smuggling his manuscripts to the West because of his disappointment with the official censor. The authorities' harassment of him culminated in a dismissal from the journalists' union, an arrest, and finally a release, prompted by Western pressure and publicity. Dovlatov immigrated to the United States in 1979.

His first published work in the United States (and in English translation) was *Nevidimaia kniga* (1977-1978; *The Invisible Book: Epilogue*, 1979), a recounting of his journalistic struggles and attempts at publishing his fictive work. This recounting, however, is not a straightforward narration but rather an opportunity for the author to hold forth on topics that interest him—including his opinions on publishing, censorship, and the tribulations of a thwarted writer. Dovlatov followed *The Invisible Book* with several more "novels," including *The Compromise* in 1981; *The Zone*, appearing in Russian in 1982 but published in English translation in 1985; and *Ours: A Russian Family Album* (also known as *Nashi*, or "the clan," in some sources) in 1983.

Dovlatov died on August 24, 1990. The translation of his novel *Chemodan* had appeared earlier the same year and is entitled *The Suitcase*, an apt symbol for his traveling spirit and his artistic life.

ANALYSIS

Many of Sergei Dovlatov's short stories have been combined and loosely gathered together into "novel" form. In fact, three of his major novels are in reality compilations of his short stories, grouped generally by theme and specifically by tone. *Ours: A Russian Family Album*, for example, includes eight short stories; these stories originally appeared in national magazines such as *Harper's*, *The New Yorker*, and *Partisan Review*. While purporting to be a novel, *The Zone* is really a series of sketches about prison life and different characters' responses to it. Dovlatov's last "novel," *The Suitcase*, has been described as a "volume of interconnected tales" and "episodes" that "are in fact short stories."

According to a 1986 article in *The Christian Sci-*

ence Monitor, "Dovlatov's considerable talent is best suited to the short story and the sketch. His first novel, 'The Compromise,' was a brilliant satire of Soviet journalism that really amounted to an ingeniously connected string of short pieces." Similarly, noting Dovlatov's talent for implying much through terse, abbreviated glimpses into Russian life, *Newsweek* stated in a review of *Ours: A Russian Family Album:*

> Famous for their long books, Russian writers can startle us with a brief one, as Sergei Dovlatov does in this deftly economical gallery of family portraits. An émigré living in New York, Dovlatov is witty in the Russian manner—which is a kind of farce played out against an open cellar door, the darkness yawning just beyond the actors' nimble feet.

"UNCLE ARON"

This sense of "farce" is evident throughout Dovlatov's stories, in probability a function of the short-story form, which is motivated by, and infused with, the need for brevity and sharp focus. Dovlatov always describes poignantly and yet sardonically the machinations of people who display the inherent contradiction of living in a Soviet state while remaining unique, individual human beings. In "Uncle Aron," Dovlatov relates how he and his aunt's husband would wage verbal political battles that were in reality name-calling stances of personal opinion. This same Uncle Aron unwittingly displays the paradox of ideology pitted against personal preference. After years of favoring Soviet heroes who were repeatedly defamed and removed from power, Uncle Aron decides to play it safe and idolize Lenin: "Lenin had died long ago and could not be removed from power. It was close to impossible even to smear his name. This meant the love could not be endangered." Yet after the years of disillusioning disappointment with a government that continually changes its mind, Uncle Aron himself comes apart, the seams of Soviet party lines and propagandist constructions unraveling in one singular life.

> At the same time, though, my uncle somehow came loose ideologically. He fell in love with Lenin but also with Solzhenitsyn. Sakharov, too—mainly because he

had helped develop the hydrogen bomb in the Soviet Union and then hadn't become a drunk but fought for the truth.

> In the last years of his life, my uncle was practically a dissident, but a moderate one. He never for an instant tolerated the anti-Communist, pro-Nazi Vlasovites; he revered Solzhenitsyn selectively.

It has been asserted that Russian literature in general is "dense" with ideological import and that this trait distinguishes Russian and Soviet writers from their "freer confreres in the West." If the concern for ideology is indeed a large part of the impetus for Russian literature, and, if Western writers are enabled to write without its heavy-handed influence, then Dovlatov is caught somewhere in the middle, in the margin, between East and West in his philosophical stance. For although Dovlatov may not exhibit the emotionalism and transcendent mysticism of Fyodor Dostoevski or the wide historical perspective of Leo Tolstoy, his stories and "sketches" exist as precious insights into both the basic humanness and ordinariness of the average Soviet citizen and the absurdities created when ideology conflicts dramatically with ordinary human concerns.

In other words, ideology, for Dovlatov, is subordinate to those elements that make human beings human, and is, in turn, often debunked in his stories by the mere interaction of the human with the supposedly acceptable state-induced attitude. What emerges as inviolable and paramount in Dovlatov's "brief glimpses" is the sense of the unique, individual, independent (as far as one was able to carry independence in the Soviet Union), and salient human being. The individual is always coupled with the dramatic, the nonindividual with the bland, gray colorlessness of the bureaucrat or Party member. Being part of the accepted Soviet Union is being part of something deadened, shameful, and yet something necessary.

"MOTHER"

In "Mother," Dovlatov reveals how at the age of six he knew the score, the true nature of living in modern Russia:

> By the age of six, I myself knew that Stalin had been responsible for the death of my grandfather, and by the

time I finished school, I knew most everything else. I knew that the newspaper printed lies. That ordinary people abroad lived better lives, were materially better off and more carefree. That to be a Party member was shameful but to one's advantage.

This is the central issue and question that runs through Dovlatov's text, like a subliminal motif or subtext in every description, observation, or satiric wisecrack: How can people live like this? How do they?

Dovlatov's "heroes" (or antiheroes) somehow manage to rebel in either blatant or quietly subversive ways. Aunt Mara, from the story "Aunt Mara," is a literary editor for the state and has volume after volume of "officially" accepted books from sanctioned authors of her day but, in the end, hoards by her bed books of "Akhmatova, Pasternak, Baratynski. . . ." Officially, her life is aligned to the state façade; unofficially, she treasures the banned and the dissident. Ironically, her "official" books with handwritten inscriptions must be censored by her relatives, who ripped out the pages of inscriptions.

"MY FIRST COUSIN"

In "My First Cousin," Dovlatov's cousin Boris is a blatant rebel who tailors the system to his own inner and psychic needs. A born achiever, he engages in self-sabotage as a means of both living in *and* out of the Soviet system. Here too, Dovlatov cannot resist the potshot at a system that he both understands and abhors: "Life turned my first cousin into a criminal. It seems to me he was lucky. Otherwise, he would inevitably have become a high-ranking Party functionary." The terrors of Dante's hell hold not a candle to the yawning abyss of Party machinations.

Boris, the reader discovers, was an "exemplary" Soviet citizen, consistently held up to the young Sergei as a role model. Readers learn of his exploits, his good grades, his dogged adherence to a Party image: "In the drama club he always played the Young Guard." Then, as if in dawning awareness, Boris strikes out on his own particular path of deviance from political acceptance, for which the narrator-author almost has "no words." What would be an insult and schoolboy prank in the United States be-

comes a most serious crime (and unheard of scandal) in Russia: Cousin Boris has urinated on a school official:

> Whereupon, my cousin climbed up onto the windowsill, asked the girls to turn around, skillfully calculated his trajectory. And doused Chebotaryov from head to foot.

This incredible stunt, however, does not stop Boris from a meteoric rise within the state film industry, at the height of which he again destroys his immediate future by committing twelve robberies. Years later, after prison camp, he again rises in his field and again subverts himself—all, it is implicitly suggested, because of the need to rebel, to have a self, to be an independent agent in a land of manipulated cogs. For Dovlatov, his cousin needed drama and "extreme situations." He "was a natural-born existentialist," able to "build a career only in prison, fight for life only on the edge of the abyss."

"UNCLE LEOPOLD"

This need for drama in the lives of individuals in an inherently dramaless state is a subtheme of Dovlatov's writing. Early in *Ours: A Russian Family Album*, he describes the price for revolt or rebellion against a capricious system in the story "Uncle Leopold." For Grandpa Isak, the price was nothing short of eradication; arrested as a spy for Belgium, Grandpa is shot.

> Specific grounds for this charge were not cited. It was enough to have relatives living abroad. Though maybe it mattered that Grandpa was not enthusiastic about the sweep of Stalin's five-year plans. Then, too, he was a little too noticeable—tall, angry, and loud-voiced. Under dictators, people who stand out do not fare well.

Yet even this is preferable to the gray, colorless, monotonous uniformity of state-dictated norms. The Soviet Union in which the adult Dovlatov finds himself may be freed of a singular, personal dictator, but in Stalin's stead stands an impersonal, vapid vacuum of mediocrity: "Life was becoming increasingly lacklustre and monotonous. Even villainy took on a kind of banal, abject quality. Goodness was transformed into apathy. People would say 'So-and-So is a good person, he doesn't inform on anyone.' "

The universe of the Soviet Union in Dovlatov's fiction is a universe that demands uniformity (and therefore loss of individuality) and a certain voice-lessness. People have no power and no means by which to assume personal responsibility for their own actions. Thus, Dovlatov can claim that goodness metamorphoses into apathy in Russia. Interestingly enough, Dovlatov, with his omnipresent ability to re-verse his perceptions and wring every drop of irony from a situation, shows how the human spirit, even under these repressive conditions, still can manage to triumph—even if only unobtrusively and covertly. When Aunt Mara palpably confronts the Russian condition of voicelessness, Dovlatov shows how the writer Mikhail Zoshchenko maintains a silent ability to assume personal responsibility for the tribulations of his life:

> She happened to meet Mikhail Zoshchenko on the street. The difficult time of official disfavor had al-ready begun for him. Zoshchenko turned his head and quickly walked past her.
>
> My aunt caught up with him and asked, "Why didn't you say hello to me?"
>
> Zoshchenko grinned and said, "Forgive me. I'm try-ing to make it easy for my friends not to talk to me."

THE COMPROMISE

Dovlatov's style, impact, topics, and format are inextricably woven from his personal history as a writer. Not only do his books describe the process of writing (and attempting to publish) what is consid-ered "dissident" material, but also they assume the format of a hounded, forbidden artist smuggling out the truth to the rest of the world. In *The Compromise*, each of the eleven chapters (displaying Dovlatov's predilection for the short, interlocking tale) is a news story (narrated by a journalist named Dovlatov), fol-lowed by a true account of what occurred. Censorship is simultaneously revealed and debunked; the hypoc-risy of Soviet news propaganda is exhibited and ridi-culed; and finally, the larger theme, made possible by eleven separate tales, is exposed: All truth is always somehow compromised.

THE ZONE

In *The Zone*, almost every chapter is punctuated with a letter to Dovlatov's "editor," a pose that pro-motes the fiction of an actual manuscript being smug-gled out of the Soviet Union in pieces, bit by bit, on microfilm. (The editor was in reality Dovlatov's edi-tor for the Russian-language edition of the novel pub-lished in the United States.)

The book becomes at once an analogy for the pro-cess of writing in Russia and, in a larger framework, an analogy for the process of writing itself—pris-matic, revealing the author bit by bit. The opening letter to the publisher highlights the three reasons why Dovlatov is having difficulty getting this particu-lar work published:

> The prison camp theme is exhausted. The reader is tired of endless prison memoirs. After Solzhenitsyn, the subject ought to be closed.
>
> This idea does not stand up to critical examination. It goes without saying that I am not Solzhenitsyn. But does that deprive me of a right to exist?
>
> Also, our books are completely different. Solzheni-tsyn describes political prison camps. I—criminal ones.
>
> Solzhenitsyn was a prisoner. I—a prison guard. Ac-cording to Solzhenitsyn, camp is hell. Whereas I think that hell is in us ourselves.

With this bit of introduction, Dovlatov, without any disparagement of Aleksandr Solzhenitsyn, defines his position (hell is personal, not a social or political con-struction) and presents a subtle critique of all types of censorship—that is, the structure of a literary canon that precludes his publication because he is too simi-lar to an already established literary giant.

Finally, Dovlatov's stories have an insightful wit that subtly comments on the action of his narrative and allows for both the ridiculous, ludicrous side of human beings and their defiant, triumphant side. Nes-tled within his short stories are nuggets of wisdom, pearls of perception that enable the reader to look newly on what is often considered the ordinary or commonplace. His stories include observations, char-acterizations, and ideas that apply universally to hu-mankind (whether Western or Eastern) and furtively ask the reader to think:

Our memory is selective, like a ballot box.

Punctuation is something every writer invents for himself.

Father . . . looked like a cross between Pushkin and an American on unemployment.

Apparently, people at the bottom of the social ladder don't care much for others like them. They prefer to love the masters, or if worst comes to worst, themselves.

Silence is an enormous power. It ought to be banned by law, like biological warfare.

Dovlatov, who emigrated in 1979, was crucially aware of the differences (and inherent likenesses) between Russians and Americans. Besides the need for drama in humdrum Soviet lives, however, and the desperate desire to express oneself both individually and as part of a coherent nation, Russians, according to Dovlatov, lack the ability to be dreamers, idealists, and are totally given over to the sense of a positivism about life.

"Freedom?" one (KGB officer) said. "You give a Russian freedom. The first thing he'll go and do is slit his mother's throat. . . ."

"Sakharov reasons like a child," another said. "His ideas are useless. What is all this nonsense about human rights? A Russian needs only one right: the right to get over his hangover." ("Glasha")

For this Soviet writer, the most obvious characteristic of Americans is not their professed democracy (after all, as a system it has its corruptions) but rather a more basic innate sense of freedom—a freedom of being that allows total unselfconsciousness—an ability simply to be and enjoy it:

What is the main quality of Americans? I immediately decided it was their optimism. In the courtyard of our building there was a man who got around in a wheelchair. If you asked him, "How are things?" he answered, "Fine," without the slightest trace of self-consciousness. Or else you saw a girl on the street, pale, disheveled, heavy-legged, wearing a T-shirt that said, "I'm Ursula Andress." Again, not the least bit self-conscious. ("Glasha")

In stories such as "Driving Gloves," "The Photo Album," and "The Colonel Says I Love You," Dovlatov satirizes Soviet life and pretensions but also moves onto a personal level that asks relevant questions about the nature and meaning of human life—outside political systems and cultural values. In "The Photo Album," the narrator (Dovlatov as himself) stumbles on an old album of photographs accumulated by his wife. Suddenly his life slaps him in the face, and he knows that his life is here and now, and real in tangible terms.

But I was morbidly agitated. . . . I saw that everything going on in our lives was for real. If I was feeling that for the first time only now, then how much love had been lost over the long years?

It is only after this internal revelation that Dovlatov admits that his wife will emigrate without him. The story ends on a questioning note, suspended in a reality that no longer applies to the author. His wife leaves him an imported Rumanian shirt. Dovlatov ends the story, ruminating: "But where would I go in it? Really, where?"

OTHER MAJOR WORKS

LONG FICTION: *Nevidimaia kniga*, 1977-1978 (*The Invisible Book: Epilogue*, 1979).

NONFICTION: *Marsh odinokikh*, 1983; *Not Just Brodsky*, 1988.

BIBLIOGRAPHY

Grimes, William. "A Novel of Crime and Freezing Punishment in Russia." *The Christian Science Monitor*, January 21, 1986, p. 26. An insightful glimpse into Dovlatov's style and intent in his novel *The Zone: A Prison Camp Guard's Story*. Although *The Zone* is a moving account of prison life, Grimes states that the book is not too disheartening: "It would take more than prison to blunt Dovlatov's comic edge."

Prescott, Peter S. "Actors, Uncles, Existentialists." Review of *Ours: A Russian Family Album*. *Newsweek*, April 24, 1989, 26. In this brief review, Prescott selects a few of the book's characters who demonstrate human failings and shows

Dovlatov's compassion in regard to their actions and his uneasiness in regard to the Party and the state.

Shragin, Boris, et al. "Writers in Exile: A Conference of Soviet and East European Dissidents." *Partisan Review* 50, no. 4 (1983): 487-525. A discussion of dissident writers including Dovlatov, Boris Shragin, Stanisław Baránczak, Erazim V. Kohak, Yuz Aleshkovsky, and others.

"Soviet Émigrés." *The Christian Science Monitor,*

October 2, 1987. A discussion of Dovlatov's position on *glasnost* and *perestroika* in terms of the reasons why he and Soviet émigrés are not published in the Soviet Union. Despite the literary freedoms that followed *glasnost*, Dovlatov believes that the outlook for Soviet émigré writers is not too positive and that total *glasnost* cannot be achieved by a state controlled by one party.

Sherry Morton-Mollo

ARTHUR CONAN DOYLE

Born: Edinburgh, Scotland; May 22, 1859
Died: Crowborough, England; July 7, 1930

PRINCIPAL SHORT FICTION

Mysteries and Adventures, 1889 (also as *The Gully of Bluemansdyke and Other Stories*)

The Captain of Polestar and Other Tales, 1890

The Adventures of Sherlock Holmes, 1892

My Friend the Murderer and Other Mysteries and Adventures, 1893

The Great Keinplatz Experiment and Other Stories, 1894

The Memoirs of Sherlock Holmes, 1894

Round the Red Lamp: Being Fact and Fancies of Medical Life, 1894

The Exploits of Brigadier Gerard, 1896

The Man from Archangel and Other Stories, 1898

The Green Flag and Other Stories of War and Sport, 1900

The Adventures of Gerard, 1903

The Return of Sherlock Holmes, 1905

Round the Fire Stories, 1908

The Last Galley: Impressions and Tales, 1911

One Crowded Hour, 1911

His Last Bow, 1917

Danger! and Other Stories, 1918

Tales of the Ring and Camp, 1922 (also as *The Croxley Master and Other Tales of the Ring and Camp*)

Tales of Terror and Mystery, 1922 (also as *The Black Doctor and Other Tales of Terror and Mystery*)

Tales of Twilight and the Unseen, 1922 (also as *The Great Keinplatz Experiment and Other Tales of Twilight and the Unseen*)

Three of Them, 1923

The Dealings of Captain Sharkey and Other Tales of Pirates, 1925

Last of the Legions and Other Tales of Long Ago, 1925

The Case-Book of Sherlock Holmes, 1927

The Maracot Deep and Other Stories, 1929

The Final Adventures of Sherlock Holmes, 1981

Uncollected Stories: The Unknown Conan Doyle, 1982

OTHER LITERARY FORMS

Arthur Conan Doyle's more than one hundred published works include novels, autobiography, political treatises, plays adapted from his fiction, and works on spiritualism as well as his short stories, for which he is best known. His character Sherlock

Holmes has been the subject of innumerable films, plays, and radio scripts and has become the archetype of the conventional detective hero.

ACHIEVEMENTS

While Doyle was not the first to write short stories featuring a detective with great analytical powers, and while he acknowledged his debt to such writers as Edgar Allan Poe and Émile Gaboriau, who had written tales of intelligent amateur detectives solving crimes through logical deduction, in Sherlock Holmes, Doyle created a character who has entered the popular imagination like no other. Sherlock Holmes is perhaps the most famous and popular character in detective fiction, if not in all modern fiction. Doyle's stories were a strong influence on writers such as Ellery Queen, Agatha Christie, John Dickson Carr, and the many others who create tightly constructed puzzles for their detectives to solve with clearly and closely reasoned analysis. Societies such as the Baker Street Irregulars have sprung up around the world to study Doyle's stories, and the name of Sherlock Holmes has become synonymous with deduction, while "Elementary, my dear Watson" is a

Arthur Conan Doyle (Library of Congress)

catchphrase even among those who have never read the stories.

BIOGRAPHY

Arthur Conan Doyle was born in Scotland of devout Irish Catholic parents and educated by the Jesuits in England and Austria. He was graduated from the medical school at the University of Edinburgh and first went to sea as a ship's surgeon on a whaler to the Arctic, later on a West African passenger liner. He opened an office in Southsea, England, and because of a dearth of patients, began writing to fill his leisure time and to supplement his income. He had previously published a few short stories anonymously, and in 1887 completed *A Study in Scarlet*, a novelette in which Sherlock Holmes, as the central character, appears for the first time. Urged on by his American editor, he wrote *The Sign of Four* (1890; also pb. as *The Sign of the Four*) and a series of Sherlock Holmes stories which appeared in the *Strand Magazine*. The popularity of Holmes enabled Doyle to give up the practice of medicine, but since the author desired to be known as a historical romancer, the character was "killed off" in a struggle with his archenemy, Professor Moriarty, in the story "The Final Problem." Ten years later, yielding to pressure from his publishers and the public, he resurrected Holmes, first in *The Hound of the Baskervilles* (1901-1902, serial; 1902, book) and later in another series of Holmes short stories. Doyle was knighted in 1902 for his political service and principally for his publications defending the conduct of the British in the Boer War. Having left Catholicism, he turned to spiritualism and devoted the rest of his life to psychic research and propagandizing his beliefs.

ANALYSIS

In spite of his desire to be acknowledged as a writer of "serious" literature, Arthur Conan Doyle is destined to be remembered as the creator of a fictional character who has taken on a life separate from the literary works in which he appears. Sherlock Holmes, as the prototype of almost all fictional detectives, has become a legend not only to his devotees but also to those who have not even read the works in which he appears, the detective being immortalized by reputation and through the media of movies, television, and radio.

Doyle claimed that the character of Sherlock Holmes was based on his memories of Dr. Joseph Bell, a teacher of anatomy at the University of Edinburgh, whose diagnostic skills he had admired as a student of medicine. Bell, however, disclaimed the honor and suggested that Doyle himself possessed the analytical acumen that more closely resembled the skills of Sherlock Holmes. Regardless of the disclaimers and acknowledgments, there is little doubt that Doyle owed a large debt to Edgar Allan Poe and other predecessors in detective fiction, such as Émile Gaboriau and François-Eugène Vidocq. Doyle records that he was familiar with *Mémoires* (1828-1829; *Memoirs of Vidocq, Principal Agent of the French Police*, 1828-1829) and had read Gaboriau's *Monsieur Lecoq* (1880). It is the influence of Poe, however, that is most in evidence in the character of Holmes and in many of his plots.

Poe's character of C. Auguste Dupin bears remarkable similarities to the Sherlock Holmes character. Both Holmes and Dupin, for example, are eccentrics; both are amateurs in the detective field; both have little regard for the official police; and both enter into investigations, not because of any overwhelming desire to bring a culprit to justice but out of the interest that the case generates and the challenge to their analytical minds. In addition, both have faithful companions who serve as the chroniclers of the exploits of their respective detective friends. While Dupin's companion remains anonymous and the reader is unable to draw any conclusions about his personality, Dr. Watson, in contrast, takes on an identity (although always in a secondary role) of his own. The reader shares with Watson his astonishment at Holmes's abilities. In effect, Watson becomes a stand-in for the reader by asking the questions that need to be asked for a complete understanding of the situation.

Generally, the Sherlock Holmes stories follow a similar pattern: There is usually a scene at the Baker Street residence, at which time a visitor appears and tells his or her story. After Holmes makes some pre-

liminary observations and speculates upon a possible solution to the puzzle, Holmes and Watson visit the scene of the crime. Holmes then solves the mystery and explains to Watson how he arrived at the solution. "The Adventure of the Speckled Band" follows this formula, and it is apparent that Poe's "The Murders in the Rue Morgue" had a direct influence on this "locked room" mystery. The murder, the locked room, and the animal killer are all variations on the ingredients in the first case in which C. Auguste Dupin appears. Even the reference to the orangutan on the grounds of the Manor House would appear to be an allusion to the murderer in Poe's story. The gothic romance influence is also apparent in this adventure of Sherlock Holmes: There is the mysterious atmosphere and the strange, looming manor house; and there is the endangered woman threatened by a male force. Changing the murderer from the ape of Poe's story to a serpent in Doyle's story suggests at least symbolically the metaphysical (or supernatural) struggle between the forces of good and evil.

Typically, this story as well as all the Holmes stories ends with the solution to the mystery. Sherlock Holmes acknowledges that, by driving the snake back into the room where Dr. Roylott, the murderer, is waiting, he is indirectly responsible for his death; yet he matter-of-factly states that it is not likely to weigh heavily on his conscience. The mystery has been solved; that has been the detective's only interest in the case. Because of this single-minded interest on the part of the detective, what happens to the criminal after discovery is no longer relevant. If the criminal is to stand trial, the story ends with the arrest and no more is heard of him. There are no trials, no dramatic courtroom scenes, and no reports of executions or prison sentences which had been popular in earlier detective stories and which were to regain immense popularity in the future.

While the solution to the "ingenious puzzle" is the prime concern for the detective and certainly of interest to the reader, it is Sherlock Holmes's character with his multifaceted personality and his limitations which makes Doyle's stories about the detective's adventures so re-readable. Holmes, for example, is an accomplished musician, a composer as well as an instrumentalist; he is an expert in chemical research and has educated himself to be an authority on blood stains; he is the author of innumerable monographs on such esoteric subjects as different types of tobacco, bicycle tire impressions, and types of perfume; and he is an exceptionally fine pugilist.

His limitations, however, are what make Sherlock Holmes so attractive to the reader. He is sometimes frighteningly ignorant; for example, after Dr. Watson has explained the Copernican system to him, he responds: "Now that I know it. . . . I shall do my best to forget it"; he considers this information trivial, since it is not useful, and he feels that retaining it will crowd practical knowledge out of his mind. Holmes can also make erroneous judgments, and, perhaps most appealing of all, he can fail as a detective. It is this capacity for the detective to fail or to be outwitted that is perhaps Doyle's most significant contribution to the detective-fiction genre. Whereas Holmes's predecessors such as Lecoq and Dupin are presented as unerring in their conclusions and infallible in solving their cases, Doyle's hero demonstrates his fallibility early in his career.

"A SCANDAL IN BOHEMIA"

It is in the first of the Sherlock Holmes short stories, "A Scandal in Bohemia," without doubt Doyle's version of Edgar Allan Poe's "The Purloined Letter," that this very human fallibility is revealed. Both stories deal with the need to recover items that are being used to blackmail a person of royal heritage. In both cases, attempts to find the items have failed and the detectives are called on for assistance; and, in both stories, a ruse is used to discover the whereabouts of the incriminating items.

While the debt to Poe is large in this story, "A Scandal in Bohemia" also displays some significant departures that establish the work as Doyle's own, artistically. The scenes in the streets of London are conveyed with convincing detail to capture effectively "the spirit of the place" of Victorian England. The characters in Poe's Dupin stories are lightly drawn, and the central interest for these tales is not in the people but in what happens to them. While the characters in Poe's stories talk about matters which are relevant only to the mystery at hand, the direct oppo-

site is true in Doyle's story. The people in the Holmes story are interesting and full of dramatic movement, and Holmes's conversations with Watson and the others are filled with comments which are not related to the case.

In addition, Doyle introduces the device of disguises in "A Scandal in Bohemia." The King of Bohemia, wearing a small face mask to hide his identity, visits Holmes in his lodgings; his disguise, however, is immediately penetrated by the detective. Sherlock Holmes also assumes a disguise in the story that is so convincing and successful that even his close friend Dr. Watson is unable to recognize him. It is the skill of Irene Adler, Holmes's antagonist in the story, in assuming another identity that leads to the detective's being foiled. Holmes's failure in this story, however, in no way detracts from him. On the contrary, this failure and his others (such as in "The Yellow Face") serve to make him only more convincing and more three-dimensional as a human being than the always successful C. Auguste Dupin. Holmes loses no status through his errors; instead, he gains in the light of his past and future successes.

"THE RED-HEADED LEAGUE"

While there will always be disagreement among Sherlock Holmes aficionados about which of the many short stories is best, there is broad agreement that one of the best-constructed stories by Arthur Conan Doyle is the second short story in the first series, "The Red-Headed League." Doyle himself ranked the story very high when he was queried, and the Victorian reading public's response attested to its popularity. This story also introduces one of the recurring themes of the short stories: that of the *Doppelgänger*, or double. The dual nature of the world and of personalities is developed in parallel manners throughout the unraveling of the mystery of Jabez Wilson's involvement with the Red-Headed League. The contemplative side of Holmes is repeatedly contrasted with his energized side, just as the orderliness of Victorian England is seen in stark relief against "the half that is evil." Repeatedly, when there is a lull in the chase or a mystery has been solved, Sherlock Holmes retreats to his contemplative side to forget at least temporarily "the miserable weather and the still more miserable ways of our fellowmen."

"The Red-Headed League" follows the traditional formula of a Sherlock Holmes story. Holmes is visited at his flat by Jabez Wilson, who relates his problem. Wilson, the owner of a small pawnshop, has been working for the Red-Headed League for eight weeks, until abruptly and under mysterious circumstances, the League has been dissolved. He qualified for the position because of his red hair, and his only duties were to remain in a room and copy the *Encyclopædia Britannica*. He has been able to perform these chores because his assistant, Vincent Spaulding, was willing to work in the pawnshop for half-wages. He has come to Sherlock Holmes because he does not want to lose such a position without a struggle.

Holmes and Watson visit the pawnshop, and Spaulding is recognized by the detective as being in reality John Clay, a master criminal and murderer. The detective is able to infer from the circumstances that the opposite of what is expected is true. He concludes that it is not the presence of Jabez Wilson in the room performing a meaningless "intellectual" task for the League that is important; rather, it is his absence from the pawnshop that gives his alter ego assistant the opportunity to perform the "physical" task of tunneling from the cellar into the nearby bank. Setting a trap, Holmes, Watson, and the police are able to capture Clay and his confederates in their criminal act.

The double theme of the story is also reinforced in Jabez Wilson's account of the applicants lining up to apply for the position with the Red-Headed League. He describes the crowd lining up on the stair; those in anticipation of employment ascending the stairs with hope; those who have been rejected descending in despair, forming a "double" stream. John Clay, Holmes's antagonist in this story, is the first in a long line of adversaries of the detective who serve in effect as *Doppelgängers* of the sleuth. Clay has an aristocratic background and possesses royal blood. Holmes also has illustrious ancestors, being descended from country squires, and his grandmother is described as being "the sister of Vernet, the French artist." Clay is well educated and urbane, characteristics Holmes re-

peatedly shows throughout his adventures. Clay is described as being "cunning" in mind as well as skillful in his fingers, again a reflection of the detective's characteristics. Clay is also gracious in his defeat and expresses admiration for the ingenuity displayed by the victorious Holmes. He is truly a worthy adversary for the detective and the direct mirror image of Sherlock Holmes.

"THE FINAL PROBLEM"

Other great master criminals and, in effect, doubles for the great detective are Colonel Sebastian Moran of "The Adventure of the Empty House," Van Bork of "His Last Bow," and, the most famous of them all, Professor Moriarty, who is described in "The Final Problem" as the "Napoleon of crime" and the "organizer of half that is evil and of nearly all that is undetected in this great city." In essence, "The Final Problem" is a departure from the formula that characterizes the previous twenty-two Holmesian short stories, basically because Doyle intended that this would be the final work in which his detective would appear. Tiring of his creation and motivated by the desire to pursue his other literary interests, he has Watson record the demise of his friend. The story has no ingenious puzzle for the detective to unravel but instead is a detailed account of Sherlock Holmes's confrontation with his nemesis. For years, Holmes, who could "see deeply into the manifold wickedness of the human heart" and who could "leave his body at will and place himself into the mind and soul" of others, had been unable to penetrate the veil that shrouded the power "which for ever stands in the way of the law, and throws its shield over the wrongdoer." In this manner, Doyle almost casually proposes a conspiracy theme in this story which, in the hands of other writers, becomes one of the overriding characteristics of the detective fiction and thriller genres.

It is the character of Professor Moriarty, however, which commands the interest of the reader, particularly when seen as a reflection of Holmes. Professor Moriarty's career, like Holmes's, "has been an extraordinary one. He is a man of good birth and excellent education, endowed by Nature with a phenomenal mathematical faculty. At the age of twenty-one he wrote a treatise upon the Binomial Theorem, which has had a European vogue." When the Professor visits Holmes at his flat, his physical appearance is described as "extremely tall and thin, his forehead domes out in a white curve, and his two eyes are deeply sunken in his head. He is clean shaven, pale, and ascetic looking." To Holmes, his appearance is quite familiar, even though he has never met the man before. It is entirely likely that Holmes's immediate recognition is intended to suggest that the detective, for the first time in his life, is viewing in the flesh the side of his nature which his great intellect has refused to allow him to acknowledge.

Even though Dr. Watson had made special efforts to characterize Holmes as being almost totally devoid of emotion in his previous chronicles of Holmes's adventures, there are many instances in which there are outbursts of extreme feelings on the part of the detective. Holmes fluctuates between ennui and expressions of delight. He is often impulsive and compassionate. He is patient and deferential to his female clients. He is moved to indignation and intends to exact a form of revenge in "The Five Orange Pips."

In this story, "The Final Problem," he shows a level of nervousness and caution which is almost akin to fear in response to the threat that the malevolent genius Moriarty poses toward his person. Professor Moriarty is too much like himself for the detective to remain scientifically detached. There is no doubt that Holmes is totally conscious of the significance of the parallels that exist between the two when the Professor states:

> It has been a duel between you and me, Mr. Holmes. You hope to place me in the dock. I tell you that I will never stand in the dock. You hope to beat me. I tell you that you will never beat me. If you are clever enough to bring destruction upon me, rest assured that I shall do as much to you.

Holmes, with Watson, flees this enemy whom he acknowledges as "being quite on the same intellectual plane" as himself. Then, at Reichenbach Falls, he is inevitably forced to come face-to-face once again with his other self. Sidney Paget, the illustrator of many of the original publications in the *Strand Magazine*, depicts the struggle between Holmes and Mori-

arty just before their dual plunge into the chasm as being entwined together.

Thus, the culmination of Holmes's illustrious career, as originally intended by Doyle, was brought about in an entirely satisfactory symbolic and literary manner. Holmes, who could idly concede, "I have always had an idea that I could have made a highly efficient criminal," and "Burglary was always an alternative profession had I cared to adopt it," had resisted those impulses. In "The Final Problem" he could say: "In over a thousand cases I am not aware that I have ever used my powers upon the wrong side." The detective, however, was keenly aware throughout this story that "if he could be assured that society was freed from Professor Moriarty he would cheerfully bring his own career to a conclusion." With the death of Moriarty, he achieves that end. While "London is the sweeter for [my] presence," the destruction of the other side of his nature in Professor Moriarty makes it all the more so. The death of Sherlock Holmes along with his nemesis is comparable to self-destruction.

"THE ADVENTURE OF THE EMPTY HOUSE"

When Doyle "killed off" his detective hero, he was in no way prepared for the public reaction that followed. He resisted almost continuous pressure from his publishers and the public until 1902, when he finally relented and resurrected Holmes in *The Hound of the Baskervilles* and later in the story "The Adventure of the Empty House." In this story, a lieutenant of Professor Moriarty, Colonel Sebastian Moran, is the culprit and functions as the alter ego for Holmes. One of the more subtle acknowledgments of the double theme in this story is the use by Holmes of a wax model of himself to mislead his adversaries. Similar to "The Final Problem," the story of the return of Sherlock Holmes does not follow the usual formula for the previous works, but the rest in the series adheres rather closely. When the stories are read in sequence, however, one can understand why the mere presence of the detective, however contrived his survival, would be cause for rejoicing by his followers. Even a lapse of more than ten years since his last appearance (three years within the stories) has in no way diminished his skill or intellectual capacity.

Sherlock Holmes remains all that he was before his showdown with Professor Moriarty. The dialogue between the characters is as crisp as ever; the scenes are portrayed as vividly as before; the careful construction of the plots and the unraveling of the mysteries are as provocative as ever; and the imagination of the author is very much in evidence. There is evidence, however, of Doyle's reluctance to take his hero as seriously as he had before.

"THE ADVENTURE OF THE DANCING MEN"

The story "The Adventure of the Dancing Men," for example, is extremely contrived, almost totally dependent on cartoons as a cipher, and the reader is left with a feeling of dissatisfaction. The stories in the first series after the "death" of Sherlock Holmes are nevertheless of generally high quality and possess many memorable scenes which remain after the mysteries have been solved.

LATER HOLMES STORIES

There is agreement that the quality of the Sherlock Holmes stories published in the two collections, *His Last Bow* and *The Case-Book of Sherlock Holmes* is significantly diminished. Published in 1917 and 1927 respectively, the books demonstrate that Doyle was tired of his detective, as the works were written casually and almost impatiently. The onset of World War I in the title story of *His Last Bow* is pointed out by Jacques Barzun as being "perhaps symbolic of the end of a world of gaslight and order in which Holmes and Watson could function so predictably." The stories in *The Case-Book of Sherlock Holmes*, published only a few years before Doyle's death, possess some fine moments, but there is a singular failure on the part of the author to re-create the vividness of the Victorian world that had lifted the previous series of short stories out of the ordinary and enabled the reader to accept and admire so readily the reasoning powers of Sherlock Holmes.

Despite the uneven quality of these works, it is a tribute to Doyle's ability that Sherlock Holmes remains a memorable character. Although Watson informs the reader that Holmes's knowledge of formal philosophy is nil, he is a philosopher in his own way. Holmes has probed the most abstract of understandings—ranging from the motivation of hu-

mans to the nature of the universe—from the study of the physical world. He possesses a peculiar morality akin to the John Stuart Mill variety: Evil is doing harm to others. When he seeks justice, he inevitably finds it; justice in the social and structured sense. Holmes has little regard for the laws of human beings; he recognizes that they do not always serve the purposes of justice, so at times he rises above them and often ignores them. For him, the distinction between right and wrong is absolute and beyond debate. It was Doyle's skill in infusing such depth into his character that makes Holmes greater than Dupin and Lecoq.

OTHER MAJOR WORKS

LONG FICTION: *A Study in Scarlet*, 1887 (serial), 1888 (book); *The Mystery of Cloomber*, 1888; *The Firm of Girdlestone*, 1889; *Micah Clarke*, 1889; *The Sign of Four*, 1890 (also pb. as *The Sign of the Four*); *Beyond the City*, 1891; *The Doings of Raffles Haw*, 1891; *The White Company*, 1891; *The Great Shadow*, 1892; *The Refugees*, 1893; *The Parasite*, 1894; *The Stark Munro Letters*, 1895; *The Surgeon of Gaster Fell*, 1895; *Rodney Stone*, 1896; *The Tragedy of the Koroska*, 1897 (also as *A Desert Drama*); *Uncle Bernac*, 1897; *A Duet, with an Occasional Chorus*, 1899, revised 1910; *The Hound of the Baskervilles*, 1901-1902 (serial), 1902 (book); *Sir Nigel*, 1905-1906 (serial), 1906 (book); *The Lost World*, 1912; *The Poison Belt*, 1913; *The Valley of Fear*, 1914-1915 (serial), 1915 (book); *The Land of Mist*, 1926.

PLAYS: *Foreign Policy*, pr. 1893; *Jane Annie: Or, the Good Conduct Prize*, pr., pb. 1893 (with J. M. Barrie); *Waterloo*, pr. 1894 (also as *A Story of Waterloo*); *Halves*, pr. 1899; *Sherlock Holmes*, pr. 1899 (with William Gillette); *A Duet*, pb. 1903; *Brigadier Gerard*, pr. 1906; *The Fires of Fate*, pr. 1909; *The House of Temperley*, pr. 1909; *The Pot of Caviare*, pr. 1910; *The Speckled Band*, pr. 1910; *The Crown Diamond*, pr. 1921; *Exile: A Drama of Christmas Eve*, pb. 1925; *It's Time Something Happened*, pb. 1925.

POETRY: *Songs of Action*, 1898; *Songs of the Road*, 1911; *The Guards Came Through and Other Poems*, 1919; *The Poems: Collected Edition*, 1922.

NONFICTION: *The Great Boer War*, 1900; *The War in South Africa: Its Causes and Conduct*, 1902; *The Case of Mr. George Edalji*, 1907; *Through the Magic Door*, 1907; *The Crime of the Congo*, 1909; *The Case of Oscar Slater*, 1912; *Great Britain and the Next War*, 1914; *In Quest of Truth, Being a Correspondence Between Sir Arthur Conan Doyle and Captain H. Stansbury*, 1914; *To Arms!*, 1914; *The German War: Some Sidelights and Reflections*, 1915; *Western Wanderings*, 1915; *The Origin and Outbreak of the War*, 1916; *A Petition to the Prime Minister on Behalf of Robert Casement*, 1916(?); *A Visit to Three Fronts*, 1916; *The British Campaign in France and Flanders*, 1916-1919 (6 volumes); *The New Revelation*, 1918; *The Vital Message*, 1919; *Our Reply to the Cleric*, 1920; *Spiritualism and Rationalism*, 1920; *A Debate on Spiritualism*, 1920 (with Joseph McCabe); *The Evidence for Fairies*, 1921; *Fairies Photographed*, 1921; *The Wanderings of a Spiritualist*, 1921; *The Coming of the Fairies*, 1922; *The Case for Spirit Photography*, 1922 (with others); *Our American Adventure*, 1923; *Memories and Adventures*, 1924; *Our Second American Adventure*, 1924; *The Early Christian Church and Modern Spiritualism*, 1925; *Psychic Experiences*, 1925; *The History of Spiritualism*, 1926 (2 volumes); *Pheneas Speaks: Direct Spirit Communications*, 1927; *What Does Spiritualism Actually Teach and Stand For?*, 1928; *A Word of Warning*, 1928; *An Open Letter to Those of My Generation*, 1929; *Our African Winter*, 1929; *The Roman Catholic Church: A Rejoinder*, 1929; *The Edge of the Unknown*, 1930; *Arthur Conan Doyle on Sherlock Holmes*, 1981; *Essays on Photography*, 1982; *Letters to the Press*, 1984.

TRANSLATION: *The Mystery of Joan of Arc*, 1924 (by Léon Denis).

EDITED TEXTS: *D. D. Home: His Life and Mission*, 1921 (by Mrs. Douglas Home); *The Spiritualist's Reader*, 1924.

EDITED TEXT: *Dreamland and Ghostland*, 1886.

BIBLIOGRAPHY

Akinson, Michael. *The Secret Marriage of Sherlock Holmes and Other Eccentric Readings*. Ann Arbor: University of Michigan Press, 1996. Attempts to read Holmes's stories in the manner in which Holmes himself might read them. "The Adventure of the Speckled Band" is read in terms of the philosophy of Kundalini yoga; "A Scandal in Bohemia" is read in terms of its use of traditional romance motifs and its debt to Edgar Allan Poe; Jungian psychology is used to read *A Study in Scarlet*; and Derridian deconstruction is used to read "The Adventure of the Copper Breeches."

Carr, John Dickson. *The Life of Sir Arthur Conan Doyle*. London: John Murray, 1949. One of the first biographies of Doyle not written by a relative. Carr's straightforward biography gives a good overview of Doyle's life. Carr quotes copiously from Doyle's letters, but there is very little discussion of the stories. Includes a list of sources and an index.

Hall, Jasmine Yong. "Ordering the Sensational: Sherlock Holmes and the Female Gothic." *Studies in Short Fiction* 28 (Summer, 1991): 295-304. Examines how gothic elements and female clients in a number of stories, including the well-known "The Speckled Band," establish the rational detective as a powerful, patriarchal hero. Argues that Holmes controls his female clients as much as the gothic villains in Doyle's stories.

Hodgson, John A., ed. *Sherlock Holmes: The Major Stories with Contemporary Critical Essays*. New York: St. Martin's Press, 1994. Includes nine essays on Holmes, from a variety of critical perspectives, including feminist, deconstruction, and discourse analysis approaches. Includes detailed discussions of such stories as "The Man with the Twisted Lip" and "The Speckled Band."

Jaffee, Jacqueline A. *Arthur Conan Doyle*. Boston: Twayne, 1987. Jaffee's solid work combines biography and a critical discussion of Doyle's stories and novels. Contains three chapters on the Sherlock Holmes stories, which closely examine the tales. Supplemented by an index, a bibliography of Doyle's work, and an annotated bibliography.

Jann, Rosemary. *The Adventures of Sherlock Holmes: Detecting Social Order*. New York: Twayne, 1995. Part of Twayne's Masterwork Series, this slim volume is divided into two parts, the first of which places the great detective in a literary and historical context, followed by Jann's own reading of Arthur Conan Doyle's Sherlockian approach to detective fiction. In addition to a selected bibliography, Jann's book includes a brief chronology of Doyle's life and work.

Kestner, Joseph A. "Real Men: Construction of Masculinity in the Sherlock Holmes Narratives." *Studies in the Literary Imagination* 29 (Spring, 1996): 73-88. Discusses the construction of masculinity in Doyle's detective stories. Claims that one peculiar value of Doyle's Sherlock Holmes stories is the exposure of the contradictory nature of the realist text and besieged late-Victorian masculinity.

Orel, Harold, ed. *Critical Essays on Sir Arthur Conan Doyle*. New York: G. K. Hall, 1992. Including both evaluations by Doyle's contemporaries and later scholarship—some of it commissioned specifically for inclusion in this collection—*Critical Essays* is divided into three sections: "Sherlock Holmes," "Other Writings," and "Spiritualism." Harold Orel opens the collections with a lengthy and comprehensive essay, which is followed by a clever and classic meditation by Dorothy L. Sayers on "Dr. Watson's Christian Name." Also included are pieces by such literary lights as George Bernard Shaw, Max Beerbohm, and Heywood Broun.

Otis, Laura. "The Empire Bites Back: Sherlock Holmes as an Imperial Immune System." *Studies in 20th Century Literature* 22 (Winter, 1998): 31-60. Argues that Sherlock Holmes acts like a bacteriologist, hunting down tiny invaders and playing a defensive role as an imperial intelligence network detecting foreigners passing themselves off as British.

Priestman, Martin. *Detective Fiction and Literature: The Figure on the Carpet*. London: Macmillan, 1990. Priestman discusses the differences and similarities of detective and conventional fiction and provides an introduction to the social, structural, and psychological implications of crime fiction. He includes two chapters on the Sherlock Holmes stories, which provide close readings of several stories.

Stashower, Daniel. *Teller of Tales: The Life of Arthur Conan Doyle*. New York: Henry Holt, 1999. An excellent biography of Doyle. Focuses less on the Holmes novels and more on the historical novels, personal crusades, and spiritualism.

Robert W. Millett, updated by
Karen M. Cleveland Marwick

THEODORE DREISER

Born: Terre Haute, Indiana; August 27, 1871
Died: Hollywood, California; December 28, 1945

PRINCIPAL SHORT FICTION
Free and Other Stories, 1918
Chains: Lesser Novels and Stories, 1927
Fine Furniture, 1930
The Best Short Stories of Theodore Dreiser, 1947
    (Howard Fast, editor)
Best Short Stories, 1956 (James T. Farrell, editor)

OTHER LITERARY FORMS

Theodore Dreiser is best known for his novels. Of the eight that he wrote, *An American Tragedy* (1925), which was twice made into a motion picture, has attracted the most continuing interest. His short fiction is subsidiary to his novels, and his stories are sometimes capsule versions of his longer fiction, or novels in miniature. Additionally, Dreiser, more interested in literature's power to educate than its ability to entertain, experimented with a variety of different forms in

Theodore Dreiser (Library of Congress)

which to express his ideas, writing several autobiographical volumes, various books of essays, sketches, and accounts of his travels, as well as two books of plays and a collection of poems.

ACHIEVEMENTS

Dreiser remains one of the foremost naturalistic writers of the early twentieth century. Best known for his novels, particularly *Sister Carrie* (1900) and *An American Tragedy*, all the other works help illuminate them. Dreiser's dark outlook and brooding style is leavened by his richness of language and compassion. His life and art have been closely examined in numerous book-length studies and critical pieces that range in the hundreds. He has been hailed as the most influential figure in American letters at the beginning of the twentieth century, the Mount Everest of American fiction, and he was considered the chief spokesman for the realistic novel. Dreiser was a finalist for the Nobel Prize in Literature in 1930, but he lost in a close and bitterly contested vote to Sinclair Lewis, a rebuff that he never forgot. In 1944, the year before his death at age seventy-four, Dreiser was given the Award of Merit from the American Academy of Arts and Letters for extraordinary achievement in his art.

BIOGRAPHY

Theodore Herman Albert Dreiser was virtually the first widely recognized American writer whose background lacked connection with the White Anglo-Saxon Protestant establishment; his father was a Catholic emigrant from Germany, and Theodore grew up, with nine siblings, in a relatively impoverished, strictly religious family. Dreiser rejected his father's religion; he maintained a sympathy for the poor and various relations with his brothers and sisters (including the writer of very popular songs, such as "My Gal Sal," Paul Dreiser), a number of whom provided him with prototypes for his fictional characters. Leaving his Indiana home at fifteen to go to Chicago, Dreiser was fascinated with the raw and vital city, where he worked at a variety of jobs, pausing to spend one term at Indiana University before beginning a career as a journalist.

From Chicago this career took him to St. Louis, Pittsburgh, and New York, where he eventually became established as a successful magazine editor. In 1908 he married his first wife; the marriage lasted until her death in 1941, with many problems, some of them reflected in stories such as "Free" and "Chains." Although his journalistic experiences had given him potential material and writing practice, Dreiser was late in turning to fiction; his first short story was not completed until he was twenty-eight, but having begun, he went on to write other stories and have his first novel, *Sister Carrie*, appear in 1900. While *Sister Carrie*, in which the heroine loses her virtue and survives, unrepentant, was in effect suppressed by its publisher because of its unconventional morality, Dreiser was launched upon his career as a writer of fiction.

Subsequent financial troubles, a partial mental breakdown, marital problems not unrelated to Dreiser's apparent constitutional aversion to monogamy, and continual attacks by the literary, moral, and economic establishments, rather than permanently halting this career, provided it with raw material. With the appearance of his novel *An American Tragedy*,

Dreiser, at fifty-four, finally achieved significant financial success and wide acceptance, although his difficult personality, sexual varietism, drinking, anti-Semitism, and communist sympathies kept him involved in controversy. Near the end of his life he both developed an interest in Eastern mysticism and joined the Communist Party. He died in 1945.

ANALYSIS

A number of Theodore Dreiser's short stories reveal skills not found in the longer works. The reader who comes to the short fiction after reading Dreiser's novels is frequently surprised by both the whimsy and humor of some of the tales, and by their concise clarity of style, hardly a prominent feature of the novels. Nevertheless, the subject matter, techniques, and especially the tone of Dreiser's short fiction more often than not mirror the novels.

Some exceptions may be noted first. "When the Old Century Was New," set in New York in 1801, presents a day in the life of William Walton, a gentleman merchant "of Colonial prestige." Although Walton does propose to, and is accepted by, the fair Mistress Beppie Cruger, very little actually happens in the sketch; its interest arises from the historical verisimilitude that Dreiser gives to the commonplace. Even further removed from the modern reality which Dreiser customarily treats are two stories, "Khat" and "The Prince Who Was a Thief," set in an indefinite time in Arabia, the first focusing on the misfortunes of Ibn Abdullah, an aged beggar, the second, subtitled "An Improvisation on the Oldest Oriental Theme," being a kind of pastiche of a tale from *The Arabian Nights' Entertainments*. A different sort of fantasy is "McEwen of the Shining Slave Makers," Dreiser's first story, in which the title figure dreams that he is a black ant engaged in a titanic struggle against red ant tribes.

Dreiser's imagination takes another turn in "The Cruise of the *Idlewild*." "Idlewild" is the name assigned to a railroad shop by the workers in it, who pretend that, rather than toiling in a stationary, unromantic workplace, they are sailing on a yacht, taking on imaginary roles as captain, bos'n, able seaman, and so forth. This is a curious tale of a kind of collec-

tive escapism, told with somewhat ponderous, but genial, humor. Finally, of Dreiser's various atypical stories, two related to his newspaper days should be noted: "A Story of Stories" and "Nigger Jeff." In both these works there is a strong emphasis on plot; the first tale involves the competition of two reporters in covering the story of a train robber; the second uses a lynching to describe the maturation of a young newspaperman. Focused on action, neither of these stories contains much of the awkward wording and sentence structure often thought characteristic of Dreiser's style. Indeed, the only aspect common to all these miscellaneous stories, by which their author does something to put his own mark on them, is the sense of the difficult, competitive nature of human existence. This sense appears even in the light sketch "When the Old Century Was New," which ends: "The crush and stress and wretchedness fast treading upon this path of loveliness he could not see"; it surfaces in "The Cruise of the 'Idlewild'" when one character, "little Ike," becomes the butt of the other men, and the humorous fantasy temporarily threatens to turn nasty.

Dreiser's fundamental view of life is more naturally expressed, however, in stories in which humor, fantasy, or action for its own sake do not dominate. His subject matter is, typically, contemporary and serious; his interest is more in character than in plot. This material and interest can be seen in "Sanctuary," a story more representative of Dreiser's work. It traces the life history of its "heroine" (the short fiction, like the novels, sometimes has a woman as protagonist), Madeline, from her upbringing in the slums through her arrest for prostitution, after which she is "turned over to the care of the Sisterhood of the Good Shepherd." After serving her time, she works at a variety of "honest" jobs, is married and abandoned by her husband, and returns, voluntarily, to find, with the Sisters, a permanent "Sanctuary." The resemblances between this tale and a famous work of naturalism, Stephen Crane's *Maggie: A Girl of the Streets* (1893), are obvious, but superficial. While both stories chronologically trace the inescapable influences of environment in warping the development of a girl not lacking sensitivity, Dreiser's tone, one of Olympian pity, differs from the ironic detachment of Crane. It is Dreiser's sense of "there but for the grace of God go I" that keeps his focus, and his reader's, on the character, whereas Crane, with his remarkable descriptive style that contrasts with Dreiser's flatness, emphasizes the background and setting.

While suggesting greater empathy with his characters than does a more typically naturalistic writer, such as Crane in *Maggie* or Frank Norris in *McTeague* (1899), Dreiser does employ techniques which produce "aesthetic distance." These techniques operate so that the reader, while reacting to the often pathetic situation of a story's protagonist, is able to see that situation in a larger "philosophic" perspective. A believer in the educational importance of literature, Dreiser had little use for the idea of "art for art's sake." His stories, while not crudely didactic, are meant to teach.

"THE OLD NEIGHBORHOOD"

"The Old Neighborhood," quite representative of Dreiser's technique, has a point to make, even if that point may ultimately reduce to a sad sigh offered in recognition of life's inescapable sorrow. This story, first appearing in 1918, but collected in Dreiser's second book of stories, *Chains*, can be seen as a dehydrated novel, in that the protagonist's whole life story is present in a relatively few pages. Unlike Dreiser's actual novels, however, which proceed in basically straightforward chronological order, this story is "framed." The central character has returned to visit his "old neighborhood"; the story begins with his walking from his car to his old apartment; it ends, shortly thereafter, with his returning to his car. Within this frame, through a series of flashbacks (a time scheme employed in a number of Dreiser's stories) which are described in the third person but limited to the protagonist's memory (also a typical device in Dreiser's short fiction), the reader learns of all the major events in the protagonist's life. The reader learns the character's reaction to these events, what his reactions were when the events occurred, and what his overall view is in retrospectively considering a life that is drawing toward a close. The reader discovers that the unnamed protagonist has struggled out of poverty, marrying a department store clerk, Marie,

when they are still both young and he has little education or apparent prospects; but he has talent as an inventor and visions of a better life. In spite of the economic pressure occasioned by fathering two children, the protagonist studies at night and on Sundays, and eventually, through his inventions, achieves fame and money. In the course of his rise, however, his two children die, and he becomes increasingly estranged from his wife, whose simple loyalty no longer satisfies him.

Driven by his ambition, he leaves his wife, and she does not share in his material success. After her death he remarries, but at the time of the story, he has returned to the scene of his earlier married days—the old neighborhood of struggle, poverty, loss, and dreams—in an attempt to lay to rest the ghosts of the past that still haunt him. In the insight that ends the story, however, he realizes "how futile this errand was" and how his actions were "not right, not fair," and that "there is something cruel and evil in it all, in all wealth, all ambition, in love of fame." He returns to his car, a symbol of "power and success," to be "whirled swiftly and gloomily away."

The moral which is drawn by the protagonist is one which the audience has been prepared by the author to accept. By means of the complex time scheme, in which the inventor's memories occur in roughly, but by no means exactly, an order corresponding to the order of the past events of his life, readers are partially "distanced" from the protagonist's attitudes, recognizing their selfishness before he does, yet maintaining some sympathy for him all the while. When, at last, he expresses a view that the audience has already approached, there is a satisfactory sense of conclusion which allows the reader to judge and pity the central figure simultaneously. A kind of catharsis that depends on "philosophical" acceptance of "the pity of it all" occurs. In some ways the story resembles James Joyce's famous work "The Dead," in which irony is also employed to lead toward an "epiphany" or revelation of a significant insight gained by both the central figure and the reader.

While Dreiser in his consistent use of imagery is certainly less impressive than is Joyce, it is worth noting that the former, often attacked for being a clumsy craftsman, does make effective use throughout the story of symbolic references to the bridge and to water. It seems that Dreiser must have decided to play with, and revitalize, the cliché "it's all water under the bridge," just as Charles Chesnutt, in his story "Baxter's Procrustes," did with the expression "don't judge a book by its cover."

If "The Old Neighborhood" is, on balance, a relatively successful story, it suffers from the attempt to cover too many events in too few pages, so that, with his novelist's inclination bound within the limitations of short fiction, Dreiser resorts to "telling" rather than "showing," and the tale produces a certain unfortunate impression of stasis. Two other stories by Dreiser, notable for avoiding this impression while still being, unlike the atypical works noted earlier, representative of his general thought and method, should be briefly mentioned. In them, Dreiser successfully integrates his philosophy of life with writing techniques adjusted to the requirements of short fiction.

"THE LOST PHOEBE"

"The Lost Phoebe," which may owe something to Norris's story, in *The Octopus* (1901), of Vanamee and his lost love, tells of an old man who, refusing to accept the death of his wife of many years, wanders over the countryside imagining her return until at last he sees her in a vision which he follows over a cliff to his death. In this work, Dreiser's view of the "terror and beauty of life" emerges through an effective balance of action, setting, and character.

"ST. COLUMBA AND THE RIVER"

Finally, "St. Columba and the River," developed from an earlier nonfiction piece Dreiser had written concerning the work of "sand-hogs," those construction workers who build underwater tunnels, may well be the author's most successful work of short fiction. The story tells of the tribulations of one such worker, McGlathery, who, driven by the need for something approaching a living wage, develops real courage in his dangerous occupation, finally surviving a cave-in through a freak of good fortune. In this work, Dreiser's naturalistic details are never tedious, because the material, involving an unusual occupation, requires them. Dreiser's frequently ponderous tone,

more out of place in short fiction than in novels, is avoided; the story is lightened with humor. Character, appropriately in a short story, is exposed more than developed, and the plot reaches a definite climax, and yet the theme is not made subservient to the plot; rather, it is integrated with it. If, as always, Dreiser teaches the reader about the strange kaleidoscope of life, here he does it while simultaneously being entertaining. With Horace, the reader can, in this story, accept the idea that art's function may be to at once delight and instruct.

In spite of such notable successes, Dreiser's short fiction remains secondary in interest to his novels, on which his reputation correctly rests. Nevertheless, not only are his short stories valuable when used to help understand his more significant work, but also they are interesting in demonstrating other sides of his remarkable talent. Most importantly, there are those successes that are, in their own right, valuable works of art.

OTHER MAJOR WORKS

LONG FICTION: *Sister Carrie*, 1900; *Jennie Gerhardt*, 1911; *The Financier*, 1912, 1927; *The Titan*, 1914; *The "Genius,"* 1915; *An American Tragedy*, 1925; *The Bulwark*, 1946; *The Stoic*, 1947.

PLAYS: *Plays of the Natural and Supernatural*, pb. 1916; *The Hand of the Potter: A Tragedy in Four Acts*, pb. 1918.

POETRY: *Moods: Cadenced and Declaimed*, 1926, 1928; *The Aspirant*, 1929; *Epitaph: A Poem*, 1929.

NONFICTION: *A Traveler at Forty*, 1913; *A Hoosier Holiday*, 1916; *Twelve Men*, 1919; *Hey, Rub-a-Dub-Dub!*, 1920; *A Book About Myself*, 1922 (revised as *Newspaper Days*, 1931; *The Color of a Great City*, 1923; *A Gallery of Women*, 1929; *My City*, 1929; *Dawn*, 1931; *Tragic America*, 1931; *America Is Worth Saving*, 1941; *Letters of Theodore Dreiser*, 1959; *Letters to Louise*, 1959; *American Diaries*, 1902-1926, 1982; *Selected Magazine Articles of Theodore Dreiser*, 1985.

BIBLIOGRAPHY

Elias, Robert H. *Theodore Dreiser: Apostle of Nature*. Ithaca, N.Y.: Cornell University Press, 1970.

An excellent scholarly biography on Dreiser, who cooperated on the work. Includes a comprehensive chapter listing a bibliography, biographies, manuscripts and letters, and criticism of the writer.

Gerber, Philip. *Theodore Dreiser Revisited*. New York: Twayne, 1992. Includes chapters on all Dreiser's major works, three chapters on the development of Dreiser studies, a chronology, notes and references, and an annotated bibliography.

Gogol, Miriam, ed. *Theodore Dreiser: Beyond Naturalism*. New York: New York University Press, 1995. Divided into sections on gender studies, psychoanalysis, philosophy, film studies, and popular literature. Gogol's introduction advances the argument that Dreiser was much more than a naturalist and deserves to be treated as a major author.

Kazin, Alfred, and Charles Shapiro. *The Stature of Theodore Dreiser: A Critical Survey of the Man and His Work*. Bloomington: Indiana University Press, 1965. Provides a good anthology of articles, essays, and personal reminiscences by noted authors and critics on Dreiser the man and the writer. Kazin's perceptive introduction sets the tone. Includes a lengthy bibliography.

Kratzke, Peter. "'Sometimes, Bad Is Bad': Teaching Theodore Dreiser's 'Typhoon' and the American Literary Canon." In *Short Stories in the Classroom*, edited by Carole L. Hamilton and Peter Kratzke. Urbana, Ill.: National Council of Teachers of English, 1999. Discusses how teaching Dreiser's story raises a number of issues about how the canon gets established; shows how an analysis of the story reveals its poor literary quality; suggests that canonical authors are not infallible.

Lydon, Michael. "Justice to Theodore Dreiser." *The Atlantic* 272 (August, 1993): 98-101. Argues that Dreiser should be seen without reservation as a giant of American letters who stood at the vanguard of modernism; argues that the incongruities and eccentricities of Dreiser's life have always affected the critical reception of his writing.

McAleer, John J. *Theodore Dreiser: An Introduction and Interpretation*. New York: Barnes & Noble Books, 1968. This volume studies the artist with the aim of helping the reader grasp the whole of Dreiser's fiction. Includes a lengthy chronology and a bibliography.

Pizer, Donald. *The Novels of Theodore Dreiser: A Critical Study*. Minneapolis: University of Minnesota Press, 1976. A solid study and introduction to Dreiser's eight published novels. Pizer examines each work as a separate unit and points out their respective merits and flaws.

Pizer, Donald, ed. *Critical Essays on Theodore Dreiser*. Boston: G. K. Hall, 1981. An excellent compilation of articles and essays. The criticism is arranged around Dreiser's works and ideas in general. A second section is reserved for individual novels.

Riggio, Thomas P. "Following Dreiser, Seventy Years Later." *The American Scholar* 65 (Autumn, 1996): 569-577. A biographical sketch that focuses on Dreiser as the most famous American to be invited to Moscow for the tenth anniversary of the Russian Revolution in 1927; describes a visit to Russia to research an edition of a diary kept by Dreiser in the late 1920's during his three months' stay in the Soviet Union.

Shapiro, Charles. *Theodore Dreiser: Our Bitter Patriot*. Carbondale: Illinois University Press, 1962. Shapiro expands his original dissertation study into the critical and illuminating examination of the underlying themes found in Dreiser's works. He believes that *An American Tragedy* is Dreiser's most important work because of its thematic richness.

Swansberg, W. A. *Dreiser*. New York: Charles Scribner's Sons, 1965. The definitive biography of Dreiser; it has stood the test of time and ranks with the best. Swansberg is less interested in Dreiser the artist, not being a literary critic, and concentrates on Dreiser the man.

William B. Stone, updated by Terry Theodore

ANDRE DUBUS

Born: Lake Charles, Louisiana; August 11, 1936
Died: Haverhill, Massachusetts; February 24, 1999

PRINCIPAL SHORT FICTION

Separate Flight, 1975
Adultery and Other Choices, 1977
Finding a Girl in America, 1980
The Times Are Never So Bad, 1983
The Last Worthless Evening, 1986
Selected Stories, 1988
Dancing After Hours: Stories, 1996

OTHER LITERARY FORMS

Although Andre Dubus wrote an early novel, *The Lieutenant* (1967), which is highly regarded by some critics and readers, and a novella, *Voices from the Moon* (1984), which has been printed separately, his most important contributions to literature are his shorter works. Besides his fiction, Dubus wrote two well-received books of autobiographical essays.

ACHIEVEMENTS

Andre Dubus's literary career is notable in the way it stands outside the shifting fashions of the American literary scene. During the 1960's and 1970's, when the "postmodernism" of Donald Barthelme, John Barth, and Thomas Pynchon was creating a highly self-conscious, self-reflective literature that often used its own craft to explore itself, Dubus remained a committed realist, at his best when he used his craft to explore the lives of his characters. During the period when the so-called minimalist stories of writers such as Raymond Carver, Bobbie Ann Mason, and Lorrie Moore came into literary prominence, Dubus remained what might be called a "maximalist" writer, who seemed most at home in the form of the long story, or novella. In a period of shifting male and female definitions, Dubus wrote often about the waywardness of people who continue to define themselves by concepts of masculinity and femininity that the world around them no longer values. Not least of all, in an age of secular values, Dubus often looks to the sacraments of the Catholic Church to find deep values.

BIOGRAPHY

Andre Dubus was born in Lake Charles, Louisiana, on August 11, 1936, and attended the Christian Brothers Catholic School in Lafayette from 1944 until 1954, after which he enrolled in McNeese State University in Lake Charles. Upon graduating from college in 1958 with a B.A. in English and journalism, he married Patricia Lowe and entered the Marine Corps with a commission as lieutenant. Over the next five years, four of the couple's children were born (Suzanne in 1958, Andre III in 1959, Jeb in 1960, and Nicole in 1963), and he was to rise to the rank of captain.

In 1963, he published his first story, "The Intruder," in *The Sewanee Review* and resigned his officer's commission to enter the M.F.A. program at the University of Iowa, the much respected Writers' Workshop program. Upon receiving his M.F.A. in 1965, he taught for one year as a lecturer at Nicholls State University in Louisiana, before accepting a position at Bradford College in Massachusetts in 1966, where he was to teach for the next fourteen years, until his retirement in 1984.

Dubus was married and divorced three times, and the pain of these broken marriages provided a source for much of his fiction. His first marriage, to Lowe in 1958, ended in divorce in 1970. His second marriage, to Tommie Gail Cotter in 1975, ended in divorce in 1977. His third marriage, to Peggy Rambach, also a writer, in 1979, produced two daughters, Cadence, born in 1982, and Madeline, born in 1987, but ended when his wife left in November, 1987, in the midst of family strain stemming from a 1986 automobile accident, which also cost Dubus a leg.

Many of Dubus's stories have been selected for the annual *The Best American Short Stories* and *Prize Stories: The O. Henry Awards* series. Among his national honors, he received a National Endowment for the Arts grant in 1985 and a John Simon Guggenheim

Memorial Foundation Fellowship in 1986. Both of these honors came after his retirement from teaching in 1984. His plans to use the monetary freedom provided by these grants to spend more time writing were violently interrupted by an accident in which he had stopped to assist two distressed motorists, only to become the victim of another car. The pain of recovering from this accident, in which he saved a life but lost a leg, is chronicled in the title essay of his collection of essays *Broken Vessels*. On February 24, 1999, Dubus died in Haverhill, Massachusetts.

ANALYSIS

Among American story writers of the twentieth century, the one to whom Andre Dubus is most often compared is Flannery O'Connor. While Dubus's works are not generally marked by the wry, ironic wit that permeates O'Connor's work, both writers are marked by what Thomas E. Kennedy, among others, has called an "existential Christian" sensibility.

"IF THEY KNEW YVONNE"

An early Dubus story, "If They Knew Yvonne," first published in *The North American Review* in 1969 and collected both in *Separate Flights* and *Selected Stories*, displays this sensibility clearly. This story traces the development of a teenager, Harry Dugal, growing into manhood and caught between two powerful forces: his emerging sexuality and his need for the absolution and communion provided by the Catholic Church. Taught by the fathers at the Christian Brothers School to regard masturbation as "self-abuse" and a mortal sin, Harry, as he discovers his own inability to resist the urge to masturbate, goes to confession at every opportunity to confess his sins. Disgusted at his own weakness and at the sexual weakness that he discovers in his family around him, including his parents, whose store of condoms he discovers, and his sister Janet, who gets married while two months pregnant, the young Harry even considers emasculating himself at one point.

At the age of nineteen, however, he has his first sexual encounter with a woman his own age, Yvonne Millet, and discovers a type of sexuality that does not disgust him. When Yvonne implores him, "Love me, Harry, love me," he begins to perceive that this type of love is not the squalid lust that he had been warned to guard against but something else, something he is not sure the Catholic fathers at his school knew anything about. The story ends shortly after he has drifted apart from Yvonne and goes to confession again. After Harry has confessed his sexual affair, the priest quotes a line from St. John, in which Christ prays, "I do not pray that You take them out of the world but that You keep them from evil," a quote that delineates the story's Christian existentialist theme. Harry begins to understand that the higher good depends not on remaining pure and safe from the world but on being a responsible, conscientious member of the world.

In his full-length study, *Andre Dubus: A Study of the Short Fiction*, Thomas Kennedy points out that almost half of Dubus's first fifty stories deal with violent themes or subjects, but he further points out that violence is only secondary to the central theme, a symptom of the greater condition of "human isolation and disconnection in . . . modern America." This is not to say that Dubus in any way excuses violence, but rather that understanding how violence grows out of an acceptance of superficial values is an important source for his fiction.

"THE PRETTY GIRL"

His novella-length story, "The Pretty Girl," collected in both *The Times Are Never So Bad* and *Selected Stories*, is one of his best extended examinations of this type of violence. One of the two point-of-view characters is Raymond Yarborough, who is presented as a wildly exploding tinderbox of violence. When the reader meets him, he is divorced from the other main character, Polly Comeau, but still obsessed by her. The reader learns early that Raymond has already raped her, though he considers that he was only "taking back my wife for a while." Before long, he beats up and severely injures a man whom he knows she has slept with and lights a fire around the house where Polly is staying, not to destroy anything but to terrorize her.

If Raymond is in many ways the antagonist in the story, he is also the most interesting, and his former wife Polly is not presented in particularly sympathetic terms. A waitress by trade, Polly is in many ways best described in the terms of the story's title as a twenty-six-year-old "pretty girl" who has used her beauty to avoid fashioning an adult identity and instead has tended to drift from one sexual affair to another, even during the course of her marriage, without much sense of responsibility or consequences.

Polly is a loner almost as much as Raymond is. She shares a house with a male acquaintance but has no close friends either male or female. Her relationships with women tend to be competitive, and her friendships with men tend to be brief, quickly sacrificed to her love affairs. She is significantly alone when Raymond breaks into her house at the end of the story to confront her about why she left him and what she really wants. Though he is unarmed, Polly, who has been ill and alone for several days, uses a gun she bought for protection to kill him when he begins to take off his clothes. Both main characters are carefully constructed to be unlikable, though only Raymond is presented as truly repugnant. The success of the story is that it compels the reader nevertheless to want to understand each of them and to appreciate each character's struggle, while not inviting the reader to forget or overlook their immature self-obsession or moral rootlessness.

"Finding a Girl in America"

A number of Dubus's stories deal with recurring characters. Two stories of the three that deal with Hank Allison, a middle-aged, philandering college professor, show Dubus's art at both its best and its worst. "Finding a Girl in America" shows both the character Hank Allison and the writer Andre Dubus at their worst. In it, Hank is presented as a divorced college professor who has been having affairs with his female students. As the story opens, he has learned that a former lover had an abortion and feels cheated because he believes that had the baby been born, it would have filled the void left in his life by his daughter growing up; the point of view of the woman who would have had a baby she did not want fathered by a man she did not love is not seriously considered. The attention to detail, which in other stories creates a convincing illusion of reality, in this story seems tedious and self-indulgent. Dubus's insistence on finding moral frameworks to understand his

characters, a tendency that in many stories uplifts his art, in this story misleads him. Hank's life is so self-indulgent that it is hard for a reader to take him half as seriously as he takes himself.

"Adultery"

The earlier story, "Adultery," is by contrast one of the finest examples of Dubus's art. To be sure, Hank Allison is the same self-centered, self-justifying man that the reader meets in the later story (as well as in "We Don't Live Here Anymore"). "Adultery," however, is carefully constructed to consider not only marital fidelity but also spiritual fidelity.

The main characters are Hank Allison, his wife Edith, and Father Joe Ritchie, a Catholic priest dying of cancer who renounces his vows and has an affair with Edith. The story also investigates the lives of a number of other men and women whom Hank and Edith choose as lovers. It is Hank who initially brings adultery into his and Edith's marriage, but when she discovers it, he immediately consents to her right to have extramarital affairs as well. The affairs they both have take their toll especially on Edith and make a sham of their marriage. The irony of the title—and the element that raises this story to the finest level of American fiction—is that Edith's adultery with a dying Catholic priest is not viewed by her or Father Ritchie as true adultery; the true adultery for her is staying in a marriage based on hypocrisy. Similarly, although this affair compromises Joe Ritchie in more ways than one, he and Edith both understand that their relationship is spiritually as well as personally the right thing to do; what worries Joe Ritchie most is that Edith might remain married to Hank, and he is relieved when she comes to him while he is dying (in the reverse of a deathbed to confession) to say that she is divorcing Hank. By deciding to divorce Hank, Edith upholds at least the *idea* of marital fidelity. Moreover, she realizes that her affair with Joe Ritchie has provided her with a new center for her life and that she would be unfaithful to herself and the belief in marriage to remain with Hank any longer.

"A Father's Story"

"A Father's Story," which was chosen by John Updike for the annual *The Best American Short Stories* in 1984, is in some respects Dubus's most important story. Smaller in scale than stories such as "The Fat Girl" or "Separate Flights," which each compress the story of several years into a few pages, "A Father's Story" focuses on a crucial incident in the life of Luke Ripley and his daughter Jennifer. Like many of Dubus's characters, Luke seems in many ways to be a version of the author, but in this case, a version that has achieved a deceptive veneer of simplicity. The opening line of the story, "My name is Luke Ripley and here is what I call my life," seems to present the voice of a direct, straightforward man. The life that Luke tells the reader about is one filled with a variety of contradictions: He is a devout Catholic but divorced; he attends Mass regularly but does not always listen; he enjoys talking to his priest but casually, preferably over a few beers, and what they discuss is mostly small talk; he is a self-described lazy man who dislikes waking up early but does so each morning to pray, not because he feels obligated to do so but because he knows he has the choice not to do so. Luke Ripley is a man who lives with contradictions and accepts them.

As such, when his daughter comes to him, frantically telling him that she hit a man with a car, he reacts almost instinctively. Rather than call the police or an ambulance, he drives to the scene of the accident to verify that the young man is in fact dead. When he knows that there is nothing that can be done to help the young man, he drives home and puts his daughter to bed, then takes her car out and runs it into a tree in front of the church to cover up the dent she had already created. The story ends with Luke recalling to the reader how he justifies himself to his God each morning, saying, "You never had a daughter and, if You had, You could not have borne her passion. . . . I love her more than I love truth." God replies, "Then you love in weakness," to which Luke responds, "As You love me."

The power of "A Father's Story" is that it captures perfectly the opposites that Dubus's fiction is constantly exploring. Luke Ripley's love for his daughter is both his strength and his weakness. Similarly, his love for his daughter moves him to deceive, even as his religion demands confession; and when he finds himself unable to confess his sin of covering up his

daughter's crime, the story itself, it is clear, is his substitute for the confession that he cannot make to a priest. Like many of Dubus's stories, "A Father's Story" shows a person caught between the confusing, ambiguous demands of his human heart and the by-no-means-clear demands of a religion in which he believes but which speaks of an absolute he can only partially understand.

OTHER MAJOR WORKS

LONG FICTION: *The Lieutenant*, 1967; *Voices from the Moon*, 1984.

NONFICTION: *Broken Vessels*, 1991; *Meditations from a Movable Chair: Essays*, 1998.

BIBLIOGRAPHY

Breslin, John B. "Playing Out of the Patterns of Sin and Grace: The Catholic Imagination of Andre Dubus." *Commonweal* 115 (December 2, 1988): 652-656. An interesting analysis of the Catholic themes in Dubus's literature, written for a lay audience. Breslin focuses particularly on Dubus's early novel, *The Lieutenant*, the trilogy of stories dealing with Hank Allison ("We Don't Live Here Anymore," "Adultery," and "Finding a Girl in America"), and "A Father's Story."

Feeney, Joseph J. "Poised for Fame: Andre Dubus at Fifty." *America* 155 (November 15, 1986): 296-299. Using the occasion of Dubus's fiftieth birthday, the author provides a general introduction to the man, his writing, and his major themes. Written for an audience he assumes to be generally unfamiliar with Dubus's fiction, this article presents the major themes of Dubus's fiction without exploring them in depth.

Kennedy, Thomas E. *Andre Dubus: A Study of the Short Fiction.* Boston: Twayne, 1988. The first full-length study of Dubus's fiction to be published, this volume is by far the most helpful work for someone interested in Dubus and his fiction. Kennedy groups Dubus's stories together by their thematic content and analyzes them in separate chapters, which are each devoted to one theme. Also included are other critical evaluations, two interviews with Dubus, an extensive bibliography of primary and secondary sources, and a helpfully designed index. If there is a flaw, it is that Kennedy sometimes seems too devoted to Dubus's work to accurately evaluate its occasional shortcomings.

Lesser, Ellen. "True Confession: Andre Dubus Talks Straight." Review of *Selected Stories*. *Village Voice* 37 (January 17, 1989): 56. Lesser claims that "Dubus writes stories like a pilot pushing the envelope—continually testing fiction's effective limits." She praises his fiction for its deliberate unfashionableness and for its unsimplified Catholic sensibility.

Miner, Madone. "Jumping from One Heart to Another: How Andre Dubus Writes About Women." *Critique* 39 (Fall, 1997): 18-31. Discusses three stories—"Anna," "Leslie in California," and "Rose"—in terms of Dubus's ability to write empathetically from a woman's perspective, to speak with a woman's voice about women's experience, while still retaining his "maleness."

Rowe, Anne E. "Andre Dubus." In *Contemporary Fiction Writers of the South*, edited by Joseph M. Flora and Robert Bain. Westport, Conn.: Greenwood Press, 1993. A general introduction to such Dubus themes as the passage from childhood to the adult world, failed friendships and marriages, and the individual's search for a meaningful center. Also includes an analytical survey of criticism of Dubus's fiction.

Todd, David Yandell. "An Interview with Andre Dubus." *Yale Review* 86 (July, 1998): 89-110. Dubus candidly discusses his decision to become a writer and the relationship between his life, his stories, and the authors who have most influenced him. He also considers what motivates his characters, creates their conflicts, and provides them with spiritual and moral significance.

Yarbrough, Steve. "Andre Dubus: From Detached Incident to Compressed Novel." *Critique: Studies in Modern Fiction* 28 (Fall, 1986); 19-27. Argues that Dubus's short stories can be categorized in three different ways, of which the largest category is the compressed novel, which follows the course of characters' lives for several years. This article focuses on a number of short stories, including "The Doctor," "The Dark Men," "Townies," "In My Life," "Separate Flights," and "The Fat Girl."

Thomas Cassidy, updated by Charles E. May

PAUL LAURENCE DUNBAR

Born: Dayton, Ohio; June 27, 1872
Died: Dayton, Ohio; February 9, 1906

PRINCIPAL SHORT FICTION

Folks from Dixie, 1898
The Strength of Gideon and Other Stories, 1900
In Old Plantation Days, 1903
The Heart of Happy Hollow, 1904
The Best Stories of Paul Laurence Dunbar, 1938

OTHER LITERARY FORMS

Known primarily for his verse, Paul Laurence Dunbar published *Lyrics of Lowly Life* in 1896; the collection vaulted him to fame as a premier dialect poet. He was the author, also, of five other volumes of original verse, three librettos written alone and with others, a drama, essays, and four novels, the most interesting of which is *The Sport of the Gods* (1902).

ACHIEVEMENTS

Paul Laurence Dunbar was America's first professional black writer and a great popular success. Championed for the dialect verse and stories of the plantation folk he was unequaled in rendering but which he himself despised as limited and compliant

Paul Laurence Dunbar (Library of Congress)

with existing stereotypes, Dunbar was hailed by the leading literary minds of his day.

BIOGRAPHY

The child of former slaves, Joshua and Matilda Glass Burton Murphy Dunbar, Paul Laurence Dunbar was raised in Dayton, Ohio; his younger sister died when he was three and his father when Paul was twelve. In high school, he was the only African American, but perhaps both despite and because of this he became president of his class, managing editor of his school newspaper, president of the school literary club, and class poet. While still in high school, he published poems in local newspapers and served as editor for the *Dayton Tattler*, published by classmate Orville Wright, coinventor of the airplane. Despite Dunbar's scholastic excellence, Dayton's discriminatory policies forced the young graduate to take a menial position as an elevator operator while

he continued to write. Encouraged by other writers and a former teacher, Dunbar published privately his first collection of poetry, *Oak and Ivy* (1893). His second collection, *Majors and Minors* (1895), won William Dean Howells's praise and sent him on the road to fame, but for Dunbar it was for all the wrong reasons.

In 1898, Dunbar married Alice Ruth Moore, a Creole writer from New Orleans; the childless couple separated in 1902. Dunbar died in 1906, at the age of thirty-three, of tuberculosis, of the effects of the alcohol prescribed to treat it, and of the melancholy brought on by his belief that his life had been a failure.

ANALYSIS

Paul Laurence Dunbar's life and writing were both impeded and tempered by the racial politics of his day. It was his greatest sorrow as an artist that his public wanted to read only his dialect verse and his stories in the plantation tradition, which were comic, sentimental, depicting black people as ignorant children. The fact that so much of his work contributed to negative stereotypes of his people has compromised his legacy and sometimes eclipsed the fact that, if he had not complied with those stereotypes, the work for which he is justly revered would not have been published at all. For African Americans of his day, his literary success was a symbol of the entire race's intellectual and creative abilities, hitherto unrecognized by white Americans, and his trials and fortunes were theirs: to suffer, to condemn, to praise.

The roots of Dunbar's short fiction are to be found in the stories his parents told him of their Kentucky home and servitude. His mother told him gentle stories about plantation community life, but his father had been a fugitive, had fought with the Massachusetts Fifty-fifth, and his stories were not sentimental. Dunbar's best short fiction is informed by the spirit and example of these stories and by the customs, traditions, and mores of the transplanted black southern community from which he came.

Dunbar's short fiction is often compared to that of his contemporary, Charles Chesnutt, who was also black and who wrote some accomplished plantation-based tales of black life. Chesnutt's stories are often peopled with characters who resist, undermine, and outsmart the white people, who think they know them. The majority of Dunbar's black characters tend instead to manipulate and subvert white opposition and gain white approval by a show of sterling character: honesty, integrity, faithfulness, loyalty, love, redemptive suffering, forgiveness. Worse, some Dunbar stories cast uneducated black people as the ignorant, minstrel buffoons his white readers preferred. Yet nestled among this packing were also great stories for which he is well remembered, stories which reveal righteous anger over ignorance and racial injustice and contempt for those who perpetuate them.

FOLKS FROM DIXIE

There's plenty of "packing" in Dunbar's first story collection. Several stories, such as "Mount Pisgah's Christmas 'Possum," represent uneducated black people as ludicrous bumpkins or grateful, indebted servants. "The Colonel's Awakening" is an extremely sentimental tale, dripping with the sort of pathos Thomas Nelson Page whipped into his plantation tales. In "Anner 'Lizer," Dunbar pokes fun at religious hypocrisy, while affirming the fact that people's emotional and spiritual needs are often deeply linked. "Jimsella," "Aunt Mandy's Investment," and "Nelse Hatton's Revenge" were written primarily for his post-Reconstruction black readers, who were still figuring out how to live now that the structure and restrictions of slavery no longer dictated their circumstances. Timely issues, which these stories address, were family responsibility, honesty, and integrity in businesses, which should serve the black community, and remembering and living the results of slavery and emancipation in ways that are not self-destructive.

"The Ordeal at Mt. Hope" and "At Shaft 11" are satisfying, well-constructed stories. The former is interesting for its autobiographical elements, its social commentary, and its "bootstrap economic" and educational philosophies as advocated by Booker T. Washington. The Reverend Howard Dokesbury steps off the train at Mt. Hope to take up his new post as Methodist preacher. The station house is run-down and filthy, like the rest of the town, and the indolent blacks, whites, and dogs view him with suspicion and malice. Dokesbury, understanding that any reconstruction of this community must happen one individual at a time, befriends 'Lias, one of the defeated young men. They collaborate on a small agricultural venture, and 'Lias gains confidence, feelings of self-reliance and self-esteem, and the financial base to go to the new industrial school to expand his skills. One by one, the townspeople are anxious to follow his example. Possibly Dunbar considered this story to be a blueprint for the betterment of the black masses, though he became increasingly critical of Washington's ideas, and by 1903 he warned of "educating the hand to the exclusion of the head." Dunbar gives Dokesbury his own physical characteristics, an occupation that Dunbar himself seriously considered, and even more importantly, some of his doubts and feelings of estrangement.

> He had always been such a loyal Negro, so proud of his honest brown . . . but . . . was he, after all, different from the majority of the people with whom he was supposed to have all thoughts, feelings, and emotions in common?

Increasingly, Dunbar discovered that education and class standing were great dividers among his people, and color-consciousness made it all much worse.

"At Shaft 11" takes place in a mining community in West Virginia where a strike is being broken with a crew of black miners. Violence erupts, and two heroes emerge: the Scottish foreman, Jason Andrews, and the black foreman, Sam Bowles, who unite for common cause and mutual benefit. Less believable than the previous story, it is a blueprint for how things might have been in a more perfect world but rarely were. Still, it is revealing as a Dunbar story: The black men fight back here, meeting violence with necessary violence, and winning their share of the American pie.

THE STRENGTH OF GIDEON AND OTHER STORIES

Dunbar's second collection of short stories reveals a wide spectrum of his thought and style. The title work and "Mammy Peggy's Pride" typify the plantation stories that champion the virtues of the race, such as honor, loyalty, dignity, faithfulness, selfless-ness, and a sense of duty and responsibility. Mammy Peggy, still the faithful, postemancipation house servant, so identifies with her owners' former aristocratic place in southern society that she almost cannot adapt to the alliances and reconciliation necessary for a new day. Gideon's strength is his sense of duty and responsibility in keeping his word to his old master, even though he loses the woman he loves and who loves him. Dunbar's intent is to glorify race relations of an earlier day in the interest of race relations of his own day, which were marked by increasing enmity and violence. It is as if he hopes to calm would-be lynchers and segregationists, and reassure potential friends of the race, with the admonition to "remember who these people are."

"The Ingrate" is based on Dunbar's father's experiences as a slave, a fugitive on the underground railroad to Canada, and a Union soldier. The former slaveholder sees his former slave's name on a Union roster and feels grievously abused that he taught "the ingrate" to read and cipher because he used these accomplishments against him. "The Case of 'Ca'line'," subtitled "A Kitchen Monologue," is a sassy piece, which anticipates Langston Hughes' Simple and Alberta K. Johnson stories.

Though there is enough melodramatic action in "The Tragedy at Three Forks" for a novel, this anti-lynching story is not entirely unsuccessful. Reflecting the usual circumstances of lynchings, the two victims are innocent, and the reader understands that this evil bloodthirst will continue as long as white people are motivated by guilt, ignorance, immorality, cruelty, base instincts, and mob violence. Other stories point out other kinds of white injustice. In "One Man's Fortunes," a worthy black college graduate goes out to get a job and, like Dunbar himself, meets defeat and deception in the white world. Others warn of the folly of migrating to the urban North, where hardship and evil await. The last story in the collection, "Silas Jackson," could have been a prototype for the beginnings of James Weldon Johnson's *Autobiography of an Ex-Coloured Man* (1912), and Ralph Ellison's *Invisible Man* (1952). Here, too, the young, country innocent has a vision of a better life, and,

through a series of ever more blinding incidents involving white "benefactors" and black charlatans, he finds himself in New York City, where he thinks he has "made something of himself." Here Silas's fortunes take a characteristic Dunbarian turn, and he returns home "spent, broken, hopeless, all contentment and simplicity gone." Portending death more than reunion with "the old folks at home," it is an ambiguous, unsettling end to the collection.

IN OLD PLANTATION DAYS

This collection is in the plantation tradition, though there are a couple stories worth reading. "The Finding of Martha" is really the second half of "The Strength of Gideon," which ended so unsatisfactorily in the previous collection, and "The Memory of Martha," which, despite certain weaknesses (omission of painful details of slavery, oversentimentality), is still an affecting love story.

THE HEART OF HAPPY HOLLOW

These stories take place during and after the Reconstruction and are concerned with the strengths and weaknesses of the southern black community in the aftermath of slavery and the strained, even violent circumstances it was forced to endure as it claimed the benefits of freedom. "The Scapegoat" is Dunbar's most successful story about how African Americans were, and are, used as America's political pawns. It is also one of the first stories by a black writer to locate an alternate, undermining seat of power in the barbershop/newsstand. "The Lynching of Jube Benson" is Dunbar's other antilynching story, this one narrated by one of the lynchers, as in James Baldwin's work. Though its impact is fueled by sentiment, it is unrelenting and unforgiving in its indictment. Other stories, primarily for a black audience, warn of the dangers of boastfulness, vanity, cowardice, self-pity, class and color consciousness, and the reactionary fear of change and difference. Stories such as "The Promoter" and "The Boy and the Bayonet" reveal that Dunbar had discovered how to use humor and pathos without sacrificing his characters' humanity. At the time of his death, his strongest work was no longer in poetry but in short fiction, a genre that allowed him to be more realistic, relevant, and true to himself and his people.

OTHER MAJOR WORKS

LONG FICTION: *The Uncalled*, 1898; *The Love of Landry*, 1900; *The Fanatics*, 1901; *The Sport of the Gods*, 1902.

POETRY: *Oak and Ivy*, 1893; *Majors and Minors*, 1895; *Lyrics of Lowly Life*, 1896; *Lyrics of the Hearthside*, 1899; *Poems of Cabin and Field*, 1899; *Lyrics of Love and Laughter*, 1903; Lyrics of *Sunshine and Shadow*, 1905; *Complete Poems*, 1913; *The Collected Poetry of Paul Laurence Dunbar*, 1993.

BIBLIOGRAPHY

Best, Felton O. *Crossing the Color Line: A Biography of Paul Laurence Dunbar*. Dubuque, Iowa: Kendall/Hunt, 1996. One of the Dunbar biographies. Short fiction is discussed as evidence of Dunbar's restrictions and intentions.

Bone, Robert. *Down Home: Origins of the Afro-American Short Story*. New York: Columbia University Press, 1988. Discusses the "strictures" of Dunbar's time and the "travesties" of his fictional response. Judges Dunbar to be a "purveyor of dead forms."

Braxton, Joanne M., ed. *The Collected Poetry of Paul Laurence Dunbar*. Charlottesville: University Press of Virginia, 1993. Though collection is of poetry, biographical introduction is insightful and useful to researchers in any Dunbar genre.

Martin, Jay, ed. *A Singer in the Dawn: Reinterpretations of Paul Laurence Dunbar*. New York: Dodd, Mead, 1975. Contains biographical "reminiscences" and essays about Dunbar's poetry and fiction, including one by Bert Bender on "The Lyrical Short Fiction of Dunbar and Chesnutt."

Turner, Darwin T. "Paul Laurence Dunbar: The Rejected Symbol." *Journal of Negro History* (January, 1967): 1-13. Provides a balanced response to the pros and cons of Dunbar's work. Points out the restrictions under which Dunbar worked and his artistic ideals. Concludes that "readers have demanded too much of Dunbar as a symbol."

Cynthia Packard Hill

LORD DUNSANY
Edward John Moreton Drax Plunkett

Born: London, England; July 24, 1878
Died: Dublin, Ireland; October 25, 1957

PRINCIPAL SHORT FICTION

The Gods of Pegāna, 1905
Time and the Gods, 1906
The Sword of Welleran and Other Stories, 1908
A Dreamer's Tales, 1910
The Book of Wonder, 1912
Fifty-one Tales, 1915
The Last Book of Wonder, 1916 (pb. in England, *Tales of Wonder*)
Tales of War, 1918
Tales of Three Hemispheres, 1919
The Travel Tales of Mr. Joseph Jorkens, 1931
Jorkens Remembers Africa, 1934
Jorkens Has a Large Whiskey, 1940
The Man Who Ate the Phoenix, 1947
The Fourth Book of Jorkens, 1948
The Little Tales of Smethers, 1952
Jorken Borrows Another Whiskey, 1954
The Food of Death: Fifty-one Tales, 1974

OTHER LITERARY FORMS

Lord Dunsany published more than fifty volumes of work, one-fourth of which are volumes of short stories and brief fictional pieces. He is best known for his plays, some of which were produced at the Abbey Theatre, of which *The Glittering Gate* (1909) is today possibly the most famous, even if only by title. Other well-known plays include *King Argimenes and the Unknown Warrior* (1911) and *The Gods of the Moun-*

Lord Dunsany (Library of Congress)

tain (1911); all were later published in *Five Plays* (1914). Dunsany also authored novels, three autobiographical works, six volumes of poetry, a translation of Horace's odes, and essays. In recent years, selected novels and stories have been reprinted or re-edited for publication.

ACHIEVEMENTS

Few authors have written as many volumes as did Lord Dunsany, but in his own era he had little influence. His settings and themes, coming out of his unique imagination, were not specifically Irish and thus his relationship with his compatriots William Butler Yeats, Lady Augusta Gregory, and John Millington Synge was tangential at best. His plays, even those produced at the Abbey Theatre, have not survived his own times. His several volumes of autobiography are well written but not revealing of the inner man; *My Ireland* (1937) only obliquely comments on the divisive political issues paramount during his times, not surprising given his pro-British bias. His

early stories and some of his novels, however, such as *The King of Elfland's Daughter* (1924), have had considerable influence on a later generation of writers. H. P. Lovecraft found Dunsany to be his major inspiration, and Dunsany was also possibly a formative source for other fantasy and science-fiction writers, such as James Branch Cabell, Robert E. Howard, Clark Ashton Smith, Arthur C. Clarke, L. Sprague De Camp, and Fletcher Pratt. In a broader sense, there is a direct line from William Morris through Dunsany to J. R. R. Tolkien in the creation of other, preindustrial worlds.

BIOGRAPHY

Although he was born in England, Lord Dunsany (Edward John Moreton Drax Plunkett) was an Irish author, having been born into an Irish family with historic roots and an ancestral castle, the author's home, in County Meath, Ireland. Lord Dunsany was the eighteenth Baron Dunsany; Sir Horace Plunkett, the Irish agricultural reformer and politician, was his uncle. It is often noted in biographical accounts of Dunsany that he claimed to have spent only three percent of his life engaged in writing; the rest of the time he was involved in such aristocratic pursuits as warfare, hunting, and playing cricket. He received his education at Cheam, Eton, and Sandhurst, and he was with the Coldstream Guards in the Boer War, with the Royal Iniskilling Fusiliers in World War I, and with the Home Guard as a volunteer in World War II. In his literary life, he was acquainted with Lady Gregory, William Butler Yeats, Rudyard Kipling, and H. G. Wells, and he did two speaking tours of the United States. Lord Dunsany died in 1957.

ANALYSIS

By Lord Dunsany's own admission, much of his writing aims at recording and sustaining moods that are dreamy, lyrical, nostalgic, anti-industrial, and, at times, wry; he preferred the outlandish products of the imagination to records of the actual as matter for art. The way in which Dunsany expresses these moods is especially important to the effect that his works produce. Modeled in part on the style of the King James Bible, his prose is rhythmic and musical. It is laden with mythically stylized names and is occasionally sentimental, but this tendency toward the saccharine is offset by the dashes of mild comic irony with which his tales are spiced. Such irony, along with the occasional use of modern details, tempers the remote and exotic quality of the experiences recounted in the stories.

To provide a groundwork for his fictional moods, Dunsany developed what is often called a "mythology." To some extent, this label is inaccurate because Dunsany did not evolve an organized theology. Yet central to much of his work is the sense that the world is ruled by various gods of Dunsany's own devising, that these gods control the works of humans but may themselves be controlled by the chief of destroyers, Time. Hence, his nostalgia is informed strongly by a sense of doom or fate, and his tales often have downbeat or elegiac conclusions. These conclusions, however, delight Dunsany's fans because they often include an unexpected twist of action or theme. Dunsany will turn some aspect of fairy tale or mythic convention back on itself; as Lin Carter suggests, he will reject the happy ending and give the reader instead one that comes nearer to the disappointments that time creates in actual experience. Perhaps the source of this technique is the advice that Yeats is reported to have given Dunsany when the latter began writing drama, that Dunsany always seek in a play to work toward surprise.

"THE SWORD OF WELLERAN"

Most of Dunsany's themes and characteristics are well represented in a story that the writer himself included in his 1954 selection of his favorite stories, "The Sword of Welleran." Like many of Dunsany's narrators, the teller of this tale is a temporary visitor to the lands of fantasy. He tells the reader about his dream of a transcendently beautiful city called Merimna, a city in the midst of a plain and opposed by enemy peoples who are kept at bay only because of their fear of the heroes of Merimna: Welleran, Soorenard, Mommolek, Rollory, Akanax, and Irain.

These heroes died more than a century before the events narrated in the story, but their statues reign over the city and fool the tribes that want to invade Merimna for her treasure. It is worth noting that, while Dunsany fills in the background to the adventure that he plans to narrate, the style and tone and pacing of the first few pages engage the reader with the story's nostalgic urgency. Like all works of fable and myth, the land of Merimna is complete in its own motivations and deeds, however highly romanticized. Hence, the reader is prepared for the strange events that befall a child named Rold, who becomes fascinated by the legend of Welleran's greatness.

The king of one of the Cyresian tribes suspects that the heroes of Merimna are dead, and he sends two spies to determine whether his suspicion is correct. When they discover that Rollory and the rest are only statues, the spies return to their king, who collaborates with three other monarchs to attack Merimna. As the enemies wait, the night before battle, Dunsany describes the fall of evening with typically slow-paced lyricism. Fortunately, in Paradise the souls of Merimna's heroes are aware of the danger to their city, so they enter the dreams of the sleeping inhabitants of Merimna to stir them to defense. In particular, Welleran causes Rold to take up his ancient sword and join the people gathered on the plain before the city. As a group, they wake, fight, and eventually massacre their enemies in the night battle.

To this point the story is a straightforward and conventional fantasy tale, but in the final page Dunsany establishes a contrast between the emotional demands of the human condition and the fairy tale justification for slaughter. When the people of Merimna see in daylight "the hideous things that the sword of Welleran had done," they share the mood of Rold, who laments over the slain enemies. Dunsany notes, "Thus wept the people of Merimna in the hour of their great victory, for men have strange moods." They mourn, too, because Welleran is dead, unaware that their dead heroes have engineered the saving of their city. Then Dunsany counters their dismay and points out their nonheroic insignificance when he ends the story with the image of the souls of Merimna's five heroes traveling back to Paradise.

Hence, one of Dunsany's recurrent points is suggested: that there is much about supernatural reality that the people of the present, even of a dream present, do not know.

Finally, it should be noted that the elegiac ending well supports the allegorical dimension of the story. At the outset, Dunsany tells us that Merimna "was a marvel of spires and figures of bronze, and marble fountains, and trophies of fabulous wars, and broad streets given over wholly to the Beautiful." In addition to the statues of ancient heroes, Welleran boasts figures of Fame, of Victory, and of Fear. These monuments protect Merimna until the tribal spies discover that they are merely made of bronze; however, Merimna's miraculous victory is a victory for Beauty and for the heroic attributes objectified by the statues. Thus, Dunsany does not suggest that such qualities are wholly dead in Merimna's present, but he does locate them as vital realities in the heroic past, recoverable mostly through dream and through the beauty of art. In fact, together these qualities make up a portrait of what Dunsany sees as the beautiful, a world in which great conflicts stir human beings to actions beyond their ordinary capacities and in which triumph is possible. Dunsany presents those aspects of modern life that are drearily unimaginative and out of touch with the fact that human beings have transcendent souls.

A story that presents similar thematic preoccupations but takes place in a modern, realistic setting is "The Kith of the Elf-folk." The story begins in late autumn in the marshlands of East Anglia, where one of the Wild Things—immortal but soulless beings who, although possessing pointed ears and the ability to leap very high, "are somewhat human in appearance, only all brown of skin and barely two feet high"—happens to wander to a great cathedral. There, during a service, the Wild Thing becomes enchanted by the music, colors, and images. Wanting to understand religion, art, and beauty, it grows sorrowful over its lack of a soul, despite the warning of the Oldest of the Wild Things that even though a soul would give the Wild Thing such understanding, with a soul comes death and knowledge of "the meaning of sorrow." Out of "grey mist," music, memories, and

the like, the Wild Things create a soul for their sorrowing friend, who accepts it and instantly becomes a young, lovely, but naked woman standing on the edge of the marsh. At first, after she has found shelter and food in the house of a farmer and his wife, the Wild Thing enjoys her experience of beauty; she feels wonder and becomes aware of the reality of Paradise. Soon, however, she begins a series of comic conflicts with modern civilization. When she tells the Dean of the cathedral that she would like to be named "Song of the Rushes," he insists that she accept the name of Mary Jane Rush. When, during a service, she tells the cathedral's young curate that she loves him, she is sent to work in a factory in the Midlands. When, mourning for the beauty of the marshes in the drab city, she tries to give her soul to one of the poor, she is told, "All the poor have souls. It is all they have."

Finally, however, even in the industrial, urban civilization that Dunsany abhors, Mary Jane's luck begins to turn. When it is discovered that she has a beautiful singing voice, she is sent to London and trained for the opera stage, and she is re-Christened Signorina Maria Russiano. Noticing that during a performance one woman in her audience remains unmoved by the yearning in her voice, Mary Jane is able to convince the woman to accept the troublesome soul. Happily freed of its human body, the Wild Thing returns to the marshes.

Although the story is charming in its plot and its blend of satire and lyricism that Dunsany uses to poke fun at the wealthy, the conventional, and the industrial, the story also provides the reader with a parable about the relationship of art and nature, of beauty and humanity. The story argues that to know fully the beauty of nature, one must be human, but being human means possessing a soul that also binds one to the experience of sorrow, to the knowledge of one's separation from God, and to the longings that are the motivation for art. Human beings are also fond of wealth and of conventional behavior, however, and these trappings of civilization always threaten to drown beauty, art, and soul.

"IDLE DAYS ON THE YANN"

It is notable that the same contrasts between the dreamy or supernaturally beautiful and ordinary, sometimes mean, reality shape many of Dunsany's tales, including the well-known "Idle Days on the Yann." In this tale, the narrator goes into the land of fantasy to travel down the Yann River as far as its entrance into the sea. He tells stories about the cities he passes, about the captain and crew of the ship on which he travels, and about the beautiful scenery along the Yann. At the end, he parts from the captain and notes, "Long we regarded one another, knowing that we should meet no more, for my fancy is weakening as the years slip by, and I go ever more seldom into the Lands of Dream." The principal attractions of this story are the evocation of a consistent mood, the lyrical language, and the invention of detail—especially of names—that mark Dunsany's style. Overall, the story celebrates the power of the imagination to create a coherent world which, ironically, the reader is forced to recognize as a fantasy.

"WHAT JORKENS HAS TO PUT UP WITH"

In addition to such fantastic stories, Dunsay wrote stories in other styles, including a series of books that centers on the tales of a group called the Billiards Club. This club includes in its membership the former great adventurer and current great whiskey-lover, Mr. Joseph Jorkens. Jorkens's incredible stories are openly disbelieved only by another member of the club, a lawyer named Terbut. Their conflict in "What Jorkens Has to Put Up With" may be taken as representative. As the story opens, a member of the club tells of their discussion one day about the relative virtues of ivory and bonzoline billiard balls. When, along the way, Jorkens is asked if he has ever seen a unicorn, he insists that he did in fact see one, even though under the unusual circumstances of having contracted malaria and of having consumed a considerable amount of vermouth for breakfast on the day that he sighted this supposedly mythical beast. He asserts that he struck the unicorn's horn with his rifle butt and knocked the horn off and suggests further that a toasting fork that he presented to the club was carved from the same horn. Ungraciously, Terbut suggests that the fork is made of bonzoline. Light, comic, and stripped of the lyricism of Dunsany's wonder tales, the Jorkens stories are of interest partly because they too embody Dunsay's biases against the modern sensibility that values drab realities over the adventurous spirit and its imaginative truths.

OTHER MAJOR WORKS

LONG FICTION: *The Chronicles of Rodriguez*, 1922; *The King of Elfland's Daughter*, 1924; *The Charwoman's Shadow*, 1926; *The Blessing of Pan*, 1927; *The Curse of the Wise Woman*, 1933; *Up in the Hills*, 1935; *My Talks with Dean Spanley*, 1936; *Rory and Bran*, 1936; *The Story of Mona Sheehy*, 1939; *Guerrilla*, 1944; *The Strange Journeys of Colonel Polders*, 1950; *The Last Revolution*, 1951; *His Fellow Men*, 1952.

PLAYS: *The Glittering Gate*, pr. 1909; *King Argimenes and the Unknown Warrior*, pr. 1911; *The Gods of the Mountain*, pr. 1911; *Five Plays*, pb. 1914; *Plays of Gods and Men*, pb. 1917; *Plays of Near and Far*, pb. 1922; *Lord Adrian*, pr. 1923; *Alexander*, pb. 1925; *Mr. Faithful*, pr. 1927; *Seven Modern Comedies*, pb. 1928; *The Old Folk of the Centuries*, pb. 1930; *Plays for Earth and Air*, pb. 1937.

POETRY: *Fifty Poems*, 1929; *Mirage Water*, 1938; *War Poems*, 1941; *Wandering Songs*, 1943; *The Year*, 1946; *To Awaken Pegasus and Other Poems*, 1949.

NONFICTION: *If I Were Dictator: The Pronouncement of the Grand Macaroni*, 1934; *My Ireland*, 1937; *Patches of Sunlight*, 1938; *While the Sirens Slept*, 1944; *The Sirens Wake*, 1945; *A Glimpse from a Watch Tower*, 1946.

BIBLIOGRAPHY

Amory, Mark. *Biography of Lord Dunsany*. London: Collins, 1972. This work is the standard modern biographical study of Dunsany. The author also successfully incorporates a discussion of Dunsany's major writings in his summary of the Irish writer's life.

Bierstadt, Edward Hale. *Dunsany the Dramatist*. Boston: Little, Brown, 1917. This work, written relatively early in Dunsany's career, is primarily a study of some of his first plays. By implication, however, it also adds to the understanding of his short stories.

Bleiler, E. F. Introduction to *Gods, Men, and Ghosts*, by Lord Dunsany. New York: Dover, 1972. In his introduction to a collection of Dunsany's short stories, Bleiler claims that Dunsany, shortly after the beginning of the twentieth century, created a new universe, out of his imagination. Admitting that much of Dunsany's work had not passed the test of time, he argues that in his best stories he created something unique in his exquisite use of language to convey a dreamlike state of fantasy.

Cahalan, James M. *The Irish Novel: A Critical History.* Boston: Twayne, 1988. The author analyzes the history of the novel in Ireland from its earliest manifestations down to the latter part of the twentieth century. In a chapter titled "Fantasia: Irish Fabulists, 1920-1955," he discusses Dunsany along with Joseph O'Neill and Austin Clarke.

Gogarty, Oliver St. John. "Lord Dunsany." *The Atlantic Monthly* 195 (March, 1955): 67-72. The author, friend of James Joyce and William Butler Yeats, as well as of Lord Dunsany, writes a personal reflection on Dunsany's long literary career. He particularly points to the influence of Dunsany's Irish heritage in explaining the core theme of his literary works.

Lobdell, Jared C. "The Man Who Didn't Write Fantasy: Lord Dunsany and the Self-Deprecatory Tradition in English Light Fiction." *Extrapolation* 35 (Spring, 1994): 33-42. Examines previous claims that Dunsany was a writer of fantasy by exploring the nature of Dunsany's fantasy and, by extension, the nature of modern fantasy as a genre. Discusses Dunsany's fiction within the self-deprecatory mode of English light fiction.

Saul, George Brandon. "Strange Gods and Far Places: The Short Stories of Lord Dunsany." *Arizona Quarterly* 19 (1963): 197-210. In this excellent discussion, the author notes the division between the early more self-indulgent fantasy stories and his later Jorkens stories, with their more bemused approach. Saul Faults Dunsany for his sentimentality and finds him a lesser figure than William Morris, but he praises him for his ingenuity and his colorful and rhythmic use of language.

Tremayne, Peter, ed. *Irish Masters of Fantasy.* Dublin: Wolfhound Press, 1979. In his introduction to Dunsany's "The Ghost in the Valley" and "Autumn Cricket," Tremayne describes Dunsany as a master of the supernatural, a dramatist who anticipated the Theater of the Absurd, and the writer who adapted the heroic fantasy to the short-story form.

Walker, Warren. "'Tales That One Never Wants to Hear': A Sample from Dunsany." *Studies in Short Fiction* 22 (Fall, 1985): 449-454. An extended analysis of "Two Bottles of Relish" as a burlesque of the detective story; argues that Dunsany maintains delicate balances in the story between horror and humor, realism and fantasy, admiration and derision.

Cheryl Herr, updated by Eugene S. Larson

STUART DYBEK

Born: Chicago, Illinois; April 10, 1942

PRINCIPAL SHORT FICTION

Childhood and Other Neighborhoods, 1980
The Coast of Chicago, 1990
The Story of Mist, 1993

OTHER LITERARY FORMS

Stuart Dybek published a volume of poetry, *Brass Knuckles*, in 1979. His short story "Death of a Right Fielder" was televised in 1991, and his play *Orchids* was produced in 1990.

ACHIEVEMENTS

Editors have chosen many of Stuart Dybek's stories for inclusion in anthologies. He won a Special Citation from the Ernest Hemingway Foundation as well as awards from the Cliff Dwellers Arts Foundation, Friends of American Writers, the Whiting Foundation, and the Society of Midland Authors. In addition, he received a Nelson Algren Award, several O. Henry Awards, and the Church and the Artist Literary Competition Award. Dybek has been the recipient of a John Simon Guggenheim Memorial Foundation Fellowship and the National Endowment for the Arts grant.

BIOGRAPHY

Stuart Dybek was born on April 10, 1942, in Chicago, the son of Stanley and Adeline Sala Dybek. He grew up in a working-class, ethnic neighborhood, a milieu that figures prominently in his writing. After graduating from a Catholic high school, he enrolled at Loyola University, but he interrupted his education to work in the Civil Rights and antiwar movements of the early 1960's. He earned a B.A. from Loyola in 1964 and an M.A. in 1968. He married Caren Bassett in 1966.

After working as a case worker with the Cook County Department of Public Aid, teaching in a Chicago-area elementary school, and teaching high school on the island of St. Thomas as a VISTA volunteer, Dybek returned to school. He earned an M.F.A.

degree from the prestigious University of Iowa Writers' Workshop in 1973. In 1974, he began teaching English and creative writing at Western Michigan University in Kalamazoo, Michigan. He served as a visiting professor at Princeton University in 1990 and began teaching in the Warren Wilson M.F.A. program for writers in 1985.

Dybek's first book-length publication was his collection of poetry and prose poems, *Brass Knuckles*. His first collection of short stories, *Childhood and Other Neighborhoods*, published in 1980, was well received by the critics. Likewise, his second collection, *The Coast of Chicago* (1990), received considerable critical praise. Since the mid-1970's, Dybek has published a steady stream of stories in such important journals as *Ploughshares* and *TriQuarterly* and such popular magazines as *The New Yorker* and *The Atlantic Monthly*.

ANALYSIS

Chicago has a long tradition of producing fine writers who use the city as their literary landscape. Gwendolyn Brooks, Carl Sandburg, Upton Sinclair, and Theodore Dreiser, among others, belong to this tradition. Stuart Dybek, while drawing heavily on the city for his settings, characters, and images, departs from the tradition with his dreamlike portrayal of life in a postmodern world. Some critics have identified his work with Magical Realism and have suggested a connection with Jorge Luis Borges and Italo Calvino. Dybek himself reports that after he wrote some of the early stories included in *Childhood and Other Neighborhoods* he began to read Franz Kafka and Gabriel García Márquez.

In addition to exploring the intersection between dreams and reality, Dybek has pioneered the genre sometimes known as "sudden" or "flash" fiction. These stories are sometimes also called "short short" stories; sudden fiction can be just a few paragraphs long, and such stories are never longer than three pages. Consequently, readers of sudden fiction often find themselves in the middle of a situation well under way, a situation that will end but not conclude. Some of the prose poems in Dybek's poetry collection, *Brass Knuckles*, could fall into this category. *The Coast of Chicago* also includes several very short stories.

Many of Dybek's stories draw on his experiences growing up in a Polish-Latino neighborhood on the south side of Chicago. His characters often have Polish surnames, attend Catholic churches, and carry with them the culture and mythology of Eastern Europe. Even when his stories are not overtly about the immigrant experience, their settings are rich with ethnic sounds, aromas, and sights. Churches frequently appear in the center of the landscape.

Dybek often places his characters in moments of transformation. Frequently this takes the form of a coming-of-age story, especially in *Childhood and Other Neighborhoods*. In a 1997 interview with Mike Nickel and Adrian Smith, Dybek says that he is always "looking for some door in the story that opens on another world." For some characters, this can be the world of adulthood; for others, it can be an entry into the world of magic or death. The entry into a different world can be a transformative moment for his characters, as well as for his readers.

CHILDHOOD AND OTHER NEIGHBORHOODS

The eleven stories of the collection are about coming-of-age. With his title, Dybek deliberately suggests that there is both a time and a space to childhood; that is, he sees childhood in the same way one would see a neighborhood, as a place where interconnected people live out their lives, bounded by streets, houses, ethnicity, and religion. The main characters in this collection are generally young people, often second- or third-generation Poles making their homes in Chicago. Dybek himself identifies the subject of the collection as "perception," reminding his readers that children perceive the world in ways that are different from the ways adults do. For many of the characters in this book, their moment of transformation comes when they leave the familiar streets of their own neighborhood and venture out into the world at large. Sometimes these adventures end tragically, sometimes humorously. Often the world outside the neighborhood is a world infused with magic or horror.

The opening story of *Childhood and Other Neighborhoods*, "The Palatski Man" is about a young girl, Mary, and her older brother John. The story opens on Palm Sunday and continues to use religious iconography and imagery throughout. At the center of the story stands the nameless Palatski Man, a vendor who dresses in white and sells taffy apples and *palatski*, a confection of wafers and honey. There is a strangeness to this treat; Mary has never seen *palatski* sold anywhere else. For Mary, eating the *palatski* reminds her of Holy Communion, an image that recurs later in the story.

John and his friend Ray Cruz are fascinated by the Ragmen, who traverse their neighborhood collecting rags. John tells Mary about following a Ragman for a long way and discovering the place where all the Ragmen live. Ray and John are discovered by the Ragmen and become separated. Later, when John calls Ray's home, Ray denies that the adventure ever happened, and John is unable to locate the Ragmen's camp again. Later, John and Mary follow the Palatski Man and find themselves once again at the Ragmen's camp. In a mystical, frightening ceremony, the young people partake of a kind of Eucharist consisting of taffy apple syrup and *palatski*, which tastes surprisingly bitter. That night, Mary discovers that John has not eaten his portion. The story closes strangely with a scene that could be a real event, a vision, or a dream. The Palatski Man comes for Mary, and she knows that she must go with him. Dybek reports that he wrote this story while listening to the music of Polish composer Zoltán Kodály. The music suggested the strange, Eastern European images. There are also undercurrents of the Persephone myth, and readers should remember that this myth was a subject of a poem in Dybek's *Brass Knuckles*. In Greek mythology, Persephone eats pomegranate seeds offered her by Hades, the ruler of the underworld. As a result, she is bound to stay with him for six months of the year. Likewise, Mary's ingestion of the minute wafer given to her by the Palatski Man makes possible the final scene.

THE COAST OF CHICAGO

The Coast of Chicago contains both longer stories and very short stories, intertwined and interconnected by theme and image. Some reviewers suggest that the very short stories are lyrical in nature and may be autobiographical. Again, Chicago provides the setting for the stories, and again, Dybek has said that he listened to music, jazz this time, as he wrote the stories. Many of the stories in the collection have a dreamlike, legendary quality to them. Art and music figure in many of the stories. For example, "Nighthawks," itself a minicollection of tales within the larger collection, uses Edward Hopper's painting by the same name as its starting point. Likewise, "Chopin in Winter" draws on the music of the Polish composer. In all, the stories are often elegiac, somber, nearly hallucinatory. Again, Dybek seems most interested in showing the reader the way characters and settings change, often subtly, often before the reader's very eyes.

"ANT"

Appearing in the Winter, 1997-1998, issue of *Ploughshares*, "Ant" is a sample of Dybek's very short fiction and an example of the blend of fantasy and realism characteristic of many of his stories. In addition, the story features entry into another world and then back into the ordinary one. The story opens with Martin lying on a blanket under a tree with his lover. When an ant begins to drag him by his toe, Martin remembers stories read to him when he was a boy by his Uncle Wayne. His uncle, a veteran of an unnamed war, acted out the stories after reading them to Martin. The most memorable for Martin was "Lonigan and the Ants." His uncle, who had pretended that he was an ant and Martin was Lonigan, had begun to pursue him. All that saved the frightened Martin from the mad pursuit by his uncle was the reminder that Lonigan does not die, and the ants do not win; the "authority of the story" is enough to change his uncle's actions. Dybek seems to be playing with the boundaries of storytelling here. In the larger story, he exerts authority over his own story and writes a version in which one ant does win. Eventually, an ant works its way up Martin's back, grabs hold of his belt, lifts him off the ground, and carries him away.

OTHER MAJOR WORKS

PLAY: *Orchids*, pr. 1990.

POETRY: *Brass Knuckles*, 1979; *Kiddie Corner*, 1981.

BIBLIOGRAPHY

Cook, Bruce. "Walks on the Southwest Side." *Washington Post Book World* (January 13, 1980): 1-2. Places Dybek in the tradition of the Chicago writers, including Nelson Algren, Gwendolyn Brooks, and Saul Bellow, in a review of *Childhood and Other Neighborhoods*.

Dybek, Stuart. "An Interview with Stuart Dybek." Interview by Mike Nickel and Adrian Smith. *Chicago Review* 43 (Winter, 1997): 87-101. A revealing interview in which Dybek reflects on what it means to be a "Chicago writer," his ethnic background and how it influences his writing, and his ideas about form and writing.

_____. "Thread." *Harper's* 297 (September, 1998): 34-37. A brief memoir by Dybek recalling his Catholic upbringing and his first Holy Communion.

Gladsky, Thomas S. "From Ethnicity to Multiculturalism: The Fiction of Stuart Dybek." *MELUS* 20 (Summer, 1995): 105-118. Offers a brief history of Polish immigration to the United States followed by a consideration of Polish American writers before turning to an examination of Stuart Dybek in this context. Connects ethnicity and memory and discusses the role of Catholicism in Dybek's prose.

Kakutani, Michiko. "Lyrical Loss and Desolation of Misfits in Chicago." *The New York Times Book Review* (April 20, 1990): C31. Draws a parallel between *The Coast of Chicago* and Sherwood Anderson's *Winesburg, Ohio* (1919), noting similarities in characters, lyricism, and "emotional forcefulness."

Lee, Don. "About Stuart Dybek." *Ploughshares* 24 (Spring, 1998): 192-198. An in-depth profile of Dybek and his subject matter. Provides biographical information as well as considering Dybek's contribution to the "short short" genre of short stories.

Shapard, Robert, and James Thomas, eds. *Sudden Fiction: American Short-Short Stories*. Salt Lake City: Gibbs M. Smith, 1986. The classic collection of the "short short" story. Includes Dybek's short short "Sunday at the Zoo" as well as an afterword by Dybek on the genre.

Ward, Robert. "A Review of *Childhood and Other Neighborhoods*." *Northwest Review* 18 (Fall, 1980): 149-157.

Weber, Katharine. "Windy City Dreaming." *The New York Times Book Review*, May 20, 1990, 30. Reviews *The Coast of Chicago*, connecting memory, dreaming, and the dreamlike nature of Dybek's stories.

Diane Andrews Henningfeld

E

MARIA EDGEWORTH

Born: Black Bourton, England; January 1, 1767
Died: Edgeworthstown, Ireland; May 22, 1849

PRINCIPAL SHORT FICTION

The Parent's Assistant: Or, Stories for Children,
1796 (3 volumes), 1800 (6 volumes)
Early Lessons, 1801 (includes parts 1-2, *Harry and
Lucy*; parts 3-5, *Rosamond*; parts 6-9, *Frank*;
and part 10, "The Little Dog Trusty," "The Or-
ange Man," and "The Cherry Orchard"; with
Richard Lovell Edgeworth)
Moral Tales for Young People, 1801
The Mental Thermometer, 1801
Popular Tales, 1804
The Modern Griselda, 1805
Tales of Fashionable Life, 1809-1812
Continuation of "Early Lessons," 1814
Rosamond: A Sequel to "Early Lessons," 1821
Frank: A Sequel to Frank in "Early Lessons," 1822
Harry and Lucy Concluded, 1825
Tales and Miscellaneous Pieces, 1825
*Garry Owen: Or, The Snow-Woman, and Poor Bob,
the Chimney-Sweeper*, 1832
Tales and Novels, 1832-1833, 1848, 1857 (18 vol-
umes), 1893 (10 volumes), 1893 (12 volumes)
Orlandino, 1848
Classic Tales, 1883
The Purple Jar and Other Stories, 1931

OTHER LITERARY FORMS

Maria Edgeworth, best known as a novelist, acquired international fame with the publication of *Castle Rackrent* in 1800. Its unique narrative technique—
the tale is told by a passive onlooker, the Rackrent
family's servant—was a fascinating innovation. Contemporary critics, comparing her novels favorably
with *Don Quixote* (1605) and *Gil Blas* (1715), be-

lieved Edgeworth was greater than Henry Fielding.
Earning more than £1,000 for each of four novels,
Edgeworth, unlike William Carleton, the Banims, and
Gerald Griffin, was financially secure. With her father, she coauthored numerous Sessays on education.
"Toys," "Tasks," "On Truth," "Wit and Judgment,"
and "Prudence and Economy" are representative topics. The comic and juvenile plays added nothing to
her fame or fortune, but they taught Edgeworth how
to write spirited dialogue. While she did not write an
autobiography, more than two thousand surviving letters describe her relationships with family, friends,
and literary acquaintances, documenting her understanding of the social, political, and economic forces
of her era.

ACHIEVEMENTS

Maria Edgeworth produced a body of work that is
distinctive for a number of important reasons. Following at somewhat of a distance the example of the
Bluestockings, or women intellectuals, of her father's
generation, she relocated many of their concerns with
race, class, and gender in a colonial society, Ireland.
Profoundly influenced by her father's intellectual interests, she evolved a fictional mode that uneasily yet
impressively sought to combine the didactic with the
comedy of manners.

The literary product of this weighty background
was fiction—largely novels—which gave Ireland a
hitherto unforeseen visibility on the cultural map.
Edgeworth's short fiction never attained the same degree of originality. It retains to a disabling degree the
pedantry and mechanical factitiousness of the French
models from which it originated, notably the *contes
moraux* of one of her father's influences, Jean-
François Marmontel. An exception must be made,
however, of *Castle Rackrent*. Generally classified as a

novel, it may be more appropriately regarded as a no-vella, and it is not only Edgeworth's most accom-plished piece of short fiction but also a work that went on to influence the development of European re-alism. In addition, the pedantic character of much of Edgeworth's short fiction helped consolidate her rep-utation as an influential educational theorist.

BIOGRAPHY

Maria Edgeworth's life, stranger than fiction, is the fountainhead of her literary work. Born at her

Maria Edgeworth (Library of Congress)

mother's home in England to Richard Lovell Edge-worth and Anna Maria Elers, Maria was one of her father's twenty-two children and her mother's five children. When, in 1773, her mother died in child-birth after an unhappy marriage (Maria recollected her crying most of the time), Edgeworth four months later married another Englishwoman, Honora Sneyd. Eight months after her death in 1780, he married her sister Elizabeth. Finally, in 1798, six months after Elizabeth's death, he married Frances Beaufort, an Anglo-Irishwoman a year younger than Maria who

had illustrated *The Parent's Assistant*. This marriage posed a considerable threat to Maria. By allowing that her father could love a new wife without altering his love for her, Maria forced Frances to wish only "to make one side with Edgeworth and Maria of an equilateral triangle." Coming to Edgeworthstown during the violent era of the 1798 Revolution, Fran-ces was welcomed by the children of the former three wives and added six of her own to complete Edge-worth's family in his sixty-fifth year.

Maria, who never married, rejected the proposal of a Swedish gentleman in Paris during her travels to England, France, and Scotland between 1802 and 1803 because she was unable to leave her father and the security of Edgeworthstown. In 1813, Maria, her father, and Frances spent a season in London, where Maria, by then a celebrated author, met Lord Byron. Her father's death in 1817 marked the beginning of Edgeworth's forced independence and the end of her literary partnership. With the exception of *Helen*, a novel published in 1834, she wrote only children's tales subsequent to the completion of *Memoirs of Richard Lovell Edgeworth Esq.* (1820).

Educated from the age of seven until 1780 in a Derby private school, Edgeworth transferred to an-other private school in London for two years, learn-ing the social graces, languages, and literature. Away from her family, including Christmas holidays at times, the young girl, feeling rejected and alienated, made supreme efforts to please her stepmothers and father. In 1782, her formal education concluded, she returned to Ireland with Edgeworth, his wife, and the children from three marriages. At fourteen years of age, Maria, helped to educate her sisters and brothers while handling the business affairs of her father.

Honora's son Lovell, a poor economist, inherited the landed property. Acquiring debts of £26,000, he would have lost the entire estate but for Maria's liter-ary earnings and her dealings with the tenants and creditors. Maria also paid for the care of William, Elizabeth's son, in a private mental institution follow-ing his breakdown. She visited Sir Walter Scott in 1823 and received him in Ireland in 1825.

This tiny woman—she was only four feet seven inches tall—suffered great personal losses. The deaths of her mother and two stepmothers, her father (the loss of whom caused the greatest pain), and seventeen brothers and sisters—only four died as infants—whom she had loved and educated, were staggering experiences for a sensitive individual. Edgeworth died as she had wished she would in the arms of Frances, her proven friend and stepmother, at Edgeworthstown House.

ANALYSIS

Maria Edgeworth's close association with children—in 1791, for example, she was responsible for the education of eight sisters and brothers while her father and stepmother Elizabeth were in England—determined the subject matter of her fiction. To amuse and instruct the children, she wrote short stories on a slate and read them aloud. Based on their critical response, she selected the best for the edition of *The Parent's Assistant*. Although she preferred her father's title *The Parent's Friend*, these stories reached the public under the publisher's inscription and remained popular throughout the nineteenth century.

Edgeworth fashioned the stories about real boys and girls. While Samuel Johnson believed that tales of giants, fairies, castles, and enchantment would stimulate children's imagination, Richard Lovell Edgeworth taught his daughter that "experience in life would soon convince them that fairies, giants, and enchanters are not to be met with in the world." She therefore avoided fantastic visions and gave her young readers useful information for successful living. The fictional tales would, Edgeworth and her father believed, teach readers about the latest scientific inventions and vocational skills while developing their characters. In the process, to Edgeworth's credit, famous child characters were introduced to the growing field of children's literature.

"SIMPLE SUSAN"

A popular story from *The Parent's Assistant*, "Simple Susan," illustrates a common technique used throughout the juvenile and adult stories: the use of contrasting characters to reveal the moral lesson. In this tale, Susan Price, the modest, loving, honest, and hardworking twelve-year-old daughter of Farmer Price, differs markedly from Barbara Case, the self-

ish, vain, devious, and indolent daughter of Attorney Case. As might be expected, the two girls are mirror images of their parents. Set in a rural English village about to celebrate May Day, the tale parallels Case's sinister attempts to oust Price from his farm with Barbara's aggressive actions against Susan.

Case, agent for the estate of Sir Arthur Somers on which the Prices live, had lent £9 to Price, taking his lease for collateral. Although the debt was paid, Case demands another £9. Simultaneously, Barbara steals Susan's guinea hen and beehive. Farmer Price looks to Sir Somers for justice and receives it with the dismissal of Case. Susan simply forgives Barbara. The most poignant scene takes place when Susan unselfishly sacrifices her pet lamb to get money for her father. The trip to the butcher and the return of her lamb by a young boy is very moving and prompted Sir Walter Scott, an early admirer, to say that there is nothing to do after that incident "but just to put down the book, and cry." R. L. Edgeworth believed that "if the tale would become known, it would be preferred to every story of the sort that has yet been written." "Simple Susan," written in 1798, is a new story from the second edition of 1800, along with "The Little Merchants," "Elton Montem," "The Basket Woman," "Waste Not, Want Not," "Forgive and Forget," "The White Pigeon," and "The Orphans."

"THE PURPLE JAR"

From the 1796 collection, "The Purple Jar," later appearing in *Rosamond* is a memorable tale. Rosamond, a literary copy of Maria Edgeworth as a child, is allowed to choose between buying a needed pair of shoes or a jar filled with purple water; she chooses the jar. Rosamond's pleasure is short-lived, since the colored water runs out, and, without proper shoes, Rosamond cannot join her father on an outing. Pained, Rosamond has learned a valuable lesson. Character development through suffering, a characteristic of these juvenile tales, is the usual experience for the young heroes and heroines.

The success of *The Parent's Assistant* led to another collection of similar stories in *Early Lessons* dramatizing the exploits of Harry, Lucy, Frank, and Rosamond. Maria Edgeworth added to the tales in 1814, 1821, 1822, and 1825. These stories, popular in

England, were used by John Ruskin's mother as a teaching tool; before the great Victorian was eight years old, he was writing his own Harry and Lucy stories revealing Harry's observational powers and geological knowledge.

FRANK, I-IV

Frank, I-IV, written for Edgeworth's six-year-old brother William, who eventually became an engineer and later suffered a nervous breakdown, introduced him to scientific knowledge supplied by their father. Social justice, agriculture, property rights, and moral precepts were taught by example in the stories. Edgeworth, not a scientist like her father, found the writing difficult, since she had to adapt pages of his scientific data to the intellectual capacity of preteen children. She reasoned that no matter how tiresome the task, "it will do good"; consequently, she happily accepted her duty and "determined to persevere."

Frank, however, modeled after her father, is a priggish character and a know-it-all; his perfection would, Emily Lawless believed, cause any spirited mother to rise up and slay him; but his mother, always under complete emotional control, loves this paragon of virtue. While other mothers offer wine to their young sons and tell dear Master Frank that "Mamma will allow you a bumper this once," she holds firm; Frank does not get the wine. Instead, he gets the finest education that doting parents can devise, acquiring a utilitarian taste for life. Frank, learning everything for a moral purpose, studies without being beaten.

Such improbable perfection in Frank's character was due to Edgeworth's belief that her father was perfect; although R. L. Edgeworth was unpopular outside his own eccentric circle—Lord Byron found him a bore while he admired Maria—she deified Edgeworth. Emotionally and intellectually, he was necessary for her health and literary productivity; after his death, she groped blindly for meaning and direction in her life. Her father, a world unto himself, never felt such indecision. Edgeworth's portrait of Frank, therefore, is not beyond reality; it is based upon her honest appraisal of the model provided by her father.

MORAL TALES FOR YOUNG PEOPLE

Moral Tales for Young People is a collection for a teenage audience. In the preface, R. L. Edgeworth states that the stories will "neither dissipate the attention, nor inflame the imagination," but will illustrate the opinions delivered in *Practical Education* (1798). They also illustrate prejudices against Jews, called to Edgeworth's attention in 1816 by Rachel Mordecai from Richmond, Virginia. *Harrington* (1817), the last work with a preface by her father, was written to illustrate a "good Jew."

"THE PRUSSIAN VASE"

"The Prussian Vase," which tells the story of a "bad Jew," is also, according to R. L. Edgeworth, a "lesson against imprudence for gentlemen intended for the bar." Remembering her father's experiences as an undergraduate law student at Oxford University, Edgeworth contrasts the English law system with that of Frederick II, King of Prussia. She also contrasts the impulsive, courageous behavior of Count Augustus Laniska, a seventeen-year-old soldier in the Prussian army, with the prudent, judicious behavior of his young lawyer friend, Albert. Accused of a crime against the King, Count Augustus is jailed at Spandau on circumstantial evidence. To demonstrate his generosity to a traveling Englishman, King Frederick allows a trial by jury; but the attorney for the defense must join his client in prison if the jury does not believe Albert's argument—an ironic twist to English justice. By a series of clever deductions and careful cross-examination following an analysis of the crime—the inscription of "Frederick, the Great tyrant" on a prize-winning vase—Albert finds that Solomon the Jew is the guilty party. Hating Count Laniska because he laughed at his son who was exercising before the King, Solomon added "tyrant" to the inscription of "Frederick, the Great" that Laniska had actually written.

Even with footnotes to identify her source of historical data, Maria Edgeworth's "The Prussian Vase" is unrealistic. The plot, never her greatest strength, is particularly weak. Sophia Mansfeld, the Dresden artist forcefully transported to Berlin to work in a pottery factory, does not relate to the other characters except in a most contrived fashion. Edgeworth wrote the story in her father's absence to have something to read to him on his return, "one of my greatest delights and strongest motives for writing." Sophia's passivity and patience must have been devised for Edgeworth's pleasure.

The other stories in *Moral Tales*, in general, are not fine literary works. Plots are labored with top-heavy moral heavyweights falling flat beside their light-headed contraries. Another Jewish villain, Aaron Carat in "The Good Aunt," gets blamed for the misdeeds of English gentlemen without being more credible than wicked Solomon from "The Prussian Vase."

"ANGELINA: OR, L'AMIE INCONNUE"

"Angelina: Or, L'Amie Inconnue" is of interest because it satirizes the romantic heroines of Mary Wollstonecraft and Mary Hays. Maria Edgeworth, the moral fabulist, diametrically opposed their frivolous romantic fiction, and "Angelina" expressed the opposition. Orphaned at fourteen, Angelina becomes the ward of Lady Diana Chillingworth, a disinterested guardian. Educating herself by reading novels from the circulating library, Angelina discovers "The Woman of Genius." She writes to the author in South Wales for almost two years before Araminta arranges for their meeting in a charming romantic cottage where Angelina "might pass her halycon days in tranquil, elegant retirement." When she finally meets her unknown friend, however, Angelina is shocked to see a vulgar, brandy-drinking woman "with a face and figure which seemed to have been intended for a man." A series of comic episodes cures Angelina of her romantic notions, and she is eventually reunited with Lady Chillingworth. In conclusion, Edgeworth tells her readers that "our heroine acquired that which is more useful than genius—good sense."

"MADEMOISELLE PANACHE"

Since Maria Edgeworth's literary canon combined fiction with morality, she ran the risk of creating "bad" characters that were greater literary creations than her "good" characters; one example is the French governess Mademoiselle Panache in "Mademoiselle Panache," Part II, from *Moral Tales*. Part I from *The Parent's Assistant* introduces the governess and her pupil Lady Augusta, while part II charts their downfall. R. L. Edgeworth describes the story as an illustration of the consequences of "imprudently

trusting the happiness of a daughter to the care of those who can teach nothing but accomplishments." Once again, the moral of the tale is illustrated through the contrasting of opposite characters. Mrs. Temple, the rather lifeless but well-educated mother of two teenage daughters, Helen and Emma, is a foil for Lady S., the card-playing, rather stupid mother of sixteen-year-old Lady Augusta. Lord George, almost twenty-one, is a cold, careless, selfish nobleman who contrasts to Mr. Mountague, a young man of about the same age but of a warm, caring nature. Each has a fine fortune. Lady Augusta's tutor-companion is Mlle Panache; Lord George's is Mr. Dashwood. Lady Augusta flirts with Lord George, Dashwood, and Mountague, while Helen quietly loves Mountague.

The French governess supplies the comic relief. When Mountague calls on Lady Augusta, she thinks he is the apothecary and engages him in a series of sharp dialogues before discovering her error. She is a source of amusement to Lord George and Dashwood because of her refusal to go into his boat, rowed by black Tom. Dashwood bets Lord George that he can get her into the boat without screaming despite her fear of blacks. Protesting to Dashwood, Mlle Panache, in "affected agony," says, "Ah! into de boat à la bonne heure; but not wid dat vilain black." Despite all her cunning and worldly wisdom, however, she is outwitted by Dashwood. By promising to marry her, he gets the governess to wait for him at the milliner's at four o'clock in the morning. With the governess out of the way, Dashwood elopes with Lady Augusta. Lady S. faints upon learning the news. When she recovers, she tries to determine why her daughter would ruin her life. Mlle Panache, recovering from her own hysterics on discovering Dashwood's duplicity, abuses him and her pupil. Finally, Lady S. orders her from the house, looking to Mrs. Temple for consolation, saying, "she was recommended to me, and how could I foresee all this?"

POPULAR TALES

Popular Tales (1804) is directed toward a diverse group. R. L. Edgeworth says in the preface that the tales were written for adults beyond the exclusively polite circles of the nobility, clergy, and professional gentlemen. Such people of "different ages, sexes, and situations in life" he hoped would not reject the stories, unless they were immoral, tiresome, or imitative. There are eleven tales: "Lame Jervas," "The Will," "The Limerick Gloves," "Out of Debt, Out of Danger," "The Lottery," "Rosanna," "Murad the Unlucky," "The Manufacturers," "The Contract," "The Grateful Negro," and "To-morrow." Each story represents vice and virtue in the lives of Cornwall miners, Lincolnshire and Monmouthshire farmers, Derby factory workers, Hereford tradesmen, London merchants, Irish farmers, land agents, and landowners, Jamaican slaves and slave owners, Philadelphian merchants, and Turkish soldiers, traders, and sultans.

As is seen in this group of characters (with the exception of the Turks in "Murad the Unlucky"), Edgeworth at the turn of the century—"The Limerick Gloves," "The Lottery," and "Lame Jervas" were actually written in 1799—was writing compassionately about the working class of the British empire. Repeating her pioneering effort in creating popular fictional children, Edgeworth successfully created a variety of characters who were workers. She, believing in the precept: "Educate them, don't hang them," earned the praise of Francis Jeffrey, editor of the *Edinburgh Review*, who viewed *Popular Tales* as superior in genius to Thomas Paine's work about the common people and to William Wordsworth's effort "to accommodate them with an appropriate vein of poetry." Edgeworth's short stories were part of the prevailing Anglo-Scottish empirical tradition which dominated the intellectual activity of the period. The Scottish Common-Sense philosophers—Archibald Alison, Hugh Blair, Lord Kames, William Robertson, Adam Smith, and the Edgeworth's family friend Dugald Steward—espoused doctrines that Edgeworth accepted, and Jeffrey, seeing dramatic instances of their philosophy in Edgeworth's tales, willingly overlooked the poor plotting and the overworked device of contrasting characters because of the social utility of the stories.

The tales illustrate the triumph of social justice and the punishment of villains. They also disclose the unfortunate lives of drinking, gambling, indolent, prejudiced, and dishonest men and women. Those who give up their bad habits survive; the others suffer misfortune and death. Helping the weak and misguided is the sole function of the many good characters in the stories, who are merely lifeless onlookers until the active, wicked characters lose their money, jobs, property, or health; then the heroes are given purpose. A promise to the faithful spouse or friend to stop drinking or gambling is a condition for the return to favor. Loss of money, a terrible moral transgression to the Edgeworths, is equivalent to a fall from grace.

"THE LOTTERY"

Of the *Popular Tales*, "The Lottery" typifies Edgeworth's concern for the cultivation of good habits among the working people. It documents her disapproval of gambling, drinking, and indolence while highlighting sound business practices for economic success and proper education of the young by happily married parents. Maurice Robinson, "one of the manufacturers employed in the cotton works at Derby," is honest, hard-working, and temperate. He is married to "industrious, prudent" Ellen and has George, who is truthful, obedient, and prudent. Mrs. Dolly Robinson, Maurice's cousin, is then introduced to the story. She "had been a laundry-maid in a great family, where she learned to love gossiping, and tea-drinking, and acquired a taste for shawls and cherry-brandy." She educates George, to his mother's horror, by coaxing and flattering him regardless of his behavior; obedience and disobedience are rewarded equally by stuffing gingerbread in his mouth. Her rival is William Deane, who, giving George a slate and pencil, taught him arithmetic. Initially, Dolly outwits Deane by convincing Maurice to buy a lottery ticket. He is to get the money from Ellen, who is "as rich as a Jew." Cheerfully, she gives Maurice her year's savings from her spinning, but, although he is tempted to buy the lottery ticket, the money goes to William so he can buy scientific books. Dolly is outraged by the affront to her power in the family. To placate her, Maurice sells the cow and buys a ticket, winning five thousand pounds.

Dolly then persuades Maurice to move to Paddington so they can live "very genteel," away from Deane, who told Maurice not to be idle despite his prize. Being genteel, to Dolly, means gossiping with acquaintances and drinking, at home and in the tavern, in an endless round of pleasure; to Maurice, it means idleness and indifference to his family. Not having worked for a year, he is a poor manager for the haberdasher's shop that Ellen has bought and stocked. Dolly's dream of the genteel life backfires when, because of Maurice's gambling, everything is lost. Rescued by Mr. Belton, a rich London carpet merchant, Maurice promises Ellen that he will never gamble again. Dolly, however, does not reform. Brought home in a drunken stupor with a broken leg and fractured skull after falling off her horse, she dies despite the surgeon's care in setting her leg and trepanning of her skull.

Following Dolly's death and Maurice's reformation—neither good George nor patient Ellen has been corrupted—the tranquil family regains its industry. Coincidentally, Maurice again meets Deane, who has become a success because of knowledge learned from the books bought by Maurice's money. George, through Deane's influence, is apprenticed to a hosier and "behaved as well as might be expected from his excellent education." The contrived tale proves Edgeworth's points: Money does not bring happiness, the pursuit of pleasure does not bring joy, and a good education leads to a job.

THE MODERN GRISELDA

It is incorrect to assume that Maria Edgeworth lacked a comic sense, despite the large quantity of didactic fiction from a fixed moral viewpoint. *The Modern Griselda*, a take-off on Geoffrey Chaucer's Griselda, is a witty, fast-moving tale of an ill-matched couple. The dialogue is funny, and the moral playfully projected. Written without her father's knowledge, it indicates Maria's own vital spirit in dramatizing Griselda Bolingbroke's conflict with her husband, "the most patient of men." Their separation, following a series of disagreements about trivial matters, occurs because Griselda persists in sacrificing her happiness because of her fear of "reforming and growing stupid."

The tales in the next collection, *Tales of Fashionable Life*, "Ennui," "Madame de Fleury," "Almeria," "The Dun," "Manoeuvring," "Vivian," "My Absentee," and "Emilie de Coulanges," dramatize the con-

flict between vice and virtue. All of the tales, however, are not short stories; although Edgeworth's dislike of contemporary frivolous novels generally precluded her use of that form, "Ennui," "Manoeuvring," "Vivian," and "The Absentee" belong to it.

"THE DUN"

Of the shorter tales, "The Dun," written in 1802 for the collection, contains some striking incidents. Debts incurred by the middle and higher social classes of English society are the subject of this twenty-five-page story. Colonel Pembroke lives beyond his income, keeping up with the spendthrift habits of his companions. Because Pembroke spends on credit, his lifestyle does not change with his fluctuation of income; the lifestyles of tradesmen awaiting his payment, however, do. His unpaid tailor cannot pay weaver John White, whose eight-year-old son accosts Pembroke on the street for a bill of £12.14. When Pembroke learns that White is dying from starvation, he curses the boy for bothering him with such a story, throws him a half-crown, and tears the bill into pieces, showering them over his head. Pembroke's gay companions laugh at the episode, which he calls "powdering a dun." Befriended by a gardener and an orange-woman with a barrow of fine fruit, the lad gets something to eat and an orange for his father.

At home, a miserable room up three flights of narrow, broken stairs, his dying father, mother, and sixteen-year-old sister Anne await him. In the dark, dank garret, his father rests on one bed; there are also two other beds and a loom in the crammed room that houses this honest English family. The descriptions of the White family and their home are exquisite, as is the dialogue between members of the family; Pembroke, on the contrary, is a flat villain.

The next incidents, Anne's employment by Mrs. Carver and her lending of money to White following his recovery, change the family's bleak future, but neither Anne nor her parents understand that Mrs. Carver is a madam, and that she is grooming Anne for the brothel. When her father discovers the truth, he tells Anne, who first suspects Mrs. Carver's identity from remarks made by the orange-woman. Anne's return of the fashionable clothes and her refusal to work for Mrs. Carver justify the family's faith in her moral standards, but the acts anger the madam, who has White jailed for debt since he has spent the borrowed money.

Returning from the prison one day, Anne receives a letter from Mrs. Carver. The eighteenth century epistolary technique is used here by Edgeworth as a convenient transitional device. This letter invites Anne to Mrs. Carver's home to make a very rich and generous gentleman happy—an action which would also relieve her family's financial distress. Anne, tempted beyond endurance, yields to necessity, and Mrs. Carver "received her with triumph." After feeding and clothing her victim, the madam leads her to the gay young gentleman.

He, by an improbable fate, is Colonel Pembroke. He does not force himself upon Anne but assures her that she will be treated "with honour and delicacy," much in the same manner that Sir Hyacinth O'Brien pleaded for Rose Gray to be his mistress in "Rosanna." Anne's response, a burst of tears and a fall to her knees before Pembroke, evokes his compassion. Upon learning of his part in her near downfall, he pays his debt to her father and reforms. He pays all his debts, sells his horses, and regulates his expenditures to his income. His diametric change in behavior is not convincing, but Edgeworth makes her point about how the evils of debt affect honest tradespeople.

In making a final judgment about Maria Edgeworth's short fiction, which spanned more than a half century of Irish life, enough evidence exists from her contemporaries and modern scholarship to establish her unique position in English and Irish literature. Like *Castle Rackrent*, the first regional novel written in English and probably in Western literature, *The Parent's Assistant* and *Early Lessons* pioneer an idea. Susan, Rosamond, Harry, Lucy, and Frank, the first literary children to exist separately from adult literature, were created solely for children's entertainment and edification.

Significantly, Edgeworth wrote specifically for preteens and teenagers because she recognized their disparate psychological needs. *Moral Tales* addresses that dichotomy. Edgeworth directed a collection of tales to the attention of the working population, just as she composed stories for the middle and upper classes. While conscious of social class, she was also aware of the classless nature of morality and its role in solving social problems. Such awareness unifies her *Popular Tales* and *Tales of Fashionable Life*.

Edgeworth's influence upon Jane Austen, John Ruskin, Sir Walter Scott, William Carleton, Ivan Turgenev, and James Fenimore Cooper substantiates her innovative role in shaping English, Scotch, Irish, Russian, and American fiction in that special mold of history, morality, and reality enlivened with a social conscience. These writers and literary critics for more than a century have established Maria Edgeworth's prominent position in Anglo-Irish literature. It is unlikely that she will lose that status.

OTHER MAJOR WORKS

LONG FICTION: *Castle Rackrent*, 1800; *Belinda*, 1801; *Leonora*, 1806; *Ennui*, 1809; *The Absentee*, 1812; *Vivian*, 1812; *Patronage*, 1814; *Harrington*, 1817; *Ormond*, 1817; *Helen*, 1834.

PLAYS: *Comic Dramas in Three Acts*, pb. 1817; *Little Plays for Children*, pb. 1827.

NONFICTION: *Letters for Literary Ladies*, 1795; *An Essay on the Noble Science of Self-Justification*, 1795; *Practical Education*, 1798 (also known as *Essays on Practical Education*, with Richard Lovell Edgeworth); *A Rational Primer*, 1799 (with Richard Lovell Edgeworth); *Essay on Irish Bulls*, 1802 (with Richard Lovell Edgeworth); *Essays on Professional Education*, 1809 (with Richard Lovell Edgeworth); *Readings on Poetry*, 1816 (with Richard Lovell Edgeworth); *Memoirs of Richard Lovell Edgeworth Esq.*, 1820 (Vol. II); *Thoughts on Bores*, 1826; *A Memoir of Maria Edgeworth*, 1867 (Francis Edgeworth, editor); *Archibald Constable and His Literary Correspondents*, 1873; *The Life and Letters of Maria Edgeworth*, 1894 (Augustus J. Hare, editor); *Chosen Letters*, 1931 (F. V. Barry, editor); *Romilly-Edgeworth Letters*, 1813-1818, 1936 (Samuel H. Romilly, editor); *Letters from England*, 1813-1844, 1971 (Christina Colvin, editor).

TRANSLATION: *Adelaide and Theodore*, 1783 (of comtesse de Stephanie Felicite Ducrest de Saint Aubin Genlis).

BIBLIOGRAPHY

Bilger, Audrey. *Laughing Feminism: Subversive Comedy in Frances Burney, Maria Edgeworth, and Jane Austen*. Detroit: Wayne State University Press, 1998. Part of the Humor in Life and Letters series, this volume reveals feminist traits of these eighteenth century writers.

Butler, Marilyn. *Maria Edgeworth: A Literary Biography*. Oxford, England: Clarendon Press, 1972. The standard biography on Edgeworth. This work is strongest when dealing with the complex and voluminously documented Edgeworth family history. Literary criticism as such is kept to a minimum. Provides a comprehensive sense of immediate family background. The overall social and cultural context of Edgeworth's work receives less detailed treatment.

_____. *Jane Austen and the War of Ideas*. Oxford, England: Clarendon Press, 1975. Despite its title, this work contains an important chapter on Edgeworth. The overall context of the Napoleonic era is taken into consideration. The obvious contrast between Edgeworth and Austen, and its consequences for the development of English fiction, results in a stimulating critique of Edgeworth's output.

Corbett, Mary Jean. "Another Tale to Tell: Postcolonial Theory and the Case of *Castle Rackrent*." *Criticism* 36 (Summer, 1994): 383-400. Examines *Castle Rackrent*, Edgeworth's novella, from a postcolonial perspective. Argues that the story comically exploits Irish and English relationships. Contends the story articulates the shifting relations of power between colonizer and colonized.

Flanagan, Thomas. *The Irish Novelists, 1800-1850*. New York: Columbia University Press, 1959. Devotes a section to Edgeworth's Irish novels. The author locates these in the context of Edgeworth's inaugurating role in Irish fiction. The emphasis is on her class, its sociopolitical context, and its influence on her writing. The methodology and some of the conclusions have been implicitly challenged by more recent criticism.

Genet, Jacqueline, ed. *The Big House in Ireland: Reality and Representation*. New York: Barnes and Noble, 1991. Discusses the story as the first so-called Big House novel in Ireland. Claims the men of Rackrent are not the victims of adverse circumstances, but of their own degeneration.

Hack, Daniel. "Inter-Nationalism: *Castle Rackrent* and Anglo-Irish Union." *Novel* 29 (Winter, 1996): 145-164. Argues that the logic of the story is the logic of Derrida's supplementarity, which fosters an understanding of Union as a continuing process of assimilation in which the absorption of Ireland into England never ends.

Harden, Elizabeth. *Maria Edgeworth*. Boston: Twayne, 1984. The author chooses the theme of education around which to organize her survey of Edgeworth's life and works. This approach reveals in broad outline the range of Edgeworth's sympathies and activities. Supplemented by an excellent bibliography.

Hollingworth, Brian. *Maria Edgeworth's Irish Writing*. New York: St. Martin's Press, 1997. A good examination of the Irish works, especially the novels *Castle Rackrent* and *Ormond* (1817). Includes detailed notes and bibliography.

Hurst, Michael. *Maria Edgeworth and the Public Scene: Intellect, Fine Feeling, and Landlordism in the Age of Reform*. London: Macmillan, 1969. This study deals with Edgeworth's artistically unproductive later years. During those years, she attempted to come to terms with the changing social and political landscape. The author provides a brisk analysis of Edgeworth's ideological commitments. This analysis may be usefully availed of to illuminate retrospectively the tensions and accommodations of Edgeworth's fiction.

Kowaleski-Wallace, Elizabeth. *Their Fathers' Daughters: Hannah More, Maria Edgeworth, and Patriarchal Complicity*. New York: Oxford, 1991. What does it mean for a female writer to identify with her father? This is the question Kowaleski-Wallace explores, devoting several chapters to Edgeworth's life and work. Includes detailed notes but no bibliography.

McCormack, W. J. *Ascendancy and Tradition in Anglo-Irish Literary History from 1789 to 1939*. Oxford, England: Clarendon Press, 1985. An intellectually far-reaching essay in the sociology of Irish literature. The ideological lineage of Edgeworth's work is firmly established, with special reference to the writings of Edmund Burke. In addition, her work's role in articulating the outlook of her class is assessed.

Eileen A. Sullivan, updated by George O'Brien

GEORGE ELIOT

Mary Ann Evans

Born: Chilvers Coton, England; November 22, 1819
Died: London, England; December 22, 1880

PRINCIPAL SHORT FICTION

Scenes of Clerical Life, 1858

OTHER LITERARY FORMS

George Eliot is known primarily for her novels: *Adam Bede* (1859), *The Mill on the Floss* (1860), *Silas Marner* (1861), *Romola* (1862-1863), *Felix Holt, the Radical* (1866), *Middlemarch* (1871-1872), and *Daniel Deronda* (1876), as well as for her poetry and essays.

ACHIEVEMENTS

George Eliot's most significant achievement is her very place in the literary canon. Despite her male pseudonym, she became a respected female writer in her own day, admired by her peers. Her novels are part of the flowering of serious writing done by women in the nineteenth century. She achieved this respect in spite of her unconventional lifestyle, having broken with her church, taken up decidedly liberal causes such as reform and women's rights, and lived openly with a married man. Such behavior was the downfall of other Victorian women, but Eliot was able to succeed and to be treated with the respect an author of her talents deserved. Eliot's works are serious, contemplative, and thoughtful, and they brought the novel to a new height, combining such philosophical seriousness with artistic handling of her subjects. Eliot and her peers were in large part responsible for the so-called rise of the novel in the mid-nineteenth century.

BIOGRAPHY

Mary Ann Evans was born on November 22, 1819, on an estate her father managed in Warwickshire. She knew from her childhood the Midlands world so lovingly portrayed yet so rigorously judged in her novels. After moving with her father to Coventry in 1841, she began reading in the sciences and German Higher Criticism, and she broke with the church in 1842. When her father died in 1849, she had the world before her, and, in 1851, she went to try her luck as a freelance writer in London, where she became friends with such notable liberals as John Chapman, Herbert Spencer, and most important, G. H. Lewes, with whom she was to live as wife in all but law from 1854 until his death in 1878. With Lewes's encouragement, George Eliot, as she styled herself, began writing her fiction. She lived with Lewes at the intellectual heart of London. In May, 1880, she married John Walter Cross, her banker. She died at Cheyne Walk, Chelsea, on December 22 of the same year.

ANALYSIS

Overshadowed by her full-length novels, George Eliot's short fiction is a writer's apprenticeship, as is that of Jane Austen. Whereas Austen's short pieces merely prefigure the themes and methods of her mature work, "Amos Barton," "Mr. Gilfil's Love Story," and "Janet's Repentance"—the three long stories that comprise *Scenes of Clerical Life*—show that from the start of her career George Eliot had identified the literary landscape that would prove so fertile under her cultivation. In this first book she records the commonplace struggles of commonplace people and the incremental blessings bestowed on society by provincial folk who "lived faithfully a hidden life and rest in unremembered tombs." Her concern with the crosscurrents that complicate the flow of even the most seemingly simple lives gives evidence that, though George Eliot had rejected orthodox Christianity, she retained her ardor for the "religion of humanity."

"Amos Barton"

For example, in "Amos Barton," George Eliot demonstrates that humble folk can attain that wisdom through suffering which in Greek tragedy is the reward only of kings and heroes. The plight of the title character, a dull, bald curate "more apt to fall into a blunder than into a sin," is too ordinary to be tragic: He has a large family, a small income, and a weak mind. The problems Barton inflicts on his congregation at Shepperton are likewise far from monstrous. An ineffective pastor, he busies himself with doctrines of salvation rather than helping his flock through the here and now. Dazzled by the patronizing attentions of the Countess Czerlaski, a cardboard aristocrat whom the villagers very sensibly mistrust, he fails to notice that his wife, Milly, a domestic angel whom Shepperton adores as much as it dislikes the countess, is literally working herself to death before his eyes. Thus, Barton alienates even his lukewarm partisans. Having lost Milly, however, he learns the one great lesson of a minister, and in George Eliot's view, of any responsible human being: that to respect and cherish one's fellow mortals is the divinest task one can perform. The parish in its turn responds sympathetically to the bereaved man as it never had to the mediocre pastor: "Amos failed to touch the spring of goodness by his sermons, but he touched it effectually by his sorrows." Still, Shepperton, as George Eliot realistically portrays it, is part of a world where fortune does not necessarily reward moral progress. Amos finds communion only to lose it. Deprived of his curacy by the holder of the living, who wants to bestow it elsewhere, Amos must leave the village he has just come to value for a new life in a large manufacturing town unsanctified by past experience.

"Mr. Gilfil's Love Story"

"Mr. Gilfil's Love Story" reminds the reader that suffering can stunt a noble nature as effectively as it can elevate a mean one. As the story opens, its protagonist, Amos Barton's predecessor at Shepperton, is an eccentric old man, generous with sarcasms and sugarplums, long on practical kindness but short on professional piety; but after a brief introduction, George Eliot's narrator takes the reader back to the end of the eighteenth century, away from prosaic Shepperton to the gothic grandeur of Cheverel Manor, and shows that Mr. Gilfil's emotions, like his body, have not forever been gnarled and crusty. A stalwart young country clergyman favored by his guardian Sir Christopher Cheverel, the young Maynard Gilfil loves Caterina Sarti, an Italian orphan whom the Cheverels have reared as half pet, half protégée. Uprooted from her native soil and caught between classes, Caterina is at the mercy of her passions and sentiments. Unfortunately, they lead her to adore a man far less worthy than Gilfil, Sir Christopher's heir Captain Anthony Wybrow, a sickly fop who, like Arthur Donnithorne in *Adam Bede*, makes idle love to stave off boredom. Frenzied by Wybrow's engagement to a lady of his own rank, Caterina goes forth to murder him only to find that a seizure has stopped his weak heart and saved her dagger some trouble.

George Eliot (Library of Congress)

The death she thought to cause only drives Caterina deeper into distraction. The constant lover Gilfil, however, is at hand to wean her slowly from the illusion of grand romance on which she has fed at Cheverel Manor to a more nourishing emotional diet, the domestic affection he can offer her at Shepperton parsonage. The delicate girl lives long enough to come to value Gilfil's love, "to find life sweet for his sake," and to reward him with a few months of happy marriage. Broken by her passion, however, she dies carrying Gilfil's child; whether she is killed by the insubstantial love or the actual one, the reader is left to decide. The effects on Maynard Gilfil, however, are unambiguous: His noblest qualities, lavished on Caterina, die with her, leaving a solid but misshapen trunk for what should have been "a grand tree spreading into liberal shade." In just this way, moralizes George Eliot,

> Many an irritating fault, many an unlovely oddity, has come of a hard sorrow, which has crushed and maimed the nature just when it was expanding into plenteous beauty; and the trivial erring life, which we visit with our harsh blame, may be but as the unsteady motion of a man whose best limb is withered.

"JANET'S REPENTANCE"

The same mixed moral judgment pervades "Janet's Repentance," the third of the *Scenes of Clerical Life*. The novella's situation is a sentimental cliché: The heroine vacillates between alternatives represented by a bad man (her husband, the lawyer Dempster) and a good one (the Evangelical minister Tynan) until the death of the good man wins her for the right. "Janet's Repentance," however, is a Victorian conversion with a difference. The story's heroine overindulges a decidedly ungenteel penchant for alcohol; its saintly paragon is a former sinner, and its villain is a good man soured; Milby village, where the action takes place, is pictured with the same carefully proportioned satire and generosity that later in George Eliot's career depict the town of Middlemarch:

> And so it was with the human life there, which at first seemed a dismal mixture of griping worldliness, vanity, ostrich feathers, and the fumes of brandy; looking closer, you found some purity, gentleness, and unselfishness, as you may have observed a scented geranium giving forth its wholesome odours amidst blasphemy and gin in a noisy pot house.

"THE LIFTED VEIL" AND "BROTHER JACOB"

If the *Scenes of Clerical Life* enabled George Eliot to find her authorial voice, her two short stories "The Lifted Veil" and "Brother Jacob" permit her to use inflections that have no place in her novels. "The Lifted Veil," George Eliot's only gothic tale, is an introverted, brooding narrative that she called a *jeu de mélancolie*. Her persona, Latimer, "cursed with an exceptional physical constitution, as I am cursed with an exceptional mental character," is as morbidly sensitive and unengaging as one of Edgar Allan Poe's aesthetic invalids. A clairvoyant, Latimer catches glimpses of his own future and, resembling the customary George Eliot narrator in perceptivity but not in sympathy, overhears the muddled, hypocritical thoughts that lie beneath the speeches of his fellow men. These gifts of insight turn Latimer in on himself rather than out toward the world. Furthermore, his mind never bears fruit to justify his self-obsession: Latimer has an artist's temperament without the corresponding talent. Married to a blonde siren who comes to despise him as completely as he has foreseen she will do, Latimer languidly waits for his death, aware that even this final experience will not relieve his boredom, for he already knows its particulars.

George Eliot is as unequivocally satiric in "Brother Jacob" as she is utterly melancholic in "The Lifted Veil." Throughout the tale she sustains the chilly irony that commences with the first sentence: "Among the many fatalities attending the bloom of young desire, that of blindly taking to the confectionary line has not, perhaps, been sufficiently considered." The aspiring young baker at the center of this *petit bourgeois* allegory, David Faux, who thinks himself deserving of great things, ineptly steals his mother's paltry savings and sets forth to make his fortune in the New World. He returns with little more than a case of malaria, sets himself up as Mr. Edward Freely, confectioner, in the dismal Midlands town of

Grimworth, begins to prosper, and finally stands revealed as a liar and impostor through his own greed and nemesis in the ungainly person of his brother, the idiot Jacob. Perhaps the story's chief merit is the literary catharsis it provided its author; for, having vented her spleen on Faux and his dreary fellows, George Eliot could view Silas Marner, her next protagonist and another superficially unlovable creature, with her characteristic magnanimity.

OTHER MAJOR WORKS

LONG FICTION: *Adam Bede*, 1859; *The Mill on the Floss*, 1860; *Silas Marner*, 1861; *Romola*, 1862-1863; *Felix Holt, the Radical*, 1866; *Middlemarch*, 1871-1872; *Daniel Deronda*, 1876.

POETRY: *The Spanish Gypsy*, 1868; *The Legend of Jubal and Other Poems*, 1874.

NONFICTION: *The Impressions of Theophrastus Such*, 1879; *Essays of George Eliot*, 1963 (Thomas Pinney, editor).

TRANSLATIONS: *The Life of Jesus Critically Examined*, 1846 (with Mrs. Charles Hennell; of D. F. Strauss's *Das Leben Jesu*); *The Essence of Christianity*, 1854 (of Ludwig Feuerbach's *Das Wesen des Christentums*).

BIBLIOGRAPHY

Ashton, Rosemary. *George Eliot: A Life*. New York: Penguin Press, 1997. An introduction to Eliot's life and work by an admirer of her fiction; interlaces discussions of Eliot's life with analysis of her fiction and the context of her work within Victorian society and social thought. Argues that her fiction most often focuses on characters out of step with their culture.

Bull, Malcolm. "Mastery and Slavery in *The Lifted Veil*." *Essays in Criticism* 48 (July, 1998): 244-261. Discusses sources of Eliot's novella in Victorian fascination with magnetism or mesmerism; discusses the relationship between Eliot's view of mesmerism and Hegel's view; considers how in both the master/slave concept can be liberating.

Dodd, Valerie A. *George Eliot: An Intellectual Life*. New York; St. Martin's Press, 1990. Part 1 gives the intellectual background of Victorian England, discussing writers such as John Stuart Mill and Thomas Carlyle. Part 2 discusses George Eliot's work in relation to that intellectual background. Includes a useful bibliography.

Dowling, Andrew. "'The Other Side of Silence': Matrimonial Conflict and the Divorce Court in George Eliot's Fiction." *Nineteenth-Century Literature* 50 (December, 1995): 322-336. Argues that there is a correlation between the legal and social changes brought about by the Matrimonial Causes Act of 1857 and the Divorce Court it created, and the emphasis on silence as a sign of matrimonial conflict in Eliot's fiction; suggests that Eliot's use of silence reflects a new social awareness of psychological cruelty in marriage.

Ermarth, Elizabeth Deeds. *George Eliot*. Boston: Twayne, 1985. An excellent short reference on Eliot. This book provides a biographical sketch and outlines Eliot's career, including a good chapter on *Scenes of Clerical Life*. The select bibliography is helpful, as is the chronology.

Flint, Kate. "Blood, Bodies, and *The Lifted Veil*." *Nineteenth-Century Literature* 51 (March, 1997): 455-473. Argues that Eliot's novella is concerned with the relationship between science and the imagination; states it was influenced by G. H. Lewes's *The Physiology of Common Life*. Claims that the blood transfusion scene is not simple gothicism but is grounded in contemporary debate about transfusion.

Hands, Timothy, *A George Eliot Chronology*. Boston: G. K. Hall, 1988. This book provides daily information about Eliot's life, particularly focusing on her writing career. Pieced together from letters and journals, this book provides a quick reference to most of the important facts of Eliot's life. A useful and interesting text.

Harvey, W. J. *The Art of George Eliot*. New York: Oxford University Press, 1962. This volume covers the structure of Eliot's work—the omniscient narrator, the treatment of time, and characterization. A helpful source for a close study of Eliot's work. Supplemented by a short bibliography.

Hutchinson, Stuart, ed. *George Eliot: Critical Assessments*. East Sussex: Helm Information, 1996. Volume 1 consists of biography, nineteenth century reviews, and responses; volume 2 contains perspectives from 1900-1970 on Eliot's work; volume 3 provides critical essays on individual works; volume 4 includes perspectives from the 1970's on.

Taylor, Ina. *A Woman of Contradictions: The Life of George Eliot*. New York: William Morrow, 1989.

Taylor claims to work from sources different from those on which all previous biographies drew—all of which, she says, come from one beginning: Eliot's husband, John Cross. An interesting and provocative book that focuses on Eliot's personal life. Includes photographs of Eliot, her family, and friends.

Peter W. Graham, updated by Kimberley L. Jacobs

STANLEY ELKIN

Born: Brooklyn, New York; May 11, 1930
Died: St. Louis, Missouri; May 31, 1995

PRINCIPAL SHORT FICTION

Criers and Kibitzers, Kibitzers and Criers, 1965
The Making of Ashenden, 1972
Searches and Seizures, 1973
The Living End, 1979
Stanley Elkin's Greatest Hits, 1980
Early Elkin, 1985
Van Gogh's Room at Arles: Three Novellas, 1993

OTHER LITERARY FORMS

In addition to his short fiction, Stanley Elkin has produced several novels, including *Boswell: A Modern Comedy* (1964), *The Dick Gibson Show* (1971), *The Franchiser* (1976), *George Mills* (1982), *Stanley Elkin's the Magic Kingdom* (1985), *The Rabbi of Lud* (1987), *The MacGuffin* (1991), *Mrs. Ted Bliss* (1995). He has also written a screenplay, *The Six-Year-Old Man* (1968), a memoir, *Why I Live Where I Live* (1983), and a collection of essays, *Pieces of Soap: Essays* (1992). In addition, Elkin has edited several collections of short fiction and has written numerous reviews and works of literary criticism for scholarly journals.

ACHIEVEMENTS

Over the course of his career, Stanley Elkin has received numerous grants and awards. In 1962, he won the Longview Foundation Award, in 1965 the *Paris*

Review prize, in 1966 a John Simon Guggenheim Memorial Foundation Fellowship, in 1968 a Rockefeller Foundation Fellowship, American Academy of Arts and Letters grant, in 1980 a Rosenthal Foundation Award, in 1981 a *Sewanee Review* award, and in 1983 a National Book Critics Circle Award. Three of his books were nominated for the National Book Award, and *Van Gogh's Room At Arles: Three Novellas* (1993) was a finalist for the PEN/Faulkner Award for Fiction.

BIOGRAPHY

Stanley Lawrence Elkin was born in Brooklyn, New York, on May 11, 1930. He grew up in Chicago and was educated at the University of Illinois at Urbana, where he earned his B.A. and M.A., and his Ph.D. in English in 1961. While still at the University of Illinois, Elkin married Joan Marion Jacobson, an artist; together they became the parents of two sons and a daughter. After serving in the armed forces for two years (1955-1957), Elkin spent several years living in London and Rome with his wife, prior to writing his first novel, *Boswell* (1964). *A Bad Man* (1967) was written on a John Simon Guggenheim Memorial Foundation Fellowship. His short fiction, much of it later integrated into his novels, has been collected in many anthologies.

In 1960, before earning his Ph.D., Elkin taught English at Washington University in St. Louis. He was assistant professor (1962-1966), associate professor (1966-1969), and became a full professor of

English in 1969. In 1983, he became a Kling Professor of Modern Letters. He was visiting lecturer and visiting professor at several institutions, including Smith College, the University of California at Santa Barbara, the University of Wisconsin at Milwaukee, Yale University, and Boston University. Death is a key subject in Elkin's fiction, as is the obverse. Perhaps his heightened sense of death and life stem from the fact that he suffered from multiple sclerosis, which was diagnosed in 1961. He died of a heart attack in St. Louis in 1995.

ANALYSIS

From the time Stanley Elkin emerged in the mid-1960's, critics applauded his novels and short fiction as some of the best satirical writing in American literature. His stories—often labeled black humor—are essentially dark, urban comedies in which unusually articulate, marginal figures struggle to define themselves in a confusing and chaotic modern world. Often, the means of definition is essentially linguistic, as the characters attempt to construct an understanding of themselves and their place in the modern world through language itself. The interplay between the characters' harsh circumstances and their ability to overcome those circumstances through language is the hallmark of Elkin's satire. Throughout his work, Elkin depicts extremes of personality—people in crisis, engaging in personal (if, from external perception, trivial) cataclysms. His characters are often grotesque; Elkin has written, "I stand in awe of the outré." His stories do not hinge on plot; in fact, often little "happens" in the stories. Rather, they delineate a situation and resolution of greater internal than external consequence. A key to Elkin's art is rhetoric. He uses a rich variety of language composed of "shoptalk," the lingo of the professions of his characters: grocers, bailbondsmen, hipsters, and collection agents. His characters, however, do not speak consistently "realistic" speech. Many magically possess the full range of rhetorical possibility, from gutter speech to learned philosophical flights. So, too, many characters are conversant with areas of knowledge far beyond their nominal experience—a metaphorical representation of their heightened consciousnesses.

Stanley Elkin (©Miriam Berkley)

Elkin does not seek literal verisimilitude in his characters' speech. This fictive rhetoric, like that of Henry James, is deliberate artifice. Elkin has written, "Rhetoric doesn't occur in life. It occurs in fiction. Fiction gives an opportunity for rhetoric to happen. It provides a stage where language can stand." Elkin's characters obsessively seek to make contact with their worlds, and their "fierce language" is both symbol and product of that aggression.

"EVERYTHING MUST GO!"

In "Everything Must Go!," a story which later became a part of *A Bad Man* along with "The Garbage Dump" and "The Merchant of New Desires," a young Jewish boy has traveled to southern Illinois with his half-mad father, who is a peddler of rags and snatches—a demented master salesman who can sell anything—who, in fact, has defined himself existentially as an archetype of the Jewish peddler fulfilling the biblical prophecy of the Diaspora. His son loves and hates his father, feeling acutely his "otherness," and is alternately amused and horrified by his father's mad intensity. The man sells everything including individual months torn from calendars: "April," he called in February, "just out. Get your April here." He sells from his wagon "old magazines, chapters from books, broken pencils, ruined pens, eraser ends in small piles, string, rope, cork scraped from the insides of bottle caps. . . ."

The man tries to educate his son in the fine art of hawking wares, insisting that the American-born lad (neither is an immigrant) sound like the archetypal peddler: "Not 'rags' not 'old *clothes*.' What are you, an announcer on the radio? You're in a street! Say 'regs,' 'all cloze.' Shout it, sing it. I want to hear steerage, Ellis Island in that throat." The boy's call decays into "Rugs, oil cloths!" and "Rex, wild clits." "Terrific, . . . wild clits is very good. We'll make our way. . . ."

The story reaches a climax when the father invades a county fair's ox-pulling contest, and in a hilarious and manic display, sells every item on a wagon towering with junk. Throughout the tale the father has referred to one "unsalable thing," which he finally reveals to his son is himself. When at last he dies of cancer, the son, metamorphosing into the true salesman, proves the father wrong. He calls the doctor to tell him that the father has died. "They argued . . . but it was no use. The doctor, on behalf of the tiny hospital, could offer him only fifteen dollars for the body."

The son, named Feldman, grows into a department store magnate, as the reader finds out in the novel, eventually turns to a life of crime, is arrested, and revolutionizes the prison to which he is sent through the use of the same gifts and manias which possessed his father. (Another story excerpted from the novel, "The Merchant of New Desires," hilariously depicts Feldman's running of the prison commissary, which has become an avatar of his father's wagon.) Together, the stories form a potent and typical introduction to Elkin's work. The language is nonstop; the "vaudeville-like patter" is continuous. The manic events mask a desperate attempt to form an identity and connect with the world. Both the situations and the rhetoric display the art of the bizarre, the grotesque manifestations of feverishly heightened consciousness and wild emotional excess.

The rhetorical aspects of Elkin's fiction combine with an exact description of every setting. Hotel rooms, for example, are described down to the texture and grain of the plastic wood veneers of the dressers and the weave of the drapes. The stark realism of locale combined with the wild multifaceted language of the characters (who often narrate their own stories) form a unique texture. Throughout, the language is not an end in itself, but rather a clue to the personality of the characters, a metaphor for their psychological states. Elkin's typical protagonists are salesmen, con men, and "consumed consumers" who may be down and out, but are struggling obsessively and subjectively, acutely conscious of their every impulse and atom of their surroundings. They exist in a world of objective, unthinking, "normal" people whose lack of engagement is a source of alienation and cause for despair. They are frequently "ordinary" characters with brutally heightened consciousnesses in discontinuity with themselves and their milieu. Their monologues and harangues, often wildly funny, at other times tragically touching, are an attempt to discover their essences through the medium of language itself. The world does not become knowable, if ever, until expressed verbally.

"IN THE ALLEY"

Fearful of losing their identities, Elkin's characters push life to its fatal limits until it retaliates. At times, they give in to their malaise with a brutal intensity. Feldman, the hero of "In the Alley" (*Criers and Kibitzers, Kibitzers and Criers*), suffering from a terminal disease, has been told that he will die in a year. He uses the time to die gracefully, stoically, with dignity; dying becomes his identity and life. His body, however, perversely refuses to die on schedule, and his new identity becomes absurd to him. He enters a hospital terminal ward to await his end and to immerse himself in his impending demise, to connect with others in the same plight. Yet his body still refuses to cooperate, and he is disabused of his self-concept of the stoic, heroic dier. There is no "fraternity among the sick."

Feldman wanders about the city, a Joycean "Nighttown" of working-class bars, enters one, and takes up conversation with a muscular Slavic woman with a tattooed wrist. He tells her of his imminent but frustratingly deferred death, at first seeking affection and solace. Finally, however, seeking release and using the woman as an agent, he brings about his own doom: He tries to seduce her, and the woman, with the help of a tough female bartender, beats him senseless. He is carried out to the alley, a sign pinned to his suit reading "STAY AWAY FROM WHITE WOMEN." Surrounded by garbage, Feldman, finally dying, thinks of his family, who had anticipated his death with admiration and compassion and "unmasked hope that it would never come to this for them, but that if it should, if it ever should, it would come with grace. But nothing came gracefully—not to heroes."

"THE BAILBONDSMAN"

One of the very best pieces of fiction Elkin has produced is "The Bailbondsman," one of the three novellas (the others are "The Making of Ashenden" and "The Condominium") in *Searches and Seizures*. Shifting effortlessly between first- and third-person narration, the story relates a day in the life of a classically obsessive Elkin protagonist, Alexander Main, a "Phoenecian" bailbondsman in Cincinnati—a member of an extinct race, practitioner of a trade which requires him to consort with all layers of life from the ermine of the bench to prostitutes. He is greedy for total immersion in his milieu and obsessed by the mystery of the meaning of his life and its relation to the world. "I have no taste, only hunger," he says—a literal pun, for he has no sense of taste—food is only fuel. He succeeds in his profession because he is a master of rhetoric and can persuade judges to set bail and persuade clients to seek his services rather than those of the competition. His Whitman like consciousness absorbs everything—history, science, the codes of the underworld, literature—with total abandon. All experience floods his consciousness with equal priority, filtered through his expansive rhetoric. He dotes on language; even Crainpool, his gray assistant, enjoys his constant patter about everything from the allegorical parasitology of the liver fluke to the prehistoric teeth Main examines in a museum, tears coursing down his face as he thinks of the fugacity of life. Everything is emblemized.

Main is obsessed with the memory of Oyp and Glyp, the only clients who have ever jumped bail. He dreams of them as grave robbers in an ornate Egyptian tomb. The dream is a profusion of opulent archeological imagery. In his dream, Main apprehends the fiends, but the Egyptian judge foils him by refusing to set bail for a crime so horrendous and then compounds the affront by setting the thieves free because there can be no appropriate punishment. Oyp and Glyp represent to Main his potential lack of control over his environment—threatened by legal changes which may make his trade obsolete—and his inability to dominate totally his world and the mystery it represents.

Main's obsession with domination leads him to his assistant's apartment, where it is revealed that Crainpool had jumped bail years ago and that Main had harbored him from prosecution by employing him. He is "the only man in the world [he is] allowed to kill." Main prepares to execute Crainpool, and the story ends as Main shoots Crainpool in the hand and chases out after him into the night. The "seizure" that ends Main's search is obsessive, cruel, and destructive, but also a crushing embrace of the life force. Like Feldman, Main is determined to register his presence in the implacable universe.

VAN GOGH'S ROOM AT ARLES

Most critics agree that the title novella in Elkin's collection of three stories is the strongest. The story centers on an undistinguished professor named Miller from a community college in Indiana, who, when granted a fellowship to attend a think tank retreat in Arles in southern France, ends up being housed in the bedroom of Vincent Van Gogh. Indeed, the room contains the nightstand, the basin and pitcher, and the cane-bottomed chair depicted in Van Gogh's famous painting entitled "Vincent's Bedroom in Arles."

Miller is something of an "innocent abroad," at first unimpressed by the famous room and obviously outclassed by his more distinguished colleagues at the retreat. However, he gradually begins to appreciate the obligation the room places on him and makes a valiant, albeit feeble, effort to do some thinking while at the think tank, cobbling together a research "project" about the attitudes university professors have toward the lowly community college.

Miller's sense of inadequacy is heightened throughout the story by the continual discovery of scenes from some of Van Gogh's most famous paintings, all of which create the illusion of Miller's moving in a world of art: "The Night Cafe in the Place Lamartine in Arles," "Fishing Boats on the Beach at Saintes-Maries," "The Langlois Bridge at Arles," and "The Railway Bridge over Avenue Montmajour, Arles." Even more challenging is the appearance of a number of Arles residents who look like characters in several Van Gogh paintings. A doctor who comes to see Miller after he faints from stress and jet-lag and who looks like Van Gogh's "Portrait of Dr. Félix Rey," tells Miller that descendants of Van Gogh's models still live in Arles. Miller is more disoriented by this mix of past and present, art and reality, when he sees a man who looks like Van Gogh's "The Seated Zouave" and a boy in a field with a great bag of seeds on his shoulder who looks like Van Gogh's "The Sower."

These encounters come to a climax when additional members of the "Club of the Portraits of the Descendants of the People Painted by Vincent Van Gogh" come to Miller's room to give him advice for what the doctor calls his "sprained soul." Miller's final encounter with a Van Gogh painting occurs when he is introduced to Madame Ginoux, who, when they meet, bends her arm at the elbow and presses the knuckles to the side of her face in a pensive salute, exactly like the gesture in Van Gogh's "Madame Ginoux with Gloves and Umbrella."

At the end of the story, although the mundane Miller has not been radically altered by his visit to the art world of Van Gogh, he is not the same either, for the world of art has made him more responsive to the mysteries and beauties of life. He understands that although one cannot create like an artist, one may still try to see as an artist sees.

OTHER MAJOR WORKS

LONG FICTION: *Boswell: A Modern Comedy*, 1964; *A Bad Man*, 1967; *The Dick Gibson Show*, 1971; *The Franchiser*, 1976; *George Mills*, 1982; *Stanley Elkin's the Magic Kingdom*, 1985; *The Rabbi of Lud*, 1987; *The MacGuffin*, 1991; *Mrs. Ted Bliss*, 1995.

SCREENPLAY: *The Six-Year-Old Man*, 1968
NONFICTION: *Why I Live Where I Live*, 1983; *Pieces of Soap: Essays*, 1992.

BIBLIOGRAPHY

Bailey, Peter J. *Reading Stanley Elkin*. Urbana: University of Illinois Press, 1985. This study of Elkin's fiction examines Elkin's major themes in order to counteract misreadings of him as another in a series of black humorists, especially given Elkin's association with black humorists of the 1960's. Each of seven chapters discusses a separate theme or thematic element in Elkin's work. A comprehensive index follows.

Bargen, Doris G. *The Fiction of Stanley Elkin*. Frankfurt, Germany: Verlag Peter D. Lang, 1980. The first book-length work of criticism on Elkin. Examines his association with the literary movements of metafiction, black humor, American Jewish writers, and popular-culture novels. Bargen argues that Elkin's work is similar in some ways to all of these but dissimilar enough to resist categorization. Her work includes an extensive biography, an interview with the author, and a comprehensive bibliography and index.

Cohen, Sarah Blacher, ed. *Comic Relief: Humor in Contemporary American Literature*. Urbana: University of Illinois Press, 1978. Several authors engage in a discussion of the role of humor in the writers who emerged in the 1960's and 1970's, with Elkin figuring prominently in the discussion. Cohen aligns Elkin with black humorists, identifying their common traits, for example their need to laugh at the absurdity of modern culture.

Dougherty, David C. *Stanley Elkin*. Boston: Twayne, 1990. Dougherty discusses all of the fiction through *The Rabbi of Lud*, including stories and novellas, emphasizing Elkin's almost poetic use of language and sense of vocation. The chronology, brief biography, bibliography of secondary works, and discussion of the uses and limitations of classifying Elkin as a Jewish-American writer, a satirist, a black humorist, and a metafictionist make this an especially useful work.

Olderman, Raymond M. *Beyond the Waste Land: The*

American Novel in the Nineteen Sixties. New Haven, Conn.: Yale University Press, 1972. Olderman's study is the first treatment of Elkin's fiction in the context of other emerging authors of the 1960's. He discusses Elkin and others of his generation, repudiating the image of modern society as the "wasteland" depicted in T. S. Eliot's landmark 1922 poem. Olderman identifies a new kind of idealism emerging in contemporary fiction.

Pinsker, Sanford. "Sickness unto Style." *Gettysburg Review* 7 (1994): 437-445. Discusses Elkin's collection of novellas *Van Gogh's Room at Arles* and his collection of essays *Pieces of Soap* primarily in terms of prose style. Discusses how the Van Gogh novella focuses on pictures within pictures and is an example of impressionism in the Van Gogh manner.

Pughe, Thomas. *Comic Sense: Reading Robert Coover, Stanley Elkin, Philip Roth*. Boston: Birkhäuser Verlag, 1994. Explores the humor in each author's fiction.

The Review of Contemporary Fiction 15 (Summer, 1995). Special issue on Elkin, with essays by Jerome Klinkowitz, Jerome Charyn, William H. Gass, and others. Features an interview with Elkin in which he discusses the mystery in his fiction, the nature of plot, the essence of story, and his prose style.

Vinson, James, ed. *Contemporary Novelists*. 2d ed. New York: St. Martin's Press, 1976. A comprehensive and broad study. Vinson includes Elkin in an overview of writers from the 1960's and 1970's. The section that covers Elkin most comprehensively is the section written by David Demarest, Jr., who discusses Elkin's place among his contemporaries.

David Sadkin, updated by Edward Huffstetler and Charles E. May

---

GEORGE P. ELLIOTT

Born: Knightstown, Indiana; June 16, 1918
Died: New York, New York; May 3, 1980

PRINCIPAL SHORT FICTION
Among the Dangs, 1961
An Hour of Last Things and Other Stories, 1968

OTHER LITERARY FORMS

George P. Elliott's published works include poetry; personal, philosophical, and literary essays (originally published in such journals as *Commentary, Commonweal, Nation, Atlantic Monthly, Harpers*, and *The Writer*); and novels. He is best known for his short stories, however, particularly those collected in *Among the Dangs*.

ACHIEVEMENTS

As an American novelist and short-story writer, George P. Elliott has proven himself as a craftsman of modern realistic fiction. His work was influenced by earlier masters of that tradition such as Henry James, Joseph Conrad, and James Joyce, as well as prose stylists of the eighteenth and nineteenth centuries. The thoughts of early modern poets such as William Butler Yeats and W. H. Auden also had an impact on his writing. While incorporating experimental elements into his work, Elliott consistently affirmed the vitality of the traditional. His honors and awards include a Hudson Review Fellowship in fiction from 1956 to 1957; a John Simon Guggenheim Memorial Foundation Fellowship from 1961 to 1962; the Indiana Authors' Day Award in 1962 for *Among the Dangs*; the D. H. Lawrence Fellowship at the University of New Mexico in 1962; a Ford Foundation fellowship for writing in connection with the theater from 1965 to 1966; and the National Institute of Arts and Letters award in 1969.

BIOGRAPHY

George Paul Elliott was the eldest of four children (he had two younger brothers and a sister), and he was born on a farm near Knightstown, Indiana, a small country town. His father, Paul Revere Elliott, descended from several generations of Quaker farmers. His mother, Nita Gregory, came from a Methodist family. Since his father did not succeed in making a living from farming in Indiana, the family moved to Southern California, near Riverside, in 1928. There, his father worked on a carob plantation. When the plantation failed in the 1930's, Elliott's father worked as an irrigator until he retired.

After reading Samuel Taylor Coleridge's *The Rime of the Ancient Mariner* (1798) when he was a child, Elliott decided that he would spend his life writing stories and poems. From the time he graduated high school in 1934 until after the war, he held a variety of jobs. Working his way through college, he first attended Riverside Junior College, then the University of California at Berkeley, where he received his M.A. in English in 1941, the year he married Mary Emma Jeffress; the couple's only child was born in 1943. Elliott was exempted from military service during the World War II for medical reasons.

In 1947, Elliott assumed his first teaching post at St. Mary's College, near Oakland, and he taught English there for eight years. He then taught for a year at Cornell University and the University of Iowa Writers' Workshop, spent one semester at Berkeley, three years at Barnard College, and finally remained at his post at Syracuse University for the remainder of his life.

Elliott, more concerned with content than form, explored his fundamentally Christian convictions in a number of novels and short stories. At the beginning of his career, his writing, according to him, consisted of "deadly naturalism, conventional versification, and bloodless fantasy." His dominant literary aim, however, later turned to the idea of infusing "poetic fantasy with the blood of life." Elliott died on May 3, 1980, in New York.

ANALYSIS

In the fictions of George P. Elliott, individuals discover the limitations or the wrongness of their beliefs or, at least, the complications in their motives, actions, and relations with the world. Quite often, the reader shares in a character's embarrassment or horror from a close distance; but at best, the characters come to revelations to which the mind, senses, and emotions all contribute, as do chance and the acts (or meddling) of other humans. Individuals struggle with various forms of pride; social, psychological, and sexual confusions; blinding imprisonment by fixed ideas; and the need for integration in a marketplace of specialists. The characters appear in groups (microcosms) which they belong to blindly or intrude upon with their motives mixed; and the strains operating upon these groups, particularly the families, make concrete universal stresses. Traditional values are never far from mind, although they are likely to be acted upon by doubting and nihilistic characters. When hope springs, it is because the characters' discoveries mute pride and zeal and unmask insecurities, causing sympathy.

Because, generally, the characters are real and their failures elicit compassion, and the reader is not put off by utter condemnations of humanity or stylistic trivialities, the experience of reading Elliott encourages questing among the mysteries of humans' nature and the world's. His message is that the way leads through appearances, complicated by the incompleteness and ambiguity of human communications. What makes the more hopeful visions convincing in their optimism is that they do not exaggerate: They show characters making small adjustments in a style that has been called "cool" and from which irony, satire, and other deflators of pretensions are never distant. The difficulties in reading this work are never great because the storytelling carries one through the complications, and close attention to the characters brings one to feel and see. Elliott called the style which achieves this moral end "formal-seeming, of a certain polish, rather distancing." He explained his didacticism as depending upon the "complex relationships among storyteller, characters and readers" and an "aesthetic distance," without which "there is not likely to be much moral clarity."

"THE NRACP"

In the popular anthology piece "The NRACP," collected in *Among the Dangs*, Elliott accomplishes this end by a satirical use of I-narration. Andrew Dixon's letters imply related and recurrent themes, the ironic disparity between appearance and reality, humans' inhumanity to humans and their misuse of thought and language to obscure the truth. Set near the present (when Christian morality is thought of as a relic to rid oneself of), the story unfolds a government plot to deal with "the negro problem in America" by exploiting prejudices at work within an apparent democracy. On the surface, the government appears to be relocating blacks, a program that does not upset more than a few dissidents; but in truth, the blacks are to be reprocessed into meat for export and for feeding to the unwitting white bureaucracy. Like Jonathan Swift's, Elliott's satire is often painfully lucid.

Andrew Dixon is one of these bureaucrats. His job, he thinks, is to rewrite the interned blacks' letters before they are sent out. By the time he discovers what is happening, he lacks the moral will to oppose it, and he struggles to put the horror from his mind. The story is chilling, first, because it is not far from other episodes in actual history, and, second, because Andy, although obtuse, is credible and not entirely unscrupulous or inhumane. He represents a middle sort between extremes, an educated Everyman. Elliott's characters are not simply allegorical, but, like the characters in moralities, they face elemental problems. It takes Andy a long time to see the truth, much longer than it takes the reader; this delay allows the irony to set its roots. To feed the irony, other characters see the truth much sooner but are incapable of acting or are unconcerned. O'Doone's suspicious nature causes him to bring invisible ink for messages, but when the truth crumbles him, he kills himself. Ruth, a secretary whom Andy marries, may know the truth, but whether she does or not matters little, unbothered, as she is, by moral scruples. Her philosophy excludes their relevance: "There are those who get it and those who dish it out"; and she intends "to be on the side of the dishers."

What blinds an apparently educated person to the nature of things? The question, implied by a number of Elliot's stories, could be answered variously; but Andy's case is representative. Although his reading suggests sophistication—including Swift, Auden, and Joyce—Andy admits that he has never known himself. This may be true, but even if it is, it sounds theatrical; indeed, a large part of his problem is his infatuation with the way he sounds. In the first letter, he enjoys sneering at the place, at those who love reading mysteries, at the black culture. In number two, he enjoys admitting his former ignorance and then congratulates himself on his newfound "largeness of spirit"; he is eating up the rhetoric. By the time Ruth enters, Andy has shown off a large vocabulary; but he has also raised some suspicions about whether he can use language truthfully. When he escalates Ruth's "dishers" and "getters" maxim into a "post-Christian golden rule" and her tired dig at his love of guilt into "Dostoevskian notions," he is, indeed, "a balloon" in a "rarefied atmosphere." Andy, like other characters in this canon, is a sentimentalist, prejudiced against blacks and peers alike and full of the sound of his own voice.

Indicative of Elliott's wisdom, he does not overwork the obtuseness of the I-narrator but develops Andy's character, thus complicating judgment by soliciting compassion. This development, is clearly on its way in the eighth letter, when Andy sees the black woman's yearning for her man and is moved by it. Andy's rhetoric is still exaggerated ("I have been discovering that the wells of pity, which have lain so long locked and frozen in my eyes, are thawed in me now"); and, in invisibility, he still allows himself to sneer. When however, he says plainly, "I cannot tell you how I pitied both these unhappy people," he has stopped taking his own pulse and felt for someone else. The last letter shows him splitting dangerously in two. Visibly, over Ruth's pregnancy, he launches into a cosmic rhetoric that apes Shakespearean flights; but, in invisibility, he recounts O'Doone's actual and his own contemplated suicide in short, deflated sentences. After the guard's indictment of his cannibalism, Andy stays invisible, disgusted but desiring to forget. Finally, he elicits some degree of sympathy because, in a world that does not encourage "felt understanding," he has known someone else's hurt, and his numbing chant masks nervousness and pain.

Elliott has a painter's or an architect's regard for form, and, as a critic of the theater, he knows how the treatment of space can effect a mood or work upon the feelings of his characters. He is a master of juxtaposition (as a cool stylist needs to be), and he can use a pattern of scenes to turn ideas nearly palpable. In "The NRACP," Andy blames his initial depression on "the rasping, blinding landscape." Retreating from the overcrowded reading room, he finds his only other choice indoors to be his "own cell" and "cot." Eventually, relief appears to come from the walks he takes "toward two" vast "realities": himself and the natural world. These walks, however, bring him also to the entrapment of long windowless sheds and fences and, finally, to enlightenment. After a dose too great to stand, he stays entrapped; even on a good day, when a bird sings outside, he thinks only of his cot and sleep, murmuring the narcotic chant, "My wife is going to have a baby, my wife is going to have a baby, my wife is going to have a baby."

AN HOUR OF LAST THINGS AND OTHER STORIES

Such images of adult humans reduced almost to fetal sleep appear increasingly in Elliott's second volume, *An Hour of Last Things and Other Stories*. For example, the reduction of hope and promise to paranoia and a pathetic death-in-life controls the nightmarish "Better to Burn." Occasionally, a good Samaritan intrudes—as Anna tries to do (but fails to help) in "Better to Burn" and as Brother Nicholas succeeds in doing in "Into the Cone of Cold," the second volume's opening story. This novella-length quest narrative, reminiscent of Joseph Conrad's *Heart of Darkness* (1902), employs the science-fiction premise that a man can be projected into the void and brought back to write about it. What occurs, however, is a blank "in his memory," an unsettling reversal of some bodily parts, and the fear that "the void has spread into" him and fills the place where his soul had been. In this world (as in the reader's) there has been a threatening complication of orders of power. The Catholic fathers of St. Anselm's, where Stuart, the central character, is teaching, are more convincing as

scientists, engineers, and bureaucrats than as Christians. Under the pall of physical and psychological reverses, the latter sort unmended by a second trip into the "anti-world," Stuart sets out to find his Kurtz, former Brother Carl, the brains behind it all. This universal genius has been so affected by his role in the experiment that he has left the order and gone off to dive into a mystery that, unlike the cone of cold, at least yields actual abalone. Still curious about the experience of the void, Carl agrees to meet with Stuart; but their verbal wrestling helps little, if at all. Then, by chance, Stuart stumbles onto where Carl dives and focuses on the "granite oceanic sculpture" Carl swims about. He feels he has "participated in a ritual of revelation"—an archetype of a man at work in the most mysterious depth *in the world* from which a man may bring back something tangible, chipped by a kind of art from stubborn stone.

When Stuart returns to his wife, Marguerite, he finds her under such a strain from his experience that she leaves him, crying that his respect for her is not enough "to think up a story" she "could at least swallow enough of to keep one little shred of self-respect." Feeling a failure, Stuart finds himself a furnished room and withdraws into bed. On the fifth day, when Stuart is nearly a bearded zombie, help comes from an unexpected source. Brother Michael intrudes, forces Stuart to clean himself and eat, and springs him from this cell. When they reach the freer space of Echo Lake, where Stuart's wife vacations, Brother Nicholas tells her a tale which she cannot understand; but she believes it. As the reunited couple settles down to sleep and she snuggles him toward intimate security, he starts to feel the stir of words, a poem on its way. A good marriage is hard to find and even harder to keep together, but it helps those who have the magic.

Through the third-person viewpoint, Elliott conveys sufficient sound and surface of the minor characters to make them credible types, and, by entering the thoughts and feelings of the main character, he conveys how an intelligent and sensitive man can cause trouble for himself. Stuart does not control his tone of voice, bad enough for anyone, but a major failing in a poet. To his superior he says, "St.

Anselm's doesn't mean too awfully much to me" and "I got my own crisis." The narrator explains,

> Because the voice in which he uttered such words was bland and slick instead of abrasive, he sort of thought no one would notice what the words implied; and he did not believe—though it had been suggested to him one way or another by a friend or two—that the smoothness of his voice made the implications of his words penetrate the deeper.

In the present case, the tension builds and the blandness flees, causing his words to come out "openly sarcastic" but "unvenomous"—*that* amounts to paying dearly for no return at all—and, later on, as "piteous bleat" and barking "No"—welcome to the pasture. Because from this viewpoint one feels the struggle and the pathos, he or she is ready to rejoice when "the sanctioned buzz of words begins."

From its position at the head, this story connects with others in the volume. "Tourist and Pilgrim" contains a search for religious fulfillment. A family experiences great strains but tolerates them in "Is He Dead?" "Words Words Words" involves intrusions with promising results; "Invasion of the Planet of Love" reveals disastrous events. There are quite a few imprisoned souls. One very much in pain haunts "Better to Burn," and one still alive enough to keep up his "complaining" speaks out from "In a Hole." This last piece, a fable of civilization's crisis, issues from what starts out as the stunned I-narrative of a forty-year-old man caught permanently within a hole after an earthquake. His reflections project an allegory of unpreparedness: The city planners built upon a fault; ancestral myths are all but gone, civilizing customs lost, and cops keep order; prayers and patriotic speeches fail. There is, however, still something that can be done. The poet, buried near the bedrock, can use "our language" in his "own way"; he can "speak" for himself and "as though" he "were being listened to." These are articles of Elliott's modernist faith, a humanism that does not scorn the mysteries. The tale is obvious, but it is a fable and short enough that one may "swallow" it yet keep his "self-respect."

"MISS CUDAHY OF STOWE'S LANDING"

The characters mentioned thus far have been face-less and almost bodiless sorts, as one might expect in a fiction focusing on thoughts and feelings, as Elliott's does. In "Miss Cudahy of Stowe's Landing," the main character, Bingham, is of this sort; but his opponent, the lady of the title, is Elliott's most vivid character, a "huge old woman" whose "heavy, pale, sensual face" makes her seem older than she is and whose "white arms" might once have called forth the admiration of men. What is most important, however, is the suggestiveness in this external portraiture. By careful selection of detail, gesture, and glance, Elliott has made a tale almost Jamesian in its ability to tease. Fitted out in the trappings of romance—the cast includes a crippled queen (the old stepmother type), a gothic troll of a gardener, a speechless maiden, and an intrusive courtier—this tale promises adventures but shuts the door with many of its mysteries intact. The self-styled courtier is discomfited. Miss Cudahy manipulates her guest: He is the mouse, her house is the trap, the girl the cheese. She offers him enough to tease him into coming back and staying longer than he had planned to do—the newel, the decorated bedroom, hints about the history of the house, statements that the girl needs some companionship; most of all, the old woman's way of touching Phoebe in his presence is sexually suggestive. At the same time, she pulls him back by attacking his unspoken motives, uttering knowing exclamations, and erupting puritanically. He knows he is flirting with a bomb but does so just the same. Finally, demanding more than he can get, he loses the girl.

Many of the mysteries remain intact. Maybe all we wanted was a picture. If he had stayed, what kind of family would this have been? Is this a mother and a daughter, or a mistress and a servant girl? Miss Cudahy can almost seem a madam selling flesh, and the complicated sexual themes of modern gothic may lurk behind that door. To these mysteries contribute the wordlessness of Phoebe, the muttering of the gardener, the speech-restraining cat and mouse of guest and hostess, and the many gestures of the hands and glances of the eyes that take the place of words. These gestures hold back as much as they express, and the reader's imagination runs forth to fill out every vein until the courting couple's touches, conveyed in language of Keatsian eroticism, leaves one tingling. Bingham is no courtly knight, however—he is more like a Peter Brench.

George P. Elliott is generally thought of as a modern realist, but he was competent in many forms, including various kinds of fables. Whatever the form, he was capable of investing it with tones that bite, amuse, and mend, thus educating mind and feelings to a life among appearances but one that casts an "affirming flame."

OTHER MAJOR WORKS

LONG FICTION: *Parktilden Village*, 1958; *David Knudsen*, 1962; *In the World*, 1965; *Muriel*, 1972.

POETRY: *Fever and Chills*, 1961; *Fourteen Poems*, 1964; *From the Berkeley Hills*, 1969; *Reaching*, 1979.

NONFICTION: *A Piece of Lettuce*, 1964; *Conversions*, 1971.

BIBLIOGRAPHY

Hills, Rust, ed. *Writer's Choice*. New York: David McKay, 1974. In the introduction to this collection of short stories by notable contemporary American writers such as John Barth and John Updike, Hills discusses the reasons why he chose to include Elliott's story "Children of Ruth" in the collection. He also mentions several reasons why the story can be considered one of Elliott's representative works.

McCormack, Thomas, ed. *Afterwords: Novelists and Their Novels*. New York: Harper & Row, 1969. In one section of this informative collection of essays written by novelists about the task of writing, Elliott offers some interesting insights about the writing of his collection *Among the Dangs*. Aside from shedding light on the general process of fiction writing, the essay also illustrates Elliott's particular blend of the personal and the universal in his writing.

Morse, J. Mitchell. "A Warm Heart and a Good Head." *The Hudson Review* 3 (Autumn, 1964): 478-480. In this review of *A Piece of Lettuce*, Morse views the work as a mix between literary criticism and autobiography. Most praiseworthy, according to Morse, is Elliott's attempt to discuss literature and politics as human activities with serious consequences.

Podhoretz, Norman. "The New Nihilism in the Novel." In *Doings and Undoings*. New York: Farrar, Straus & Giroux, 1964. In this chapter, Podhoretz comments on the novel *Parktilden Village*, stating that it is a revealing document about contemporary religious values. He also points out that the protagonist reveals sheer habituation to the nihilism of American life. Elliott treats a religious solution to the problem with mild irony and controlled outrage.

Sale, Roger. "High Mass and Low Requiem." *The Hudson Review* 1 (Spring, 1966): 124-138. In this article, Sale reviews *In the World*, among other works by prominent twentieth century authors. He asserts that the work's strength derives from the impact of William Makepeace Thackeray rather than Leo Tolstoy, as Elliott had professed. He complains that Elliott does not illustrate or describe what it means to be "in the world," other than in the academic world.

Solotaroff, Theodore. "The Fallout of the Age." In *The Red Hot Vacuum and Other Pieces on the Writing of the Sixties*. New York: Atheneum Press, 1970. The author discusses the novel *David Knudsen* as a topical novel deserving more critical attention than it has received. He argues that the novel is concerned, in a concrete and sensitive way, with the contemporary problems of what it means to live in the nuclear age—a topic little discussed in previous fiction.

Tisdale, Lyn Camire. "George P. Elliott and the Common Reader." *The American Scholar* 58 (Summer, 1989): 421-428. A general discussion of the life and work of Elliott; discusses Elliott's love of literature and his belief in the power of literature to create both anguish and delight in the reader.

William P. Keen, updated by Genevieve Slomski

HARLAN ELLISON

Born: Cleveland, Ohio; May 27, 1934

PRINCIPAL SHORT FICTION

The Deadly Streets, 1975
A Touch of Infinity, 1960
Gentleman Junkie and Other Stories of the Hung-Up Generation, 1961
The Juvies, 1961
Ellison Wonderland, 1962 (also published as *Earthman, Go Home*, 1964)
Paingod and Other Delusions, 1965
I Have No Mouth and I Must Scream, 1967
From the Land of Fear, 1967
Perhaps Impossible, 1967
Love Ain't Nothing but Sex Misspelled, 1968
The Beast That Shouted Love at the Heart of the World, 1969
Over the Edge: Stories from Somewhere Else, 1970
Alone Against Tomorrow: Stories of Alienation in Speculative Fiction, 1971 (published in England as *All the Sounds of Fear*, 1973)
The Time of the Eye, 1971
Approaching Oblivion: Road Signs on the Treadmill Towards Tomorrow, 1974
Deathbird Stories: A Pantheon of Modern Gods, 1975
Partners in Wonder, 1975
The Illustrated Harlan Ellison, 1978
Strange Wine: Fifteen New Stories from the Nightside of the World, 1978
The Fantasies of Harlan Ellison, 1979
Shatterday, 1980
Stalking the Nightmare, 1982
Angry Candy, 1988
Footsteps, 1989
Dreams with Sharp Teeth, 1991
Mefisto in Onyx, 1993
Mind Fields: The Art of Jacek Yerka, the Fiction of Harlan Ellison, 1993
"Repent, Harlequin!" Said the Ticktockman: The Classic Story, 1997

Slippage: Precariously Poised, Previously Uncollected Stories, 1997

OTHER LITERARY FORMS

Though his reputation rests primarily with the short story, Harlan Ellison has abundantly produced novels, essays, anthologies, and scripts for the motion-picture industry and television. Two highly influential anthologies, *Dangerous Visions* (1967) and *Again, Dangerous Visions* (1972), critique his own work and that of others. He contributed scripts to many popular television series in the 1960's and 1970's and adapted his story "A Boy and His Dog" for film in 1975. His essays, which comment on a broad range of social issues, have been collected in a number of volumes, including *The Glass Teat: Essays of Opinion on the Subject of Television* (1969), *An Edge in My Voice* (1986), *Harlan Ellison's Watching* (1989), and *The Harlan Ellison Hornbook* (1990). He also published *I, Robot: The Illustrated Screenplay*, an adaptation of Isaac Asimov's novel, in 1994.

ACHIEVEMENTS

As the author of more than thirteen hundred published pieces and more than forty-five volumes, Harlan Ellison was perhaps the most influential writer of science fiction and fantasy to emerge in the 1960's. His stories have won numerous Nebula and Hugo awards and a Writers Guild of America award for a television script. Acclaimed as a leader of the New Wave writers who sought greater sophistication for science fiction—a movement that he has hotly rejected as nonexistent—Ellison nevertheless brought "crossover" qualities to genre fiction, winning new audiences and exploring new literary possibilities. His talent most definitely lies in the short story. As an artist, he is a risk taker, seeking out a preposterous central image vital enough to contain his moral outrage and screaming rhetoric. When he succeeds—and he has succeeded often enough to contribute several of the best modern stories—then he casts a memorable metaphor, "do you remember the story in which . . . ?" When he fails, as risk takers often do, he comes up empty and shrill.

BIOGRAPHY

Harlan Jay Ellison's fiction often seems like an extension of the author's vibrant and dominating personality. His stories are frequently dressed up with long titles, quotations, and other paraphernalia, as if they did not stand by themselves but as the basis for platform performances. Ellison has been a much-sought-after participant at fan conventions and academic groups, where he characteristically strews insults and abuse upon audiences, who howl for more. His friends and associates nevertheless find him charming, witty, and generous.

Despite his enormous energy and productivity, Ellison developed slowly as a writer. Born in Cleveland, Ohio, on May 27, 1934, he attended Ohio State University and was soon asked to leave, one reason being his insults to a creative writing instructor who told him that he could not write. In Cleveland, he edited a science-fiction "fanzine," showing a hero worship of writers that is still reflected in his work. In New York, he joined a street gang to get authentic material and poured out stories to establish himself, publishing his first, "Glowworm," in 1956. After two years in the army, he supported himself for a time as an editor. His first novel, *The Man with Nine Lives*, appeared in 1959. In 1962, he moved to the Los Angeles area, where he continued to live.

In the 1960's, Ellison became a successful television writer, contributing scripts to *Route Sixty-six, The Alfred Hitchcock Hour, The Untouchables, The Outer Limits, Star Trek*, and *The Man from U.N.C.L.E.* In the same period, he began writing the stories upon which his reputation is based. Hugo and Nebula awards were presented to him for "'Repent, Harlequin!' Said the Ticktockman" in 1966, and thereafter critical acclaim flowed to him in a remarkable string of honors. His activities continued to be energetic and broad, both socially and intellectually, leaving him surrounded by many friends and thirty-seven thousand books, while observers wondered when he could possibly find time to write. In his Cali-

fornia period, he has been a book reviewer for *The Los Angeles Times* (1969 to 1982), an editorial commentator for the Canadian Broadcasting Corporation (1972 to 1978), a columnist, a commercial spokesperson for General Electric, and a television writer, while continuing to write short fiction.

ANALYSIS

Harlan Ellison is a stern moralist. Despite his adopted role as a Hollywood pacesetter, professional bad boy, and outrageous commentator, he is at heart thoroughly conventional, a description he may not want to hear. He declares the necessity of love, loyalty, discipline, personal responsibility, and a puritan world of work, outside which life decays into horror, a wasteland depicted in violent and grotesque imagery. Despite his antireligion, he is resolutely on the side of the angels, his standards often as simple as the message on a bumper sticker. His successes use that simplicity to make clear images and dramatic patterns in which eternal truths once more become vivid. Of his hundreds of stories, the five considered here are all highly praised and frequently anthologized. They represent his work at its best and show his range of themes, images, and methods. Three of these come from *Deathbird Stories*, the most central of his collections and a good place to begin.

"SHATTERED LIKE A GLASS GOBLIN"

"Shattered Like a Glass Goblin" (from *Deathbird Stories*) shows the expressionist at work, using images and dramatic patterns to express his disgust for the drug culture's special claims about morality and its hypocritical expropriation of "love." Seeking his girlfriend, who has been missing for eight months, Rudy finally locates her in a decaying Los Angeles house, a hippie commune of eleven persons who drift in and out with little attachment to one another. Kris, the girlfriend, is strung out on drugs and tells him to leave. Rudy stays nevertheless and is steadily absorbed into the character of the house.

It was a self-contained little universe, bordered on the north by acid and mescaline, on the south by pot and peyote, on the east by speed and redballs, on the west by downers and amphetamines.

From the beginning, he hears strange noises. The inhabitants, who care about nothing except their own sensations, are degenerating into beasts: "[He] had heard squeaking from the attic. It had sounded to him like the shrieking of mice being torn to pieces." Far from being committed to love, the members of the commune cannot extend the simplest commitment to one another. In time, Rudy notices that some of them have disappeared. Changes have started to come upon him too: "He wore only underpants. His hands and feet hurt. The knuckles of his fingers were larger, from cracking them, and they were always angry crimson."

Eventually, he cannot find any of the inhabitants and goes into the basement and upstairs to explore.

> On the first floor he found the one who was the blonde girl. . . . She lay out thin and white as a tablecloth on the dining room table as three of the others he had not seen in a very long while put their teeth into her, and through their hollow sharp teeth they drank up the yellow fluid from the bloated pus-pockets that had been her breasts and her buttocks.

Rudy, locating Kris "sucking out the moist brains of a thing that giggled like a harpsichord," pleads with her to escape with him. By this time, however, he discovers that he has turned into a glass goblin. Showing little concern, the werewolf behind him says to the glass goblin "Have you ever grooved heavy behind *anything* except love?" and then smashes him into a thousand pieces. The vision of hell, which is both felt and believed, earns the intense language and grotesque violence.

This vision of hell frequently uses the city—New York, Los Angeles, New Orleans, or elsewhere—as the threatening habitation of demons and strange gods lusting for the souls of those who falter. Again and again, Ellison invents his own pantheon of the supernatural, rejecting ordinary religious imagery but nevertheless showing a fundamental puritanism that emphasizes humankind's moral weakness and the eternal damnation that follows it. "Croatoan" (collected in *Strange Wine*), illustrates the constantly repeated connection between individual morality, a vivid central image, and the mythological creatures underlying the story.

Carol, having had an abortion and having flushed the fetus down the toilet, quarrels with her boyfriend, Gabe. She demands that he go down into the sewer to retrieve the fetus. To please her, he goes out into the street and lifts the manhole cover.

> It had finally overtaken me; the years of casual liaisons, careless lies, the guilt I suppose I'd *always* known would mount up till it could no longer be denied.

Gabe is so completely irresponsible that his abortionists regard him as a steady customer. He therefore feels compelled to enter the sewer, and he proceeds deeply into the bowels of the earth, fascinated by the smell of rot and his guilty reflections about Carol and his long string of abandoned girlfriends. He passes a group of bums, and one of them follows him, pleading that he should go back and leave this world to its inhabitants. The man has no hands, only chewed stumps. He comes upon an alligator, with no feet, chewing up a nest of rats. (Gabe remembers the legend that the sewers are occupied by alligators originally bought as children's curiosities and then disposed of down the toilet, as he had once done, paralleling the treatment of the fetus.) Gabe follows the hideous animal and is finally stopped by a heavy door, with "CROATOAN" carved on it in heavy gothic lettering. He finally remembers that this was the one word carved in a tree left by the vanished community at Roanoke, Virginia, in 1590, never to be found again and which sponsored the legend of Virginia Dare. He enters the door and realizes that he is surrounded by alligators. Then he sees the children: "And the light came nearer, and the light was many lights. Torches, held aloft by the children who rode the alligators." He stays in the sewer, the only adult among them, and, he says, "They call me father." In this story, as he does in other successful pieces, Ellison, far from resting upon clever imagery, builds his narrative with several degrees of accretions. He combines moral indignation about personal irresponsibility leading to abortion, the sewers underlying the city as a central image of moral disgust, the popular belief that alligators remained alive after being disposed of in toilets, the historical legend of Roanoke and Virginia Dare, and finally, a translation of the action into a personal mythology, with the children riding on the backs of the alligators.

"THE FACE OF HELENE BOURNOUW"

"The Face of Helene Bournouw" continues the pattern of connecting moral responsibility to a central image and ultimately to the supernatural, though the language is quieter and subtler (the reader may feel relief when Ellison stops banging the drum and writes a page without an apocalypse). A celebrated model, Helene is the withered hag made beautiful, "the most beautiful woman who had ever seen man through eyes of wonder." She creates adoration in whomever she touches, "the most memorable succubus he had ever encountered," according to a gossip columnist. Readers follow her throughout her day. Her first engagement is with her lover, Jimmy, at lunch at Lindy's. She tells him that their affair, which seemed perfect to him, is finished. Later that day, he commits suicide, and Helene goes on to her second appointment. Quentin Deane is a struggling artist for whom she had been a patron. Now she ridicules his latest work, which had been important to him, and tells him she is going to withdraw her support if he persists with these ideas. He rips up his canvases and returns to Ohio.

Her third appointment is with a Catholic priest who is alarmed to see her because she knows his weakness. She dresses up as a little girl and indulges his sexual fantasies. Her day, however, is not over. She leaves her fashionable Sutton Place apartment and takes a cab to the Bowery. In a filthy alley, she knocks on a door and is admitted to a room containing eight hideous demons from hell. Then they turn her off, for Helene is only a machine: "Ba'al, wipe her off; you know we've got to keep the rolling stock in good condition." The technological detail itself pushes the reader over the fine line separating fantasy from science fiction.

> Later, when they wearied of formulating their new image, when they sighed with the responsibility of market trends and saturation levels and optimum penetration campaigns, they would suck on their long teeth and use her, all of them, at the same time.

"ON THE DOWNHILL SIDE"

"On the Downhill Side," a modern ghost story and a fantasy without science-fiction elements, has much greater delicacy in its images than most of Ellison's gothic horror but is insistently moral nevertheless. The action takes the reader through the Vieux Carré of New Orleans, using familiar landmarks. Paul, accompanied by his unicorn, meets the beautiful Lizette on the street (she must be a virgin because she is able to stroke the mane of his unicorn, a symbol of moral perfection, with its ivory horn and platinum hoofs clattering on the pavement), and as they wander from place to place, they tell their stories without directly responding to each other, as if they were talking at cross-purposes. Their lives are at opposite ends of a scale: She has been silly and selfish and trivial, rejecting love; he, on the other hand, has overcommitted himself to his insane wife and demanding mother-in-law, smothering himself in guilt. They have but one night out of all eternity to redeem themselves and to escape their fate. Now it is already after midnight, "on the downhill side."

After her flirtation with a flamenco dancer in a café and hearing her pleas about her hopeless condition, Paul reluctantly allows her to go her own way. With dawn approaching, however, he and the unicorn fly over the fence of the Saint Louis Cemetery, that archetype of all cemeteries, because they know that Lizette must return there. The naked Lizette lies upon an altar, attended by eyeless creatures, the agents of the god of love, who are about to claim her. He cries out to her in one last effort, and she comes to him at last in an act of love. As she does, however, the faithful unicorn disappears in the mist, symbolizing his abandonment of "loving too much," in contrast to Lizette, who "loved too little." Thus, the lovers meet on a middle ground in which their damning faults are worked through in compromise. Though the resolution is too abstract, its concluding imagery too vague to support the moral action, the story nevertheless has a fine touch and a restraint often lacking elsewhere. One can remember especially the unicorn, with its "silken mane and rainbow colors, platinum hoofs and spiral horn." The pattern remains much the same as that of other stories: a moral preoccupation tied to a vivid central image and realistic elements giving way to a supernatural override.

"JEFFTY IS FIVE"

"Jeffty Is Five," winner of the Nebula Award for the best science-fiction story of 1977, brilliantly uses nostalgia to attack the empty vulgarity of modern technology, especially television, one of the author's favorite essay targets. Donny and Jeffty are both five when they meet. As friends, they engage in activities familiar to their age, which Donny lovingly recalls: eating nickel Clark Bars covered with real chocolate, attending Saturday matinees that featured Lash LaRue and Wild Bill Elliott, listening to radio programs such as *The Lone Ranger* and *The Shadow*. They all form a flood of memories made real by the author's absorption into popular culture. Donny moves away and comes back several times. He continues to grow up, but Jeffty mysteriously remains at age five—not retarded but with the interests and concerns of a lively child of that age. When Donny returns from college to go into business at his own electronics store, he continues to befriend the child, frequently taking him to see a film. Jeffty's parents have been terrified by his lack of development and have left him in limbo, without love.

Donny then discovers Jeffty's radio, which plays programs long since discontinued. Furthermore, Jeffty receives a *new* Captain Midnight Secret Decoder Badge in the mail, buys *new* versions of old comic books, and is even able to project at a local theater a film from James Blish's *The Demolished Man*, which ought to exist but does not. He is reordering others' reality, especially Donny's. One Saturday, Donny is forced to send Jeffty on to the theater alone because his store is busy selling color television sets. While waiting in line at the theater, Jeffty takes the radio of another to listen to one of his favorite programs. This causes a fight, and Jeffty is seriously injured. Thereafter, he lies in his room upstairs, listening to rock music on his radio, the old programs no longer available. His escape into the past is clearly tied to the indifference of the parents, and Donny's placing of business before Jeffty is a betrayal that he lives to regret. A paragraph of science-fiction boilerplate, mentioning that "the laws of the con-servation of energy occasionally break," unnecessarily tries to hold the story within the science-fiction genre.

Ellison's explosive imagination scores often enough to believe that his best work will live after him. If, as the poet Randall Jarrell said, a great poet is one for whom lightning has struck half a dozen times, all the rest being mere competence, then Ellison may already have won his place. Other noteworthy stories that should be mentioned here are "A Boy and His Dog," which won a Nebula best novelette in 1969; two stories that Ellison names as his personal favorites, "Pretty Maggie Monyeyes" and "At the Mouse Circus"; "O Ye of Little Faith," which Ellison wrote in one hour on the basis of three words given to him in the central hall of a science-fiction convention, only to see if it could be done; "I Have No Mouth and I Must Scream," a Hugo Award winner in 1968; and "The Deathbird," which Ellison has said best represents his work.

OTHER MAJOR WORKS

LONG FICTION: *Rumble*, 1958 (published as *The Web of the City*, 1975); *The Man with Nine Lives*, 1959; *Spider Kiss*, 1961, 1991 (originally pb. as *Rockabilly*); *All the Lies That Are My Life*, 1980; *Run for the Stars*, 1991.

NONFICTION: *Memos from Purgatory*, 1961; *The Glass Teat: Essays of Opinion on the Subject of Television*, 1969; *The Other Glass Teat*, 1975; *Sleepless Nights in the Procrustean Bed*, 1984; *An Edge in My Voice*, 1985; *Harlan Ellison's Watching*, 1989; *The Harlan Ellison Hornbook*, 1990.

SCREENPLAY: *I, Robot: The Illustrated Screenplay*, 1994 (adaptation of Isaac Asimov's novel).

EDITED TEXTS: *Dangerous Visions*, 1967; *Again, Dangerous Visions*, 1972.

MISCELLANEOUS: *The Essential Ellison: A Thirty-five Year Retrospective*, 1987; *The Essential Ellison: A Fifty Year Retrospective*, 2000.

BIBLIOGRAPHY

Adams, Stephen. "The Heroic and Mock-Heroic in Harlan Ellison's 'Harlequin.'" *Extrapolation* 26 (1985): 285-289. The often-anthologized "'Repent, Harlequin!' Said the Ticktockman" is convincingly viewed as a mock-heroic epic, parodying epic conventions through the central character and the narrator: "They both upset established rules (social or literary) and interject spontaneous, anarchic humor into an otherwise joyless, predictable, over-regulated world."

Atheling, William Jr. *More Issues at Hand*. Chicago: Advent, 1970. An early view of Ellison's impact upon science fiction, especially concerning the anthology *Dangerous Visions*, its significance being that it consisted entirely of literary experiments then called "New Wave." Ellison is highly (but skeptically) praised: "a born writer, almost entirely without taste and control but with so much fire, originality and drive, as well as compassion, that he makes the conventional virtues of the artist seem almost irrelevant."

Ellison, Harlan. "An Ill-Begotten Enterprise." *Harper's* 294 (May, 1997): 31-32. Describes the controversy over a 1966 *Star Trek* episode that Ellison wrote, "The City on the Edge of Forever." According to Ellison, Gene Roddenberry, the creator of the series, claimed in public that he had rescued the episode from the original script; Ellison strongly criticizes the various people who have claimed that they saved the teleplay.

Fredericks, Casey. *The Future of Eternity*. Bloomington: Indiana University Press, 1982. Contains an analysis of Ellison's mythmaking capacity, especially the story "The Place with No Name," which apparently allows no settled interpretation.

McMurran, Kristin. "Harlan Ellison." *People Weekly* 24 (December 2, 1985): 97-100. A biographical sketch that claims that Ellison's genius is often overshadowed by his big mouth; discusses how Ellison's childhood was marred by anti-Semitic insults, how he went through a bout of depression for several years, and how he is driven to work harder.

Nicholls, Peter, ed. *The Science Fiction Encyclopedia*. Garden City, N.Y.: Doubleday, 1979. An excellent, fact-filled summary of Ellison's career, which carries the reader through the period of Ellison's greatest accomplishments. The mere list of his activities demonstrates his extraordinary energy and ambition. The article emphasizes, however, that he will be remembered largely for his short fiction.

Platt, Charles. *Dream Makers*. New York: Berkeley Books, 1980. In this book of interviews and interpretations, Platt talks to Ellison in his Los Angeles home, crowded with books and memorabilia. The discussion covers the wide ground of Ellison's interests and serves as a good introduction to his personality.

Slusser, George Edgar. *Harlan Ellison: Unrepentant Harlequin*. San Bernardino, Calif.: Borgo Press, 1977. In this interview, Ellison reflects on his early life as a writer and in a lively manner offers an analysis of how the genre magazines operated in the 1950's.

Bruce Olsen

RALPH ELLISON

Born: Oklahoma City, Oklahoma; March 1, 1914
Died: Harlem, New York; April 16, 1994

PRINCIPAL SHORT FICTION
Flying Home and Other Stories, 1996

OTHER LITERARY FORMS

Invisible Man, Ralph Ellison's 1952 novel, is one of the most important American novels of the twentieth century. He also published two well-received collections of essays, *Shadow and Act* (1964) and *Going to the Territory* (1986), which were combined into one volume in *The Collected Essays of Ralph Ellison* (1995). In 1999, a posthumous edition of his long-awaited second novel was published as *Juneteenth: A Novel*.

ACHIEVEMENTS

Though he won a Rosenwald grant in 1945 on the strength of his short fiction, and though two of his short stories, "Flying Home" and "King of the Bingo Game," are among the most commonly anthologized short stories in twentieth century American literature, Ralph Ellison is best known for his 1952 novel *Invisible Man*, which won the National Book Award and the Russwurm Award. In 1975 he was elected to the American Academy of Arts and Letters, which in 1955 awarded him a Prix de Rome Fellowship. He received the French Chevalier de l'Ordre des Arts et des Lettres in 1970 and the National Medal of Arts in 1985. In 1984 he was awarded the Langston Hughes medallion by City College in New York for his contributions to arts and letters.

BIOGRAPHY

Ralph Waldo Ellison was born March 1, 1914, in Oklahoma City to Ida and Lewis Alfred Ellison, who had moved out of the South in search of a more progressive place to live. An ambitious student, he distinguished himself locally and was rewarded with a scholarship to attend the Tuskegee Institute, in part because the local white population did not want Ellison, an African American, to integrate the white colleges in Oklahoma. Unable to afford the fare to Alabama, he rode a freight train to Tuskegee, in which he enrolled in 1933. A voracious reader in college, he pursued interests in literature, history, and folklore. At the end of his junior year, Ellison, like the narrator of *Invisible Man*, was refused financial aid and so traveled to New York City, where he hoped to make enough money to finish his studies. While in New York, he met another African American author, Richard Wright, who encouraged Ellison's literary ambitions, and instead of returning to Tuskegee, he began to contribute short stories and essays to various literary journals and anthologies. From 1938 to 1944, he worked with the Federal Writers Project, and in 1945, he was a awarded a Rosenwald grant to write a novel. The result was *Invisible Man* (1952), a landmark work in African American fiction that won for its author numerous honorary degrees, literary awards, and worldwide fame.

Though Ellison would publish two well-received collections of essays, *Shadow and Act* and *Going to the Territory*, he would never follow up his first novel with a second in his lifetime. He began writing his next novel around 1958, and over the years he was to publish numerous excerpts from it as a work-in-progress. A fire at his Plainsfield, Massachusetts, summer home destroyed much of the manuscript in 1967, causing him to have to painstakingly reconstruct it. Though he was to work on this project for the rest of his life, he never found a final form for the novel with which he felt comfortable, and it remained unfinished when he died of a heart attack in 1994. His literary executor, John F. Callahan, published his short fiction in one volume as *Flying Home and Other Stories* in 1996 and a self-contained portion of his final novel as *Juneteenth* in 1999.

ANALYSIS

Because most of Ralph Ellison's short fiction was written before his career as a novelist began, his short stories are often analyzed biographically, as the train-

Ralph Ellison (National Archives)

ing ground for the novelist he was to become. This is not entirely unjustified because a biographical overview of his literary output reveals that he tried out the voices, techniques, and ideas that he was to present so boldly in *Invisible Man* and almost completely abandoned the form after his success as a novelist, devoting himself to his essays and to his never-to-be-completed second novel.

It is true that in his two most accomplished stories, "The King of the Bingo Game" and "Flying Home," he develops themes of the chaos of the modern world and the affliction of racial conflict that would later be combined and expanded in his famous novel. On the other hand, his earlier stories show him working out many of the same ideas from different perspectives. While the voice that informs his most accomplished work is a mature voice that is uniquely Ellison's own, the voices in his other stories show more clearly the influences of Ernest Hemingway, Richard Wright, and James Joyce.

In relating his short fiction to his overall work, Edith Schor in *Visible Ellison: A Study of Ralph Ellison's Fiction* (1993) has aptly observed that

Ellison's short stories provided experimental laboratories for testing the translation of the forms and experiences of African American life into literature. In evaluating the stories themselves, however, Robert Bone best summarized their lasting value when he observed in "Ralph Ellison and the Uses of Imagination" (1966) that Ellison's short stories are about "adventurers" testing "the fixed boundaries of southern life."

FLYING HOME AND OTHER STORIES

Flying Home and Other Stories is a posthumous collection of stories edited by Ralph Ellison's literary executor, John F. Callahan, which brings together in one volume all of the principal short fiction Ellison wrote (excepting pieces that were published as excerpts of his novels). Callahan arranged the stories according to the age of the main characters, thereby highlighting the stories' thematic unity regarding the growth of young persons' ideologies, which might not otherwise be evident.

The collection opens with "A Party Down by the Square," a story told in an intentionally flat style by a young man from Cincinnati who visits his uncle in Alabama and witnesses a lynching on a stormy night. Confused by the cyclone that moves through the town, an airplane pilot mistakes the fire of the lynching for an airport flare and flies too low through the town, knocking loose a wire and electrocuting a white woman. Undaunted, the crowd continues with the lynching and the anonymous narrator watches a nameless black man being burned, marveling at the victim's resiliency but showing no moral awareness of the horror of the act.

Four of the stories in the collection focus on two young friends, Buster and Riley, as they explore their world and their friendship. The first story, "Mister Toussan," finds them making up imaginary exploits for Haitian liberator Toussaint L'Ouverture, a name they have heard but with which they have only vague associations and upon which they hang various fantasies. Similarly, "Afternoon" and "That I Had Wings" find the boys involved in imaginative games to stave off boredom. "A Coupla Scalped Indians" focuses on Riley, who has just been "scalped" (circumcised) at the age of eleven, having a sexually charged encounter with old Aunt Mack, an eccentric healer Riley sees naked in her shack as he is making his way home from a carnival. "All was real," Riley tells the reader after leaving her shack, in wonderment about his discovery of the encroaching adult reality.

"Hymie's Bull" and "I Did Not Learn Their Names" are stories about riding freight trains, and together with "The Black Ball" and "A Hard Time Keeping Up," they are about young men finding their way in a world that can be violent and harsh but that can also contain friendship and tenderness in unexpected places. The importance of learning to discern the tenderness amid the harshness of the world becomes the central theme of two of the most important stories in the collection, "In a Strange Land" and "Flying Home." "King of the Bingo Game," by contrast, is a story about a young man trying to make his way in a world that offers little in the way of tenderness and much in the way of danger. Though "Flying Home" and "King of the Bingo Game" are the most significant stories in this collection, the collection offers a startling group of works, each of which is a semiprecious jewel and which, when taken together, mark the growth of the author's artistry.

"KING OF THE BINGO GAME"

One of Ellison's most durable statements about the harsh chaos of the modern world can be found in "King of the Bingo Game." The main character is an unnamed black North Carolina man living in Harlem, who has wandered into a cinema in the hope of winning the door prize that might pay for a doctor for his wife. By playing his own and several discarded Bingo cards simultaneously, he manages to win the bingo portion of the game, which gives him the opportunity to spin the bingo wheel. While on stage, he spins the bingo wheel by pressing a button but is then unable to take the chance of letting the button go. Only double zero will win the jackpot of $36.90, and he realizes that so long as he keeps the wheel spinning, he has not lost, so he refuses to let the wheel stop. The wheel takes on the symbolic importance of a mandala, a wheel of life, something the main character realizes when he exclaims, "This is God!" Because he has taken much too long to let go of the button, security guards try to take it from him and knock him out in

an altercation. The wheel stops at double zero, but as he fades into unconsciousness, he realizes that he will not get the prize he sought. Though this story is among Ellison's harsher fictions, it is also one of his most poetic presentations of the unfeeling chaos of the modern world.

"IN A STRANGE COUNTRY"

Though not as artistically satisfying as the longer "Flying Home," "In a Strange Country" tells a similar tale of self-discovery through the acceptance of a previously despised group identity. Parker is an intelligent black merchant seaman who lands in Wales during World War II only to be promptly attacked by a group of American soldiers simply for being a black man. A group of Welshmen, led by Mr. Catti, rescues him but not before his eye is injured and begins to swell. Over several drafts of ale, Catti learns that Parker is a music enthusiast and takes him to a singing club. There, Parker is swept up in the emotions of the songs about Welsh national pride but reminds himself that he is from Harlem, not Wales. He feels at first alienated and then deeply connected to the men around him, who, he believes, see his humanity much more clearly than do his fellow Americans who are white. As the evening is ending, the band begins to play "The Star-Spangled Banner" in his honor, and he finds himself singing along with deep feeling.

On one hand, the "strange country" of the title is Wales, but on a deeper level, it is the part of himself that is opened up by the bonding of common humanity he shares with these Welshmen and which, for the first time in his life, disallows any easy cynicism.

"FLYING HOME"

Ralph Ellison's longest short story, "Flying Home," is also his most richly satisfying accomplishment in the form. At the center of the story is Todd, a young black man whose lifelong dream of becoming a pilot crashes along with his plane when he flies into a buzzard on a training flight. Jefferson, an old black man who comes to Todd's rescue after the crash, tells him the buzzards are called "jim crows" locally, setting up an important level of symbolism about what has really caused Todd's crash. In fact, Todd has been training with the Tuskegee Airmen, a group of black World War II pilots who trained at the famed Tuskegee Institute but were only reluctantly deployed for combat missions. For Todd, this crash landing on a routine flight almost certainly means he will never get another chance to fly and, in his mind, will become the common black man he considers Jefferson to be, the worst fate he can imagine for himself.

Despite the younger man's hostility, Jefferson distracts the injured Todd by telling him a story about dying, going to heaven, and flying around so fast as to cause "a storm and a couple of lynchings down here in Macon County." In his story-within-a-story, Jefferson is stripped of his wings for flying too fast and is sent down to earth with a parachute and a map of Alabama. Todd, seeing only that this story has been twisted to mirror his own situation, snaps, "Why are you making fun of me?"—which, in fact, the old man is not doing. A feverish dream into which Todd drifts reveals not only the depth of his lifelong desire to fly but also the power of his grandmother's admonition:

> Young man, young man
> Yo arm's too short
> To box with God.

To Todd, becoming a pilot means taking a position higher than the majority white culture wants to allow black men of his time to occupy; it is the equivalent of boxing with God in his mind. To have failed as a pilot means not only to have made a mistake but also to have let his entire race down, something he cannot allow to happen.

So when Dabney Graves, the racist landowner on whose property Todd has crashed, arrives at the site, Todd snaps at the man and places his own life in danger. Jefferson, though, saves him by intervening and telling Graves that the army told Todd never to abandon his ship. Graves's temper is assuaged, and Jefferson and a young boy are allowed to take Todd to safety in a stretcher. The final image is of Todd watching a buzzard flying against the sun, glowing like a bird of flaming gold. This image suggests that though Todd will never fly again, his spirit will rise up like a phoenix from the ashes of his defeat, a victory made possible by the current of goodwill he can now allow himself to feel for Jefferson. Todd will be-

gin to learn to love himself for who he is by loving others for who they are.

OTHER MAJOR WORKS

LONG FICTION: *Invisible Man*, 1952; *Juneteenth: A Novel*, 1999.

NONFICTION: *Shadow and Act*, 1964; *The Writer's Experience*, 1964 (with Karl Shapiro); *The City in Crisis*, 1968 (with Whitney M. Young and Herbert Gans); *Going to the Territory*, 1986; *The Collected Essays of Ralph Ellison*, 1995; *Trading Twelves: The Selected Letters of Ralph Ellison and Albert Murray*, 2000.

MISCELLANEOUS: *Conversations with Ralph Ellison*, 1995 (Maryemma Graham and Amritjit Singh, editors).

BIBLIOGRAPHY

Bloom, Harold, ed. *Modern Critical Views: Ralph Ellison*. New York: Chelsea House, 1986. Though this widely available collection of essays focuses mainly on *Invisible Man*, it provides insights from which any reader of Ralph Ellison may profit, and Berndt Ostendor's essay, "Anthropology, Modernism, and Jazz," offers much to the reader of "Flying Home."

Bone, Robert. "Ralph Ellison and the Uses of Imagination." *Triquarterly* 6 (1966): 39-54. An important essay on the uses of transcendentalism and jazz in Ellison's fiction and of his writing's importance to the Civil Rights movement and black culture in general.

Callahan, John F. Introduction to *Flying Home and Other Stories*, by Ralph Ellison. Edited by John F. Callahan. New York: Random House, 1996. Callahan's introduction to this collection of fiction is essential reading for anyone interested in Ellison's fiction, not only for the literary insights it provides but also for the basic editorial information about how these stories were selected and edited.

Schor, Edith. *Visible Ellison: A Study of Ralph Ellison's Fiction*. Westport, Conn.: Greenwood, 1993. Published a year before Ellison's death, this is an excellent full-length study of the fiction that was generally available at the time, including his short fiction, which had not yet been collected in book form. This is probably the best place for the serious scholar of Ralph Ellison to begin.

Skerret, Joseph. "Ralph Ellison and the Example of

Richard Wright." *Studies in Short Fiction* 15 (Spring, 1978): 145-153. An examination of the influence of Richard Wright on Ralph Ellison's short fiction.

Thomas Cassidy

SHŪSAKU ENDŌ

Born: Tokyo, Japan; March 27, 1923
Died: Tokyo, Japan; September 29, 1996

PRINCIPAL SHORT FICTION

Aden made, 1954 (novella)
Endō Shūsaku shū, 1960
Aika, 1965
Endō Shūsaku yūmoa shōsetsu shū, 1969-1973
   (2 volumes)
Gekkō no domina, 1972
Endō Shūsaku misuteri shōsetu shū, 1975
Juichi no irogarasu, 1979
Stained-Glass Elegies, 1984
The Final Martyrs, 1993
Five by Endo: Stories, 2000

OTHER LITERARY FORMS

Although Shūsaku Endō wrote first-rate short fiction, he is better known as the leading Roman Catholic writer of Japan and as a novelist and essayist. Of his novels, the best known are *Obakasan* (1959; *Wonderful Fool*, 1974), *Kazan* (1959; *Volcano*, 1978), *Chimmoku* (1966; *Silence*, 1969), *Kuchibue o fuku toki* (1974; *When I Whistle*, 1979), *Samurai* (1980; *The Samurai*, 1982), *Sukyandaru* (1986; *Scandal*, 1988), *Dipu riba* (1993; *Deep River*, 1994), and *Shukuteki* (1995). Two of these, *Silence* and *The Samurai*, are historical, the rest contemporary. In addition to these important works, Endō wrote plays, biographies, essays, diaries, interviews, and accounts of his travels. As for essays, he wrote on morality, religion, art, literature, and history; specifically, he treated of

Jesus, Christian martyrs, medieval castles, women and the family, and love.

ACHIEVEMENTS

Shūsaku Endō wrote several volumes of short stories, about twenty novels, some plays, and numerous essays. He is regarded in Japan not merely as its leading Catholic author but also as one of its most important literary figures. Western critics have compared Endō with the British authors Graham Greene and Evelyn Waugh and with the French writers François Mauriac and Georges Bernanos. Such comparisons, however, are misleading: as a Japanese Catholic, Endō's ethos is quite different from any of theirs. In Japan, Catholics are an insignificant minority, and Endō himself held that Japanese culture and Christianity are incompatible.

Endō received virtually every important literary prize awarded in Japan: the Akutagawa Prize, the Sincho Award, the Mainichi Press Cultural Award, the Tanizaki Prize, and the Noma Prize. These prizes were awarded respectively for the following novels: *Shiroi hito* (1954; white man), *Umi to dokuyaku* (1957; *The Sea and Poison*, 1972), *Silence*, and *The Samurai*. These and other basically serious works are often infiltrated with humor. Endō has also written straight comic novels such as *Taihen da* (1969; good grief). His biography of Christ represents Jesus as a maternal and compassionate figure. Endō was editor of the literary journal *Mita bungaku*. His *Life of Jesus* won the Dag Hammarskjöld Prize in 1978. He was scheduled to receive the Culture Prize from the Emperor in 1995 but was too ill to attend the ceremonies at the Imperial Palace and was awarded the prize *in absentia*. Nominated for the Nobel Prize more than once, he was expected to win in 1994, but lost to his colleague Kenzaburō Ōe.

BIOGRAPHY

Shūsaku Endō, the future Catholic convert and prominent writer, was born in Tokyo, Japan, on March 27, 1923. Four years later, his parents moved to Dairen, a city in southern Manchuria. Six years later, Endō's mother, a domineering woman, left her husband and returned with Endō and his elder brother to Japan. She, together with her family, took up residence with her Catholic sister in Tokyo. After his mother became a Catholic convert, Endō was persuaded, at the age of eleven, to be baptized in the Catholic faith. For a long time, however, he felt uncomfortable with this foreign religion. To him, as Van C. Gessel has written, Catholicism felt like "an ill-fitting suit of Western-style clothes," which he attempted through his future writing "to retailor . . . into native Japanese attire."

Pleurisy kept Endō out of World War II. Later in life, he was often hospitalized for respiratory ailments, culminating in the removal of a lung. His hospital experiences often figure in his fiction. In 1945, he entered Keio University in Tokyo, a prestigious private institution, where he majored in French literature. In 1950, he went to France, the first Japanese to study abroad after the war. There, he attended the University of Lyons, specializing in French Catholic authors such as Paul Claudel, Mauriac, and Bernanos. In Europe, Endō hoped to recover from the "anguish of an alien," which he had felt since his religious conversion. His entry into an environment in which Christianity was both dominant and pervasive, however, only increased the tension that he felt between East and West. He decided to become a novelist and, in his writings, to attempt to reconcile the two selves that divided him.

In 1953, Endō left France and returned to Japan in a mood of discouragement and depression. His desire to write and to express himself in regard to his inner conflicts, however, served to sustain him and to reshape his life. His first book, *Furansu no Daigakusei* (a French collegian), was published in 1953. His first fiction, the novella *Aden made* (to Aden), came out the following year, causing no stir. His second novel, however, *Shiroi hito*, won the Akutagawa Prize, which is awarded to promising Japanese writers. As a writer of imaginative literature, *Endō* was on his way. The conflict within him of his ideals, on the one hand, and of his obligations, on the other, continued, being acerbated at the same time by his poor health, the result of lung disease. Bogged down in what he referred to as his Japanese "mudswamp," he sought escape by carrying a banner on which was pictured his own *imago Christi*. In addition, he felt an absolute obligation not to betray his Catholic mother by abandoning her faith or by leaving the house of the wife whom she had arranged for him to marry, even though he had no love for this woman. According to Jean Higgins, it was not until the writing of his prize-winning novel *Silence* that he began to reconcile himself with himself, with the cosmos, and with Christ. His well-known contemplative biography of Jesus, *Iseu no Shōgai* (1973; *A Life of Jesus*, 1973), has had a considerable impact on Western theologians and the church. His fiction has received the praise of his own compatriot Yukio Mishima and also of the Western writers Greene and John Updike. Having suffered poor health all his life, Endō died September 29, 1996, in Tokyo, of kidney ailments. He was survived by his wife and son.

ANALYSIS

Shūsaku Endō's writings in general reflect his Roman Catholic beliefs and his peculiarly Japanese attitude toward the foreign religion to which he was converted at the age of eleven by virtue of his mother's will. For years, a conflict simmered within him: Feeling betrayed by his mother, he also felt guilty because of his own arrogant but silent disobedience. For years, he also felt uncomfortable wearing his Western "monkey suit" while tramping about the "mudswamp" that he considered modern Japan to be. As time went on, however, his commitment to Roman Catholicism gradually crystallized and became hardcore, yet the hallmarks of his writings are wisdom, tolerance, and compassion.

Endō's short stories have been collected principally in two volumes: *Aika* (elegies) and *Juichi no irogarasu* (eleven stained-glass windows). Van C. Gessel has translated twelve stories selected from these volumes into English under the title *Stained-Glass Elegies*. The protagonists, who are usually observers rather than actors, tend to be personae—that is, masks that the author himself has donned to disguise his own identity, whatever pseudonyms he has conferred on them. Most of Endō's short stories treat of themes similar to those found in his novels: sickness, fear of dying, the changes brought about in a person from growing old, alienation from society, religious doubt and faith, treason, apostasy, good and evil, failure, disappointment, the gulf between Eastern and Western ideals, torture and physical suffering, Christian conscience and sin, the Christian life—especially of monks and priests—the Japanese view of Jesus, and the many Christian martyrs of the times of proscription as well as the trials of the *kakure Kirishitan* (clandestine Christians)—Japanese Christians who managed by a subterfuge to escape the prohibition edicts during successive waves of persecution. Apart from those persons who have followed Saint Paul's admonition to become "fools for Christ," there are no heroics in Endō's fiction, and apart from the short stories that recall historical events of the seventeenth century, most of them are contemporary or recall the World War II period. Most of the stories are set in Japan, mainly in Tokyo and its environs, although one is set in the prefecture of Nagasaki, another in Manchuria, and a third in Lyons, France.

In a good number of short stories—at least seven or eight—Endō has created a protagonist named Suguro who is very much like his creator: He has been troubled by lung disease, has been hospitalized, and has had an operation. He has a dumpy wife whom he does not love but to whom he remains loyal. After the war, he studied in France. He returned home to become a Catholic novelist interested in the problems of contemporary Japanese Christians and in the historic sufferings of Christian martyrs during the periods of persecution. He is a keen observer of human life and of the characters of human beings, especially of troubled persons, for whom he has compassion in

respect to their loneliness. He feels that the sad eyes of birds and dogs express these creatures' sympathy for the human condition. Realizing that he himself is a mixture of good and evil, that every man has an evil *Doppelgänger* as a constant companion, he shrugs his shoulders at others' sins, his Christ having urged Judas to do quickly what he was bent on doing; it is his Jesus who kisses the lips of the Grand Inquisitor in Fyodor Dostoevski's *Bratya Karamazovy* (1879-1880; *The Brothers Karamazov*, 1912).

"A FORTY-YEAR-OLD MAN"

In the story "Shi-jū sai no dan" ("A Forty-Year-Old Man"), Suguro is the middle-aged man who is hospitalized and operated on for lung disease. Depressed and fearing physical suffering and possible death, he is also racked by guilt, having committed sins of adultery and abortion. He is unable to confess these sins to a priest, and he is unable to communicate his feelings to other persons, neither to his wife, to whom he sticks despite his lack of love for her, nor to his sister-in-law, who has been his mistress and has aborted his child. He does think that he will be able to communicate with, and get solace from, a pet bird, so he requests that his wife purchase a mynah bird for him because such a bird has the ability to mimic human speech. Although such a bird is expensive, his wife fulfills his request. He tries to get the bird to say "Good morning" (*O hayō gozaimasu*), but it cannot say this any more than he can confess his sins and ask God's forgiveness. The ending of this story is an ironical tour de force.

"RETREATING FIGURES"

In "Rashiroshi" ("Retreating Figures"), Endō, through his surrogate Suguro, seeks to evoke a tragic sense of life—a perception, according to Suguro, that becomes especially evident after a man passes into his fifties. On a sleepless night, Suguro recalls several casual acquaintances whom he knew only briefly before they departed; he never saw them again. One such person is Mrs. Horiguchi, a patient in the room next to Suguro when, fifteen years previously, he was hospitalized to undergo a third operation. She is a frail, pale-faced, middle-aged invalid of ten years and the wife of a famous Kabuki actor. She decides to leave the hospital to benefit her husband despite her doctor's warning that absence of further treatment would soon result in her death. When she bids Suguro good-bye, he watches her walk away "with her head bowed down the long, silent corridor," but "even after she was gone, the afterimage of her retreating figure remained before" Suguro's eyes. She died three years later.

In several other stories, the narrator or protagonist is not identified by name but is referred to simply as "I," "he," or "the man." In these cases, however, the text strongly suggests that the unidentified person can be no one other than Endō's persona Suguro.

"THE DAY BEFORE" AND "THE SHADOW FIGURE"

In "The Day Before," the narrator is hospitalized, and it is "the day before" his third and most serious operation. He has sent his friend, Father Inouye, to Nagasaki, to fetch back an antique *fumie*, a copper engraving of the crucified Christ on which Christians were obliged to stamp their feet as proof of their apostasy, which had been used during the persecutions at Urakami during the second half of the nineteenth century. While the narrator is waiting anxiously to view the image of Jesus before facing his operation, a peddler of pornographic photographs drops into his room seeking to interest him in buying sex pictures. Also, having read a Catholic tract about the fourth siege of Urakami, the narrator tells the story of the apostate Tōgorō, who was ashamed of his treason but could not help himself.

"The Shadow Figure" is written in epistolary form. A Catholic novelist explains his attitude toward a former Spanish priest whom he has just seen (without being seen) for the first time in years. He knew this priest well when a schoolboy because the priest was his mother's spiritual adviser. His mother revered the priest—a handsome, impeccably dressed, vigorous man—and considered him a model for her son to follow. After the writer's mother died, however, the priest became the lover of a Japanese woman—much to the writer's disillusionment—and married her. Hence the priest was defrocked and became separated from the Christian community.

Endō's persona Suguro is the protagonist of his novel *Scandal*. Here, Suguro finds his reputation as a Catholic novelist is on the line by virtue of allegations that he is in the habit of indulging in sordid sex. At first, he thinks that some unknown enemy is seeking to scandalize him, but after visiting Tokyo's pleasure quarters in an effort to discover the impostor, he concludes that his supposed double is none other than himself, his face of innocence having masked his inner depravity.

"DESPICABLE BASTARD"

Endō's short stories that do not present or suggest the author's surrogate Suguro include "Hiretsuna-kan" ("Despicable Bastard") and "Kusuteki kokai" ("Incredible Voyage"). In "Despicable Bastard," the bastard and contemptible fellow is Egi. He is a university student in Tokyo during World War II and lives in a dormitory occupied mostly by Christians. The classes at the school are not being held because the students are being required to work in a war factory that is under military discipline. Egi is a noncooperative type, a slacker and a goldbricker. Not respectful enough to satisfy a military police officer, he is beaten and his knee is wounded.

Every year, the Christian students organize a program at the leper asylum in Gotemba. Part of the program consists of a baseball game with the healthier lepers. Egi is asked to take part in the game, but he does so with considerable trepidation. He is particularly fearful of being infected because of his wounded knee. Having gone up to bat, he hits a fair ball and rounds first base to find himself trapped between first and second. Egi stops and fearfully awaits the tag of the ball in the hand of the leper. The leper baseman's eyes, however, flicker plaintively, and the patient says softly: "Go ahead. I won't touch you." When Egi was by himself, he felt like crying. By contrast, this story echoes Gustave Flaubert's legend of Saint Julian the Hospitaler who, having granted a leper a kiss, found himself face to face with Jesus.

"INCREDIBLE VOYAGE"

"Incredible Voyage" is generally a Rabelaisian parody of science fiction, but specifically it is a parody of a 1966 American science-fiction film called *Fantasic Voyage*. Like the film, the story is set in the twenty-first century, after it has become possible to miniaturize any object to microscopic size. As in the film, a team of doctors and a boat are miniaturized and injected into the bloodstream of a patient needing critical surgery. In the film, the patient is a scientist important to the defense establishment, and the complication is that one of the doctors is a traitor. In the story, the patient is also the fiancé of one of the doctors, and the complication is that in exiting after the operation, the doctors mistakenly get into the girl's intestines, where they discover that her attendants have neglected to give her an enema prior to her operation. The story is therefore broadly and coarsely humorous.

"THE FINAL MARTYRS"

The title story of Endō's collection *The Final Martyrs* is a moral exemplum told in a simple narrative fashion. Set in the nineteenth century during a time of persecution of Japanese Christians, the story focuses on son Kisuke, a giant of a man, who is clumsy, ineffectual, and easily frightened. When his village is raided by government agents seeking to punish anyone who has violated the prohibition against Christianity, Kisuke's cowardice makes him quickly recant his religion, an act that transforms him into a Judas figure who has betrayed his savior. Unable to bear the guilt of his betrayal, two years later, Kisuke, now a beggar, returns to the prison where his friends, who held firm to their religion, are kept, for he has heard a voice telling him what he has to do to be with the others. Kisuke's return, in spite of his terror, reaffirms to the others that they have been right to uphold their faith, for it reflects the power of Christian forgiveness. Thus Kisuke becomes one of the most beloved of all the final martyrs, because he came back even though he was the most frightened.

"THE BOX"

"The Box," a mystical treatment of Christian eschatology, focuses on a central symbolic object and takes place in a world that is at once both real and in the realm of desire. The central theme is stated emphatically when, after relating an anecdote about talking to his plants, the narrator says that humans and animals are not the only ones that have hearts and language and faculties; even things humans think of as simple objects—sticks and stones—have some kind of power living inside them. The story begins

when the narrator, a writer, finds an old wooden box in an antique shop containing a Bible with some postcards and a photograph album. The narrator evinces a writerly curiosity about the postcards addressed to a Mademoiselle Louge and some photographs of an old deserted road. He learns that the woman has been tortured by the Japanese military police for not agreeing to spy for them. When the narrator notices that the return addresses of the postcards are actually references to passages in the Bible, which are in turn allusions to the war and peace efforts sent to Mademoiselle Louge and then passed on to others, he believes the postcards have taken on a will of their own, waiting for someone like him to reveal their truth. He explains that this is why he speaks to plants, for he thinks that plants must talk to each other and that trees and rocks and even postcards are saturated with the thoughts of people.

Although Endō holds himself a Catholic and clings stubbornly to his Christianity, his faith is flavored with intellectual doubt and is neither doctrinaire nor fanatical. He is ever humble and compassionate. Without arrogant pride, he realizes that all humans are to some degree a compact of good and evil and that they all need forgiveness, whether its source be Jesus or the universe.

OTHER MAJOR WORKS

LONG FICTION: *Shiroi hito*, 1954; *Kiiroi hito*, 1955; *Umi to dokuyaku*, 1957 (*The Sea and Poison*, 1972); *Kazan*, 1959 (*Volcano*, 1978); *Obakasan*, 1959 (*Wonderful Fool*, 1974); *Watashi ga suteta onna*, 1963 (*The Girl I Left Behind*, 1994); *Chimmoku*, 1966 (*Silence*, 1969); *Taihen da*, 1969; *Kuchibue o fuku toki*, 1974 (*When I Whistle*, 1979); *Samuri*, 1980 (*The Samurai*, 1982); *Sukyandaru*, 1986 (*Scandal*, 1988); *Hangyaku*, 1989; *Kessen no tiki*, 1991; *Otoko no issho*, 1991; *Yojo no gotoku*, 1991 (mystery novel); *Aio chiisana budo*, 1993; *Dipu riba*, 1993 (*Deep River*, 1994); *Shukuteki*, 1995.

PLAYS: *Ogon no kuni*, pr. 1966, pb. 1969 (*The Golden Country*, 1970).

NONFICTION: *Furansu no Daigakusei*, 1953; *Gūtara seikatsu nyūmon*, 1967; *Iesu no shōgai*, 1973 (*A Life of Jesus*, 1973); *Seisho no naka no joseitachi*,

1975; *Tetsu no kukikase*, 1976; *Watakushi no Iesu*, 1976; *Kirisuto no tanjō*, 1977; *Ningan no naka no X*, 1978; *Jū to jūjika*, 1979; *Haru wa basha ni notte*, 1989 (essays); *Honto no watakushi o motomete*, 1990; *Iesu ni atta onnatachi*, 1990; *Ihojin no tachiba kara*, 1990 (essays); *Kirishitan jidai: Junkyo to kikyo*, 1992; *Kokoro no sunadokei*, 1992 (essays).

MISCELLANEOUS: *To Friends from Other Lands: A Shūsaku Endō Miscellany*, 1992.

BIBLIOGRAPHY

Beverly, Elizabeth. "A Silence That Is Not Hollow." *Commonweal* 116 (September 22, 1989): 491-494. Claims that Endō's writing is inspired by two elemental aspects of his identity: the Japanese culture and Catholicism; argues that Endō's embrace of both has often made his life difficult and perilous, but that the labor of fiction has made it bearable.

Cavanaugh, William T. "The God of Silence: Shūsaku Endō's Reading of the Passion." *Commonweal* 125 (March 13, 1998): 10-12. Argues that Endō's work can be seen as a profound exploration of the twisted logic of the Incarnation—the trajectory of God from heaven to earthly flesh and the assumption of weakness by omnipotence; asserts that Endō weaves together the spiritual anguish of his characters with an embattled and paradoxically orthodox theology.

Gessel, Van C., trans. Introduction to *Stained-Glass Elegies: Stories by Shūsaku Endō*. New York: Dodd, Mead, 1984. An explanation of Endō's talents and position as a writer in Japan and the West plus a brief but comprehensive rundown on each of the stories translated in the volume: dates of composition, sources or occasions inspiring the stories, and analyses of their themes.

_____. "The Voice of the Doppelgänger." *Japan Quarterly*, no. 38 (1991): 198-213. Gessel examines four postwar Japanese novelists, including Endō, and notes how the postwar fiction differs from the prewar tradition of the "I story," in which author and persona are one. He selects Endō's *Scandal* as a model of the new treatment in which the *Doppelgänger* actually mocks the protagonist

who represents the novelist, thus introducing aesthetic distance and irony.

Higgins, Jean. "The Inner Agon of Endō Shūsaku." *Cross Currents*, no. 34 (1984/1985): 414-416. Higgins seeks to explain the conflicts that have made Endō the writer he is: one is the guilt and sense of betrayal he felt toward the mother who persuaded him to become a Christian and his lack of a full acceptance of Christianity; the other is the confusion and dismay he felt in attempting to absorb the extent and richness of Western culture which works against the Japanese grain.

Mathy, Francis. "Endō Shūsaku: White Man, Yellow Man." *Comparative Literature Studies* 23, no. 1 (1967): 58. A Jesuit, Mathy explores Endō's fiction and essays and produces a clear and comprehensive treatment of the cultural conflict between Japan and Western Europe, especially as this conflict relates to religion and notions of beauty and morality. Mathy shows how Endō has experienced strong opposition between his Japanese heritage and the Christian view of life that he was taught by his mother and by Christian missionaries.

_____. "Shūsaku Endō: Japanese Catholic Novelist." *America* 167 (August 1-8, 1992): 66-71. A biographical account of Endō's life, from his childhood and his education up through the development of his most important works; surveys Endō's work and analyzes the themes presented in two early essays, "God and Gods" and "The Problems of a Catholic Writer."

Netland, John T. "From Resistance to Kenosis: Reconciling Cultural Difference in the Fiction of Shūsaku Endō." *Christianity and Literature* 48 (Winter, 1999): 177-194. Discusses Endō's translation of the polemics of cultural difference into art; claims that his works replace a simple binary postcolonial tension with a three-dimensional configuration of Christianity, Easter, and European perspectives.

Quinn, P. L. "Tragic Dilemmas, Suffering Love, and Christian Life." *Journal of Religious Ethics* 17 (1989): 151-183. A comprehensive description and analysis of Endō's *Silence*, in which the life of the Portuguese priest, Sebastian Rodrigues, who became an apostate by trampling on an image of Christ to save his parishioners from torture and death by the governmental authorities, is reflected upon in the hope of enriching ethical thought.

Reinsma, Luke M. "Shūsaku Endō's River of Life." *Christianity and Literature* 48 (Winter, 1999): 195-211. In this special issue on Endō, Reinsma discusses the natural world, particularly the river, as a metaphorical backdrop for his work. Claims that Endō has shifted from landscapes and waters ravaged by a Father God in his early work to the lush vegetation of his later.

Williams, Mark. *Endō Shūsaku: A Literature of Reconciliation*. New York: Routledge, 1999. An interesting study of Endō's fictive technique. Includes bibliographical references.

Richard P. Benton, updated by Charles E. May

LOUISE ERDRICH

Born: Little Falls, Minnesota; June 7, 1954

PRINCIPAL SHORT FICTION

"The Red Convertible," 1981
"Scales," 1982
"The World's Greatest Fisherman," 1982
"American Horse," 1983
"Destiny," 1985
"Saint Marie," 1985
"Fleur," 1987
"Snares," 1987
"Matchimanito," 1988

OTHER LITERARY FORMS

Louise Erdrich is perhaps best known for her novels, which include *Love Medicine* (1984), *The Beet Queen* (1986), *Tracks* (1988), *The Bingo Palace* (1994), *Tales of Burning Love* (1996), and *The Antelope Wife* (1998). She is also the author of several collections of poetry and a number of children's books.

ACHIEVEMENTS

Several of Louise Erdrich's stories have appeared in the annual *The Best American Short Stories* and *Prize Stories: The O. Henry Awards* series. She received a Nelson Algren Fiction Award as well as a National Endowment for the Arts Fellowship in 1982, the Pushcart Prize and the National Magazine Award for Fiction in 1983, a John Simon Guggenheim Memorial Foundation Fellowship in 1985, and a Western Literary Association Award in 1992. Her *Love Medicine* received the Virginia McCormack Scully Prize, the National Book Critics Circle Award, the *Los Angeles Times* award for best novel, the Sue Kaufman Prize, the American Book Award and was named one of the best eleven books of 1985 by *The New York Times Book Review*.

BIOGRAPHY

Karen Louise Erdrich was born in Little Falls, Minnesota, on June 7, 1954, the first of seven children of a German father and Chippewa mother. A member of the first coeducational class at Dartmouth College in 1972, she received her B.A. in 1976. While teaching expository and creative writing on a fellowship at The Johns Hopkins University, she earned an M.A. from The Johns Hopkins Writing Program in 1979. In 1980 she was a textbook writer for the Charles Merrill Company, and a year later, she became a visiting fellow at Dartmouth. On October 10, 1981, she married the writer Michael Dorris.

In 1981, Louise Erdrich published her first short story, "The Red Convertible," in *Mississippi Valley Review*. Over the next two years, she published such award-winning stories as "The World's Greatest Fisherman" and "Scales." In 1984, she published her first collection of poetry, *Jacklight*, as well as her first novel, *Love Medicine*. In 1991, she coauthored *The Crown of Columbus* with her husband.

Since 1981, Erdrich has been Writer-in-Residence at Dartmouth's Native American Studies Program. Erdrich has said that the success of her works is due in great part to the collaboration of her husband. However, despite his death in 1997, Erdrich continued to write successful works of fiction.

ANALYSIS

Just as fiction in general has opened up to a diverse ethnic spectrum of writers, so too has short fiction, and Louise Erdrich's stories stand as excellent examples of contemporary Native American literature. Like Leslie Silko, Linda Hogan, and Paula Gunn Allen, Erdrich has taken a place as one of the prominent female Native American authors of short fiction. Even among American Indian stories, Erdrich's stand out for their multiethnic nature. Erdrich's stories include not only Native American characters but also characters of German, Swedish, and other European descent. Likewise, many of the stories' themes are not specifically Native American themes. Indeed, the themes of Erdrich's stories range from the effects of war on families and personal identity to loss of heritage and family and personal relationships.

Stylistically, Erdrich's stories reveal many similarities to the stories of writers she has said had significant influence on her. The distinct sense of place, of character, and of history that colors the works of Toni Morrison, William Faulkner, and Italo Calvino is similarly prominent in Erdrich's stories. She has said of Calvino that "the magic in his work is something that has been an influence," which is clear especially in stories like "Fleur" and "Snares." As Faulkner does with Yoknapatawpha County, Erdrich creates a world of the Chippewa reservation and the town of Argus, in which and around which nearly all of her stories occur. Many of her characters are employed repeatedly in her stories. Minor characters in one story may be the central characters in another or relatives of characters in one story are featured in later stories. Thus, most of Erdrich's stories connect to create a fictional world, which appears as true as the real world.

Louise Erdrich (Michael Dorris)

Erdrich has said that "the story starts to take over if it is good." Her stories fulfill this criterion, capturing readers' imagination and carrying them along on an intense mental ride. Her stories truly "touch some universals" that embrace readers of all ages, cultures, and beliefs.

"THE RED CONVERTIBLE"

"The Red Convertible" is Erdrich's first published story. Like many of her stories, this tale of two brothers later became a chapter in the novel *Love Medicine*. On the surface, the story appears to be merely a simple tale of two brothers and the car they share. Lyman Lamartine, a young Indian man with a "touch" for money, and his brother Henry save enough money to buy a used, red Oldsmobile convertible. Lyman tells the story, describing the early adventures he and his brother shared in the car. However, as the story progresses, it becomes clear that much more than the car is important in this story. Lyman describes how Henry changed when he returned home from the Vietnam War. While the family tries to help the deeply depressed Henry, Lyman tricks his brother into fixing up the car that he damaged. While Henry does improve, even the car cannot save him as he commits suicide in the end. In this story, the red convertible represents the freedom and innocence of youth, yet once those things are lost due to war in Henry's case and due to the altered Henry in Lyman's case, they cannot be regained; they must be let go. While the story unfolds mainly on the reservation, part of its success is that the topic itself (the loss of innocence, the effects of war) is universal, which allows any reader to understand and be intrigued by the tale.

"SAINT MARIE"

Like many of Erdrich's stories, "Saint Marie" also became a chapter in *Love Medicine*. "Saint Marie" is the story of a young Indian girl, who goes to the Catholic convent near the reservation so she might prove she is better than the other heathen Indians. Marie tries very hard to keep Satan out of her life, yet one of the nuns, Sister Leopolda, believes Marie to be completely under the devil's control. Leopolda proceeds to torture Marie to the point of stabbing her with a fork in order to expunge the evil. Yet to cover her madness, Leopolda lies to the other nuns, telling them that Marie must be touched by God as she has the signs of the stigmata on her hand; Marie must be a saint. However, Marie uses her knowledge of the truth of what happened to intimidate and humble Leopolda. Once again, this is a story about loss of innocence, about the psychological effects of a traumatic event in a young person's life. Similarly, Marie's struggle with her beliefs and Leopolda's madness are not necessarily specific to Native Americans, so many readers can access the story and enjoy it.

"DESTINY"

A story which later became part of *The Beet Queen*, "Destiny" describes Celestine Duval's visit to see her granddaughter's Christmas play. Wallacette, Celestine's granddaughter, is a large, strong, impulsive girl, who intimidates the other children in her school and town. The destiny of the title is Wallacette's destiny to be strong and independent, just like her grandmother. Celestine adores Wallacette, though she does not get along with Wallacette's parents very well. In particular, there is bad blood between Celestine and her daughter-in-law,

whose gelatin molds with vegetables in them are a source of great disgust for Celestine. The story turns comic when Wallacette hits a little boy she likes when he does not cooperate in the play, and it ends on a humorous note as Celestine reveals that the secret dish she had taken to the play with her daughter-in-law's name on it was a gelatin mold with nuts and bolts in it. This story is very entertaining and universal in its depictions of family struggles and the pains of growing up. The psychological element still exists in this story, but some of the intense emotional pains are absent, which allows a humorous tone to come through.

"FLEUR"

"Fleur" presents the story of one woman's multiple drowning experiences and her influence on the people around her. Told from the point of view of Pauline Puyat, this story later became a chapter in *Tracks* (1988). Pauline describes how Fleur Pillager drowned several times, and every man who rescued her ended up either crazy or dead. Pauline believes that Fleur has special magic powers, and she tells the story of the time Fleur left the reservation and went to the town of Argus. After beating a group of men at cards for a number of weeks, Fleur is attacked by the men in a smokehouse. Pauline stands by and watches the event, doing nothing to help Fleur. However, Fleur has her revenge when, in the midst of a storm that came from nowhere and touched nothing that Fleur valued, the men become locked in a meat freezer. Pauline believes that Fleur called up the storm. While the story is about Fleur, it is also about Pauline. Pauline voices her own feelings and thoughts throughout the story, revealing the guilt she feels for not helping Fleur as well as the envy she feels toward this strong woman. Fleur is an enigma to Pauline, but she is also what Pauline seems to want to be in this story.

"MATCHIMANITO"

Though it was published after "Fleur," "Matchimanito" is the story of how Fleur came to be the last living member of her family and what happened to her when she came back to the reservation from Argus. An old man, Nanapush, tells how he found Fleur amid her dead family and took her away to recover from the "spotted sickness." This story reveals that Fleur is different from everyone else from the beginning. She is quiet yet powerful. Upon returning from Argus, she lives alone in a cabin next to Matchimanito, the lake, which fuels rumors about her relationship with the lake monster, Mishepeshu. However, Fleur soon attracts a young man, Eli Kashpaw, and they live as husband and wife by the lake. Fleur becomes pregnant, and her pregnancy sparks more rumors, as the child's paternity is questioned. The birth of the child is difficult, and though many people believe that Fleur and her baby are dead, both live to prove them wrong. This is a powerful story because it demonstrates the strength of Fleur, the mixing of the old Indian ways with the new ones, the interaction of the community and individuals, and the history of both one person and a people. This story is particularly successful in its ability to show all of these things without force-feeding them to the reader.

OTHER MAJOR WORKS

LONG FICTION: *Love Medicine*, 1984 (revised and expanded 1993); *The Beet Queen*, 1986; *Tracks*, 1988; *The Crown of Columbus*, 1991 (with Michael Dorris); *The Bingo Palace*, 1994; *Tales of Burning Love*, 1996; *The Antelope Wife*, 1998.

POETRY: *Jacklight*, 1984; *Baptism of Desire: Poems*, 1989.

NONFICTION: *Route Two*, 1990 (with Michael Dorris); *The Blue Jay's Dance: A Birth Year*, 1995; *The Birthbark House*, 1999.

CHILDREN'S FICTION: *Grandmother's Pigeon*, 1996; *The Birchbark House*, 1999.

BIBLIOGRAPHY

Bruchac, Joseph. "Whatever Is Really Yours: An Interview with Louise Erdrich." In *Survival This Way: Interviews with American Indian Poets*. Tucson: University of Arizona Press, 1987. Erdrich discusses her poetry in particular but also her inspirations for her stories and her philosophy on what makes a good story. She explains how the characters and their stories are formed as well.

Coltelli, Laura. *Winged Words: American Indian Writers Speak* Lincoln: University of Nebraska Press, 1990. Erdrich and Michael Dorris discuss their collaborations with each other, their stories, novels, and poems, and their views on American Indian literature. They explain how a number of Erdrich's short stories are the genesis for her novels and how they create the connections between short and long fiction.

Davis, Rocío G. "Identity in Community in Ethnic Short Story Cycles: Amy Tan's *The Joy Luck Club*, Louise Erdrich's *Love Medicine*, Gloria Naylor's *The Women of Brewster Place*." In *Ethnicity and the American Short Story*, edited by Julia Brown. New York: Garland, 1997. Discusses how Erdrich's *Love Medicine* is in fact a cycle of short stories. Suggests that each chapter is a story with a different narrator, but the narrators' voices combine to present a communal protagonist. This variety of narration and collection of short stories present the confusion and disconnectedness of the people that Erdrich depicts. An interesting concept and a useful way of understanding the stories as they stand on their own.

Erdrich, Louise. *Conversations with Louise Erdrich and Michael Dorris*. Edited by Allan Chavkin and Nancy Feyl Chavkin. Jackson: University Press of Mississippi, 1994. Erdrich discusses her work.

Ferguson, Suzanne. "The Short Stories of Louise Erdrich's Novels." *Studies in Short Fiction* 33 (1996): 541-555. An excellent discussion of four short stories—"Saint Marie," "Scales," "Fleur," and "Snares"—and how they were modified when they became chapters in the novels. Ferguson also argues that alone the short stories should be read differently than when they are presented as chapters in a novel. This is a good article for clarifying the differences between the short stories and their counterpart chapters in the novels.

Stone, Brad. "Scenes from a Marriage: Louise Erdrich's New Novel—and Her Life." *Newsweek* 131, no. 12 (March 23, 1998): 69. Discusses Erdrich's *The Antelope Wife* and the suicide of her husband Michael Dorris.

Keri L. Overall

CRITICAL SURVEY
OF
SHORT FICTION

GEOGRAPHICAL INDEX

GEOGRAPHICAL INDEX

CATEGORY INDEX

REGIONAL STORIES. *See also* **LOCAL COLOR**

RELIGIOUS STORIES

ROMANCE

ROMANTICISM

RUSSIAN CULTURE

SATIRE. *See also* **MANNERS, FICTION OF, SOCIAL SATIRE**

CATEGORY INDEX

SOCIAL SATIRE. *See also* MANNERS, FICTION OF, SOCIAL REALISM

SOUTH AFRICAN CULTURE

SOUTHERN UNITED STATES

SOUTHWESTERN UNITED STATES

SPANISH CULTURE

SUPERNATURAL STORIES. *See also* GHOST, GOTHIC, GROTESQUE STORIES, HORROR, MAGICAL REALISM, OCCULT, SUSPENSE

CATEGORY INDEX